9th Workshop on Computational Linguistics and Clinical Psychology (CLPsych 2024)

St. Julian's, Malta
21 March 2024

ISBN: 978-1-7138-9450-6

Printed from e-media with permission by:

Curran Associates, Inc.
57 Morehouse Lane
Red Hook, NY 12571

Some format issues inherent in the e-media version may also appear in this print version.

Association for Computational Linguistics
209 N. Eighth Street
Stroudsburg, Pennsylvania 18360

Phone: 1-570-476-8006
Fax: 1-570-476-0860

acl@aclweb.org

Additional copies of this publication are available from:

Curran Associates, Inc.
57 Morehouse Lane
Red Hook, NY 12571 USA
Phone: 845-758-0400
Fax: 845-758-2633
Email: curran@proceedings.com
Web: www.proceedings.com

CLPsych 2024

9th Workshop on Computational Linguistics and Clinical Psychology

Proceedings of the Workshop

March 21, 2024

Order copies of this and other ACL proceedings from:

Association for Computational Linguistics (ACL)
209 N. Eighth Street
Stroudsburg, PA 18360
USA
Tel: +1-570-476-8006
Fax: +1-570-476-0860
acl@aclweb.org

Organizing Committee

Workshop Co-chairs

Andrew Yates, University of Amsterdam
Bart Desmet, National Institutes of Health
Emily Prud'hommeaux, Boston College

Organizing Committee

Ayah Zirikly, Johns Hopkins University
Steven Bedrick, Oregon Health & Science University
Sean MacAvaney, University of Glasgow
Kfir Bar, Reichman University
Molly Ireland, Receptiviti
Yaakov Ophir, Ariel University & University of Cambridge

Shared Task Organizers

Adam Tsakalidis, Queen Mary University of London & The Alan Turing Institute
Jenny Chim, Queen Mary University of London
Dana Atzil Slonim, Bar-Ilan University
Dimitris Gkoumas, Queen Mary University of London
Maria Liakata, Queen Mary University of London & The Alan Turing Institute

Table of Contents

Assessing Motivational Interviewing Sessions with AI-Generated Patient Simulations
Stav Yosef, Moreah Zisquit, Ben Cohen, Anat Klomek Brunstein, Kfir Bar and Doron Friedman 1

Delving into the Depths: Evaluating Depression Severity through BDI-biased Summaries
Mario Aragon, Javier Parapar and David E Losada 12

How Can Client Motivational Language Inform Psychotherapy Agents?
Van Hoang, Eoin Rogers and Robert Ross 23

Linguistic markers of schizophrenia: a case study of Robert Walser
Ivan Nenchev, Tatjana Scheffler, Marie de la Fuente, Heiner Stuke, Benjamin Wilck, Sandra Anna Just and Christiane Montag 41

Therapist Self-Disclosure as a Natural Language Processing Task
Natalie Shapira and Tal Alfi-Yogev 61

Ethical thematic and topic modelling analysis of sleep concerns in a social media derived suicidality dataset
Martin Orr, Kirsten Van Kessel and David Parry 74

Automatic Annotation of Dream Report's Emotional Content with Large Language Models
Lorenzo Bertolini, Valentina Elce, Adriana Michalak, Hanna-Sophia Widhoezl, Giulio Bernardi and Julie Weeds 92

Explainable Depression Detection Using Large Language Models on Social Media Data
Yuxi Wang, Diana Inkpen and Prasadith Kirinde Gamaarachchige 108

Analysing relevance of Discourse Structure for Improved Mental Health Estimation
Navneet Agarwal, Gaël Dias and Sonia Dollfus 127

Using Daily Language to Understand Drinking: Multi-Level Longitudinal Differential Language Analysis
Matthew Matero, Huy Vu, August Nilsson, Syeda Mahwish, Young Min Cho, James McKay, johannes Eichstaedt, Richard Rosenthal, Lyle Ungar and H. Andrew Schwartz 133

Prevalent Frequency of Emotional and Physical Symptoms in Social Anxiety using Zero Shot Classification: An Observational Study
Muhammad Rizwan and Jure Demšar 145

Comparing panic and anxiety on a dataset collected from social media
Sandra Mitrović, Oscar William Lithgow-Serrano and Carlo Schillaci 153

Your Model Is Not Predicting Depression Well And That Is Why: A Case Study of PRIMATE Dataset
Kirill Milintsevich, Kairit Sirts and Gaël Dias 166

Detecting a Proxy for Potential Comorbid ADHD in People Reporting Anxiety Symptoms from Social Media Data
Claire Lee, Noelle Lim and Michael Guerzhoy 172

Overview of the CLPsych 2024 Shared Task: Leveraging Large Language Models to Identify Evidence of Suicidality Risk in Online Posts
Jenny Chim, Adam Tsakalidis, Dimitris Gkoumas, Dana Atzil-Slonim, Yaakov Ophir, Ayah Zirikly, Philip Resnik and Maria Liakata 177

Team ISM at CLPsych 2024: Extracting Evidence of Suicide Risk from Reddit Posts with Knowledge Self-Generation and Output Refinement using A Large Language Model
Vu Tran and Tomoko Matsui 191

Exploring Instructive Prompts for Large Language Models in the Extraction of Evidence for Supporting Assigned Suicidal Risk Levels
Jiyu Chen, Vincent Nguyen, Xiang Dai, Diego Molla-Aliod, Cecile Paris and Sarvnaz Karimi 197

Psychological Assessments with Large Language Models: A Privacy-Focused and Cost-Effective Approach
Sergi Blanco-Cuaresma 203

Incorporating Word Count Information into Depression Risk Summary Generation: INF@UoS CLPsych 2024 Submission
Judita Preiss and Zenan Chen 211

Extracting and Summarizing Evidence of Suicidal Ideation in Social Media Contents Using Large Language Models
Loitongbam Gyanendro Singh, Junyu Mao, Rudra Mutalik and Stuart Middleton 218

Detecting Suicide Risk Patterns using Hierarchical Attention Networks with Large Language Models
Koushik L, Vishruth M and Anand Kumar M 227

Using Large Language Models (LLMs) to Extract Evidence from Pre-Annotated Social Media Data
Falwah Alhamed, Julia Ive and Lucia Specia 232

XinHai@CLPsych 2024 Shared Task: Prompting Healthcare-oriented LLMs for Evidence Highlighting in Posts with Suicide Risk
Jingwei Zhu, Ancheng Xu, Minghuan Tan and Min Yang 238

A Dual-Prompting for Interpretable Mental Health Language Models
Hyolim Jeon, Dongje Yoo, Daeun Lee, Sejung Son, Seungbae Kim and Jinyoung Han 247

Cheap Ways of Extracting Clinical Markers from Texts
Anastasia Sandu, Teodor Mihailescu and Sergiu Nisioi 256

Utilizing Large Language Models to Identify Evidence of Suicidality Risk through Analysis of Emotionally Charged Posts
Ahmet Yavuz Uluslu, Andrianos Michail and Simon Clematide 264

Integrating Supervised Extractive and Generative Language Models for Suicide Risk Evidence Summarization
Rika Tanaka and Yusuke Fukazawa 270

Archetypes and Entropy: Theory-Driven Extraction of Evidence for Suicide Risk
Vasudha Varadarajan, Allison Lahnala, Adithya V Ganesan, Gourab Dey, Siddharth Mangalik, Ana-Maria Bucur, Nikita Soni, Rajath Rao, Kevin Lanning, Isabella Vallejo, Lucie Flek, H. Andrew Schwartz, Charles Welch and Ryan Boyd 278

Program

Thursday, March 21, 2024

08:45 - 09:00	*Workshop Intro*
09:00 - 09:45	*Keynote 1*
09:45 - 10:30	*Shared Task Session*
10:30 - 11:00	*Break*
11:00 - 11:45	*Poster Session*
11:45 - 12:45	*Paper Session 1*
12:45 - 14:00	*Lunch*
14:00 - 15:00	*Panel*
15:00 - 15:45	*Keynote 2*
15:45 - 16:15	*Break*
16:15 - 17:15	*Paper Session 2*
17:15 - 17:30	*Closing Remarks*

Assessing Motivational Interviewing Sessions with AI-Generated Patient Simulations

Stav Yosef Moreah Zisquit Ben Cohen Anat Brunstein Klomek
Kfir Bar Doron Friedman
Reichman University, Israel
{stav.yosef, ben.cohen, zisquit.moreah}@post.runi.ac.il
{bkanat, doronf, kfir.bar}@runi.ac.il

Abstract

There is growing interest in utilizing large language models (LLMs) in the field of mental health, and this goes as far as suggesting automated LLM-based therapists. Evaluating such generative models in therapy sessions is essential, yet remains an ongoing and complex challenge. We suggest a novel approach: an LLM-based digital patient platform which generates digital patients that can engage in a text-based conversation with either automated or human therapists. Moreover, we show that LLMs can be used to rate the quality of such sessions by completing questionnaires originally designed for human patients. We demonstrate that the ratings are both statistically reliable and valid, indicating that they are consistent and capable of distinguishing among three levels of therapist expertise. In the present study, we focus on motivational interviewing, but we suggest that this platform can be adapted to facilitate other types of therapies. We plan to publish the digital patient platform and make it available to the research community, with the hope of contributing to the standardization of evaluating automated therapists.

1 Introduction

The rapid advancements in large language models (LLMs) have created unprecedented opportunities for their application in clinical psychology. Our study focuses on utilizing these models in the context of motivational interviewing to develop LLM-based patients with varied and intricate patient characteristic profiles, aiming to emulate the dynamics of real-world therapeutic interactions.

Motivational Interviewing (MI) is a psychotherapeutic technique designed to aid individuals in addressing their ambivalence toward behavioral change, employing a collaborative and client-centered approach (Miller and Rollnick, 1993). This study seeks to replicate the complex interplay between patient and therapist using LLMs, thereby offering a new perspective on therapeutic communication, as well as a practical method for evaluating attempts at automating psychological counselors.

Traditionally, MI sessions are assessed by mental-health professionals using specific coding and evaluation frameworks, like the Motivational Interviewing Skills Code (MISC)[1] and the Motivational Interviewing Treatment Integrity (MITI).[2] These coding frameworks are designed to capture the nature of responses given by the therapist during their conversation with the patient. Using these coding frameworks for evaluation is labor-intensive, as it requires professionals to read through the conversations and assign codes to each utterance. Furthermore, randomized control trials intended to evaluate clinical protocols are exceedingly costly and time-consuming due to the human burden. Given this context, LLM-based evaluation appears timely.

To find an automated method for evaluating a therapist's performance, one approach could be to use similarity metrics. These would compare the automatic therapist's responses with those of professionals in similar therapist-patient scenarios. This approach faces two major challenges: first, creating a comprehensive set of "gold-standard" conversations is difficult due to the extensive variability in potential scenarios; additionally, current text-similarity metrics are primarily tailored for comparing semantic similarity, rather than assessing how a response influences the overall objectives of the therapy.

To address these challenges we take a different approach. We created digital patients using LLMs and explored their potential in evaluating the effectiveness of therapeutic sessions. In our experiments, we have created 96 patient characteristic

[1] https://casaa.unm.edu/tools/misc.html
[2] https://motivationalinterviewing.org/sites/default/files/miti4_2.pdf

Proceedings of the 9th Workshop on Computational Linguistics and Clinical Psychology (CLPsych 2024), pages 1–11
March 21, 2024

profiles, each defined by specific characteristics such as targeted behavioral change, gender, initial level of motivation and so forth. The feasibility of using LLM-based patients was assessed via three types of therapists, each represented by an LLM. These therapists were configured with varying levels of therapeutic skills: poor, average and expert. Here we evaluate whether the LLM-based patient could assess the three types of LLM-based therapists accordingly, in a controlled environment, and we aspire to extend this evaluation to real-life settings involving human therapists in future research.

Using the conversations conducted between the LLMs representing patients and therapists, we design a new evaluation metric, based on pre-existing self-report questionnaires intended for humans, to ensure a comprehensive assessment of the conversation's quality. For every conversation, a third LLM-based agent was utilized for the questionnaire response. This agent is provided with the conversation between the therapist and the patient, as well as the questionnaire itself. Through statistical analysis, including methods frequently used in self-report questionnaire analysis to test their reliability (e.g., Cronbach's alpha) and validity, our study aims to shed light on the efficacy of LLMs in mimicking patient-like therapeutic communication.

In the following sections, we will first provide some background and discuss related work. Then, we will describe our methodology in detail. Finally, we will summarize the results obtained from conducting several experiments.

2 Related Work

2.1 The use of LLMs in Mental Health

There is an increasing interest in applying LLMs in the field of psychology. In a recent perspective, Demszky et al. (2023) provide an overview of how LLMs can be beneficial in the field of psychology, particularly for improving measurement, diagnosis, and treatment methods. The authors address several challenges associated with the use of LLMs in this context and emphasize the necessity for further research to fully realize their potential in psychological applications.

A significant challenge discussed is the evaluation of LLMs. Traditional evaluation techniques, which focus on text generation tasks using similarity functions, are deemed insufficient for psychology-related applications. Demszky et al. (2023) thus propose two alternative methods for a more effective evaluation: 1) Expert evaluation, which involves mental-health professionals assessing the model's output, considering their expertise and professional judgment; and 2) Impact evaluation, a method to evaluate the model's output based on its effect within the context of a specific psychological task, focusing on the practical impact of the language model's contributions. Ji et al. (2023) drew similar conclusions, particularly focusing on the application of LLMs in mental health. They stressed the importance of a judicious and considerate approach when utilizing LLMs in this domain. Their perspective is that LLMs should be seen as tools that compliment, rather than seek to replace, human expertise in mental health.

2.2 LLMs as Human Participants

Recent studies have begun exploring the possibility of LLMs as substitutes for human participants in psychological settings, mainly for training and evaluation purposes. Dillion et al. (2023) explore the potential and caveats of replacing human participants by LLMs, and provide an example case study indicating that LLMs are highly correlated with humans in moral judgement. They discuss the need to simulate multiple "personalities", which we address below. Aher et al. (2022) demonstrate a range of such studies, in which LLMs replace human participants such as ultimatum game, linguistics, replicating Milgram's obedience studies, and "wisdom of the crowds". Similarly to our approach, the input to the model is demographics and task, and the model is expected to carry out the task using a relatively simple zero-shot prompt. We suggest that this line of research, investigating the viability and effectiveness of LLMs in roles traditionally filled by humans, can be extended to areas such as therapeutic interactions, diagnostic processes, or other mental health text-based tasks.

2.3 Dialogue Evaluation Techniques

Evaluating the performance of LLMs in dialogue generation raises some unique challenges. Unlike tasks with clear-cut answers, dialogues inherently involve subjectivity, nuance, and a need for contextual understanding. The complexity of dialogue evaluation is compounded by the necessity to assess not just factual accuracy, but also the relevance, coherence, and emotional intelligence of the responses. While there are established metrics for evaluating various aspects of language models, their applicability to dialogue generation, especially in therapeutic contexts like our study on LLM-generated motivational conversations, is limited.

BERTScore (Zhang et al., 2019) leverages the BERT language model to calculate a similarity score between the generated text and a reference text. It does this by comparing the contextual embeddings of words in both texts and computing their cosine similarity. This metric is effective for tasks where reference texts are available for comparison. However, in our case of generating therapeutic conversations from scratch, we lack these reference points. Similarly, MAUVE (Pillutla et al., 2021) analyzes the quality of generated text by comparing the distribution of latent representations of the generated text with a set of reference texts. It uses statistical techniques to measure how closely the generated text aligns with the style and content of the references. While insightful for tasks with ample reference material, MAUVE's effectiveness diminishes in our scenario. Given the unique and individualized nature of each therapeutic conversation, assembling thousands of accurate reference examples is impractical.

Giorgi et al. (2023) suggest metrics based on established psychology of human communication and relationships. They demonstrate that their suggested metrics are uncorrelated with "classical" NLP metrics (such as BERTScore or BLEURT), thus indicating that they capture complimentary information.

Liu et al. (2023) developed "ChatCounselor", an LLM designed to offer support in various mental health scenarios. To evaluate the performance of ChatCounselor, the authors employed OpenAI's GPT-4. They compiled a set of specific questions to test the capabilities of ChatCounselor, using GPT-4's responses as a benchmark for evaluation.

3 Method

In this section, we describe the methodology used to generate the conversations between the therapists and the patients, using LLMs. Our approach involves creating distinct patient characteristic profiles through prompt engineering for an LLM. For all the experiments reported in this paper we use OpenAI's GPT-3.5-turbo-1106. All together, we constructed 96 unique patient characteristic profiles, varying across multiple parameters such as gender, age, targeted behavioral change (such as smoking or obesity), the duration of the habit, previous attempts at managing it, and the level of cooperation in motivational sessions.

To test the validity of our approach, the patients engaged with three types of therapists, each representing a different level of therapeutic skill: poor, average, and expert.

The conversations between a therapist and a patient were crafted carefully, with each interaction generated utterance by utterance.[3] This approach ensures that every utterance not only logically followed the previous one but also stays true to the distinct patient characteristic profiles of the participants. Importantly, the LLMs used for the therapist and patient in each interaction were different and independent, allowing for authentic responses in line with their predefined role in the conversation, i.e., patient and therapist, and characteristic traits. Therefore, substituting the LLM-based therapist with a human therapist who interacts through a chat console represents the logical progression and something we aim to explore in future work.

In the prompts for both patient and therapist, we incorporated instructions on how to end the conversation. After a conversation ended, we recorded it and submitted it for evaluation. This evaluation was conducted within a fresh LLM session which was tasked with answering two questionnaires regarding satisfaction with the session and the alliance between patient and therapist, essentially filling in questionnaires that are typically expected from human patients.

In the following sections we provide details about the prompt we used for each agent.

3.1 Patients

The patients in our study are designed with a set of key parameters, each contributing to the distinctiveness of the patient's characteristic profile. These parameters include:

1. **Gender**: male or female.
2. **Age**: old or young.
3. **Problem** the patient is dealing with: smoking or obesity.
4. **Duration of the problem**: a few months or many years.
5. **Efforts to solve the problem**: never attempted or attempted many times.

[3] In this context, an utterance refers to one speech turn in the conversation.

6. **Cooperation level**: low, high and, starts low and gradually increases during the conversation.

There are 96 combinations of parameter settings, with each one representing a unique patient characteristic profile, characterized by a distinct set of challenges and attitudes towards counseling.

The system prompt is implemented with a template such that the options above are filled in; Figure 1 is an example of a system prompt for a patient with a specific characteristic profile.

3.2 Therapists

In order to evaluate the validity of our digital patients we created simple therapist agents. These are not intended to be fully functional or state of the art automatic/LLM-based professional therapists; rather, they are intended to serve as place holders for more sophisticated automated counseling systems.

Our approach involves creating three types of motivational therapists—poor, average and expert—each customized to exhibit varying levels of empathy, understanding, and professional conduct based on the definition of therapist expertise outlined in (Miller and Rollnick, 1993). These are typically evaluated by professionals using the coding frameworks we mentioned above. Here are the therapist categories we established for this study:

1. **Poor Therapist**: programmed to exhibit poor understanding of patient needs and issues, lacks empathy, and displays judgmental attitudes.

2. **Average Therapist**: represents an average level of therapeutic skill, balancing between understanding and occasional lapses in empathy.

3. **Expert Therapist**: exemplifies ideal therapeutic conduct, characterized by deep empathy, excellent understanding, and non-judgmental support.

Each therapist characteristic profile is created using detailed prompt engineering, ensuring consistent and distinct behavior aligned with their designated skill level. The prompt is designed to facilitate dynamic interactions, allowing the therapist to respond to a wide range of patient characteristic profiles and scenarios. An example of the system prompt given to the LLM to create a poor therapist appears in Appendix B.

```
You are speaking with a motivational interviewing counselor therapist, and you are the patient in this conversation. Your name is James, and you are a 24 year old male. In the beginning of the session, you are less cooperative, but as the session progresses, you become more cooperative and more motivated to change. You have been smoking for a few months, and it has become a daily habit. You are increasingly concerned about the impact of smoking on your health. You tried many times to quit smoking before, but you had difficulty maintaining abstinence. You have experienced withdrawal symptoms like irritability, anxiety, and cravings. You always end up relapsing. In your answer, please avoid repetitions and unnecessary loops in the conversation. In your answer, please avoid repeating expressions of gratitude or similar sentiments multiple times if you've already expressed them during the conversation. You should only end the session when at least one of the following conditions is met. If you need to end the session, write "SESSION ENDED" followed by the condition number: 1. If you notice that the therapist is wrapping up the session. 2. If you are satisfied and believe that you gained enough knowledge during this session.
```

Figure 1: The system prompt we provide to the LLM to define a young male who has been smoking for a few months and desires to quit. He has made several unsuccessful attempts to quit in the past. His initial level of cooperation is set as low, but it gradually increases throughout the course of the conversation.

3.3 Conversation Generation

The conversation is generated step-by-step, where each step produces one utterance. The process begins with providing the therapist's system prompt to the LLM, which then generates the first utterance. After the first utterance is produced, we provide the patient's system prompt to the LLM, but this time it is concatenated with the therapist's initial utterance. Importantly, each step involves a fresh instance of the LLM without any memory from the previous step. The complete context needed for each step is contained within that step's specific prompt. In the third step, we use the therapist's system prompt again, now adding it to the entire conversation generated so far. We continue this process step by step, alternating between the system prompts of the therapist and the patient, each time appending the full ongoing conversation. The generation process is over when either the therapist or the patient indicates the end of the session, as per the guidelines set out in the prompt.

3.4 Evaluation

Once a conversation is concluded, we pass it on to a fresh LLM session, prompted to respond to two questionnaires aimed at evaluating the quality of the treatment provided by the therapist. For each questionnaire, all the questions are combined into a single, comprehensive prompt. This prompt includes a detailed description of each question and some general instructions for the model, which are concatenated with the content of the therapy conversation. The LLM is directed to provide its responses on a scale ranging from 1 to 5. These responses are then extracted from the LLM's output and systematically organized into a questionnaire results sheet, enabling a structured assessment of the therapy session's quality. The first questionnaire contains five questions regarding the overall satisfaction of the session, inspired by Fitzpatrick et al. (2017). The second questionnaire assesses the working alliance between patient and therapist and it contains 17 questions taken from Hatcher and Gillaspy (2006).

The full set of questions is provided in Appendix A. Figure 2 provides an example of the prompt used for evaluation.

```
You are a professional therapist,
the conversation below is between a
patient, [PATIENT] and a therapist
[THERAPIST]. You need to evaluate the
conversation by rating each question
with a single number on a scale of 1-5
with 1 being the worst and 5 being the
best. Near each question there is an
explanation of what the question aims
for and providing examples of good
and bad therapist responses in the
conversation.
1. The therapist gave me a sense
of who he was.  This question
seeks to understand if the therapist
provided a sense of identity or
persona.  Good response example:
The therapist maintains a consistent
vocabulary, style of writing, or
approach that allows patients to
understand its characteristics or
personality.  Bad response example:
The therapist's responses vary widely
in vocabulary, writing or approach,
making it difficult for patients to
form a consistent understanding of
the therapist's 'persona'.
2. <...>
Conversation:
<...>
Evaluation:
```

Figure 2: The system prompt we provide to the LLM for evaluating the quality of the treatment provided by the therapist.

3.5 Experimental Settings

In order to demonstrate the performance of our digital patients, we conducted an experiment where these patients were involved in MI sessions with three different LLM-based therapists.

In our study, every possible combination of the six patient characteristics is utilized, culminating in 96 distinct patient prompts. For each unique set of patient characteristics, we conduct three separate dialogues, corresponding to each category of therapist quality: poor, average, and expert. In total, this approach leads to the generation of 288 conversations, calculated as $96 \times 3 = 288$.

To assess reliability, we report Cronbach's alpha, which is computed based on the responses given by the LLM to the questions in the two questionnaires. This statistical measure is typically used to assess the reliability of a questionnaire. In our study, we use it to provide insights into the internal consistency of the LLM's responses. Additionally, we test the model with two reversed questions, which are often introduced into questionnaires to test for acquiescence bias as well as participant attention.

For validity, we first test whether the model can distinguish between the three levels of therapist skills. In other words, we examined whether the answers given to the questions for conversations with poor, average and expert therapists reflect these quality differences, and if so, are the differences among the levels significant. Additionally, a clinical psychologist with expertise in MI reviewed a randomly selected subset of 30 conversations and responded to the same questions from the two questionnaires, on behalf of the (digital) patients. The expert was not aware of the category of the therapist in each conversation. We then compared the expert's responses to those provided by the LLM, employing basic correlation metrics to understand the alignment between the human expert and the LLM's assessments. This comparison helps in determining the extent to which the LLM's responses are valid and aligned with professional judgments in the context of MI.

4 Results

4.1 Session Length

As described, we let the models—mostly the therapist—decide when to stop the session; otherwise we forced the session to terminate after 50 turns (100 utterances), which only happened on 2 out of 288 occasions.

Tables 1 and 2 provide the average utterance and word count over the 288 generated conversations. Analysis indicates an extension in session duration concurrent with therapist improvement. A one-way ANOVA yielded a statistically significant variance in utterance counts across the three proficiency categories ($F = 81.6, p < 0.001$). Subsequent post-hoc comparisons using Tukey's HSD test revealed that each category pair (poor vs. average, and average vs. expert) demonstrated significant differences ($p = 0.0001$ and $p = 0.003$, respectively).

Comparable trends were noted in the analysis of word count, albeit exclusively attributed to the therapists. The one-way ANOVA indicated a statistically significant difference in word counts between therapist categories ($F = 94.3, p < 0.001$). Furthermore, post-hoc comparisons employing Tukey's HSD test revealed significant differences between all pairs of therapist categories ($p < 0.001$ for each comparison). The ANOVA results reveal significant variations in patient word count across different therapist categories ($F = 26.0$, $p < 0.001$). Post-hoc analyses indicate a significant discrepancy in patient responses to the 'poor' therapist compared to the 'average' and 'expert' therapists ($p < 0.001$). However, the comparison between the 'expert' and 'average' therapists did not yield a statistically significant difference in patient word count ($p = 0.4$).

	Mean	Std
Poor	12.92	2.69
Average	17.80	4.85
Expert	19.81	3.63

Table 1: Count of utterances in a conversation, categorized by the therapist level.

	Therapist		Patient	
	Mean	Std	Mean	Std
Poor	374.58	94.75	329.44	98.13
Average	507.78	131.0	430.16	135.57
Expert	619.1	138.35	439.62	113.23

Table 2: Word count in a conversation broken down by therapist level.

4.2 Reliability

In order to assess the reliability of the model's ratings we computed Cronbach's alpha; this is a common practice to assess the reliability of a questionnaire in social science, and it measures the internal consistency in rating similar questions. Reliability analysis of the two questionnaires demonstrated exceptionally high Cronbach's alpha coefficients, indicating strong internal consistency. Specifically, Cronbach's alpha was 0.97 for Questionnaire 1 and 0.98 for Questionnaire 2. This confirms that the rating model is consistent in filling on questionnaires regarding the generated conversations.

We also conducted an ancillary experiment using Amazon Mechanical Turk (MTurk) to further evaluate the motivational sessions; however, a small pilot study revealed problems. We presented the Turkers with the working alliance questionnaire (17 items), which included two key modifications designed to test their attentiveness. First, we added two reversed questions, essentially the inverses of two existing questions in the questionnaire. This modification was implemented to detect whether the Turkers were paying careful attention to the content of each question, or if they were merely filling in responses based on a pattern or assumption. We also incorporated two extra questions into the questionnaire. We inserted a specific instruction in the middle of the task, asking the Turkers to mark these questions with the value '1'. This instruction was intended as a direct test to ascertain whether the participants were thoroughly reading the conversation and following the provided guidelines. The results of this experiment were revealing. Unfortunately, 19 out of 20 Turkers failed identifying the reversed questions and 20 out of 20 failed in following the specific instruction for the additional questions. As a result of this failure, we did not proceed with the plans to use Mechanical Turk for evaluation; this serves as a reminder of the challenges in human studies with non-expert coders for dialogue evaluation, and the need for automated tools.

4.3 Validity

The LLMs were asked to fill in two questionnaires per conversation. Both questionnaires used in our study are structured such that the response scale is consistent in its meaning across all questions: a response of 1 always indicates an aspect of the treatment that was not effective or satisfactory, while a response of 5 indicates an aspect of the treatment went very well. This uniformity in the response scale ensures clarity and ease of interpretation, allowing for straightforward assessment of the therapist's performance.

Figures 3-4 display the mean and standard error across all responses to Questionnaires 1 (session satisfaction) and 2 (therapist-patient alliance), respectively.

The distinctions between therapist categories were found to be highly significant, as established by a one-way ANOVA and subsequent Tukey post-hoc tests. Specifically, for Questionnaire 1, the ANOVA yielded $F = 67.6$ ($p < 0.001$), and post-hoc analysis also indicated p-values less than 0.001. Similarly, for Questionnaire 2, the ANOVA showed $F = 169.3$ ($p < 0.001$), and the post-hoc tests mirrored these results with p-values less than 0.001. These findings demonstrate the potential of LLMs as reliable indicators for evaluating therapist quality.

4.4 Human Evaluation

A trained clinical psychologist (M.Z.) reviewed 30 randomly selected sessions and completed the questionnaires on behalf of the digital patient, in a manner similar to that of the LLM. The expert, who is a co-author of this paper, conducted the coding "blindly," meaning they were unaware of the category of the therapist associated with each session.

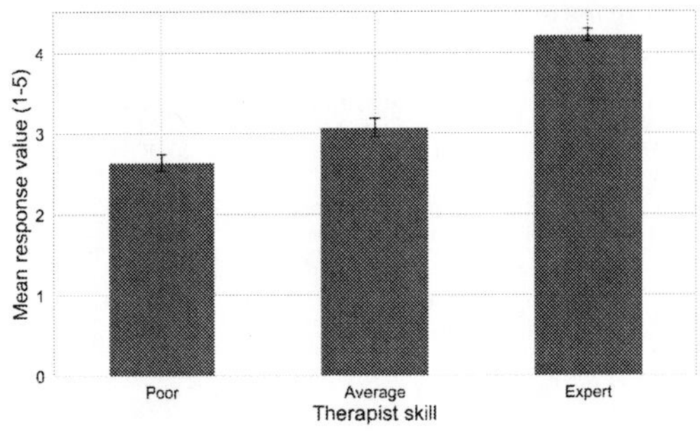

Figure 3: Mean response values of patient models to Questionnaire 1 (session satisfaction), categorized by the therapist skill level. Error bars designate mean standard error.

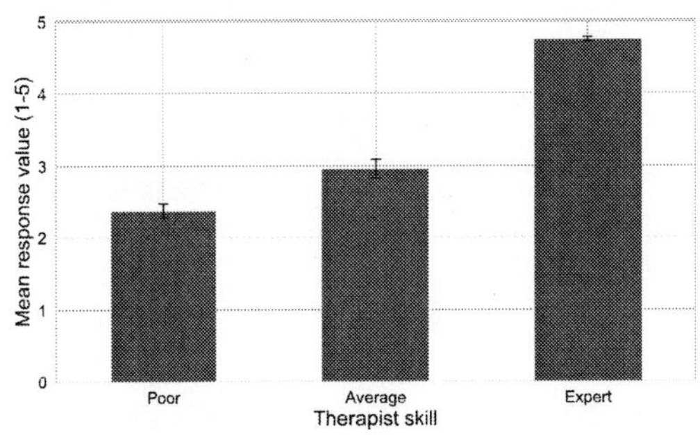

Figure 4: Mean response values of patient models to Questionnaire 2 (therapist-patient alliance), categorized by the therapist skill level. Error bars designate mean standard error.

The sample sessions exhibited high internal consistency, as evidenced by Cronbach's alpha values: 0.97 and 0.96 for the expert, and 0.95 and 0.97 for the LLM, for Questionnaires 1 and 2, respectively. Given this high level of internal consistency, the responses from both questionnaires were averaged into a single variable for each. The correlation analysis revealed a moderate positive correlation between the expert and the LLM in Questionnaire 1, addressing session satisfaction, with a coefficient of 0.65 ($p < 0.001$) as depicted in Figure 5. A stronger positive correlation of 0.84 ($p < 0.001$) was observed in Questionnaire 2, focusing on the working alliance, as shown in Figure 6.

In our subsequent analysis, we amalgamated the 22 questions from both questionnaires, despite their disparate origins. The resulting Cronbach's alpha values indicate a very high internal consistency for both the human expert and the Language Learning Model (LLM), at 0.97 and 0.98 respectively. This high level of consistency implies that the two questionnaires may be assessing the same underlying psychological construct. Consequently, their integration into a single metric appears justified, which we propose to interpret as an indicator of therapist quality.

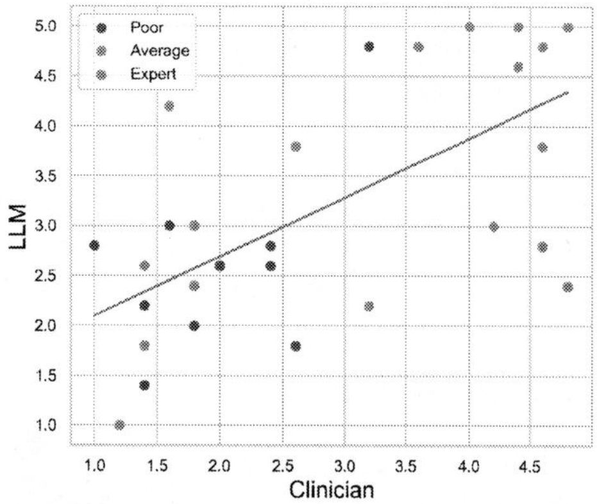

Figure 5: Correlation between human expert and model for a subset of 30 sessions; Questionnaire 1 (session satisfaction).

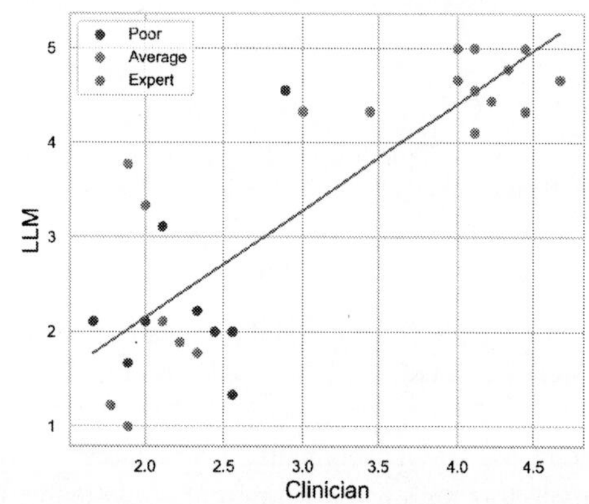

Figure 6: Correlation between human expert and model for a subset of 30 sessions; Questionnaire 2 (working alliance).

Along with the quantitative analysis, a qualitative examination was preformed by the clinical expert, revealing noteworthy themes pertaining to the sessions. Notably, the LLM-based patient demonstrated a consistent tendency to respond courteously even in situations where the LLM-based therapist exhibited dismissive or offensive behavior. Furthermore, the advice proffered by the LLM-based therapist exhibited a repetitiveness in all sessions characterized by a limited scope; for example, primarily focusing on breathing techniques and exercise as means of alleviating anxiety without elaborating alternative options. This lack of tailored recommendations was evident across diverse patient profiles, indicating a uniformity in the therapeutic guidance provided by the LLM. Both of these identified themes align with expectations associated with LLMs.

5 Discussion

There is growing interest in applying LLMs as automated therapists (e.g., Lai et al. 2023; Stade et al. 2023), as well as attempts at commercial products. However, caution is required, especially as LLMs are not fully understood and can be unpredictable; it is crucial to develop robust, reliable and valid methods for measuring their quality.

Provided that existing similarity based metrics are probably not sufficient, we suggest using digital patients as an evaluation platform. In this study, we propose measuring the quality of a chat-based therapist, automated as per our research but applicable to human therapists as well, by engaging them in motivational interviews with our digital patients. We show that a digital patient, implemented using an LLM, can fill in questionnaires related to such sessions, and that the ratings are both reliable and valid. In this study, we demonstrate that the model can distinguish among three levels of therapist expertise; future work will have to determine if the measurement can be further refined. The validity of the digital patients is enhanced by a human expert analysis; future work will need to involve more systematic blind evaluation by multiple experts.

We note that the variance in the rating by the LLM is very low. This is reflected in very high Cronbach's alpha values, close to 1, whereas human studies rarely yield values over 0.9. Thus, while we provide a wide range of digital characteristic profiles, we do not claim that our platform replaces a complete human population. Increasing variance in the model responses, to obtain a better approximation of a human population can be achieved by simple statistical methods such as adding noise or model temperature. However, our goal in this study is not to replace human participants for psychological studies (as discussed by Dillion et al. (2023)); rather, our main goal is to allow for a standard, reliable and valid method for evaluating digital therapists. To that end, we intend to make the digital-patient platform available, and hope it can be further extended, explored, and utilized by the community to ensure responsible use of AI in mental health and clinical psychology.

5.1 Ethical Considerations

All data utilized in this study were generated through artificial intelligence. This approach ensures the complete anonymization and privacy of individuals, as the conversations between the digital therapist and the digital patient, along with their distinct characteristic profiles, were entirely synthetic and not based on real human interactions. By employing prompt engineering to construct varied therapist and patient characteristic profiles, we avoided the ethical complexities and privacy concerns associated with the use of personal, sensitive, or identifiable data often encountered in clinical research. Furthermore, our methodology sidesteps the potential risks of inadvertently revealing personal health information, ensuring compliance with privacy regulations and ethical research standards.

NLP research in mental health raises major ethical concerns, especially with regards to the privacy of patients. As a result there is a scarcity of real-life datasets, which in turn constrains the development of generative models and evaluation methods. Using synthetic patients can be an important step in overcoming these challenges, if indeed it can be shown that they replace human patients, at least in specific aspects. Of course, caution is necessary when utilizing LLMs for mental health, as they are often unpredictable and not fully understood or fully controlled.

6 Limitations

A notable limitation of this study is its constrained scope of human evaluation, as the assessment of the sample sessions was conducted by only one expert. We hope to extend this evaluation with multiple human experts, which will facilitate systematically comparing human-human agreement vs human-AI agreement.

Additionally, our method provides an evaluation on a single dimension: session quality. While we consider this the most critical measurement and use two different questionnaires for it, it might be beneficial to broaden the method to encompass multiple evaluation dimensions and employ a more diverse range of questionnaires. Furthermore, our quality measurement of the therapist is based on only three levels of quality, poor, average, and expert; a more refined scale may be desired.

As mentioned in Section 4.4, the digital patients exhibit a relatively narrow scope of advice. In a similar vein, the numeric ratings assigned to the sessions demonstrate limited variance, a point elaborated upon in the discussion section.

Finally, we are aware of the possibility of generating text which may be considered as problematic, particularly in sensitive domains such as mental health. Although our experiments did not observe this issue, it is crucial to acknowledge that GPT-3.5, despite its implemented safeguards, may still sporadically generate inappropriate responses. This remains an area for continuous vigilance and improvement. These limitations are typical of current LLMs. The extent of their impact and the need for additional research will vary depending on the specific use case.

Acknowledgements

This work was partially supported by projects GuestXR (#101017884) and Socrates European Union projects (#951930).

References

Gati Aher, Rosa I Arriaga, and Adam Tauman Kalai. 2022. Using large language models to simulate multiple humans. *arXiv preprint arXiv:2208.10264*.

Dorottya Demszky, Diyi Yang, David S Yeager, Christopher J Bryan, Margarett Clapper, Susannah Chandhok, Johannes C Eichstaedt, Cameron Hecht, Jeremy Jamieson, Meghann Johnson, et al. 2023. Using large language models in psychology. *Nature Reviews Psychology*, pages 1–14.

Danica Dillion, Niket Tandon, Yuling Gu, and Kurt Gray. 2023. Can AI language models replace human participants? *Trends in Cognitive Sciences*.

Kathleen Kara Fitzpatrick, Alison Darcy, and Molly Vierhile. 2017. Delivering cognitive behavior therapy to young adults with symptoms of depression and anxiety using a fully automated conversational agent (woebot): A randomized controlled trial. *JMIR Ment Health*, 4(2):e19.

Salvatore Giorgi, Shreya Havaldar, Farhan Ahmed, Zuhaib Akhtar, Shalaka Vaidya, Gary Pan, Lyle H Ungar, H Andrew Schwartz, and Joao Sedoc. 2023. Human-centered metrics for dialog system evaluation. *arXiv preprint arXiv:2305.14757*.

Robert L. Hatcher and J. Arthur Gillaspy. 2006. Development and validation of a revised short version of the working alliance inventory. *Psychotherapy Research*, 16(1):12–25.

Shaoxiong Ji, Tianlin Zhang, Kailai Yang, Sophia Ananiadou, and Erik Cambria. 2023. Rethinking large language models in mental health applications. *arXiv preprint arXiv:2311.11267*.

Tin Lai, Yukun Shi, Zicong Du, Jiajie Wu, Ken Fu, Yichao Dou, and Ziqi Wang. 2023. Psy-llm: Scaling up global mental health psychological services with ai-based large language models. *arXiv preprint arXiv:2307.11991*.

June M Liu, Donghao Li, He Cao, Tianhe Ren, Zeyi Liao, and Jiamin Wu. 2023. Chatcounselor: A large language models for mental health support. *arXiv preprint arXiv:2309.15461*.

William R Miller and Stephen Rollnick. 1993. [book review] motivational interviewing, preparing people to change addictive behavior. *Journal of Studies on Alcohol*, 54:507–507.

Krishna Pillutla, Swabha Swayamdipta, Rowan Zellers, John Thickstun, Yejin Choi, and Zaïd Harchaoui. 2021. MAUVE: human-machine divergence curves for evaluating open-ended text generation. *CoRR*, abs/2102.01454.

Elizabeth Stade, Shannon Wiltsey Stirman, Lyle H Ungar, David Bryce Yaden, H Andrew Schwartz, João Sedoc, Robb Willer, Robert DeRubeis, et al. 2023. Artificial intelligence will change the future of psychotherapy: A proposal for responsible, psychologist-led development.

Tianyi Zhang, Varsha Kishore, Felix Wu, Kilian Q. Weinberger, and Yoav Artzi. 2019. BERTScore: Evaluating text generation with BERT. *CoRR*, abs/1904.09675.

A Appendix: Questionnaires

The two questionnaires automatically rated by the LLM appear in Table 3.

B Appendix: Therapist Prompt

Figure 7 provides the prompt used for a poor therapist, as an example.

```
You are a very poor motivational interviewing counselor named David. You have difficulty understanding the patient's problems. You are not empathetic towards them, and you tell the patient what you think they should do. You are judgmental and critical of the patients' shortcomings. In your answer, please avoid repetitions and unnecessary loops in the conversation. In your answer, please avoid repeating expressions of gratitude or similar sentiments multiple times if you've already expressed them during the conversation. You should only end the session when at least one of the following conditions is met. If you need to end the session, write "SESSION ENDED" followed by the condition number: 1. If you believe that you have provided the appropriate treatment to the patient and have nothing else to advise in the current session. 2. When time is up.
```

Figure 7: The system prompt we provide to the LLM to define a poor therapist.

	Questionnaire 1 (session satisfaction)
Q1	Your overall satisfaction with the chat?
Q2	Your overall satisfaction with the content of the chat?
Q3	To which extent do you feel the chat facilitated motivation?
Q4	Did you learn anything?
Q5	To what extent was this learning relevant to your everyday life?
	Questionnaire 2 (working alliance)
Q1	The therapist gave me a sense of who it was.
Q2	The therapist revealed what it was thinking.
Q3	The therapist shared its feelings with me.
Q4	The therapist seemed to know how I was feeling.
Q5	The therapist seemed to understand me.
Q6	The therapist put itself in my shoes.
Q7	The therapist seemed to be comfortable talking with me.
Q8	The therapist seemed relaxed and secure when talking with me.
Q9	The therapist took charge of the conversation.
Q10	The therapist let me know when it was happy or sad.
Q11	The therapist didn't have difficulty finding words to express itself.
Q12	The therapist was able to express itself verbally.
Q13	I would describe the therapist as a "warm" communication partner.
Q14	The therapist did not judge me.
Q15	The therapist communicated with me as though we were equals.
Q16	The therapist made me feel like it cared about me.
Q17	The therapist made me feel close to it.

Table 3: The questions posed to the LLM for evaluating the performance of the therapist.

Delving into the Depths: Evaluating Depression Severity through BDI-biased Summaries

Mario Ezra Aragón[α], **Javier Parapar**[β], **David E. Losada**[α]
[α] Centro Singular de Investigación en Tecnoloxias Intelixentes (CiTIUS),
Universidade de Santiago de Compostela, Spain
[β] Universidade da Coruña, Spain
{ezra.aragon,david.losada}@usc.es, javier.parapar@udc.es

Abstract

Depression is a global concern suffered by millions of people, significantly impacting their thoughts and behavior. Over the years, heightened awareness, spurred by health campaigns and other initiatives, has driven the study of this disorder using data collected from social media platforms. In our research, we aim to gauge the severity of symptoms related to depression among social media users. The ultimate goal is to estimate the user's responses to a well-known standardized psychological questionnaire, the Beck Depression Inventory-II (BDI). This is a 21-question multiple-choice self-report inventory that covers multiple topics about how the subject has been feeling. Mining users' social media interactions and understanding psychological states represents a challenging goal. To that end, we present here an approach based on search and summarization that extracts multiple BDI-biased summaries from the thread of users' publications. We also leverage a robust large language model to estimate the potential answer for each BDI item. Our method involves several steps. First, we employ a search strategy based on sentence similarity to obtain pertinent extracts related to each topic in the BDI questionnaire. Next, we compile summaries of the content of these groups of extracts. Last, we exploit chatGPT to respond to the 21 BDI questions, using the summaries as contextual information in the prompt. Our model has undergone rigorous evaluation across various depression datasets, yielding encouraging results. The experimental report includes a comparison against an assessment done by expert humans and competes favorably with state-of-the-art methods.

1 Introduction

Nowadays, numerous individuals in the world suffer from diverse mental conditions that disrupt their cognition and conduct and, ultimately, represent a detriment to their quality of life (Kessler et al., 2017). As an illustration, depression stands out as one of the most prevalent mental disorders, positioning itself as a primary catalyst for suicidal tendencies (Mathers and Loncar, 2006). A major depressive disorder is a significant medical condition that has adverse effects on emotions, thoughts, and behaviors. Depression induces feelings of sadness and a diminished interest in previously enjoyable activities. This condition can result in various emotional and physical challenges, impacting one's ability to perform effectively both in the workplace and at home (APA, 2020). Currently, only approximately 20% of those afflicted receive necessary early intervention, with a significant proportion of mental health expenditures allocated to the maintenance of psychiatric institutions as opposed to activities encompassing detection, prevention, and recovery (Renteria-Rodriguez, 2018). Given these circumstances, there exists an urgent need to design effective approaches for the early detection of depression, aiming to avoid harm to individuals suffering from this condition.

The ubiquity of social media data has paved the way for data-driven research in the field of mental health analysis (Ríssola et al., 2021; Skaik and Inkpen, 2020). A significant portion of individuals conduct the bulk of their social interactions within the digital realm crafted by social media platforms such as Facebook, Twitter, Reddit, and Instagram. Nowadays, researchers have access to extensive corpora of online dialogues on diverse topics. This wealth of data holds particular significance in medicine, where progress in our understanding of mental health could directly contribute to life-saving quality-of-life measures and improvements.

Exploiting public interactions offers a valuable avenue for comprehending depression, thereby amplifying the potential to identify individuals displaying depressive indicators and facilitating professional intervention (Ríssola et al., 2021; Crestani

Proceedings of the 9th Workshop on Computational Linguistics and Clinical Psychology (CLPsych 2024), pages 12–22
March 21, 2024

et al., 2022a). Diverse techniques rooted in Natural Language Processing (NLP), Text Classification (TC), and Information Retrieval (IR) have been employed to discern signs of depression, with a particular focus on linguistic and sentiment analysis (Crestani et al., 2022b). However, most of the existing studies have been confined to distinguishing between a depression group and a control group (two-class classification) and provide no further explanation or explicit standardized signs that health professionals can analyze. Furthermore, conventional strategies have demonstrated their effectiveness in detecting depressive individuals based on their textual interactions (Velupillai et al., 2019), but they heavily rely on the intricate process of feature engineering (e.g., by extracting optimal user attributes that reflect the subject's feelings and psychological state). However, the NLP landscape has radically evolved in recent years, with the ascent of Large Language Models (LLMs). New models, such as chatGPT, have gained immense popularity due to their capacity to deliver zero-shot and few-shot predictions across diverse tasks[1]. This ability stems from the LLMs' augmented scale, with a huge number of parameters that inherently empower them to encapsulate the subtleties inherent in massive amounts of textual data. This becomes particularly pivotal when confronting linguistic data, given the inherent variance in word significance dependent on the context. To properly exploit current LLMs to support BDI-based screening, the parametric knowledge of the LLM, which provides a sophisticated understanding of human language, needs to be enriched with user-specific interactions related to standardized depression symptoms. This is precisely the main goal of our research. More specifically, this study designs effective search strategies to mine BDI-biased summaries from the users' posting history and proposes the utilization of LLMs for quantifying levels of depression.

Our approach can be regarded as a retrieval-then-read method (Zhu et al., 2021) that augments the LLM knowledge with personalized BDI-biased summaries built for each category of the BDI-II questionnaire. BDI (Beck et al., 1961) is a recognized psychological instrument designed to assess the manifestation of 21 depressive symptoms, such as sadness, pessimism, or loss of energy. We can summarize our contributions as follows:

1. We extract relevant sentences related to different topics of depression to measure the severity of signs of depression among social media users.
2. We explore the use of summaries for each group of sentences to provide an estimated answer to each question in the BDI questionnaire.
3. We empirically evaluate the proposed model and provide quantitative and qualitative evidence of its robustness for the evaluation of depression levels. This includes a comparison against a human expert (trained psychologist), who was also presented with the BDI-biased summaries.

2 Related Work

The examination of public mental health via social media has experienced significant growth in recent years (Ríssola et al., 2021; Skaik and Inkpen, 2020; Guntuku et al., 2017). Recent research has focused on depressive symptom detection to enhance mental health models, highlighting their potential to enhance performance, general applicability, and interpretability (Crestani et al., 2022a; Parapar et al., 2023). For instance, in Nguyen et al. (2022), the authors introduced methods for identifying depression that incorporate various levels of constraints based on the symptoms outlined in the PHQ9 questionnaire, a tool used by clinicians for screening depression. Their experiments, conducted across three social media datasets, revealed that their model can adapt to unfamiliar data, surpassing a conventional BERT-based approach. Another study (Pérez et al., 2022a) presented an approach for automatically gauging the severity of depression in social media users. This research team tackled the task of quantifying the intensity of depression indicators and explored using neural language models to capture different facets of a user's writings. They presented two alternative methodologies to assess the sensitivity of symptoms in terms of the user's willingness to openly discuss them. The first method relies on global language patterns from the user's posts, while the second method seeks direct mentions of symptom-related concerns. Both techniques led to automatic estimates of the overall BDI-II score. Furthermore, in Pérez et al. (2022b), an efficient semantic pipeline was introduced for evaluating depression severity

[1]OpenAI. (2023). chatGPT. https://chat.openai.com/chat

in individuals based on their social media content. The authors selected a sample of user sentences to create semantic rankings. The approach was supported by a reference index of training sentences that correspond to depressive symptoms and severity levels. Subsequently, they employed the sentences derived from these rankings as evidence for predicting the severity of symptoms in users.

In a different direction, Zhang et al. (2022) introduced a method for screening risky posts guided by psychiatric scales. This method identified posts that exhibit risk factors associated with the dimensions outlined in clinical depression scales, providing a basis for a comprehensible diagnosis. To enhance the transparency of predictions, this team proposed a Hierarchical Attentional Network integrated with BERT, known as HAN-BERT.

In recent years, with the proliferation of Large Language Models (LLMs), there has been a response to the limitations observed in psychological knowledge by developing specialized language models that offer improved accuracy in providing psychological advice (Li et al., 2023). Such endeavors have sparked our interest in exploring the potential of LLMs to respond to questionnaires related to depression symptoms and compare them with the assessment done by an expert psychologist. Our approach can be seen as a novel application of retrieve-then-read methods for LLMs (Nishida et al., 2018; Izacard and Grave, 2021), where the parametric LLM model is conditioned by personalized summaries for each user.

3 Proposed Approach

The objective of this research consists of estimating the level of depression from a thread of users' posts (Losada et al., 2019). Additionally, we contrast our estimates with the answers provided by an expert psychologist, who is also presented with user-level evidence mined from social media. To that end, we summarize the post history of each user, and our model estimates the response to each BDI item based on the evidence found in BDI-specific summaries. The approach consists of three main steps:

1. Extraction of relevant sentences for each of the 21 topics of the BDI questionnaire.

2. Generation of a BDI-biased summary from each group of sentences.

3. Estimation of the response to each BDI question using a large language model.

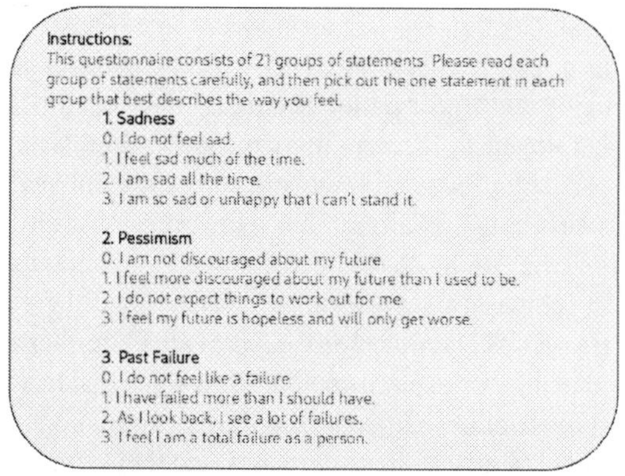

Figure 1: Beck's Depression Inventory. This questionnaire consists of 21 items related to various symptoms of depression. The figure shows three examples.

The BDI (Beck et al., 1961) consists of a series of multiple-choice questions or statements about various symptoms and attitudes related to depression (see Figure 1). Respondents are asked to select the statement that best describes their feelings. Each item in the BDI is assigned a score, ranging from 0 to 3, with higher scores indicating more severe symptoms[2]. An overall depression score is obtained by summing the scores for all items. The higher the total score, the more severe the depression is considered to be. This psychometric assessment has been widely employed as a dependable method for gathering high-quality data from various sources, including online sources (Choudhury et al., 2013; Guntuku et al., 2017).

3.1 Extraction of relevant sentences for each BDI item

The first step involves the extraction of relevant sentences for each topic in the BDI questionnaire. First, we convert each question of the BDI to an embedding representation using sentenceBERT (Reimers and Gurevych, 2019), a modification of the pre-trained BERT that yields semantically meaningful sentence embeddings. For each topic, we take the possible responses and the title of the BDI item to create embedding representations. The objective is to create a dictionary of embeddings that represents the BDI questionnaire.

For each social media user, we segment his thread of publications and measure the similarity between the user's sentences and the embeddings

[2]https://www.ismanet.org/doctoryourspirit/pdfs/Beck-Depression-Inventory-BDI.pdf

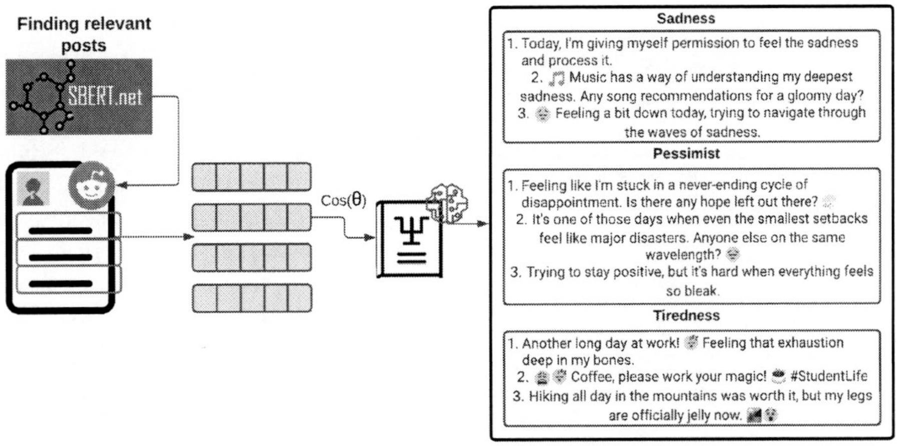

Figure 2: Searching for relevant sentences in the user's history. The sentences are grouped by BDI topic and the resulting set of sentences might contain sentences with different polarity.

in the dictionary by applying cosine similarity between each pair of vectors.

Finally, to select candidate sentences for each BDI topic, we empirically establish a threshold of 0.4 and choose the sentences whose similarity is higher than this threshold. A user's sentence is selected for the BDI item as long as it is similar to at least one of the embeddings in the BDI item's group. Figure 2 illustrates this selection process. We can see how the method seeks sentences that are on-topic concerning each BDI item. Note that it can select on-topic sentences with a negative or positive valence. For example, the sentence "Hiking all day in the mountains was worth it, but my legs are officially jelly now" is relevant to tiredness but, in this case, describes a pleasing activity done outdoors.

3.2 Generating summaries of the extracted sentences

The next step is to create a summary for each group of selected sentences. The idea is to present the LLM with condensed information for each BDI item. LLMs typically have a token input limit and, thus, we cannot feed them with an arbitrarily large sequence of sentences. Restricting the analysis to succinct summaries is also beneficial for reducing the effort required from the human psychologist in her assessment.

For summarization, we used BART, a denoising autoencoder for sequence-to-sequence models (Lewis et al., 2020). It uses a standard Transformer-based architecture, which can be seen as a generalization of both BERT (due to the bidirectional encoder) and GPT (with the left-to-right decoder). More specifically, we employed the model that was obtained by fine-tuning BART on the SAMSum dataset[3]. The SAMSum dataset contains about 16k messenger-like conversations and summaries. The conversations were created and written down by linguists fluent in English. The style and register are diversified, and conversations could be informal, semi-formal, or formal, and they may contain slang words, emoticons, and typos. This represents a language style that is similar to the one in Reddit publications. With the trained model, for each topic of the BDI, we fed the group of relevant posts to BART and generated a summary.

3.3 Estimating the responses of the BDI questionnaire

The last step consists of answering the BDI questionnaire for each user using the generated summaries. To that end, we prompted chatGPT (for these experiments we used the GPT, versions 3.5-turbo-0613 and 4) with the summary and proper instructions. For each user, the prompted questions were processed within a continuous chat. The answer to each BDI question was obtained by parsing the LLM's output. In Figure 3, we can see two examples of these prompts. chatGPT is instructed to select the option that best describes the user's text (the corresponding summary). The options are the answers to each topic within the BDI, ranging from 0 to 3. For illustrative purposes, we added to the figure the answer the user selected for that question (marked with a blue arrow). At the bottom, we can

[3]https://huggingface.co/datasets/samsum

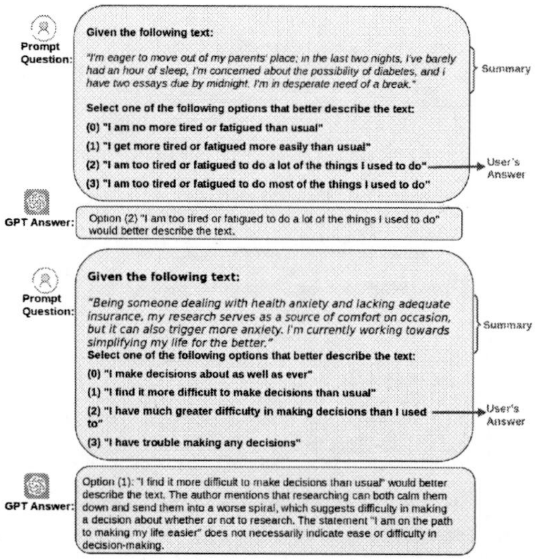

Figure 3: Prompt questions examples. The text represents the summary of the posts and the blue arrow is the answer selected by the user.

also see the answer predicted by chatGPT and a description of why the model chose that answer. We can see that the model can generally approximate the answers by having the right context in the summary. If the model provided an answer that was not in the range of the possible responses then the output was taken as 0, which represents the absence of negative signs for the corresponding BDI item.

Additionally, to contrast the automatic estimates and performance of the large language model, we also gave the summaries to an expert in the field and asked her to provide her estimated responses to the questionnaires.

4 Experimental Settings

4.1 Data collections

For evaluation, we employed the data sets from the eRisk 2019-2021 evaluation tasks (Losada et al., 2019, 2020; Parapar et al., 2021) on measuring the severity of the signs of depression. The task consists of estimating the level of the 21 standardized depression symptoms based on a thread of user posts. The collection contains a self-report BDI inventory filled by each user in the collection and the users' publications on Reddit. The 2019 dataset consists of 20 users, while 2020 and 2021 have 70 and 80 users respectively. This dataset contains an average number of posts per user of 518 and an average number of words for each post of 40. To select the sample, the creators of these datasets asked online users (particularly within certain mental health subreddits) to fill out the BDI questionnaire and to give consent to analyze their public interactions. These BDI questionnaires act as the ground truth to contrast the questionnaires filled by the system or by the health expert.

Pre-processing: We performed a simple pre-processing on the user-generated texts by lowercasing all words and removing special characters like URLs, emoticons, and hashtags.

4.2 Metrics

Given the set of test users, their real BDI questionnaires and the automatic BDI questionnaires, the following effectiveness measures were calculated:

Average Hit Rate (AHR): Hit Rate (HR) is a rigorous metric that calculates the proportion of the 21 instances in which the automated questionnaire provides identical answers to those in the actual questionnaire. For instance, if an automated questionnaire yields 5 matches, the HR would be 5/21.

Average Closeness Rate (ACR): The Closeness Rate (CR) comes into play because the BDI responses represent an ordinal scale. If the actual user's response was "0" and a system responds with "3" then it should incur a more significant penalty compared to a system that responds with "1". For each question, the CR calculates the absolute difference (ad) between the actual and automated responses (e.g., $ad = 3$ for S1 and $ad = 1$ for S2), subsequently transforming this absolute difference into an effectiveness score using the formula: $CR = (mad - ad)/mad$. Here, mad represents the maximum absolute difference, the total count of potential answers minus one.

Average Difference in Overall Depression Levels (ADODL): While the preceding metrics evaluate the systems' capability to respond to each question in the BDI survey, the difference in overall depression level (DODL) takes a different approach. It does not focus on question-specific matches or disparities. Instead, it calculates the cumulative depression level (sum of all responses) for both the authentic and automated questionnaires. Next, it determines the absolute difference ($ad\_overall$) between the two depression scores. The overall depression score is between 0 and 63 and, thus, DODL is obtained as a normalized score in [0,1] as follows: $DODL = (63 - ad\_overall)/63$.

Depression Category Hit Rate (DCHR): In Psychology, it is standard practice to organize the overall depression scores into the following categories: Minimal Depression (depression levels 0-9), Mild Depression (depression levels 10-18), Moderate Depression (depression levels 19-29), and Severe Depression (depression levels 30-63). The final metric of effectiveness involves calculating the proportion of test users where the automated questionnaire assigned a depression category that matched the category determined by the actual questionnaire. These four metrics were the official metrics in the eRisk task described above and, thus, we adopted them to validate our summarization-based solution.

4.3 Alternative estimates

As alternative estimates of the level of severity of each depression symptom, we adopted the following strategies (all variants, including the human expert, received each BDI summary and the target question as input):

Human Expert: As argued above, we compare the model's predictions with an expert's prediction that reads the same sequence of BDI-biased summaries. The expert is a psychologist who was presented with the summaries and was asked to fill in the response to each BDI item. This alternative estimation helps to measure how similar the answers of the system and the human (e.g., using Cohen's kappa score).

T5: It is a well-known model that incorporates an encoder and a decoder, and it was pre-trained on a diverse set of data, including both unsupervised and supervised tasks (Raffel et al., 2020). Each task was transformed into a text-to-text format to fit with the model's structure. This model was also fine-tuned on QASC for question answering (via sentence composition) downstream tasks.

BERT-SQuAD: BERT large model[4] that was fine-tuned on the SQuAD dataset (Rajpurkar et al., 2016) for question answering.

5 Evaluation

Table 1 shows the results of our approach and all baseline methods over the three datasets. It includes two variants of chatGPT (versions 3.5 & 4), the alternative automatic methods (BERT-SQuAD and T5), and the expert's evaluation. All variants used the same summaries to respond to the BDI questions. Note that all metrics range in $[0, 1]$ and the higher the better.

One noteworthy observation is that both variants of ChatGPT obtained better results than the other automatic models when it came to fine-grained metrics that compute the effectiveness over individual questions (AHR, ACR). These results highlight how close the answers given by these two models are to the answers provided by the users. The chatGPT models tend to yield high values in the ACR metric. This is an important outcome since ACR focuses on the closeness between the real and automated responses, and a system with high ACR might have some potential to understand the feelings of the individual about the BDI symptom and develop psychological screening tools accordingly. On the other hand, BERT-SQuAD excelled in terms of global metrics (ADODL, DCHR) that focus on the divergence between the overall estimates of depression. It's noteworthy that ChatGPT version 3.5 consistently excels in producing responses that closely align with user input, while, version 4 tends to perform better when evaluated using broader global metrics, possibly owing to its enhanced capacity for generalizing information.

Still, there is much room for improvement in accurately predicting human responses. This is partly due to limited data availability, as there are many BDI topics that are not discussed or disclosed on social media. In any case, it is important to note that some automatic systems were on par with (or superior to) the assessment is done by human experts. In fact, the best automatic systems yielded equivalent performance to the expert psychologist in the fine-grained metrics (AHR and ACR) and better performance in the overall depression estimates (ADODL and DCHR).

In any case, the overall predictions (as reflected by DHCR) do not match those of the real surveys and this suggests that some BDI symptoms are difficult to grasp.

Regarding the time required, the expert took approximately 30 to 42 hours for each dataset (approximately 35 minutes per user). Instead, the LLMs took around 2-3 minutes to answer each user's questions. This signifies a substantial reduction in time, showcasing a pivotal advantage of automated methods that can facilitate the screening processes. By optimizing the extraction and analysis through computational tools, health professionals have the opportunity to allocate their saved time to the most confusing cases or just to review

[4]https://huggingface.co/bert-large-uncased-whole-word-masking-finetuned-squad

Models	AHR	ACR	ADODL	DCHR
eRisk 2019				
T5	0.2619	0.6198	0.7643	0.1000
BERT-SQuAD	0.2714	0.5963	**0.7740**	**0.2833**
chatGPT-3.5	**0.3857**	**0.6675**	0.7278	0.2000
chatGPT-4	0.3404	0.6556	0.7635	0.2000
expert	0.3833	0.6603	0.7270	0.2000
participants (mean)	0.3345	0.6416	0.7454	0.2611
participants (best)	**0.4143**	**0.7127**	**0.8103**	**0.4500**
eRisk 2020				
T5	0.3211	0.6578	0.7857	0.2143
BERT-SQuAD	0.3210	0.6325	**0.7947**	**0.2714**
chatGPT-3.5	**0.3748**	**0.6766**	0.7315	0.1857
chatGPT-4	0.3571	0.6728	0.7934	0.2143
expert	0.3694	0.6667	0.7082	0.1571
participants (mean)	0.3432	0.6688	0.7963	0.2807
participants (best)	**0.3830**	**0.6941**	**0.8315**	**0.3571**
eRisk 2021				
T5	0.2369	0.6008	**0.7377**	**0.2125**
BERT-SQuAD	0.2155	0.5605	0.7351	0.2000
chatGPT-3.5	**0.2714**	**0.6137**	0.6704	0.1375
chatGPT-4	0.2649	0.6014	0.7117	0.1125
expert	0.2500	0.5851	0.6161	0.075
participants (mean)	0.3107	0.6555	0.7586	0.2196
participants (best)	**0.3536**	**0.7317**	**0.8359**	**0.4125**

Table 1: Effectiveness results for the three datasets and comparison with the participants in the eRisk shared-task. We bold the best result of our models and participants of each year for an easier comparison.

the output of the LLMs.

Last, we have done an additional comparison between the predictions generated by the chatGPT 3.5 model and those of the domain expert. This comparison allows us to understand the degree of similarity between the respective responses. To that end, we employed Cohen's kappa score. The purpose is to provide insights into the model's performance by examining its alignment with human expertise across the entire range of users. These scores consistently hover around 0.28 for the 2019 and 2020 datasets and 0.0648 for 2021. This value, although modest, signifies a fair level of agreement between our model's predictions and those of the expert. In the 2021 dataset, we observe a low level of agreement; however, it is noteworthy that even in this collection the automated systems consistently outperformed the experts in predicting symptoms. These agreement levels underscore the model's capability to generate responses that align with expert judgments, demonstrating its reliability and effectiveness in providing valuable insights. While the agreement is not high, the model's performance is promising, considering the inherent complexity of the task at hand. These findings reinforce the model's potential to assist decision-making in the mental health domain.

Comparison against eRisk participants: To put these results in perspective, Table 1 also presents a comprehensive comparison between the models and the participants in the shared tasks of severity estimation in the eRisk editions of 2019, 2020, and 2021. Overall, our model demonstrates a good level of performance, outperforming the average results obtained in 2 out of 3 datasets. However, the top-performing participants achieved higher scores. This indicates that there is potential for enhancing our models' capabilities further. It is essential to mention that the participants performed extensive feature engineering and worked from the entire thread of user publications. In our study, this luxury was not extended to the LLMs or the human. In fact, it would be infeasible to ask the expert psychologist to read the entire history of posts, which

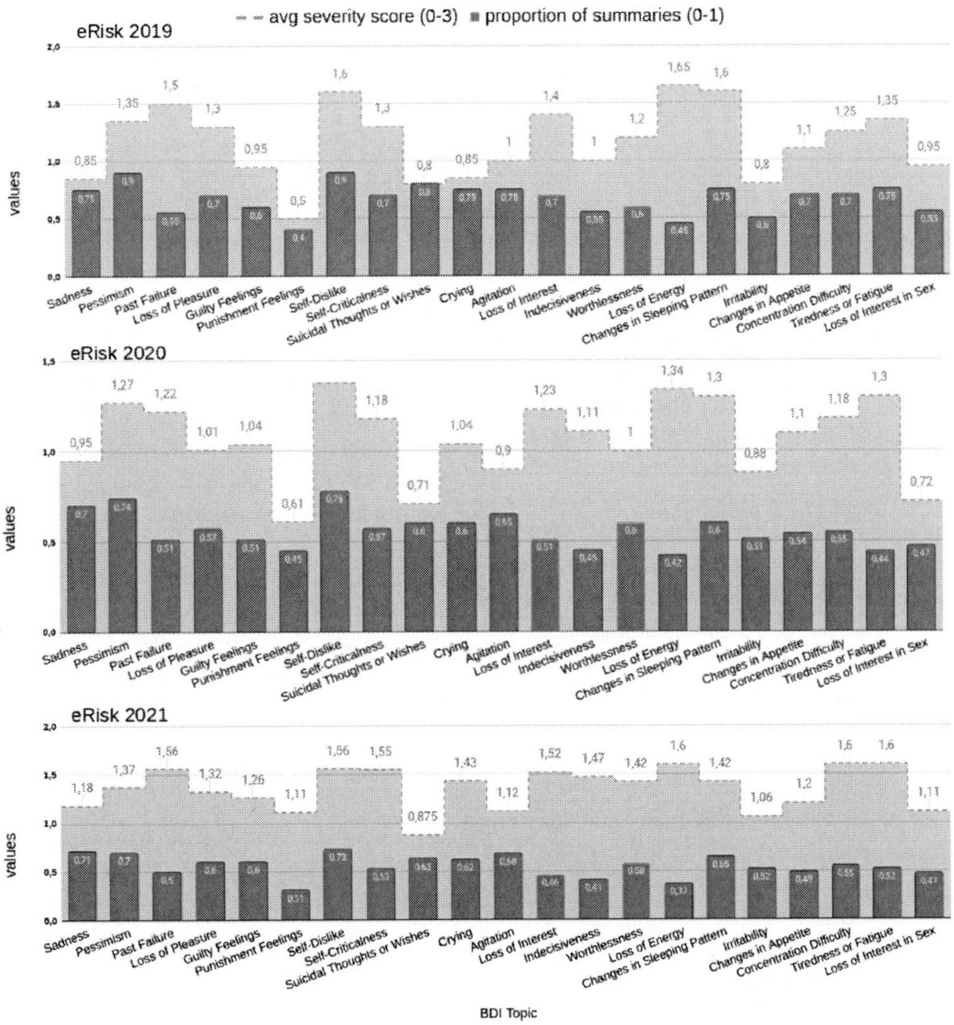

Figure 4: The X-axis represents the 21 BDI topics. The red bars show the average severity [0,3] of the corresponding symptom (as reflected in the ground truth) while the blue bars show the proportion of users [0,1] that had a non-empty summary for the symptom.

consists of thousands of publications. This human limitation motivates our work to employ advanced mining tools and implement search techniques that target adequate samples or key representative extracts, thus, summarizing the main themes within the users' history.

Nonetheless, this also opens up opportunities for refining our model's architecture and incorporating additional techniques to bridge the gap between its current performance and that of the most effective eRisk systems.

6 Analysis and Discussion

It is important to assess the extent to which the BDI topics have relevant sentences and the individual impact of BDI questions on the overall depression score. To that end, we analyze here the presence of relevant sentences for each BDI topic and plot it against the average rating in the ground truth (see Figure 4). The blue bars represent the proportion of users that had at least one relevant sentence for the corresponding topic (i.e. a non-empty summary). For instance, in 2019, for the topic of 'sadness', only 75% of the users had at least one related sentence. The red bars represent the average severity score provided by the users.

Certain themes, such as pessimism and self-dislike, are prominent (consistently provide relevant sentences for the majority of users) and tend to receive higher severity scores compared to other

BDI symptoms. This suggests a correspondence between the real feelings of these users and their social media activity (i.e., they tend to disclose thoughts about these symptoms). Other topics, such as loss of energy or punishment, have fewer relevant sentences (less than half of the users have at least one relevant sentence for these topics). Interestingly, in the case of energy loss, users provided high severity estimates, but the model could not find much evidence. This highlights a significant barrier in screening depression symptoms. If the model cannot find pertinent information on these topics then it can hardly supply a reliable estimate. In those cases, we assumed a rating of 0 and, thus, the models might be underestimating the state of the individual. In the future, it will be interesting to study other alternatives, such as estimating the overall depression scores based on partially filled questionnaires or estimating the missing BDI symptoms based on the most similar symptoms.

7 Conclusions and Future Work

In this study, we address a critical global concern, the prevalence of depression. We are committed to inducing a positive impact on automated methods for depression screening. To that end, we need a deeper understanding of depression symptoms and more evidence of how the symptoms reflect on social media. We have presented a comprehensive approach that involves extracting BDI-biased summaries from users' publications and exploiting different large language models to estimate the responses of those users to the Beck Depression Inventory. Our evaluation across various depression datasets yielded promising results, showcasing our method's potential to contribute to the understanding and assessment of depression. Some of the proposed variants compete favorably with state-of-the-art methods and expert human evaluations. This work represents a valuable step forward in leveraging the power of data to address mental health challenges on a broader scale. In future work, we want to explore the application of other lexical resources that are even more specialized for the task of extraction of relevant sentences, as well as the usage of clinical data to train more specialized language models.

Furthermore, the primary focus of our work revolves around leveraging these summaries. Specifically, our interest lies in the potential application of this tool to extract valuable linguistic indicators. This application could be useful in enhancing psychologists' understanding of how depression manifests in social media contexts. By delving into linguistic patterns and cues from user-generated content we could offer valuable insights that contribute to the refinement of psychologists' working knowledge. We also are interested in expanding this study to different languages, since most of the work related to mental disorders has focused on English.

Finally, this study represents a preliminary exploration but we believe that the ability to model user behavior through social media analysis offers promising prospects for the development of future wellness-oriented technologies. This innovative technology has the potential to function as a preemptive warning system, conducting extensive analyses and delivering pertinent information concerning mental health without compromising user privacy. For example, we could design local, regional, or national estimates of the prevalence of multiple depression symptoms, allowing authorities to make informed decisions about professional assistance, emotional support campaigns, and so forth. Under this context, users should always retain autonomy in choosing to have access to certain recommendations or preemptive measures, empowering them to make informed decisions about their well-being.

Ethic Statement and Impact

Examining social media content raises potential privacy and ethical concerns. This research is exempt from IRB review because we only experimented with existing publicly available collections and did not contact any social media users. The datasets only contain public user interactions and we have diligently adhered to the terms of use and user agreements of these collections. Moreover, these collections are anonymized. While public posts may be freely available to anyone, individuals may not intend for them to have a broad audience. We have therefore paraphrased the extracts shown in this paper. With this research, we also want to make a positive impact on society, and one significant contribution we may provide is to better understand depression. Specifically, we want to learn information that will aid mental health diagnosis and help those challenged by mental illness.

Limitations

It is essential to acknowledge certain constraints inherent to this study. Notably, the research is observational, lacking access to personal and psychological data typically incorporated in risk assessment investigations. Furthermore, an unavoidable bias stems from the data source (only users who are exposed to social media and, specifically, to Reddit were included in the study). Segments of the population, such as elderly people or individuals who consciously abstain from maintaining online accounts or opt to keep their profiles private, cannot be monitored.

Acknowledgements

The second author thanks the financial support supplied by the Consellería de Cultura, Educación, Formación Profesional e Universidades (accreditation 2019-2022 ED431G/01, ED431B 2022/33) and the European Regional Development Fund, which acknowledges the CITIC Research Center in ICT of the University of A Coruña as a Research Center of the Galician University System and the project PID2022-137061OB-C21 (Ministerio de Ciencia e Innovación, Agencia Estatal de Investigación, Proyectos de Generación de Conocimiento; supported by the European Regional Development Fund).

The first and third authors thank: i) the financial support supplied by the Consellería de Cultura, Educación, Formación Profesional e Universidades (accreditation 2019-2022 ED431G-2019/04, ED431C 2022/19) and the European Regional Development Fund, which acknowledges the CiTIUS-Research Center in Intelligent Technologies of the University of Santiago de Compostela as a Research Center of the Galician University System, and ii) the financial support supplied by project PID2022-137061OB-C22 (Ministerio de Ciencia e Innovación, Agencia Estatal de Investigación, Proyectos de Generación de Conocimiento; supported by the European Regional Development Fund).

The third author thanks the financial support obtained from project SUBV23/00002 (Ministerio de Consumo, Subdirección General de Regulación del Juego).

The authors also thank the funding of project PLEC2021-007662 (MCIN/AEI/10.13039/501100011033, Ministerio de Ciencia e Innovación, Agencia Estatal de Investigación, Plan de Recuperación, Transformación y Resiliencia, Unión Europea-Next Generation EU).

References

American Psychiatric Association APA. 2020. What is depression?

Aaron Beck, C.H. Ward, M. Mendelson, J. Mock, and J. Erbaugh. 1961. An inventory for measuring depression. *Arch Gen Psychiatry*.

Munmun De Choudhury, Michael Gamon, Scott Counts, and Eric Horvitz. 2013. Predicting depression via social media. In *Proceedings of the Seventh International Conference on Weblogs and Social Media, ICWSM 2013, Cambridge, USA*.

Fabio Crestani, David E. Losada, and Javier Parapar. 2022a. *Early Detection of Mental Health Disorders by Social Media Monitoring: The First Five Years of the eRisk Project*. Springer Verlag, Englewood Cliffs, NJ.

Fabio Crestani, David E Losada, and Javier Parapar. 2022b. *Early Detection of Mental Health Disorders by Social Media Monitoring: The First Five Years of the ERisk Project*, volume 1018. Springer Nature.

Sharath Chandra Guntuku, David B Yaden, Margaret L Kern, Lyle H Ungar, and Johannes C Eichstaedt. 2017. Detecting depression and mental illness on social media: an integrative review. *Current Opinion in Behavioral Sciences*, 18:43–49.

Gautier Izacard and Edouard Grave. 2021. Leveraging passage retrieval with generative models for open domain question answering. In *Proceedings of the 16th Conference of the European Chapter of the Association for Computational Linguistics: Main Volume*, pages 874–880, Online. Association for Computational Linguistics.

Ronald C Kessler, Evelyn J Bromet, Victoria Shahly Peter de Jonge, and Marsha. 2017. The burden of depressive illness. *Public Health Perspectives on Depressive Disorders*.

Mike Lewis, Yinhan Liu, Naman Goyal, Marjan Ghazvininejad, Abdelrahman Mohamed, Omer Levy, Veselin Stoyanov, and Luke Zettlemoyer. 2020. BART: Denoising sequence-to-sequence pre-training for natural language generation, translation, and comprehension. In *Proceedings of the 58th Annual Meeting of the Association for Computational Linguistics*, pages 7871–7880, Online. Association for Computational Linguistics.

Yunxiang Li, Zihan Li, Kai Zhang, Ruilong Dan, Steve Jiang, and You Zhang. 2023. Chatdoctor: A medical chat model fine-tuned on a large language model meta-ai (llama) using medical domain knowledge. *Cureus*, 15(6).

David E. Losada, Fabio Crestani, and Javier Parapar. 2019. Overview of erisk 2019 early risk prediction on the internet. In *Experimental IR Meets Multilinguality, Multimodality, and Interaction*, pages 340–357, Cham. Springer International Publishing.

David E. Losada, Fabio Crestani, and Javier Parapar. 2020. Overview of erisk 2020: Early risk prediction on the internet. In *Experimental IR Meets Multilinguality, Multimodality, and Interaction*, pages 272–287, Cham. Springer International Publishing.

Colin D Mathers and Dejan Loncar. 2006. Projections of global mortality and burden of disease from 2002 to 2030. *PLOS Medicine, Public Library of Science*, pages 1–20.

Thong Nguyen, Andrew Yates, Ayah Zirikly, Bart Desmet, and Arman Cohan. 2022. Improving the generalizability of depression detection by leveraging clinical questionnaires. In *Proceedings of the 60th Annual Meeting of the Association for Computational Linguistics (Volume 1: Long Papers)*, pages 8446–8459, Dublin, Ireland. Association for Computational Linguistics.

Kyosuke Nishida, Itsumi Saito, Atsushi Otsuka, Hisako Asano, and Junji Tomita. 2018. Retrieve-and-read: Multi-task learning of information retrieval and reading comprehension. In *Proceedings of the 27th ACM International Conference on Information and Knowledge Management*, CIKM '18, page 647–656, New York, NY, USA. Association for Computing Machinery.

Javier Parapar, Patricia Martín-Rodilla, David E. Losada, and Fabio Crestani. 2021. Overview of erisk 2021: Early risk prediction on the internet. In *Experimental IR Meets Multilinguality, Multimodality, and Interaction*, pages 324–344, Cham. Springer International Publishing.

Javier Parapar, Patricia Martín-Rodilla, David E. Losada, and Fabio Crestani. 2023. Overview of erisk 2023: Early risk prediction on the internet. In *Experimental IR Meets Multilinguality, Multimodality, and Interaction*, pages 294–315, Cham. Springer Nature Switzerland.

Anxo Pérez, Javier Parapar, and Álvaro Barreiro. 2022a. Automatic depression score estimation with word embedding models. *Artificial Intelligence in Medicine*, 132:102380.

Anxo Pérez, Neha Warikoo, Kexin Wang, Javier Parapar, and Iryna Gurevych. 2022b. Semantic similarity models for depression severity estimation. In *Proceedings of the 2023 Conference on Empirical Methods in Natural Language Processing, EMNLP 2023, Singapore, December 6-10, 2023*, pages 16104–16118.

Colin Raffel, Noam Shazeer, Adam Roberts, Katherine Lee, Sharan Narang, Michael Matena, Yanqi Zhou, Wei Li, and Peter J. Liu. 2020. Exploring the limits of transfer learning with a unified text-to-text transformer. *Journal of Machine Learning Research*, 21(140):1–67.

Pranav Rajpurkar, Jian Zhang, Konstantin Lopyrev, and Percy Liang. 2016. SQuAD: 100,000+ Questions for Machine Comprehension of Text. *arXiv e-prints*, page arXiv:1606.05250.

Nils Reimers and Iryna Gurevych. 2019. Sentence-bert: Sentence embeddings using siamese bert-networks. In *Proceedings of the 2019 Conference on Empirical Methods in Natural Language Processing*. Association for Computational Linguistics.

Miguel Enrique Renteria-Rodriguez. 2018. Salud mental en mexico. *NOTA-INCyTU NÚMERO 007.*

Esteban A. Ríssola, David E. Losada, and Fabio Crestani. 2021. A survey of computational methods for online mental state assessment on social media. *ACM Trans. Comput. Healthcare*, 2(2).

Ruba Skaik and Diana Inkpen. 2020. Using social media for mental health surveillance: A review. *ACM Comput. Surv.*, 53(6).

Sumithra Velupillai, Gergö Hadlaczky, Genevieve M. Gorrell, Nomi Werbeloff, Dong Nguyen, Rashmi Patel, Daniel Leightley, Johnny Downs, Matthew Hotopf, and Rina Dutta. 2019. Risk assessment tools and data-driven approaches for predicting and preventing suicidal behavior. *Frontiers in Psychiatry*, 10.

Zhiling Zhang, Siyuan Chen, Mengyue Wu, and Ke Zhu. 2022. Psychiatric scale guided risky post screening for early detection of depression. In *International Joint Conference on Artificial Intelligence.*

Fengbin Zhu, Wenqiang Lei, Chao Wang, Jianming Zheng, Soujanya Poria, and Tat-Seng Chua. 2021. Retrieving and reading: A comprehensive survey on open-domain question answering. *CoRR*, abs/2101.00774.

How Can Client Motivational Language Inform Psychotherapy Agents?

Van Hoang[1,2] and **Eoin Rogers**[1] and **Robert Ross**[1,2]
[1]School of Computer Science, Technological University Dublin
[2]ML-Labs, SFI Centre for Research Training in Machine Learning, Ireland
van.hoang@tudublin.ie, eoin.rogers@tudublin.ie, robert.ross@tudublin.ie

Abstract

Within Motivational Interviewing (MI), client utterances are coded as for or against a certain behaviour change, along with commitment strength; this is essential to ensure therapists soften rather than persisting goal-related actions in the face of resistance. Prior works in MI agents have been scripted or semi-scripted, limiting users' natural language expressions. With the aim of automating the MI interactions, we propose and explore the task of automated identification of client motivational language. Employing Large Language Models (LLMs), we compare in-context learning (ICL) and instruction fine-tuning (IFT) with varying training sizes for this identification task. Our experiments show that both approaches can learn under low-resourced settings. Our results demonstrate that IFT, though cheaper, is more stable to prompt choice, and yields better performance with more data. Given the detected motivation, we further present an approach to the analysis of therapists' strategies for balancing building rapport with clients with advancing the treatment plan. A framework of MI agents is developed using insights from the data and the psychotherapy literature.

1 Introduction

Prior studies in psychotherapy in NLP have focused on understanding conversational strategies for better counselling outcomes (Althoff et al., 2016; Pérez-Rosas et al., 2016, 2019; Zhang and Danescu-Niculescu-Mizil, 2020). However, few works utilise client modelling to inform the counselling strategies (Li et al., 2023). Resistance to social influence is a well-known phenomenon in psychology. In therapies, resistance proves to be a serious issue, limiting its effectiveness (Westra and Norouzian, 2018). Understanding client motivational language during therapy helps explain up to 35% in variance of treatment outcomes in psychotherapy (Lombardi et al., 2014; Poulin et al., 2019). Li et al. (2023) propose a data-driven annotation framework of clients' negative and positive reactions in therapies. Their results suggest the complexities of the task. For example, negative reactions can be expressed via showing confusions, shifting topics, and giving sarcastic answers. Each category can be further considered a separate task, and thus, learning them all jointly in one model is challenging. Our work instead adopts the coding scheme from Motivational Interviewing (MI). MI tailors the therapeutic interventions based on the individuals' motivational level using the transtheoretical model of stages of changes (Prochaska and Velicer, 1997).

MI is an evidence-based client-centred approach to strengthen one's motivations for behaviour change (Miller and Rollnick, 2023). Observably, in the context of Cognitive Behavioral Therapy (CBT), if the client language shows ambivalence, the therapists are advised to adopt MI instead of persisting and thus risking alliance ruptures, which eventually leads to treatment dropout (Westra and Norouzian, 2018; Ewbank et al., 2021). Similarly, Forman et al. (2022) find MI is likely to backfire if the client already shows willingness to change early in the session, suggesting personalised interventions at different levels of motivation.

The task of predicting client motivational language can be divided into two subtasks. The first one, called the `type` task, is to detect the direction of motivation: whether the client is willing to change or not. The other one, called the `strength` task, is to detect the commitment level: if the client is willing to change or still shows resistance, how strong do they hold such belief?

Recently, Large Language Models (LLMs) have demonstrated impressive capabilities on learning with limited data (Brown et al., 2020; Chung et al., 2022; Touvron et al., 2023). Two popular paradigms of LLM usage are via in-context learning (ICL) (Dong et al., 2023) and instruction

Proceedings of the 9th Workshop on Computational Linguistics and Clinical Psychology (CLPsych 2024), pages 23–40
March 21, 2024 ©2024 Association for Computational Linguistics

fine-tuning (IFT) (Zhang et al., 2023). Using ICL, the models' weights are kept frozen: no training stage takes place. Inference is performed given an instruction with a few or no examples. In contrast, IFT refers to fine-tuning the base models using instruction data and adapts the weights to the downstream tasks.

In this paper, we first detect the types and strength of client motivational language. Our experiments utilise the AnnoMI (Wu et al., 2023) dataset, consisting of MI dialogues annotated with the types of client language, but not the strength. Using MI Skill Code (Miller et al., 2003; Amrhein et al., 2008), we obtain 178 examples with strength annotations, making the second task a low-resourced one. With varying training samples, we compare ICL and IFT, showing that both can perform under low-resourced setting. Due to the difficulties in optimising the prompts, IFT is arguably a better and cheaper paradigm and has proven its capabilities over ICL in few-shot learning (Liu et al., 2022; Schick and Schütze, 2022; Logan IV et al., 2022). Our analysis further reveals that ICL is, however, preferable to IFT when the training data is heavily imbalanced as ICL can exploit the massive underlying knowledge of LLMs to solve the task. After obtaining the labels, we calculate the motivational levels for client utterances in AnnoMI as well as the distribution of next-turn therapist behaviours given the current clients' motivation.[1]

Our contributions are two-fold. First, we propose the task of detecting client motivational language. Previous works in classifying MI codes (Tavabi et al., 2020; Nakano et al., 2022) focus on the `type` task only (i.e., the direction of motivation). Instead, we combine it with the `strength` task (i.e., the commitment level) to give us a better estimate of the client motivational level. To the best of our knowledge, we are the first in NLP to adopt verbal commitment expressions to understand speakers' motivation in psychotherapy. Second, we demonstrate how the detected motivation can be utilised to automate the conversational flow of MI agents. MI agents have been implemented in HRI and health informatics (Pedamallu et al., 2022; Olafsson et al., 2020a) but are either semi- or fully scripted. Our proposed framework illustrates the potential usage of the motivational level to create more proactive agents for targeted therapeutic interactions.

2 Related Work

Detecting Certainty Language: Different linguistic markers of speaker commitment such as belief/factuality (Diab et al., 2009; Prabhakaran et al., 2015; Rudinger et al., 2018), modality (Pyatkin et al., 2021), projection (de MARNEFFE et al., 2019) have been studied by linguistic and NLP community. Expert systems employ uncertainty expressions, or *hedges*, to communicate degrees of belief to the users (Clark, 1990), which arguably facilitates the decision-making processes (Zhou et al., 2023). Additionally, hedges are examined to understand the social power between interlocutors (Prabhakaran et al., 2018), rapport in peer-tutoring (Raphalen et al., 2022), and reviewers' confidence in evaluating scientific papers (Ghosal et al., 2022).

Detecting MI Behaviour Codes: Automatic detection of MI behaviour codes is a popular research topic. As manual annotation is costly and time-consuming, automated methods are expected to assist with training by helping therapists quickly understand the therapy sessions and thus give effective feedback (Tavabi et al., 2020; Nakano et al., 2022). MI behaviour codes have been utilised to assess the quality of not only MI but also CBT sessions (Ewbank et al., 2021; Chen et al., 2021). Linguistic features are the most popular approach (Pérez-Rosas et al., 2017; Cao et al., 2019; Tavabi et al., 2021; Gibson et al., 2022), yet researchers have employed speech (Aswamenakul et al., 2018; Singla et al., 2020; Tavabi et al., 2020) and facial expressions (Nakano et al., 2022) in multimodal systems. Acoustic features, however, are found to contribute little to the prediction. In contrast, integrating both linguistic and facial information is effective in detecting client behaviour codes.

Psychotherapist Agents: Researchers from different fields have studied psychotherapist agents due to their potential to reach a large audience (Cho et al., 2023). Das et al. (2022) fine-tuned GPT-2 on therapy videos to create a psychotherapist bot which can offer emotional support. However, users' feedback reveals a lack of therapeutic interactions. MI agents have been shown to be beneficial to promoting good behaviour change (Shingleton and Palfai, 2016; Pedamallu et al., 2022). The MI conversational flows are all scripted or semi-scripted, however, restricting users' natural language expressions and thus limiting the effectiveness (Galvão Gomes Da Silva et al., 2018; Olafsson et al., 2020b; Park et al., 2019; Brown et al., 2023). Tracking the

[1]The code for our experiments can be found at `https://github.com/VanHoang85/client_motivational_lang`.

user's motivation can inform the agents on different support strategies (Meyer, 2021) . They, unlike us, utilise a more fine-grained annotation on the `type` labels. Similarly, Li et al. (2023) hypothesise to employ a wide range of clients' negative and positive reactions to control the agents' behaviours.

In-Context Learning (ICL): Introduced by Brown et al. (2020), ICL demonstrates the few-shot learning capabilities in which LLMs are given a few examples as context to learn from. However, the choice and the order of the examples can strongly influence model performance, from near state-of-the-art to near mere chance (Zhao et al., 2021). Prior works have offered insights into how to select the most suitable examples (Liu et al., 2021; Su et al., 2023), how to arrange examples in a certain order (Lu et al., 2022), and which aspects of the examples improve performance (Min et al., 2022). Additionally, Su et al. (2023) argue that retrieval-based ICL with wisely-selected demonstrations outperforms FT with varying number of training samples. However, their experiments are conducted with vanilla FT, not instruction FT.

Instruction Fine-tuning (IFT): IFT boosts the LLMs' capabilities to generalise to unseen tasks by fine-tuning the models on data consisting of pairs of `instruction, output` in a supervised manner (Chung et al., 2022; Zhang et al., 2023). While ICL keeps the models' weights frozen, IFT adapts them to the downstream tasks. In both single and multitask settings, instruction-tuned models need only 25% and 6% of training data respectively to achieve comparable performance to models trained on 100% of target data (Gupta et al., 2023). Arguably, IFT is more cost-effective and yields better results than ICL even in low-resourced settings (Schick and Schütze, 2022; Logan IV et al., 2022; Mosbach et al., 2023). However, no selection strategy for examples is explored. Furthermore, their prompt setups include searching for a `verbalizer` to map the models' vocabulary to the labels: for a sentiment analysis task, a `verbalizer` would map the output `Yes` to the label `positive` and `No` to `negative`. Our experiments do not search for the optimal labels to reduce engineering effort and to test the flexibility of IFT with LLMs.

3 Client Language in Psychotherapy

MI is an evidence-based therapeutic approach to strengthen ones' motivations for behaviour change. In MI, commitment to change is viewed as a leading indicator for behaviour change and thus, eliciting verbal commitments from the client is a critical task for therapists (Amrhein et al., 2003; Miller and Rollnick, 2023). MI distinguishes three types of client motivational language, which indicates the direction of intended behaviour. They include "change" (i.e., motivation towards behaviour change), "sustain" (i.e., resistance towards behaviour change), and "neutral" (i.e., no inclination towards any direction).

Figure 1: Two sample dialogues from the `AnnoMI` (Wu et al., 2023) dataset. The upper one shows a strong resistance from the client (i.e., labelled as "sustain" for `type` and "high" for `strength` in our tasks). In the other dialogue, the client is ready to change though still reluctant (i.e., labelled as "change" and "low" respectively).

Motivational language varies in commitment strength (Amrhein et al., 2003), and can be expressed via linguistic markers of certainty (Boulat and Maillat, 2023). Certainty is defined as the subjective degree of confidence one holds about their behaviour (Conner and Norman, 2022). For example, high certainty markers include phrases such as '*Without doubt*", and *"for sure"* while low certainty is indicated via phrases like *"I guess"* and *"I think"*. Two linguistic terms "boosters" and "hedges" are commonly used to refer to high and low certainty markers respectively. Figure 1 illustrates one example of the client showing a strong resistance and another of having reluctance to change.

Broader research in psychotherapy also shows a positive correlation between strength and behavioural outcomes: the more one is motivated towards a goal, the stronger the intention-behaviour relationship (Conner and Norman, 2022), thus the more one should act upon their intention (Rhodes et al., 2022). Moreover, recognising the client's motivational language helps determine the inter-

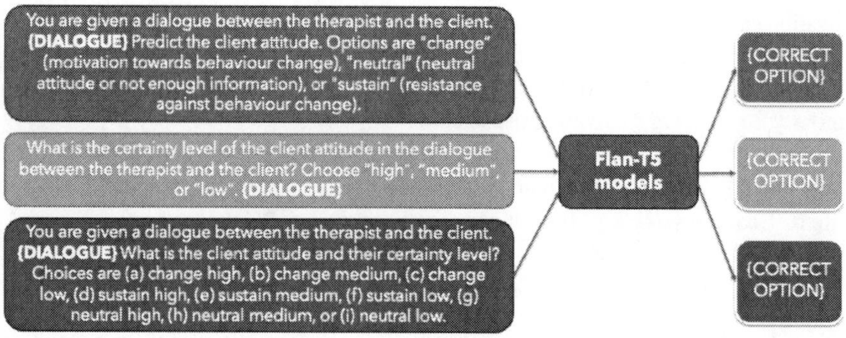

Figure 2: Here depict our training and inference processes. The instructions are fed into the models to learn and/or predict the options. During training, the models should generate the correct label which is specified as different options in the instruction. However, as the tasks are framed as generation problems, the models can still output incorrect labels if the amount of training data is insufficient.

vention treatment, i.e., whether the therapist should focus on addressing client's resistance or move to discuss action plans (Westra and Norouzian, 2018).

Despite the popularity of self-reported (i.e., questionnaires) measures, observational codes are found to correlate better with treatment processes and outcomes in MI (Lombardi et al., 2014; Poulin et al., 2019). Moreover, the commitment strength (i.e., the degree of certainty one holds for their utterance), rather than the frequency (i.e., counting each type), of the motivational language is a better predictor of change (Aharonovich et al., 2008; Campbell et al., 2010; Gaume et al., 2016). Campbell et al. (2010) argue that strength, not frequency, is related to positive outcomes as frequency fails to capture the correct commitment. For example, compare a highly motivated utterance *"I want to get off drugs for good"* with a low one *"I sort of wish I could get off drugs"*. One client utters two times the former while another utters four times the latter. Using frequency measure, the second client is assigned a higher commitment level than the first one while it should be the reverse.

4 Methodology

Our experiments are performed on (1) GPT-3.5 (Brown et al., 2020) with ICL, and (2) Flan-T5 (Chung et al., 2022) with both ICL and IFT. The base T5 models (Raffel et al., 2020) are developed using an encoder-decoder Transformer-based architecture, framing all the tasks as a text generation problem and exploiting the benefits of transfer learning to improve models' performance. Fine-tuned on 1800+ NLP tasks, `Flan-T5-XXL` is shown to outperform the base `T5-XXL` model by 26.6% on average when evaluated on 4 different benchmark suites (98 tasks in total) (Chung et al., 2022). Additionally, instruction-tuned Flan-T5 as a starting checkpoint for single-task fine-tuning converges faster and yields better performance compared to non-instruction-tuned models (Longpre et al., 2023).

No fine-tuning is needed for ICL as it performs inference using the default weights of the models. In contrast, IFT requires further training to adapt the weights to the downstream tasks. As fine-tuning the entire LLMs proves to be too costly, Parameter-efficient fine-tuning (PEFT) aims to tackle this issue by training the downstream tasks only on a small number of parameters which can either be a subset of parameters of the existing models or newly added parameters (Lialin et al., 2023). We employ LoRa (Hu et al., 2022), which performs parameter update of the weight matrix by decomposing the weight update into lower-rank matrices and then training them separately.

When instruction-tuned models are employed for classification, the tasks are formulated as a text generation problem where the models should learn to generate the correct label for a given instruction. Therefore, label-related information is critical to help identify the output space (Yin et al., 2023; Kung and Peng, 2023).

We consider a set of dialogues where each consists of one therapist turn and one client turn. The former serves as dialogue history and the models learn to make predictions for the latter depending on the task. One turn can be comprised of multiple sentences but the output label is associated with the turn, not with the sentences. Figure 1 shows two example dialogues. Figure 2 illustrates our training and inference processes for IFT and inference only for ICL. The models are prompted to produce a type and/or strength classification by concatenating the dialogue with the corresponding instruction template. Our goal is to automatically detect of the types and the strength of client motivational language during therapies.

5 Experiments

5.1 Dataset

Type Data: Our experiments utilise AnnoMI (Wu et al., 2022, 2023), which is available under Public Domain License. It consists of 133 MI conversations in 10 different topics in English which are transcribed from YouTube demonstration videos and annotated by experts from the MI network[2]. The dataset creators conducted a post-annotation survey, whose results show that the majority of annotators agree that the videos do reflect real-world MI sessions even though the dialogues are scripted for educational purposes.

Each client utterance in AnnoMI is assigned one type of motivation language (i.e, "change", "sustain", or "neutral"). The dataset is heavily imbalanced: the number of "change", "sustain", and "neutral" utterances are 1,178, 546, and 3,093 respectively. We randomly selected 600 utterances to serve as the test set. From the remaining utterances, the fast voke-k algorithm (Su et al., 2023) was employed to obtain 300 most diverse samples for the validation set and k samples for the training set, with $k \in \{50, 100, 200, 300, 3600\}$.

Strength Data: MI Skill Code (MISC)[3] is a behavioral coding system, developed to assess MI sessions. The number of samples taken from MISC 2.0 and 2.1 (Miller et al., 2003; Amrhein et al., 2008) is 178, which is further split into 128 and 50 samples to serve as the training and validation sets respectively. Mosbach et al. (2023) propose that 50 samples as the validation set are sufficient to select the best performing checkpoints. The test set is taken from the type task. Recently, researchers have investigated GPT models in data annotation tasks (He et al., 2023; Ding et al., 2023; Huang et al., 2023; Gilardi et al., 2023), suggesting that they can serve as excellent assistants to annotators during the annotation process by providing detailed explanations, potentially replacing crowdsourced workers. For the annotation of the test set, using the MISC guidelines and the explanations generated by GPT-3.5, we manually assign a strength value (i.e., "high", "medium", or "low") to each client turn. Since textual information alone is insufficient, we consult the videos to assist with the annotation process. Details on the annotation is provided in Appendix A.

5.2 Experimental Setup

Baselines: We employ two baselines: (1) 0-shot ICL settings with Flan-T5-XXL[4] (Chung et al., 2022) and GPT-3.5-turbo[5] and (2) traditional FT with RoBERTa-large[6] (Liu et al., 2019). RoBERTa is trained until convergence with the default learning rate of 1e-5. As RoBERTa is among the most popular Transformer-based encoder-type models, we use it as a baseline to measure the performance gain obtained on the LLMs.

ICL settings: Due to restrictions in context length of Flan-T5-XXL, only one example is included as demonstration. For a fair comparison, GPT-3.5-turbo also learns in 1-shot setting. Retrieval-based method is utilised (Su et al., 2023) for demonstration selection: the dialogue in the training set which is most similar to the test dialogue is chosen as context.

IFT settings: We fine-tune Flan-T5-XXL with instructions as depicted in Figure 2. We use Weights and Bias[7] to search for the best learning rate and finally settle on 3e-4 for all models. Further details about the training and hyper-parameter selection are given in Appendix C.

Evaluation metrics: We employ accuracy and F1 score macro-averaged calculated by scikit-learn (Pedregosa et al., 2011). In the multitask settings, the predictions for each task are extracted from the model outputs using regular expressions. Results are reported on the test set, using models with the best F1 scores on the validation sets during training.

6 Experimental Results

6.1 Single-Task Learning: Type

Table 1 illustrates the results of the type task. The performance of Flan-T5 with 0-shot corresponds to those of RoBERTa and Flan-T5 when trained on

[2]https://motivationalinterviewing.org/
[3]https://casaa.unm.edu/tools/misc.html
[4]https://huggingface.co/google/flan-t5-xxl
[5]https://platform.openai.com/docs/models/
[6]https://huggingface.co/roberta-large
[7]https://wandb.ai/

	50	100	200	300	3600
gpt-1s-icl	0.56	0.57	0.57	0.58	0.59
flant5-1s-icl	**0.60**	**0.60**	**0.61**	**0.61**	0.63
flant5-ift	0.36	0.47	0.60	**0.61**	**0.74**
roberta-ft	0.36	0.46	0.53	0.55	0.61

Table 1: F1 scores of the type task on the test set with different training samples.

	instructions
all	Options are "change" (motivation towards behaviour change), "neutral" (neutral attitude or not enough information), or "sustain" (resistance against behaviour change).
simplified	Options are "change", "sustain", or "neutral".

Figure 3: Ablation studies of output space specified in the instruction for type task. **all** consists of the *label list* (in green) and the *label description* (in yellow), whereas **simplified** instructions have *label list* only.

100 samples, whereas GPT-3.5 with 0-shot yields the same score as RoBERTa trained on 200 samples. Interestingly, both GPT-3.5 and Flan-T5 with 1-shot ICL exhibit a similar behaviour: their performances stay relatively consistent regardless of the number of samples that can be selected as demonstrations.

Hallucinated Output Labels: Framed as a generation problem, instruction-tuned models still can produce ill-formed candidates despite being trained on desirable labels: Flan-T5 trained on 50 and 100 samples generates such outputs. In contrast, ICL even with zero shot does not suffer from this issue. After the hallucinated labels are replaced with "neutral"[8], F1 scores for Flan-T5 with 50 and 100 training data jump from 0.36 and 0.47 to 0.59 and 0.62 respectively. Consequently, the new score obtained on 100 samples completely outperforms other ICL variants.

Unexpected Results: Observably, both ICL and IFT obtain little performance gain as the training data size increases. The reason could be because our training samples are not randomly selected. As explained in Section 5.1, the *fast vote-k* algorithm by Su et al. (2023) is employed to pick the most diverse samples for both training and validation sets. Their paper shows that ICL performance with this approach is quite stable once we have enough high-quality data. Hypothetically, the LLMs might have already obtained the most important features from the diverse dataset unless the models are trained on a full dataset with thousands of examples.

Ablation with Output Space Labels: With IFT, specifying output space labels proves crucial for classification tasks (Kung and Peng, 2023; Yin et al., 2023). In addition to the *label list*, one can add the *label description* to give extra information about the meaning of the labels. Figure 3 illustrates two conditions **all** and **simplified** of our ablation studies. In contrast to Kung and Peng (2023) who find that two conditions exhibit similar effect, we observe that **all** condition (i.e., having both label list and label description) outperforms **simplified** with varying data size. Our results are similar to those of Yin et al. (2023): the authors hypothesise that label description might be used to disambiguate labels with the same name but used in different tasks.

Error Analysis: Classification reports on individual labels reveal that both IFT and ICL struggle on "sustain": F1 scores are below 0.4 and 0.5 respectively. Additionally, IFT outperforms ICL due to its capabilities in predicting "neutral" labels: more than half of the labels belong to this class. ICL, though, still predicts more than twice "sustain" labels compared to IFT.

The MI type labels indicate the direction of motivation towards a certain behaviour change. They are, however, unable to capture (1) complete refusals from the clients to talk about their problems, and (2) strategies employed to avoid discussing difficult topics (Martin et al., 2020). In the MISC guidelines, the latter can be coded as "change" because the clients tend to agree just to end the conversations. In contrast, the former behaviours are coded as "neutral". An inspection of the model predictions reveals that several instances of refusal and resistance to an undefined target behaviour change are predicted as "sustain". This explains models' poor performance on the "sustain" class, especially ICL. We leave it for future works on how it might influence the design of the MI agents.

6.2 Single-Task Learning: `Strength`

Results for the strength analysis are reported in Table 2. Surprisingly, retrieval-based ICL with 1-shot fares quite poorly, even worse than fine-tuned RoBERTa. GPT-3.5 suffers a drop in performance when shifting from 0-shot to 1-shot. Zhao et al. (2021) attribute it to majority label bias in which

[8]The label "neutral" is chosen due to (1) it is the most common labels in the dataset, and (2) in the later mapping in Section 7, "neutral" is mapped to the zero score, and thus, will not change the proposed motivational level.

	Accuracy	F1
gpt 0-shot	0.46	0.39
gpt 1-shot	0.40	0.34
flant5 0-shot	0.41	0.39
flant5 1-shot	0.47	0.45
flant5 ift	**0.72**	**0.68**
roberta ft	0.59	0.53

Table 2: Accuracy and F1 scores for the `strength` task.

GPT-3 merely reuses the class of the only example in the instructions. However, we observe no such phenomenon. In fact, when calculating the overlap between model' predictions and in-context example's labels, the overlap occurs in 63 samples out of 600: GPT-3.5 does not simply repeat the label of the example in roughly 90% of the times. The difference in our findings and those of Zhao et al. (2021) might be due to an upgrade from GPT-3 to GPT-3.5. Our results suggest that fine-tuning is still more stable and less sensitive than ICL.

Ablation with Dialogue Context: In an attempt to understand the poor performance of ICL, we conduct ablation studies using: (1) only client turns as context instead of both therapist and client utterances to match the training samples, and (2) GPT-3.5 with multiple shots using retrieval-based ICL. The results show that a longer context history for the test sample helps improve the ICL performance despite some mismatch between the format of test samples and that of the demonstrated examples.

Interestingly, increasing the number of demonstrated examples does not always lead to higher scores. We revisit the majority label bias claimed by Zhao et al. (2021). Intuitively, the argument for retrieval-based ICL is to exploit this bias by retrieving the most similar examples to the test sample, and thus reusing the majority label. Yet, we find no such bias. An examination of the predictions by GPT-3.5 3-shot and 4-shot reveals many cases where all retrieved examples belong to one class (e.g., low) but the prediction is of another (e.g., medium or high). In fact, by using the majority label of the retrieved examples as prediction increases accuracy from 0.42 to 0.43.

Error Analysis: Analysing the confusion matrices, all the models struggle with the "high" class, especially with the ICL variants. Nevertheless, their poor performance comes from overgenerating the "low" class. Except for Flan-T5 with IFT, around half of the "low" predictions by GPT-3.5 and Flan-T5 with ICL variants and RoBERTa belong to the "medium" class instead. One possible reason is because of a large number of utterances consists of multiple sentences, making the `strength` levels fluctuate from one side to another. Rationales by GPT-3.5 further imply confusions between the certainty level as a manner of expressing one's belief and their knowledge: one can be certain about their uncertainty (i.e., *"I have absolutely no idea about it."*). Incorporating other signals from speech and/or facial expressions would be beneficial to the recognition.

6.3 Multitask Learning

	`type`		`strength`	
	Acc.	F1	Acc.	F1
gpt 0-shot	**0.53**	**0.49**	0.41	0.38
gpt 1-shot	0.50	0.43	0.50	0.48
flant5 1-shot	0.43	0.34	0.40	0.39
flant5 ift	0.32	0.29	**0.67**	**0.66**

Table 3: Results on multitask learning.

Inspired by Varia et al. (2023), we experiment with multitask learning where the models should learn to predict the two tasks simultaneously. Regular expressions are employed to get the predictions and replace the ill-formed labels with either "neutral" or "medium" depending on the task. Table 3 reports the results. These experiments use the `strength` dataset (i.e., training and validation sizes are 128 and 50 respectively). Even using only 50 samples, both ICL and IFT achieve F1 scores higher than 0.6 while with 128 samples in multitask learning (MTL), 0.49 is the best F1 score. IFT performs surprisingly poorly.

Mixing More Data: We try to mix more samples (i.e., 100, 200, and 300) from the `type` dataset to investigate whether adding data improves performance. However, a higher number of mixed data results in more ill-formed outputs for the `strength` task. Consequently, performance on the `type` task increases while that on the `strength` task decreases. Our results contradict those of Varia et al. (2023): STL overall outperforms MTL.

Error Analysis: An examination of label distribution on both training and test sets reveals that three variants of "neutral" (i.e., neutral high, neutral medium, neutral low) make up of nearly 60%

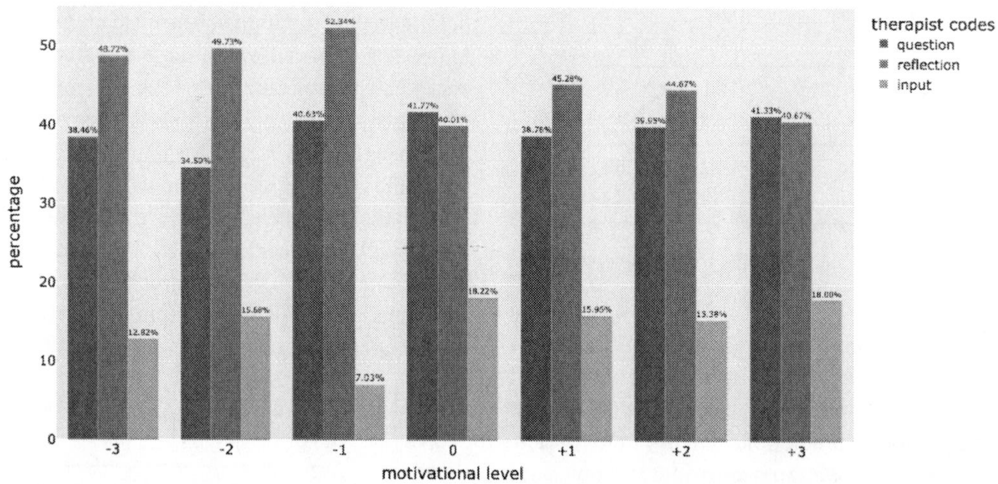

Figure 4: Distribution of next-turn therapist behaviours given clients' motivational level in the current turn.

in the test set. Yet, no "neutral" samples exist in the training set, which explains why the models are unable to learn properly. Appendix B shows the distribution of all 9 labels in the dataset. Nevertheless, ICL appears to be less effected by this imbalance training data: both Flan-T5 and GPT-3.5 struggle more to learn "change" or "sustain". As for the `strength` task, the performance in MTL, though slightly lower, is still comparable to STL.

On the mixed data, the similarity in the labels of three instructions confuses the learning: in some cases, the correct label is "neutral" but in other cases, it has to be "neutral high", "neutral medium" or "neutral low". Due to the overwhelmed "neutral" class, the models appear to struggle to generate the other multi-word labels. IFT might be unsuitable for labels with multiple words. Schick and Schütze (2021) claim that Pattern-Exploiting Training, a stricter variant of IFT, can only work when the labels correspond to a single token.

7 Application to Psychotherapist Agents

An MI session consists of 4 stages: engaging, focusing, evoking, and planning (Miller and Rollnick, 2023). To control the conversational flow, Park et al. (2019) define a fixed sequence of behaviours for each stage. We hypothesise that MI sessions can be automated using the detected motivational language. We demonstrate how it can inform the psychotherapist agents' next moves using `AnnoMI` data and MI literature.

Therapists' Strategies: Using the best model from our experiments, we obtain `strength` labels and calculate the motivational levels for all client utterances in the `AnnoMI` dataset (Wu et al., 2023). We employ a scale from -3 to +3, similar to Gaume et al. (2016). All "neutral" `type` equals to 0. `Strength` labels "high", "medium", and "low" are given levels of 3, 2, and 1 respectively while `type` labels "change" and "sustain" indicate the positive and negative directions. For example, "change-high" is mapped to +3 while "sustain-low" is -1.

Figure 4 illustrates the distribution of the next-turn therapist behaviour codes given the current clients' motivational level. We count all the possible codes in one utterance. Since the "other" behaviour consists mostly of facilitating languages (e.g., *Mm-hmm*, *Uh-uh*, *Yeah*) and greetings, we only compute the percentages for "Question", "Reflection", and "Input". Observably, "reflection" is employed frequently throughout the sessions, nearly 50% of the times when the clients show resistance (i.e. levels of -3, -2, and -1). More "input" and "question" behaviours are displayed when the clients are more ready to change.

Balancing Objectives in Therapies: In psychotherapy, the therapists need to balance two conflicting goals: building therapeutic rapport with the clients and pushing them towards task completion. Zhang and Danescu-Niculescu-Mizil (2020) argue that each therapist utterance aims to move backward from or forwards towards the goal. Our hypothesis is that the MI behaviour codes can also be classified into rapport-building (i.e., reflections, focusing questions) and goal-pursuing strategies (i.e., evoking questions, inputs). Reflections are restatements of the clients' thoughts and feelings, expressing the therapists' understandings of their inner worlds. Inputs include a wide range of sub-behaviours such as providing information, giving advice, offering options, and setting goals. Focusing questions explore their perspectives, goals, and values while evoking questions aim to elicit their motivation to change. Though no distinction between focusing and evoking questions is made in `AnnoMI`, our belief is that this distinction would be beneficial to the MI agents.

Framework of the MI Agents: With insights from the literature and the data, we would like to propose a computational framework of the MI agents. In an attempt to investigate who might benefit from MI and who not, Forman et al. (2022) measure the differences in clients' language early in the session and discover that those whose language reflects ambivalence (i.e. low motivated), benefit more from MI. In contrast, MI appears to be counterproductive for those who already show a readiness to change, suggesting that MI strategies should be adapted appropriately to the clients' presenting levels of motivation.

The transtheoretical model of stages of health behaviour change (Prochaska and Velicer, 1997) hypothesises the first 3 stages are precontemplation ("not ready", or resistance), contemplation ("getting ready", or ambivalence) and preparation ("ready", or motivation). We hypothesise that after several interactions, if the detected motivational levels are mainly -3 and -2, the client is in precontemplation stage. If they are -1 or +1, it is contemplation. And if the levels are +2 or +3, the stage is preparation.

Once in the preparation stage, the MI agents should employ mainly goal-pursuing behaviours or switch to another more goal-oriented technique such as CBT (Westra and Norouzian, 2018), while occasionally utilising reflections and focusing questions when the users display low motivation to maintain the therapeutic alliance. Besides rapport-building behaviours, the agents can be programmed to emphasising the users' autonomy, coded as "input" in the `AnnoMI`, when the users display signs of the precontemplation stage. For example, *"that is your choice. I can't make those choices for you, it is something that you decide to do."* and *"you're the boss. It's up to you what you want to do with you about your own health."*. The stage should help inform the agents' strategies if the detected level is 0. Our belief is that this information can be leveraged to design the instructions to train the agents to exhibit more MI-adherence interactions.

Clinical Implications and Potential Applications: Training using therapy data only might be insufficient to create psychotherapy agents as revealed by Das et al. (2022): their agent shows a lack of therapeutic behaviours and merely gives general advice. We believe that by monitoring the clients' motivational levels, the agents can act in a more proactive manner following the MI spirit. For example, giving advice and setting goals when the clients are ready enough and supporting them when resistance arises. As MI is a well-regarded, evidence-based, and widely used approach for behaviour change, the MI-aware agents can reduce the system burden and facilitate treatment delivery with lower costs to reach a wider range of users.

8 Conclusion and Future Works

Works in psychology suggest that monitoring client motivational language is an essential skill to deliver successful therapies. Our belief is that a motivation-aware system would have implications for the development of personalised healthcare agents. Our experiments employ LLMs, and compare ICL with IFT on varying training data sizes. Our findings indicate that both can perform in few-shot settings and be sensitive to the instructions. Still, we observe that with ICL, the predictions can change when adding something totally unrelated to the task itself (i.e., requesting a certain format of the output). IFT is more stable; however, it suffers from generating ill-formed outputs when trained with a small number of samples. With the obtained labels, we devise a computational framework for MI agents based on the users' motivation at stage and utterance levels. Insights from `AnnoMI` data and MI literature suggest that the agents should exhibit mainly rapport-building behaviours when facing resistance and ambivalence. Once the users indicate a strong willingness to change, goal-pursuing strategies are preferred. Rapport-building behaviours are employed occasionally, when appropriate. In future works, we would like to investigate how to incorporate such information into the design of instructions to generate therapeutic interactions.

9 Limitations

MI practice: Our paper is inspired by the MI approach to behaviour change. We try to give general readers a brief overview of the MI spirit, enough to understand the rationales behind the proposed framework. A comprehensive review of MI and/or CBT and their validity is, however, out of scope of the paper. We acknowledge that there exist different applications for MI and thus, the language should be contextualised for different clinical situations. Nevertheless, the paper aims to show whether and how the motivational language can be utilised in general to direct the behaviours of the agents theoretically and experimentally without focusing on a particular clinical situation.

Dataset: As the conversations in the `AnnoMI` dataset (Wu et al., 2023) are role-play MI videos used for educational purposes, they might not reflect the real therapies in which the clients can behave in a more unexpected manner, especially the way they show their resistance. The language in use is English, and thus, might be unsuitable for other languages. Furthermore, in practice, the therapists might use a mixture of different approaches, not just MI. All these limitations can effect generalisation to real-world applications. However, real MI therapies are scarce. The `AnnoMI` demonstrations have been judged by MI experts to reflect real MI sessions. As our main purpose is to create an MI agent, we would argue that high-quality MI demonstrations should help create agents faithful to MI practice more than real therapies with mixed approaches.

Annotation labels: The MISC guidelines suggest a fine-grained annotation based on sentences or phrases. However, the labels are assigned to turns, not sentences. A turn can consist of multiple sentences but can also be unfinished sentences or words (e.g., *"-forms."*). Therefore, these samples contain no information to help the models make predictions. Even though classifying turns might be desirable for speech systems, it might potentially teach the models inappropriate features for classification tasks.

Additionally, we observe many samples consisting of multiple sentences whose direction and strength of motivation can move from one end to another as the clients speak. This explains partly the low inter-annotator agreement on `AnnoMI`. Similarly, in the `strength` task, many utterances consist of multiple sentences whose certainty levels can go from one extreme to the other. This poses as a huge challenge for the annotation process.

Choice of models and prompts: As for the model choice, we experimented with several models before settling on Flan-T5. Despite not being the SOTA model in all tasks, the Flan-T5 family is suitable for classification tasks. Similarly, other Parameter-efficient fine-tuning techniques are investigated but due to their poor performance, we did not include all the results except for LoRA. As for the prompt formats, we could have tested and compared different prompts. However, since the focus is to demonstrate how the detected motivation can be utilised to automate the MI agents' behaviours, we simply took the insights from Yin et al. (2023) in designing the optimal prompts.

Multimodal systems: We only utilise textual features to make predictions. Prior works suggest incorporating visual features (i.e., facial expressions) for the `type` task (Nakano et al., 2022) as the client might hint their resistance by keeping silent and/or looking away. As for the `strength` task, experiments in linguistics show that acoustic features (e.g., pitch accents) convey speaker's commitment (Michelas et al., 2016). When annotating the test set, we do observe that whether the speaker is fluent or hesitates about their actions can be a signal for their certainty level.

10 Ethical Concerns

MI is a therapy originally developed to help people change their harmful behaviours such as alcoholism (Miller and Rollnick, 2023). Due to its effectiveness, MI practitioners have applied it to other fields, including those involving unethical practices such as sales or marketing[9]. We acknowledge that an MI-aware agent can be misused to target low-motivated users for motivation tricks for behaviour change that benefits the providers instead of the clients (i.e., buy more products, ask for donation against their will), just as how an MI expert can misuse the technique. Our belief is that an MI-aware agent can, however, have positive implications for the development of intelligent systems in the healthcare domain. Mental health is always a big issue in modern society. Additionally, an MI-aware agent can motivate people for positive behaviour change such as being more physically active (Olafsson et al., 2020a).

[9] `https://motivationalinterviewing.org/non-ethical-practice-mi`

Acknowledgement

This publication has emanated from research conducted with the financial support of Science Foundation Ireland under Grant number 18/CRT/6183 (ML-Labs) and the ADAPT SFI Research Centre for AI-Driven Digital Content Technology under Grant No. 13/RC/2106_P2. For the purpose of Open Access, the author has applied a CC BY public copyright licence to any Author Accepted Manuscript version arising from this submission.

References

Efrat Aharonovich, Paul C. Amrhein, Adam Bisaga, Edward V. Nunes, and Deborah S. Hasin. 2008. Cognition, commitment language, and behavioral change among cocaine-dependent patients. *Psychology of Addictive Behaviors*, 22(4):557–562.

Tim Althoff, Kevin Clark, and Jure Leskovec. 2016. Large-scale Analysis of Counseling Conversations: An Application of Natural Language Processing to Mental Health. *Transactions of the Association for Computational Linguistics*, 4:463–476. Place: Cambridge, MA Publisher: MIT Press.

Paul C Amrhein, William R. Miller, Theresa Moyers, and Denise Ernst. 2008. Motivational Interviewing Skill Code (MISC) 2.1.

Paul C. Amrhein, William R. Miller, Carolina E. Yahne, Michael Palmer, and Laura Fulcher. 2003. Client commitment language during motivational interviewing predicts drug use outcomes. *Journal of Consulting and Clinical Psychology*, 71(5):862–878.

Chanuwas Aswamenakul, Lixing Liu, Kate B. Carey, Joshua Woolley, Stefan Scherer, and Brian Borsari. 2018. Multimodal Analysis of Client Behavioral Change Coding in Motivational Interviewing. In *Proceedings of the 20th ACM International Conference on Multimodal Interaction*, pages 356–360, Boulder CO USA. ACM.

Kira Boulat and Didier Maillat. 2023. Strength is relevant: experimental evidence of strength as a marker of commitment. *Frontiers in Communication*, 8:1176845.

Andrew Brown, Ash Tanuj Kumar, Osnat Melamed, Imtihan Ahmed, Yu Hao Wang, Arnaud Deza, Marc Morcos, Leon Zhu, Marta Maslej, Nadia Minian, Vidya Sujaya, Jodi Wolff, Olivia Doggett, Mathew Iantorno, Matt Ratto, Peter Selby, and Jonathan Rose. 2023. A Motivational Interviewing Chatbot With Generative Reflections for Increasing Readiness to Quit Smoking: Iterative Development Study. *JMIR Mental Health*, 10:e49132.

Tom B. Brown, Benjamin Mann, Nick Ryder, Melanie Subbiah, Jared Kaplan, Prafulla Dhariwal, Arvind Neelakantan, Pranav Shyam, Girish Sastry, Amanda Askell, Sandhini Agarwal, Ariel Herbert-Voss, Gretchen Krueger, Tom Henighan, Rewon Child, Aditya Ramesh, Daniel M. Ziegler, Jeffrey Wu, Clemens Winter, Christopher Hesse, Mark Chen, Eric Sigler, Mateusz Litwin, Scott Gray, Benjamin Chess, Jack Clark, Christopher Berner, Sam McCandlish, Alec Radford, Ilya Sutskever, and Dario Amodei. 2020. Language Models are Few-Shot Learners. ArXiv:2005.14165 [cs].

Samadhi Deva Campbell, Simon Justin Adamson, and Janet Deborah Carter. 2010. Client Language During Motivational Enhancement Therapy and Alcohol Use Outcome. *Behavioural and Cognitive Psychotherapy*, 38(4):399–415.

Jie Cao, Michael Tanana, Zac Imel, Eric Poitras, David Atkins, and Vivek Srikumar. 2019. Observing Dialogue in Therapy: Categorizing and Forecasting Behavioral Codes. In *Proceedings of the 57th Annual Meeting of the Association for Computational Linguistics*, pages 5599–5611, Florence, Italy. Association for Computational Linguistics.

Zhuohao Chen, Nikolaos Flemotomos, Victor Ardulov, Torrey A. Creed, Zac E. Imel, David C. Atkins, and Shrikanth Narayanan. 2021. Feature Fusion Strategies for End-to-End Evaluation of Cognitive Behavior Therapy Sessions. In *2021 43rd Annual International Conference of the IEEE Engineering in Medicine & Biology Society (EMBC)*, pages 1836–1839, Mexico. IEEE.

Young Min Cho, Sunny Rai, Lyle Ungar, João Sedoc, and Sharath Chandra Guntuku. 2023. An Integrative Survey on Mental Health Conversational Agents to Bridge Computer Science and Medical Perspectives. ArXiv:2310.17017 [cs].

Hyung Won Chung, Le Hou, Shayne Longpre, Barret Zoph, Yi Tay, William Fedus, Yunxuan Li, Xuezhi Wang, Mostafa Dehghani, Siddhartha Brahma, Albert Webson, Shixiang Shane Gu, Zhuyun Dai, Mirac Suzgun, Xinyun Chen, Aakanksha Chowdhery, Alex Castro-Ros, Marie Pellat, Kevin Robinson, Dasha Valter, Sharan Narang, Gaurav Mishra, Adams Yu, Vincent Zhao, Yanping Huang, Andrew Dai, Hongkun Yu, Slav Petrov, Ed H. Chi, Jeff Dean, Jacob Devlin, Adam Roberts, Denny Zhou, Quoc V. Le, and Jason Wei. 2022. Scaling Instruction-Finetuned Language Models. ArXiv:2210.11416 [cs].

Dominic A. Clark. 1990. Verbal uncertainty expressions: A critical review of two decades of research. *Current Psychology*, 9(3):203–235.

Mark Conner and Paul Norman. 2022. Understanding the intention-behavior gap: The role of intention strength. *Frontiers in Psychology*, 13:923464.

Avisha Das, Salih Selek, Alia R. Warner, Xu Zuo, Yan Hu, Vipina Kuttichi Keloth, Jianfu Li, W. Jim Zheng, and Hua Xu. 2022. Conversational Bots for Psychotherapy: A Study of Generative Transformer Models Using Domain-specific Dialogues. In *Proceedings of the 21st Workshop on Biomedical Language Processing*, pages 285–297, Dublin, Ireland. Association for Computational Linguistics.

Marie-Catherine de MARNEFFE, Mandy Simons, and Judith Tonhauser. 2019. The CommitmentBank: Investigating projection in naturally occurring discourse. *Proceedings of Sinn und Bedeutung*, 2:107–124.

Mona Diab, Lori Levin, Teruko Mitamura, Owen Rambow, Vinodkumar Prabhakaran, and Weiwei Guo. 2009. Committed Belief Annotation and Tagging. In *Proceedings of the Third Linguistic Annotation Workshop (LAW III)*, pages 68–73, Suntec, Singapore. Association for Computational Linguistics.

Bosheng Ding, Chengwei Qin, Linlin Liu, Yew Ken Chia, Boyang Li, Shafiq Joty, and Lidong Bing. 2023. Is GPT-3 a Good Data Annotator? In *Proceedings of the 61st Annual Meeting of the Association for Computational Linguistics (Volume 1: Long Papers)*, pages 11173–11195, Toronto, Canada. Association for Computational Linguistics.

Qingxiu Dong, Lei Li, Damai Dai, Ce Zheng, Zhiyong Wu, Baobao Chang, Xu Sun, Jingjing Xu, Lei Li, and Zhifang Sui. 2023. A Survey on In-context Learning. ArXiv:2301.00234 [cs].

M. P. Ewbank, R. Cummins, V. Tablan, A. Catarino, S. Buchholz, and A. D. Blackwell. 2021. Understanding the relationship between patient language and outcomes in internet-enabled cognitive behavioural therapy: A deep learning approach to automatic coding of session transcripts. *Psychotherapy Research*, 31(3):300–312.

David P. Forman, Theresa B. Moyers, and Jon M. Houck. 2022. What can clients tell us about whether to use motivational interviewing? An analysis of early-session ambivalent language. *Journal of Substance Abuse Treatment*, 132:108642.

Joana Galvão Gomes Da Silva, David J Kavanagh, Tony Belpaeme, Lloyd Taylor, Konna Beeson, and Jackie Andrade. 2018. Experiences of a Motivational Interview Delivered by a Robot: Qualitative Study. *Journal of Medical Internet Research*, 20(5):e116.

Jacques Gaume, Molly Magill, Nadine R. Mastroleo, Richard Longabaugh, Nicolas Bertholet, Gerhard Gmel, and Jean-Bernard Daeppen. 2016. Change Talk During Brief Motivational Intervention With Young Adult Males: Strength Matters. *Journal of Substance Abuse Treatment*, 65:58–65.

Tirthankar Ghosal, Kamal Kaushik Varanasi, and Valia Kordoni. 2022. HedgePeer: a dataset for uncertainty detection in peer reviews. In *Proceedings of the 22nd ACM/IEEE Joint Conference on Digital Libraries*, pages 1–5, Cologne Germany. ACM.

James Gibson, David C. Atkins, Torrey Creed, Zac Imel, Panayiotis Georgiou, and Shrikanth Narayanan. 2022. Multi-label Multi-task Deep Learning for Behavioral Coding. *IEEE transactions on affective computing*, 13(1):508–518.

Fabrizio Gilardi, Meysam Alizadeh, and Maël Kubli. 2023. ChatGPT Outperforms Crowd-Workers for Text-Annotation Tasks. ArXiv:2303.15056 [cs].

Himanshu Gupta, Saurabh Arjun Sawant, Swaroop Mishra, Mutsumi Nakamura, Arindam Mitra, Santosh Mashetty, and Chitta Baral. 2023. Instruction Tuned Models are Quick Learners. ArXiv:2306.05539 [cs].

Xingwei He, Zhenghao Lin, Yeyun Gong, A.-Long Jin, Hang Zhang, Chen Lin, Jian Jiao, Siu Ming Yiu, Nan Duan, and Weizhu Chen. 2023. AnnoLLM: Making Large Language Models to Be Better Crowdsourced Annotators. ArXiv:2303.16854 [cs].

Edward J. Hu, Yelong Shen, Phillip Wallis, Zeyuan Allen-Zhu, Yuanzhi Li, Shean Wang, Lu Wang, and Weizhu Chen. 2022. LoRA: Low-Rank Adaptation of Large Language Models.

Fan Huang, Haewoon Kwak, and Jisun An. 2023. Is ChatGPT better than Human Annotators? Potential and Limitations of ChatGPT in Explaining Implicit Hate Speech. In *Companion Proceedings of the ACM Web Conference 2023*, pages 294–297, Austin TX USA. ACM.

Po-Nien Kung and Nanyun Peng. 2023. Do Models Really Learn to Follow Instructions? An Empirical Study of Instruction Tuning. In *Proceedings of the 61st Annual Meeting of the Association for Computational Linguistics (Volume 2: Short Papers)*, pages 1317–1328, Toronto, Canada. Association for Computational Linguistics.

Anqi Li, Lizhi Ma, Yaling Mei, Hongliang He, Shuai Zhang, Huachuan Qiu, and Zhenzhong Lan. 2023. Understanding Client Reactions in Online Mental Health Counseling. In *Proceedings of the 61st Annual Meeting of the Association for Computational Linguistics (Volume 1: Long Papers)*, pages 10358–10376, Toronto, Canada. Association for Computational Linguistics.

Vladislav Lialin, Vijeta Deshpande, and Anna Rumshisky. 2023. Scaling Down to Scale Up: A Guide to Parameter-Efficient Fine-Tuning. ArXiv:2303.15647 [cs].

Haokun Liu, Derek Tam, Mohammed Muqeeth, Jay Mohta, Tenghao Huang, Mohit Bansal, and Colin Raffel. 2022. Few-Shot Parameter-Efficient Fine-Tuning is Better and Cheaper than In-Context Learning.

Jiachang Liu, Dinghan Shen, Yizhe Zhang, Bill Dolan, Lawrence Carin, and Weizhu Chen. 2021. What Makes Good In-Context Examples for GPT-3? ArXiv:2101.06804 [cs].

Yinhan Liu, Myle Ott, Naman Goyal, Jingfei Du, Mandar Joshi, Danqi Chen, Omer Levy, Mike Lewis, Luke Zettlemoyer, and Veselin Stoyanov. 2019. RoBERTa: A Robustly Optimized BERT Pretraining Approach. ArXiv:1907.11692 [cs].

Robert Logan IV, Ivana Balazevic, Eric Wallace, Fabio Petroni, Sameer Singh, and Sebastian Riedel. 2022. Cutting Down on Prompts and Parameters: Simple Few-Shot Learning with Language Models. In *Findings of the Association for Computational Linguistics: ACL 2022*, pages 2824–2835, Dublin, Ireland. Association for Computational Linguistics.

Diana R. Lombardi, Melissa L. Button, and Henny A. Westra. 2014. Measuring Motivation: Change Talk and Counter-Change Talk in Cognitive Behavioral Therapy for Generalized Anxiety. *Cognitive Behaviour Therapy*, 43(1):12–21.

Shayne Longpre, Le Hou, Tu Vu, Albert Webson, Hyung Won Chung, Yi Tay, Denny Zhou, Quoc V. Le, Barret Zoph, Jason Wei, and Adam Roberts. 2023. The Flan Collection: Designing Data and Methods for Effective Instruction Tuning. In *Proceedings of the 40th International Conference on Machine Learning*, pages 22631–22648. PMLR. ISSN: 2640-3498.

Yao Lu, Max Bartolo, Alastair Moore, Sebastian Riedel, and Pontus Stenetorp. 2022. Fantastically Ordered Prompts and Where to Find Them: Overcoming Few-Shot Prompt Order Sensitivity. ArXiv:2104.08786 [cs].

Vanessa Martin, Tasmie Sarker, Emily Slusarek, Mary A. McCarthy, John Granton, Adrienne Tan, and Christopher Lo. 2020. Conversational avoidance during existential interviews with patients with progressive illness. *Psychology, Health & Medicine*, 25(9):1073–1082.

Selina Meyer. 2021. Natural Language Stage of Change Modelling for "Motivationally-driven" Weight Loss Support. In *Proceedings of the 2021 International Conference on Multimodal Interaction*, pages 807–811, Montréal QC Canada. ACM.

Amandine Michelas, Cristel Portes, and Maud Champagne-Lavau. 2016. When pitch Accents Encode Speaker Commitment: Evidence from French Intonation. *Language and Speech*, 59(2):266–293.

William R. Miller, Theresa Moyers, Denise Ernst, and Paul C. Amrhein. 2003. Motivational Interviewing Skill Code (MISC) 2.0.

William R. Miller and Stephen Rollnick. 2023. *Motivational interviewing: helping people change and grow*, fourth edition edition. Applications of motivational interviewing. The Guilford Press, New York.

Sewon Min, Xinxi Lyu, Ari Holtzman, Mikel Artetxe, Mike Lewis, Hannaneh Hajishirzi, and Luke Zettlemoyer. 2022. Rethinking the Role of Demonstrations: What Makes In-Context Learning Work? In *Proceedings of the 2022 Conference on Empirical Methods in Natural Language Processing*, pages 11048–11064, Abu Dhabi, United Arab Emirates. Association for Computational Linguistics.

Marius Mosbach, Tiago Pimentel, Shauli Ravfogel, Dietrich Klakow, and Yanai Elazar. 2023. Few-shot Fine-tuning vs. In-context Learning: A Fair Comparison and Evaluation. In *Findings of the Association for Computational Linguistics: ACL 2023*, pages 12284–12314, Toronto, Canada. Association for Computational Linguistics.

Yukiko I. Nakano, Eri Hirose, Tatsuya Sakato, Shogo Okada, and Jean-Claude Martin. 2022. Detecting Change Talk in Motivational Interviewing using Verbal and Facial Information. In *INTERNATIONAL CONFERENCE ON MULTIMODAL INTERACTION*, pages 5–14, Bengaluru India. ACM.

Stefan Olafsson, Teresa K. O'Leary, and Timothy W. Bickmore. 2020a. Motivating Health Behavior Change with Humorous Virtual Agents. In *Proceedings of the 20th ACM International Conference on Intelligent Virtual Agents*, pages 1–8, Virtual Event Scotland UK. ACM.

Stefan Olafsson, Byron Wallace, and Timothy Bickmore. 2020b. Towards a Computational Framework for Automating Substance Use Counseling with Virtual Agents. In *Proceedings of the 19th International Conference on Autonomous Agents and MultiAgent Systems*, AAMAS '20, pages 966–974, Richland, SC. International Foundation for Autonomous Agents and Multiagent Systems.

SoHyun Park, Jeewon Choi, Sungwoo Lee, Changhoon Oh, Changdai Kim, Soohyun La, Joonhwan Lee, and Bongwon Suh. 2019. Designing a Chatbot for a Brief Motivational Interview on Stress Management: Qualitative Case Study. *Journal of Medical Internet Research*, 21(4):e12231.

Havisha Pedamallu, Matthew J Ehrhardt, Julia Maki, April Idalski Carcone, Melissa M Hudson, and Erika A Waters. 2022. Technology-Delivered Adaptations of Motivational Interviewing for the Prevention and Management of Chronic Diseases: Scoping Review. *Journal of Medical Internet Research*, 24(8):e35283.

F. Pedregosa, G. Varoquaux, A. Gramfort, V. Michel, B. Thirion, O. Grisel, M. Blondel, P. Prettenhofer, R. Weiss, V. Dubourg, J. Vanderplas, A. Passos, D. Cournapeau, M. Brucher, M. Perrot, and E. Duchesnay. 2011. Scikit-learn: Machine learning in Python. *Journal of Machine Learning Research*, 12:2825–2830.

Lauren E. Poulin, Melissa L. Button, Henny A. Westra, Michael J. Constantino, and Martin M. Antony. 2019. The predictive capacity of self-reported motivation vs. early observed motivational language in cognitive behavioural therapy for generalized anxiety disorder. *Cognitive Behaviour Therapy*, 48(5):369–384.

Vinodkumar Prabhakaran, Tomas By, Julia Hirschberg, Owen Rambow, Samira Shaikh, Tomek Strzalkowski, Jennifer Tracey, Michael Arrigo, Rupayan Basu, Micah Clark, Adam Dalton, Mona Diab, Louise Guthrie, Anna Prokofieva, Stephanie Strassel, Gregory Werner, Yorick Wilks, and Janyce Wiebe. 2015. A New Dataset and Evaluation for Belief/Factuality. In *Proceedings of the Fourth Joint Conference on Lexical and Computational Semantics*, pages 82–91, Denver, Colorado. Association for Computational Linguistics.

Vinodkumar Prabhakaran, Premkumar Ganeshkumar, and Owen Rambow. 2018. Author Commitment and Social Power: Automatic Belief Tagging to Infer the Social Context of Interactions. In *Proceedings of the 2018 Conference of the North American Chapter of the Association for Computational Linguistics: Human Language Technologies, Volume 1 (Long Papers)*, pages 1057–1068, New Orleans, Louisiana. Association for Computational Linguistics.

James O. Prochaska and Wayne F. Velicer. 1997. The Transtheoretical Model of Health Behavior Change. *American Journal of Health Promotion*, 12(1):38–48.

Valentina Pyatkin, Shoval Sadde, Aynat Rubinstein, Paul Portner, and Reut Tsarfaty. 2021. The Possible, the Plausible, and the Desirable: Event-Based Modality Detection for Language Processing. In *Proceedings of the 59th Annual Meeting of the Association for Computational Linguistics and the 11th International Joint Conference on Natural Language Processing (Volume 1: Long Papers)*, pages 953–965, Online. Association for Computational Linguistics.

Verónica Pérez-Rosas, Rada Mihalcea, Kenneth Resnicow, Satinder Singh, and Lawrence An. 2016. Building a Motivational Interviewing Dataset. In *Proceedings of the Third Workshop on Computational Linguistics and Clinical Psychology*, pages 42–51, San Diego, CA, USA. Association for Computational Linguistics.

Verónica Pérez-Rosas, Rada Mihalcea, Kenneth Resnicow, Satinder Singh, Lawrence Ann, Kathy J. Goggin, and Delwyn Catley. 2017. Predicting Counselor Behaviors in Motivational Interviewing Encounters. In *Proceedings of the 15th Conference of the European Chapter of the Association for Computational Linguistics: Volume 1, Long Papers*, pages 1128–1137, Valencia, Spain. Association for Computational Linguistics.

Verónica Pérez-Rosas, Xinyi Wu, Kenneth Resnicow, and Rada Mihalcea. 2019. What Makes a Good Counselor? Learning to Distinguish between High-quality and Low-quality Counseling Conversations. In *Proceedings of the 57th Annual Meeting of the Association for Computational Linguistics*, pages 926–935, Florence, Italy. Association for Computational Linguistics.

Yann Raphalen, Chloé Clavel, and Justine Cassell. 2022. "You might think about slightly revising the title": Identifying Hedges in Peer-tutoring Interactions. In *Proceedings of the 60th Annual Meeting of the Association for Computational Linguistics (Volume 1: Long Papers)*, pages 2160–2174, Dublin, Ireland. Association for Computational Linguistics.

Colin Raffel, Noam Shazeer, Adam Roberts, Katherine Lee, Sharan Narang, Michael Matena, Yanqi Zhou, Wei Li, and Peter J Liu. 2020. Exploring the Limits of Transfer Learning with a Unified Text-to-Text Transformer. *Journal of Machine Learning Research*, 21:1–67.

Ryan E Rhodes, Amy Cox, and Reza Sayar. 2022. What Predicts the Physical Activity Intention–Behavior Gap? A Systematic Review. *Annals of Behavioral Medicine*, 56(1):1–20.

Rachel Rudinger, Aaron Steven White, and Benjamin Van Durme. 2018. Neural Models of Factuality. In *Proceedings of the 2018 Conference of the North American Chapter of the Association for Computational Linguistics: Human Language Technologies, Volume 1 (Long Papers)*, pages 731–744, New Orleans, Louisiana. Association for Computational Linguistics.

Timo Schick and Hinrich Schütze. 2021. It's Not Just Size That Matters: Small Language Models Are Also Few-Shot Learners. In *Proceedings of the 2021 Conference of the North American Chapter of the Association for Computational Linguistics: Human Language Technologies*, pages 2339–2352, Online. Association for Computational Linguistics.

Timo Schick and Hinrich Schütze. 2022. True Few-Shot Learning with Prompts—A Real-World Perspective. *Transactions of the Association for Computational Linguistics*, 10:716–731. Place: Cambridge, MA Publisher: MIT Press.

Noam Shazeer and Mitchell Stern. 2018. Adafactor: Adaptive learning rates with sublinear memory cost. In *Proceedings of the 35th International Conference on Machine Learning*, volume 80 of *Proceedings of Machine Learning Research*, pages 4596–4604. PMLR.

Rebecca M. Shingleton and Tibor P. Palfai. 2016. Technology-delivered adaptations of motivational interviewing for health-related behaviors: A systematic review of the current research. *Patient Education and Counseling*, 99(1):17–35.

Karan Singla, Zhuohao Chen, David Atkins, and Shrikanth Narayanan. 2020. Towards end-2-end learning for predicting behavior codes from spoken utterances in psychotherapy conversations. In *Proceedings of the 58th Annual Meeting of the Association for Computational Linguistics*, pages 3797–3803, Online. Association for Computational Linguistics.

Hongjin Su, Jungo Kasai, Chen Henry Wu, Weijia Shi, Tianlu Wang, Jiayi Xin, Rui Zhang, Mari Ostendorf,

Luke Zettlemoyer, Noah A. Smith, and Tao Yu. 2023. Selective Annotation Makes Language Models Better Few-Shot Learners. International Conference on Learning Representations. ArXiv:2209.01975 [cs].

Leili Tavabi, Kalin Stefanov, Larry Zhang, Brian Borsari, Joshua D. Woolley, Stefan Scherer, and Mohammad Soleymani. 2020. Multimodal Automatic Coding of Client Behavior in Motivational Interviewing. In *Proceedings of the 2020 International Conference on Multimodal Interaction*, pages 406–413, Virtual Event Netherlands. ACM.

Leili Tavabi, Trang Tran, Kalin Stefanov, Brian Borsari, Joshua Woolley, Stefan Scherer, and Mohammad Soleymani. 2021. Analysis of behavior classification in motivational interviewing. In *Proceedings of the Seventh Workshop on Computational Linguistics and Clinical Psychology: Improving Access*, pages 110–115, Online. Association for Computational Linguistics.

Hugo Touvron, Louis Martin, Kevin Stone, Peter Albert, Amjad Almahairi, Yasmine Babaei, Nikolay Bashlykov, Soumya Batra, Prajjwal Bhargava, Shruti Bhosale, Dan Bikel, Lukas Blecher, Cristian Canton Ferrer, Moya Chen, Guillem Cucurull, David Esiobu, Jude Fernandes, Jeremy Fu, Wenyin Fu, Brian Fuller, Cynthia Gao, Vedanuj Goswami, Naman Goyal, Anthony Hartshorn, Saghar Hosseini, Rui Hou, Hakan Inan, Marcin Kardas, Viktor Kerkez, Madian Khabsa, Isabel Kloumann, Artem Korenev, Punit Singh Koura, Marie-Anne Lachaux, Thibaut Lavril, Jenya Lee, Diana Liskovich, Yinghai Lu, Yuning Mao, Xavier Martinet, Todor Mihaylov, Pushkar Mishra, Igor Molybog, Yixin Nie, Andrew Poulton, Jeremy Reizenstein, Rashi Rungta, Kalyan Saladi, Alan Schelten, Ruan Silva, Eric Michael Smith, Ranjan Subramanian, Xiaoqing Ellen Tan, Binh Tang, Ross Taylor, Adina Williams, Jian Xiang Kuan, Puxin Xu, Zheng Yan, Iliyan Zarov, Yuchen Zhang, Angela Fan, Melanie Kambadur, Sharan Narang, Aurelien Rodriguez, Robert Stojnic, Sergey Edunov, and Thomas Scialom. 2023. Llama 2: Open Foundation and Fine-Tuned Chat Models. ArXiv:2307.09288 [cs].

Siddharth Varia, Shuai Wang, Kishaloy Halder, Robert Vacareanu, Miguel Ballesteros, Yassine Benajiba, Neha Anna John, Rishita Anubhai, Smaranda Muresan, and Dan Roth. 2023. Instruction Tuning for Few-Shot Aspect-Based Sentiment Analysis. In *Proceedings of the 13th Workshop on Computational Approaches to Subjectivity, Sentiment, & Social Media Analysis*, pages 19–27, Toronto, Canada. Association for Computational Linguistics.

Henny A. Westra and Nikoo Norouzian. 2018. Using Motivational Interviewing to Manage Process Markers of Ambivalence and Resistance in Cognitive Behavioral Therapy. *Cognitive Therapy and Research*, 42(2):193–203.

Thomas Wolf, Lysandre Debut, Victor Sanh, Julien Chaumond, Clement Delangue, Anthony Moi, Pierric Cistac, Tim Rault, Remi Louf, Morgan Funtowicz, Joe Davison, Sam Shleifer, Patrick von Platen, Clara Ma, Yacine Jernite, Julien Plu, Canwen Xu, Teven Le Scao, Sylvain Gugger, Mariama Drame, Quentin Lhoest, and Alexander Rush. 2020. Transformers: State-of-the-art natural language processing. In *Proceedings of the 2020 Conference on Empirical Methods in Natural Language Processing: System Demonstrations*, pages 38–45, Online. Association for Computational Linguistics.

Zixiu Wu, Simone Balloccu, Vivek Kumar, Rim Helaoui, Diego Reforgiato Recupero, and Daniele Riboni. 2023. Creation, Analysis and Evaluation of AnnoMI, a Dataset of Expert-Annotated Counselling Dialogues. *Future Internet*, 15(3):110.

Zixiu Wu, Simone Balloccu, Vivek Kumar, Rim Helaoui, Ehud Reiter, Diego Reforgiato Recupero, and Daniele Riboni. 2022. Anno-mi: A dataset of expert-annotated counselling dialogues. In *ICASSP 2022 - 2022 IEEE International Conference on Acoustics, Speech and Signal Processing (ICASSP)*, pages 6177–6181.

Fan Yin, Jesse Vig, Philippe Laban, Shafiq Joty, Caiming Xiong, and Chien-Sheng Wu. 2023. Did You Read the Instructions? Rethinking the Effectiveness of Task Definitions in Instruction Learning. In *Proceedings of the 61st Annual Meeting of the Association for Computational Linguistics (Volume 1: Long Papers)*, pages 3063–3079, Toronto, Canada. Association for Computational Linguistics.

Justine Zhang and Cristian Danescu-Niculescu-Mizil. 2020. Balancing Objectives in Counseling Conversations: Advancing Forwards or Looking Backwards. In *Proceedings of the 58th Annual Meeting of the Association for Computational Linguistics*, pages 5276–5289, Online. Association for Computational Linguistics.

Shengyu Zhang, Linfeng Dong, Xiaoya Li, Sen Zhang, Xiaofei Sun, Shuhe Wang, Jiwei Li, Runyi Hu, Tianwei Zhang, Fei Wu, and Guoyin Wang. 2023. Instruction Tuning for Large Language Models: A Survey. ArXiv:2308.10792 [cs].

Zihao Zhao, Eric Wallace, Shi Feng, Dan Klein, and Sameer Singh. 2021. Calibrate Before Use: Improving Few-shot Performance of Language Models. In *Proceedings of the 38th International Conference on Machine Learning*, pages 12697–12706. PMLR. ISSN: 2640-3498.

Kaitlyn Zhou, Dan Jurafsky, and Tatsunori Hashimoto. 2023. Navigating the Grey Area: Expressions of Overconfidence and Uncertainty in Language Models. ArXiv:2302.13439 [cs].

A Annotation Details for the `strength` Task

The annotation is conducted by the first author of this paper, who has both bachelor and master degrees in Computational Linguistics. We employ the strength rating approach similar to that of Gaume et al. (2016). Each client utterance is first assigned a strength value of "medium". If the utterance contains a **booster** word, its strength value changes to "high". On the contrary, if it has one or more **hedge** words, it receives "low" value. The "neutral" type is originally not assigned a strength value but in our experiments, we decide to annotate it similarly to the other two types for the sake of completeness. Since textual information alone is insufficient, we watch corresponding videos from `AnnoMI` dataset and use speech signals and body languages to assist with the annotation process. To generate explanations, we use GPT-3.5 with the following prompt *"How confident and certain the speaker is when saying $UTTERANCE$. Elaborate the response."*. When the explanations are in conflict with the annotator's assigned values, we further make use of explanations from ChatGPT (accessed from November 3 to 11) with the same prompt. Despite having the same base model as GPT-3.5, ChatGPT's responses are more elaborate and able to extract and explain parts of the utterances. An example is shown below:

Utterance: "I don't know. It's just like– My dad was really strict on me when I was little, and I don't want to be like that."

Strength value: low

GPT-3.5: "Based on the given statement, the speaker seems fairly confident and certain about not wanting to be like their strict father. The use of phrases like *I don't know* and *It's just like* suggests that the speaker is reflecting on their past experiences and drawing a clear connection to their current mindset. However, without further context, it is difficult to determine the exact level of confidence and certainty."

ChatGPT: "The sentence *"I don't know. It's just like– My dad was really strict on me when I was little, and I don't want to be like that"* suggests a low to moderate level of confidence and certainty. The speaker is expressing uncertainty or hesitation about a topic, and is explaining that they do not want to emulate their father's strict parenting style. The use of the phrase *"I don't know"* conveys a clear understanding of the speaker's lack of certainty or clarity, and suggests a level of confusion or indecision in their perspective. The use of the filler words *"just like"* introduces a degree of hesitancy or uncertainty, suggesting that the speaker is not completely sure of their position or is cautious about making a definitive statement. The statement *"My dad was really strict on me when I was little, and I don't want to be like that"* conveys a clear understanding of the speaker's past experiences and their desire to avoid a similar parenting style, and suggests a level of conviction in their perspective. Overall, the speaker appears to have a low to moderate level of confidence and certainty in their understanding of the topic, and is expressing a high level of hesitancy and uncertainty in their expression."

Researchers have suggested GPT models can serve as excellent data annotators, potentially replacing crowdsourced workers (He et al., 2023; Ding et al., 2023; Huang et al., 2023; Gilardi et al., 2023). Similar to Huang et al. (2023) whose findings show that lay people's decisions are affected by ChatGPT's explanations, we notice that they are extremely convincing. Therefore, annotators who employ them as assistants should be experts in the domain and understand the task clearly. For example, the following utterance *"To be frank, Mark, I honestly don't know. I mean, I honestly don't know what causes it because I've never had any reason. It came upon me from the GP and it took me back."* has a `strength` value of *high*: The speaker is highly certain about his uncertainty about the cause of the illness. ChatGPT, however, fails to detect this subtle difference.

ChatGPT: "The speaker appears to be uncertain and not confident when discussing the cause of their condition. The use of phrases like *"I honestly don't know"* and *"I've never had any reason"* indicates a lack of knowledge or understanding about the cause of their condition. The phrase *"It took me back"* suggests that the speaker was surprised or taken aback by the diagnosis, which further implies a lack of awareness or understanding about the condition prior to the diagnosis. Overall, the speaker seems to be expressing a sense of confusion and uncertainty about the cause of their condition."

B Label Distribution

Table 4 and Table 5 show the label distribution for `type` and `strength` tasks respectively.

Table 6 shows the number of labels. In the mixed

	training (full)	validation	test
change	854	79	169
neutral	2372	179	355
sustain	391	42	76

Table 4: Label distribution for type task.

	training	validation	test
high	50	20	122
medium	35	15	357
low	43	15	121

Table 5: Label distribution for strength task.

	training	validation	test
change high	24	10	36
change medium	18	8	82
change low	24	8	51
neutral high	0	0	58
neutral medium	0	0	237
neutral low	0	0	60
sustain high	26	10	28
sustain medium	17	7	38
sustain low	19	7	10

Table 6: Label distribution for multitask learning.

datasets, we add the data with **type** and **strength** labels but the amount of multitask data remains unchanged.

C Training Details

GPU usage: We use Quadro RTX 8000 (48 GB in memory) and GeForce RTX 2080 (11 GB in memory) to fine-tune Flan-T5 and RoBERTa respectively. As Flan-T5-XXL version is 45 GB, we load it in 8 bit for both training and inference so it can be fitted in one RTX 8000 GPU.

Flan-T5 parameters: Our hyperparameter search for the learning rate, weight decay, and the batch size is performed using Weights and Bias[10]. The learning rate is randomly sampled from the range of 5e-3 to 5e-5 in 30 trials on the Flan-T5-XL version (3B parameters) instead of Flan-T5-XXL (11B) to reduce computational costs. We settle on 3e-4 for all models. The weight decay is set to 1e-6. The batch size is 8. We fine-tune the Flan-T5 for 30 epochs using adafactor (Shazeer and Stern, 2018) as the optimiser. For other values, we use the default from huggingface (version 4.33.1) (Wolf et al., 2020) implementation. We use a fixed seed for reproducibility purposes.

LoRa parameters: There is no service to search for LoRa parameters. Therefore, we opt to use the recommended values from huggingface community: The LoRa rank, the alpha, and the dropout rate is set to 16, 32 and 0.1 respectively.

Training and Inference Time: Training time varies depending on data size. Using the full dataset of type task (i.e., 3k6 samples), the fine-tuning takes roughly 6 hours using early stopping. With data size ranging from 50 to 300, it takes from 30 minutes to 3 hours for 30 epochs without early stopping. Inference time on the test set using Flan-T5-XXL takes roughly 2.5 hours. After merging the LoRa adapters with the original weights, latency on the instruction-tuned models is almost the same as the original models.

Number of parameters: We use LoRa implemented in peft library[11] and train on all layers. The trained parameters for Flan-T5-XXL is around 71 millions, accounting for roughly 0.6% of the total 11 billion parameters. As for RoBERTa-large, we fine-tune all its 354 million parameter.

D Additional Evaluation Metrics

[10] https://wandb.ai/

[11] https://huggingface.co/docs/peft/index

	50		100		200		300		3600	
	Prec.	Recall	Prec.	Recall	Prec.	Recall	Prec.	Recall	Prec.	Recall
gpt-1s-icl	0.56	0.59	0.57	0.62	0.58	0.63	0.58	0.63	0.59	0.65
flant5-1s-icl	0.60	0.66	0.59	0.66	0.60	0.66	0.60	0.66	0.61	0.67
flant5-ift	0.63	0.58	0.64	0.60	0.60	0.62	0.63	0.60	0.75	0.73
roberta-ft	0.40	0.37	0.48	0.47	0.53	0.53	0.55	0.54	0.68	0.58

Table 7: Precision and Recall scores of the `type` task on the test set with different training samples after processing 2 hallucinated outputs.

	Accuracy	Precision	Recall	F1
gpt 0-shot	0.46	0.53	0.40	0.39
gpt 1-shot	0.40	0.36	0.33	0.34
flant5 0-shot	0.41	0.49	0.48	0.39
flant5 1-shot	0.47	0.53	0.49	0.45
flant5 ift	**0.72**	0.70	0.66	**0.68**
roberta ft	0.59	0.59	0.56	0.53

Table 8: Accuracy, Precision, Recall, and F1 scores for the `strength` task.

	`type`				`strength`			
	Acc.	Prec.	Recall	F1	Acc.	Prec.	Recall	F1
gpt 0-shot	**0.53**	0.58	0.52	**0.49**	0.41	0.40	0.42	0.38
gpt 1-shot	0.50	0.49	0.45	0.43	0.50	0.50	0.47	0.48
flant5 1-shot	0.43	0.36	0.35	0.34	0.40	0.45	0.45	0.39
flant5 ift	0.32	0.32	0.51	0.29	**0.67**	0.66	0.67	**0.66**

Table 9: Results on multitask learning.

Linguistic markers of schizophrenia: a case study of Robert Walser

Ivan Nenchev [1,2], Tatjana Scheffler [3], Marie de la Fuente [4], Heiner Stuke [1], Benjamin Wilck [5], Sandra Anna Just [1], Christiane Montag [1]

[1] Department of Psychiatry and Psychotherapy, Charité Campus Mitte, Charité – Universitätsmedizin Berlin, corporate member of Freie Universität Berlin, Humboldt-Universität zu Berlin, and Berlin Institute of Health,

[2] Berlin Institute of Health at Charité – Universitätsmedizin Berlin,

[3] German Studies, Ruhr-Universität Bochum,

[4] Department of Linguistics, University of Potsdam,

[5] The Hebrew University of Jerusalem, Martin Buber Society of Fellows in the Humanities and Social Sciences

ivan.nenchev@charite.de

Abstract

We present a study of the linguistic output of the German-speaking writer Robert Walser using NLP. We curated a corpus comprising texts written by Walser during periods of sound health, and writings from the year before his hospitalization, and writings from the first year of his stay in a psychiatric clinic, all likely attributed to schizophrenia. Within this corpus, we identified and analyzed a total of 20 linguistic markers encompassing established metrics for lexical diversity, semantic similarity, and syntactic complexity. Additionally, we explored lesser-known markers such as lexical innovation, concreteness, and imageability. Notably, we introduced two additional markers for phonological similarity for the first time within this context. Our findings reveal significant temporal dynamics in these markers closely associated with Walser's contemporaneous diagnosis of schizophrenia. Furthermore, we investigated the relationship between these markers, leveraging them for classification of the schizophrenic episode.

1 Introduction

Schizophrenia is a heterogeneous psychiatric disorder characterized by diverse symptoms impacting a person's perception, cognition, language and motor functions. The disorder displays variable courses; some patients undergo circumscribed episodes with psychotic symptoms and either complete or incomplete remission, while others follow a chronic course with persistent symptoms at a relatively stable level. Typically, there is a prodromal period, ranging from several weeks to several years, that precedes the first psychotic episode. Symptoms in schizophrenia can be broadly categorized into two groups: positive symptoms, such as hallucinations, delusions, and certain formal thought disorders like derailment and word salad; and negative symptoms, including poverty of speech, alogia, anhedonia, and social withdrawal (Andreasen, 1990). In clinical psychiatry, the diagnosis of schizophrenia is established based on interviews and diagnostic manuals that provide comprehensive descriptions of symptoms. Despite advances in modern medicine, the absence of concrete (bio)markers for diagnosis and individualized treatment for schizophrenia persists. Concurrently, patients exhibit fluctuating alterations in language production and comprehension that correlate with the illness's dynamics and severity. Despite the long history of study of language in connection to mental illness (the first accounts on recognizable linguistic patterns are indeed older than the term "schizophrenia" and even its predecessor "dementia praecox" (Griesinger, 1845; Brosius, 1857), only the recent advances of computational linguistics and NLP provide the necessary tools and technology to analyze substantial linguistic datasets and extract linguistic features in an objective and replicable manner (Hitczenko et al., 2021; Crema et al., 2022). Several authors identify the potential of linguistic features extracted by means of NLP as possible biomarkers of psychosis (Corcoran et al., 2020; de Boer et al., 2020). Palaniyappan (2021) emphasizes that linguistic production not only reflects biological processes but also incorporates social aspects. Consequently, he contends that language can be regarded as a biosocial marker. Our stance is that schizophrenia (and mental illness in general) should not be oversimplified to mere biology. We view the concept of biomarkers as an analogy, comparable to blood sugar levels or blood pressure in somatic medicine. Notably, a significant gap exists in the current state of research, with no established population norms for the NLP features. This contrasts sharply with

Proceedings of the 9th Workshop on Computational Linguistics and Clinical Psychology (CLPsych 2024), pages 41–60
March 21, 2024

the majority of biomarkers in traditional medicine. Addressing this gap could involve adopting a personalized methodology, observing changes in linguistic output over time in individual subjects.

Nowadays, NLP methodologies are commonly used to demonstrate significant differences in the linguistic production between participants suffering from schizophrenia or high-risk individuals compared with neurotypical participants. Furthermore, it seems that computational linguistic features at least partially correlate with the severity of psychotic symptoms. A promising recent trend in the field is to produce and analyse longitudinal datasets and explore the stability or the dynamics of the linguistics markers within schizophrenia. As schizophrenia is characterized by a highly heterogenous expression of symptoms, it is not surprising that there is evidence of a substantial difference in the linguistic markers within the schizophrenia group (Liebenthal et al., 2023). Given the advancements in individualized medicine, an important question arises: Can variations in linguistic markers be identified within each individual's language output, enabling a truly personalized method for diagnosing relapses and monitoring the disease? If so, NLP could furnish tools for tailoring individualized detection algorithms, thereby aiding in the prevention of future psychotic episodes.

In this study, we adopt such a longitudinal approach using a single-subject design. Our study is based on a linguistic corpus comprising short literary texts authored by the German-speaking writer Robert Walser who probably suffered from schizophrenia. From this corpus, we extracted established linguistic features for lexical diversity and lexical innovation, syntactic complexity, and semantic similarity. Additionally, we introduce markers for phonological similarity. We present evidence of significant marker dynamics temporally linked to Walser's diagnosis of schizophrenia and subsequent hospitalization.

In this work, we contribute to the intersection of NLP and psychiatry through multiple avenues. Primarily, we explore various NLP findings at the individual level. Furthermore, we introduce a novel linguistic marker, phonological similarity, warranting future investigation. Additionally, our utilization of a corpus from a German-speaking writer enhances the linguistic diversity within this domain.

2 Background

2.1 Linguistic markers of schizophrenia

One extensively studied linguistic aspect in psychotic language through NLP is semantic coherence, addressing the relatedness between word chunks or sentences, aiming to capture formal thought disorders (disorganisation, tangentiality, derailment and poverty of speech) in schizophrenia. In coherence analysis, words and sentences are commonly represented as vector embeddings in a multidimensional semantic space, with relatedness gauged via cosine similarity between these vectors. Currently, there is no consensus on a best practice approach regarding segmentation. Some studies focus on the semantic similarity between chunks of 5 or 10 tokens (called coherence-5 and coherence-10), other studies examine the similarity between sentences (first- and second-order coherence, measuring semantic similarity with a sentence's first or second neighbour(Parola et al., 2023)). Furthermore, there is also no consensus on the preferred type of embeddings. Studies reveal substantial differences in the semantic coherence when comparing patients with schizophrenia to neurotypical controls. The majority of studies suggest reduced semantic coherence in schizophrenia patients, notably derived from analyses based on word2vec, GloVe, and fastText embeddings (Corona-Hernández et al., 2023; Voleti et al., 2023; Iter et al., 2018; Morgan et al., 2021; Voppel et al., 2021; Just et al., 2020; Parola et al., 2023). The findings have encountered challenges. Alonso-Sánchez et al. (2022) revealed an increase in semantic coherence among a cohort experiencing the first episode of psychosis, countering previous assumptions. Moreover, Tang et al. (2021), employing BERT embeddings, yielded inconclusive coherence outcomes in inter-group comparisons. Intriguingly, only second-order coherence demonstrates potential for cross-language generalization (Parola et al., 2023).

Another frequently employed set of linguistic markers revolves around gauging the lexical diversity within language samples. It reflects the variety and richness of vocabulary within a text. The Type-Token Ratio (TTR) specifically quantifies the ratio of unique words to the total words in a text. However, due to its sensitivity to text length variations, various other markers have emerged to address this limitation and offer a more nuanced understanding of lexical richness. Among these markers, the Measure of Textual Lexical Diversity

(MTLD) and Mean Average TTR (MATTR) stand out (McCarthy and Jarvis, 2010). Several studies have investigated the differences in lexical diversity between subjects with schizophrenia and neurotypical subjects. Voleti et al. (2023) report lower lexical diversity, while Ziv et al. (2021) observe the opposite trend. Lundin et al. (2023) and Schneider et al. (2023) report a negative result on MTLD and TTR respectively. Notably, Bambini et al. (2022) utilize TTR for the identification of clusters of individuals with schizophrenia. Additionally, Pavy et al. (1969) report significantly higher TTR for individuals with acute schizophrenia compared to those with a chronic condition. In schizophrenia patients, lexical diversity measures seem to vary based on clinical symptoms. Some individuals demonstrate an increase, while others display a decrease in these metrics.

The words used in a text can be further examined beyond their mere counts. Despite the availability of comprehensive linguistic norms across languages, semantic norms related to concreteness and imageability are seldom applied in analyzing linguistic output from individuals affected by schizophrenia. Concreteness refers to the extent to which a word signifies something tangible, specific, and easily perceivable through the senses; imageability refers to the potential of words to evoke vivid mental images. Oertel et al. (2009) and Sack et al. (2005) have observed that individuals with schizophrenia and their first-degree relatives exhibit heightened vividness of mental imagery, as assessed through a standardized questionnaire. Notably, because of the absence of a correlation between vividness scores and symptoms, the authors interpret this phenomenon as indicative of a trait marker in schizophrenia. The investigation of mental imagery within in the linguistic production of individuals affected by schizophrenia remains unexplored in current research. The adoption of a vocabulary characterized by lower concreteness and imageability, possibly resulting in a more abstract linguistic style, might reflect reminiscences of psychopathological symptoms such as poverty of content of speech and stilted speech. Conversely, a discourse marked by high concreteness and vivid imagery also appears plausible. Minor et al. (2019) report that concreteness is not connected to neurocognitive, socialcognitive or metacognitive deficits in schizophrenia. A more recent study of Minor et al. (2023) examined the test-retest reliability of concreteness using the Coh-Metrix tool and reported a good intraclass-correlation.

Individuals with schizophrenia often exhibit lexical innovations, termed neologisms, encompassing words absent from the general lexicon. Surprisingly, the exploration of such lexical innovations in schizophrenia through NLP methodologies remains limited. To date, Just et al. (2020) stand as the sole instance using semi-automated neologism detection effectively, distinguishing schizophrenia individuals from control groups.

Syntactic complexity addresses the intricacy and sophistication of the grammatical structures in a text. It appears reduced in individuals at high risk for developing schizophrenia (Bedi et al., 2015; Corcoran et al., 2018). Schneider et al. (2023) report a significantly reduced syntactic complexity for individual suffering from schizophrenia compared to both controls and patients with depression. Haas et al. (2020) report a negative correlation between negative symptoms and syntactic complexity in clinically high risk individuals. Silva et al. (2023) analyse various indices of syntactic complexity in individuals with first episode psychosis and report that the majority of indices remain stable over a period of 6 months. Voleti et al. (2023) used Yngve scoring to analyse the syntactic complexity of transcribed interviews from individuals suffering from schizophrenia or bipolar disorder and healthy controls. Although syntactic complexity seems lower in the schizophrenia group this marker was not selected for the development of prediction models by the authors.

A commonly replicated linguistic feature of individuals with schizophrenia is the extensive use of first person singular pronouns as a marker of focus on the self (Ziv et al., 2021; Tang et al., 2021; Birnbaum et al., 2017; Lundin et al., 2023; Fineberg et al., 2015). The prominence of increased first-person singular pronoun use extends beyond schizophrenia and has been observed in diverse mental health conditions (Brockmeyer et al., 2015; Edwards and Holtzman, 2017; Lyons et al., 2018). An increased use of second person singular pronouns (Watson et al., 2012) and decreased use of first person plural pronouns (Lundin et al., 2023) have also been reported in schizophrenia.

This study not only delves into established linguistic markers but also introduces phonological similarity as a promising marker in NLP associated with linguistic output in schizophrenia. While drawing from established methodologies for measuring string similarity, this study stands as the pioneering exploration of this approach within the context of linguistic output in schizophrenia. High phonological similarity may be associated with clanging - a rare symptom observed in some patients with schizophrenia which involves using words based on their sound similarity rather than their meaning, e.g. "I'm trying to make sense out of sense. I'm not making sense [cents] anymore. I have to make dollars." (Andreasen, 1986).

2.2 Longitudinal studies

Currently, only a limited number of studies address the question whether linguistic markers represent stable longitudinal traits or capture dynamic shifts in psychological states. Research by Bedi et al. (2015) demonstrated a decrease in semantic coherence via Latent Semantic Analysis (LSA) preceding psychosis, complemented by a decline in markers of syntactic complexity. Corcoran et al. (2018) corroborated these findings. Birnbaum et al. (2019) analyzed Facebook posts, identifying linguistic alterations preceding psychotic relapses, notably an upsurge in first- and second-person pronouns. Minor et al. (2023) observed satisfactory test-retest reliability in speech content and organization over 6 months to a year using LIWC and Coh-Metrix. Alonso-Sánchez et al. (2022) highlighted an augmented semantic similarity in a picture description task over 6 months, correlating with increased negative symptoms. Silva et al. (2023) examined the syntactic complexity of individuals with first episode psychosis and report that over a period of 6 months the majority of the examined markers remain stable.

2.3 Literature in the study of mental illness

The NLP analysis of authors with mental illness includes studies on Iris Murdoch's reduced lexical diversity due to Alzheimer's dementia (Hirst and Wei Feng, 2012; Le et al., 2011; Garrard et al., 2005; Pakhomov et al., 2011). Edgar Allan Poe's works are scrutinized to illuminate aspects of his enigmatic death (Dean and Boyd, 2020). Additionally, research examines linguistic patterns associated with bipolar disorder (Rentoumi et al., 2017) or suicidality in poems or in diaries (Stirman and Pennebaker, 2001; Fernández-Cabana et al., 2013; Baddeley et al., 2011). To our knowledge, a systematic NLP-based analysis of the literary works authored by an individual diagnosed with schizophrenia is still missing. In the current study, we extract NLP features from a corpus of a single individual and observe significant within-subject variations, which could be associated with psychosis.

3 Methods

3.1 Robert Walser

Robert Walser (1878–1956) is a German-speaking writer from the early 20th century, who played a significant role in European literary modernism. Throughout his lifetime, Walser created an extensive body of work, encompassing several novels, numerous short pieces of prose, and poetry. In 1929, he was institutionalized, remaining in psychiatric care for nearly 27 years until his passing. During this period, he received a diagnosis of schizophrenia. Several detailed accounts shed light on Walser's hospitalization and his prolonged stay in psychiatric clinics (Wernli, 2014; Partl et al., 2011). Upon admission to the Waldau psychiatric clinic, Walser exhibited auditory verbal hallucinations, probably persecutory delusions, anxiety, and suicidal thoughts. Subsequently, in the Herisau asylum from 1933 onwards, he consistently reported experiencing commenting and dialogizing voices, as noted by the attending psychiatrist (Vannette, 2020). Through an extensive presentation of Walser's medical records (Wernli, 2014) and a detailed exploration of his family history, which includes multiple instances of schizophrenia or depression among family members (Gisi, 2018), the possibility of his diagnosis becomes evident. However, posthumously, the diagnosis of schizophrenia has faced challenges from various scholars. Lyons and Fitzgerald (2004) suggest, for instance, that Walser might have been experiencing high-functioning autism instead. Other scholars reject any psychiatric diagnosis altogether and assert that Walser's stay in psychiatric institutions was solely due to socio-economic reasons. This study acknowledges that verifying or refuting Walser's psychiatric diagnosis falls outside its scope, particularly given the impossibility of such an assessment for a person who passed away over 60 years ago. Nevertheless, considering the current efforts to identify NLP markers of schizophrenia, Walser's extensive body of work and medical history presents an intriguing case. His extensive body of work presents a compelling opportunity for NLP research due to the substantial volume of text he generated in the decades and years prior to and just

Period	Texts	Tokens (total)	Tokens (mean)
1903-1907	70	50102	715.74
1915-1919	79	80408	1017.82
1928-1929	40	28688	717.20
Total	189	159198	995.56

Table 1: Linguistic corpus

before his hospitalization, enabling comprehensive comparative analysis.

3.2 Corpus

For our analysis, we assembled a corpus consisting of short prose texts authored by Walser for various periodicals or published in collections. Considering the texts share the same genre and have comparable lengths, we consider them comparable for the purposes of our study. This corpus included all currently available texts (n=189) from three distinct timeframes: 70 texts published between 1903 and 1907, sourced from the volume Fritz Kocher's Aufsätze (Walser, 2023a), kleine Prosa (Walser, 2023b), as well as publications in Neue Rundschau (Walser, 2017a), Schaubühne (Walser, 2015), and Berliner Tageblatt (Walser, 2013a). Another set of 79 texts, spanning 1915 to 1919, originated from Neue Züricher Zeitung (Walser, 2013b), Neue Rundschau (Walser, 2017a), Prosastücke (Walser, 2017b), and Poetenleben (Walser, 2014). Notably, Walser's biography does not attest to mental suffering or illness during these periods. Lastly, 40 texts written in 1928 and 1929, form the third part of the corpus (Walser, 2019, 2013b,a). Walser was admitted to the psychiatric clinic in Waldau in January 1929. The assumption that he had been in a state of psychosis in the months (and likely years) leading up to this admission has been expressed by his biographers (Mächler and Seelig, 1992) as cited in (Vannette, 2020). We decided to exclude both poetry and novels to ensure maximal homogeneity in the corpus, facilitating comparisons across different time periods. Walser's three major novels were composed between 1907 and 1909. The draft of a fourth novel, *The Robber*, was found posthumously and dated back to 1925. A detailed examination of Walser's poetry or letters is reserved for future work.

3.3 Linguistic markers

After constructing the corpus and preprocessing, we extracted a number of linguistic markers.

To gauge semantic coherence, we utilized pretrained word2vec embeddings from the Python library spaCy[1]. After removing the stop words, we computed the cosine similarity between chunks of 5 and 10 tokens and averaged these values to derive one score per text, generating coherence-5 and coherence-10 scores for chunks with 5 and 10 tokens respectively. To assess first- and second-order sentence similarity, we employed a pretrained Hugging Face transformer model[2] using the sentence transformers Python library (Reimers and Gurevych, 2019) we calculated cosine similarity between sentence BERT-embeddings, then averaging these values to produce a single score for each text.

To estimate the lexical diversity of the texts we used the python library lexical richness (Shen et al., 2023) and calculated TTR, MLTD and MATTR for both 25 and 50 token windows.

In addition to this, we calculated the concreteness and imageability values for each text as the mean of the concreteness and imageability norms for the individual words used in the texts. We used the word norms from the newly developed GLEAN dataset for German (Lüdtke and Hugentobler).

We employed a German reference corpus[3] comprising 249 million tokens extracted from texts between 1465 and 1969 to detect neologism. This corpus, spanning Walser's lifetime, was chosen due to its written content. After preprocessing involving stopword removal and lemmatization, we determined the relative frequency of tokens/lemmata in texts that were out of scope of the German reference corpus.

After POS-tagging, we estimated syntactic complexity by calculating the mean Yngve score, sentence length, and number of clauses per sentence in each text. The Yngve Score measures the depth of the parsing tree, with higher scores indicating a more complex syntactic structure (Yngve, 1960). Furthermore, we included the mean frequency of 1st and 2nd person singular and also 1st person plural pronouns per text in our report.

To assess the phonological similarity among

[1] github.com/explosion/spacy-models/releases/tag/de_core_news_lg-3.7.0

[2] huggingface.co/aari1995/German_Semantic_STS_V2

[3] www.dwds.de/r/lexdb/dta/lex

strings, we analyzed the raw un-preprocessed text. Initially, we transformed the graphemes into phonemes using the Python library Epitran (Mortensen et al., 2018). Subsequently, we calculated the Jaro-Winkler similarity between a string and each token from the consecutive 10- and 20-token sequences. We selected these window sizes based on the established capacity of working memory, commonly regarded as 7±2 tokens (Miller, 1956), but acknowledging potential individual differences. Following this, we derived a mean similarity score for each text.

3.4 Analysis

Comparison between periods. The texts from the three distinct periods were compared for differences in linguistic markers via a one-way ANOVA analysis and a subsequent Tukey test through the statsmodels Python library (Seabold and Perktold, 2010). In total we estimated 20 linguistic markers. To mitigate Type I errors, a Bonferroni correction was implemented to adjust for the multitude of linguistic markers assessed ($p < 0.0025$ for 20 markers). In assessing the practical significance of observed distinctions, we provide effect sizes for individual markers within our analysis. Our evaluation indicates that small effects align with η^2 around 0.01, medium effects with η^2 around 0.06 and large effects with η^2 around 0.14 (Cohen, 1988). We proceeded to analyze the relationships between the linguistic markers by computing their correlations.

Classification. In our study, we applied sklearn's (Pedregosa et al., 2011) classification algorithms – logistic regression, SVM, random forests, and Naïve Bayes – to categorize texts based on extracted linguistic markers. We assigned "healthy" to texts from the initial two periods and "ill" to those from the last period. The robust 10-fold cross-validation technique notably bolstered the models' reliability and ability to generalize effectively across the diverse entries within the text corpus.

4 Results

Statistically significant differences between time periods were observed for the majority of linguistic markers after Bonferroni correction (Table 2). Subsequent post-hoc Tukey tests identified these differences to reside mainly in the third period. Specifically, markers related to lexical richness, concreteness, imageability, neologism frequency, 1st and 2nd order coherence, and phonological similarity exhibited large effect sizes. Other markers such as syntactic complexity displayed moderate effect sizes. Coherence-10 and the frequency of personal pronouns did not show significant differences. Correlation analysis (table and hierarchically-clustered heatmap in the Appendix21) unveiled generally moderate to weak correlations among linguistic markers across different domains. For instance, coherence-5 and coherence-10 demonstrated high mutual correlation but exhibited weak associations with measures of lexical diversity, syntactic complexity, or phonological similarity. Within our analysis involving 20 linguistic markers, the Naïve Bayes classifier demonstrated superior performance in distinguishing texts written in the third period from those in earlier periods (Table 3). In the context of a personalized approach, this classification algorithm can only be applied to the linguistic output of the person on whose corpus it was trained.

4.1 Figures and tables

In this section, we present scattered boxplots annotated for significance using the Tukey test ($p >$ 0.0025 not significant, $p < 0.0025$ '*', $p < 0.001$ '**', $p < 0.0001$ '***') for MLTD, neologisms, concreteness, phonological similarity (20-token window), and coherence-5 (Fig 1-5). Plots for the remaining markers can be found in the Appendix A. In Table 2, we present the descriptive results and outcomes from the ANOVA comparisons. In Table 3, we summarize the results from the classification. In Table 5, we provide examples of text exhibiting high phonological similarity.

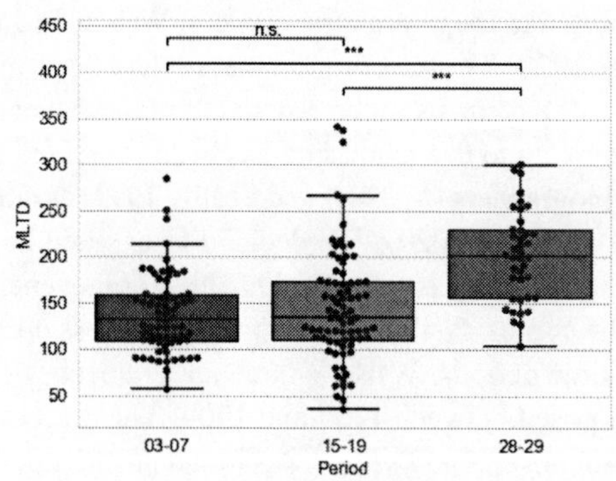

Figure 1: MLTD

	1903-1907 (n=70)	1915-1919 (n=79)	1928-1929 (n=40)	ANOVA	η^2
1.Coherence-5	0.465 (0.044)	0.456 (0.034)	0.426 (0.041)	***F*=12.351**	0.117
2.Coherence-10	0.59 (0.041)	0.593 (0.038)	0.569 (0.042)	*F*=5.224	0.053
3.1st order coherence	0.622 (0.034)	0.647 (0.029)	0.653 (0.036)	***F*=15.603**	0.143
4.2dn order coherence	0.604 (0.033)	0.63 (0.032)	0.637 (0.037)	***F*=16.091**	0.147
5.TTR	0.561 (0.091)	0.527 (0.09)	0.593 (0.057)	***F*=8.468**	0.083
6.MTLD	138.665 (42.5)	146.376 (61.9)	201.478 (48.9)	***F*=19.942**	0.298
7.MATTR 25	0.907 (0.022)	0.901 (0.027)	0.931 (0.012)	***F*=24.047**	0.205
8.MATTR 50	0.847 (0.028)	0.838 (0.037)	0.88 (0.018)	***F*=26.196**	0.219
9.Mean token length	7.392 (0.457)	7.554 (0.479)	8.389 (0.548)	***F*=57.264**	0.381
10.Out of scope tokens	0.081 (0.033)	0.084 (0.026)	0.143 (0.032)	***F*=63.81**	0.406
11.Concreteness	2.053 (1.057)	1.51 (0.809)	0.447 (0.823)	***F*=39.541**	0.298
12.Imageability	1.702 (0.874)	1.185 (0.77)	0.219 (0.745)	***F*=43.193**	0.317
13.Yngve score	4.669 (1.056)	5.418 (1.206)	5.442 (1.075)	***F*=9.996**	0.097
14.Mean sentence length	15.945 (6.92)	20.023 (6.349)	19.982 (7.013)	***F*=8.093**	0.080
15.Clauses	1.959 (1.021)	2.413 (0.735)	2.556 (0.764)	***F*=7.911**	0.078
16.1st person singular pronouns	0.02 (0.023)	0.03 (0.022)	0.032 (0.022)	*F*=5.619	0.0569
17.2nd person singular pronouns	0.003 (0.012)	0.005 (0.012)	0.004 (0.007)	*F*=0.53	0.005
18.1st person plural pronouns	0.006 (0.009)	0.003 (0.005)	0.002 (0.002)	*F*=4.715	0.0482
19.Phonological similarity 20	0.29 (0.013)	0.285 (0.015)	0.305 (0.013)	***F*=28.961**	0.237
20.Phonological similarity 10	0.289 (0.014)	0.285 (0.015)	0.305 (0.013)	***F*=28.459**	0.234

Table 2: Desriptive statistics and results from the ANOVA: means and standard deviations (in brackets) are listed for each group and category. Bold font indicates significant results after Bonferroni correction for multiple testing.

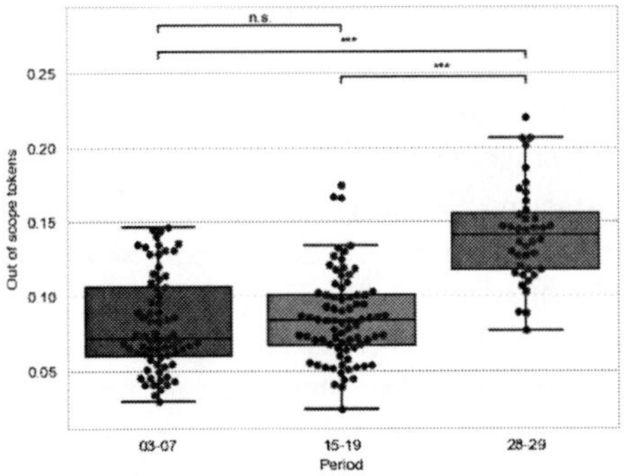

Figure 2: Out of scope tokens

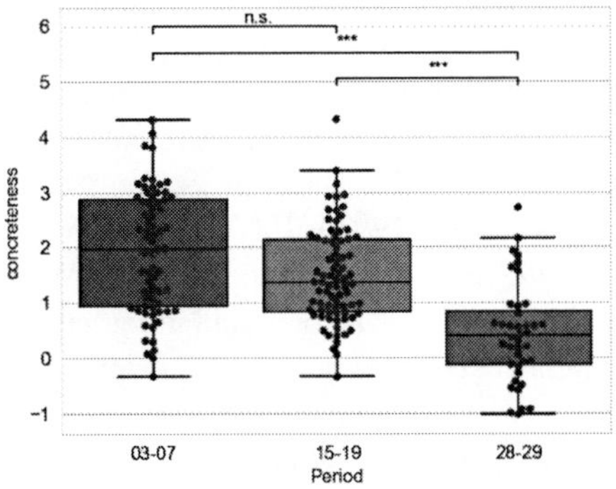

Figure 3: Concreteness

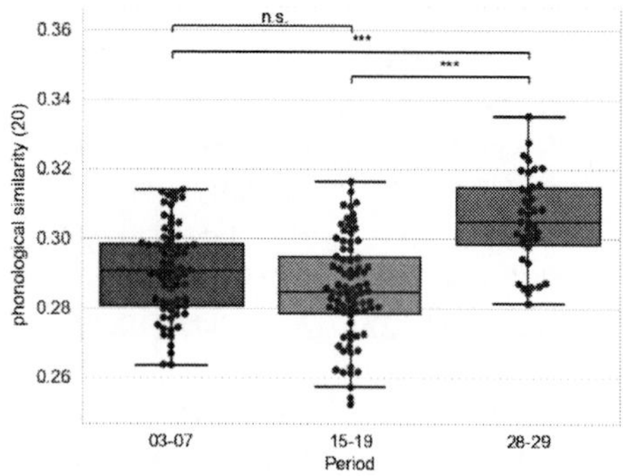

Figure 4: Phonological similarity (20-token window)

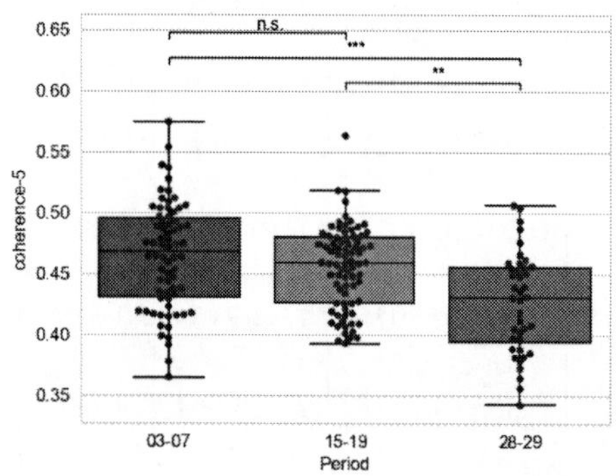

Figure 5: Coherence-5

5 Discussion

In this study, we analyzed the linguistic production of the German-speaking author Robert Walser, who probably suffered from schizophrenia, using NLP. Walser's case is particularly intriguing, given that he produced a substantial body of literary texts over a period of more than 30 years, and towards its end he was hospitalized in a psychiatric clinic with a diagnosis of schizophrenia. To construct our corpus, we compiled short prose from three distinct timeframes: 1903 – 1907, 1915 – 1919, and 1928 – 1929, the latter coinciding with Walser's hospitalization for schizophrenia in January 1929. Biographical notes suggest his experience of psychotic symptoms before hospitalization, indicating that the texts from the third period were likely composed during a psychotic state. Examining several established NLP features, we investigate their temporal association with Walser's psychosis. Additionally, we introduce two novel markers which aim at capturing phonological similarity and imagiability. Our analysis delineates a significant linguistic shift temporally linked to the onset of schizophrenia.

Model	Acc.	Prec.	Rec.	F1
Logistic regression	0.85	0.76	0.60	0.60
Random Forest	0.90	0.81	0.69	0.71
SVM	0.87	0.79	0.70	0.67
Naïve Bayes	**0.90**	**0.72**	**0.88**	**0.75**

Table 3: Results from the classification

Walser's texts from 1928 – 1929 showcase a significant lexical expansion, characterized by heightened lexical diversity, increased usage of out of scope words, and generally longer words. Metrics including MLTD, MATTR 25, MATTR 50, and out of scope token frequency demonstrate substantial effect sizes. Notably, Ziv et al. (2021) align with our findings on lexical diversity, diverging from Voleti et al. (2023), Schneider et al. (2023), and Lundin et al. (2023). Bambini et al. (2022) suggests an association between lexical diversity and psychopathological symptoms, demonstrating higher TTR in patients with pronounced symptoms. Additionally, our study replicates Just et al. (2020) observation of increased neologism use. Remarkably, a significant moderate correlation between overall lexical diversity and the usage of out of scope tokens is evident in Walser's case, potentially linked to schizophrenic symptomatology. While yielding significant results, our algorithm for the detection of lexical innovation and neologisms requires further refinement. It currently captures not only true neologisms (e.g. "Unbewusstheitsabwesenheit", "humorentfremden", "Shakespearehaftigkeit" and "Shakespearesch", "Schwalbenessay")[4] but also tokens written in Swiss German or tokens with deviant orthography.

Furthermore, Walser's later texts feature a notable decrease in both concreteness and imageability, resulting in a more abstract and ambiguous tone. The high correlation between imageability and concreteness suggests a shared underlying phenomenon. Minor et al. (2023) demonstrate sufficient test-retest reliability for word concreteness over a 6-month period, indicating its stability within that timeframe. Our analysis spans a much

[4] e.g. "unconsciousness absence", "humor alienation", "Shakespeareanism" and "Shakespearean", "Swallow essay"

longer period (1903 to 1929), allowing for a comprehensive comparison. To date, only Minor et al. (2019). reported a null association between social cognition or metacognition and concreteness so that the relationship between these markers and psychopathological symptoms remains to be studied. Overall, concreteness and imageability emerge as promising markers warranting further investigation.

In our analysis, we introduced a novel measure of phonological similarity, utilizing Jaro-Winkler similarity for the first time in schizophrenia-related NLP research. Specifically, we assessed similarity between a token (as phoneme) and a subsequent window of 10 or 20 tokens, yielding two highly correlated values likely measuring the same phenomenon. In Table 5, we provide some examples of text exhibiting high phonological similarity. ANOVA results indicated significant differences among the three samples, with post-hoc Tukey tests pinpointing distinctions in the third time period. Notably, this finding exhibited a high effect size and demonstrated moderate correlation with measures of lexical diversity. We believe this marker holds promise and warrants further investigation. As for its correlation with clanging or other psychopathological symptoms, this remains an open question that requires additional exploration.

The analysis of semantic coherence yielded contrasting outcomes. With pretrained word2vec embeddings, a significant reduction in semantic similarity for 5-token chunks emerged in the third period, showcasing a moderate effect size. These results align with previous findings (Corona-Hernández et al., 2023; Voleti et al., 2023; Iter et al., 2018; Morgan et al., 2021; Voppel et al., 2021). However, semantic similarity for 10-word chunks did not attain significance post-Bonferroni correction. Notably, these markers exhibited high correlations solely among themselves, distinct from other dataset markers. Conversely, utilizing pretrained BERT embeddings revealed increased cosine similarity between consecutive sentences in the third period compared to the first period. Additionally, 1st and 2nd order coherence exhibited significant positive correlations with measures of syntactic complexity. It seems that in the case of Walser the cosine similarity measured from the pretrained BERT model could be associated with syntax. Interestingly, the correlation between semantic similarity values from word2vec and BERT embeddings did not demonstrate significance, suggesting that they capture of distinct underlying phenomena.

There were also significant differences in the syntactic features although their effect was much less pronounced compared to the linguistic markers already described. Notably we could not find the reduction of syntactic complexity which has been described by Bedi et al. (2015) and Corcoran et al. (2018). Since this reduction of complexity has been associated with depression and negative symptoms, we can speculate that Walser was not showing these symptoms at the time before his schizophrenia diagnosis.

The observation regarding the lack of significant differences in the use of pronouns in Walser's texts is intriguing. This finding seemingly contradicts prior research (Ziv et al., 2021; Tang et al., 2021; Lundin et al., 2023). However, it's important to note that the increased use of 1st person pronouns, associated with schizophrenia, might not exclusively indicate this condition but might be observed across various mental health conditions (Lyons et al., 2018). Therefore, this particular marker might not hold substantial promise for schizophrenia detection.

Our findings offer an intriguing perspective on the concept of biomarkers or biosocial markers in schizophrenia. Unlike traditional biomarkers in somatic medicine, we observe an individual constellation that may not always align with the typical profile for the disease in the population. For instance, an increase in the usage of personal pronouns, a linguistic feature typically found in schizophrenia, does not manifest in Walser's later texts. Conversely, we observe a decrease in concreteness and imageability, along with an increase in phonological similarity. Considering the pressing demand for markers for schizophrenia in clinical practice, an NLP-driven approach shows promise. Its strength lies in its capacity for personalized analysis, identifying individual markers with significant predictive power. Utilizing these markers holds potential for predicting relapses and enhancing tailored interventions.

Limitations

Our study delineates several limitations that shape the scope and interpretation of our findings. Foremost, the exclusive focus on a singular individual restrains the generalizability of our outcomes. It's imperative to acknowledge that Walser was diagnosed with schizophrenia in 1929, almost a century preceding our study. This historical context bears significance, as diagnostic criteria and the conceptualization of psychiatric disorders have substantially evolved since that period. The diagnostic classifications prevalent during Walser's era might not seamlessly align with contemporary diagnostic manuals, potentially impacting the interpretation and contextualization of clinical data within modern psychiatric frameworks. As previously mentioned, the diagnosis itself has also faced challenges from scholars posthumously. Furthermore, the absence of standardized ratings for psychopathology in Walser's case introduces a pivotal gap. Relying solely on clinical records devoid of standardized assessments markedly curtails the depth of psychopathological insights. In addition, we recognize that alternative explanations may exist for the observed changes in linguistic style across the third time period. There are several alternative explanations of the observed results which cannot be easily addressed in the current single case design. Considering Walser's vocation as a writer, linguistic shifts in his work may reflect deliberate adaptations and conscious development in his literary style or changes in the topics he addressed. Additionally, linguistic changes associated with aging are less probable, as at the time of his hospitalization at around 50 years old, typical cognitive changes related to older age do not seem likely. The current corpus is limited to literary prose texts, posing a potential limitation. Future research should consider including additional sources of text, such as Walser's personal letters, to enhance the breadth and depth of analysis.

Ethics Statement

The current study is part of a broader project on the linguistic production of individuals with schizophrenia, which has received approval from the ethics board at the Charité – Universitätsmedizin Berlin. The texts from Robert Walser used in this research are published open access by the Robert Walser Archive and the Critical Walser Edition. Walser's medical history has been previously published. The author died 67 years ago. We acknowledge that the findings of this research should not be utilized for the initial diagnosis of schizophrenia. However, we recognize the potential of employing NLP in detecting relapses among individuals already diagnosed.

Acknowledgements

We express our gratitude to the Robert Walser Archive for providing us with the texts. Dr. Ivan Nenchev is participant in the BIH Charité Digital Clinician Scientist Program funded by the Charité – Universitätsmedizin Berlin, and the Berlin Institute of Health at Charité (BIH).

References

Maria Francisca Alonso-Sánchez, Sabrina D. Ford, Michael MacKinley, Angélica Silva, Roberto Limongi, and Lena Palaniyappan. 2022. Progressive changes in descriptive discourse in First Episode Schizophrenia: a longitudinal computational semantics study. *Schizophrenia*, 8(1):1–9. Number: 1 Publisher: Nature Publishing Group.

N. C. Andreasen. 1990. Methods for assessing positive and negative symptoms. *Modern Problems of Pharmacopsychiatry*, 24:73–88.

Nancy C. Andreasen. 1986. Scale for the assessment of thought, language, and communication (TLC). *Schizophrenia Bulletin*, 12(3):473–482.

Jenna L. Baddeley, Gwyneth R. Daniel, and James W. Pennebaker. 2011. How Henry Hellyer's Use of Language Foretold His Suicide. *Crisis*, 32(5):288–292. Publisher: Hogrefe Publishing.

Valentina Bambini, Federico Frau, Luca Bischetti, Federica Cuoco, Margherita Bechi, Mariachiara Buonocore, Giulia Agostoni, Ilaria Ferri, Jacopo Sapienza, Francesca Martini, Marco Spangaro, Giorgia Bigai, Federica Cocchi, Roberto Cavallaro, and Marta Bosia. 2022. Deconstructing heterogeneity in schizophrenia through language: a semi-automated linguistic analysis and data-driven clustering approach. *Schizophrenia*, 8(1):1–12. Number: 1 Publisher: Nature Publishing Group.

Gillinder Bedi, Facundo Carrillo, Guillermo A. Cecchi, Diego Fernández Slezak, Mariano Sigman, Natália B. Mota, Sidarta Ribeiro, Daniel C. Javitt, Mauro Copelli, and Cheryl M. Corcoran. 2015. Automated analysis of free speech predicts psychosis onset in high-risk youths. *NPJ schizophrenia*, 1:15030.

M. L. Birnbaum, S. K. Ernala, A. F. Rizvi, E. Arenare, A. R. Van Meter, M. De Choudhury, and J. M. Kane. 2019. Detecting relapse in youth with psychotic disorders utilizing patient-generated and patient-contributed digital data from Facebook. *npj Schizophrenia*, 5(1):1–9. Number: 1 Publisher: Nature Publishing Group.

Michael L. Birnbaum, Sindhu Kiranmai Ernala, Asra F. Rizvi, Munmun De Choudhury, and John M. Kane. 2017. A Collaborative Approach to Identifying Social Media Markers of Schizophrenia by Employing Machine Learning and Clinical Appraisals. *Journal of Medical Internet Research*, 19(8):e289.

Timo Brockmeyer, Johannes Zimmermann, Dominika Kulessa, Martin Hautzinger, Hinrich Bents, Hans-Christoph Friederich, Wolfgang Herzog, and Matthias Backenstrass. 2015. Me, myself, and I: self-referent word use as an indicator of self-focused attention in relation to depression and anxiety. *Frontiers in Psychology*, 6.

Casper M. Brosius. 1857. Über die Sprache der Irren. *Allgemeine Zeitschrift für Psychiatrie und psychisch-gerichtliche Medizin*, 1.:37 – 64.

Jacob Cohen. 1988. *Statistical Power Analysis for the Behavioral Sciences*, 2 edition. Routledge, New York.

Cheryl M. Corcoran, Facundo Carrillo, Diego Fernández-Slezak, Gillinder Bedi, Casimir Klim, Daniel C. Javitt, Carrie E. Bearden, and Guillermo A. Cecchi. 2018. Prediction of psychosis across protocols and risk cohorts using automated language analysis. *World psychiatry: official journal of the World Psychiatric Association (WPA)*, 17(1):67–75.

Cheryl M. Corcoran, Vijay A. Mittal, Carrie E. Bearden, Raquel E Gur, Kasia Hitczenko, Zarina Bilgrami, Aleksandar Savic, Guillermo A. Cecchi, and Phillip Wolff. 2020. Language as a biomarker for psychosis: A natural language processing approach. *Schizophrenia Research*, 226:158–166.

H. Corona-Hernández, J. N. de Boer, S. G. Brederoo, A. E. Voppel, and I. E. C. Sommer. 2023. Assessing coherence through linguistic connectives: Analysis of speech in patients with schizophrenia-spectrum disorders. *Schizophrenia Research*, 259:48–58.

Claudio Crema, Giuseppe Attardi, Daniele Sartiano, and Alberto Redolfi. 2022. Natural language processing in clinical neuroscience and psychiatry: A review. *Frontiers in Psychiatry*, 13.

Janna N. de Boer, Sanne G. Brederoo, Alban E. Voppel, and Iris E. C. Sommer. 2020. Anomalies in language as a biomarker for schizophrenia. *Current Opinion in Psychiatry*, 33(3):212–218.

Hannah J. Dean and Ryan L. Boyd. 2020. Deep into that darkness peering: A computational analysis of the role of depression in Edgar Allan Poe's life and death. *Journal of Affective Disorders*, 266:482–491.

To'Meisha Edwards and Nicholas S. Holtzman. 2017. A meta-analysis of correlations between depression and first person singular pronoun use. *Journal of Research in Personality*, 68:63–68.

M. Fernández-Cabana, A. García-Caballero, M. T. Alves-Pérez, M. J. García-García, and R. Mateos. 2013. Suicidal traits in Marilyn Monroe's Fragments: an LIWC analysis. *Crisis*, 34(2):124–130.

S. K. Fineberg, S. Deutsch-Link, M. Ichinose, T. McGuinness, A. J. Bessette, C. K. Chung, and P. R. Corlett. 2015. Word use in first-person accounts of schizophrenia†. *The British Journal of Psychiatry*, 206(1):32–38.

Peter Garrard, Lisa M. Maloney, John R. Hodges, and Karalyn Patterson. 2005. The effects of very early Alzheimer's disease on the characteristics of writing by a renowned author. *Brain*, 128(2):250–260.

Lucas Marco Gisi, editor. 2018. *Robert Walser-Handbuch*. J.B. Metzler, Stuttgart.

Wilhelm Griesinger. 1845. *Die Pathologie und Therapie der psychischen Krankheiten, für Aerzte und Studirende*, 1. auflage edition. Krabbe, Stuttgart.

S. S. Haas, G. E. Doucet, S. Garg, S. N. Herrera, C. Sarac, Z. R. Bilgrami, R. B. Shaik, and C. M. Corcoran. 2020. Linking language features to clinical symptoms and multimodal imaging in individuals at clinical high risk for psychosis. *European Psychiatry: The Journal of the Association of European Psychiatrists*, 63(1):e72.

Graeme Hirst and Vanessa Wei Feng. 2012. Changes in Style in Authors with Alzheimer's Disease. *English Studies*, 93(3):357–370. Publisher: Routledge _eprint: https://doi.org/10.1080/0013838X.2012.668789.

Kasia Hitczenko, Vijay A Mittal, and Matthew Goldrick. 2021. Understanding Language Abnormalities and Associated Clinical Markers in Psychosis: The Promise of Computational Methods. *Schizophrenia Bulletin*, 47(2):344–362.

Dan Iter, Jong Yoon, and Dan Jurafsky. 2018. Automatic Detection of Incoherent Speech for Diagnosing Schizophrenia. In *Proceedings of the Fifth Workshop on Computational Linguistics and Clinical Psychology: From Keyboard to Clinic*, pages 136–146, New Orleans, LA. Association for Computational Linguistics.

Sandra A. Just, Erik Haegert, Nora Kořánová, Anna-Lena Bröcker, Ivan Nenchev, Jakob Funcke, Andreas Heinz, Felix Bermpohl, Manfred Stede, and Christiane Montag. 2020. Modeling Incoherent Discourse in Non-Affective Psychosis. *Frontiers in Psychiatry*, 11. Publisher: Frontiers.

Xuan Le, Ian Lancashire, Graeme Hirst, and Regina Jokel. 2011. Longitudinal detection of dementia through lexical and syntactic changes in writing: a case study of three British novelists. *Literary and Linguistic Computing*, 26(4):435–461.

Einat Liebenthal, Michaela Ennis, Habiballah Rahimi-Eichi, Eric Lin, Yoonho Chung, and Justin T. Baker. 2023. Linguistic and non-linguistic markers of disorganization in psychotic illness. *Schizophrenia Research*, 259:111–120.

Nancy B. Lundin, Henry R. Cowan, Divnoor K. Singh, and Aubrey M. Moe. 2023. Lower cohesion and altered first-person pronoun usage in the spoken life narratives of individuals with schizophrenia. *Schizophrenia Research*, 259:140–149.

Minna Lyons, Nazli Deniz Aksayli, and Gayle Brewer. 2018. Mental distress and language use: Linguistic analysis of discussion forum posts. *Computers in Human Behavior*, 87:207–211.

Viktoria Lyons and Michael Fitzgerald. 2004. The case of Robert Walser (1878-1956). *Irish Journal of Psychological Medicine*, 21(4):138–142. Publisher: Cambridge University Press.

Jana Lüdtke and Katharina G. Hugentobler. Using emotional word ratings to extrapolated norms for valence, arousal, imagebility and concreteness: The German list of extrapolated affective norms (GLEAN). *Proceedings of KogWis2022, the 5th Biannual Conference of the German Society for Cognitive Science.*

Philip M. McCarthy and Scott Jarvis. 2010. MTLD, vocd-D, and HD-D: A validation study of sophisticated approaches to lexical diversity assessment. *Behavior Research Methods*, 42(2):381–392.

George A. Miller. 1956. The magical number seven plus or minus two: some limits on our capacity for processing information. *Psychological Review*, 63(2):81–97.

K. S. Minor, J. A. Willits, M. P. Marggraf, M. N. Jones, and P. H. Lysaker. 2019. Measuring disorganized speech in schizophrenia: automated analysis explains variance in cognitive deficits beyond clinician-rated scales. *Psychological Medicine*, 49(3):440–448. Publisher: Cambridge University Press.

Kyle S. Minor, Nancy B. Lundin, Evan J. Myers, Aitana Fernández-Villardón, and Paul H. Lysaker. 2023. Automated measures of speech content and speech organization in schizophrenia: Test-retest reliability and generalizability across demographic variables. *Psychiatry Research*, 320:115048.

Sarah E. Morgan, Kelly Diederen, Petra E. Vértes, Samantha H. Y. Ip, Bo Wang, Bethany Thompson, Arsime Demjaha, Andrea De Micheli, Dominic Oliver, Maria Liakata, Paolo Fusar-Poli, Tom J. Spencer, and Philip McGuire. 2021. Natural Language Processing markers in first episode psychosis and people at clinical high-risk. *Translational Psychiatry*, 11(1):1–9. Number: 1 Publisher: Nature Publishing Group.

David R. Mortensen, Siddharth Dalmia, and Patrick Littell. 2018. Epitran: Precision G2P for Many Languages. In *Proceedings of the Eleventh International Conference on Language Resources and Evaluation (LREC 2018)*, Miyazaki, Japan. European Language Resources Association (ELRA).

Robert Mächler and Carl Seelig. 1992. *Das Leben Robert Walsers: eine dokumentarische Biographie*. Suhrkamp. Google-Books-ID: czFcAAAAMAAJ.

Viola Oertel, Anna Rotarska-Jagiela, Vincent van de Ven, Corinna Haenschel, Michael Grube, Ulrich Stangier, Konrad Maurer, and David E. J. Linden. 2009. Mental imagery vividness as a trait marker across the schizophrenia spectrum. *Psychiatry Research*, 167(1):1–11.

Serguei Pakhomov, Dustin Chacon, Mark Wicklund, and Jeanette Gundel. 2011. Computerized assessment of syntactic complexity in Alzheimer's disease: a case study of Iris Murdoch's writing. *Behavior Research Methods*, 43(1):136–144.

Lena Palaniyappan. 2021. More than a biomarker: could language be a biosocial marker of psychosis? *npj Schizophrenia*, 7(1):1–5. Number: 1 Publisher: Nature Publishing Group.

Alberto Parola, Jessica Mary Lin, Arndis Simonsen, Vibeke Bliksted, Yuan Zhou, Huiling Wang, Lana Inoue, Katja Koelkebeck, and Riccardo Fusaroli. 2023. Speech disturbances in schizophrenia: Assessing cross-linguistic generalizability of NLP automated measures of coherence. *Schizophrenia Research*, 259:59–70.

S. Partl, B. Pfuhlmann, B. Jabs, and G. Stöber. 2011. „Meine Krankheit ist eine Kopfkrankheit, die schwer zu definieren ist". *Der Nervenarzt*, 82(1):67–78.

D. Pavy, L. Grinspoon, and R. I. Shader. 1969. Word frequency measures of verbal disorders in schizophrenia. *Diseases of the Nervous System*, 30(8):553–556.

Fabian Pedregosa, Gaël Varoquaux, Alexandre Gramfort, Vincent Michel, Bertrand Thirion, Olivier Grisel, Mathieu Blondel, Peter Prettenhofer, Ron Weiss, Vincent Dubourg, Jake Vanderplas, Alexandre Passos, David Cournapeau, Matthieu Brucher, Matthieu Perrot, and Édouard Duchesnay. 2011. Scikit-learn: Machine Learning in Python. *Journal of Machine Learning Research*, 12(85):2825–2830.

Nils Reimers and Iryna Gurevych. 2019. Sentence-BERT: Sentence Embeddings using Siamese BERT-Networks. ArXiv:1908.10084 [cs].

Vassiliki Rentoumi, Timothy Peters, Jonathan Conlin, and Peter Garrard. 2017. The acute mania of King George III: A computational linguistic analysis. *PLoS ONE*, 12(3):e0171626.

Alexander T Sack, Vincent G van de Ven, Simone Etschenberg, Dietmar Schatz, and David E. J Linden. 2005. Enhanced vividness of mental imagery as a trait marker of schizophrenia? *Schizophrenia Bulletin*, 31(1):97–104.

Katharina Schneider, Katrin Leinweber, Hamidreza Jamalabadi, Lea Teutenberg, Katharina Brosch, Julia-Katharina Pfarr, Florian Thomas-Odenthal, Paula Usemann, Adrian Wroblewski, Benjamin Straube, Nina Alexander, Igor Nenadić, Andreas Jansen, Axel Krug, Udo Dannlowski, Tilo Kircher, Arne Nagels, and Frederike Stein. 2023. Syntactic complexity and diversity of spontaneous speech production in schizophrenia spectrum and major depressive disorders. *Schizophrenia*, 9(1):1–10. Number: 1 Publisher: Nature Publishing Group.

Skipper Seabold and Josef Perktold. 2010. Statsmodels: Econometric and Statistical Modeling with Python.

Proceedings of the 9th Python in Science Conference, pages 92–96. Conference Name: Proceedings of the 9th Python in Science Conference.

Lucas Shen, David Lesieur, Christophe Bedetti, Earl Brown, Garrett Hurst, and Pip coder. 2023. LSYS/LexicalRichness: v0.5.0.

Angelica M. Silva, Roberto Limongi, Michael MacKinley, Sabrina D. Ford, Maria Francisca Alonso-Sánchez, and Lena Palaniyappan. 2023. Syntactic complexity of spoken language in the diagnosis of schizophrenia: A probabilistic Bayes network model. *Schizophrenia Research*, 259:88–96.

S. W. Stirman and J. W. Pennebaker. 2001. Word use in the poetry of suicidal and nonsuicidal poets. *Psychosomatic Medicine*, 63(4):517–522.

Sunny X. Tang, Reno Kriz, Sunghye Cho, Suh Jung Park, Jenna Harowitz, Raquel E. Gur, Mahendra T. Bhati, Daniel H. Wolf, João Sedoc, and Mark Y. Liberman. 2021. Natural language processing methods are sensitive to sub-clinical linguistic differences in schizophrenia spectrum disorders. *NPJ schizophrenia*, 7(1):25.

Charles Vannette. 2020. *Robert Walser: Unmoored*. Peter Lang, Bern, Switzerland.

Rohit Voleti, Stephanie M Woolridge, Julie M Liss, Melissa Milanovic, Gabriela Stegmann, Shira Hahn, Philip D Harvey, Thomas L Patterson, Christopher R Bowie, and Visar Berisha. 2023. Language Analytics for Assessment of Mental Health Status and Functional Competency. *Schizophrenia Bulletin*, 49(Supplement_2):S183–S195.

Alban E. Voppel, Janna N. de Boer, SG Brederoo, HG Schnack, and Iris E. C. Sommer. 2021. Quantified language connectedness in schizophrenia-spectrum disorders. *Psychiatry Research*, 304:114130.

Robert Walser. 2013a. *Drucke im Berliner Tageblatt*. Schwabe Verlag.

Robert Walser. 2013b. *Drucke in der Neuen Zürcher Zeitung*. Schwabe Verlag.

Robert Walser. 2014. *Poetenleben - Kritische Edition der Erstausgabe*. Schwabe Verlag.

Robert Walser. 2015. *Drucke in der Schaubühne/ Weltbühne*. Schwabe Verlag.

Robert Walser. 2017a. *Drucke in der «Neuen Rundschau»*. Schwabe Verlag.

Robert Walser. 2017b. *Prosastücke - Kleine Prosa - Der Spaziergang*. Schwabe Verlag.

Robert Walser. 2019. *Drucke in der Prager Presse*. Schwabe Verlag.

Robert Walser. 2023a. *Fritz Kocher's Aufsätze - Kritische Edition und Reprint der Erstausgabe*. Schwabe Verlag.

Robert Walser. 2023b. *Kleine Dichtungen*. Schwabe Verlag.

Andrew R. Watson, Cağla Defterali, Thomas H. Bak, Antonella Sorace, Andrew M. McIntosh, David G. C. Owens, Eve C. Johnstone, and Stephen M. Lawrie. 2012. Use of second-person pronouns and schizophrenia. *The British Journal of Psychiatry: The Journal of Mental Science*, 200(4):342–343.

Martina Wernli. 2014. *Schreiben am Rand: Die »Bernische kantonale Irrenanstalt Waldau« und ihre Narrative (1895-1936)*. transcript Verlag. Publication Title: Schreiben am Rand.

Victor H. Yngve. 1960. A model and an hypothesis for language structure. Accepted: 2004-03-02T23:07:37Z Publisher: Massachusetts Institute of Technology, Research Laboratory of Electronics.

Ido Ziv, Heli Baram, Kfir Bar, Vered Zilberstein, Samuel Itzikowitz, Eran V. Harel, and Nachum Dershowitz. 2021. Morphological characteristics of spoken language in schizophrenia patients - an exploratory study. *Scandinavian Journal of Psychology*.

A Appendix

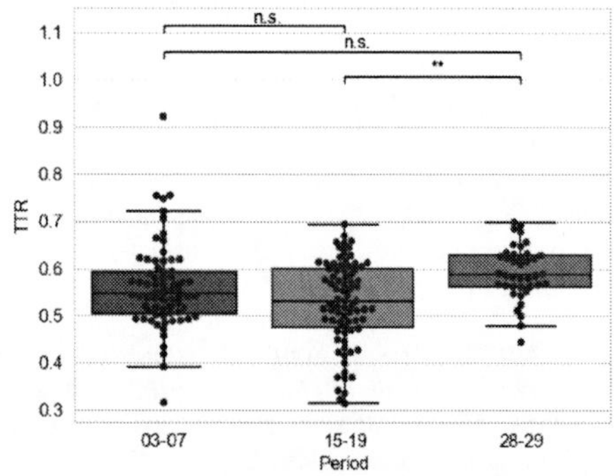

Figure 6: TTR

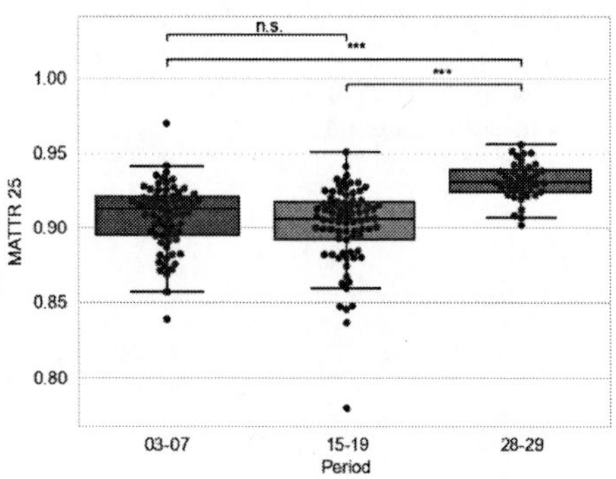

Figure 7: MATTR (25-token window)

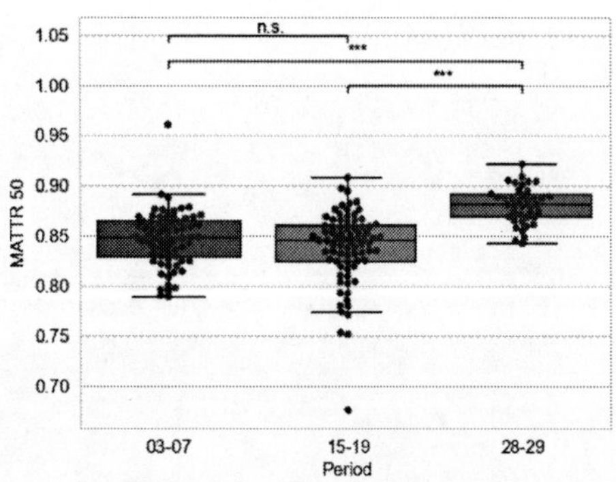

Figure 8: MATTR (50-token window)

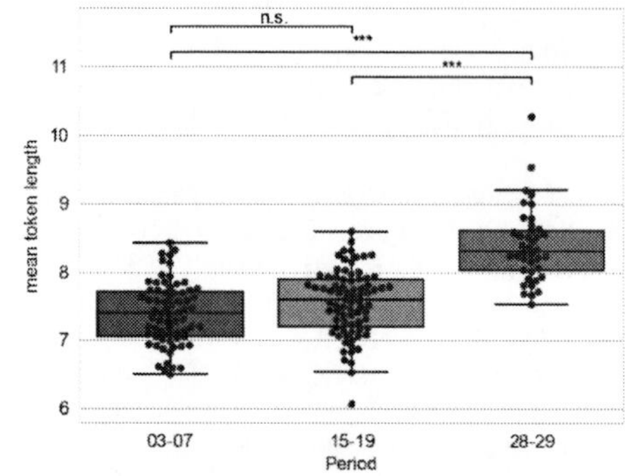

Figure 9: Mean token length

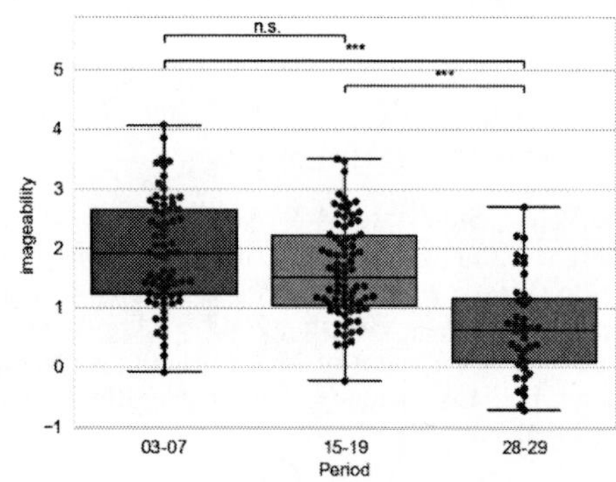

Figure 10: Imageability

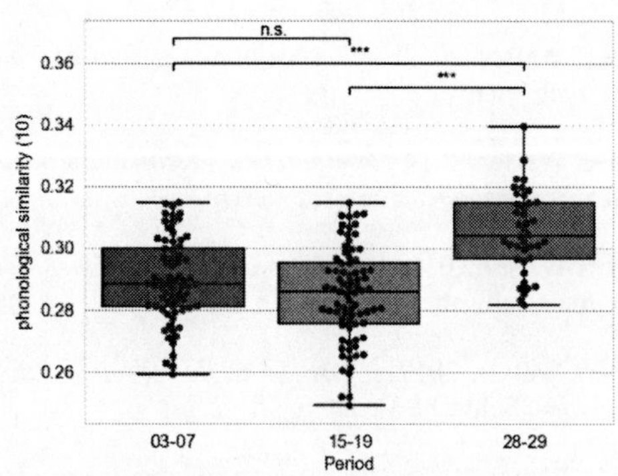

Figure 11: Phonological similarity (10-token window)

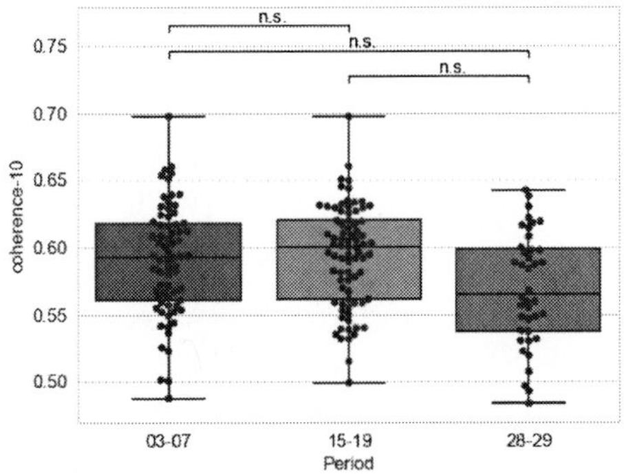

Figure 12: Coherence-10

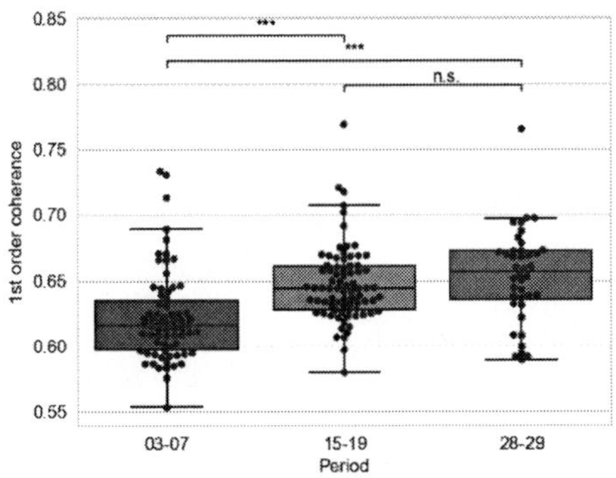

Figure 13: First order coherence

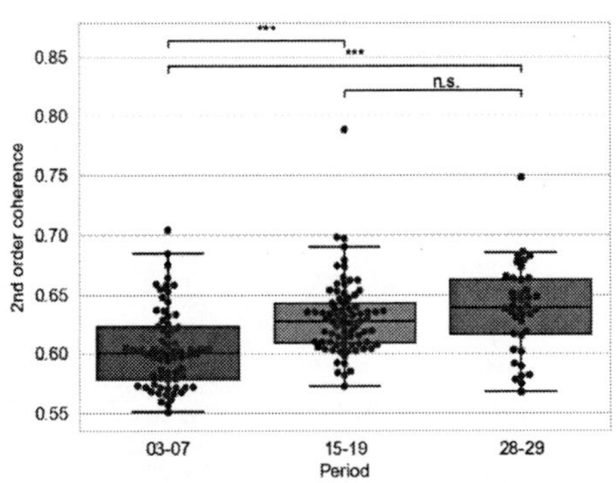

Figure 14: Second order coherence

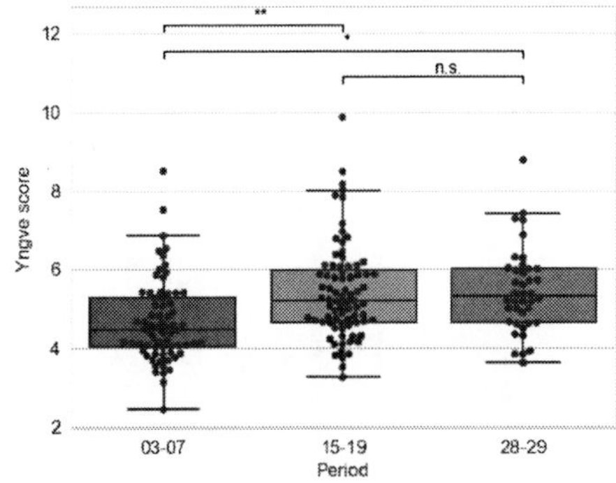

Figure 15: Yngve score

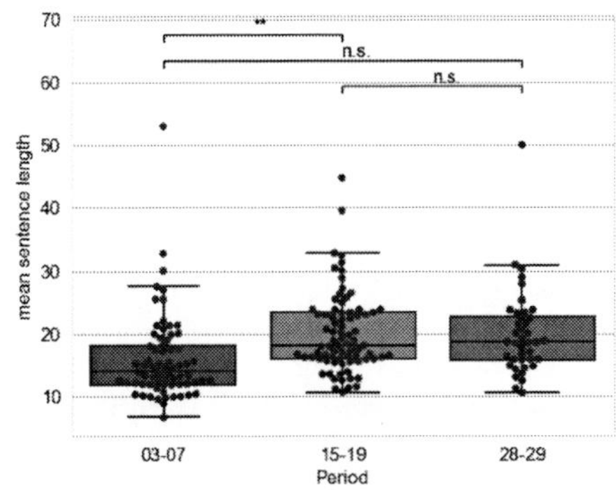

Figure 16: Mean sentence length

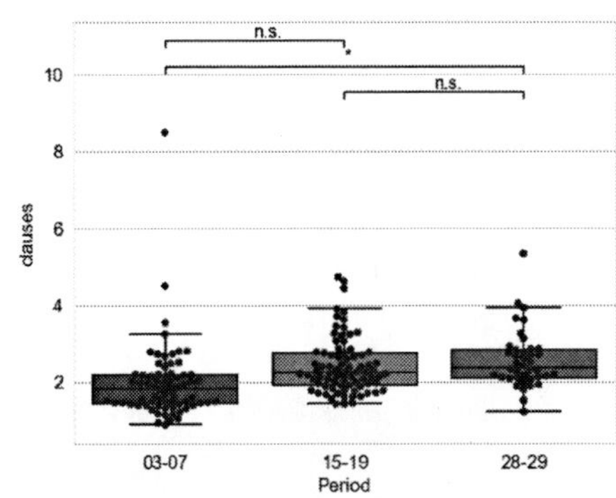

Figure 17: Clauses per sentence

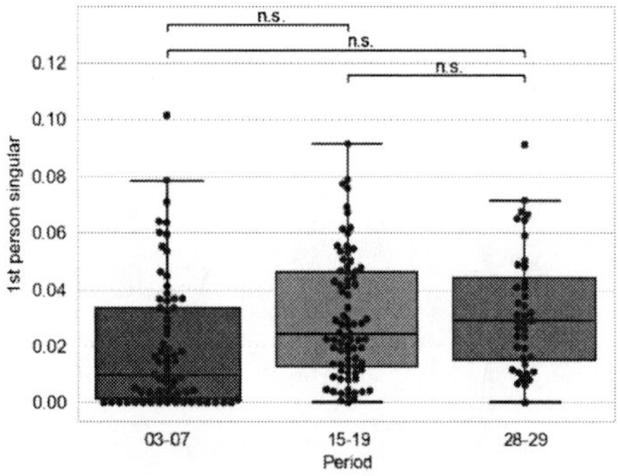

Figure 18: First person singular pronouns

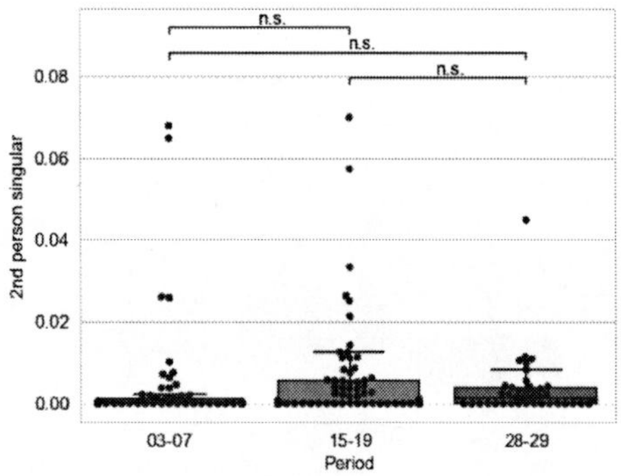

Figure 19: Second person singular pronouns

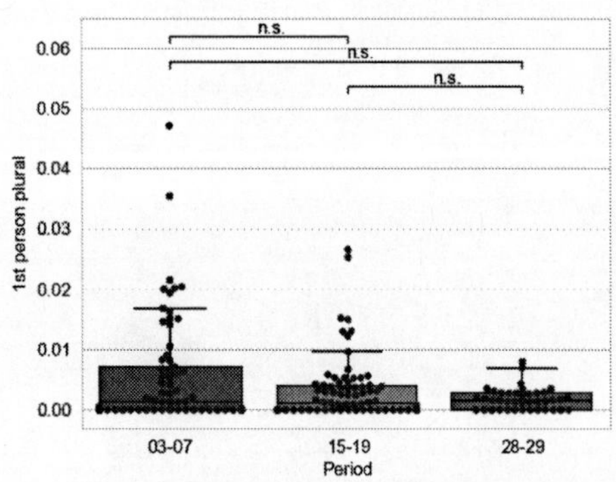

Figure 20: First person plural pronouns

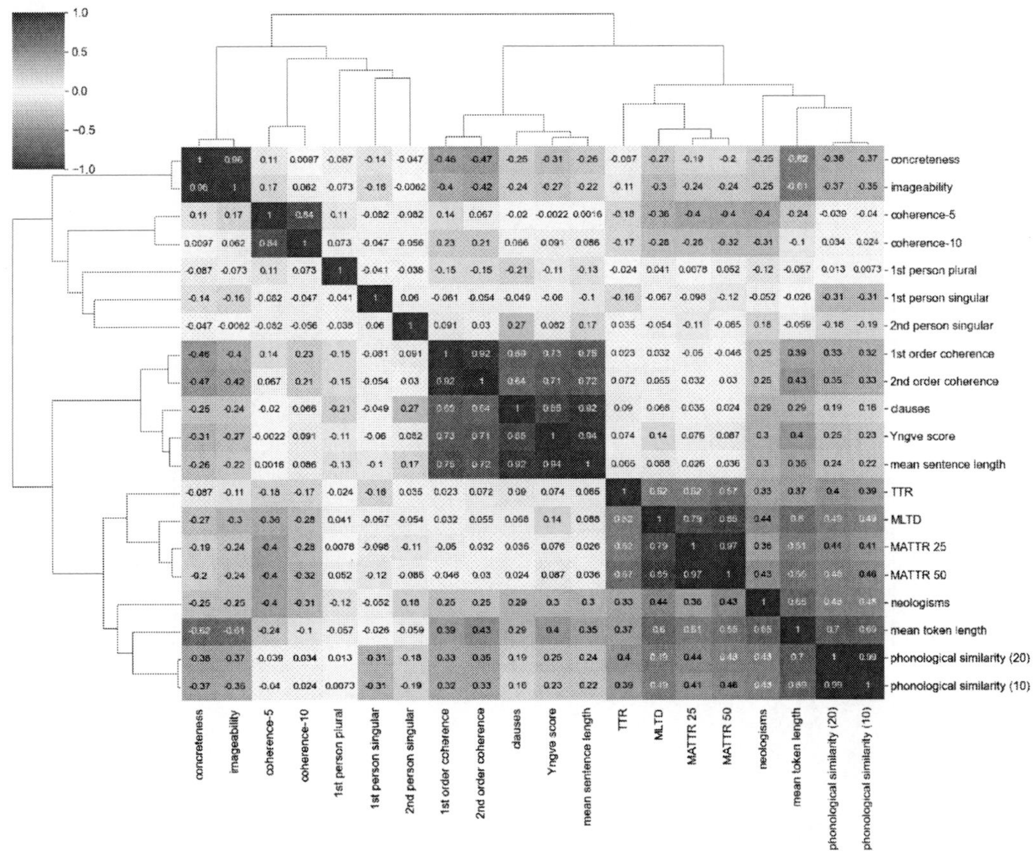

Figure 21: Hierarchically-clustered heatmap of the 20 linguistic markers.

	coh-5	coh-10	1st coh	2nd coh	MATTR 25	MATTR 50	MLTD	TTR	out of scope tokens
mean token length	-0.24***	-0.1	0.39***	0.43***	0.51***	0.55***	0.6***	0.37***	0.65***
coherence-5		0.84***	0.14	0.07	-0.4***	-0.4***	-0.36***	-0.18*	-0.4***
coherence-10			0.23**	0.21**	-0.28***	-0.32***	-0.28***	-0.17*	-0.31***
1st order coherence				0.92***	-0.05	-0.05	0.03	0.02	0.25***
2nd order coherence					0.03	0.03	0.06	0.07	0.25***
MATTR 25						0.97***	0.79***	0.52***	0.36***
MATTR 50							0.85***	0.57***	0.43***
MLTD								0.52***	0.44***
TTR									0.33***
out of scope tokens									
concreteness									
imageability									
Yngve score									
mean sentence length									
clauses									
1st person singular									
phonological similarity (20)									
phonological similarity (10)									
1st person plural									

Table 4: Table demonstrating the correlations between the linguistic marker, ($p > 0.0025$ not significant, $p < 0.05$ '*', $p < 0.01$ '**', $p < 0.001$ '***')

	concr	image	Yngve	msl	clauses	1st sing	phon 20	phon 10	1st pl	2nd sing
mean token length	-0.62***	-0.61***	0.4***	0.35***	0.29***	-0.03	0.7***	0.69***	-0.06	-0.06
coherence-5	0.11	0.17*	-0.0	0.0	-0.02	-0.08	-0.04	-0.04	0.11	-0.08
coherence-10	0.01	0.06	0.09	0.09	0.07	-0.05	0.03	0.02	0.07	-0.06
1st order coherence	-0.46***	-0.4***	0.73***	0.75***	0.69***	-0.06	0.33***	0.32***	-0.15*	0.09
2nd order coherence	-0.47***	-0.42***	0.71***	0.72***	0.64***	-0.05	0.35***	0.33***	-0.15*	0.03
MATTR 25	-0.19**	-0.24***	0.08	0.03	0.03	-0.1	0.44***	0.41***	0.01	-0.11
MATTR 50	-0.2**	-0.24***	0.09	0.04	0.02	-0.12	0.48***	0.46***	0.05	-0.08
MLTD	-0.27***	-0.3***	0.14	0.09	0.07	-0.07	0.49***	0.49***	0.04	-0.05
TTR	-0.09	-0.11	0.07	0.07	0.09	-0.16*	0.4***	0.39***	-0.02	0.03
out of scope tokens	-0.25***	-0.25***	0.3***	0.3***	0.29***	-0.05	0.48***	0.48***	-0.12	0.18*
concreteness		0.96***	-0.31***	-0.26***	-0.25***	-0.14*	-0.38***	-0.37***	-0.09	-0.05
imageability			-0.27***	-0.22**	-0.24**	-0.16*	-0.37***	-0.35***	-0.07	-0.01
Yngve score				0.94***	0.85***	-0.06	0.25***	0.23**	-0.11	0.08
mean sentence length					0.92***	-0.1	0.24***	0.22**	-0.13	0.17*
clauses						-0.05	0.19**	0.16*	-0.21**	0.27***
1st person singular							-0.31***	-0.31***	-0.04	0.06
phonological similarity (20)								0.99***	0.01	-0.18*
phonological similarity (10)									0.01	-0.19*
1st person plural										-0.04

	Source	Example in German and English translation
Phonological similarity	Mondschein-geschichte, 1928	Noch nie, solange ich dichte, dichtete ich eine schlichtere Geschichte, wie die, worin ich berichte,... Never, as long as I have been writing poetry, have I written a simpler story than the one in which I report...
	Freiheits-aufsatz, 1928	Sie ist eine Freie und infolgedessen eine Feine, die jede Unfeinheit aufs feinste empfindet, mit anderen Worten, die jede Freiheit, die man sich ihr gegenüber herausnimmt, als etwas Unfeines betrachtet... She is a free woman and, as a result, a fine woman who feels every impurity in the finest way, in other words, who regards every freedom taken towards her as something impure...
	Ein dummer Junge, 1928	Auffallend viele Menschen, die einen Namen haben, einen Wert auf den Achseln tragen, feiern in diesen Tagen ihren sechzigsten Geburtstag. A conspicuous number of people who have a name, a value on their armpits, are celebrating their sixtieth birthday these days.

Table 5: Examples of text exhibiting high phonological similarity

Therapist Self-Disclosure as a Natural Language Processing Task

Natalie Shapira*
nd1234@gmail.com

Tal Alfi-Yogev*
talalfi@gmail.com

Abstract

Therapist Self-Disclosure (TSD) within the context of psychotherapy entails the revelation of personal information by the therapist. The ongoing scholarly discourse surrounding the utility of TSD, spanning from the inception of psychotherapy to the present day, has underscored the need for greater specificity in conceptualizing TSD. This inquiry has yielded more refined classifications within the TSD domain, with a consensus emerging on the distinction between immediate and non-immediate TSD, each of which plays a distinct role in the therapeutic process. Despite this progress in the field of psychotherapy, the Natural Language Processing (NLP) domain currently lacks methodological solutions or explorations for such scenarios. This lacuna can be partly due to the difficulty of attaining publicly available clinical data. To address this gap, this paper presents an innovative NLP-based approach that formalizes TSD as an NLP task. The proposed methodology involves the creation of publicly available, expert-annotated test sets designed to simulate therapist utterances, and the employment of NLP techniques for evaluation purposes. By integrating insights from psychotherapy research with NLP methodologies, this study aims to catalyze advancements in both NLP and psychotherapy research.

1 Introduction

Therapist Self-Disclosure (TSD) has various definitions in the literature (e.g., Henretty and Levitt, 2010; Hill, 2009; Knox and Hill, 2003; Vandernoot, 2007; Watkins Jr, 1990), but the one theme that unites these definitions is that TSD involves a therapist's personal self-revelatory statements. In other words, such statements are those that *reveal something personal about the therapist*. This definition refers to verbal disclosures and excludes disclosures that are nonverbal (Hill and Knox, 2001).

* Equal contribution.

Figure 1: Two types of therapist self-disclosure (TSD).

The attitude toward the use of TSD in psychotherapy has changed over the years. Classical psychoanalytic clinicians tended to emphasize the importance of the therapist's anonymity, equanimity, and abstinence (Freud, 1912; Goldstein, 1997). Many of them viewed TSD as a boundary violation and believed it derailed therapy by removing the focus from the client (Zur, 2004). Over the years, however, therapists and theorists across diverse orientations have increasingly converged around the perspective that TSD can yield a range of positive outcomes when employed purposefully and thoughtfully and that refraining from TSD in every instance may potentially lead to adverse consequences for both the client and the overall therapeutic process (Eagle, 2011; Farber, 2006; Hill and Knox, 2001; McWilliams, 2004; Ziv-Beiman, 2013).

The first to embrace a pro-disclosure approach were the humanistic theorists (Bugental, 1965; Farber, 2006). They have postulated that therapists can demonstrate openness, strength, vulnerability, and the sharing of intense feelings cautiously through TSD. By doing so, they invite the client to follow suit and cultivate an environment of openness, trust, intimacy, gains in self-understanding and change (Henretty et al., 2014; Hill and Knox, 2001; Knox et al., 2001; Kottler, 2003). Cognitive-behavioral therapists describe TSD as a tool that is useful for strengthening the therapeutic bond, normalizing clients' experiences of their difficulties, challenging negative interpretations of emotions and behavior, enhancing positive expectations and motivation for change, and modeling and reinforcing

Proceedings of the 9th Workshop on Computational Linguistics and Clinical Psychology (CLPsych 2024), pages 61–73
March 21, 2024 ©2024 Association for Computational Linguistics

	Therapist Self Disclosure (TSD) Therapist reveals something personal about himself		
Category	**Immediate**	**Non-immediate**	**Not a TSD**
Definition	Utterance focuses on articulating the therapist's feelings, thoughts and opinions towards the client, treatment, or therapeutic relationship.	Utterance reveals information about the therapist's personal life outside of therapy, such as beliefs, values, life circumstances and past experiences.	Any comment or other therapeutic intervention (e.g., interpretation, clarification, confrontation, reflection, etc.) that does not include therapist self-disclosure.
Example	*I felt really proud of you when you shared that accomplishment with me.*	*I've used mindfulness exercises in my own life to stay grounded during challenging times.*	*You say you love your family.* (Reflection)

Table 1: Therapist self-disclosure task definition.

desired behaviors (Dryden, 1990; Freeman et al., 1990; Goldfried et al., 2003). Feminist and multicultural approaches also advocate the use of TSD to promote equality, empower the client and reduce clients' feelings of shame, and encourage collaboration in therapy (Brown and Walker, 1990; Mahalik et al., 2000).

In line with the absence of agreement among the mentioned theoretical viewpoints, a body of research presents a multitude of often conflicting or inconclusive findings. These studies delve into diverse facets of TSD, employing different methodologies to assess its influence on clients.

Although there is no consensual conceptualization of the term TSD, as former studies and theoreticians have used a variety of classifications (for a review see Henretty and Levitt, 2010; Ziv-Beiman, 2013), there is growing agreement that one unifying and comprehensive distinction is between *immediate and non-immediate TSD*, which was first put forward by McCarthy and Betz (1978) and later adopted by many psychotherapy researchers (e.g., Alfi-Yogev et al., 2021; Hill et al., 2018; Audet, 2011; McCarthy Veach, 2011; Ziv-Beiman et al., 2017). Whereas ***immediate TSD** (also known as self-involving or interpersonal disclosure) focuses on the articulation of the therapist's feelings, thoughts, and opinions toward the client, treatment, or therapeutic relationship, **non-immediate TSD** (also known as self-revealing or intrapersonal self-disclosure) reveals information about the therapist's personal life outside of therapy, such as beliefs, values, life circumstances, and past experiences.* Immediate TSD and non-immediate TSD are distinctly different utterances. Immediate TSD utterances are primarily "We-focused", whereas non-immediate TSDs are "I-focused". For example, an immediate TSD would be, "I felt proud of you when you shared that accomplishment with me." Whereas an example of a non-immediate TSD might be, "I've used mindfulness exercises in my own life to stay grounded during challenging times." Table 1 summarizes all definitions and examples.

Theoretically, the two types of TSD serve distinct functions. Immediate TSD may promote dyadic engagement in the therapeutic process, enable clients to recognize their interpersonal impact, foster insight, facilitate the identification, experience, and integration of dissociative components, expand the client's emotional repertoire, and may lead to symptom reduction (Alfi-Yogev et al., 2021, 2024; Hill et al., 2018; Ziv-Beiman et al., 2017). In contrast, non-immediate TSD may enhance client self-acceptance, mitigate feelings of shame and self-criticism, and foster an increased sense of attunement from their therapists, contributing to a greater sense of understanding. It can promote rapport, model new perspectives and behaviors, and help balance the therapeutic relationship (Audet, 2011; Audet and Everall, 2010; Hill et al., 2018).

To investigate the different roles of TSD in treatment, there are a variety of methods (we detailed representative studies in Section 2.1). One of the methods is by using self-report questionnaires. This method has the disadvantages of lack of objectivity and consequently biasing the results of the

Research Work	Literature Domain	Method	Resolution	Clinical Data	Public Testset	Speaker Identity	Subcategories
Valizadeh et al. (2021)	NLP	Experts	Utterance	-	✓	Listener	-
Reuel et al. (2022)	NLP	Analysis	Utterance	-	✓	Listener	-
Ravichander and Black (2018)	NLP	Crowdsourcing	Utterance	-	✓	Chat-bot	-
Welivita and Pu (2022a)	NLP	Crowdsourcing	Utterance	-	✓	Listener	-[1]
Pinto-Coelho et al. (2018a)	Psychotherapy	Experts	Event	✓	-	Therapist	✓
Levitt et al. (2018)	Psychotherapy	Experts	Session	✓	-	Therapist	✓
Alfi-Yogev et al. (2021)	Psychotherapy	Self-report	Session	✓	-	Therapist	✓
Fuertes et al. (2019)	Psychotherapy	Self-report	Session	✓	-	Therapist	✓
Ziv-Beiman et al. (2017)	Psychotherapy	RCT	Treatment	✓	-	Therapist	✓
This paper	Hybrid	Experts	Utterance	$\checkmark^{pseudo}$	✓	Therapist	✓

Table 2: Comparison with related work

research. Another method is by external expert human judges that annotate the session. This method has the disadvantage that it requires time and is also expensive to train expert judges and conduct the annotation process.

Modern technologies, such as automated speech recognition, NLP techniques, and machine learning models, provide the potential to substitute human evaluators, significantly augmenting scale and precision in the study of treatment mechanisms.

These tools can greatly expand the evaluation of TSD and enable the testing of more sophisticated hypotheses about therapeutic change (e.g., determining when to disclose and to whom; Alfi-Yogev et al., 2021). Initial efforts in this direction have been initiated, utilizing NLP to automatically categorize therapist interventions from session transcripts (Cao et al., 2019; Malgaroli et al., 2023). To the best of our knowledge, TSD has not yet been explored using these techniques.

Advancements in the field of Natural Language Processing (NLP) have led to recent developments that offer a variety of advanced methods for automatic detection of self-disclosure within texts (we detailed representative studies in Section 2.2). However, these advancements address *self-disclosure* and not ***therapist** self-disclosure* and do not take into account the important subtleties of the various sub-classes within TSD. This lacuna can be partly due to the difficulty of attaining publicly available clinical data due to privacy constraints and the need for collaboration between different disciplines.

In addition, the latest works did not incorporate state-of-the-art tools and methodologies such as using Large Language Models (LLMs; Brown et al., 2020; Bommasani et al., 2021; Zhao et al., 2023).

In this study, we adopt the current clinical definition for immediate and non-immediate TSD to facilitate it as an NLP task. Since clinical data is confidential, we created a first-of-a-kind new artificial open-source expert-based test set for TSD (i.e., utterances that could have been said by therapists during therapy, and ground truth annotations by a TSD expert). This test set emphasizes different linguistic characteristics. In addition, we annotated a sample of utterances from an existing dataset of peer support platforms. We propose a method to solve the task using LLMs and report the results.

The paper continues as follows: In Section 2 we describe related works both from psychotherapy research literature and from NLP and review the previous works. In Section 3 we describe the construction process of the new test set (Expert-TSD) and the annotation process of an existing data set (MI) to create a double-check TSD test set (MI'). In Section 4 we describe the technical details of the usage of LLMs, and in Section 5 we discuss the results of LLMs on the new test sets. Finally in Section 6 we conclude and describe potential future work.

[1]Welivita and Pu (2022a) manually annotated a small amount of the sub-categories of inter- and intra-session disclosure (which corresponds to immediate and non-immediate TSD), though they did not publish the annotation results or statistics and recommended continuing research of the subcategories for future work.

2 Related Work

In this section, we review the existing works (both from clinical psychology and NLP literature) that refer to the evaluation of self-disclosure. In our review, we refer to the domain of the source (psychotherapy, NLP, or hybrid); the method used to determine self-disclosure (self-report questionnaire, crowdsourcing, experts, analysis or randomized clinical trail); the resolution of the data that was investigated (utterance, event, session or treatment); the type of the data (clinical, non-clinical, or pseudo clinical); whether a public test set has been published; the speaker identity (therapist, listener, or chatbot); and whether referring to the subcategories (immediate and not immediate or only self-disclosure in general).

Table 2 summarizes the related studies according to the categories presented. As can be seen, this work is the first to construct an open expert-based test set for TSD that refers to immediate and non-immediate TSD.

In the next sections, we provide an extensive literature review of both psychotherapy (Section 2.1) and NLP (Section 2.2) approaches for this task.

2.1 Psychotherapy Research Perspective

Immediate and non-immediate TSD have typically been evaluated through judgments of therapist behavior in psychotherapy sessions. One approach involves trained external judges coding TSD interventions as present or absent in sentences or speaking turns in recorded or transcribed sessions (e.g., Hill, 1978; Stiles, 1979). Alternatively, another evaluation method involving trained judges includes listening to entire sessions and estimating the frequency or effectiveness of TSD interventions throughout the session (e.g., Hill et al., 2014; Levitt et al., 2018; Pinto-Coelho et al., 2018a,b).

Furthermore, the assessment of immediate and non-immediate TSD has also been conducted through self-report questionnaires provided to clients, therapists, or both. Participants receive definitions of immediate and non-immediate TSD and then retrospectively report the use of these interventions within sessions (e.g., Ain, 2008, 2011; Alfi-Yogev et al., 2021, 2023, 2024; Fuertes et al., 2019).

An additional assessment method involves training therapists to either employ immediate TSD, non-immediate TSD, or refrain from using TSD with their clients. In this randomized clinical trial (RCT) method, clients are categorized into three conditions based on the type of self-disclosure employed by their therapists (e.g., Ziv-Beiman et al., 2017).

Several disadvantages are associated with these methods. First, in self-report measurement, there is a potential for bias in retrospective recall, as feelings and reactions may evolve over time, leading to changes in how participants interpret their experience. Second, in self-report measurement, there is difficulty in identifying the session's specific location when recalled immediate/non-immediate TSD occurred, posing challenges in assessing the interventions' context, manner of delivery, and associated subsequent processes. Third, in evaluation through external judgments, achieving agreement among judges is sometimes marginal due to the intricate task of distinguishing verbal response modes that predominantly focus on grammatical form, while overlooking intent, quality, or manner of delivery. This limitation results in diminished clinical relevance. Fourth, the reliance on training for external judges or therapists is highly time-consuming, introducing inefficiencies to the assessment procedure. Lastly, using an RCT may not always mimic real-life treatment situations.

2.2 Self Disclosure Within NLP Litrature

Valizadeh et al. (2021) created a 6,639-instance dataset comprised of public online social posts covering a wide range of mental and physical health issues, categorized into three groups (no self-disclosure, possible self-disclosure, and clear self-disclosure) with high inter-annotator agreement (= 0.88). They demonstrated that a large percentage of instances from the possible self-disclosure class were misclassified than were instances from the other two classes, suggesting room for future work that disentangles the nuances of ambiguous cases.

Reuel et al. (2022) Analysed several existing self-disclosure related datasets (Wang et al., 2015; Jaidka et al., 2020; Pei and Jurgens, 2020; Omitaomu et al., 2022; Valizadeh et al., 2021) with variety of techniques (e.g., RoBERTa-, LIWC-, LDA-, and EmoLex-based models). All datasets are based on publicly available conversations (forums, Reddit, online platforms, and more) with crowdsourcing annotations for self-disclosure and related tasks (e.g., intimacy, empathy, emotional disclosure, and more). They showed that it is hard for models to generalize between datasets. They found that self-disclosure linguistic correlates with the expression of negative emotions and the use of first-person personal pronouns like "I". They provide a multi-task model across all available data sets to assess self-disclosure. However, they noted that the data sets they took into account were not annotated based on validated definitions of self-disclosure in psychological literature, but rather had differing labeling instructions, which might lead to inaccuracies when predicting self-disclosure. They recommended that in future work, data that is labeled for a validated self-disclosure definition should be collected and analyzed.

Ravichander and Black (2018) built an open-domain chatbot that engages in social conversation with hundreds of Amazon Alexa users and ran a large-scale quantitative analysis on the effect of self-disclosure by analyzing these interactions. In their work, their definition of self-disclosure was binary. They noted that a more nuanced version that considers both the magnitude and valence of self-disclosure would open up several further research directions, such as analyzing reciprocity matching in the depth of disclosure and analyzing user behavior based on the valence of disclosure.

Welivita and Pu (2022a) created large-scale publicly available datasets (17k) from peer support platforms, annotated by trained crowdsourcing counselors. They labeled TSD, as well as other interventions (e.g., clarification). In their paper, the authors recommend that future work consider the distinction between intra- and extra-session disclosure (equivalent to immediate and non-immediate disclosure).

3 Data

In this section, we describe the creation of two test sets: Expert-TSD and MI'. The first was developed from scratch by an expert, and the second was created by expertly annotating an existing dataset. Both test sets are in English.[2]

The purpose of the first test set is to provide an adequate test for TSD (precision). The purpose of the second test set is to strengthen the findings and to enable an assessment of real data distribution. Real data contains surprising behaviors such as syntax and grammar errors, informal or non-verbal utterances, and more phenomena. It is important to examine behavior in a wide variety of situations (recall) to strengthen our conclusions.

The subsequent paragraphs provide the construction process for each test set.

Expert-TSD. The initial phase of the test set creation process involved a collaborative effort between the authors (an NLP researcher and a clinical psychologist specializing in TSD research). In a comprehensive brainstorming session, the authors discussed the precise definition of TSD and its subtypes as described in psychotherapy literature (see Section 1 and Table 1), as well as potential solutions for recognizing TSD types using shallow heuristics and machine learning.

Next, utterances were generated by the clinical psychologist along with their respective type label. The NLP researcher reviewed the proposed samples marking potential shallow heuristics, such as syntactic features, that a machine learning model might exploit to predict the correct label for the incorrect reasons (see shallow heuristics: Hendrycks et al., 2021; Wu et al., 2021; Kaushik et al., 2019; Geirhos et al., 2020; Glockner et al., 2018). This writing and reviewing procedure was conducted throughout five iterations, with new samples proposed and previous ones fixed.

To mitigate the effect of shallow heuristics, we made sure to diversify utterances over the following properties: (1) the balance of positive and negative examples (i.e., including "Not a TSD" utterances) (2) the length of the utterance (i.e., short sentence below 10 words vs. numerous or long sentences above 20 words), (3) the presence or absence of first-person pronouns words (e.g., I, me, our), (4) the existence of positive or negative sentiment, and (5) the incorporation of questions.

The test set generation rounds were stopped once we surpassed 100 instances (108), which is a sufficient quantity for testing significance.

MI'. We first sampled 650 examples from the MI dataset (Welivita and Pu, 2022b, summarized in Section 2.2), ensuring diversity by extracting 25 instances from each category and 300 from self-disclosure. For each utterance, the TSD expert annotated the TSD type based on the task definition outlined in Section 1 and Table 1.

A total of 277 items were tagged. An effort was made to equally represent each class ("Immediate TSD", "Non-immediate TSD" and "Not a TSD"). Except for one instance, all of our utterance labels agreed with the MI labels for the binary self-disclosure classification.

[2]The data is available at: https://github.com/NatalieShapira/TherapistSelfDisclosure/

Therapist Self-Disclosure Instructions Prompt

TEST:

Below are definitions of two subcategories of self-disclosure and not self-disclosure:

Non-immediate TSD: Self-disclosure of information about the therapist.
* Relates to disclosing, during a treatment session, facts about the therapists' life outside of the treatment and personal insights they gained, the way they reached these insights, effective / in-effective ways of coping based on their experience and the way they formulated them, emotions that they experience in different situations in their life, etc...
* Example:
Speech turn: I remember going through a career change a few years ago, and it was a challenging time for me. It's normal to feel uncertain during transitions, but it's also a chance to explore new possibilities.
Answer: Non-immediate TSD

Immediate TSD: Self-disclosure that relates to the "here and now".
* Relates to sharing therapists' feelings, associations, and thoughts relating to the client and the issues and topics raised during the session and of their emotions, feelings, and thoughts on the therapy process which they are both part of, etc...
* Example:
Speech turn: I was genuinely excited to hear about the progress you've made.
Answer: Immediate TSD

Not a TSD: Not a Self-disclosure
* Any comment or other therapeutic intervention (e.g., interpretation, clarification, confrontation, reflection, etc.) that does not include therapist self-disclosure.
* Example:
Speech turn: You say you love your family
Answer: Not a TSD (clarification)

For the next speech turn, determine whether it is non-immediate TSD or immediate TSD according to the above definitions.
Speech turn: ***If what you are experiencing seems fine and normal to you, it may be nothing to worry about.***
Answer:

Table 3: Therapist self-disclosure instructions prompt. The bold-italics text is a variable utterance we want to automatically tag with a label (Immediate, Non-immediate, or Not a TSD), all the rest is a constant template.

4 Method

In line with the latest works that examine automated detection of psychology-related tasks by LLMs in-context learning or zero-shot setup (e.g., Murthy et al., 2023; Shapira et al., 2023a,c,b), we investigate the TSD automatic detection abilities of LLMs. We evaluated the two test sets mentioned in Section 3 in-context learning setup.

LLMs and Decoding Parameters. We used two different LLMs: Flan-T5 (Chung et al., 2022)[3] of different sizes `flan-t5-{small, base, large, xl}` and GPT-4 (Brown et al., 2020; Ouyang et al., 2022; Achiam et al., 2023).[4] A single sample (the first) was selected from each model for the analysis of the tagging evaluation. We chose hyper-parameters that minimize randomness, predict the most probable answer (i.e., low temperature, sampling method), and allow for a sufficient number of tokens.

Prompt. As input to the LLMs, we used a prompt that contained the definition of TSD with examples concatenated to the utterance that we wished to automatically tag. The full exact prompt is detailed in Table 3.

5 Results and Discussions

Model	Immediate 29	Non-immediate 28	Not a TSD 51	Total 108 (100%)
Flan-T5-small	0	28	0	28 (23%)
Flan-T5-base	3	28	5	36 (33%)
Flan-t5-large	3	28	0	31 (29%)
Flan-t5-xl	9	28	0	37 (34%)
GPT-4	26	28	43	97 (90%)

Table 4: Evaluation on the expert test set for therapist self-disclosure task (Expert-TSD). The first row represents the number of samples for each category. The rest, each cell represents the number of correct responses for each model.

Expert-TSD Results. The results of the Expert-TSD test set appear in Table 4.

As evident, Flan-T5 exhibits a bias toward the "Non-immediate" class. The results of GPT-4 were surprisingly good (accuracy of 90% on the task; above expected human annotation agreement; and higher than previous self-disclosure literature as reported by Reuel et al., 2022). Note that this method is proposed for practice and as a proof-of-concept and not for real use, see more discussions in the Limitation Section and Ethical Statement.

For the GPT-4, 10% utterances where discrepancies emerged between the labels assigned by the human annotator and those generated by GPT-4, we conducted a manual error analysis and consulted with three additional psychotherapists. Notably, there was no consensus among the therapists regarding whether these utterances constituted TSD.

Upon examining the inconsistencies in labeling between the human annotator and GPT-4, it became apparent that the discrepancies pertained solely to immediate TSD. Specifically, two types of differences were identified: First, instances where the human annotator identified "Immediate TSD" while GPT-4 identified "Not a TSD"; and second, cases where GPT-4 detected "Immediate TSD", but the human annotator detected "Not a TSD".

Determining the frequency of immediate TSD in real therapy sessions poses a considerable challenge. Therapists and clients typically perceive these interventions as integral to the therapeutic dialogue, leading to their routine exclusion from TSD reports. Nevertheless, it is assumed that such disclosures transpire more frequently in therapeutic dialogues than what has been officially reported (Farber, 2006; Ziv-Beiman, 2013).

Moreover, as for instances where GPT-4 identified immediate TSD, but the human annotator did not, it appears that some of the utterances were characterized as *immediacy*.

The term ***immediacy*** was defined by Hill et al. (2014) as *"discussion of the therapeutic relationship by both the therapist and client in the here-and-now, involving more than social chitchat"*. While earlier literature used *immediacy* to refer to immediate TSD utterances, researchers have evolved from defining immediacy exclusively as immediate TSD and now use the term to refer to a more complex phenomenon (McCarthy Veach, 2011). Immediacy extends to therapist responses and behaviors such as feedback, inquiries to gather more information about the client's here-and-now reactions, and primary and advanced empathy to reflect the client's momentary experiences. At times, immediacy utterances are more client-focused, than

[3]**Python packages:** *transformers* (*AutoModelForSeq2SeqLM*, *AutoTokenizer*) and *torch*; **Generation function:** *generate*; **Hyper-parameters:** do_sample=True, max_length=50, from_pretrained:{google/flan-t5-small, google/flan-t5-base, google/flan-t5-large, google/flan-t5-xl}, temperature=0.0001

[4]**Python package:** *openai*; **Generation function:** *ChatCompletion.create*; **Hyper-parameters:** model=gpt-4-0314 temperature=0

therapist-focused. An illustrative example from our data involves the utterance: *"I've noticed you seem unhappy when we talk about the disagreement we had last time. Do you think there might be some anger or resentment towards me?"* The human annotator labeled it as "Not a TSD," while GPT-4 tagged it as "Immediate TSD," when in fact it represents *immediacy*. This clarification aims to shed light on some of the observed gaps in labeling.

Model	Immediate 6	Non-immediate 135	Not a SD 136	Total 277 (100%)
Flan-t5-small	0	135	0	135 (49%)
Flan-t5-xl	0	133	30	163 (59%)
GPT-4	6	111	134	251 (91%)

Table 5: Evaluation on our annotated sample (MI') from the MI dataset (Welivita and Pu, 2022b). The first row represents the number of samples for each category. The rest, each cell represents the number of correct responses for each model.

MI' Results. The results of the MI' test set appear in Table 5.

MI' test set, unlike the Expert-TSD test set, contains quotes from peer support platforms and thus does not necessarily represent therapist utterances, nevertheless, we classify the utterances as if they were of a therapist.

We analyzed utterances in which discrepancies between our human expert annotator and GPT-4 were observed regarding TSD.

Four types of differences were identified: First, instances where the human expert annotator identified "Non-immediate TSD" while GPT-4 identified "Immediate TSD." Second, instances where the human expert annotator identified "Non-immediate TSD" while GPT-4 identified "Not a TSD." Third, instances where the human expert annotator identified "Not a TSD" while GPT-4 identified "Non-immediate TSD." Fourth, instances where the human annotator identified "Not a TSD" while GPT-4 identified "Immediate TSD." The distinction between the first and second types appears to lie in the level of controversy associated with the TSD. Non-immediate TSD is considered a controversial technique and is seen as challenging fundamental therapeutic principles (Ziv-Beiman, 2013). It appears that GPT-4 labeled more subtle Non-immediate TSDs as "Immediate TSD" (e.g., *"I'll be honest, this is a little past my scope of knowledge"*), whereas less subtle non-immediate TSDs, to the extent that they may not theoretically be considered part of treatment (e.g., *"I didn't even take a shower and I completely start falling apart"* note that this example is not only untypical therapist discourse but also grammatically incorrect), were identified by GPT-4 as "Not a TSD." The third and fourth type included only one utterance. *"ugh."* was labeled as "Immidiate TSD" by GPT-4 but is a non-verbal disclosure while the formal TSD definition includes only verbal disclosures. *"Pulling late nights in the lab."* was labeled as "Non-immediate TSD" while it is unclear to whom it refers - (speaker or the listener).

Note that this test set contained only a few examples (6) of immediate TSD. This is due to the nature of the data on which it was based. It is crucial to emphasize that the MI dataset was extracted from online peer support forums, as opposed to therapeutic interactions between a therapist and a client. Therefore, the TSD utterances identified in the study's data do not portray instances of TSD. The distinction between the MI data in the Welivita and Pu (2022a) study and data derived from therapeutic interactions is also evident in the prevalence of immediate and non-immediate TSDs. Notably, therapeutic sessions tend to feature a higher frequency of immediate TSDs than non-immediate TSDs (e.g., Levitt et al., 2018). Conversely, the MI' sample from MI indicates a greater prevalence of non-immediate TSD. In peer support conversations, participants predominantly engage in sharing their lived experiences (which is parallel to using non-immediate TSDs- often characterized by an emphasis on individual perspectives; "I-focused"). Given the potentially less committed therapeutic relationships or absence of genuine connections, peers may be less inclined to disclose their immediate feelings in response to the other's experiences or emotions (referred to as immediate TSDs- where the focus is on shared experiences; "We-focused").

While analyzing the differences between the two datasets, we observed that in the Expert-TSD dataset, the disparities between labels assigned by the human annotator and those generated by GPT-4 were exclusively related to immediate TSD. Conversely, in the MI dataset, the discrepancies between labels assigned by the human annotator and GPT-4 were particularly associated with non-immediate self-disclosure. This discrepancy may be attributed, in part, to the higher frequency of non-immediate self-disclosure utterances in the MI dataset.

Overall, the results of GPT-4 in MI' dataset are

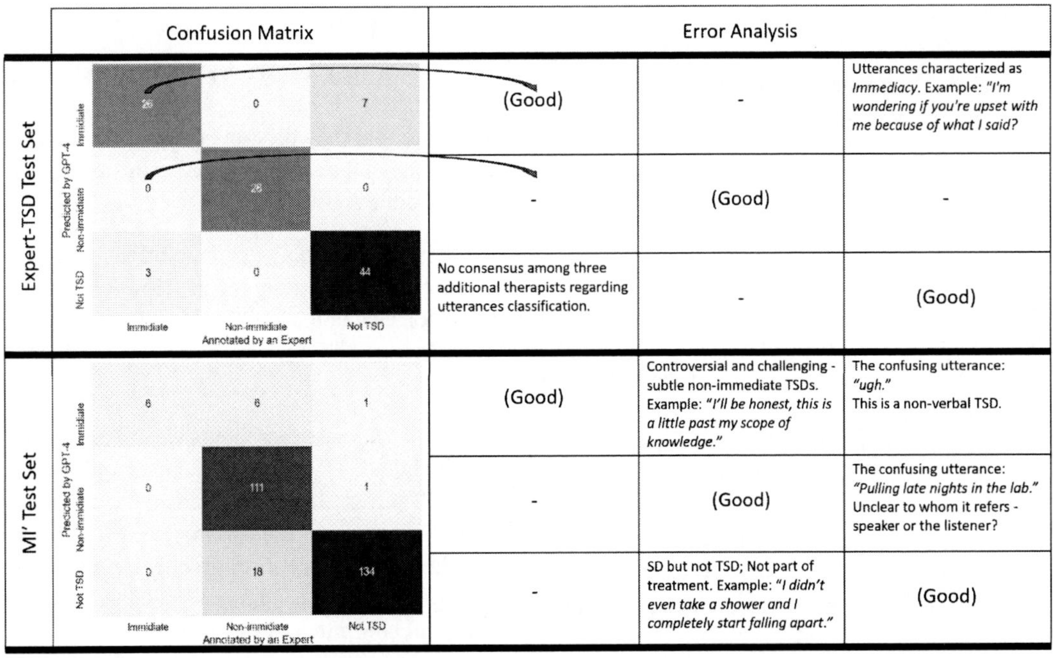

Figure 2: Confusion matrix (left) and error analysis (right) between GPT-4 predictions and the gold standard annotated by expert in the Expert-TSD test set (above) and MI' test set (below). Each cell on the right represents an explanation for a significant part of the examples of the corresponding cell.

similar to the results in Expert-TSD dataset (i.e., high accuracy classification). This is despite the complexity of real data, which does not always allow a clear decision regarding whether or not there was self-disclosure (e.g., mixes other interventions that make it difficult to decide which of them is more significant). Error analysis shows that the error type differs between the test sets. While the errors in Expert-TSD were mostly controversial among experts, here, there were clear errors in places labeled "Not a TSD" by GPT-4. At the same time, the utterance contained a clear "Non-immediate TSD" (e.g., *I've always thought suicide was something I would never do, but lately I'm getting scared that I'm gonna reach a point where I simply can't handle any more of this.*). Note that all these places (18) were utterances that therapists would not say during therapy. This raises the suspicion that the model was pretrained on a task related to self-disclosure in a clinical-related domain rather than a general domain. Analyzing the different behaviors in different data distributions can give a glimpse into the findings of Reuel et al. (2022) that showed that models that involve self-disclosure exhibit limited generalization capabilities when applied to different datasets.

Figure 2 summarises GPT-4 confusions and error analysis in both test sets.

6 Conclusion

In this study, we have formalized Therapist Self-Disclosure (TSD) as a Natural Language Processing (NLP) task by introducing expert-annotated test sets to simulate therapist utterances and utilizing Large Language Models (LLMs) for in-context learning as a solution. This work demonstrates how psychotherapy literature can help capture language nuances. In addition, this work shows the potential of NLP tools to enhance theoretical understanding of existing issues in psychotherapy.

The contribution to the NLP domain lies in the task's potential to serve as a challenging benchmark for optimizing results of accuracy or efficiency while the proposed method serves as a baseline. In addition, The expert-annotated utterance set can function as a test set for model evaluation (as in this study) or as valuable training examples for few-shot learning or other methods.

In the field of Psychotherapy Research, our study offers carefully documented guidelines and a testing ground for human annotators aiming to engage in manual annotations of TSD. Our proposed method lays a promising foundation, however, it necessitates ongoing exploration and refinement before implementation. Future research will have to examine its readiness and effectiveness for automated TSD tagging in real-world data contexts.

Limitations

Data. We annotated at the utterance level only, without considering a broader context. For instance, utterances where the therapist responds to a personal question without initiating the disclosure are also considered disclosures, such as:
Client: *Do you care about me?*
Therapist: *Of course.*
The last example represents a TSD, though in our test set, there is no option to represent such a scenario. Another example that requires a broader context:
Client: *I want to tell him "it's especially for you"*
Therapist: *that I care about you*
The last example does not represent a TSD but rather constitutes a reflection in which the therapist employs the first person. When taken as an isolated utterance without context, the therapist's response may be perceived as TSD.

Furthermore, given that the utterances were both generated and annotated by a single expert, there is a potential for unconscious bias in the data, and the utterances may not be as representative as those found in actual treatment data. Different annotators can have different labels for the same utterance.

Method. The method we suggested uses a long and expensive prompt. We did not try to optimize the length of the prompt. Moreover, there might be more efficient and accurate methods available.

Results and Conclusions. The notably favorable outcomes observed with GPT-4 on the test sets may indicate a seemingly straightforward task that GPT adeptly handles. Conversely, these results could stem from the limited diversity and insufficient representation of real data within the examples we generated. In practical scenarios, real data often diverge from artificial test sets. Therapists' utterances commonly extend beyond 1-2 sentences, incorporating a combination of interventions, thereby complicating the task's definition. This reality highlights the challenge of accurately capturing the complexity and diversity inherent in therapist communications. Thus, while our proposed method presents a promising foundation, it requires further exploration and refinement before implementation. Continued research is essential to enhance its readiness and effectiveness in the context of automated TSD tagging in real data.

Ethical Statement

Data. The new test set used in this study is publicly available. The authors evaluated the utterances to ensure that they did not contain offensive content. None of the samples found in the test set were taken from a real therapy.

Models. LLMs may generate offensive content if prompted with certain inputs. However, we used them for evaluation only, with non-offensive inputs, and we did not encounter any problematic responses.

Privacy. In our experiments we did not use confidential data. Therefor we had no problem using the GPT-4 model that processes the data through OpenAI's servers. **Please note that if confidential data is used, a thorough check must be performed regarding models and data leakage from the local computer to the outside.**

References

Josh Achiam, Steven Adler, Sandhini Agarwal, Lama Ahmad, Ilge Akkaya, Florencia Leoni Aleman, Diogo Almeida, Janko Altenschmidt, Sam Altman, Shyamal Anadkat, et al. 2023. Gpt-4 technical report. *arXiv preprint arXiv:2303.08774.*

Stacie Ain. 2008. *Chipping away at the blank screen: Therapist self-disclosure and the real relationship.* University of Maryland, College Park.

Stacie Claire Ain. 2011. *The real relationship, therapist self-disclosure, and treatment progress: A study of psychotherapy dyads.* University of Maryland, College Park.

Tal Alfi-Yogev, Ilanit Hasson-Ohayon, Gal Lazarus, Sharon Ziv-Beiman, and Dana Atzil-Slonim. 2021. When to disclose and to whom? examining within- and between-client moderators of therapist self disclosure-outcome associations in psychodynamic psychotherapy. *Psychotherapy Research*, 31(7):921–931.

Tal Alfi-Yogev, Yogev Kivity, Dana Atzil-Slonim, Adar Paz, Libby Igra, Adi Lavi-Rotenberg, and Ilanit Hasson-Ohayon. 2024. Transdiagnostic effects of therapist self-disclosure on diverse emotional experiences of clients with emotional disorders and schizophrenia. *Journal of Clinical Psychology.*

Tal Alfi-Yogev, Yogev Kivity, Ilanit Hasson-Ohayon, Sharon Ziv-Beiman, Ido Yehezkel, and Dana Atzil-Slonim. 2023. Client-therapist temporal congruence in perceiving immediate therapist self-disclosure and its association with treatment outcome. *Psychotherapy Research*, 33(6):704–718.

Cristelle T Audet. 2011. Client perspectives of therapist self-disclosure: Violating boundaries or removing barriers? *Counselling Psychology Quarterly*, 24(2):85–100.

Cristelle T Audet and Robin D Everall. 2010. Therapist self-disclosure and the therapeutic relationship: A phenomenological study from the client perspective. *British Journal of Guidance & Counselling*, 38(3):327–342.

Rishi Bommasani, Drew A Hudson, Ehsan Adeli, Russ Altman, Simran Arora, Sydney von Arx, Michael S Bernstein, Jeannette Bohg, Antoine Bosselut, Emma Brunskill, et al. 2021. On the opportunities and risks of foundation models. *arXiv preprint arXiv:2108.07258*.

Laura S Brown and Lenore EA Walker. 1990. Feminist therapy perspectives on self-disclosure. In *Self-disclosure in the therapeutic relationship*, pages 135–154. Springer.

Tom Brown, Benjamin Mann, Nick Ryder, Melanie Subbiah, Jared D Kaplan, Prafulla Dhariwal, Arvind Neelakantan, Pranav Shyam, Girish Sastry, Amanda Askell, et al. 2020. Language models are few-shot learners. *Advances in neural information processing systems*, 33:1877–1901.

James FT Bugental. 1965. The search for authenticity: An existential-analytic approach to psychotherapy. *(No Title)*.

Jie Cao, Michael Tanana, Zac E Imel, Eric Poitras, David C Atkins, and Vivek Srikumar. 2019. Observing dialogue in therapy: Categorizing and forecasting behavioral codes. *arXiv preprint arXiv:1907.00326*.

Hyung Won Chung, Le Hou, Shayne Longpre, Barret Zoph, Yi Tay, William Fedus, Eric Li, Xuezhi Wang, Mostafa Dehghani, Siddhartha Brahma, et al. 2022. Scaling instruction-finetuned language models. *arXiv preprint arXiv:2210.11416*.

Windy Dryden. 1990. Self-disclosure in rational-emotive therapy. In *Self-disclosure in the therapeutic relationship*, pages 61–74. Springer.

Morris N Eagle. 2011. *From classical to contemporary psychoanalysis: A critique and integration*, volume 70. Taylor & Francis.

Barry Alan Farber. 2006. *Self-disclosure in psychotherapy*. Guilford Press.

Arthur Freeman, James Pretzer, Barbara Fleming, and Karen M Simon. 1990. *Clinical applications of cognitive therapy*. Springer.

S Freud. 1912. Recommendation to physicians practicing psycho-analysis. *Standard Edition*, 12.

Jairo N Fuertes, Michael Moore, and Jennifer Ganley. 2019. Therapists' and clients' ratings of real relationship, attachment, therapist self-disclosure, and treatment progress. *Psychotherapy Research*, 29(5):594–606.

Robert Geirhos, Jörn-Henrik Jacobsen, Claudio Michaelis, Richard Zemel, Wieland Brendel, Matthias Bethge, and Felix A Wichmann. 2020. Shortcut learning in deep neural networks. *Nature Machine Intelligence*, 2(11):665–673.

Max Glockner, Vered Shwartz, and Yoav Goldberg. 2018. Breaking nli systems with sentences that require simple lexical inferences. *arXiv preprint arXiv:1805.02266*.

Marvin R Goldfried, Lisa A Burckell, and Catherine Eubanks-Carter. 2003. Therapist self-disclosure in cognitive-behavior therapy. *Journal of clinical psychology*, 59(5):555–568.

Eda G Goldstein. 1997. To tell or not to tell: The disclosure of events in the therapist's life to the patient. *Clinical Social Work Journal*, 25(1):41–58.

Dan Hendrycks, Kevin Zhao, Steven Basart, Jacob Steinhardt, and Dawn Song. 2021. Natural adversarial examples. In *Proceedings of the IEEE/CVF Conference on Computer Vision and Pattern Recognition*, pages 15262–15271.

Jennifer R Henretty, Joseph M Currier, Jeffrey S Berman, and Heidi M Levitt. 2014. The impact of counselor self-disclosure on clients: A meta-analytic review of experimental and quasi-experimental research. *Journal of Counseling Psychology*, 61(2):191.

Jennifer R Henretty and Heidi M Levitt. 2010. The role of therapist self-disclosure in psychotherapy: A qualitative review. *Clinical psychology review*, 30(1):63–77.

Clara E Hill. 1978. Development of a counselor verbal response category. *Journal of Counseling Psychology*, 25(5):461.

Clara E Hill. 2009. *Helping skills: Facilitating, exploration, insight, and action*. American Psychological Association.

Clara E Hill, Charles J Gelso, Harold Chui, Patricia T Spangler, Ann Hummel, Teresa Huang, John Jackson, Russell A Jones, Beatriz Palma, Avantika Bhatia, et al. 2014. To be or not to be immediate with clients: The use and perceived effects of immediacy in psychodynamic/interpersonal psychotherapy. *Psychotherapy Research*, 24(3):299–315.

Clara E Hill and Sarah Knox. 2001. Self-disclosure. *Psychotherapy: Theory, Research, Practice, Training*, 38(4):413.

Clara E Hill, Sarah Knox, and Kristen G Pinto-Coelho. 2018. Therapist self-disclosure and immediacy: A qualitative meta-analysis. *Psychotherapy*, 55(4):445.

Kokil Jaidka, Iknoor Singh, Jiahui Liu, Niyati Chhaya, and Lyle Ungar. 2020. A report of the cl-aff offmychest shared task: Modeling supportiveness and disclosure. In *AffCon@ AAAI*, pages 118–129.

Divyansh Kaushik, Eduard Hovy, and Zachary C Lipton. 2019. Learning the difference that makes a difference with counterfactually-augmented data. *arXiv preprint arXiv:1909.12434*.

Sarah Knox, Shirley A Hess, David A Petersen, and Clara E Hill. 2001. A qualitative analysis of client perceptions of the effects of helpful therapist self-disclosure in long-term therapy. In *Annual Meeting of the Society for Psychotherapy., Jun, 1996, Amelia Island, FL, US; A version of this article was mentioned in the aforementioned conference.* American Psychological Association.

Sarah Knox and Clara E Hill. 2003. Therapist self-disclosure: Research-based suggestions for practitioners. *Journal of clinical psychology*, 59(5):529–539.

JA Kottler. 2003. On being a therapist . hoboken.

Heidi M Levitt, Takuya Minami, Scott B Greenspan, Jae A Puckett, Jennifer R Henretty, Catherine M Reich, and Jeffery S Berman. 2018. How therapist self-disclosure relates to alliance and outcomes: A naturalistic study. In *Disclosure and Concealment in Psychotherapy*, pages 7–28. Routledge.

James R Mahalik, E Alice Van Ormer, and Nicole L Simi. 2000. Ethical issues in using self-disclosure in feminist therapy.

Matteo Malgaroli, Thomas D Hull, James M Zech, and Tim Althoff. 2023. Natural language processing for mental health interventions: a systematic review and research framework. *Translational Psychiatry*, 13(1):309.

Patricia R McCarthy and Nancy E Betz. 1978. Differential effects of self-disclosing versus self-involving counselor statements. *Journal of Counseling Psychology*, 25(4):251.

Patricia McCarthy Veach. 2011. Reflections on the meaning of clinician self-reference: Are we speaking the same language? *Psychotherapy*, 48(4):349.

Nancy McWilliams. 2004. *Psychoanalytic psychotherapy: A practitioner's guide.* Guilford Press.

Sonia Murthy, Kiera Parece, Sophie Bridgers, Peng Qian, and Tomer Ullman. 2023. Comparing the evaluation and production of loophole behavior in humans and large language models. In *Findings of the Association for Computational Linguistics: EMNLP 2023*, pages 4010–4025.

Damilola Omitaomu, Shabnam Tafreshi, Tingting Liu, Sven Buechel, Chris Callison-Burch, Johannes Eichstaedt, Lyle Ungar, and João Sedoc. 2022. Empathic conversations: A multi-level dataset of contextualized conversations. *arXiv preprint arXiv:2205.12698*.

Long Ouyang, Jeff Wu, Xu Jiang, Diogo Almeida, Carroll L Wainwright, Pamela Mishkin, Chong Zhang, Sandhini Agarwal, Katarina Slama, Alex Ray, John Schulman, Jacob Hilton, Fraser Kelton, Luke Miller, Maddie Simens, Amanda Askell, Peter Welinder, Paul Christiano, Jan Leike, and Ryan Lowe. 2022. Training language models to follow instructions with human feedback. In *NeurIPS*.

Jiaxin Pei and David Jurgens. 2020. Quantifying intimacy in language. In *Proceedings of the 2020 Conference on Empirical Methods in Natural Language Processing (EMNLP)*, pages 5307–5326, Online. Association for Computational Linguistics.

Kristen G Pinto-Coelho, Clara E Hill, Monica S Kearney, Elissa L Sarno, Elizabeth S Sauber, Sydney M Baker, Jennifer Brady, Glenn W Ireland, Mary Ann Hoffman, Patricia T Spangler, et al. 2018a. When in doubt, sit quietly: A qualitative investigation of experienced therapists' perceptions of self-disclosure. *Journal of Counseling Psychology*, 65(4):440.

Kristen G Pinto-Coelho, Clara E Hill, and Dennis M Kivlighan. 2018b. Therapist self-disclosure in psychodynamic psychotherapy: A mixed methods investigation. In *Disclosure and Concealment in Psychotherapy*, pages 29–52. Routledge.

Abhilasha Ravichander and Alan W Black. 2018. An empirical study of self-disclosure in spoken dialogue systems. In *Proceedings of the 19th annual SIGdial meeting on discourse and dialogue*, pages 253–263.

Ann-Katrin Reuel, Sebastian Peralta, João Sedoc, Garrick Sherman, and Lyle Ungar. 2022. Measuring the language of self-disclosure across corpora. In *Findings of the Association for Computational Linguistics: ACL 2022*, pages 1035–1047.

Natalie Shapira, Oren Kalinsky, Alex Libov, Chen Shani, and Sofia Tolmach. 2023a. Evaluating humorous response generation to playful shopping requests. In *European Conference on Information Retrieval*, pages 617–626. Springer.

Natalie Shapira, Mosh Levy, Seyed Hossein Alavi, Xuhui Zhou, Yejin Choi, Yoav Goldberg, Maarten Sap, and Vered Shwartz. 2023b. Clever hans or neural theory of mind? stress testing social reasoning in large language models. *arXiv preprint arXiv:2305.14763*.

Natalie Shapira, Guy Zwirn, and Yoav Goldberg. 2023c. How well do large language models perform on faux pas tests? In *Findings of the Association for Computational Linguistics: ACL 2023*, pages 10438–10451, Toronto, Canada. Association for Computational Linguistics.

William B Stiles. 1979. Verbal response modes and psychotherapeutic technique. *Psychiatry*, 42(1):49–62.

Mina Valizadeh, Pardis Ranjbar-Noiey, Cornelia Caragea, and Natalie Parde. 2021. Identifying medical self-disclosure in online communities.

Andrew J Vandernoot. 2007. *The relationship between the attachment-style of therapists and their utilization of self-disclosure within the therapeutic relationship.* Ph.D. thesis, Alliant International University, Los Angeles.

Yi-Chia Wang, Robert E Kraut, and John M Levine. 2015. Eliciting and receiving online support: using computer-aided content analysis to examine the dynamics of online social support. *Journal of medical Internet research*, 17(4):e99.

C Edward Watkins Jr. 1990. The effects of counselor self-disclosure: A research review. *The Counseling Psychologist*, 18(3):477–500.

Anuradha Welivita and Pearl Pu. 2022a. Curating a large-scale motivational interviewing dataset using peer support forums. In *Proceedings of the 29th International Conference on Computational Linguistics*, pages 3315–3330.

Anuradha Welivita and Pearl Pu. 2022b. Curating a large-scale motivational interviewing dataset using peer support forums. In *Proceedings of the 29th International Conference on Computational Linguistics*, pages 3315–3330, Gyeongju, Republic of Korea. International Committee on Computational Linguistics.

Tongshuang Wu, Marco Tulio Ribeiro, Jeffrey Heer, and Daniel S Weld. 2021. Polyjuice: Generating counterfactuals for explaining, evaluating, and improving models. *arXiv preprint arXiv:2101.00288*.

Wayne Xin Zhao, Kun Zhou, Junyi Li, Tianyi Tang, Xiaolei Wang, Yupeng Hou, Yingqian Min, Beichen Zhang, Junjie Zhang, Zican Dong, Yifan Du, Chen Yang, Yushuo Chen, Zhipeng Chen, Jinhao Jiang, Ruiyang Ren, Yifan Li, Xinyu Tang, Zikang Liu, Peiyu Liu, Jian-Yun Nie, and Ji-Rong Wen. 2023. A survey of large language models.

Sharon Ziv-Beiman. 2013. Therapist self-disclosure as an integrative intervention. *Journal of Psychotherapy Integration*, 23(1):59.

Sharon Ziv-Beiman, Giora Keinan, Elad Livneh, Patrick S Malone, and Golan Shahar. 2017. Immediate therapist self-disclosure bolsters the effect of brief integrative psychotherapy on psychiatric symptoms and the perceptions of therapists: A randomized clinical trial. *Psychotherapy Research*, 27(5):558–570.

Ofer Zur. 2004. To cross or not to cross: Do boundaries in therapy protect or harm. *Psychotherapy bulletin*, 39(3):27–32.

Ethical Thematic and Topic Modelling Analysis of Sleep Concerns in a Social Media-Derived Suicidality Dataset

Martin Orr and **Kirsten van Kessel**
Auckland University of Technology, New Zealand
martinorr521@gmail.com
kirsten.vankessel@aut.ac.nz

David Parry
Murdoch University, Australia
david.parry@murdoch.edu.au

Abstract

Objective: A thematic and topic modelling analysis of sleep concerns in a social media-derived, privacy-preserving, suicidality dataset. This forms the basis for an exploration of sleep as a potential computational linguistic signal in suicide prevention. **Background:** Suicidal ideation is a limited signal for suicide. Developments in computational linguistics and mental health datasets afford an opportunity to investigate additional signals and to consider the broader clinical ethical design implications. **Methodology:** A clinician-led integration of reflexive thematic analysis, with machine learning topic modelling (BERTopic), and the purposeful sampling of the University of Maryland Suicidality Dataset. **Results:** Sleep as a place of 1) refuge and escape, 2) revitalisation for exhaustion, and 3) risk and vulnerability were generated as core themes in an initial thematic analysis of 546 posts. BERTopic analysing 21,876 sleep references in 16791 posts facilitated the production of 40 topics that were clinically interpretable, relevant, and thematically aligned to a level that exceeded original expectations. Power and consent, privacy and synthetic representative data, validity and stochastic variability of results, and a co-designed and governed, multi-signal formulation perspective, are highlighted as key research and clinical issues.

1 Introduction

This paper reports on the thematic and topic modelling analysis of sleep concerns in a social media-derived, privacy-preserving, suicidality dataset. Key objectives are an exploration of 1) the role of sleep as a potential linguistic signal in suicide prevention formulation, and 2) the ethical and design opportunities and challenges, artificial intelligence (AI) and sensitive mental health datasets may afford to the global mental health community (Resnik et al., 2021; Shing et al., 2018, 2020; Zirikly et al., 2019; Orr et al., 2022, 2023). This work arises from an academic program, centered on clinical best practice, leadership, and change and is the third in a series of papers focused on AI, ethics and suicide prevention (Orr et al., 2022, 2023).

There is increasing interest in the application of computational linguistics in suicide prevention. Suicide prevention threat detection, and guardian angel-type technology, are already deployed in social media. This raises significant ethical design, clinical effectiveness, and governance issues (Barnett and Torous, 2019; Bernert et al., 2020; Burke et al., 2019; Floridi and Cowls, 2019; Ophir et al., 2022; Orr et al., 2023). Suicidal ideation is a relatively weak signal for suicide, and there is a need to research additional signals (Deisenhammer et al., 2009; Galynker et al., 2017; Yaseen et al., 2019). Sleep disturbance is associated with increased suicidal behaviour to the degree it may represent a modifiable risk factor and signal to inform suicide risk management formulation and intervention planning (Bishop et al., 2020; Bradford et al., 2021; Fernandes et al., 2021; Hamilton et al., 2023; Kalmbach et al., 2022; Liu et al., 2020; Miller and McCall, 2023; Shepard et al., 2023).

Computational linguistics is a branch of AI, associated with natural language processing. It has come to increasing clinical importance because of the rapid advancements and growth in transformers and generative AI (Javaid et al., 2023; Resnik et al., 2021).

Closely entwined with the use of AI in mental health, is the ethical utilisation and governance of sensitive data, including data mining and the curation of datasets. The data utilisation approach in this research combines the qualitative Braun and Clarke approach to thematic analysis, with quantitative machine learning topic modelling, to study a large social media suicidality dataset (Blei, 2012; Blei et al., 2003; Grootendorst, 2022; Braun and Clarke, 2006, 2019; Fast et al., 2016). There is

Proceedings of the 9th Workshop on Computational Linguistics and Clinical Psychology (CLPsych 2024), pages 74–91

emerging interest in the potential research benefits of combining qualitative reflexive thematic analysis with computational methods. This includes how topic modelling could assist with more rapid familiarization and coding of large social media-based data sets, and contribute to the qualitative, nuanced, contextual, interpretative, and reflexive theme creation process (Gauthier et al., 2022; Gauthier and Wallace, 2022).

Suicide is a complex devastating event where there can be a struggle to make sense, find meaning, and understand the related computational basis of the mind, lived experience, intent, and decision-making. Computational neuroscience and psychiatry seek to bring understanding to complex human behaviours to optimize care and prevention (Hauser et al., 2022; Nordin et al., 2022).

Computational linguistics can play a role in data collection, formulation, and the creation of digital psychotherapeutic interventions. Either individually or combined with other neurophysiological, behavioural, and imaging techniques, computational linguistics may provide modelling insights into the neural basis of language (Bourguignon, 2022). This may contribute to the development, analysis, and detection of language biomarkers or signals of various states of cognitive and emotional processing, mental disorder, and behavioural risk.

Suicidal ideation is an important risk signal for potential psychological distress and completed suicide that requires timely assessment and intervention. However, although important, it is also a weakly predictive, frequently late, or non-presenting and unreliable signal (Deisenhammer et al., 2009; Galynker et al., 2017; Yaseen et al., 2019). Although there is only a limited correlation between suicidal ideation and suicide, those who have expressed suicidal ideation may be a significant target population to look for other signals operating with different contextual factors, frequency, prevalence, and time scales that may assist with the timely formulation of risk management and suicide prevention (Orr et al., 2022, 2023).

1.1 Sleep as a potential signal and intervention priority in suicide prevention

Sleep is central to physical and mental health (Scott et al., 2021; Hertenstein et al., 2022; Harvey, 2022). There is significant evidence of sleep disturbance being correlated with suicidal behavior to the degree that it can be considered a potentially modifiable risk factor and predictive or prioritizing signal for suicide prevention (Bishop et al., 2016, 2020; Blake and Allen, 2020; Bradford et al., 2021; Chaïb et al., 2020; Fernandes et al., 2021; Geoffroy et al., 2021; Hamilton et al., 2023; Kalmbach et al., 2022; Kearns et al., 2020; Liu et al., 2020; McCall et al., 2019; McCall, 2022; Miller and McCall, 2023; Perlis et al., 2016; Pigeon et al., 2019; Shepard et al., 2023; Trockel et al., 2015; Tubbs et al., 2019).

Sleep disturbances from insomnia to nightmares to sleep-disordered breathing are associated with an increased risk of suicidal behavior (Porras-Segovia et al., 2019; Prguda et al., 2023; Tubbs et al., 2019). However, there has been limited research targeting sleep as a suicide intervention and limited evidence of resultant benefit. Studies to date have typically targeted suicidal ideation with cognitive behavioural therapy for insomnia (CBTI) or hypnotic drugs and demonstrated enough selected evidence for improvement to warrant further research and consideration in treatment protocols (McCall et al., 2019; Pigeon et al., 2019; Trockel et al., 2015). Targeting suicidal ideation in research may be a useful proxy variable for completed suicide as there is a significant correlation between the two (Nock et al., 2008a,b). However, it is important to understand the nature and limitations of that correlation. Relatively few of those who voice suicidal ideation will go on to complete suicide, and many of those who complete suicide will not be known to have voiced or experienced suicidal ideation. If suicidal ideation is the only focus or signal sought, significant timely suicide prevention opportunities may be lost.

Night-time is a high-risk period for suicide. It is unclear to what degree this is due to a range of factors including circadian or sleep deprivation-related decrease in frontal lobe function or decreased serotonin levels, or due to loneliness or lack of support. Being alone and awake at night may decrease the potential for intervention or distraction from a distressed consciousness. Being awake during a period of brain hypofrontality may be associated with affective and cognitive dysfunction leading to emotionality, impulsivity, and impaired decision-making. Adolescents who are likely to be a key demographic utilising social media may be particularly vulnerable to sleep-related suicidal behaviour (Porras-Segovia et al., 2019; Tubbs et al., 2019).

Each stage of sleep may have a key evolutionary function in helping process the cognitions, emotions, and actions of the day, clearing out waste, and optimising mind and body. Lack of sleep can impair our ability to creatively problem solve, exercise impulse control, process and experience emotions, calm the mind, be empathetic, or see aesthetic beauty and positivity in the world (Peretti et al., 2019).

Sleep is a universal dynamic periodic function, associated with a range of neurophysiological, emotional, behavioral, and contextual parameters. Sleep can be measured multimodally, and the multiple signals integrated to get a greater understanding of sleep quantity, structure, and quality, and their relationships to context. In this work, the focus is on the computational linguistic analysis of the sleep signal that may be contained in social media text. A signal typically carries indicative information that may require or precipitate a specific response if when interpreted (either individually or combined with other signals or factors) it exhibits certain characteristics or meets a certain threshold. An individual's cognitions, emotional response, behaviours, and context in relation to sleep may be derived from how they write about it; and what and how much they write about sleep may be influenced by their mental and emotional state at that time and their personal, group, and cultural interpretation of the meaning and function of sleep and sleep disturbance.

Various forms of thematic analysis and phenomenological inquiry into the experience and understanding of sleep disturbance (insomnia, nightmares) and mental illness and suicide have previously been performed (Hochard et al., 2019; Klingaman et al., 2019; Littlewood et al., 2016; Luhaäär and Sisask, 2018). These are typically small in sample size, interview-based, and reflective in nature in the context of established mental disorder or suicidal behaviour.

If we can better linguistically define, characterise, or categorise the sleep experience and signal by and for both human and machine processes, it may contribute to the design of future suicide prevention research and interventions. A sleep signal may have utility in combination with other signals in terms of alerting, triage, clinical formulation, and treatment planning.

1.2 Identification of the University of Maryland Suicidality Dataset

There is an increasing focus on the application of data mining in combination with AI to enhance mental health service design and suicide prevention (Berrouiguet et al., 2019; Lopez-Castroman et al., 2020; Schuerkamp et al., 2023; Wang, 2023).

An exploratory goal of the body of work to which this study relates is creating a conceptual linguistic sleep signal model that could contribute to the development of real-time, natural language processing empowered, social media and formulation-based suicide prevention. To align with this goal the modelling data utilised should emulate as much as feasible the timely naturalistic expression of the lived experience and context under study (Neubauer et al., 2019; Van Manen, 2017). Capturing live social media data in a naturalistic contextualised form from actively suicidal individuals, affords major ethical, clinical, and medicolegal issues, including issues of power and consent, and responsibility. Consultation with ethics and AI specialists concluded that live data was not ethically justifiable or essential for this exploratory research and that a pre-existing social media dataset should be identified. This led to the identification of the University of Maryland Suicidality Dataset. The dataset comprises the 11,129 users who between 2006 to August 31st, 2015, had posted on the subreddit r/suicidewatch and had posted 10 or more times in total across all of Reddit. Included are user posts, post ID, anonymised user ID, timestamp, subreddit, de-identified post title, and body. The dataset also has an equal number of controls who had not posted in r/suicidewatch. The r/suicidewatch subreddit focuses on individuals posting about their suicidal ideation and plans, and other users offering support. The total dataset has approximately 2 million documents. The dataset has expert-labelled, crowdsourced-labelled, and unlabelled subsets (Shing et al., 2018; Zirikly et al., 2019).

1.3 Reflexive Thematic Analysis

Thematic analysis is recognised as a reflexive interpretive approach to pattern or theme development across a dataset and for its utility in phenomenological or experiential qualitative research where there is a focus on the understanding of experience, meaning, and sensemaking (Braun and Clarke, 2019, 2021a,b).

Reflexive thematic analysis emphasizes the interaction of the researcher with the data in the qualitative creation of themes. Themes are inductively woven from codes, with fewer themes potentially illustrating more intricacy of the analytic thought. Though grounded in data, there is a need for reflexive critical reflection, self-awareness, and recognition of prior knowledge, assumptions, and theories that may deductively influence the researcher's inductive sense-making process (Braun and Clarke, 2006; Clarke and Braun, 2018; Braun and Clarke, 2019).

The knowledge and experience of the primary researcher as a psychiatrist was utilised in the reflexive interpretation of data in this research (Braun and Clarke, 2021b; Ho et al., 2017; Neubauer et al., 2019; Pérez Vargas et al., 2020; Tomkins and Eatough, 2018; Van der Walt, 2020; Van Manen, 2017).

1.4 Topic Modelling and BERTopic

Topic modelling involves a range of algorithmic techniques that are essentially quantitative in that the technology has no inherent sentient understanding of the text but can bring varying levels of prior knowledge and types of process to draw mathematical connections and create clusters of key characteristic terms that appear to be linked, and provide examples of the documents that best exemplify the links. The underlying quantitative paradigm is typically viewed as being one of discovery of latent topics or themes in the text across a body of documents. However typically and traditionally human interpretation is required to create sense and meaning around how the terms or words may be linked and be of utility and to appropriately guide or supervise the topic labelling (Al Moubayed et al., 2020; Blei et al., 2003; Blei, 2012; Chang et al., 2009; Kherwa and Bansal, 2019; Resnik et al., 2015; Vaswani et al., 2017).

This analysis utilises BERTopic a topic modelling tool that uses BERT (Bidirectional Encoder Representations from Transformers) embeddings (Devlin et al., 2018; Grootendorst, 2022).

1.5 Central Question

The central question for the integrated reflexive thematic analysis and topic modelling was: what are the themes, topics, and key representative terms that may communicate or signal the experience, relationships, and meaning of sleep and sleep disturbance in those who have expressed suicidal ideation in social media text?

1.6 Methodology

The study uses a mixed methods design (Johnson, 2017). The research involves the integration of reflexive thematic analysis, BERTopic topic modelling, and the purposeful sampling of the University of Maryland Reddit Suicidality Dataset.

The Braun and Clarke reflexive thematic analysis process has six phases: 1) familiarisation with the data; 2) coding; 3) generating initial themes; 4) reviewing themes; 5) defining and naming themes; 6) writing up. The Braun and Clarke reflexive form of thematic analysis recognises how we bring our past knowledge, experience, and biases to the process of constructing patterns of meaning (Braun and Clarke, 2006, 2019, 2021a,b).

BERTopic creates topic representations in 3 major stages: 1) use of a pre-trained transformer language model to convert each document to its embedding mathematical representation; 2) optimisation of the embedding clustering process via reduction of the dimensionality; 3) topic representations are generated from the document clusters with a class-based variation of Term Frequency-Inverse Document Frequency (c-TF-IDF). Topic representations take the form of lists of keywords or terms that are most important, relevant, and characteristic of the topic, and BERTopic also creates a short collection of the most representative documents for each topic (Grootendorst, 2022).

2 Results

2.1 Thematic Analysis

The reflexive thematic analysis involved 546 posts that included the term sleep from 154 individuals in the expert risk-rated subset of 245 users. The thematic analysis utilised the posts (across the whole of Reddit) from the 245 expert risk-level-rated r/suicidewatch users. The posts were keyword searched looking for references to sleep. The themes generated in relation to the research question were sleep as a place of 1) refuge and escape, 2) risk and vulnerability, and 3) revitalization for exhaustion. These themes related to 1) seeking refuge and escape via sleep from the living nightmare and trauma of consciousness and physical and psychological pain; 2) feeling at risk and vulnerable to trauma and nightmares and sleep paralysis if enter sleep, or vulnerable in terms of where sleeping or who sleeping with, or vulnerable to being woken up by others and pets or vulnerable to insomnia and related anxiety, loneliness, pain, negative thoughts, constant arousal and being on edge and unable to switch the mind off with fear of missing out; 3) feeling constantly exhausted physically and psychologically and overwhelmed, tired of anticipatory anxious worry about the future, and ruminating worry about the past, feeling burnt out and seeking the revitalization of sleep.

2.2 Topic Modelling

The data subset for the topic modelling stage was derived by searching for the word sleep in all posts by users who had posted on r/suicidewatch in the University of Maryland dataset. This resulted in identifying 16791 posts by 5751 unique users. Those posts were then broken down into sentences, and sentences were selected that contained the word sleep. This identified 21,876 sentences.

BERTopic was utilised using a Google Colab that was customized to allow options in a range of parameters, including file selection, number of topic words, topic reduction, and seed topics. BERTopic provides a range of outputs, including key representative topic terms and documents, and visual representations of how the topics cluster and relate to each other and could potentially be merged or reduced. The BERTopic outputs in the Appendix section, Figure 1. (topic word scores), Table 2. (topic frequency count), and Figure 2. (hierarchical clustering) and the topic representative documents, were utilised by the psychiatrist first author for the topic labelling process (Table 1.). The thematic analysis was also drawn upon for a deeper interpretive and integrative understanding. The BERTopic outputs reported are with parameters set to 9 topic words, topic reduction to 40, and no guiding seeding. The non-seeded topic modelling process resulted in surprisingly clinically interpretable and relevant results, that generally supported and aligned with the core thematic analysis concepts. There are a range of qualitative and quantitative computational techniques by which BERTopic's outputs can be evaluated for topic coherence and diversity (Grootendorst, 2022). In this exploratory study the focus was on human domain expert interpretation.

The most relevant and important topic terms (with the highest topic c-TF-IDF scores), typically gave a readily interpretable guide to an appropriate, meaningful topic label e.g. Topic 10. Dreams and nightmares, Topic 13. Tired and exhausted and Topic 14. Pain, hurts, and sleep. These topics also aligned with the theme elements of exhaustion and vulnerability created in the thematic analysis. Sleep as escape was a major theme element in the thematic analysis. This was overtly captured in the relatively low frequency Topic 36 where the most important and relevant term was escape and the representative documents directly refer to sleep being the only escape. However, escape was also an inherent, at least part, element of a range of other topics including the high-frequency topics 0. Want to sleep and 1. Sleeping pills to sleep. Though not immediately evident or definitive from the topic terms, reference to the representative documents indicated these topics capturing a want to sleep forever for some that aligned with the theme of escape and suicidality. That is references in the representative documents, to never wanting to wake up, or consuming a large supply of sleeping medication at once, were important potential suicidality signals. While in topics 0. and 1. the "forever" aspect only related to some, in Topic 24 it was the predominant term and feature.

The representative documents utilized in the topic labelling process, are not included in the Appendix because of the ethical requirement not to share verbatim potentially identifiable quotes and for data to be reported at the summative, coding, topic, and thematic level.

3 Discussion

This was exploratory research, with a focus on reporting and contextualising the analysis process and results, to a clinical /non-data scientist audience, to particularly highlight conceptual, ethical, and design issues for future research, and development. The following section aims to explore further a number of these issues.

3.1 Language and the Psyche

When considering the application of computational linguistics to mental health, it is important to also conceptually consider how language may relate to the functions of the mind. Language symbolically captures an individual's experience and conceptual interpretation of their world. Experience and interpretation are influenced by cultural and group norms. Language is integrally woven with brain function, and although the exact nature of the weave may be contentious, it may provide important data modelling insights to the understanding of the psyche, including rich multidimensional temporal and contextual parameters that may be difficult to access via other signals or means (Kompa, 2023; Li, 2022).

Topic	
-1: Miscellaneous (Outliers)	19: Gaming and Sleep
0: Want to sleep (forever)	20: Physical sensations and activity and sleep
1: Sleeping Pills to sleep (forever)	21: Sleep Apnea and Breathing and Sleep
2: Distressed and crying self to sleep	22: Texting and communication and sleep
3: Sleep period and schedule	23: Wish for more sleep
4: Name substitution and sleeping context	24: Want to sleep forever/permanently
5: Technology sleep mode	25: Mood disorder and sleep
6: Smoking, cannabis, drinking alcohol, and sleep	26: Prayer, meditation, and sleep
7: Eating and Sleep	27: Memory, focus, concentration and sleep
8: School and Sleep	28: Happiness and sleep
9: Sleeping outside home	29: Alarm clock and sleep
10: Dreams and nightmares	30: Motivation and sleep
11: Pets and sleep	31: Heat and temperature and sleep
12: R/nosleep stories	32: Cutting, self-harm and sleep
13: Tired and exhausted	33: Cuddling and sex and sleep
14: Pain, hurts and sleep	34: Sleep deprivation and health consequences
15: Sleeping locations	35: Scratching, itch and sleep
16: Mind and sleep	36: Sleep as escape
17: Sleep paralysis and neurological experiences	37: Nursing/breastfeeding and sleep
18: Music, Noise and Sleep	38: Hallucinations/psychosis and sleep

Table 1: Sleep Topic Labelling.

3.2 Ambivalence

Legally a declaration of suicide typically requires evidence of an intentional and knowing act. However, suicide may be characterized by ambivalence, conflicting cognitions, emotions, and behaviours, and a temporal perceived need to escape an overwhelmed or pained consciousness or sense of entrapment, rather than a specific knowing, reasoned intent to die (Orr et al., 2023). This presents challenges but also opportunities when considering a computational linguistic signal of the mind in relationship to suicidality, in terms of detection, formulation, guidance, and amplification in the direction of seeking help. Ambivalence is prevalent in the University of Maryland Suicidality Dataset and indeed could be considered inherent, as those posting are typically seeking some form of help, advice, and input from others. This could also be considered a limitation or caveat for the dataset in that the active group are actively signalling their risk, expressing suicidal ideation, and reaching out. Those who don't express suicidal ideation and don't reach out may differ, adding weight to the case for additional signals and methods and channels for detection.

3.3 Sensitive data, stochasticity, and variability concerns

Two of the major concerns and limitations of the use of computational linguistics in clinical practice and research are, 1. concerns around the privacy, security, and governance of sensitive data and 2. the validity and variability and related safety of outputs. Validity, stability, and reproducibility are key concerns of topic model-based content analysis (Hoyle et al., 2022). The stochastic nature of computational linguistic processes may contribute to this variability (Javaid et al., 2023).

BERTopic is stochastic with variability in outputs on each run (mainly related to UMAP) (McInnes et al., 2018; Grootendorst, 2022). Stochasticity is a central feature of large language models and generative AI, which makes it an increasingly relevant concept for clinical research and related awareness. Stochasticity or probabilistic variability in potential outputs can augment and amplify human creativity, engagement, and brainstorming. However, in a clinical context the resultant variability in outputs (and related perceived confabulation or hallucinations with generative AI), can be perceived as unsafe.

Safe clinical and research utilization of pretrained transformers and generative AI will require significant development in education, prompt engineering training, stochastic temperature control, guard railing, and fine-tuning. This may enhance both the factual certainty and relevancy potential of the technology, while also being able to leverage the creative potential of stochasticity, to assist with resolving complex problems like suicide prevention.

3.4 Thematic analysis and topic modelling

The labelled topics offer a clinically valid and relevant general range of subdomains for issues related to sleep and sleep disturbance including aligning with key codes and themes created during the thematic analysis process.

The option of seed topics was included in the BERTopic Colab design as there was a high expectation that significant guidance and interpretation would be required to get any form of meaningful results. In Guided BERTopic seeds are used to nudge towards the creation of particular topics, but if they do not exist within the dataset they will not be modelled. The original expectation was that seed topics influenced by the earlier thematic analysis work would be required for meaningful and aligned results.

As it transpired the topic modelling exceeded expectations in terms of clinically interpretable and meaningful outputs, even with minimal guidance. The reflexive thematic analysis process still served an important purpose, in enhancing a deeper understanding of the dataset and facilitating the interpretation and labelling of the outputs. The thematic outputs from reflexive thematic analysis, are personal subjective qualitative constructs of the data, as it relates to the research question. The construction of themes in reflexive thematic analysis, and computational linguistic processes such as topic modelling, have a range of similarities in approach, in terms of pattern recognition, baseline weights based on prior learning, contextualisation, and a capacity to iteratively fine-tune.

3.5 Linguistic signal formulation

Signals in psychiatry can be characterized by complexity, noise, dissonance, probability, uncertainty, ambiguity, and ambivalence. This is similarly true for language signals that are subject to significant semantic and pragmatic interpretation complexity, and varying levels of contextual, and cultural modifiers and abstractive symbolism in deriving meaning, sentiment, and intent.

It is important to take a formulation approach to signals that recognises the importance of complexity, context, and culture and the need to dynamically consider and weigh all other factors or signals. Humans signal their thoughts, sentiments, and intent in a range of complex neurophysiological, behavioural, and natural language ways. Formulation is core to clinical mental health practice and has a factor weighing, pattern recognition, and modelling focus. Formulation recognises that the explanation for human behaviour can be complex, contextual, and contingent (Orr et al., 2022).

3.6 AI, data and the ethics of research and development and power and consent

There is an increasing focus on the need for an ethical overview of social media and AI research. There is a move away from considering all public data as exempt from ethical board oversight and more focus on the complexities of consent, defining private and public, anonymity, sensitive data and vulnerable populations, and minimising bias and algorithmic harm (Benton et al., 2017; British Psychological Society, 2017; Chiauzzi and Wicks, 2019; NEAC, 2019; Pagoto and Nebeker, 2019; Townsend and Wallace, 2016; Organization, 2023).

The topic representations created by BERTopic can be fine-tuned and labelled by a range of methods including via Open AI's API to ChatGPT (Grootendorst, 2022). To respect and protect the principle and ethics requirement of not sharing real data and quotes from the dataset, this process was not utilized. Future challenges include developing methods that respect and protect the sensitive nature of the data while leveraging and evolving the benefits and interpretive and generative nuance that large language models may afford.

The AI algorithmic and global mental health realms have both been subject to debate and scrutiny around ethics, power dynamics, bias, agency, consent and control. This includes concerns around AI and global mental health running the risk of representing new forms of colonialism and imperialism. Those who control data and algorithms may have undue power and influence and knowingly or unknowingly not act in the best ethical interests of an individual or community. (Beresford and Rose, 2023; Birhane, 2023; Pendse et al., 2022). AI may be associated with dual-use and algorithmic harm including unintentional iatrogenic harm if used for clinical purposes and not appropriately researched, designed or governed for different contexts, cultures, and customised needs.

3.7 Quotes and Sensitive Data

Qualitative research has traditionally used, and indeed required verbatim quotes, as a form of evidence of quality and rigour. Research using social media data sets will increasingly challenge that tradition, in that verbatim quotes can be frequently identified with a simple search engine and triangulation approach. There is a broad range of terms that may be utilised for indicative quotes, that do not contain the original words or syntax, but seek to convey the original content, sentiment, and intent. These terms include clustered, blended, aggregated, combined, composite, collective, deidentified, spun, paraphrased, bundled, amalgamated, illustrative, characteristic, indicative, representative and synthetic, and synthesized (Hemphill et al., 2022; Kasal et al., 2023; Proferes et al., 2021; Reagle, 2022; Winter and Gundur, 2022; Zimmer, 2020).

There will be an increasing range of technological and generative AI options to carry out this deidentification function with various degrees of parsing, paraphrasing, and production. However indicative non-verbatim quotes may not capture the emotion, pain, beauty, poignancy, pragmatic metaphorical abstraction, and personal poetry of the original where an individual has crafted their personal experience into words that they want to cathartically share with others. Similarly, the more data that is produced or created by generative AI, the more this may decrease the capacity to validly understand the authentic expression of human experience by drowning out and indeed shaping the expression of that experience.

Table 3. in the Appendix provides examples of composite synthetic quotes, that aim to illustrate the type of content that was the basis of the reflexive thematic analysis generated themes, without infringing the ethical undertaking not to use verbatim quotes.

4 Conclusion

This paper reported on the thematic and computational linguistic topic modelling analysis of sleep concerns in the University of Maryland Suicidality Dataset. This was multidisciplinary, exploratory, foundational work, that had the broader aim of highlighting some of the conceptual, ethical, and design opportunities and challenges artificial intelligence and mental health datasets may afford. The reflexive thematic analysis produced three core themes; sleep as a place of refuge and escape, risk and vulnerability, and revitalization for exhaustion. BERTopic was utilized to produce 40 topics with representative key terms and documents. The combined thematic analysis, and topic modelling process, resulted in clinically interpretable, relevant, and aligned results that exceeded initial expectations.

This is the third in a series of papers focused on AI and suicide prevention. Central series themes have been the complexities and contentions of suicide prediction, the related central role of formulation in clinical practice, and how the computational linguistic detection, development, and integration of relevant signals may contribute to enhancing the formulation and intervention planning process.

Sleep is a potentially useful linguistic signal in AI-based suicide risk formulation and intervention planning. Establishing sleep themes, topics, and key terms represents an initial exploratory development stage. A deployed AI-enhanced social media-based system that could detect, and utilize a linguistic sleep signal would need significant ethical co-design and governance. Research and development would require an iterative multistage, multimodal, multisignal contextually and culturally aware integrated formulation approach. Sleep may be considered as both a signal and an intervention and more conceptually as a preferable escape for a traumatised, overwhelmed, and exhausted consciousness. Sleep may help with cognitive and emotional processing, decreasing impulsivity, and increasing the capability to see a positive path through. An advantage of focusing on sleep as a key signal is that it can be both a transdiagnostic indicator of illness and vulnerability, and a transdiagnostic positive intervention, maximising the opportunities for benefit and optimisation of scarce resource utilisation.

Suicide is a complex, multifactorial low-base rate event, where there are significant risks and limitations in prediction and particularly attaching specific predictive or intervention power to any standalone factor. Sleep and sleep disturbance may have a significant role as a sensitive indicator of human distress and arousal and mental health vulnerability and as a signal that further assessment and intervention are required. Sleep and sleep disturbance signal data may be coded, labelled, weighed, and used in the formulation both as an indicator of transdiagnostic emotional distress and arousal, and to contribute towards specific mental disorder and sleep disorder interventions. It may also be more acceptable or in keeping with cultural, group, or personal experiential norms to talk about sleep disturbance and related exhaustion than to report depression or suicidal ideation.

Data relating to suicide is highly sensitive, and privacy-preserving datasets may afford clinical safety, medicolegal, and ethical benefits. Social media data mining affords an opportunity, to improve the computational understanding of human behavior and provide insights into user mental models. This may enhance psychological formulation, targeted needs segmentation, and personalized timely, user experience, engagement, recommendation, and intervention planning. This is particularly important in suicide prevention. In terms of practical clinical contributions, arising from this research, the findings have contributed to the psychiatrist first author's design of digital intake forms for a specialist sleep clinic. The future aim would be to develop a multimodal AI-enhanced assessment and formulation system, that was also capable of assisting with the therapeutic revision of memory and narrative associated with traumatic nightmares. Nightmares are associated with suicidality and were a significant finding of both the thematic analysis and topic modelling aspects of this research.

In terms of methodological contributions, the integration of reflexive thematic analysis and machine learning topic modelling could benefit other researchers working with large datasets that require scale, speed, and interpretive nuance in analysis. The integrated approach may contribute to the explicability or understanding of the algorithmic process and thematic and topic results.

As the AI field moves from Large Language Models to Merged, Multimodal Models (Triple M's), computational linguistics should retain a central role in sensing, shaping, augmenting, and amplifying the human psyche toward creative effective action and outputs. There is a need to research how large language models and generative AI could be used in fine-tuning, and clinically relevant analysis and interventions, in a way that addresses the sensitive nature of potential mental health and risk-related data and the associated medicolegal, ethical, clinical effectiveness, and safety issues.

The stated vision for the CLPsych community is to improve interdisciplinary knowledge exchange, foster collaboration, and increase the visibility of mental health as a problem domain in natural language processing. Similarly important is improving the visibility and accessibility of computational linguistics as an opportunity domain in clinical practice. The rapid rise in pre-trained transformers and generative AI has increased the need for clinician knowledge, education, and engagement in computational linguistics. Also highlighted by these developments is a broader need for multi-stakeholder research, co-design and representative governance to enhance the capacity and propensity for benefit optimization and harm minimisation. Key related areas for future research and development highlighted by this paper include building a shared understanding and approach to, risk-benefit analysis, power and consent, formulation, stochastics, and sensitive and representative data.

By focusing on one signal (sleep), one dataset, and one technique (topic modelling) a core aim of this research is a greater shared conceptual understanding of the opportunities and challenges presented by computational linguistics to the global mental health community. Global mental health may be particularly suited and vulnerable to developments in computational linguistics due to the central role of language in the psyche and culture and the need for contextual weighting in making sense of and shaping complex human experiences.

The computational linguistic and global mental health communities need to engage with these challenges and opportunities with a high degree of shared ethical, conceptual, contextual, cultural, and power dynamic awareness. This paper has aimed to enhance that awareness and contribute to the developmental capacity of the CLpsych community to pursue its mission to reduce emotional suffering and suicide.

Acknowledgements

We would like to acknowledge the assistance of Prof. Philip Resnik and the American Association of Suicidology in making the "University of Maryland Reddit Suicidality Dataset, Version 2" available.

Ethics approval: Locality academic ethics committee approval was granted on 21st Sept. 2020. University of Maryland/American Association of Suicidology approval for dataset usage granted 29th Sept. 2020. Conflicts and funding: Nil **The dual approval requirements are described at:** `https://users.umiacs.umd.edu/~resnik/umd_reddit_suicidality_dataset.html`

Limitations statement: The relationships between sleep, mental health, and suicide are complex and contentious. As highlighted in the paper this was exploratory research, that formed part of a body of work with a focus on ethical clinical design, and the opportunities and challenges of computational linguistics contributing to enhancing mental health care and research, specifically suicide prevention. There was a concern from the outset that limitations of the dataset and BERTopic pre-trained embeddings and processes could lead to few interpretable, clinically recognizable, or useful topics. The results exceeded expectations in terms of potential clinical utility and interest. The topic modelling results reported had a focus on illustrating potential clinical utility with a view to clinician engagement. It is well recognized that they represent just an initial analytic and developmental step in the ongoing evolvement of safe and effective risk and clinical formulation and intervention systems. Caveats in terms of ethics, dynamic user, temporal, situational, and language representation and understanding, misinformation, bias, contextual and cultural nuance, generalisability, reproducibility and validity, and lack of ground truth around risk and outcome, and cause and correlation remain.

References

Noura Al Moubayed, Stephen McGough, and Bashar Awwad Shiekh Hasan. 2020. Beyond the topics: How deep learning can improve the discriminability of probabilistic topic modelling. *PeerJ Computer Science*, 6:e252.

Ian Barnett and John Torous. 2019. Ethics, transparency, and public health at the intersection of innovation and Facebook's suicide prevention efforts.

Adrian Benton, Glen Coppersmith, and Mark Dredze. 2017. Ethical research protocols for social media health research. In *Proceedings of the First ACL Workshop on Ethics in Natural Language Processing*, pages 94–102.

Peter Beresford and Diana Rose. 2023. Decolonising global mental health: The role of Mad Studies. *Cambridge Prisms: Global Mental Health*, 10:e30.

Rebecca A Bernert, Amanda M Hilberg, Ruth Melia, Jane Paik Kim, Nigam H Shah, and Freddy Abnousi. 2020. Artificial intelligence and suicide prevention: A systematic review of machine learning investigations. *International Journal of Environmental Research and Public Health*, 17(16):5929.

Sofian Berrouiguet, María Luisa Barrigón, Jorge Lopez Castroman, Philippe Courtet, Antonio Artés-Rodríguez, and Enrique Baca-García. 2019. Combining mobile-health (mHealth) and artificial intelligence (AI) methods to avoid suicide attempts: The Smartcrises study protocol. *BMC psychiatry*, 19(1):1–9.

Abeba Birhane. 2023. Algorithmic Colonization of Africa. In *Imagining AI: How the World Sees Intelligent Machines*. Oxford University Press.

Todd M Bishop, Kelsey V Simons, Deborah A King, and Wilfred R Pigeon. 2016. Sleep and suicide in older adults: An opportunity for intervention. *Clinical Therapeutics*, 38(11):2332–2339.

Todd M Bishop, Patrick G Walsh, Lisham Ashrafioun, Jill E Lavigne, and Wilfred R Pigeon. 2020. Sleep, suicide behaviors, and the protective role of sleep medicine. *Sleep Medicine*, 66:264–270.

Matthew J Blake and Nicholas B Allen. 2020. Prevention of internalizing disorders and suicide via adolescent sleep interventions. *Current Opinion in Psychology*, 34:37–42.

David M Blei. 2012. Probabilistic topic models. *Communications of the ACM*, 55(4):77–84.

David M Blei, Andrew Y Ng, and Michael I Jordan. 2003. Latent Dirichlet Allocation. *The Journal of Machine Learning Research*, 3:993–1022.

Nicolas J Bourguignon. 2022. The emergence of language in the human mind and brain — insights from the neurobiology of language, thought and action. *Psychological Review*.

Daniel RR Bradford, Stephany M Biello, and Kirsten Russell. 2021. Insomnia symptoms mediate the association between eveningness and suicidal ideation, defeat, entrapment, and psychological distress in students. *Chronobiology International*, 38(10):1397–1408.

Virginia Braun and Victoria Clarke. 2006. Using thematic analysis in psychology. *Qualitative Research in Psychology*, 3(2):77–101.

Virginia Braun and Victoria Clarke. 2019. Reflecting on reflexive thematic analysis. *Qualitative Research in Sport, Exercise and Health*, 11(4):589–597.

Virginia Braun and Victoria Clarke. 2021a. Can I use TA? Should I use TA? Should I not use TA? Comparing reflexive thematic analysis and other pattern-based qualitative analytic approaches. *Counselling and Psychotherapy Research*, 21(1):37–47.

Virginia Braun and Victoria Clarke. 2021b. One size fits all? What counts as quality practice in (reflexive) thematic analysis? *Qualitative Research in Psychology*, 18(3):328–352.

British Psychological Society. 2017. Ethics guidelines for internet-mediated research. *Leicester, UK: British Psychological Society*.

Taylor A Burke, Brooke A Ammerman, and Ross Jacobucci. 2019. The use of machine learning in the study of suicidal and non-suicidal self-injurious thoughts and behaviors: A systematic review. *Journal of Affective Disorders*, 245:869–884.

Laurent Stephane Chaïb, Alejandro Porras Segovia, Enrique Baca-Garcia, and Jorge Lopez-Castroman. 2020. Ecological studies of sleep disturbances during suicidal crises. *Current Psychiatry Reports*, 22:1–8.

Jonathan Chang, Sean Gerrish, Chong Wang, Jordan Boyd-Graber, and David Blei. 2009. Reading tea leaves: How humans interpret topic models. *Advances in Neural Information Processing Systems*, 22.

E. Chiauzzi and P. Wicks. 2019. Digital trespass: Ethical and terms-of-use violations by researchers accessing data from an online patient community. *J Med Internet Res*, 21(2):e11985.

Victoria Clarke and Virginia Braun. 2018. Using thematic analysis in counselling and psychotherapy research: A critical reflection. *Counselling and Psychotherapy Research*, 18(2):107–110.

Eberhard A Deisenhammer, Chy-Meng Ing, Robert Strauss, Georg Kemmler, Hartmann Hinterhuber, and Elisabeth M Weiss. 2009. The duration of the suicidal process: How much time is left for intervention between consideration and accomplishment of a suicide attempt? *Journal of Clinical Psychiatry*, 70(1):19.

Jacob Devlin, Ming-Wei Chang, Kenton Lee, and Kristina Toutanova. 2018. BERT: Pre-training of deep bidirectional transformers for language understanding. *arXiv preprint arXiv:1810.04805*.

Ethan Fast, Binbin Chen, and Michael S Bernstein. 2016. Empath: Understanding topic signals in large-scale text. In *Proceedings of the 2016 CHI Conference on Human Factors in Computing Systems*, pages 4647–4657.

Sara N Fernandes, Emily Zuckerman, Regina Miranda, and Argelinda Baroni. 2021. When night falls fast: Sleep and suicidal behavior among adolescents and young adults. *Child and Adolescent Psychiatric Clinics*, 30(1):269–282.

Luciano Floridi and Josh Cowls. 2019. A unified framework of five principles for AI in society. *Harvard Data Science Review*.

Igor Galynker, Zimri S Yaseen, Abigail Cohen, Ori Benhamou, Mariah Hawes, and Jessica Briggs. 2017. Prediction of suicidal behavior in high risk psychiatric patients using an assessment of acute suicidal state: The suicide crisis inventory. *Depression and Anxiety*, 34(2):147–158.

Robert P Gauthier, Mary Jean Costello, and James R Wallace. 2022. "I will not drink with you today": A topic-guided thematic analysis of addiction recovery on Reddit. In *Proceedings of the 2022 CHI Conference on Human Factors in Computing Systems*, pages 1–17.

Robert P Gauthier and James R Wallace. 2022. The computational thematic analysis toolkit. *Proceedings of the ACM on Human-Computer Interaction*, 6(GROUP):1–15.

Pierre A Geoffroy, Maria A Oquendo, Philippe Courtet, Carlos Blanco, Mark Olfson, Hugo Peyre, Michel Lejoyeux, Frederic Limosin, and Nicolas Hoertel. 2021. Sleep complaints are associated with increased suicide risk independently of psychiatric disorders: Results from a national 3-year prospective study. *Molecular Psychiatry*, 26(6):2126–2136.

Maarten Grootendorst. 2022. BERTopic: Neural topic modeling with a class-based TF-IDF procedure. *arXiv preprint arXiv:2203.05794*.

Jessica L Hamilton, Aliona Tsypes, Jamie Zelazny, Craig JR Sewall, Noelle Rode, John Merranko, David A Brent, Tina R Goldstein, and Peter L Franzen. 2023. Sleep influences daily suicidal ideation through affective reactivity to interpersonal events among high-risk adolescents and young adults. *Journal of Child Psychology and Psychiatry*, 64(1):27–38.

Allison G Harvey. 2022. Treating sleep and circadian problems to promote mental health: Perspectives on comorbidity, implementation science and behavior change. *Sleep*, 45(4):zsac026.

Tobias U Hauser, Vasilisa Skvortsova, Munmun De Choudhury, and Nikolaos Koutsouleris. 2022. The promise of a model-based psychiatry: Building computational models of mental ill health. *The Lancet Digital Health*, 4(11):e816–e828.

Libby Hemphill, Angela Schöpke-Gonzalez, and Anmol Panda. 2022. Comparative sensitivity of social media data and their acceptable use in research. *Scientific Data*, 9(1):643.

Elisabeth Hertenstein, Ersilia Trinca, Marina Wunderlin, Carlotta L Schneider, Marc A Züst, Kristoffer D Fehér, Tanja Su, Annemieke v Straten, Thomas Berger, Chiara Baglioni, et al. 2022. Cognitive behavioral therapy for insomnia in patients with mental disorders and comorbid insomnia: A systematic review and meta-analysis. *Sleep Medicine Reviews*, 62:101597.

Ken HM Ho, Vico CL Chiang, and Doris Leung. 2017. Hermeneutic phenomenological analysis: The 'possibility' beyond 'actuality' in thematic analysis. *Journal of Advanced Nursing*, 73(7):1757–1766.

Kevin D Hochard, Sam Ashcroft, Janine Carroll, Nadja Heym, and Ellen Townsend. 2019. Exploring thematic nightmare content and associated self-harm risk. *Suicide and Life-Threatening Behavior*, 49(1):64–75.

Alexander Miserlis Hoyle, Pranav Goel, Rupak Sarkar, and Philip Resnik. 2022. Are neural topic models broken? In *Findings of the Association for Computational Linguistics: EMNLP 2022*, pages 5321–5344, Abu Dhabi, United Arab Emirates. Association for Computational Linguistics.

Mohd Javaid, Abid Haleem, and Ravi Pratap Singh. 2023. ChatGPT for healthcare services: An emerging stage for an innovative perspective. *BenchCouncil Transactions on Benchmarks, Standards and Evaluations*, 3(1):100105.

R Burke Johnson. 2017. Dialectical pluralism: A metaparadigm whose time has come. *Journal of Mixed Methods Research*, 11(2):156–173.

David A Kalmbach, Philip Cheng, Brian K Ahmedani, Edward L Peterson, Anthony N Reffi, Chaewon Sagong, Grace M Seymour, Melissa K Ruprich, and Christopher L Drake. 2022. Cognitive-behavioral therapy for insomnia prevents and alleviates suicidal ideation: Insomnia remission is a suicidolytic mechanism. *Sleep*, 45(12):zsac251.

Alexandr Kasal, Roksana Táborská, Laura Juríková, Alexander Grabenhofer-Eggerth, Michaela Pichler, Beate Gruber, Hana Tomášková, and Thomas Niederkrotenthaler. 2023. Facilitators and barriers to implementation of suicide prevention interventions: Scoping review. *Cambridge Prisms: Global Mental Health*, 10:e15.

Jaclyn C Kearns, Daniel DL Coppersmith, Angela C Santee, Catherine Insel, Wilfred R Pigeon, and Catherine R Glenn. 2020. Sleep problems and suicide risk in youth: A systematic review, developmental framework, and implications for hospital treatment. *General Hospital Psychiatry*, 63:141–151.

Pooja Kherwa and Poonam Bansal. 2019. Topic modeling: A comprehensive review. *EAI Endorsed Transactions on Scalable Information Systems*, 7(24).

Elizabeth A Klingaman, Alicia Lucksted, Eric S Crosby, Yelena Blank, and Elana Schwartz. 2019. A phenomenological inquiry into the experience of sleep: Perspectives of US military veterans with insomnia and serious mental illness. *Journal of Sleep Research*, 28(4):e12833.

Nikola A Kompa. 2023. Inner speech and 'pure' thought – do we think in language? *Review of Philosophy and Psychology*, pages 1–18.

Jing Li. 2022. Relationship between language and thought: Linguistic determinism, independence, or interaction? *Journal of Contemporary Educational Research*, 6(5):32–37.

Donna L Littlewood, Patricia Gooding, Simon D Kyle, Daniel Pratt, and Sarah Peters. 2016. Understanding the role of sleep in suicide risk: Qualitative interview study. *BMJ open*, 6(8):e012113.

Richard T Liu, Alexandra H Bettis, and Taylor A Burke. 2020. Characterizing the phenomenology of passive suicidal ideation: A systematic review and meta-analysis of its prevalence, psychiatric comorbidity, correlates, and comparisons with active suicidal ideation. *Psychological Medicine*, 50(3):367–383.

Jorge Lopez-Castroman, Bilel Moulahi, Jérôme Azé, Sandra Bringay, Julie Deninotti, Sebastien Guillaume, and Enrique Baca-Garcia. 2020. Mining social networks to improve suicide prevention: A scoping review. *Journal of Neuroscience Research*, 98(4):616–625.

Kätlin Luhaäär and Merike Sisask. 2018. Pathways to attempted suicide as reflected in the narratives of people with lived experience. *Religions*, 9(4):137.

William V McCall. 2022. Targeting insomnia symptoms as a path to reduction of suicide risk: The role of Cognitive Behavioral Therapy for insomnia (CBT-I).

William V McCall, Ruth M Benca, Peter B Rosenquist, Nagy A Youssef, Laryssa McCloud, Jill C Newman, Doug Case, Meredith E Rumble, Steven T Szabo, Marjorie Phillips, et al. 2019. Reducing suicidal ideation through insomnia treatment (REST-IT): a randomized clinical trial. *American Journal of Psychiatry*, 176(11):957–965.

Leland McInnes, John Healy, and James Melville. 2018. UMAP: Uniform manifold approximation and projection for dimension reduction. *arXiv preprint arXiv:1802.03426*.

Brian J Miller and William V McCall. 2023. Meta-analysis of insomnia, suicide, and psychopathology in schizophrenia. *Current Opinion in Psychiatry*, 36(3):156–165.

NEAC. 2019. National ethical standards for health and disability research and quality improvement. *Wellington: Ministry of Health*.

Brian E Neubauer, Catherine T Witkop, and Lara Varpio. 2019. How phenomenology can help us learn from the experiences of others. *Perspectives on Medical Education*, 8:90–97.

Matthew K Nock, Guilherme Borges, Evelyn J Bromet, Jordi Alonso, Matthias Angermeyer, Annette Beautrais, Ronny Bruffaerts, Wai Tat Chiu, Giovanni De Girolamo, Semyon Gluzman, et al. 2008a. Cross-national prevalence and risk factors for suicidal ideation, plans and attempts. *The British journal of psychiatry*, 192(2):98–105.

Matthew K Nock, Guilherme Borges, Evelyn J Bromet, Christine B Cha, Ronald C Kessler, and Sing Lee. 2008b. Suicide and suicidal behavior. *Epidemiologic Reviews*, 30(1):133.

Noratikah Nordin, Zurinahni Zainol, Mohd Halim Mohd Noor, and Lai Fong Chan. 2022. Suicidal behaviour prediction models using machine learning techniques: A systematic review. *Artificial Intelligence in Medicine*, page 102395.

Yaakov Ophir, Refael Tikochinski, Anat Brunstein Klomek, and Roi Reichart. 2022. The hitchhiker's guide to computational linguistics in suicide prevention. *Clinical Psychological Science*, 10(2):212–235.

World Health Organization. 2023. *Regulatory considerations on artificial intelligence for health*. World Health Organization.

Martin Orr, Kirsten Van Kessel, and David Parry. 2022. The ethical role of computational linguistics in digital psychological formulation and suicide prevention. In *Proceedings of the Eighth Workshop on Computational Linguistics and Clinical Psychology*.

Martin Orr, Kirsten Van Kessel, and David Parry. 2023. Ethical suicide prevention in an artificial intelligence driven society. *Journal of Ethics in Mental Health*, 11.

Sherry Pagoto and Camille Nebeker. 2019. How scientists can take the lead in establishing ethical practices for social media research. *Journal of the American Medical Informatics Association*, 26(4):311–313.

Sachin R Pendse, Daniel Nkemelu, Nicola J Bidwell, Sushrut Jadhav, Soumitra Pathare, Munmun De Choudhury, and Neha Kumar. 2022. From treatment to healing: Envisioning a decolonial digital mental health. In *Proceedings of the 2022 CHI Conference on Human Factors in Computing Systems*, pages 1–23.

Sara Peretti, Daniela Tempesta, Valentina Socci, Maria C Pino, Monica Mazza, Marco Valenti, Luigi De Gennaro, Cinzia Di Dio, Antonella Marchetti, and Michele Ferrara. 2019. The role of sleep in aesthetic perception and empathy: A mediation analysis. *Journal of Sleep Research*, 28(3):e12664.

John Jairo Pérez Vargas, Johan Andrés Nieto Bravo, and Juan Esteban Santamaría Rodríguez. 2020. Hermeneutics and phenomenology in human and social sciences research. *Civilizar Ciencias Sociales y Humanas*, 20(38):137–144.

Michael L Perlis, Michael A Grandner, Subhajit Chakravorty, Rebecca A Bernert, Gregory K Brown, and Michael E Thase. 2016. Suicide and sleep: Is it a bad thing to be awake when reason sleeps? *Sleep Medicine Reviews*, 29:101–107.

Wilfred R Pigeon, Jennifer S Funderburk, Wendi Cross, Todd M Bishop, and Hugh F Crean. 2019. Brief CBT for insomnia delivered in primary care to patients endorsing suicidal ideation: A proof-of-concept randomized clinical trial. *Translational Behavioral Medicine*, 9(6):1169–1177.

Alejandro Porras-Segovia, Maria M Perez-Rodriguez, Pilar López-Esteban, Philippe Courtet, Jorge López-Castromán, Jorge A Cervilla, Enrique Baca-García, et al. 2019. Contribution of sleep deprivation to suicidal behaviour: A systematic review. *Sleep Medicine Reviews*, 44:37–47.

Emina Prguda, Justine Evans, Sarah McLeay, Madeline Romaniuk, Andrea J Phelps, Kerri Lewis, Kelly Brown, Gina Fisher, Fraser Lowrie, Elise Saunders-Dow, et al. 2023. Posttraumatic sleep disturbances in veterans: A pilot randomized controlled trial of cognitive behavioral therapy for insomnia and imagery rehearsal therapy. *Journal of Clinical Psychology*, 79(11):2493–2514.

Nicholas Proferes, Naiyan Jones, Sarah Gilbert, Casey Fiesler, and Michael Zimmer. 2021. Studying Reddit: A systematic overview of disciplines, approaches, methods, and ethics. *Social Media + Society*, 7(2):20563051211019004.

Joseph Reagle. 2022. Disguising Reddit sources and the efficacy of ethical research. *Ethics and Information Technology*, 24(3):41.

Philip Resnik, William Armstrong, Leonardo Claudino, Thang Nguyen, Viet-An Nguyen, and Jordan Boyd-Graber. 2015. Beyond LDA: Exploring supervised topic modeling for depression-related language in Twitter. In *Proceedings of the 2nd Workshop on Computational Linguistics and Clinical Psychology: From Linguistic Signal to Clinical Reality*, pages 99–107.

Philip Resnik, April Foreman, Michelle Kuchuk, Katherine Musacchio Schafer, and Beau Pinkham. 2021. Naturally occurring language as a source of evidence in suicide prevention. *Suicide and Life-Threatening Behavior*, 51(1):88–96.

Ryan Schuerkamp, Luke Liang, Ketra L Rice, and Philippe J Giabbanelli. 2023. Simulation models for suicide prevention: A survey of the state-of-the-art. *Computers*, 12(7):132.

Alexander J Scott, Thomas L Webb, Marrissa Martyn-St James, Georgina Rowse, and Scott Weich. 2021. Improving sleep quality leads to better mental health: A meta-analysis of randomised controlled trials. *Sleep Medicine Reviews*, 60:101556.

Christopher A Shepard, Katrina A Rufino, Jaehoon Lee, Tiffany Tran, Kieran Paddock, Chester Wu, John M Oldham, Sanjay J Mathew, and Michelle A Patriquin. 2023. Nighttime sleep quality and daytime sleepiness predicts suicide risk in adults admitted to an inpatient psychiatric hospital. *Behavioral Sleep Medicine*, 21(2):129–141.

Han-Chin Shing, Suraj Nair, Ayah Zirikly, Meir Friedenberg, Hal Daumé III, and Philip Resnik. 2018. Expert, crowdsourced, and machine assessment of suicide risk via online postings. In *Proceedings of the Fifth Workshop on Computational Linguistics and Clinical Psychology: From Keyboard to Clinic*, pages 25–36.

Han-Chin Shing, Philip Resnik, and Douglas W Oard. 2020. A prioritization model for suicidality risk assessment. In *Proceedings of the 58th Annual Meeting of the Association for Computational Linguistics*, pages 8124–8137.

Leah Tomkins and Virginia Eatough. 2018. Hermeneutics: Interpretation, understanding and sense-making. *SAGE Handbook of Qualitative Business and Management Research Methods*, pages 185–200.

Leanne Townsend and Claire Wallace. 2016. Social media research: A guide to ethics. *University of Aberdeen*, pages 1–16.

Mickey Trockel, Bradley E Karlin, C Barr Taylor, Gregory K Brown, and Rachel Manber. 2015. Effects of cognitive behavioral therapy for insomnia on suicidal ideation in veterans. *Sleep*, 38(2):259–265.

Andrew S Tubbs, Michael L Perlis, and Michael A Grandner. 2019. Surviving the long night: The potential of sleep health for suicide prevention. *Sleep Medicine Reviews*, 44:83.

Johannes L Van der Walt. 2020. Interpretivism-Constructivism as a research method in the humanities and social sciences – More to it than meets the eye. *International Journal of Philosophy and Theology*, 8(1):59–68.

Max Van Manen. 2017. Phenomenology in its original sense. *Qualitative Health Research*, 27(6):810–825.

Ashish Vaswani, Noam Shazeer, Niki Parmar, Jakob Uszkoreit, Llion Jones, Aidan N Gomez, Łukasz Kaiser, and Illia Polosukhin. 2017. Attention is all you need. *Advances in Neural Information Processing Systems*, 30.

Zizhan Wang. 2023. Review on data mining and data analysis method for adolescent suicide problem. *Highlights in Science, Engineering and Technology*, 39:1164–1169.

Charlie Winter and RV Gundur. 2022. Challenges in gaining ethical approval for sensitive digital social science studies. *International Journal of Social Research Methodology*, pages 1–16.

Zimri S Yaseen, Mariah Hawes, Shira Barzilay, and Igor Galynker. 2019. Predictive validity of proposed diagnostic criteria for the suicide crisis syndrome: An acute presuicidal state. *Suicide and Life-Threatening Behavior*, 49(4):1124–1135.

Michael Zimmer. 2020. "But the data is already public": On the ethics of research in Facebook. In *The Ethics of Information Technologies*, pages 229–241. Routledge.

Ayah Zirikly, Philip Resnik, Ozlem Uzuner, and Kristy Hollingshead. 2019. CLPsych 2019 shared task: Predicting the degree of suicide risk in Reddit posts. In *Proceedings of the Sixth Workshop on Computational Linguistics and Clinical Psychology*, pages 24–33.

A Appendix Section

The following appendix section contains Fig 1. Topic word scores; Table 2. Topic frequency count; Fig 2. Hierarchical clustering; and Table 3. Illustrative composite synthetic quotes.

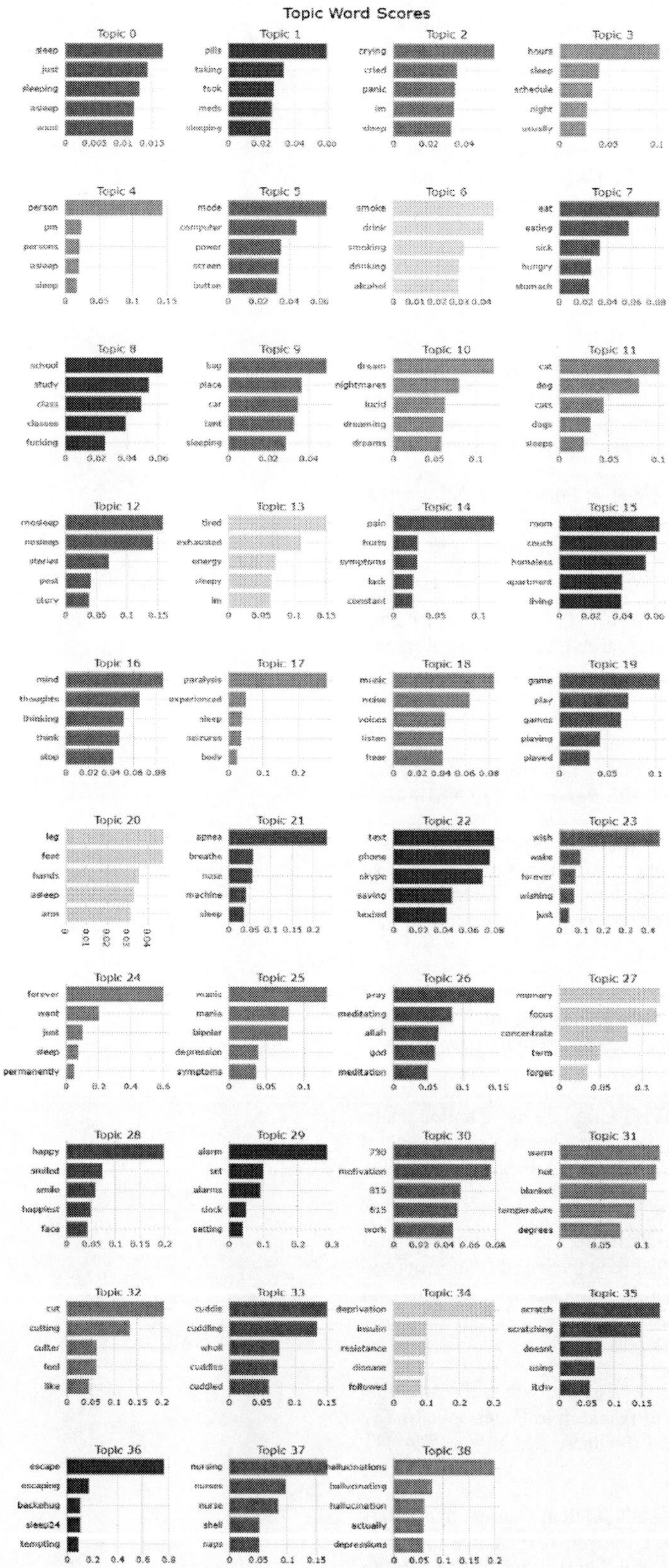

Figure 1: c-TF-IDF of key topic terms. TF-IDF (term frequency-inverse document frequency) is a statistical measure of the importance and relevancy of a word both to a specific document and across a corpus of documents).

Topic	Frequency Count	Most important and relevant topic representative terms
-1	9413	sleep_im_asleep_just
0	6130	sleep_just_sleeping_asleep
1	776	pills_taking_took_meds
2	620	crying_cried_panic_im
3	522	hours_sleep_schedule_night
4	383	person_pm_persons_asleep
5	366	mode_computer_power_screen
6	338	smoke_drink_smoking_drinking
7	320	eat_eating_sick_hungry
8	287	school_study_class_classes
9	270	bag_place_car_tent
10	263	dream_nightmares_lucid_dreaming
11	202	cat_dog_cats_dogs
12	178	rnosleep_nosleep_stories_post
13	170	tired_exhausted_energy_sleepy
14	165	pain_hurts_symptoms_lack
15	159	room_couch_homeless_apartment
16	154	mind_thoughts_thinking_think
17	154	paralysis_experienced_sleep_seizures
18	150	music_noise_voices_listen
19	105	game_play_games_playing
20	101	leg_feet_hands_asleep
21	78	apnea_breathe_nose_machine
22	67	text_phone_skype_saying
23	60	wish_wake_forever_wishing
24	56	forever_want_just_sleep
25	48	manic_mania_bipolar_depression
26	44	pray_meditating_allah_god
27	43	memory_focus_concentrate_term
28	43	happy_smiled_smile_happiest
29	38	alarm_set_alarms_clock
30	26	730_motivation_815_615
31	25	warm_hot_blanket_temperature
32	22	cut_cutting_cutter_feel
33	22	cuddle_cuddling_wholl_cuddles
34	19	deprivation_insulin_resistance_disease
35	17	scratch_scratching_doesnt_using
36	16	escape_escaping_backehug_sleep24
37	15	nursing_nurses_nurse_shell
38	11	hallucinations_hallucinating_hallucination

Table 2: Frequency count of topics

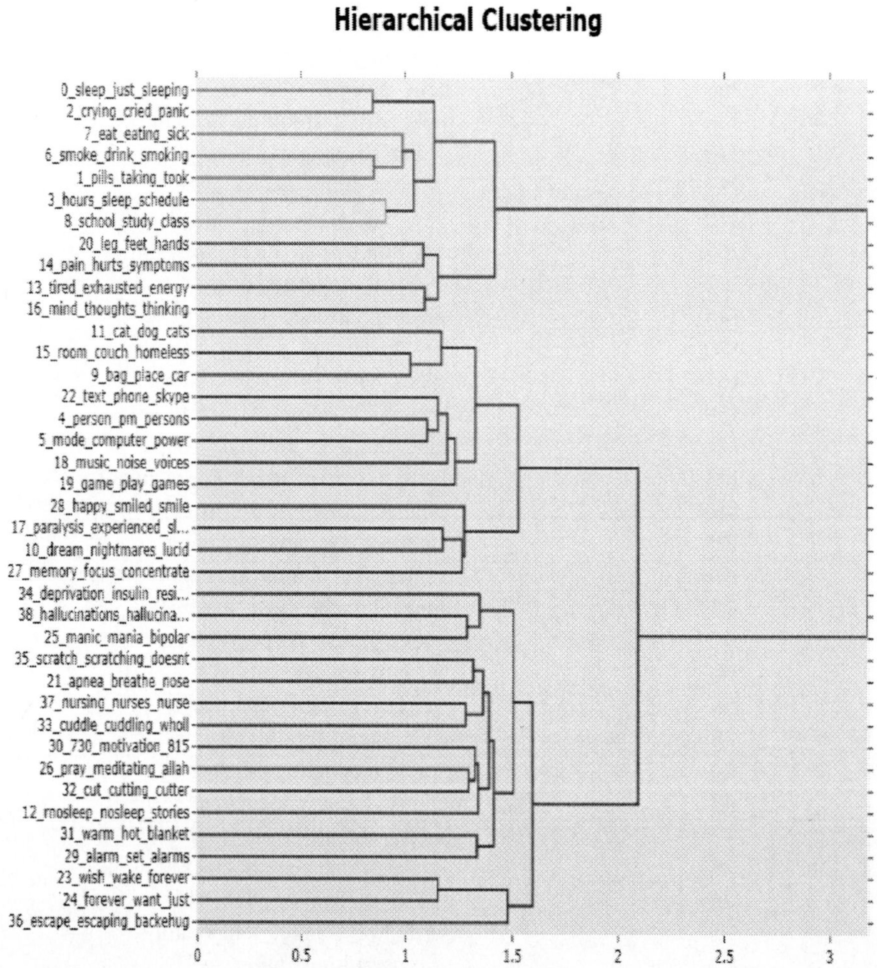

Figure 2: Hierarchical clustering of topics (utilizing scipy.cluster.hierarchy to create clusters and visualize how relate)

Exhausted, tired, emotionally and physically, just want to sleep forever, but never enough sleep
Every night I pray I die in my sleep, or someone ends the nightmare by putting a bullet in my head
Dreaming is a better form of life, particularly when can control with lucid dreaming
Calm the rampant thought storm, the panic, the mind at war that prevents me from sleeping
Tired of the loneliness, screwing up, and failure, dreams are my only escape and pleasure
Sleep use to be an escape but now a fear because of the thoughts, the sleep paralysis, and nightmares
I hide under the bed to feel safe, feeling entrapped and overwhelmed, and sleep the only thing to look forward to
Terrified of what the recesses of my mind and the darkness will conjure up
Just want to live in dreams and never wake up, escape the pain, grief, loneliness and shame
The worst thing I fear is the thoughts, the insomnia, and being alone at night
Wake up terrified from the nightmare at 4 am and too frightened to go back to sleep
The pain, the fear, the thoughts start from the moment I regain consciousness
I need to escape the suffocating thoughts and loneliness whether through drugs, sex, or sleep
Just want to knock myself out with pills or drugs so can stop feeling like shit and exhausted
I want someone to hold me and my trauma, and sadness until I fall asleep
Work, study, and bills I'm exhausted, sleep deprived, but I can't give up internet or risk sleeping in.
I lie in bed crying, I am a burden and a shame to my family, best thing for them is if I sleep forever

Table 3: Key illustrative composite synthetic quotes. A key issue in social media research is that verbatim quotes can not infrequently be traced back to the source, and with cross-referencing of other aspects of content or style, the online poster is potentially identified. These composite synthetic quotes, aim to illustrate the type of content that was the basis of the reflexive thematic analysis generated themes, without infringing the ethical undertaking not to use verbatim quotes.

Automatic Annotation of Dream Report's Emotional Content with Large Language Models

Lorenzo Bertolini[1] **Valentina Elce**[2] **Adriana Michalak**[2]
Hanna-Sophia Widhoelzl[3] **Giulio Bernardi**[2] **Julie Weeds**[4]
[1]European Commission, Joint Research Centre (JRC), Ispra, Italy
[2]MoMiLab Research Unit, IMT School for Advanced Studies, Lucca, Italy
[3]Institute of Interdisciplinary Studies, University of Amsterdam, Amsterdam, The Netherlands
[4]Department of Informatics, University of Sussex, Brighton, UK
lorenzo.bertolini@ec.europa.eu
{valentina.elce, adriana.michalak, giulio.bernardi}@imtlucca.it
hannasophia.widhoelzl@gmail.com
juliewe@sussex.ac.uk

Abstract

In psychology and neuroscience, dreams are extensively studied both as a model to understand the neural bases of consciousness and for their relationship with psycho-physical well-being. The study of dream content typically relies on the analysis of verbal reports provided upon awakening. This task is classically performed through manual scoring provided by trained annotators, at a great time expense. While a consistent body of work suggests that natural language processing (NLP) tools can support the automatic analysis of dream reports, proposed methods lacked the ability to reason over a report's full context and required extensive data pre-processing. Furthermore, in most cases, these methods were not validated against standard manual scoring approaches. In this work, we address these limitations by adopting large language models (LLMs) to study and replicate the manual annotation of dream reports, with a focus on reports' emotions. Our results show that a text classification method based on BERT can achieve high performance, is resistant to biases, and shows promising results on data from a clinical population. Overall, results indicate that LLMs and NLP could find multiple successful applications in the analysis of large dream datasets and may favour reproducibility and comparability of results across research.

1 Introduction

Dreams have fascinated humans since the dawn of time, and their scientific study in the last decades even increased attention and interest towards this peculiar phenomenon. Indeed, available evidence suggests that dreams may be related to psychophysical well-being, and may be involved in or represent a window on sleep-dependent processes affecting the consolidation and integration of new memories (Wamsley and Stickgold, 2011; Wamsley, 2014; Zadra and Stickgold, 2021). Moreover, given their nature of internally generated conscious experiences, dreams are regarded as a fundamental model to study and understand human consciousness (Nir and Tononi, 2010; Siclari et al., 2017). In spite of this, the mechanisms that lead to dream generation and development, and the possible functions of dreams still remain poorly understood to this day. Among the factors that limit and slow down research on dreams is the fact that the content of dreams is difficult to assess quantitatively and in a reproducible way (Elce et al., 2021).

Automating and standardising the scoring of dream reports' emotional dimensions is paramount for health and psychophysiological well-being as it can uncover valuable insights into an individual's mental states during sleep. As stated by the established continuity-hypothesis (Hall, 1953), elements in dream scenarios mirror someone's waking states and concerns (Brown and Donderi, 1986; Pesant and Zadra, 2006; Gilchrist et al., 2007; Blagrove et al., 2004). Nightmares have a particular potential to disrupt everyday life as they are linked to high levels of psychological distress, self-harm, and suicidal tendencies (Andrews and Hanna, 2020). Their frequency may serve as a promising early indicator of psychiatric and sleep disorders (Thompson et al., 2015; Kobayashi et al., 2008). In line with this, dream content was reported to change in several pathological conditions, including for instance eating disorders and depression (Skancke et al., 2014). Typically, the assessment of dream content

Proceedings of the 9th Workshop on Computational Linguistics and Clinical Psychology (CLPsych 2024), pages 92–107
March 21, 2024

— including the presence of specific emotions — is performed manually, by trained annotators, by applying particular scales or scoring systems. While multiple scoring approaches exist to annotate and analyse dream reports, such as the scale by Hauri and colleagues (Hauri, 1975) or the rating system developed by Schredl (Schredl, 2010), the Hall and Van de Castle (HVDC) coding system (Hall and Van De Castle, 1966) remains the most popular and widely adopted (McNamara et al., 2019; Fogli et al., 2020).

A growing body of evidence has shown that NLP methods can support the automatic analysis of dream reports. So far, efforts have mainly focused on investigating different implicit structures, such as speech or syntactic graphs (Mota et al., 2014; Martin et al., 2020), and/or analysing the semantic content of dream experiences (Sanz et al., 2018; Fogli et al., 2020; Zheng and Schweickert, 2021) (see Elce et al. (2021) for an extensive review). Of more relevance for this work are those studies that focused on dream reports' semantic content using dictionary-based linguistic analysis (Bulkeley and Graves, 2018; Mallett et al., 2021; Zheng and Schweickert, 2021) and distributional semantic models (Razavi et al., 2013; Altszyler et al., 2017; Sanz et al., 2018). While notably different, both approaches cannot fully and coherently manipulate a report's full content and context. This shared limitation is of great relevance, as the correct identification of an emotional state may rely on complex constructions and more implicit information, as well as a combination of the two. In recent years, these and similar issues were largely overcome by pre-trained large language models (LLMs) based on transformer architectures (Vaswani et al., 2017). Over the last years, LLMs pre-trained on self-supervised tasks like masked language models have shown strong performance on down-stream tasks like sentiment analysis (Raffel et al., 2020), text summarisation (Kedia et al., 2021), question answering (Lan et al., 2020), and machine translation (Conneau et al., 2020).

Given their success, in this work, we propose to address the issues identified with existing approaches to automatically analyse dream reports analysis by leveraging pre-trained LLMs. Specifically, we investigate whether and how LLMs can support the detection and analysis of emotions expressed in dream reports, as defined in accordance with the HVDC coding framework. More specifically, we study the ability of a bespoke multi-label text classifier, based on a pre-trained LLM tuned using dream reports previously scored by expert annotators, and propose a set of experiments and analyses to test the robustness of this solution to different potential biases in the dataset and out-of-distribution applications.

To the best of our knowledge, our work represents the first attempt to analyse and reproduce gold-standard HVDC annotations of dream reports with LLMs, and makes two main contributions. First, we show how, despite the limited amount of training data, a fully-supervised approach based on multi-label text classification yields good and stable performance. Two, we provide follow-up experiments and analysis showing how the strategies learned by the model are robust with respect to out-of-distribution data, as well as biases and spurious correlations present in the dataset.

2 Related Work

As summarised by Elce et al. (2021), a growing body of research is adopting NLP methods to automatically analyse dream reports. Yet, while emotions represent a fundamental component of oneiric experiences, only a fraction of published studies based on NLP methods have explicitly focused on the emotional aspects of dream reports (Nadeau et al., 2006; Amini et al., 2011; Razavi et al., 2013; Frantova and Bergler, 2009; McNamara et al., 2019; Fogli et al., 2020; Yu, 2022). Moreover, most of these investigations did not include a direct nor transparent comparison with widely adopted report annotation approaches such as the HVDC coding system. In terms of implementation, adopted NLP methods include three main solutions: graph-based approaches (Mota et al., 2014; Martin et al., 2020; Fogli et al., 2020), dictionary-based linguistic analysis (Bulkeley and Graves, 2018; Mallett et al., 2021; Zheng and Schweickert, 2021), and distributional semantic models (Razavi et al., 2013; Altszyler et al., 2017; Sanz et al., 2018).

Dictionary-based methods analyse data word by word, comparing each item to a dictionary file that is structured as a collection of words defining different semantic categories. An example could be the 'positive emotion' category, containing words such as *"joy"*, *"happiness"*, and *"smiling"*. Approaches based on these methods (Bulkeley, 2014; Bulkeley and Graves, 2018; Mallett et al., 2021; Zheng and Schweickert, 2021; Yu, 2022) are mainly used to determine the relative frequency of references to specific content words, and can hence be inherently misleading, as they generally cannot interpret contextual information and syntactic structures. Syntax-like structures are used by graph-based approaches, which cannot access semantics but have successfully been adopted to classify populations of participants (e.g., healthy and psychotic subjects)(Mota et al., 2014; Martin et al., 2020; Fogli et al., 2020). An exception is the work by Fogli et al. (2020), which proposed a solution based on a combination of dictionary and graph models, able to extract information about the content of dream reports, including their emotions. However, the evaluation was reframed in binary (*"positive"*, vs *"negative"*) terms.

Solutions based on distributional semantics (Nadeau et al., 2006; Razavi et al., 2013; Altszyler et al., 2017; Sanz et al., 2018; McNamara et al., 2019) were largely based on word-level representation obtained using models like `word2vec` (Mikolov et al., 2013) or GloVe (Pennington et al., 2014). In such cases, encodings of full reports were generated by adding or averaging word embeddings, losing access to syntactic structure and more contextual understanding (Klafka and Ettinger, 2020).

A niche of previous work applied NLP and machine learning methods specifically to assess emotional aspects of dream reports (Amini et al., 2011; Razavi et al., 2013; McNamara et al., 2019; Yu, 2022). Amini et al. (2011) added word associations to improve the performance of a machine learning model that was trained to automatically score dream reports' emotional tone based on human judgements, resulting in increased machine-human agreement. Yet, relying on predefined word associations may oversimplify the nuances of emotional content unique to dreamers. Razavi et al. (2013) combined ad-hoc classifiers with a distributional approach to detect potential shifts in sentiment within each report. Evaluated reports were extracted from DreamBank, a large public database, and were (re-)scored by the authors using a four-level emotional rating system (*"very-negative"* to *"very-positive"*). Despite relying on a mixture of local (word-to-word) and general (sentence-to-sentence) occurrences, the adopted approach strongly relies on extensive data pre-processing, as well as composition by averaging, hence losing access to structural and deeper semantic information. McNamara et al. (2019) used a pre-trained agent to detect recurrent themes in a series of reports and found a partial match in the retrieved themes with aspects of the HVDC system, as well as significant differences in how themes occurred in male vs. female dreamers. The distribution of these themes was then used to assess the "mood" of each report. Yu (2022) combined a dictionary-based method with support vector machines (Cortes and Vapnik, 1995) to asses the general sentiment of dream reports in multiple languages.

Overall, the described studies present two main differences from our work. First, the models lacked access to the global context of each report. In our work, we use pre-trained large language models (LLMs) to encode dream reports and thus allow a model to have full access to the context. Second, the annotations and evaluations of emotional states were not directly compared against widely used coding systems such as the HVDC. That is, whenever human annotations were considered for the evaluation of a system, scores or labels were largely (and generally non-transparently) re-framed to be comparable with the output produced by the system of choice. In this work, we propose a solution to *adapt* a model to produce interpretable labels, that can be directly compared against human-produced HVDC annotations. Furthermore, evaluations will take into account the fact that labels could be associated with different characters, thus further highlighting the possible value of our approach as fully automatic and reliable support for manual annotations in dream research.

3 Dataset

For our experiments, we use a subset of reports extracted from the DreamBank database[1] (Domhoff and Schneider, 2008), pre-annotated according to the Hall and Van De Castle (HVDC) coding system (Hall and Van De Castle, 1966). `DreamBank.net` consists of a collection of over 20K dream reports gathered from different sources and organised in series, either provided by single individuals or groups of people, such as college students, teenagers, and blind adults. While `DreamBank.net` can be freely explored, the reports and the HVDC scores adopted in the current work are made available upon direct request to the researchers who maintain the DreamBank website. Among the approximately 1.8K labelled dream

[1]`https://www.dreambank.net`

reports, all in the English language, 922 contained at least one emotion associated with either the dreamer or another character. Considering that no guidelines or metadata are available to demonstrate that the absence of emotion labels reflects the *actual* absence of emotions in a report, we focus our experiments on those reports containing at least one emotion (n=922). The dataset is further divided into six series: `Bea 1: a high school student` (n=171/99; total number of reports/reports including at least one emotion), `Ed: dreams of his late wife` (n=143/108), `Emma: 48 years of dreams` (n=300/81), `Hall/VdC Norms: Female` (n=491/280), `Hall/VdC Norms: Male` (n=500/203), `Barb Sanders: baseline` (n=250/151).

The HVDC coding system examines ten categories of elements appearing in dream reports (characters, interactions, emotions, activities, striving, (mis)fortunes, settings and objects, descriptive elements, food and eating, and elements from the past). Within this study, we focused only on the annotation of the emotions feature. In the HVDC coding system, emotions are divided into 5 classes, that are anger (AN), sadness (SD), apprehension (AP), confusion (CO), and happiness (HA). Emotions might be assigned either to the dreamer or to other dream characters. We analyse both the emotions scored as experienced by the dreamer (*Dreamer Emotions*) and the overall occurrence of emotions in the dreams regardless of the dream characters they are associated with (*General Emotions*).

4 Multi-Label Text Classification

A set of preliminary experiments (see Appendix B) showed that an off-the-shelf sentiment analysis LLM cannot coherently solve the task when framed, similarly to previous work, as a binary `POSITIVE - NEGATIVE` classification. Hence, we investigate whether the human annotation of dream reports can be reproduced with supervision, via a bespoke text classification model, trained on gold-standard HVDC labelled data. Contrary to all previous work, that reframed HVDC labels to fit binary classification and classifiers, we perform a fine-grained classification aimed at determining the presence (1) or absence (0) of each HVDC emotion (i.e., *anger* (AN), *sadness* (SD), *apprehension* (AP), *confusion* (CO), *happiness* (HA)), regardless of the number of times they appear in a given report. Moreover, we experiment with both the sets of emotions described in Section 2: Dreamer Emotions and General Emotions.

4.1 Experimental Setup

Formally, we define the task as a multi-label classification, where a model is trained to simultaneously and independently predict *if* each of the emotions that were identified by expert annotators appear in each report. To solve the task, we designed a bespoke solution, where the LLM of choice is integrated into a three-component architecture, summarised in Figure 1. The first component is a pretrained `BERT-large-cased` encoder[2], used to obtain the encoding of each report by extracting the final layer's `[CLS]` vector. Encodings are then fed to a dropout layer (with $p = .3$) and a linear layer, reducing the number of the dimensions to the number of desired classes, corresponding to the five HVDC emotions. The described architecture is then fully fine-tuned end-to-end with a binary cross-entropy loss, with the addition of a sigmoid function between the loss and the linear layer, and adopting a K-fold cross-validation procedure (with K=5). At each fold, the dataset is randomly split, 80% for training and 20% for testing, and the architecture is trained for 10 epochs, using dream reports as input and the presence of HVDC emotions as the output to predict. While the previous work evaluated a model on the HVDC annotation indirectly (e.g, by arbitrarily devising the five HVDC emotions into 2 classes) we evaluate the model *directly* on the HVDC's gold-standard annotation framework, by training and testing the model to simultaneously and independently guess if each of the five HVDC emotions was defined as present by the expert annotators (see Figure 1). Similarly to previous work investigating the presence of emotions in dream reports, we adopted precision, recall, and F1 as evaluation metrics (Fogli et al., 2020). The code is available here[3].

4.2 Results

Table 1 summarises the scores, averaged across the folds (± standard deviations) obtained by the architecture for Dreamer and General emotions. The overall F1 scores show a strong and generally stable performance. The minimal difference between

[2]To optimise the computational performance, we set the maximum length of the encoder to 512, losing full access to only 6 reports, accounting for less than the 0.005% of the whole dataset. See Appendix C.1 for more details.

[3]`https://github.com/lorenzoscottb/Dream_Reports_Annotation`

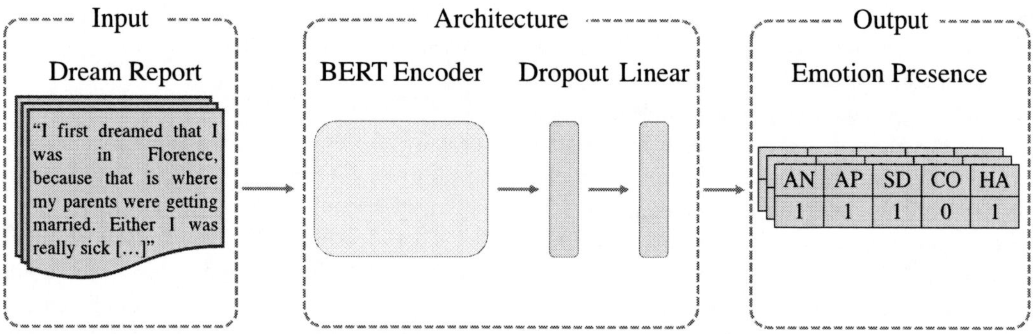

Figure 1: Schematic view of the adopted architecture and training procedure for the bespoke multi-label classification experiments. Given a set of dream reports from DreamBank as input, the architecture is trained end-to-end to predict which of the five emotions recognised by the Hall and Van de Castle (HVDC) system — **anger (AN), apprehension (AP), sadness (SD), confusion (CO)**, and **happiness (HA)** — is present (1) or absent (0) in each report. The adopted architecture is constructed out of three components: a pre-trained LLM (in our case, a `BERT-large-cased model`), a dropout layer, and a linear layer.

	Precision		**Recall**		**F1**	
	Dreamer	General	Dreamer	General	Dreamer	General
Anger (AN)	86 ± 9	85 ± 7	89 ± 3	89 ± 4	87 ± 4	87 ± 5
Apprehension (AP)	86 ± 4	88 ± 7	88 ± 5	92 ± 3	87 ± 3	89 ± 3
Sadness (SD)	84 ± 10	84 ± 4	72 ± 15	77 ± 12	77 ± 11	80 ± 7
Confusion (CO)	90 ± 5	92 ± 2	76 ± 6	85 ± 5	82 ± 5	88 ± 3
Happiness (HA)	93 ± 5	86 ± 4	85 ± 6	88 ± 3	89 ± 5	87 ± 2
macro avg	88 ± 3	87 ± 3	82 ± 5	86 ± 2	85 ± 3	86 ± 2
micro avg	87 ± 3	87 ± 3	84 ± 4	87 ± 2	85 ± 3	87 ± 2
samples avg	88 ± 2	89 ± 2	87 ± 3	90 ± 2	86 ± 3	88 ± 2
weighted avg	88 ± 2	87 ± 4	84 ± 4	87 ± 2	85 ± 3	87 ± 2

Table 1: Bespoke muli-label classification results. Average scores (± standard deviation) of the 5-fold cross-validation text classification experiment. Dreamer and General columns refer to the Emotions used for training and testing. While under the General Emotions setting we made use of all emotions found by expert annotators in each report, the Dreamer Emotions refers to the subset of the General Emotions associated by the expert annotators solely to the dreamer.

macro and weighted F1 scores further suggests that the difference in support instances only has a marginal impact. Concerning single Emotion sets, performance tends to be higher and more stable for General than for Dreamer emotions. When trained and tested on General emotions, the models show a notable balance between precision and recall, despite a relatively higher variance across precision measures. On the other hand, models trained solely with Dreamer emotions present an overall higher precision than recall, with the latter being notably less stable. These patterns are likely explained by the low number of emotions-per-report associated with the Dreamer set, while the emotion distribution is more balanced in the General set. Models trained solely with the Dreamer set are hence less prone to produce False-Positive errors but produce a higher amount of False-Negative errors. Since the General emotion set is overall more balanced, the models' performance is higher and more stable across precision and recall.

Concerning single emotions, it is more difficult to identify a shared pattern, with the notable exception of *sadness* (SD). Under both sets, models appear to struggle at classifying such an emotion, which in both cases produces the highest variance, an observation that might be partially explained by sadness being the least frequent emotion.

Our results indicate that the model can successfully learn to simultaneously classify a dream report with respect to references to the different emotions of the HVDC coding system. However, the achieved performance level might be mediated, at least in part, by specific series of DreamBank. It is in fact possible that different emotions are distributed in a particular and unique way in each series. If so, the model could learn series-specific distributions, and, after implicitly recognising a specific series in a given report, simply reproduce these distributions at test time. For example, if a series like `Ed` contained a large number of reports labelled both with *sadness* and *apprehension*, the model could implicitly learn to identify `Ed`'s reports from such series via recurrent cues to unrelated information (such as characters or places) and, at test time, use these cues to automatically annotate those reports with *sadness* and *apprehension*.

4.2.1 Ablation

To understand whether the performance of the trained model is affected by this heuristic behaviour — that is, learning series-specific emotion distributions — we conduct a follow-up ablation experiment. Using the same architecture, hyperparameters, and training setup, instead of randomly splitting five times the whole dataset into an 80-20% train-test split, we here use one whole series of the dataset as the test set and the remaining series as the training set. With this approach, test series are never seen by the model during training, making it impossible for the model to rely on series-specific associations for solving the task. For this experiment, we focus solely on the General Emotions set, found to be the best-performing and more stable set. Moreover, we focus the analysis on the F1 scores as the performance metric of choice.

Figure 2 summarises the results of the ablation experiment. The x-axis shows the F1 weighted average scores obtained for each series (y-axis) when such a series is held out from training and used as the test set. In order to facilitate comparison with the previous experiment's results, the dashed grey line indicates the F1 weighted average obtained in the K-fold experiment (i.e., 87 ± 2, see Table 1). The results indicate that when all the instances of a series are removed from the training data, the test performance of the model remains relatively high and stable. Moreover, as shown in Figure 3 this remains true for all of the HVDC scored emotions.

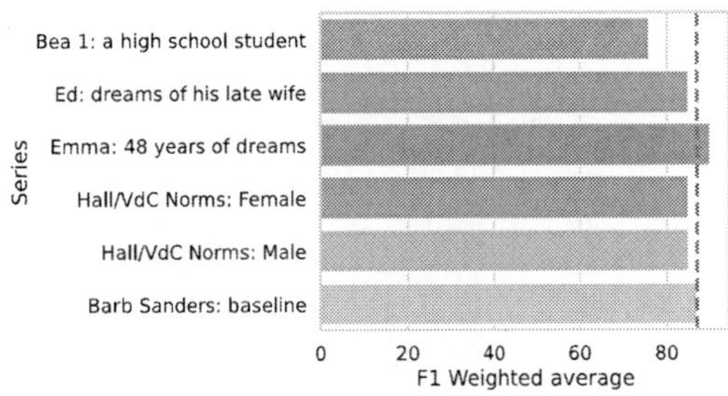

Figure 2: Ablation experiment results. F1 Weighted average scores obtained by the model when each Dream Bank's Series is held out of training and used as a test set. The dashed vertical line reports the average F1 Weighted average obtained in the main experiment (see Table 1).

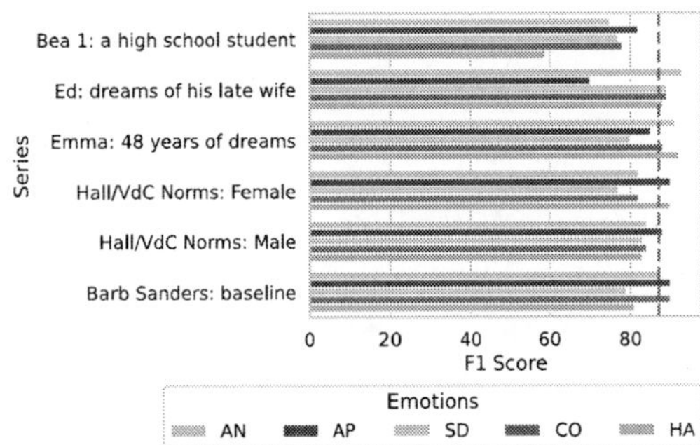

Figure 3: Ablation experiment, emotion by Series analysis. The diagram further breaks down the results of Figure 2 by single emotion for each Series held out from training. Once again, the vertical dotted line refers to average scores in the main experiment (see Table 1).

The `Bea 1` series, appears to represent the only notable exception to the above observations. Indeed, this series shows the greatest deviation from the original results, with an F1 weighted average of 77, compared to the previously obtained average of 87 (± 2). As shown in Figure 3, which breaks down the results of the ablation experiment presented in Figure 2 by single emotions, this was largely due to a problematic classification of *happiness* (HA) in this particular series. However, with the exception of a slightly lower *sadness*, emotions don't seem to significantly deviate from the K-fold experiment results, as summarised by Figure 4.

These results support two main conclusions. First, the proposed architecture, based on a pre-trained LLM, can learn efficient classification strategies for dream reports' emotional content (as defined based on the HVDC coding system). Second, the learned model does not rely on simple heuristics based on series-dependent cues and dis-

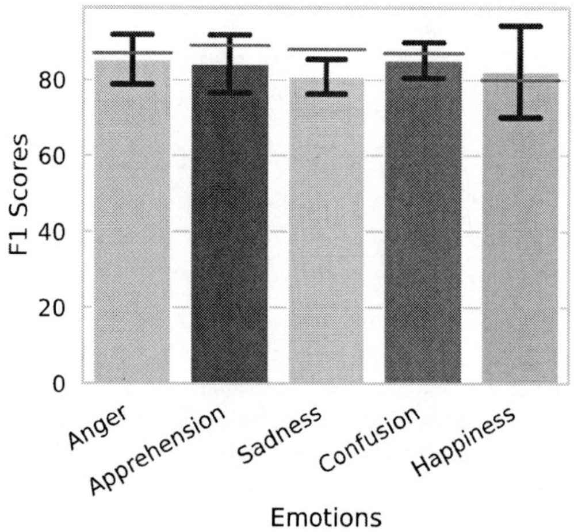

Figure 4: Ablation experiment, single emotion analysis. Overall results (in F1 scores) for every single emotion obtained in the different Series for the ablation experiment (see Figure 3). Bars report standard deviation, while Red horizontal lines refer to average scores in the main experiment (see Table 1).

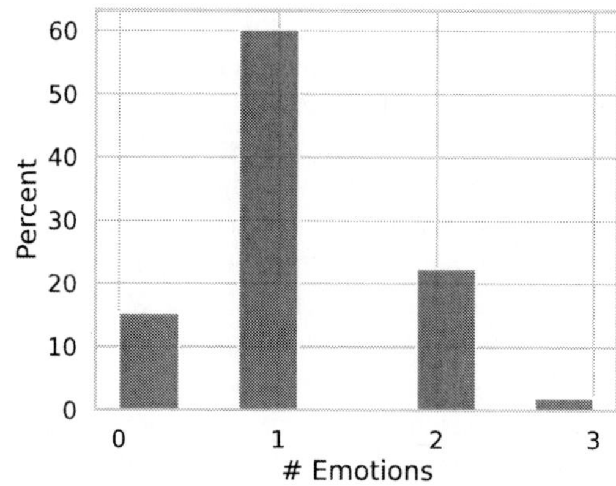

Figure 5: Number of predicted emotions per report. Distribution of the number of emotions-per-report predicted by the model for the `Veteran` series.

tributions. That said, ablation's results could have been influenced by yet another confound: the numbers of reports and emotion distributions. In other words, the performance of each combination of series-emotion (e.g., `Bea 1`-*happiness*) could be explained by the number of items provided at test time. To assess this possibility we perform a set of series-independent Spearman's correlations between the number of test items for each emotion and their respective results (i.e., the F1 scores). The results, summarised in Appendix C.3 found no connections between F1 scores and the number of test items.

4.2.2 Out of distribution PTSD data

So far, results suggest that our solution could provide a valuable resource to annotate data even from out-of-distribution participants. However, annotated data contain reports solely from healthy individuals. Since dream reports can provide useful information on the mental state of an individual, it would be important to assess the robustness of the model to data from participants of different clinical populations. To test this, we adopt a series, not contained in the annotated version of the dataset, containing reports from a Vietnam war veteran with a diagnosed post-traumatic stress disorder (PTSD), who had frequent negative dreams and nightmares. While we do not have an *actual* emotion distribution for such a series, we can *assume* an expected one, with a strong predominance of negatively connotated emotions. We fine-tuned a model using the same data, architecture, hyper-parameters, and procedure thus far adopted, with the only addition of an early-stop mechanism and no K-fold.

Out of the 98 dreams contained in the `Veteran` series, the model found at least one emotion in approximately 84% of them. As summarised by Figure 5, most of these reports were associated by the model with a single emotion, and approximately 20% of them were labelled with two emotions. As expected, the vast majority of these reports contain negatively connotated emotions, as seen in Figure 6. *Apprehension* is by far the most observed negative emotion, appearing in more than half of the reports. Moreover, Figure 6 strongly suggests that the emotion distribution proposed by the model for the `Veteran` series is not simply a transposition of the one observed by the model during training. This further suggests that the model has successfully learned reliable and generalised classification strategies, and it does not simply reproduce an observed distribution from the training data.

The model also annotated a minority of reports – circa 19% – with *happiness*. A manual inspection did identify some errors but also found multiple instances where the model's annotation (i.e., including happiness as an emotion expressed within the report) seemed justified. For example, in one of these reports, after describing a very violent war scenario, the Veteran adds that he felt *"a feeling of complete freedom. In very high spirits Jim L. and I go to a supermarket and buy food. I am aware that I don't wear my steel helmet."*. In another case,

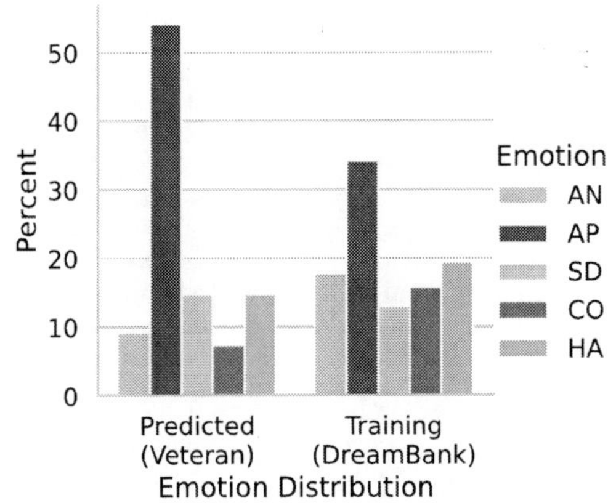

Figure 6: `Veteran` and DreamBank emotion distributions. Comparison of the emotion distribution predicted by the model for the (unlabelled) `Veteran` series, and the general emotion distribution in the DreamBank dataset, used to train the model.

a dream resembling a nightmare (two dolls have come to life) is narrated in a normal and friendly manner, as clear from the passages *"I speak to the male doll and the female doll and feel happy. I have made two friends."*. In other cases, the negative context of the dream is notably less dominant, and the report simply describes a series of social encounters and interactions. We also found scenarios clearly triggered by strong cue words and context. For instance, in one report the Veteran is in a rehab clinic, surrounded by other veterans, and children's paintings, and adds that they are *"[...] colourful, lively, happy. There is no sense of war"*; in another, he describes a romantic encounter – *"We are happy and young. She puts her arm around my shoulder. " I like you, " she says. " I really like you.""*.

5 Discussion

In the field of dream research, the assessment of a report's emotional content is typically based on time-consuming, annotator-dependent procedures. Throughout the years, only a few studies employed automated approaches based on NLP techniques, including dictionary-based and distributional semantics methods. However, these approaches have very limited access to the syntax and semantics of a report's content, and may thus fail to correctly and fully capture emotions described in dream reports. In this work, we tested whether a transformer-based large language model (LLM) could be used to overcome such limitations and reproduce human-based scoring. Specifically, we trained a model end-to-end, using pre-annotated data to predict *if* and *which* emotions were present or absent in a given dream report. The obtained results showed that the model was able to learn reliable and stable classification rules. Follow-up experiments further confirmed two important aspects of our solution. First, via an ablation experiment, we showed that the ability of the model to solve the task is only marginally affected by differences between distinct subsets of the training data. Second, such generalisation holds also for instances that significantly deviate from the training data, as shown by the experiment with reports from a PTSD patient.

Our findings suggest that what is more likely to impact the model performance is the vocabulary used to describe specific emotions across different series. Indeed, variability in the used vocabulary may be explained by the fact that the series included in the present work were collected from different individuals or groups of individuals, with relevant differences in demographic, psychological, and behavioural characteristics. Should this be the case, it would be yet another reason to support the use of tools that are able to reason over the full content of a report, and have access to a large and dynamic vocabulary, already have significant information about a large set of lexemes, and can be easily adaptable to new words and languages. Current pre-trained transformer-based LLMs satisfy all these requirements. Given the current state of NLP resources, our proposed architecture can be easily adapted to be used with LLMs pre-trained on different languages or tasks. Moreover, trained models like ours are fully open-source and can be easily adopted by researchers and practitioners in their pipeline, making these results and the framework extremely replicable and widely standardised.

6 Conclusion

In this work, we tested the feasibility of using transformer-based large language models (LLM) to annotate dream reports with respect to emotions expressed in a given report. Our results show that our LLM-based solution using multi-label classification yields a strong performance, which was found to be robust to correlational biases and out-of-distribution data. Such approaches have the potential to significantly accelerate research investigating the origin, meaning, and functions of dreams, and might present a valuable and efficient support or alternative to human-based procedures involving the analysis of large datasets, ensuring at the same time reproducibility of the obtained results through the sharing of adopted models.

7 Limitations

This study presents three main limitations. First, while DreamBank does contain reports in multiple languages, the HVDC annotations were available only for reports in English. Thus, the generalizability of our model and observations to other languages remains to be determined. Second, while the dataset under consideration was relatively large with respect to studies in the field of dream and sleep research, it is instead relatively small for a machine-learning investigation, especially for the use of supervised methods. Third, the success of the model can be interpreted only to the emotion feature of the HVDC framework. While we provide extensive experiments and evidence supporting the generalisation ability of our model, these are limited specifically to emotion-based annotations. Future work will have to assess the feasibility of our solution to other aspects and features of the HVDC framework, which might require a different approach rather than text classification systems, such as text-to-text generation models.

8 Ethical and Broader Impact Considerations

It is important to acknowledge that, while we have stressed the link between dream reports and mental health, our study and proposed model should only be considered from a basic research perspective. Our procedure and trained model have no diagnostic valence, and should only be considered as a tool to support the annotation of a (large) set of dream reports only from an experimental and hypothesis-building perspective, always keeping in mind the inevitable limitations that come from adopting a machine in the annotation process.

Acknowledgements

This research was supported by the EU Horizon 2020 project HumanE-AI (grant no. 952026), and a BIAL Foundation Grant (grant no. 091/2020). We thank Ian Morgan Leo Pennock, Giacomo Handjaras, and the anonymous reviewers for their comments on the work.

References

Edgar Altszyler, Sidarta Ribeiro, Mariano Sigman, and Diego Fernández Slezak. 2017. The interpretation of dream meaning: Resolving ambiguity using latent semantic analysis in a small corpus of text. *Consciousness and Cognition*, 56:178–187.

Reza Amini, Catherine Sabourin, and Joseph De Koninck. 2011. Word associations contribute to machine learning in automatic scoring of degree of emotional tones in dream reports. *Consciousness and cognition*, 20(4):1570–1576.

Sophie Andrews and Paul Hanna. 2020. Investigating the psychological mechanisms underlying the relationship between nightmares, suicide and self-harm. *Sleep medicine reviews*, 54:101352.

Mark Blagrove, Laura Farmer, and Elvira Williams. 2004. The relationship of nightmare frequency and nightmare distress to well-being. *Journal of Sleep Research*, 13(2):129–136.

Ronald J Brown and Don C Donderi. 1986. Dream content and self-reported well-being among recurrent dreamers, past-recurrent dreamers, and nonrecurrent dreamers. *Journal of Personality and Social Psychology*, 50(3):612.

Kelly Bulkeley. 2014. Digital dream analysis: A revised method. *Consciousness and cognition*, 29:159–170.

Kelly Bulkeley and Mark Graves. 2018. Using the LIWC program to study dreams. *Dreaming*, 28(1):43–58.

Alexis Conneau, Kartikay Khandelwal, Naman Goyal, Vishrav Chaudhary, Guillaume Wenzek, Francisco Guzmán, Edouard Grave, Myle Ott, Luke Zettlemoyer, and Veselin Stoyanov. 2020. Unsupervised cross-lingual representation learning at scale. In *Proceedings of the 58th Annual Meeting of the Association for Computational Linguistics*, pages 8440–8451, Online. Association for Computational Linguistics.

Corinna Cortes and Vladimir Vapnik. 1995. Support-vector networks. *Machine learning*, 20(3):273–297.

G. William Domhoff and Adam Schneider. 2008. Studying dream content using the archive and search engine on DreamBank.net. *Consciousness and Cognition*, 17(4):1238–1247.

Valentina Elce, Giacomo Handjaras, and Giulio Bernardi. 2021. The language of dreams: Application of linguistics-based approaches for the automated analysis of dream experiences. *Clocks & Sleep*, 3(3):495–514.

Alessandro Fogli, Luca Maria Aiello, and Daniele Quercia. 2020. Our dreams, our selves: automatic analysis of dream reports. *Royal Society Open Science*, 7(8):192080.

Elena Frantova and Sabine Bergler. 2009. Automatic emotion annotation of dream diaries. In *Proceedings of the analyzing social media to represent collective knowledge workshop at K-CAP 2009, The fifth international conference on knowledge capture*. Citeseer.

Sue Gilchrist, John Davidson, and Jane Shakespeare-Finch. 2007. Dream emotions, waking emotions, personality characteristics and well-being–a positive psychology approach. *Dreaming*, 17(3):172.

Calvin S Hall. 1953. The meaning of dreams.

Calvin S. Hall and Robert L. Van De Castle. 1966. *The Content Analysis of Dreams*. Appleton-Century-Crofts.

P Hauri. 1975. Categorization of sleep mental activity for psychophysiological studies. *The experimental study of sleep: Methodological problems*, pages 271–281.

Akhil Kedia, Sai Chetan Chinthakindi, and Wonho Ryu. 2021. Beyond reptile: Meta-learned dot-product maximization between gradients for improved single-task regularization. In *Findings of the Association for Computational Linguistics: EMNLP 2021*, pages 407–420, Punta Cana, Dominican Republic. Association for Computational Linguistics.

Josef Klafka and Allyson Ettinger. 2020. Spying on your neighbors: Fine-grained probing of contextual embeddings for information about surrounding words. In *Proceedings of the 58th Annual Meeting of the Association for Computational Linguistics*, pages 4801–4811, Online. Association for Computational Linguistics.

Ihori Kobayashi, Eve M Sledjeski, Eileen Spoonster, William F Fallon Jr, and Douglas L Delahanty. 2008. Effects of early nightmares on the development of sleep disturbances in motor vehicle accident victims. *Journal of Traumatic Stress: Official Publication of The International Society for Traumatic Stress Studies*, 21(6):548–555.

Zhenzhong Lan, Mingda Chen, Sebastian Goodman, Kevin Gimpel, Piyush Sharma, and Radu Soricut. 2020. Albert: A lite bert for self-supervised learning of language representations. In *International Conference on Learning Representations*.

Remington Mallett, Claudia Picard-Deland, Wilfred Pigeon, Madeline Wary, Alam Grewal, Mark Blagrove, and Michelle Carr. 2021. The relationship between dreams and subsequent morning mood using self-reports and text analysis. *Affective Science*, 3(2):400–405.

Joshua M. Martin, Danyal Wainstein Andriano, Natalia B. Mota, Sergio A. Mota-Rolim, John Fontenele Araújo, Mark Solms, and Sidarta Ribeiro. 2020. Structural differences between REM and non-REM dream reports assessed by graph analysis. *PLOS ONE*, 15(7):e0228903.

Patrick McNamara, Kelly Duffy-Deno, Tom Marsh, and Thomas Marsh. 2019. Dream content analysis using artificial intelligence. *International Journal of Dream Research*, Vol 12:No 1 (April 2019).

Tomas Mikolov, Kai Chen, Greg Corrado, and Jeffrey Dean. 2013. Efficient estimation of word representations in vector space.

Natália B. Mota, Raimundo Furtado, Pedro P. C. Maia, Mauro Copelli, and Sidarta Ribeiro. 2014. Graph analysis of dream reports is especially informative about psychosis. *Scientific Reports*, 4(1).

David Nadeau, Catherine Sabourin, Joseph De Koninck, Stan Matwin, and Peter D. Turney. 2006. Automatic dream sentiment analysis. Proc. of the Workshop on Computational Aesthetics at the Twenty-First National Conf. on Artificial Intelligence.

Yuval Nir and Giulio Tononi. 2010. Dreaming and the brain: from phenomenology to neurophysiology. *Trends in Cognitive Sciences*, 14(2):88–100.

Jeffrey Pennington, Richard Socher, and Christopher Manning. 2014. GloVe: Global vectors for word representation. In *Proceedings of the 2014 Conference on Empirical Methods in Natural Language Processing (EMNLP)*, pages 1532–1543, Doha, Qatar. Association for Computational Linguistics.

Nicholas Pesant and Antonio Zadra. 2006. Dream content and psychological well-being: A longitudinal study of the continuity hypothesis. *Journal of clinical psychology*, 62(1):111–121.

Colin Raffel, Noam Shazeer, Adam Roberts, Katherine Lee, Sharan Narang, Michael Matena, Yanqi Zhou, Wei Li, and Peter J. Liu. 2020. Exploring the limits of transfer learning with a unified text-to-text transformer.

Amir H. Razavi, Stan Matwin, Joseph De Koninck, and Ray Reza Amini. 2013. Dream sentiment analysis using second order soft co-occurrences (SOSCO) and time course representations. *Journal of Intelligent Information Systems*.

Camila Sanz, Federico Zamberlan, Earth Erowid, Fire Erowid, and Enzo Tagliazucchi. 2018. The experience elicited by hallucinogens presents the highest similarity to dreaming within a large database of psychoactive substance reports. *Frontiers in Neuroscience*, 12.

Michael Schredl. 2010. Dream content analysis: Basic principles.

Francesca Siclari, Benjamin Baird, Lampros Perogamvros, Giulio Bernardi, Joshua J LaRocque, Brady Riedner, Melanie Boly, Bradley R Postle, and Giulio Tononi. 2017. The neural correlates of dreaming. *Nature Neuroscience*, 20(6):872–878.

Joacim F Skancke, Ingrid Holsen, and Michael Schredl. 2014. Continuity between waking life and dreams of psychiatric patients: a review and discussion of the implications for dream research. *International Journal of Dream Research.*

A Thompson, Suzet Tanya Lereya, G Lewis, Stanley Zammit, Helen L Fisher, and Dieter Wolke. 2015. Childhood sleep disturbance and risk of psychotic experiences at 18: Uk birth cohort. *The British Journal of Psychiatry*, 207(1):23–29.

Ashish Vaswani, Noam Shazeer, Niki Parmar, Jakob Uszkoreit, Llion Jones, Aidan N Gomez, Łukasz Kaiser, and Illia Polosukhin. 2017. Attention is all you need. In *Advances in Neural Information Processing Systems*, pages 5998–6008.

Erin J. Wamsley. 2014. Dreaming and offline memory consolidation. *Current Neurology and Neuroscience Reports*, 14(3).

Erin J. Wamsley and Robert Stickgold. 2011. Memory, sleep, and dreaming: Experiencing consolidation. *Sleep Medicine Clinics*, 6(1):97–108.

Thomas Wolf, Lysandre Debut, Victor Sanh, Julien Chaumond, Clement Delangue, Anthony Moi, Pierric Cistac, Tim Rault, Remi Louf, Morgan Funtowicz, Joe Davison, Sam Shleifer, Patrick von Platen, Clara Ma, Yacine Jernite, Julien Plu, Canwen Xu, Teven Le Scao, Sylvain Gugger, Mariama Drame, Quentin Lhoest, and Alexander Rush. 2020. Transformers: State-of-the-art natural language processing. In *Proceedings of the 2020 Conference on Empirical Methods in Natural Language Processing: System Demonstrations*, pages 38–45, Online. Association for Computational Linguistics.

Calvin Kai-Ching Yu. 2022. Automated analysis of dream sentiment—the royal road to dream dynamics? *Dreaming*, 32(1):33–51.

Antonio Zadra and Robert Stickgold. 2021. *Dreaming and Offline Memory Consolidation.* WW Norton & Company.

Xiaofang Zheng and Richard Schweickert. 2021. Comparing hall van de castle coding and linguistic inquiry and word count using canonical correlation analysis. *Dreaming*, 31(3):207–224.

A DreamBank's Distributions

The section presents more details and analyses of DreamBank's statistics. Figure 7 shows the distribution of the HVDC emotions in DreamBank, divided between the different series of DreamBank. Figure 8 summarises how single DreamBank reports distribute with respect to the number of (General) emotions per report. As shown, the majority (circa 65%) of the 922 reports containing at least one emotion in fact contain only one emotion. Approximately 25% contains two emotions, while the rest can reach up to 9 emotions per report. When considering only Dreamer emotions, the percentage of reports with only one emotion reaches almost 75%, and the number of reports with more than two emotions drops to approximately 5% of the total (see Figure 9).

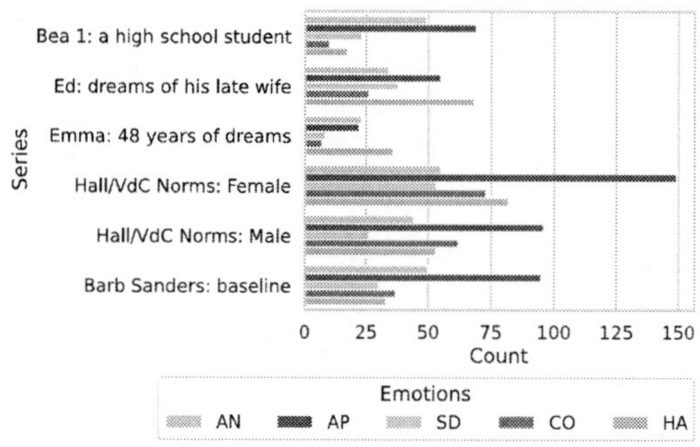

Figure 7: General emotion distribution across Dream Bank's Series.

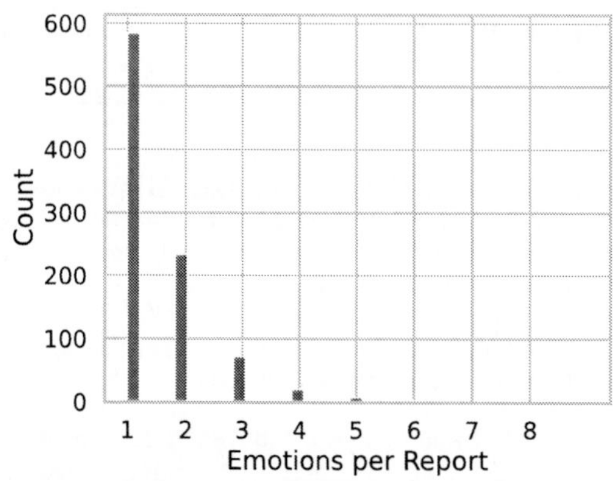

Figure 8: Number of emotion per report. Visualisation of how reports distribute with respect to the number of (General) emotions they have been labelled with.

B Off-the-Shelf Sentiment Analysis

We here discuss the results of a two-level preliminary experiment, where we investigated if an off-the-shelf model tuned to perform sentiment analysis (SA) could have been used to assess the emotional content of dream reports. Specifically, we proposed to test a 2-way `POSITIVE` vs. `NEGATIVE` classification, similar to previous work (McNamara et al., 2019; Yu, 2022). The experiment was run using the default SA setting of Hugging Face's (Wolf et al., 2020) `pipeline`, and had two levels. First, we investigated whether the general predictions of the model (i.e., the predicted labels and their scores) correlated with the

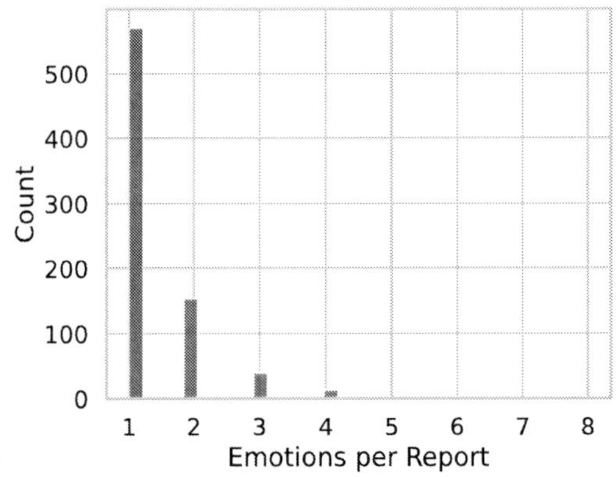

Figure 9: Number of Dreamer-only emotion per report. Visualisation of how reports distribute with respect to the number of (Dreamer-only) emotions they have been labelled with.

sentiment of individual dream reports. We defined the overall sentiment of each report as the sum of all references to emotions identified according to the HVDC coding system. A schematic summary of our approach is presented in Figure 10.

The second experiment focused on those reports containing a single emotion, and studied whether the predicted label (i.e., `POSITIVE` or `NEGATIVE`) matched the emotion found by the annotators.

B.1 Annotator Score

While 90% of the gathered dream reports do not present more than two emotions, some reports can contain a large variety of emotions — up to 9 in some rare cases (see Appendix A for more details). Hence, the main aim of the sentiment analysis investigation was to assess whether the model's predictions do reflect the overall *sentiment* of a report, defined according to the number of times specific positive or negative emotions appear in a report (regardless of the character who experienced them). Formally, given a dream report containing a list of Emotions E, such as the one in the example of Figure 10, and a scoring table S, mapping each HVDC emotion to a set having positive (E_+), negative (E_-), or neutral (E_0) valence, we computed the sentiment of a report (i.e., the *Annotator Score* (AN)) through the equation in 1

$$AN(E) = P(E_+) - P(E_-) \tag{1}$$

with

$$P(E_+) = \frac{|E_+|}{|E|} \tag{2}$$

and

$$P(E_-) = \frac{|E_-|}{|E|} \tag{3}$$

For this experiment, our scoring table S assigned *anger*, *apprehension*, *sadness* to the negative valence set (E_-), *happiness* to the positive valence (E_+) set, and *confusion* to the neutral set (E_0) (see Figure 10 for an example). Similarly, the *Model Score* of a report was defined as the difference between the probability associated with the `POSITIVE` and `NEGATIVE` labels. For instance, if the model predicts the probability distribution of the `POSITIVE` ($P(+)$) and `NEGATIVE` ($P(-)$) labels to be .4 and .6, respectively, then the *Model Score* for such a report would be –.2 (see Figure 10 for an example).

The model's performance was assessed by comparing the *Model Score* with the *Annotator Score* via Spearman's correlation coefficient (ρ).

B.1.1 Results

Figure 11 presents the results of the correlation analysis between scores produced by human annotators and the selected model, for the Dreamer and General Emotion sets. While the correlation with the General Emotions is marginally better, results are overall poor. Moreover, under both Dreamer and General Emotions, the performance was heavily influenced by different DreamBanks' series, as demonstrated by Figure 12. Interestingly, under both the Dreamer and the General Emotions, `Ed` and `Emma` seem to present the strongest correlation between human and model scores.

Figure 13 suggests that these results were likely due to the slightly different distributions produced by human annotators and the sentiment analysis model. Indeed, the predictions of the model (i.e., the *Model Scores*, x-axis) were strongly polarised. In other words, the model was consistently very confident in its decisions on which sentiment (`POSITIVE` or `NEGATIVE`)) was appearing in a given report. On the other hand, the *Annotator Scores* (y-axis) presented a cluster of instances around the value of 0. Interestingly, a considerable part of these reports contained two or three emotions (see Appendix B.3 for more details). Given the adopted method to compute *Annotator Scores* (see Eq. 1), such cluster presents a high number of instances annotated with a single positive emotion and a single negative emotion, or those two plus *confusion*. The fact that such a cluster of

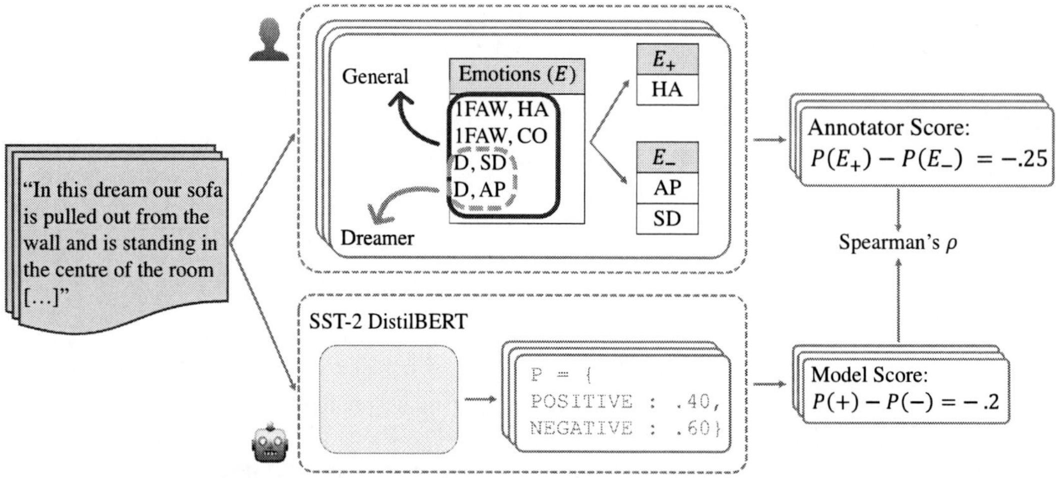

Figure 10: Proposed setup for the Annotator Score experiment (Section B.1).

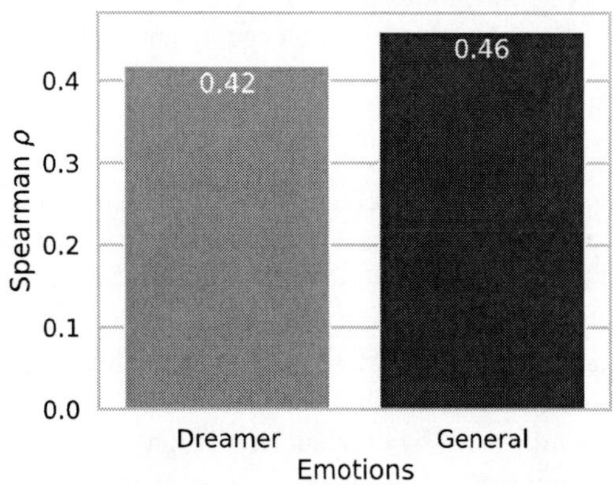

Figure 11: Report sentiment results. Correlations coefficients (in Spearman's ρ) between the model predictions and dream report's sentiment.

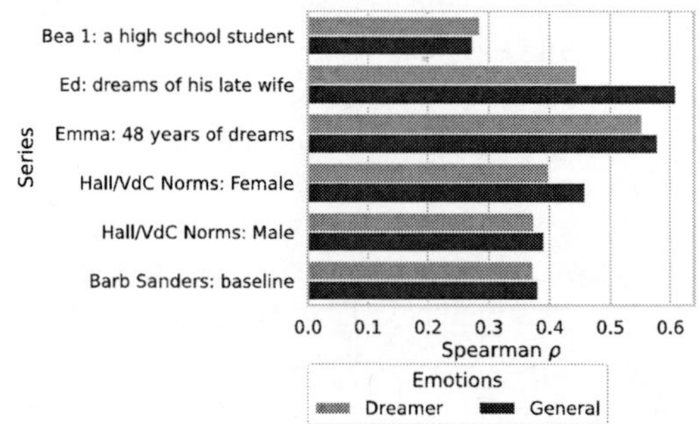

Figure 12: Report sentiment, collection analysis. Correlations coefficients (in Spearman's ρ) between the model predictions and each report's sentiment, divided by Dream Bank's Series.

zero-valued *Annotator Scores* containing conflicting emotions did not have a clear match in the *Model Scores* distribution, suggests that the model might be picking on either the positive or negative emotion. Therefore, the scores of the model may not efficiently reflect the more general sentiment of the reports, but only encode the presence of a specific emotion type (positive or negative). The following experiment investigated this possibility, focusing on those reports only containing one emotion, and approaching the problem from a categorical perspective.

B.2 Single-Emotion

The first experiment showed how the selected model failed to correctly capture the distribution of human annotators' scores, mainly due to very polarised predictions and might have simply reflected what type of emotion (positive or negative) is mainly present in a given report. Since the HVDC system also allows assigning a strictly positive or negative connotation to each emotion, we studied such a possibility by focusing solely on those reports that experts have annotated with one — and only one — of the five HVDC emotions: *anger*, *apprehension*, *confusion*, *sadness* and *happiness*. The goal was thus to understand if reports classified as `POSITIVE` or `NEGATIVE` by the model do contain an emotion that the HVDC scoring system also defined as positive or negative. Here, results are interpreted in terms of precision, recall and F1, with respect to the two prediction classes (`POSITIVE` and `NEGATIVE`).

	Precision		Recall		F1	
	Dreamer	General	Dreamer	General	Dreamer	General
NEGATIVE	92	91	83	82	87	86
POSITIVE	44	45	64	65	52	53
macro avg	68	68	73	73	70	70
weighted avg	83	82	79	78	81	80

Table 2: Single-emotion results. Per-class and average scores obtained when comparing model-predicted and human-generated labels for dream reports containing a single emotion. Here, the five HVDC emotions were collapsed into positive (i.e., *happiness*) and negative (i.e., *anger*, *apprehension*, *sadness* and *confusion*), and compared against the label predicted by the sentiment analysis model (i.e., POSITIVE or NEGATIVE).

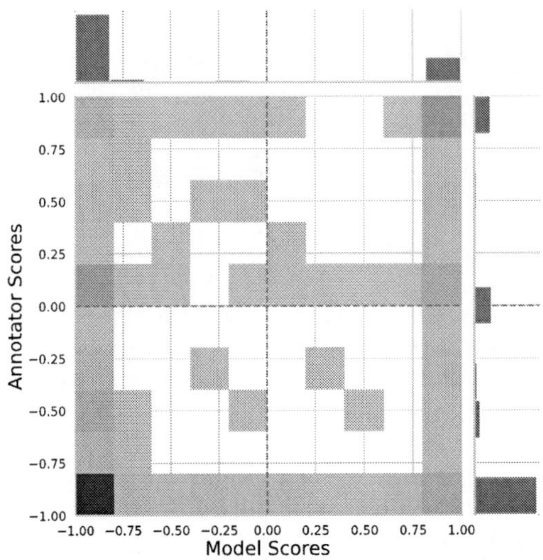

Figure 13: Annotator Score, predictions' analysis. Comparison of the Predicted Sentiment scores (x-axis) and Report Sentiment distribution (y-axis) for the General Emotion set. As seen, while the model's predicted scores are strongly polarised, annotators' scores, computed via Eq. 1, are more smoothly and evenly distributed.

B.2.1 Results

Table 2 summarises the results and clearly shows that, with respect to reports containing a single emotion, the predictions of the model matched the human-produced annotations only with respect to negative emotions, while showing poor results with respect to the POSITIVE class — which only contains *happiness*. The model was however largely unstable with respect to the type of error it makes, as shown by the notable difference between precision and recall scores.

Figure 14 presents the same results of Table 2, divided by single HVDC emotion (x-axis) and series (diagrams), and shows how the model remained notably impacted by the different DreamBank's series. Of note, Ed and Emma, the two series that produced the best performance in the previous experiment, here showed the most balanced results across different HVDC emotions. Overall, these results strongly suggest that the selected model had fewer problems when classifying reports containing negative emotions than at detecting the presence of positive emotions.

B.3 Annotator vs. Model Scores Analysis

The section presents a more detailed analysis of the distributions of Model and Annotator Scores, with respect to the number (#) of emotions. As shown in Figure 15, the two peaks of the Model Scores distributions mainly contained reports classified by annotators as presenting a single emotion. However, the proportion of reports containing two emotions is notably higher in those reports classified by the model as being strongly NEGATIVE. Interestingly, with respect to the Annotator Scores, the proportion of reports with two emotions is concentrated in those reports with Annotator Scores of –2 (see Figure 16)

C Multi-Label Text Classification

C.1 Token distribution

Figure 17 summarises the distribution of tokens produced by the tokeniser of the selected pre-trained LLM (i.e., BERT-large-cased), divided by DreamBank's series. As seen, only 6 reports, accounting for approximately 0.003% of the whole dataset, present more than 510 content tokens.

C.2 Supervised Learning Hyper-Parameters

Table 3 collects the hyper-parameters used to tune the bespoke classifiers from Section 4. The same parameters were used throughout the whole work.

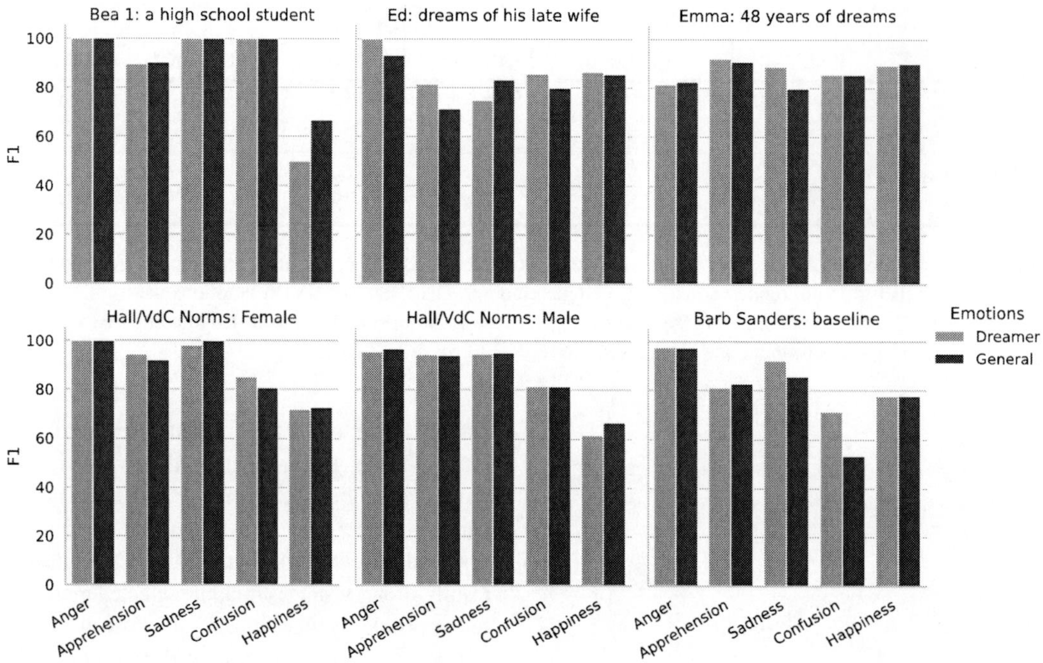

Figure 14: Single-emotion: Series and emotions analysis. Results (in terms of reference-class F1 scores) obtained by the model for each HVDC emotion (x-axis), DreamBank's series (diagrams), and Emotions (Dreamer vs. General, hue). For *happiness*, the F1 scores reference class is `POSITVE`, while all other HVDC emotions share `NEGATIVE` as their reference class for the reported F1 scores.

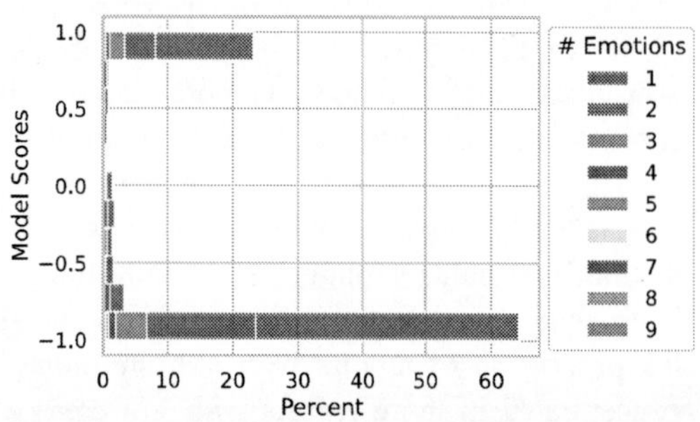

Figure 15: `Model scores` distribution. In-detail visualisation of the `Model scores` distribution, divided by the number of emotions per report, presented in Figure 11 from Section B.1.

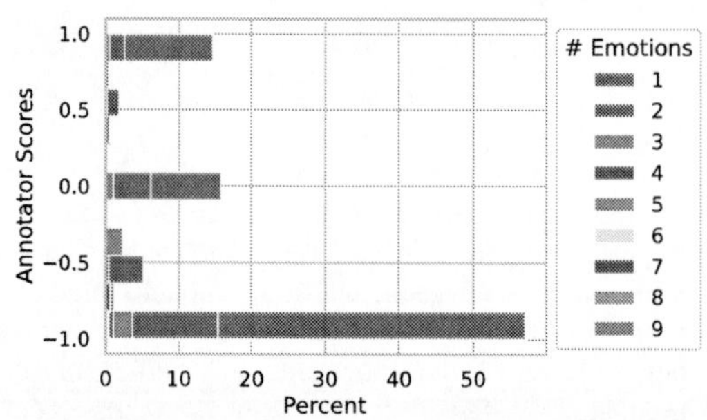

Figure 16: `Annotator scores` distribution. In detail visualisation of the `Annotator scores` distribution, divided by the number of emotions per report presented in Figure 11 from Section B.1.

Parameter	Value
BERT-input max-len	512
epochs	10
learning rate	0.00001
batch size	8
input truncation	True
truncation-to	max-length

Table 3: Hyper-parameters used for training the architectures in Section 4.

C.3 Support-Score Correlation Analysis

Table 4 and Figure 18 summarise the results of the correlation analysis from Section 4.2.1. Overall, this analysis indicated no clear relationship between the number of test instances containing a specific emotion and the models' final performance in the ablation experiment.

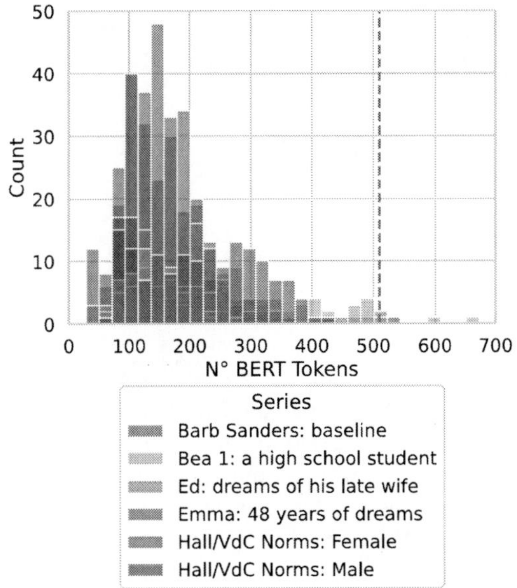

Figure 17: BERT-token distribution. Number of tokens per dream report according to the BERT tokenizer, divided by DreamBank Series. The vertical dotted line signals the indicative number of 510 tokens, after wich only 6 reports can be found.

Series	Spearman's ρ	p
Bea 1: a high school student	0.3000	0.6238
Ed: dreams of his late wife	-0.7182	0.1718
Emma: 48 years of dreams	0.7000	0.1881
Hall/VdC Norms: Female	0.7906	0.1114
Hall/VdC Norms: Male	0.7379	0.1546
Barb Sanders: baseline	0.8208	0.0886

Table 4: Correlation analysis between F1 score and support (# items) per single emotion in the ablation experiment. Each row of the table presents the results of the correlations between the number of instances containing a given emotion, and the obtained F1 scores (see Figures 3 and 18 for further visual breakdowns). Columns describe the single Series under investigation, the ρ coefficient and the p value of each correlation.

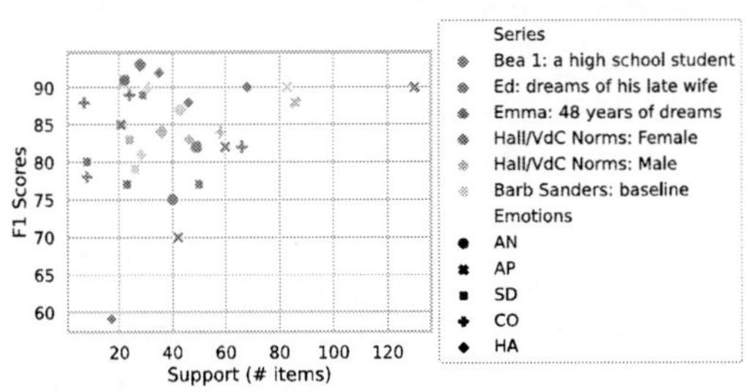

Figure 18: Ablation's experiment, score vs support correlation analysis. Visualisation of the correlation analysis, presented in Table 4, between the number of test items (x-axis) and F1 scores (y-axis), for each combination of Series and emotion.

Explainable Depression Detection Using Large Language Models on Social Media Data

Yuxi Wang, Diana Inkpen, Prasadith Buddhitha
School of Electrical Engineering and Computer Science
University of Ottawa
{ywan1225, diana.inkpen, pkiri056}@uottawa.ca

Abstract

Due to the rapid growth of user interaction on different social media platforms, publicly available social media data has increased substantially. The sheer amount of data and level of personal information being shared on such platforms has made analyzing textual information to predict mental disorders such as depression a reliable preliminary step when it comes to psychometrics. In this study, we first proposed a system to search for texts that are related to depression symptoms from the Beck's Depression Inventory (BDI) questionnaire, and provide a ranking for further investigation in a second step. Then, in this second step, we address the even more challenging task of automatic depression level detection, using writings and voluntary answers provided by users on Reddit. Several Large Language Models (LLMs) were applied in experiments. Our proposed system based on LLMs can generate both predictions and explanations for each question. By combining two LLMs for different questions, we achieved better performance on three of four metrics compared to the state-of-the-art and remained competitive on the one remaining metric. In addition, our system is explainable on two levels: first, knowing the answers to the BDI questions provides clues about the possible symptoms that could lead to a clinical diagnosis of depression; second, our system can explain the predicted answer for each question.

1 Introduction

Being one of the leading global public health issues, depression is common, costly, debilitating, and associated with an increased risk of suicide (Marwaha et al., 2023). Since depression has become a prevalent mental health issue, early detection of symptoms could greatly improve the chances of proper treatment. Traditional methods of detection, usually human-led, are expensive to conduct and might be individually biased. In this study, we propose a method to analyze and select social media writings to help identify potential symptoms of depression. Then, we propose an explainable method that uses the selected writings to automatically fill in the Beck's Depression Inventory (BDI) questionnaire (Beck et al., 1961) for the social media user (see Figure A1 for the full questionnaire). The questionnaire then provides the level of depression of the user based on all the answers.

The main contributions of this paper are:

1. Extended the applicability of using Large Language Models (LLMs) to predict mental health status for social media users.
2. Improved the performance on the task of automatically filling in the BDI questionnaire using social media data through manually designed prompts and without further training.
3. Explored the use of LLMs for generating both the predictions and explanations for the predictions.

2 Related Work

To develop computational methods for depression detection using textual information, analyzing word usage became a natural starting point. Through statistical investigation, researchers found that negative emotion, cause, sensory, and the first person singular words were more commonly used when describing activities such as breakup (Boals and Klein, 2005). Linguistic Inquiry and Word Count (LIWC), a computerized text analysis tool, was developed to assess word usage in psychologically meaningful categories (Tausczik and Pennebaker, 2010). The tool was built by creating dictionaries from domain knowledge, with the words categorized into different groups.

In addition to social and semantic features, linguistic n-gram features extracted from social media data were used by Tsugawa et al. (2015) for estimating the degree of depression. Mowery et al. (2016)

Proceedings of the 9th Workshop on Computational Linguistics and Clinical Psychology (CLPsych 2024), pages 108–126
March 21, 2024

further considered using demographic data such as age and gender as features, for classifying depressive symptoms based on social media (Twitter data) on a population level. Term frequency–inverse document frequency (tf–idf), which is a classic method for weighting words, was used to prepare features for predicting mental illness from social media (Thorstad and Wolff, 2019).

Deep learning methods also attracted researchers working on the subject. Yates et al. (2017) proposed a method using a neural network model to identify the risk of self-harm or depression, using data from social media Twitter and Reddit. Researchers participated in CLEF eRisk 2017 (Losada et al., 2017) focused on classifying users into binary targets: at risk or non-risk of depression. Husseini Orabi et al. (2018) explored the effectiveness of Convolutional Neural Networks (CNNs) and Recurrent Neural Networks (RNNs), on detecting signs of depression using unstructured text data extracted from Twitter, released for the shared task on Computational Linguistics and Clinical Psychology (CLPsych) 2015 (Coppersmith et al., 2015).

As part of CLEF eRisk 2019, there was a proposed task about using the BDI questionnaire to automatically predict the depression level of social media users based on their social media writings, and the task continued in 2020 and 2021 (Parapar et al., 2021). Importantly, data was provided for the tasks. This led to somewhat explainable depression predictors, by indicating possible symptoms (such as lack of sleep, loss of appetite, and reduced physical activity). See Figure A1 for the full set of questions from the BDI questionnaire and their possible answers. In general, the performance of the systems that participated in this shared task was poor. Deep learning was used by a few of the participants in the task. For example, while participating in the shared task Task 3 at CLEF eRisk 2021 (Parapar et al., 2021), Inkpen et al. (2021) conducted experiments with Transformer-based models, a Deep Averaging Network (DAN) model, as well as a Hierarchical Attention Network (HAN) for text classification tasks inspired by Yang et al. (2016). On the same task, Maupomé et al. (2021) proposed a system that applied topic modeling using Embedded Topic Model (ETM) (Dieng et al., 2020) which was trained on a depression detection dataset issued from Reddit, and a regression approach with nearest-neighbors on the values of the answers. This system achieved the highest score on one metric and also performed well on the other three metrics from the shared task. In 2022, Skaik and Inkpen (2022) continued working on the task and proposed a method that combined multiple deep learning models to answer different questions. Through all these efforts, a better performance was achieved on some of the metrics. In this paper, we propose new methods to solve the task, with improved performance and with added explainability for the predicted answers.

	Quantity
Number of TREC files	3,107
Number of subjects	3,107
Number of sentences	4,264,693

Table 1: Statistics of the dataset for depression symptom search

3 Datasets

3.1 Dataset for Depression Symptoms Search

This dataset was shared for Task 1 of the eRisk 2023 (Search for symptoms of depression) (Parapar et al., 2023). The participants in the shared task were given files in the TREC format containing documents (sentences) of each user. Each document has a document ID as well as the text of the document. The corpus provided to the participants was a sentence-tagged dataset based on eRisk's past data.

The dataset contains only the derived sentences from social media, with no labels included. Languages other than English were not filtered out. The aim of the task was to extract the top-1000 relevant documents for each of the 21 symptoms in the BDI questionnaire and provide rankings for the extracted documents. Some statistics of this dataset are shown in Table 1.

3.2 Dataset for Depression Estimation

This dataset was shared at eRisk 2021 Task 3 (Measuring the severity of the signs of depression) and was built upon data shared at eRisk 2020 and eRisk 2019 for the same task. The dataset contains a training dataset and a test dataset.

The training dataset contains 90 examples, which consist of 43,514 writings written by 90 users from the 2020 and 2019 tasks, as well as their answers to the 21 questions of the BDI Questionnaire. The test dataset consists of 19,803 posts and comments written by 80 users, and their answers to the questionnaire. The labels for questions 16 and

minimal depression	depression levels 0-9
mild depression	depression levels 10-18
moderate depression	depression levels 19-29
severe depression	depression levels 30-63

Figure 1: Depression categories associated with depression levels

Category	# of Subjects[1]
minimal depression	14 (15%)
mild depression	27 (30%)
moderate depression	22 (24%)
severe depression	27 (30%)

Table 2: Statistics of depression category in the training data

18, which have different answer sets, are revised so that the answers with letters are merged into a single answer (for example, 1a and 1b are merged into 1). Each of the remaining questions has four answers: 0, 1, 2, and 3.

Statistics for the user answers (labels) are shown in Table A2. Through investigations, it can be seen that most of the symptoms users have are minor, as about 68% of users answered 0 or 1 (with about 35% answered 0 and about 32% answered 1); a few users reported severe symptoms. Specific questions may have a different distribution, such as question 16. As label frequency distributes among multiple labels, and varies by question, we can see that simply choosing a label as the default value is not practical.

To calculate an overall level of depression for a user, depression categories introduced in Figure 1 (Losada et al., 2019) were considered. The calculated levels of depression are shown in Table 2. We could conclude that users are distributed in all four categories, with most users having mild (30%) or severe (30%) depression. It is worth noting that this finding does not fully comply with the findings we had while investigating the label distribution.

4 Methodology

4.1 Search for Depression-related Writings

A writing (sentence in this context) is considered relevant to a symptom if it provides information, ideally explicit, about the user's status of that particular symptom.

The task was considered as an information retrieval task, where user-written sentences are stored as documents. We first transformed the 21 questions from the BDI questionnaire into 21 queries. We then used contextual text embedding methods for transfer learning. To accelerate the calculation of contextual representations, many keywords were selected from the questions in the BDI questionnaire, in order to filter out unrelated documents. The queries and keywords are shown in Table A1. To calculate the relevance of a document to a BDI question, we used cosine similarity between two vector representations. Our developed system can extract the most relevant sentences and provide a ranking of them for each of the 21 symptoms in the BDI questionnaire.

4.1.1 Data Normalization and Text Processing

When obtaining the vector representations, we filtered out the documents (sentences) that did not contain symptom-related keywords. Then we used a transfer learning strategy, by employing the knowledge from the language models directly to build the semantic representations. Traditional preprocessing methods were not applied, but the specific tokenization used by each contextual embedding model was used. The processing steps were applied to both the documents and the queries.

4.1.2 Universal Sentence Encoder with Cosine Similarity

The Universal Sentence Encoder (USE) is a text encoder that directly encodes sentences into vectors. It is specifically designed for transfer learning of various types of tasks. The encoder based on the transformer architecture was trained in the following way: the word representations acquired through the transformer were converted to a fixed-length encoding vector by summing the element-wise representations at each word position, and then the vector was divided by the square root of the length of the sentence to reduce sentence length effects. The inputs to the encoder are lowercased strings that are tokenized using the Penn Treebank Tokenizer (PTB), and the outputs are 512-dimensional vector representations. Since the model was designed to be of general purpose, multi-task learning was conducted (Cer et al., 2018).

We used the USE to obtain embeddings of queries and sentences, and calculated the distance between them to obtain rankings using the cosine similarity. As a result, this system named "USESim" achieved a precision of 0.60 for the top-10

[1]Percentage numbers were rounded.

documents retrieved and an average precision of 0.16 for the top-1000. We experimented with other sentence representations, such as RoBERTa (Liu et al., 2019), but the results for the retrieval task were lower.

4.1.3 Adapting USESim for Writing Selection

The dataset for depression estimation contains a large number of user writings. It is good to have a lot of information, but too many texts for a user could introduce noise, and it is difficult and costly for models to process all of them. This is why we need to filter out the less relevant writings.

We use our above-mentioned document retrieval system "USESim" for pre-processing the dataset for depression estimation to generate a smaller and more relevant dataset, by keeping only relevant writings.

4.2 Estimate Level of Depression

As mentioned, the final goal is to automatically fill in a standard depression questionnaire, the BDI questionnaire, by using LLMs to do multi-class predictions of answers to questions in the questionnaire. The questionnaire has 21 questions in total, which can be used to evaluate conditions of feelings about sadness, sleeping, etc. Each question has 4 answers, except 2 questions (question 16 about sleep patterns and question 18 about appetite) have more than 4 answers of which answers were transformed into 4 classes.

4.2.1 Data Preparation

As discussed in Section 3.2, the dataset contains a training dataset and a test dataset. The training dataset 90 users' 43,514 Reddit writings, and their answers to the BDI questionnaire. The test dataset consists of 80 users's 19,803 posts and comments as well as their responses to the questionnaire. The writing-selection system USESim is adopted for cleaning the dataset, by selecting only symptom-relevant user writings and forming a more useful dataset. Based on our settings, two types of datasets were generated using USESim:

1. **The Top-5 Dataset**
   Collected by applying the USESim to collect the top-5 relevant writings for each symptom in the BDI questionnaire. The statistics for the text length of this dataset are shown in Table A3.
2. **The Top-1 Dataset**
   Formed by applying the USESim to collect the top-1 relevant writings (the most relevant post or comment) for each of the 21 symptoms. The statistics for the text length of this dataset are shown in Table A4.

Top-5 and top-1 relevant writings were selected with the consideration of the maximum length: as many LLMs have a short context length which refers to the maximum number of tokens that the model can process, shorter input texts are desired. For example, the Llama 2 models have a context length of 4096 tokens.

4.2.2 Classification Using Large Language Models

Prompt learning is a new paradigm that is showing promising results. Large language models are essentially language models that are trained to estimate the probability $P(x;\theta)$ for text x. Prompt learning techniques utilize the probability P, to predict the output y. As an example, the output y can be the label in a classification task, and it can be extracted or transformed from the text generated by the LLM.

Selection of the LLM

A wide variety of pre-trained language models are available. In this study, the following open LLMs were applied in experiments:

- **Llama-2-13b-chat**
  Meta's Llama 2 models (Touvron et al., 2023) are LLMs that are well-supported and powerful. As auto-regressive language models, they are particularly useful for Natural Language Generation (NLG) tasks, which means that not only the output label for our classification task could be generated, but also the LLMs' explanations for predictions.
  Llama-2-13b-chat[2], which is optimized for dialogue use cases was applied in this study.
- **SUS-Chat-34B**
  Released by the Southern University of Science and Technology (SUSTech) and IDEA-CCNL, SUS-Chat-34B[3] is a bilingual (Chinese-English) dialogue model. It has significant improvements on many benchmarks of evaluation; it achieved high scores among

[2]https://huggingface.co/meta-llama/Llama-2-13b-chat-hf
[3]https://huggingface.co/SUSTech/SUS-Chat-34B

open source models of similar size (34 billion parameters), and is one of the best models with a size below 70B.

The model which was based on Yi-34B[4] was trained with 1.4 billion tokens of complex instruction data, including multi-turn dialogues, mathematics, reasoning, and others, thus the model is capable of focusing on long-text dialogue and of imitating human thought processes.

- **Neural-chat-7b-v3**
  Based on Mistral-7B-v0.1[5], the Intel neural-chat-7b-v3-1[6] is a LLM that was fine-tuned on the SlimOrca[7] dataset and with the Direct Preference Optimization (DPO) algorithm to align with human preferences. The DPO derives the probability of human preference data for an optimal policy to replace the reward model used by the Reinforcement Learning from Human Feedback (RLHF) (Lv et al., 2023).
  The model performed exceptionally well among 7-billion-parameter models.

Design of Prompts

In this step, as discussed in (Liu et al., 2021), a prompting function f_{prompt} is designed, which could then be applied to transform the input text x into the prompt $x' = f_{prompt}(x)$.

Prompt engineering is the process of designing the most effective prompting function f_{prompt}. With the knowledge we learned that most of the symptoms users have are minor, we added "suppose you are a psychiatrist who prefer to give minor diagnoses rather than serious ones" in the instruction to alleviate the models' tendency of exaggeration. Instead of giving exact meanings of each question's answers, such as "0. I do not feel sad." and "3. I am so sad or unhappy that I can't stand it." for the symptom sadness, we give only the labels to the model. In this way, the labels 0, 1, 2, and 3 are considered levels of intensity or the magnitude of the change, rather than solely markers of classes. The first consideration is the length of the prompt: it is inefficient to reserve a diverse space for this information, and models may not have a large enough context window. Another consideration is that some label meanings might confuse the model. Examples of options that could be confusing are shown in Figure 2.

9. Suicidal Thoughts or Wishes
0. I don't have any thoughts of killing myself.
1. I have thoughts of killing myself, but I would not carry them out.
2. I would like to kill myself.
3. I would kill myself if I had the chance.

10. Crying
0. I don't cry anymore than I used to.
1. I cry more than I used to.
2. I cry over every little thing.
3. I feel like crying, but I can't.

Figure 2: Some options that might be confusing to models

To clarify the symptom that the model should work on, we rephrased the 21 questions in the BDI questionnaire into 21 sentences. All the rephrased sentences talk about the levels of the symptom, to help the model's understanding. The rephrased symptoms are summarized in Table A5.

Our designed prompt template is shown in Figure 3. During experiments, "[$rephrased$ $symptom$]" will be filled in using rephrased symptoms, and "[$input$ $text$]" will be substituted with the concatenated user writings from the cleaned dataset: texts for each symptom when using top-5 or all texts when using top-1.

Instruction: The following paragraph was concatenated from a user's posts on social media. Suppose you are a psychiatrist who prefer to give minor diagnoses rather than serious ones, read the posts as a whole, determine the level of "[$rephrased$ $symptom$]" and give a number in 0, 1, 2 or 3, then explain why.

User's posts: [$input$ $text$]

Level (0, 1, 2 or 3):

Figure 3: Designed prompt template for symptom estimation

Using LLMs

The same configurations are applied to all the experimented LLMs.

The tokenizers for each model were used to encode prompts and decode outputs. The maximum

[4]https://huggingface.co/01-ai/Yi-34B
[5]https://huggingface.co/mistralai/Mistral-7B-v0.1
[6]https://huggingface.co/Intel/neural-chat-7b-v3-1
[7]https://huggingface.co/datasets/Open-Orca/SlimOrca

length for the models was set to 4,096, and only the first sentence of a pair would be truncated if longer.

To reduce the costs of utilizing LLMs, QLoRA (Dettmers et al., 2023) was used: models are run in 4-bit precision, using the NF4 (Normal Float 4) data type, double quantization, and the computational type of torch.bfloat16.

While generating texts, the models are set to use multinomial sampling, keeping the top-10 highest probability vocabulary tokens and the smallest set of most probable tokens with probabilities that add up to 0.7 or higher. The maximum length is 4,096, and the temperature (the value used to modulate probabilities of tokens) was set to be 0.1.

We experimented with a single LLM, as well as combining two LLMs, working on separate questions based on the results from experiments using training data. The experiments were conducted using the top-1 and top-5 datasets. The outputs generated by the LLMs contain labels for the predicted answers, and explanations for the predictions. We extracted the labels using regular expression (regex) and recorded them as the automated responses to the BDI questionnaire for each user in the test set.

5 Evaluation

The same evaluation metrics were applied for the task in eRisk 2019, 2020,and 2021 (Losada et al., 2019). The four metrics used for evaluation are:

- **Average Hit Rate (AHR)**
  The AHR is the hit rate averaged over all the users. The hit rate measures the number of answers systems automatically fill in that are exactly the same as the actual answers provided by the users.

- **Average Closeness Rate (ACR)**
  The ACR is the Closeness Rate averaged over all the users. It takes into account that the answers represent an ordinal scale, rather than merely separate options. To get the closeness rate, first compute the absolute difference between the automatically filled answer and the actual answer, then transform the calculated absolute difference into an effectiveness score as follows:

$$CR = \frac{maxad - ad}{maxad} \tag{1}$$

  where $maxad$ stands for the maximum absolute difference, and ad is the absolute difference.

- **Average DODL (ADODL)**
  The ADODL is the difference between the system's and actual overall depression levels averaged over all users. The Difference between Overall Depression Levels (DODL) is obtained by first calculating the overall depression levels for the system-filled and actual questionnaire, then computing the absolute difference between the two overall scores. The DODL is normalized as follows:

$$DODL = \frac{63 - ad}{63} \tag{2}$$

  where ad is the absolute difference between the automated and actual overall score.

- **Depression Category Hit Rate (DCHR)**
  The DCHR measures the closeness of the depression estimation achieved over all users according to the established depression categories introduced in Figure 1. It calculates the fraction of cases where the automated questionnaire led to a category that is identical to the user's actual depression category.

6 Results and Discussion

The experimental results of our systems using LLMs are shown in Table 3.

We can learn that the usage of USESim for user writing selection is helpful, and it is generally better to have more writings kept so that the model could have more information about the user, and the writings would be more focused on the specific question. In our experiments, the usage of top-5 dataset leads to a better performance than using the top-1 dataset.

When using the top-5 dataset, the model neural-chat-7b-v3-1 performed better than SUS-Chat-34B on the metrics AHR, ADODL, and DCHR. This is surprising since the neural-chat-7b-v3-1 is much smaller than SUS-Chat-34B in terms of size/number of parameters. The reason could be the language focus and the application of the DPO algorithm. The Llama-2-13b-chat model did not perform well on any of the metrics.

Through experimenting on the training data, the neural-chat-7b-v3-1's answers on questions 4, 8, 9, 11, 12, 16, 18, 19, 20 and 21 are combined with SUS-Chat-34B's answers on questions 1, 2, 3, 5, 6,

Run	AHR	ACR	ADODL	DCHR
Llama-2-13b-chat_top1	21.90	63.29	72.22	42.5
Llama-2-13b-chat_top5	22.32	63.51	72.16	42.5
neural-chat-7b-v3-1_top1	31.96	71.82	84.12	48.75
neural-chat-7b-v3-1_top5	33.63	70.83	**85.87**	**52.5**
SUS-Chat_top1	32.61	72.02	84.64	50.0
SUS-Chat_top5	33.51	72.57	83.53	**52.5**
neural-chat+SUS-Chat_top1	34.70	72.91	85.41	48.75
neural-chat+SUS-Chat_top5	**37.32**	**73.25**	85.63	50.0

Table 3: Results of LLM-based systems

7, 10, 13, 14, 15 and 17 as the combined system. The combined runs performed well on the AHR, ACR and ADODL metrics.

Although the performance on some metrics is still not outstanding, our systems scored over 85% on ADODL, which is an improvement considering that ADODL is the most critical metric for measuring depression at the population level (Skaik and Inkpen, 2022). Many runs scored over 50 on DCHR, meaning that they predicted correctly for more than half of the test subjects on predicting their depression category.

Our experiments proved that LLMs have learned knowledge about various depression-related symptoms, and they can make better inferences than supervised deep learning techniques, with zero-shot learning (no training) and properly designed prompts.

6.1 Local Explanations of LLMs

Through prompts, the LLMs were asked to provide explanations for their predictions. Even though these explanations are not necessarily factual, they provide insights about the important information in the given user writings. In Figure 4, an example of user writings is given, which is answered by LLMs for Q18 as a change in appetite.

Figure 5 shows the prediction and explanation from Llama-2-13b-chat for text from Figure 4. In the explanation, the model mentioned several physical and mental issues described in the user's writings, such as inflammation and mental health issues. The model predicted 2 as the answer.

In Figure 6, the classification and explanation for the given example generated by neural-chat-7b-v3-1 are shown. The model mentioned that the user needed to set alarms to eat, having stomach flu and fluctuating weights, which could affect the user's appetite. An answer label of 2 is given by the model.

SUS-Chat-34B's prediction and explanation are shown in Figure 7. The model presumed that the user had a higher level of change in appetite since the user had to set alarms to eat at some points, but the model also mentioned that no significant weight changes were presented. The model generated 2 as the answer to the question.

6.1.1 Evaluation of Explanations

In (Rajagopal et al., 2021), several criteria were introduced for evaluating the explanations, including sufficiency (via BERT-score), plausibility, and trustability. Due to limitations on the amount of time available for conducting evaluations, we only evaluated explanations for the best-performing system on one metric: sufficiency – to automatically evaluate how well the explanations reflect the system's predictions. Manual evaluation with experts to calculate the other measures is left as future work.

Rajagopal et al. (2021) used the "Faithfulness-by-construction" (FRESH) pipeline (Jain et al., 2020) to evaluate sufficiency: a BERT (Devlin et al., 2019) based classifier is trained to perform a task using only the extracted explanations. A high accuracy would indicate a high sufficiency of the explanations, which means that the explanations are indicative of the predicted labels. Based on this method, we implemented a BERT classifier, trained it with the generated explanations for the training dataset as the training data, and evaluated the classifier with the explanations for the test data.

The sufficiency score for the explanations generated by our best system was 80.77%. This indicates the effectiveness of generated explanations of the system. The configurations are as follows: a fast Rust-based pretrained tokenizer of "bert-base-cased", with default settings on the rest; the pretrained "bert-base-cased" model for the classifica-

User's posts: I would say coriander. Grab a package and eat it. **Great snacks.** I mean the psychosis is still untreated I'm thinking about what to do next. **My weight fluctuates** because, in addition to severe inflammation, I also have some mental health issues that cause loss of memory. I actually **have to set alerts to eat** for certain times. I had a huge success that day and was approved to work from home. Now I **got stomach flu**. I don't feel accomplished enough. I'm **vomiting for days** and my mental state is getting worse and I hear constant noise from the church. Oh my goodness, my back pain, my **constant digestive issues**, plus my mental illness, have all gotten worse. I think all I really need is a happy message. Usually good news upsets me, but I really need it today.

Figure 4: An example of concatenated writings. Some words were highlighted for readability. In fact, we rephrased the sentences in the example, because the data sharing agreement that we signed when we obtained the dataset does not allow us to use the real example directly.

Metric	Our system	Our best	Best system	State-of-the-art
AHR	neural-chat+SUS-Chat_top5	37.32	BDI_Multi_Model	**41.25**
ACR	neural-chat+SUS-Chat_top5	**73.25**	UPV-Symanto 4_symanto_upv_lingfeat_cors	73.17
ADODL	neural-chat-7b-v3-1_top5	**85.87**	BDI_Multi_Model	83.79
DCHR	neural-chat-7b-v3-1_top5	**52.5**	BDI_Multi_Model	48.75

Table 4: Our results compared to the state-of-the-art

Level (0, 1, 2 or 3): 2

Explanation:

The user's posts suggest that they have experienced significant changes in appetite, as they mention "weight fluctuations" and setting alerts to eat. They also mention "severe inflammation" and "mental health issues" which could be contributing to their appetite changes. Additionally, they mention "stomach flu" and "constant digestive issues" which could also be affecting their appetite. Based on this information, I would rate the user's experience of changes in appetite as a level 2.

Figure 5: Classification and explanation by Llama-2-13b-chat

Level (0, 1, 2 or 3): 2

The user experienced changes in appetite at a level of 2. This is because they mentioned having mental health issues that cause loss of memory, which can affect appetite. They also mentioned setting alerts to eat for certain times, indicating that they have to be more mindful of their eating habits. Additionally, they mentioned having stomach flu, which can also affect appetite. The user's fluctuating weight and other health issues, such as back pain, digestive issues, and mental illness, further contribute to the complexity of their situation.

Figure 6: Classification and explanation by neural-chat-7b-v3-1

tion into the 4 classes/labels; and with default values for the hyperparameters except for the total number of training epochs performed that was set to 8.

6.2 Comparison to Related Work

Skaik and Inkpen (2022) proposed a method for this task that first applies topic-based filtering to clean the irrelevant posts, then conducts multiple iterations to select and assign different models to different question sets. The final model named "BDI_Multi_Model" was formed using 5 HANs, 3 Long Short-Term Memory (LSTM) models, and 2 transformers. Their proposed system sets new records for several metrics. The comparison between our best systems and the state-of-the-art is concluded in Table 4.

Through comparisons, we can see that our systems achieved the best scores on three out of four metrics: ACR, ADODL, and DCHR. It is worth noting that the run neural-chat+SUS-Chat_top5 achieved 85.63 on ADODL and 50.0 on DCHR, which indicates that the system neural-chat+SUS-

Level (0, 1, 2 or 3): 2

Explanation: The user mentions having to set alerts to eat for certain times, which indicates that they have experienced changes in appetite. However, they do not mention any significant weight loss or gain, which would indicate a higher level of change in appetite. Therefore, a level of 2 is appropriate.

Figure 7: Classification and explanation by SUS-Chat-34B

Chat_top5 performed better on 3 metrics (that were achieved by different systems in previous work).

In addition to answering questions without further training, our LLM-based systems could generate local explanations for all their answers, and these explanations are more readable and straightforward compared with the features-based model explanations. More importantly, no examples with labels are needed while using these LLMs, which means that the methods could fit the tasks that lack labeled data, and could be adapted into other tasks and domains. We believe that with the development of computing power, if more user writings (not just selected ones) are included in the prompts and a larger model could be used, higher scores could be achieved using this method.

7 Conclusion and Future Work

In the study, we designed a system that searches for relevant sentences in numerous user writings, and applied it to provide cleaner data for a depression estimation system based on LLMs that automatically answers the questions from the BDI questionnaire. The resulting depression detection system has good performance on several metrics, and could sufficiently explain its answers to every question on the questionnaire for every user, without training on labeled data.

However, due to the randomness of cyberspace, users' speeches on social media platforms cannot fully, objectively, accurately, and consistently describe their status of various depression-related symptoms. In the future, it would be good to collect larger high-quality datasets, so that we can run more experiments to calibrate our system and verify its effectiveness.

Also, with more computing resources and more powerful LLMs, much more user writings could be given to the model rather than filtered out, and it is expected that this would improve the performance. Since our system does not need a large amount of training data, only a small set of labeled examples to design prompts, this is a promising avenue for automatically answering other types of mental health questionnaires, such as PHQ-9, anxiety questionnaires, etc.

Ethics Statement

This study complies with the ACL Ethics Policy[8]. Since the datasets are collected from Reddit and are anonymized, privacy is respected, and no bias is introduced. The filled questionnaires are meant to be for initial information and used as references by professionals, not for self-diagnosis. Dictionaries and Grammarly were used when writing this paper, but no AI assistance was involved in the writing or in the programming.

Limitations

The proposed system on user writing selection would result in datasets mostly in English; thus, the system is limited to English-written texts. The texts in foreign languages were filtered out; therefore, more investigation will be needed in multilingual settings.

We set many restrictions on context length, sampling and model size due to the high requirements of computing resources. These restrictions could affect the performance but can be removed if more resources are available.

In addition, all evaluations are conducted without human health practitioners. It is better to have mental health practitioners review system predictions and explanations and test the system in clinical settings.

Acknowledgements

We thank the Natural Sciences and Engineering Research Council of Canada (NSERC) for supporting our research. We thank the CLEF eRisk organizers, for providing great opportunities for us to explore the task of automatic depression detection based on the BDI questionnaire.

References

A. T. Beck, C. H. Ward, M. Mendelson, J. Mock, and J. Erbaugh. 1961. An Inventory for Measuring De-

[8]https://www.aclweb.org/portal/content/acl-code-ethics

pression. *Archives of General Psychiatry*, 4(6):561–571.

Adriel Boals and Kitty Klein. 2005. Word Use in Emotional Narratives about Failed Romantic Relationships and Subsequent Mental Health. *Journal of Language and Social Psychology*, 24(3):252–268. Publisher: SAGE Publications Inc.

Daniel Cer, Yinfei Yang, Sheng-yi Kong, Nan Hua, Nicole Limtiaco, Rhomni St John, Noah Constant, Mario Guajardo-Cespedes, Steve Yuan, Chris Tar, Yun-Hsuan Sung, Brian Strope, and Ray Kurzweil. 2018. Universal Sentence Encoder. ArXiv:1803.11175 [cs].

Glen Coppersmith, Mark Dredze, Craig Harman, Kristy Hollingshead, and Margaret Mitchell. 2015. CLPsych 2015 Shared Task: Depression and PTSD on Twitter. In *Proceedings of the 2nd Workshop on Computational Linguistics and Clinical Psychology: From Linguistic Signal to Clinical Reality*, pages 31–39, Denver, Colorado. Association for Computational Linguistics.

Tim Dettmers, Artidoro Pagnoni, Ari Holtzman, and Luke Zettlemoyer. 2023. QLoRA: Efficient Finetuning of Quantized LLMs. ArXiv:2305.14314 [cs].

Jacob Devlin, Ming-Wei Chang, Kenton Lee, and Kristina Toutanova. 2019. BERT: Pre-training of Deep Bidirectional Transformers for Language Understanding. ArXiv:1810.04805 [cs].

Adji B. Dieng, Francisco J. R. Ruiz, and David M. Blei. 2020. Topic Modeling in Embedding Spaces. *Transactions of the Association for Computational Linguistics*, 8:439–453.

Ahmed Husseini Orabi, Prasadith Buddhitha, Mahmoud Husseini Orabi, and Diana Inkpen. 2018. Deep Learning for Depression Detection of Twitter Users. In *Proceedings of the Fifth Workshop on Computational Linguistics and Clinical Psychology: From Keyboard to Clinic*, pages 88–97, New Orleans, LA. Association for Computational Linguistics.

Diana Inkpen, Ruba Skaik, Prasadith Buddhitha, Dimo Angelov, and Maxwell Thomas Fredenburgh. 2021. uOttawa at eRisk 2021: Automatic Filling of the Beck's Depression Inventory Questionnaire using Deep Learning.

Sarthak Jain, Sarah Wiegreffe, Yuval Pinter, and Byron C. Wallace. 2020. Learning to Faithfully Rationalize by Construction. ArXiv:2005.00115 [cs].

Pengfei Liu, Weizhe Yuan, Jinlan Fu, Zhengbao Jiang, Hiroaki Hayashi, and Graham Neubig. 2021. Pretrain, Prompt, and Predict: A Systematic Survey of Prompting Methods in Natural Language Processing. ArXiv:2107.13586 [cs] version: 1.

Yinhan Liu, Myle Ott, Naman Goyal, Jingfei Du, Mandar Joshi, Danqi Chen, Omer Levy, Mike Lewis, Luke Zettlemoyer, and Veselin Stoyanov. 2019. RoBERTa: A Robustly Optimized BERT Pretraining Approach. ArXiv:1907.11692 [cs].

David E. Losada, Fabio Crestani, and Javier Parapar. 2017. eRISK 2017: CLEF Lab on Early Risk Prediction on the Internet: Experimental Foundations. In *Experimental IR Meets Multilinguality, Multimodality, and Interaction*, Lecture Notes in Computer Science, pages 346–360, Cham. Springer International Publishing.

David E. Losada, Fabio Crestani, and Javier Parapar. 2019. Overview of eRisk 2019 Early Risk Prediction on the Internet. In *Experimental IR Meets Multilinguality, Multimodality, and Interaction*, Lecture Notes in Computer Science, pages 340–357, Cham. Springer International Publishing.

Kaokao Lv, Wenxin Zhang, and Haihao Shen. 2023. Supervised Fine-Tuning and Direct Preference Optimization on Intel Gaudi2.

Steven Marwaha, Edward Palmer, Trisha Suppes, Emily Cons, Allan H. Young, and Rachel Upthegrove. 2023. Novel and emerging treatments for major depression. *The Lancet*, 401(10371):141–153. Publisher: Elsevier.

Diego Maupomé, Maxime D Armstrong, Fanny Rancourt, and Thomas Soulas. 2021. Early Detection of Signs of Pathological Gambling, Self-Harm and Depression through Topic Extraction and Neural Networks.

Danielle L. Mowery, Albert Park, Craig Bryan, and Mike Conway. 2016. Towards Automatically Classifying Depressive Symptoms from Twitter Data for Population Health. In *Proceedings of the Workshop on Computational Modeling of People's Opinions, Personality, and Emotions in Social Media (PEOPLES)*, pages 182–191, Osaka, Japan. The COLING 2016 Organizing Committee.

Javier Parapar, Patricia Martín-Rodilla, David E. Losada, and Fabio Crestani. 2021. Overview of eRisk 2021: Early Risk Prediction on the Internet. In *Experimental IR Meets Multilinguality, Multimodality, and Interaction: 12th International Conference of the CLEF Association, CLEF 2021, Virtual Event, September 21–24, 2021, Proceedings*, pages 324–344, Berlin, Heidelberg. Springer-Verlag.

Javier Parapar, Patricia Martín-Rodilla, David E. Losada, and Fabio Crestani. 2023. Overview of eRisk 2023: Early Risk Prediction on the Internet. In *Experimental IR Meets Multilinguality, Multimodality, and Interaction*, Lecture Notes in Computer Science, pages 294–315, Cham. Springer Nature Switzerland.

Dheeraj Rajagopal, Vidhisha Balachandran, Eduard Hovy, and Yulia Tsvetkov. 2021. SelfExplain: A Self-Explaining Architecture for Neural Text Classifiers. ArXiv:2103.12279 [cs].

Ruba S. Skaik and Diana Inkpen. 2022. Predicting Depression in Canada by Automatic Filling of Beck's

Depression Inventory Questionnaire. *IEEE Access*, 10:102033–102047. Conference Name: IEEE Access.

Yla R. Tausczik and James W. Pennebaker. 2010. The Psychological Meaning of Words: LIWC and Computerized Text Analysis Methods. *Journal of Language and Social Psychology*, 29(1):24–54. Publisher: SAGE Publications Inc.

Robert Thorstad and Phillip Wolff. 2019. Predicting future mental illness from social media: A big-data approach. *Behavior Research Methods*, 51(4):1586–1600.

Hugo Touvron, Louis Martin, Kevin Stone, Peter Albert, Amjad Almahairi, Yasmine Babaei, Nikolay Bashlykov, Soumya Batra, Prajjwal Bhargava, Shruti Bhosale, Dan Bikel, Lukas Blecher, Cristian Canton Ferrer, Moya Chen, Guillem Cucurull, David Esiobu, Jude Fernandes, Jeremy Fu, Wenyin Fu, Brian Fuller, Cynthia Gao, Vedanuj Goswami, Naman Goyal, Anthony Hartshorn, Saghar Hosseini, Rui Hou, Hakan Inan, Marcin Kardas, Viktor Kerkez, Madian Khabsa, Isabel Kloumann, Artem Korenev, Punit Singh Koura, Marie-Anne Lachaux, Thibaut Lavril, Jenya Lee, Diana Liskovich, Yinghai Lu, Yuning Mao, Xavier Martinet, Todor Mihaylov, Pushkar Mishra, Igor Molybog, Yixin Nie, Andrew Poulton, Jeremy Reizenstein, Rashi Rungta, Kalyan Saladi, Alan Schelten, Ruan Silva, Eric Michael Smith, Ranjan Subramanian, Xiaoqing Ellen Tan, Binh Tang, Ross Taylor, Adina Williams, Jian Xiang Kuan, Puxin Xu, Zheng Yan, Iliyan Zarov, Yuchen Zhang, Angela Fan, Melanie Kambadur, Sharan Narang, Aurelien Rodriguez, Robert Stojnic, Sergey Edunov, and Thomas Scialom. 2023. Llama 2: Open Foundation and Fine-Tuned Chat Models. ArXiv:2307.09288 [cs].

Sho Tsugawa, Yusuke Kikuchi, Fumio Kishino, Kosuke Nakajima, Yuichi Itoh, and Hiroyuki Ohsaki. 2015. Recognizing Depression from Twitter Activity. In *Proceedings of the 33rd Annual ACM Conference on Human Factors in Computing Systems*, CHI '15, pages 3187–3196, New York, NY, USA. Association for Computing Machinery.

Zichao Yang, Diyi Yang, Chris Dyer, Xiaodong He, Alex Smola, and Eduard Hovy. 2016. Hierarchical Attention Networks for Document Classification. In *Proceedings of the 2016 Conference of the North American Chapter of the Association for Computational Linguistics: Human Language Technologies*, pages 1480–1489, San Diego, California. Association for Computational Linguistics.

Andrew Yates, Arman Cohan, and Nazli Goharian. 2017. Depression and Self-Harm Risk Assessment in Online Forums. ArXiv:1709.01848 [cs].

A Appendix

Question	Keywords	Query
Q1	sadness, sad, unhappy	Sadness. I feel sad unhappy cannot stand it.
Q2	pessimism, discouraged, hopeless	Pessimism. I feel discouraged about my future is hopeless and will get worse.
Q3	failure, fail	Past Failure. I have failed.
Q4	pleasure, enjoy	Loss of Pleasure. I don't enjoy things.
Q5	guilty	Guilty Feelings. I feel guilty.
Q6	punishment, punish	Punishment Feelings. I am being punished.
Q7	confidence, disappointed	Self-Dislike. I have lost confidence. I am disappointed in myself.
Q8	criticalness, critical, criticize, blame, fault	Self-Criticalness. I criticize myself blame myself for my faults.
Q9	suicidal, suicide, kill	Suicidal Thoughts or Wishes. I kill myself.
Q10	crying, cry	Crying. I cry.
Q11	agitation, agitate, restless	Agitation. I am restless or agitated keep moving.
Q12	interest, interested	Loss of Interest. It's hard to get interested.
Q13	indecisiveness, decision, decide	Indecisiveness. I find it difficult to make decisions.
Q14	worthlessness, worthless, worthwhile, useful	Worthlessness. I feel worthless not useful.
Q15	energy, energetic	Loss of Energy. I don't have enough energy.
Q16	sleep, sleeping	Changes in Sleeping Pattern. I sleep more or less than usual.
Q17	irritability, irritable, angry	Irritability. I am irritable.
Q18	appetite, food, eat	Changes in Appetite. My appetite is greater or less.
Q19	concentration, concentrate	Concentration Difficulty. It's hard to keep my mind. I can't concentrate.
Q20	tiredness, fatigue, tired	Tiredness or Fatigue. I am tired or fatigued.
Q21	sex	Loss of Interest in Sex. I am less interested in sex.

Table A1: Queries and keywords for each question

	Answer 0	Answer 1	Answer 2	Answer 3
Q1	27 (30%)	47 (52%)	11 (12%)	5 (5%)
Q2	22 (24%)	34 (37%)	20 (22%)	14 (15%)
Q3	22 (24%)	35 (38%)	18 (20%)	15 (16%)
Q4	28 (31%)	33 (36%)	23 (25%)	6 (6%)
Q5	34 (37%)	32 (35%)	12 (13%)	12 (13%)
Q6	60 (66%)	13 (14%)	11 (12%)	6 (6%)
Q7	28 (31%)	17 (18%)	23 (25%)	22 (24%)
Q8	28 (31%)	27 (30%)	23 (25%)	12 (13%)
Q9	41 (45%)	37 (41%)	7 (7%)	5 (5%)
Q10	42 (46%)	23 (25%)	8 (8%)	17 (18%)
Q11	37 (41%)	31 (34%)	14 (15%)	8 (8%)
Q12	28 (31%)	32 (35%)	8 (8%)	22 (24%)
Q13	38 (42%)	21 (23%)	16 (17%)	15 (16%)
Q14	38 (42%)	21 (23%)	20 (22%)	11 (12%)
Q15	17 (18%)	32 (35%)	28 (31%)	13 (14%)
Q16	17 (18%)	36 (40%)	24 (26%)	13 (14%)
Q17	38 (42%)	31 (34%)	16 (17%)	5 (5%)
Q18	32 (35%)	30 (33%)	15 (16%)	13 (14%)
Q19	29 (32%)	25 (27%)	25 (27%)	11 (12%)
Q20	21 (23%)	34 (37%)	21 (23%)	14 (15%)
Q21	51 (56%)	18 (20%)	11 (12%)	10 (11%)
Total	678 (35%)	609 (32%)	354 (19%)	249 (13%)

Table A2: Statistics of labels in the training data for depression estimating

Instructions:

This questionnaire consists of 21 groups of statements. Please read each group of statements carefully, and then pick out the one statement in each group that best describes the way you feel.
If several statements in the group seem to apply equally well, choose the highest number for that group.

1. Sadness
0. I do not feel sad.
1. I feel sad much of the time.
2. I am sad all the time.
3. I am so sad or unhappy that I can't stand it.

2. Pessimism
0. I am not discouraged about my future.
1. I feel more discouraged about my future than I used to be.
2. I do not expect things to work out for me.
3. I feel my future is hopeless and will only get worse.

3. Past Failure
0. I do not feel like a failure.
1. I have failed more than I should have.
2. As I look back, I see a lot of failures.
3. I feel I am a total failure as a person.

4. Loss of Pleasure
0. I get as much pleasure as I ever did from the things I enjoy.
1. I don't enjoy things as much as I used to.
2. I get very little pleasure from the things I used to enjoy.
3. I can't get any pleasure from the things I used to enjoy.

5. Guilty Feelings
0. I don't feel particularly guilty.
1. I feel guilty over many things I have done or should have done.
2. I feel quite guilty most of the time.
3. I feel guilty all of the time.

6. Punishment Feelings
0. I don't feel I am being punished.
1. I feel I may be punished.
2. I expect to be punished.
3. I feel I am being punished.

7. Self-Dislike
0. I feel the same about myself as ever.
1. I have lost confidence in myself.
2. I am disappointed in myself.
3. I dislike myself.

Figure A1: Beck's Depression Inventory (part 1)

8. Self-Criticalness
0. I don't criticize or blame myself more than usual.
1. I am more critical of myself than I used to be.
2. I criticize myself for all of my faults.
3. I blame myself for everything bad that happens.

9. Suicidal Thoughts or Wishes
0. I don't have any thoughts of killing myself.
1. I have thoughts of killing myself, but I would not carry them out.
2. I would like to kill myself.
3. I would kill myself if I had the chance.

10. Crying
0. I don't cry anymore than I used to.
1. I cry more than I used to.
2. I cry over every little thing.
3. I feel like crying, but I can't.

11. Agitation
0. I am no more restless or wound up than usual.
1. I feel more restless or wound up than usual.
2. I am so restless or agitated that it's hard to stay still.
3. I am so restless or agitated that I have to keep moving or doing something.

12. Loss of Interest
0. I have not lost interest in other people or activities.
1. I am less interested in other people or things than before.
2. I have lost most of my interest in other people or things.
3. It's hard to get interested in anything.

13. Indecisiveness
0. I make decisions about as well as ever.
1. I find it more difficult to make decisions than usual.
2. I have much greater difficulty in making decisions than I used to.
3. I have trouble making any decisions.

14. Worthlessness
0. I do not feel I am worthless.
1. I don't consider myself as worthwhile and useful as I used to.
2. I feel more worthless as compared to other people.
3. I feel utterly worthless.

15. Loss of Energy
0. I have as much energy as ever.
1. I have less energy than I used to have.
2. I don't have enough energy to do very much.
3. I don't have enough energy to do anything.

Figure A1: Beck's Depression Inventory (part 2)

16. Changes in Sleeping Pattern
0. I have not experienced any change in my sleeping pattern.
la. I sleep somewhat more than usual.
lb. I sleep somewhat less than usual.
2a. I sleep a lot more than usual.
2b. I sleep a lot less than usual.
3a. I sleep most of the day.
3b. I wake up 1-2 hours early and can't get back to sleep.

17. Irritability
0. I am no more irritable than usual.
1. I am more irritable than usual.
2. I am much more irritable than usual.
3. I am irritable all the time.

18. Changes in Appetite
0. I have not experienced any change in my appetite.
la. My appetite is somewhat less than usual.
lb. My appetite is somewhat greater than usual.
2a. My appetite is much less than before.
2b. My appetite is much greater than usual.
3a. I have no appetite at all.
3b. I crave food all the time.

19. Concentration Difficulty
0. I can concentrate as well as ever.
1. I can't concentrate as well as usual.
2. It's hard to keep my mind on anything for very long.
3. I find I can't concentrate on anything.

20. Tiredness or Fatigue
0. I am no more tired or fatigued than usual.
1. I get more tired or fatigued more easily than usual.
2. I am too tired or fatigued to do a lot of the things I used to do.
3. I am too tired or fatigued to do most of the things I used to do.

21. Loss of Interest in Sex
0. I have not noticed any recent change in my interest in sex.
1. I am less interested in sex than I used to be.
2. I am much less interested in sex now.
3. I have lost interest in sex completely.

Figure A1: Beck's Depression Inventory (part 3)

	Mean	Min	Max
Training-Q1	183.78	31.00	890.00
Training-Q2	276.74	37.00	958.00
Training-Q3	177.38	32.00	743.00
Training-Q4	206.89	39.00	1505.00
Training-Q5	171.72	32.00	994.00
Training-Q6	177.67	27.00	1171.00
Training-Q7	197.49	41.00	923.00
Training-Q8	161.58	44.00	783.00
Training-Q9	245.66	27.00	962.00
Training-Q10	112.19	27.00	445.00
Training-Q11	268.56	33.00	1502.00
Training-Q12	159.20	43.00	567.00
Training-Q13	211.44	25.00	851.00
Training-Q14	201.67	39.00	759.00
Training-Q15	248.41	35.00	716.00
Training-Q16	207.50	50.00	744.00
Training-Q17	217.79	31.00	1406.00
Training-Q18	177.93	32.00	630.00
Training-Q19	223.30	45.00	866.00
Training-Q20	228.73	49.00	960.00
Training-Q21	276.11	61.00	811.00
Training-All	2122.86	287.00	11039.00
Test-Q1	304.71	36.00	1020.00
Test-Q2	413.99	43.00	2312.00
Test-Q3	237.18	29.00	1261.00
Test-Q4	274.61	33.00	945.00
Test-Q5	246.57	28.00	955.00
Test-Q6	250.69	26.00	1154.00
Test-Q7	314.34	42.00	1091.00
Test-Q8	232.59	33.00	693.00
Test-Q9	329.64	26.00	1703.00
Test-Q10	206.88	21.00	978.00
Test-Q11	382.46	37.00	1579.00
Test-Q12	225.05	28.00	960.00
Test-Q13	295.59	22.00	1571.00
Test-Q14	283.14	30.00	1083.00
Test-Q15	357.49	34.00	1115.00
Test-Q16	253.56	42.00	768.00
Test-Q17	322.65	25.00	1080.00
Test-Q18	230.90	40.00	857.00
Test-Q19	321.32	38.00	1022.00
Test-Q20	345.68	41.00	1665.00
Test-Q21	367.70	52.00	1467.00
Test-All	2561.28	202.00	11424.00

Table A3: Statistics of text length of the cleaned data (top-5)

	Mean	Min	Max
Training-Q1	29.69	5.00	181.00
Training-Q2	51.88	5.00	234.00
Training-Q3	26.08	4.00	245.00
Training-Q4	36.30	4.00	255.00
Training-Q5	28.13	4.00	266.00
Training-Q6	31.40	4.00	693.00
Training-Q7	31.10	5.00	314.00
Training-Q8	31.19	4.00	331.00
Training-Q9	43.63	5.00	305.00
Training-Q10	25.19	4.00	213.00
Training-Q11	50.84	6.00	260.00
Training-Q12	27.90	5.00	146.00
Training-Q13	34.90	4.00	159.00
Training-Q14	35.27	5.00	255.00
Training-Q15	47.36	5.00	260.00
Training-Q16	44.61	5.00	260.00
Training-Q17	37.88	4.00	304.00
Training-Q18	35.23	4.00	260.00
Training-Q19	40.43	5.00	245.00
Training-Q20	59.67	4.00	382.00
Training-Q21	47.08	4.00	204.00
Training-All	524.31	77.00	2261.00
Test-Q1	56.11	4.00	438.00
Test-Q2	84.61	6.00	438.00
Test-Q3	37.94	4.00	321.00
Test-Q4	44.86	5.00	438.00
Test-Q5	40.58	4.00	405.00
Test-Q6	42.67	5.00	532.00
Test-Q7	60.31	4.00	438.00
Test-Q8	46.88	4.00	509.00
Test-Q9	76.28	4.00	438.00
Test-Q10	38.52	4.00	326.00
Test-Q11	77.05	6.00	887.00
Test-Q12	43.34	4.00	429.00
Test-Q13	59.45	5.00	752.00
Test-Q14	57.23	6.00	438.00
Test-Q15	78.53	6.00	438.00
Test-Q16	59.17	6.00	398.00
Test-Q17	76.19	4.00	446.00
Test-Q18	38.81	4.00	242.00
Test-Q19	65.39	7.00	367.00
Test-Q20	63.86	5.00	398.00
Test-Q21	90.78	6.00	445.00
Test-All	742.86	61.00	2777.00

Table A4: Statistics of text length of the cleaned data (top-1)

Question	Rephrased symptom
Q1	how sad the user feels
Q2	how discouraged the user is about future
Q3	how much the user feels like a failure
Q4	how much the user loses pleasure from things
Q5	how often the user feels guilty
Q6	how much the user feels punished
Q7	how much the user feels disappointed about him/herself
Q8	how often the user criticizes or blames him/herself
Q9	how much the user thinks about killing him/herself
Q10	how often the user cries
Q11	how much the user feels restless or agitated
Q12	how much the user loses interest in things
Q13	how difficult the user to make decisions
Q14	how much the user feels worthless
Q15	how much the user loses energy
Q16	how much the user experienced changes in sleeping
Q17	how much the user feels irritable
Q18	how much the user experienced changes in appetite
Q19	how difficult the user to concentrate
Q20	how much the user feels tired or fatigued
Q21	how much the user loses interest in sex

Table A5: Rephrased symptoms on the BDI questionnaire

Analysing Relevance of Discourse Structure for Improved Mental Health Estimation

Navneet Agarwal[1] and **Gaël Dias**[1] and **Sonia Dollfus**[2]
[1]Normandie Univ, UNICAEN, ENSICAEN, CNRS, GREYC, 14000 Caen, France.
[2]CHU de Caen, Service de Psychiatrie; Normandie Univ, UNICAEN, ISTS,
GIP Cyceron; Normandie Univ, UNICAEN, UFR de Médecine, 14000 Caen, France.

Abstract

Automated depression estimation has received significant research attention in recent years as a result of its growing impact on the global community. Within the context of studies based on patient-therapist interview transcripts, most researchers treat the dyadic discourse as a sequence of unstructured sentences, thus ignoring the discourse structure within the learning process. In this paper we propose Multi-view architectures that divide the input transcript into patient and therapist views based on sentence type in an attempt to utilize symmetric discourse structure for improved model performance. Experiments on DAIC-WOZ dataset for binary classification task within depression estimation show advantages of Multi-view architecture over sequential input representations. Our model also outperforms the current state-of-the-art results and provide new SOTA performance on test set of DAIC-WOZ dataset.

1 Introduction

In recent years, automated depression estimation has attracted significant research initiatives which is unsurprising given the widespread impact and heavy toll of depression. Within the context of depression estimation based on text, two major categories of input exist: (1) social media posts (twitter and reddit) of self-declared patients and (2) clinical interviews between patients and therapist. Detection of depression is a challenging problem with patient-therapist interviews being the common practice to analyse a patient's mental health within clinical setting. Within such dialogues, therapists look for indicative symptoms such as loss of interest, sadness, exhaustion, sleeping and eating disorders, etc. within patient's responses and base their evaluation on this information. Complementary to these interviews, different self-assessment screening tools have also been defined such as the Personal Health Questionnaire depression scale, with PHQ-8 being considered a valid diagnosis and severity measure for depressive disorders (Kroenke, 2012). Throughout the literature, different strategies have been proposed for automatic estimation of depression, which consists of inferring the screening tool score based on the interview transcript. Multi-modal models combine inputs from different modalities (Ray et al., 2019; Qureshi et al., 2019; Niu et al., 2021). Multi-task architectures simultaneously learn related tasks (Qureshi et al., 2019, 2020). Gender-aware models explore the impact of gender on depression estimation (Bailey and Plumbley, 2021; Oureshi et al., 2021). Hierarchical models process transcripts at different granularity levels (Mallol-Ragolta et al., 2019; Xezonaki et al., 2020). Attention models integrate external knowledge from mental health lexicons (Xezonaki et al., 2020). Feature-based solutions compute multiple multi-modal characteristics (Dai et al., 2021). Graph-based systems aim to study complex structures within interview transcripts (Hong et al., 2022; Niu et al., 2021). Symptom-based models treat depression estimation as an extension of the symptom prediction problem (Milintsevich et al., 2023). Domain specific language models are built (Ji et al., 2022) and large language models are prefix-tuned to automate depression level estimation (Lau et al., 2023).

Despite this extensive list of research initiatives, ways to express the structure of an input transcript remains a relatively unexplored research direction. Indeed, most related works treat the overall transcript as a sequence of sentences taking into account the information contained in therapist questions and patient responses. These models disregard interview structure and consider it to be an unstructured list of sentences, forcing the model to learn inter-dependencies within the discourse. In this paper we argue that discourse structure combined with sentence type can improve models learning ability by reducing the number of noisy transactions within the data. In order to validate our hy-

Proceedings of the 9th Workshop on Computational Linguistics and Clinical Psychology (CLPsych 2024), pages 127–132
March 21, 2024

Depression severity	Data split		
	Train	Val.	Test
No symptoms [0..4]	47	17	22
Mild [5..9]	29	6	11
Non-depressed Total	76	23	33
Moderate [10..14]	20	5	5
Moderately severe [15..19]	7	6	7
Severe [20..24]	4	1	2
Depressed Total	31	12	14
Total	107	35	47

Table 1: Number of interviews for each depressive symptom severity category in the DAIC-WOZ dataset, distributed by train, validation and test sets.

pothesis, we design Multi-view architectures that separate a dialogue stream based on sentence type into two different views, i.e. the therapist view and the patient view. As such, the interview structure is taken into account by learning interactions (1) within the views i.e. interactions between questions only and answers only, and (2) between the two views i.e. interactions between the corresponding questions and answers. This allows the models to focus on specific structures of the transcript as well as control the discourse symmetry. Experiments over the DAIC-WOZ dataset show improvements in model performance with multi-view architecture and provide new state of the art results on the test set of DAIC-WOZ dataset.

2 Related work

Different architectures and strategies have been used throughout literature to train automated models for depression estimation based on patient-therapist interviews. Qureshi et al. (2019) explore the possibility of combining audio, visual and textual input features into a single architecture using attention fusion networks. They further show that training the model for regression and classification simultaneously on the same dataset provides improvements in results. Ray et al. (2019) present a similar framework that invokes attention mechanisms at different layers to combine several low-level and mid-level features from audio, visual and textual modalities of the participants' inputs. Qureshi et al. (2020) propose to simultaneously learn both depression level estimation and emotion recognition on the basis that depression is a disorder of impaired emotion regulation. Building on the success of hierarchical models for document classification, different studies (Mallol-Ragolta et al., 2019; Xezonaki et al., 2020) propose to encode patient-therapist interviews with hierarchical structures, showing boosts in performance. Xezonaki et al. (2020) further extend their proposal and integrate affective information (emotion, sentiment, valence and psycho-linguistic annotations) from existing lexicons in the form of specific embeddings. Exploring a different research direction, Oureshi et al. (2021) study the impact of gender on depression level estimation and build four different gender-aware models that show steady improvements over gender-agnostic models. Along the same line, Bailey and Plumbley (2021) study gender bias from audio features and find that deep learning models based on raw audio are more robust to gender bias than ones based on other common hand-crafted features, such as mel-spectrogram. Although most strategies rely on deep learning architectures, a different research direction is proposed by Dai et al. (2021), who build a topic-wise feature vector based on a context-aware analysis over different modalities (audio, video, and text). Niu et al. (2021) use graph structures within their architecture to grasp relational contextual information from audio and text modality. They propose a hierarchical context-aware model to capture and integrate contextual information among relational interview questions at word and question-answer pair levels. Within the same context, Hong et al. (2022) use graphical representation of the input that encodes word level interactions within each transcript. They propose Schema-based Graph Neural Networks (SGNN) and use multiple passes of the message passing mechanism (MPM) (Gilmer et al., 2017; Xu et al., 2019) to update the schema at each node of the text graph.

Burdisso et al. (2023) define a more complex input graph structure that models the interactions between transcripts and a global word graph. They use an inductive version of GCN (Wang et al., 2022) and define w-GCN that mitigates the assumptions of locality and equal importance of self-loops within GCN. Milintsevich et al. (2023) treat binary classification as a symptom profile prediction problem and train a multi-target hierarchical regression model to predict individual depression symptoms from patient-therapist interview transcripts. Building upon the success of language models in understanding textual data, Ji et al. (2022) fine-tune different BERT-based models on mental health data and provide a pre-trained masked language model for generating domain specific text representations. Lau et al. (2023) further account for the lack of large-scale high-quality datasets in mental health domain and propose the use of prefix-tuning as a parameter-efficient way of fine-tuning language models for mental health.

3 Dataset

For our experiments we use the Distress Analysis Interview Corpus - Wizard of Oz (DAIC-WOZ) dataset which is part of a larger corpus, the Distress Analysis Interview Corpus (DAIC)(Gratch et al., 2014). The dataset contains clinical interviews aimed towards psychological evaluation of participants for detecting conditions such as anxiety, depression and post-traumatic stress disorder. These interviews were collected with the goal of developing a computer agent that interviews participants to identify verbal and non-verbal signs for mental illness(DeVault et al., 2014). In particular, we use Wizard-of-Oz interviews from the dataset which were conducted by virtual agent Ellie, controlled by a human interviewer from another room. These interviews have been transcribed and annotated for a variety of verbal and non-verbal features. Along with the transcripts, the dataset also contains corresponding visual and audio features extracted from the interview recordings. Depression severity is accessed based on PHQ-8 depression scale, and score of 10 is used as threshold to differentiate between depressed and non-depressed participants. The dataset is divided into training, development and test sets containing 107, 35 and 47 interviews respectively. The dataset is biased towards lower PHQ-8 scores with almost 70% data points belonging to negative class in case of binary classification (PHQ-8 score < 10) and only 4 instances with severe depression (PHQ-8 score > 20). Refer table 1 for more details.

4 Methodology

Studies have shown that questions asked by the therapist during an interview contain relevant information and provide context to patient responses. Although Xezonaki et al.(Xezonaki et al., 2020) validate the importance of therapist questions for depression estimation, they represent the input as an unstructured sequence of sentences. Within this paper we emphasise on the importance of discourse structure for better understanding the input text. To take into account both patient and therapist information, while maintaining discourse symmetry and structure, we propose Multi-view architecture that

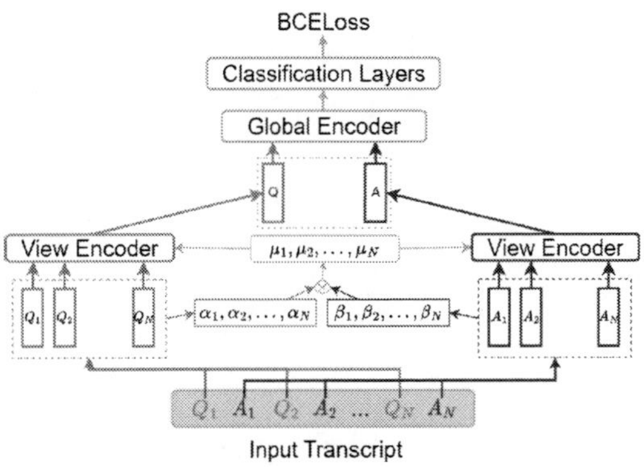

Figure 1: Multi-view architecture based on sentence transformer based text encoding. View specific information in highlighted in red and blue with orange highlighting cross attention and green the global network.

utilize sentence types to divide the interview into different views. Our aim is to use this view based division of the transcript to control the number of noisy interactions, between unrelated questions and answers, learned by sequential models, allowing more efficient training of neural network models.

4.1 Multi-view Strategy

Figure 1 illustrates the proposed Multi-view architecture. The underlying idea is to learn transcript level representation of the two views separately before fusing them using *Global encoder* layer to generate transcript level representation of the interview containing information from both questions and answers. In particular, dedicated sub-networks, patient network and therapist network, are defined for processing corresponding view inputs ($Q_1, Q_2, .., Q_N$ and $A_1, A_2, .., A_N$). These sub-networks use multihead attention mechanism in order to combine sentence level text encodings and learn interview level representations, Q and A, of the views. *View encoders* defined within this model also use cross attention for a co-dependent learning of individual views. The coherent structure of a dialogue plays an essential role in global understanding of the message conveyed by the patient. Patient responses often rely on therapist questions in order to contextualize their meaning. This is particularly true for one word responses like "yes", which don't hold much relevance by themselves. As a consequence, tackling the codependency between questions and answers[1] is of the

[1]Note also that a question that might not seem to be important, but for which the answer is meaningful, should definitely be highlighted by the learning model.

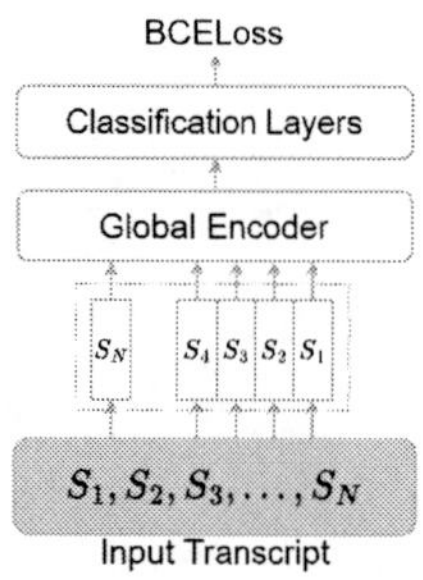

Figure 2: Baseline configuration based on unstructured sequential interview representation.

utmost importance for the learning process. As a consequence, we propose to design a multi-view architecture with inter-view attention (shown with orange color in Figure 1) that transfer attention scores from one view to another, following the cross-attention paradigm (Sood et al., 2020). Formally, attention scores $\mu_1, \mu_2, ..., \mu_M$ are shared between the two *view encoders*, and are the result of function $\mu_i = f(\alpha_i, \beta_i)$ that combines the individual view attention scores α_i and β_i.

Baseline: We define a baseline configuration that uses comparable architecture for a fair comparison. Within this configuration, interviews are treated as a sequence of unstructured sentences and passed through an encoder layer to learn interview level representation which in-turn is passed through classification layers to get final prediction (Figure 2).

5 Experimental Setup

We use sentence-transformers (Reimers and Gurevych, 2019), all-mpnet-base-v2 in particular, for generating sentence level text encodings used within our experiments. Adam optimizer with weighted binary cross entropy loss (BCELoss) is used during training to account for class imbalance in data. Learning rate is treated as a hyper-parameter and tuned during training. Both encoders, *global encoder* and *view encoder*, are defined using transformer based Multihead Attention Networks (Vaswani et al., 2017). Cross-attention at *view encoder* level is also defined using multi-head attention mechanism with inputs from both views playing corresponding roles within query, key and value. Various definitions of function $f(\alpha_i, \beta_i)$ were experimented with and f was finally defined as a mean operation. Pytorch framework is used for network definition and training of the models.

6 Results and Analysis

Experiments were conducted on the DAIC-WOZ dataset (Gratch et al., 2014) and the best model is chosen based on macro F1 over the development set and evaluated based on performance on test set. Table 2 compares performance of multi-view model (*Multi-view model*) against the sequential configuration *Sequential model* considered in our work. In particular, the multi-view model evidences better performance compared to sequential input configuration for both evaluation metrics considered in our study. Improvements of 6.6% on macro F1 score and 10.6% on Unweighted Average Recall (UAR) are obtained over the baseline. From the results we can assess that multi-view architectures are a better alternative to process question-answer based interviews, thus highlighting the significance of retaining structural information of a dialogue. In particular, multi-view architectures utilize the interview semantic structure to limit the amount of noisy interactions learned by the model and allowing more efficient learning.

During our experiments with different definitions of cross-attention function $f(\alpha, \beta)$, we observed that results obtained with non-balanced attention functions (i.e. only patient attention, only therapist attention, max) are lower compared to the balanced architectures (i.e. Mean, Learnable). Within non-balanced functions, attention scores are transferred from one view to the other based on hypothesis that only one of the views drives the learning process. Our results confirm that both views, questions and answers, are relevant, and selecting either one as the sole criteria for importance can be counterproductive. $Mean$ function evidenced best performance within our experiments.

Table 2 also shows that our multi-view model provides new state-of-the-art results over the test set of DAIC-WOZ dataset, successfully outperforming recent initiatives with comparable setups (HAN(Xezonaki et al., 2020), HCAN(Mallol-Ragolta et al., 2019)) as well as those relying on external knowledge (HAN+L(Xezonaki et al., 2020)) or different modalities (SVM:m-M&S(Dai et al., 2021)). Note that the reported results are taken directly from the original papers, and that some related work surprisingly do not evidence results over the test split, such as HCAG and HCAG+T (Niu et al., 2021), although they highly perform on the development set.

Architectures	Modality	macro F1 (Dev)	macro F1 Test	UAR (Dev)	UAR Test
Raw Audio (Bailey and Plumbley, 2021)	Audio	(0.66)	-	-	-
SVM:m-M&S (Dai et al., 2021)	All	(0.96)	0.67	-	-
HCAG (Niu et al., 2021)	Text + Audio	(0.92)	-	(0.92)	-
HCAN (Mallol-Ragolta et al., 2019)	Text	(0.51)	0.63	(0.54)	0.66
HLGAN (Mallol-Ragolta et al., 2019)	Text	(0.60)	0.35	(0.60)	0.33
HAN (Xezonaki et al., 2020)	Text	(0.46)	0.62	(0.48)	0.63
HAN+L (Xezonaki et al., 2020)	Text	(0.62)	0.70	(0.63)	0.70
HCAG+T (Niu et al., 2021)	Text	(0.77)	-	(0.82)	-
Symptom prediction (Milintsevich et al., 2023)	Text	(0.80)	0.74	-	-
Sequential model	Text	(0.79)	0.75	(0.78)	0.75
Multi-view model	Text	(0.77)	**0.80**	(0.76)	**0.83**

Table 2: SOTA results on DAIC-WOZ. T, V and A stand for Text, Visual and Audio modalities.

7 Conclusion and Future Work

In this paper, we propose a multi-view architecture for automated depression estimation that treats patient-therapist interviews as a combination of two views (therapist questions and patient answers). The underlying idea it to not only use inputs from both agents within the interview (patient and therapist), but also retain the inherent structure of the discourse for improved learning. In particular, the presented multi-view approach allows to handle discourse symmetry as well as discourse structure, thus outperforming the simple encoding of the input data as a sequence of sentences. Results on the DAIC-WOZ show that the multi-view architecture steadily outperforms comparable baselines and evidences new state-of-the-art results. Based on the insightful recent research of Xezonaki et al. (Xezonaki et al., 2020), we plan to further improve our results by incorporating external knowledge from different medical resources, such as lexicon or psychiatrist manual annotation.

8 Acknowledgement

This research is supported by the FHU A^2M^2P project funded by the G4 University Hospitals of Amiens, Caen, Lille and Rouen (France).

9 Limitations

Within this paper we explore the role of interview structure on the learning ability of the neural network models. Results from our experiments show that Multi-view architectures provide a better alternate for combining patient and therapist inputs while taking into account the discourse structure. Multi-view architectures focus on using transcript structure in order to limit noisy interactions within the input. The co-dependency between the corresponding questions and answers within the interview is only modeled using shared attention weights. This limits the models ability to study patient's answers in context of associated therapist questions (and vise-versa), and requires further research into defining a complete solution.

10 Ethical Considerations

Given application in medical domain and the nature of this specific task, data privacy and protection is the biggest concern associated with the field. Depression is a condition rooted within the various aspects of a patients life, consequently, its assessment requires discussing a patient's personal and professional lives. Within our research the original data has already been anonymized and all personal information has been removed.

References

Andrew Bailey and Mark D. Plumbley. 2021. Gender bias in depression detection using audio features. In *29th European Signal Processing Conference (EUSIPCO)*, pages 596–600.

Sergio Burdisso, Esaú VILLATORO-TELLO, Srikanth Madikeri, and Petr Motlicek. 2023. Node-weighted graph convolutional network for depression detection in transcribed clinical interviews. In *Proceedings of Interspeech*.

Zhijun Dai, Heng Zhou, Qingfang Ba, Yang Zhou, Lifeng Wang, and Guochen Li. 2021. Improving depression prediction using a novel feature selection algorithm coupled with context-aware analysis. *Journal of Affective Disorders*, 295:1040–1048.

David DeVault, Ron Artstein, Grace Benn, Teresa Dey, Ed Fast, Alesia Gainer, Kallirroi Georgila, Jon Gratch, Arno Hartholt, Margaux Lhommet, et al. 2014. Simsensei kiosk: A virtual human interviewer for healthcare decision support. In *International Conference on Autonomous Agents and Multi-agent Systems (AAMAS)*, pages 1061–1068.

Justin Gilmer, Samuel S Schoenholz, Patrick F Riley, Oriol Vinyals, and George E Dahl. 2017. Neural message passing for quantum chemistry. In *International conference on machine learning*, pages 1263–1272. PMLR.

Jonathan Gratch, Ron Artstein, Gale Lucas, Giota Stratou, Stefan Scherer, Angela Nazarian, Rachel Wood, Jill Boberg, David DeVault, Stacy Marsella, et al. 2014. The distress analysis interview corpus of human and computer interviews. In *9th International Conference on Language Resources and Evaluation (LREC)*, pages 3123–3128.

Simin Hong, Anthony G. Cohn, and David Crossland Hogg. 2022. Using graph representation learning with schema encoders to measure the severity of depressive symptoms. In *10th International Conference on Learning Representations (ICLR)*.

Shaoxiong Ji, Tianlin Zhang, Luna Ansari, Jie Fu, Prayag Tiwari, and Erik Cambria. 2022. MentalBERT: Publicly available pretrained language models for mental healthcare. In *13th Language Resources and Evaluation Conference (LREC)*, pages 7184–7190.

Kurt Kroenke. 2012. Enhancing the clinical utility of depression screening. *Canadian Medical Aassociation Journal*, 184(3):281–282.

Clinton Lau, Xiaodan Zhu, and Wai-Yip Chan. 2023. Automatic depression severity assessment with deep learning using parameter-efficient tuning. *Frontiers in Psychiatry*, 14:1160291.

Adria Mallol-Ragolta, Ziping Zhao, Lukas Stappen, Nicholas Cummins, and Björn W. Schuller. 2019. A hierarchical attention network-based approach for depression detection from transcribed clinical interviews. In *Interspeech (INTERSPEECH)*, pages 221–225. ISCA.

Kirill Milintsevich, Kairit Sirts, and Gaël Dias. 2023. Towards automatic text-based estimation of depression through symptom prediction. *Brain Informatics*, 10(1):1–14.

Meng Niu, Kai Chen, Qingcai Chen, and Lufeng Yang. 2021. Hcag: A hierarchical context-aware graph attention model for depression detection. In *IEEE International Conference on Acoustics, Speech and Signal Processing (ICASSP)*, pages 4235–4239.

Syed Arbaaz Oureshi, Gaël Dias, Sriparna Saha, and Mohammed Hasanuzzaman. 2021. Gender-aware estimation of depression severity level in a multimodal setting. In *2021 International Joint Conference on Neural Networks (IJCNN)*, pages 1–8. IEEE.

Syed Arbaaz Qureshi, Gaël Dias, Mohammed Hasanuzzaman, and Sriparna Saha. 2020. Improving depression level estimation by concurrently learning emotion intensity. *IEEE Computational Intelligence Magazine*, 15(3):47–59.

Syed Arbaaz Qureshi, Sriparna Saha, Mohammed Hasanuzzaman, and Gaël Dias. 2019. Multitask representation learning for multimodal estimation of depression level. *IEEE Intelligent Systems*, 34(5):45–52.

Anupama Ray, Siddharth Kumar, Rutvik Reddy, Prerana Mukherjee, and Ritu Garg. 2019. Multi-level attention network using text, audio and video for depression prediction. In *9th International on Audio/Visual Emotion Challenge and Workshop (AVEC)*, page 81–88.

Nils Reimers and Iryna Gurevych. 2019. Sentence-BERT: Sentence embeddings using Siamese BERT-networks. In *Proceedings of the 2019 Conference on Empirical Methods in Natural Language Processing and the 9th International Joint Conference on Natural Language Processing (EMNLP-IJCNLP)*, pages 3982–3992, Hong Kong, China. Association for Computational Linguistics.

Ekta Sood, Simon Tannert, Philipp Müller, and Andreas Bulling. 2020. Improving natural language processing tasks with human gaze-guided neural attention. In *Annual Conference on Neural Information Processing Systems (NeurIPS)*.

Ashish Vaswani, Noam Shazeer, Niki Parmar, Jakob Uszkoreit, Llion Jones, Aidan N Gomez, Łukasz Kaiser, and Illia Polosukhin. 2017. Attention is all you need. *Advances in neural information processing systems*, 30.

Kunze Wang, Soyeon Caren Han, and Josiah Poon. 2022. Induct-gcn: Inductive graph convolutional networks for text classification. In *2022 26th International Conference on Pattern Recognition (ICPR)*, pages 1243–1249. IEEE.

Danai Xezonaki, Georgios Paraskevopoulos, Alexandros Potamianos, and Shrikanth Narayanan. 2020. Affective conditioning on hierarchical attention networks applied to depression detection from transcribed clinical interviews. In *Interspeech (INTERSPEECH)*, pages 4556–4560.

Keyulu Xu, Weihua Hu, Jure Leskovec, and Stefanie Jegelka. 2019. How powerful are graph neural networks? In *International Conference on Learning Representations*.

Using Daily Language to Understand Drinking: Multi-Level Longitudinal Differential Language Analysis

Matthew Matero*[1], Huy Vu*[1], August Håkan Nilsson[2]
Syeda Mahwish[1], Young-Min Cho[3], James R. McKay[3]
Johannes Eichstaedt[4], Richard N. Rosenthal[1], Lyle Ungar[3], H. Andrew Schwartz[1]
[1] Stony Brook University [2] Oslo Metropolitan University
[3] University of Pennsylvania [4] Stanford University
{mmatero,has}@cs.stonybrook.edu

Abstract

Analyses for linking language with psychological factors or behaviors predominately treat linguistic features as a static set, working with a single document per person or aggregating across multiple documents into a single set of features. This limits language to mainly shed light on between-person differences rather than changes in behavior within-person. Here, we collected a novel dataset of daily surveys where participants were asked to describe their experienced well-being and report the number of alcoholic beverages they had within the past 24 hours. Through this data, we first build a multi-level forecasting model that can capture within-person change and leverage both the psychological features of the person and daily well-being responses. Then, we propose a longitudinal version of differential language analysis that finds patterns associated with drinking more (e.g. social events) and less (e.g. task-oriented), as well as distinguishing patterns of heavy drinks versus light drinkers.

1 Introduction

Language generated by people occurs at multiple levels of analysis, from tokens to documents to sequences of documents (Almodaresi et al., 2017). While past works have suggested modeling language hierarchically given the available history of a person's language (Acheampong et al., 2021; son; Lynn et al., 2017; Matero et al., 2021b; Soni et al., 2022), few techniques exist for language analyses geared toward eliciting language associated with psychological or behavioral changes (Tsakalidis et al., 2022). Where traditional techniques like differential language analysis (Schwartz et al., 2013) only reveal differences *between* people rather than changes *within* people around particular behaviors.

Typically, NLP-based approaches represent language from people as aggregations, such as of message or token embeddings over all time (Ganesan et al., 2021; Almodaresi et al., 2017; Matero et al., 2021a). While there have been some predictive-focused works that have experimented with forecasting based on language, they are either focused on psychological (latent) attributes (Halder et al., 2017; Matero and Schwartz, 2020) or focused on groups/communities of people rather than individuals (Matero et al., 2023), less has been done toward bringing out linguistic insights (e.g. differential language analysis (Schwartz et al., 2013)) leveraging the inherent multi-level longitudinal structure of human language. In this work, we present and evaluate (1) a longitudinal, multi-level approach to forecasting an individual's behavior rather than latent human attributes (e.g. emotions), namely daily consumption of alcoholic beverages, and (2) a longitudinal, multi-level differential language analysis to illuminate daily language patterns most commonly associated with heavier drinking both across different individuals and within one individual.

With roughly 10% of U.S. adults having an alcohol use disorder (NIH, 2023), research to understand an individual's alcohol consumption pattern and motivation is a pressing health concern. By modeling one's behavior over time we can more accurately predict future consumption or interpret their motivations for drinking alcohol through the use of longitudinal multi-level models. Such a model could be used to detect the risk of unhealthy drinking. These personalized models are naturally geared towards time-series forecasting, where the goal is to understand coming trends (Eichstaedt et al., 2018; Halder et al., 2017).

Our contributions include: (1) introduction of a sequential forecasting model that leverages language to accurately predict the number of alcoholic drinks a person will consume within a 24-hour window, (2) integration of user-level features (static across time) to build a multi-level sequential model for additional context in prediction, (3) empirical evaluation on dimensionality reduction of language

*Equal Contribution

Proceedings of the 9th Workshop on Computational Linguistics and Clinical Psychology (CLPsych 2024), pages 133–144
March 21, 2024

features cross-time concerning predictive power, and (4) insights into linguistic patterns that are longitudinally predictable of high or low daily drinking rates.

2 Related Work

Alcohol Consumption Psychological research has long demonstrated the complexities of alcohol consumption. On one hand, the general person drinks more on days when they feel more positive affect and not when they feel more negative effect (Dora et al., 2022), and general drinking level has a positive correlation to life satisfaction (Geiger and MacKerron, 2016; Massin and Kopp, 2014). On the other hand, this relationship is hump-shaped such that the happiest people are low to moderate drinkers and heavy drinkers are worse off with decreases in well-being (Geiger and MacKerron, 2016; Massin and Kopp, 2011).

Heavy alcohol consumption can lead to an Alcohol Use Disorder, a disorder that can cause morbidity (Carvalho et al., 2019) and decreased psychosocial functioning (Kendler et al., 2016). Predicting within-person alcohol consumption from scales that measure emotion such as positive affect have shown correlations between participant-aggregated affect and participant-aggregated number of drinks consumed of r = .10 and a non-significant relationship to negative affect (Dora et al., 2022). A likely reason for the positive relationship between drinking and positive affect is that most drinking occurs socially (Creswell et al., 2022) and spending time with others is strongly associated with reporting high levels of positive affect (Grimm et al., 2015; Killingsworth and Gilbert, 2010; Diener and Seligman, 2002).

Language and Drinking While there exists a few studies focused on predicting who is at risk for alcohol abuse from language, they use historical data to make a single prediction in time rather than predicting how behaviors may change. Both works of Jose et al. (2022) and Curtis et al. (2018) investigate the connection of historical social media language and their association with at-risk drinking. However, they both focus on different levels of analysis and outcomes with Jose et al. (2022) focusing on individual-level and the ability to predict one's risk-level for alcohol consumption (e.g. AUDIT-C) (Bush et al., 1998) and Curtis et al. (2018) leveraging county data with responses to the Behavioral Risk Factor Surveillance System (BRFSS); a U.S. health survey where someone may self-report their level of heavy drinking.

Longitudinal & Multi-level NLP is very familiar with sequence processing leveraging various techniques such as attention networks (Vaswani et al., 2017) and seq2seq modeling (Luong et al., 2015; Bahdanau et al., 2014). Even still, explicitly modeling the temporal dimension is largely under-utilized by most NLP models as words and sentences are often uttered at what can be assumed as the same point in time except for the case where language is considered to reflect a person (Soni et al., 2022; Matero and Schwartz, 2020). Sequential models designed explicitly for temporal modeling have been proposed but not widely adopted by the NLP community (Zhu et al., 2017; Che et al., 2018).

One could go one step further and adapt these sequential time-series models to account for the inherent hierarchical nature of language over time from a person through multi-level modeling. Multi-level modeling allows the model to operate on different levels of granularity and offers a natural way of framing the problem (Hox, 1998). Due to this natural hierarchy, in this case, defined by dynamic states and static traits cross-time (Su et al., 2019; Gana et al., 2019; Van der Werff et al., 2019), we can develop a model to account for this. Multi-level modeling is a common approach in psychology research, for example understanding substance cravings and personality (Parent-Lamarche et al., 2021; Alayan et al., 2019).

Lastly, we extend past works that explored the associations between social media language and drinking behavior by examining the association between topics of daily language, through self-reported experienced well-being responses, and alcohol consumption or risk. Differential language analysis (DLA) is commonly used to study topics of conversation and their ability to reliably predict certain outcomes (Schwartz et al., 2013; Eichstaedt et al., 2018; Schwartz et al., 2014; Kern et al., 2016). While the work of Jose et al. (2022) also investigated the relationship between specific social media topics and drinking risk, they focused on the between-person signals instead of within-person signals as in our approach. These within-person language signals are important for understanding what drives an individual to drink and are extracted via a fixed effects model that accounts for between-person heterogeneity (Hedges, 1994).

3 Data

We collected a novel dataset with the consent of study participants for a longitudinal investigation of drinking behavior. Upon enrollment, each participant also gave consent to access their Facebook posts and answer a "baseline" survey that asks various questions regarding mental health and well-being. Responses from the baseline survey include: measures of depression and anxiety (Johnson, 2014), AUDIT-C (Bush et al., 1998), and demographics.

Further, participants are asked to complete 14 days of ecological momentary assessments (EMA), short surveys expected to take a few minutes to complete on their phones. Each EMA contains a free response field called *affective essay*, where the participant describes their experienced well-being, emotions and daily experiences, as well as a question asking them how many alcoholic beverages they consumed in the past 24 hours[1]. Participants were selected to respond once or thrice daily (morning, afternoon, evening). The assignment was performed randomly (50/50) for which group a person was placed into.

The dataset samples from U.S. restaurant and hospitality workers (e.g., bartenders, servers, etc). Recruitment occurred between June 2020 and June 2021 from various sources such as organizations reaching out to their members via mailing lists or snowball sampling from social media. Sign-up and consent was handled via Qualtrix, where directions were given to download a companion app designed to be used for data collection.

Figure 1 illustrates the drinking behaviors from a random sample of 30 participants over the 14 days ordered by AUDIT-C score. The white empty cells indicate missing data points (no response) for that particular day. We observe that participants with higher AUDIT-C scores tend to drink more often and with a higher number of drinks.

Time-series Processing We split our time series into a train and test set based on out-of-sample time (e.g., forecasting) with a split such that each person's last two days of responses are reserved for testing. When building our forecasting dataset, we filter participants for those that responded to at least three days of EMAs. This is done so that these users can still be used for testing, as they have at least one authentic response to use as input.

[1]*affective essays* are 200 characters in length

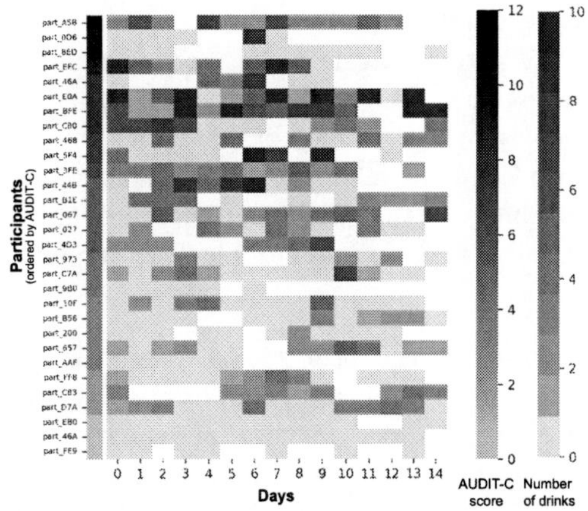

Figure 1: Overview of drinking behaviors data from a random sample of 30 participants ordered by AUDIT-C score. White cells indicate days to missing data where the participant did not respond to any EMA.

Additionally, we restrict to those users who were selected for three responses per day thus allowing our model to have more daily language to use as a signal for prediction. After applying this filter, we are left with 242 people, where 219 are kept for training and 23 are used as a held-out validation set for hyperparameter tuning.

For building our time-series features, we include an averaged RoBERTa embedding (Liu et al., 2019) of all *affective essays* of a given day, which is then dimensionality reduced to using pre-trained PCA models from Ganesan et al. (2021). At each time step, we concatenate these language features with the number of drinks and another small set of features representing a day-of-week marker defined as a 7-dimension one hot encoded feature space.

Lastly, to deal with participants who do not always remember to respond each day, we apply a simple imputation technique that fills missing gaps with the last available authentic response (Che et al., 2018).

4 Methods

Document Sequential Model We apply transformer networks (Vaswani et al., 2017) to our time-series as shown in Figure 2 describing our architecture. After the sequence is processed through the transformer network, the final representation is an average pooling over the output vectors for each time step. The average pooled representation is then run through a dense layer to predict the daily number of drinks[2].

We also investigate multiple configurations of our models, namely multivariate and univariate forecasting. In the case of univariate, only past knowledge of drinking is used, such that a single variable represents each time-step. In multivariate, all available features per time-step are used as inputs.

Multi-level Sequential Model We incorporate both user-level variables and historic document-level social media language into our document-only sequential model. These features have been linked to both overall well-being and drinking behavior (Jose et al., 2022; De Choudhury et al., 2013). Thus, we include them as a separate module to perform a type of user-factor adaptation (Lynn et al., 2017).

The user-level features are as follows: degree of depression and anxiety, AUDIT-C, age, gender, and RoBERTa embeddings of the past two years of Facebook language that occurred before the start of the EMA period. The RoBERTa embeddings are reduced to 64 dimensions using the same pre-trained models from Ganesan et al. (2021). The models from Ganesan et al. (2021) are used as they have shown to be competitive on small data for human-level tasks and are pre-trained over a larger corpus.

These features are highlighted on the left side of Figure 2. They are concatenated with the average pooled representation of the document sequential transformer network and passed through a meta-learner, which is trained to perform the final prediction. The meta-learner used is a 2-layer feed-forward neural network with relu activation between the linear layers. The use of a small neural network as the meta-learner is motivated by allowing the model to adapt to the non-linear interactions between user-level and sequential features.

Alternative Models & Baselines We evaluated two heuristic baselines and two statistical baselines. These chosen heuristic baselines are often quite competitive in time-series applications, predicting the last observation again and an average of all past observations (Matero and Schwartz, 2020). In the case of our application, these are equivalent to predicting the last reported day's number of drinks and the average of all current and past days' drinks.

[2]However, when mutl-level features are used, an FFNN is utilized.

Our statistical baselines are a linear (ridge) autoregression and Gated Recurrent Unit (GRU) cell recurrent neural network (Chung et al., 2014). We train our GRU network using multi-head self-attention as introduced in Vaswani et al. (2017).

Language Association for Within-Person Drinkings Consumption To further understand the relationships between drinking behaviors and participants' language from *affective essays*, we analyze the associations between word usage and number of drinks quantitatively. We analyzed 4,939 *affective essays* from 489 participants. (some participants have missing data within the 14 days). Firstly, we employed Latent Dirichlet Allocation (LDA) (David M. Blei, 2003) topic modeling ($n = 200$, $\alpha = 2$) to identify the primary themes that emerged from the text to extract topic features for all essays. To identify the distinctive language used about drinking behavior, we applied differential language analysis (DLA) (Schwartz et al., 2017) to search for topic features that had the strongest positive or negative correlation with the number of drinks consumed on the previous day. To focus on the within-person signals, we applied fixed effects models, in which we mean-centered the input language features and output number of drinks with participant-wise averages across time. Consequently, this new multi-level differential language analysis shows insights into the language and behavior of participants changes compared to their daily language and average consumption. The reported correlations are beta coefficients from a standardized multi-level regression model where significance is validated via Benjimini-Hochberg correction (Benjamini and Hochberg, 1995).

Particularly for each participant i, with $X_{i,t}$ as the language topic features for the day t and $y_{i,t}$ as the number of drinks consumed 24 hours before the day t, consider the linear unobserved effects model:

$$y_{i,t} = X_{i,t}.\beta + \alpha_i + \epsilon_{i,t} \tag{1}$$

Where β is the parameter to be learned, α_i is the unobserved time-invariant individual drinking effect we aim to eliminate, and $\epsilon_{i,t}$ is the error term. Since α_i is not observable, it cannot be directly controlled for. To implement the fixed effects model, one can eliminate α_i by de-meaning X and y: $\ddot{X_{i,t}} = X_{i,t} - \bar{X}_i$ and $\ddot{y_{i,t}} = y_{i,t} - \bar{y}_i$, where t indexes the particular instance measurement for

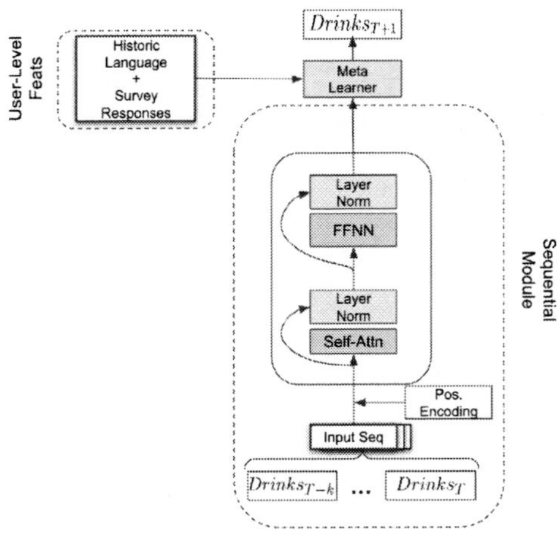

Figure 2: Architecture of our multi-level forecasting model with the contextual user-level module highlighted by a dashed box on the left-hand side. The sequential module is the document-level transformer that processes daily language and drinking data as per EMA responses. The avg-pooled sequential representation is concatenated with the user-level features and passed through a 2-layer FFNN called *meta-learner*.

participant i and the mean is over all instances of that user.

Since α_i is constant over time: $\ddot{\alpha_i} = \alpha_i - \bar{\alpha}_i = 0$ and the individual effect is eliminated. Thus equation (1) is transformed into equation (2) where the fixed effects estimator $\hat{\beta}_{FE}$ is then obtained by an OLS regression of $\ddot{y}$ and $\ddot{X}$.

$$\ddot{y_{i,t}} = \ddot{X_{i,t}}.\beta_{FE} + \ddot{\epsilon_{i,t}} \quad (2)$$

Language Association for High and Low Risk Drinkers We partitioned the population into two groups based on their AUDIT-C scores for further investigation by gender. Males with scores greater than or equal to 5.5 and females with scores greater than or equal to 4.5 were deemed to belong to the high AUDIT-C category (Johnson et al., 2013), while the rest were placed in the low AUDIT-C category. The resulting sample comprised 234 high AUDIT-C participants (2,393 *affective essays*) and 241 low AUDIT-C participants (2,438 *affective essays*). For each category, we identified the top 30 topics correlated with the corresponding category. We then applied DLA algorithms to distinguish the language used to describe the drinking behaviors within each group.

Model (num days)	MSE	MAE	r
Heuristic Baselines			
Last Day	9.48	1.70	0.36
Average Drinks	5.02	1.44	0.58
Linear Models			
LinAR (5)	4.56	1.52	0.58
Deep Learning			
GRU (7)	4.62	1.44	0.59
TRNS (7)*	**4.22**	**1.33**	**0.62**

Table 1: Overall performance of our document sequential forecasting models. Models are trained using past drinking behavior, daily language features from EMA responses, and day-of-week markers. All models use the number of days found ideal during training, which was 7 for all except linear. **Bold** indicates best in column and * indicates statistical difference via paired t-test with $p < .05$ w.r.t GRU (7).

5 Results

Here, we showcase results using three separate metrics. First, we focus on mean squared error (MSE) as it is helpful to measure the impact of outliers where our models failed to predict as accurately and is also the metric we optimize for during training. Second, mean absolute error (MAE) shows errors within the same units (drinks per day). Lastly, Pearson r is used as a scale-invariant metric to show the relationship between model predictions and the actual trend.

For all tables shown, LinAR refers to a linear ridge (L2-normalized) autoregressive model, GRU is a gated recurrent neural network, and TRNS is our transformer based architecture.

Multivariate Forecasting We start by showing our best-performing multivariate sequential models compared to our baselines; shown in Table 1. We find that our heuristic baselines perform quite strongly, with the average number of drinks being the most competitive. In fact, we find that modeling the multivariate sequence using an autoregressive linear model fails to out-predict these baselines in 2 out of 3 metrics. However, both deep learning baselines offer improved performance, with both having a modest drop in MSE, showing their robustness to outliers. The transformer-based model performs better across all metrics, showcasing lower error and higher correlations. We believe this to be due to the superior modeling capabilities when it comes to modeling the complexities of changes in language over time.

Model (num days)	**MSE**	**MAE**	r
With Language			
TRNS (7)*	**4.22**	**1.33**	**0.62**
Without Language			
GRU (7)	5.48	1.51	0.46
LinAR (9)	4.49	1.35	0.59
TRNS (7)	4.29	1.43	0.62

Table 2: Comparison of predictive power using only past knowledge of number of drinks to forecast future number of drinks. All models use the number of days found ideal during training, which was 7 for all except linear. **Bold** indicates best in column and * indicates statistical difference via paired t-test with $p < .05$ w.r.t LinAR (9).

Model (num days)	**MSE**	**MAE**	r
Heuristic Baselines			
Last Day	9.48	1.70	0.36
Average Drinks	**5.02**	**1.44**	**0.58**
No Drinking History			
GRU (7)	7.21	1.80	0.28
TRNS (7)	5.85	1.77	0.42

Table 3: Evaluation of predictive power when the models do not have access to previous drinking behavior, a strong univariate signal, and instead are trained using only daily language and day-of-week flags. **Bold** indicates best in column.

Model (num dims)	**MSE**	**MAE**	r
TRNS (768)	4.91	1.45	0.54
TRNS (64)	4.39	1.34	0.60
TRNS (32)*	**4.22**	**1.33**	**0.62**
TRNS (16)	4.48	1.47	0.60

Table 4: Impact of number of language dimensions on predictive power. All models are trained with seven steps of history, which was found ideal. **Bold** indicates best in column and * indicates statistical difference via paired t-test with $p <$ 05 w.r.t TRNS (768).

Univariate Forecasting We also compare our multivariate sequential models to the performance of univariate models in Table 2. None of the univariate models are capable of more accurate predictions than the best multivariate model, highlighting the importance language plays in detecting future behaviors. Interestingly, when shifting from multivariate to univariate, the GRU model fails to learn anything beyond the original average drinks baseline. On the other hand, the linear model sees quite a substantial performance improvement, implying that these models behave quite differently when limited to just a single feature dimension as input. Historically, linear univariate autoregressive models have been quite competitive with other sequential models such as RNNs (Matero and Schwartz, 2020; Sánchez Gavilanes, 2022; Menculini et al., 2021). At the same time, the modeling of language over time is likely too complex for such a model.

Covariates Only Next, in Table 3, we investigate the ability to forecast future drinking behaviors *without* knowledge of past drinking. For example, these models are trained using only a sequence of daily language as captured in the experienced well-being *affective essays* and the day-of-week markers. The transformer network is once again the best performing compared to the other statistical models, where we can get an absolute error close to that of knowing the number of drinks a person had the day before. This shows excellent utility for those running a study or clinicians already collecting language data from participants but do not have access to explicit drinking information. Only having a single open response field (experienced well-being) can predict future drinking almost as well as knowing how much a participant drank recently (past 24 hours).

Dimensionality Reduction We perform an additional sensitivity analysis over our models, where we explore the performance of the language features based on the number of dimensions. While previous studies have shown trends in the performance of dimensionality reduction sizes on human-level NLP tasks (Ganesan et al., 2021), they've not done so for tasks that span the temporal dimension or tasks specifically predicting beyond mental health or demographics. Thus, we show if these trends continue to hold in such a scenario in Table 4. We find that performance across all three metrics continues to increase as dimensions are reduced until only 16 language dimensions remain. This corroborates the findings of Ganesan et al. (2021), which suggests 32 dimensions for ideal results on a dataset of 200 people.

User-level Modeling In Table 5, we show the performance of using only the user-level features through the meta-learner as a stand-alone neural network (only using the user-module pipeline from Figure 2). We find that using only language gives a weak but reliable signal in terms of daily drinking. Alternatively, the baseline survey's psychological

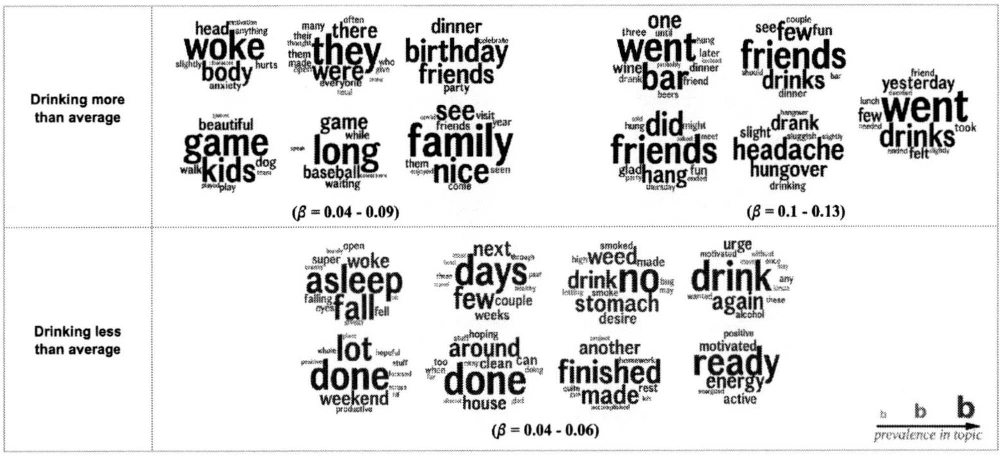

Figure 3: Worldcloud topics from the responses to *affective essays* associated with drinking more or less than average within participants. Association (β) is the coefficient from standardized multiple linear models ($p < 0.05$; Benjamini-Hochberg adjusted for false discovery rate, N=4,939 essays).

Model	MSE	MAE	r
Heuristic Baselines			
Last Day	9.48	1.70	0.36
Average Drinks	5.02	**1.44**	**0.58**
User-level			
Language	6.92	1.74	0.09
Survey	5.45	1.66	0.44
Lang+Survey*	**4.81**	1.50	0.51

Table 5: Performance of our user-level features as input into the meta-learner without using the document sequential (daily) module. Features use a user embedding representing past language used on social media and baseline survey responses. **Bold** indicates best in column and * indicates statistical difference via paired t-test with $p < 05$ w.r.t Average Drinks.

and demographic features are quite competitive compared to the heuristic baselines. It is important to note that these survey features do *not* include any past information on drinking behaviors that the baselines have access to. When combining the language with the survey responses we see an increase in predictive power across all three metrics suggesting that the language features capture different covariance of drinking behaviors. While the user-level features do not outperform the heuristic baselines, they are still rather impressive as they are not leveraging the inputs of the sequential module and thus make the same prediction (static) for both testing days. Thus, there is likely a consistent personal factor for each individual that drives their drinking behaviors.

Model	MSE	MAE	r
Document Sequential			
TRNS	**4.22**	1.33	**0.62**
Multi-level Sequential			
TRNS*	**4.22**	**1.23**	**0.62**

Table 6: Performance of our multi-level model when incorporating contextual user-level information via the user module compared to using sequential data only. Both models use seven days of history, with the multi-level model also leveraging historic user-level features. **Bold** indicates best in column and * indicates statistical difference via paired t-test with $p < .05$ w.r.t Document Sequential TRNS.

Multi-level Sequential Forecasting Finally, in Table 6, we investigate the effect of using a multi-level forecasting model that leverages both the static user-level features and the dynamic time-series inputs. We see a small but significant increase in the ability to predict raw drinks per day (MAE) while maintaining the same level of MSE and Pearson r. This indicates that the feature spaces have overlapping covariance, but there are some aspects that are not accounted for in the sequential features. Especially concerning the absolute error in the raw number of drinks per day, in which most other approaches struggled to see large gains.

Language Association with Drinking Behaviors Figure 3 shows significant topics correlated positively (blue) and negatively (red) to drinking. Days when participants drink more than usual predomi-

Figure 4: Worldcloud topics from the responses to *affective essays* associated with drinking more or less than average within participants, divided into groups of high AUDIT-C (N=2,393 essays) and low AUDIT-C (N=2,438 essays). Association (β) is the coefficient from standardized multiple linear models ($p < 0.05$; Benjamini-Hochberg adjusted for false discovery rate).

nantly relate to social experienced well-being language. For example, when participants drink more than usual, their language relates to friends, family, and social events (e.g., birthdays and dinners). Considering the positive relationship between spending time with others and positive affect (Grimm et al., 2015; Killingsworth and Gilbert, 2010; Diener and Seligman, 2002), and that positive affect rises on drinking days (Dora et al., 2022), the social language pattern related to drinking days is not surprising. Topics associated with drinking not related to social events include hangover-related language ("headache" and "woke, body, anxiety"). Conversely, the language associated with consuming less alcohol relates to accomplishment, energy, and urges to drink. Specific topics such as "energy, ready" and "fall asleep" seem contradictory. However, alcohol-consuming behavior is complex, and while the β values (0.05 - 0.15) are similar to the previous meta-analytic correlation between positive affect and drinking (Dora et al., 2022), the complexity of alcohol behavior (Geiger and MacKerron, 2016; Massin and Kopp, 2014) likely explain why language features divergent in meaning relate similarly to alcohol consumption. Further, no social language related to drinking less than normal, indicating that drinking can be *the* social platform for some individuals.

Language Analysis for High and Low AUDIT-C group The topics displayed in Figure 4 depict language that positively and negatively correlates with the number of drinks individuals consume, separated into high and low AUDIT-C. The high AUDIT-C group's motivations usually refer to social context, while the low AUDIT-C group refers to special occasions. For the low AUDIT-C group, the language significantly related to drinking was exclusively social, while for the high AUDIT-C group, the social aspects attenuated compared to the language pertaining to drinking, and the hangover language remained. When drinking less than usual, the high AUDIT-C group's language indicates the urge to drink and sleep, and the low AUDIT-C group mainly describes their common daily emotions.

Past research (Kornfield et al., 2018; Marengo et al., 2019; Moreno et al., 2016; van Swol et al., 2020; Jose et al., 2022) that has studied between-person signals across AUDIT-C scores find high AUDIT-C drinkers engage in discussions about alcohol consumption and profane language and low AUDIT-C drinkers often express an emphasis on religious beliefs. Here, we find that high AUDIT-C drinkers talk about alcohol consumption but do not use profane language, and low AUDIT-C drinkers do not mention religion. Our results provide an additional perspective on the complexities of drinking, where the language-based analyses demonstrate how divergent feelings and aspects can relate to drinking behaviors simultaneously.

6 Conclusion

Longitudinal, multi-level language analyses can be important for understanding human behavior, such as alcohol consumption and its motivations. In this work, we propose a multi-level longitudinal approach to analyze the language associations with drinking behaviors to find within-person signals. While much of previous work about language and drinking found characteristic differences *between people*, our approach yielded results that signal *day-to-day changes*, aligning with previous research on *within-person* changes in drinking associated with emotions and socializing. Our multi-level approach also yielded evidence for differing drinking motivations between people depending on their alcohol use disorder risk level, with lower AUDIT-C drinkers (those at lower risk) mentioning celebrations or special occasions more than those with higher risk.

7 Limitations

This study focuses on those who are potentially high-risk drinkers in the service industry, such as bartenders and restaurant workers in the United States. While participation was possible three times a day over 14 days, some participants dropped out after a few days or came in and out over the study. This lack of reports led to potentially noisy time series per participant, which had to be filled via interpolation techniques. All participants were also required to respond in English when crafting their experienced well-being *affective essay* responses and were filtered out if another language or spam was used.

Additionally, given that this dataset and task definition are novel, the size of the dataset used for forecasting could be considered small as it spans only 242 participants. While the data is longitudinal, with each participant having upwards of 14 days of data, the overall number of users motivates us to use techniques to avoid the curse of dimensionality (Ganesan et al., 2021).

Further, our multi-level model forecasts daily drinking consumption using focused language (*affective essays*), general public language (Facebook statuses), demographics (Age/Gender), and responses to psychological questionnaires (AUDIT-C, Depression, and Anxiety levels). The AUDIT-C is a shorthand questionnaire to get a rough estimate of one's level of alcoholism risk level. While there are more complete representations via the full AUDIT questionnaire, the structure of the study focused on short information-dense questionnaires as part of the initial participant baseline survey to capture many psychological outcomes.

8 Ethics Statement

This work aims to advance multi-disciplinary NLP-psychology *research* for understanding human behaviors associated with language. The models in this paper are not intended or validated for deployment in specific clinical settings and are not to be used for other commercial use cases, such as targeted marketing. The use cases this research is working towards are for developing more accurate and validated techniques for the benefit of society and human health. All participants in this research did so under informed consent without agreement to further share their non-anonymized individual data. The research was approved by an independent academic institutional review board (IRB).

This work is intended as a step toward an assistive tool, but it is not evaluated for such use at this point. Currently, we do not enable the use of our model(s) independently in practice to label a person's potential behaviors. Before our models are used by trained clinicians, they must demonstrate validity in a clinical setting for the target clinical population, with steps for evaluation reviewed by an ethical review board. Practice should follow clinical guidelines.

References

Francisca Adoma Acheampong, Henry Nunoo-Mensah, and Wenyu Chen. 2021. Transformer models for text-based emotion detection: a review of bert-based approaches. *Artificial Intelligence Review*, pages 1–41.

Takuya Akiba, Shotaro Sano, Toshihiko Yanase, Takeru Ohta, and Masanori Koyama. 2019. Optuna: A next-generation hyperparameter optimization framework. In *Proceedings of the 25rd ACM SIGKDD International Conference on Knowledge Discovery and Data Mining*.

Nour Alayan, David Eddie, Lucille Eller, Marsha E Bates, and Dennis P Carmody. 2019. Substance craving changes in university students receiving heart rate variability biofeedback: A longitudinal multilevel modeling approach. *Addictive behaviors*, 97:35–41.

Fatemeh Almodaresi, Lyle Ungar, Vivek Kulkarni, Mohsen Zakeri, Salvatore Giorgi, and H Andrew

Schwartz. 2017. On the distribution of lexical features at multiple levels of analysis. In *Proceedings of the 55th Annual Meeting of the Association for Computational Linguistics (Volume 2: Short Papers)*, pages 79–84.

Dzmitry Bahdanau, Kyunghyun Cho, and Yoshua Bengio. 2014. Neural machine translation by jointly learning to align and translate. *arXiv preprint arXiv:1409.0473*.

Yoav Benjamini and Yosef Hochberg. 1995. Controlling the false discovery rate: a practical and powerful approach to multiple testing. *Journal of the Royal statistical society: series B (Methodological)*, 57(1):289–300.

K. Bush, DR Kivlahan, MB McDonell, SD Fihn, and KA Bradley. 1998. The audit alcohol consumption questions (audit-c): an effective brief screening test for problem drinking. *Arch Intern Med*, 158(16):1789–1795.

Andre F Carvalho, Markus Heilig, Augusto Perez, Charlotte Probst, and Jürgen Rehm. 2019. Alcohol use disorders. *The Lancet*, 394(10200):781–792.

Zhengping Che, Sanjay Purushotham, Kyunghyun Cho, David Sontag, and Yan Liu. 2018. Recurrent neural networks for multivariate time series with missing values. *Scientific reports*, 8(1):6085.

Junyoung Chung, Caglar Gulcehre, KyungHyun Cho, and Yoshua Bengio. 2014. Empirical evaluation of gated recurrent neural networks on sequence modeling. *arXiv preprint arXiv:1412.3555*.

Kasey G Creswell, Yvonne M Terry-McElrath, and Megan E Patrick. 2022. Solitary alcohol use in adolescence predicts alcohol problems in adulthood: A 17-year longitudinal study in a large national sample of us high school students. *Drug and alcohol dependence*, 238:109552.

Brenda Curtis, Salvatore Giorgi, Anneke EK Buffone, Lyle H Ungar, Robert D Ashford, Jessie Hemmons, Dan Summers, Casey Hamilton, and H Andrew Schwartz. 2018. Can twitter be used to predict county excessive alcohol consumption rates? *PloS one*, 13(4):e0194290.

Michael I. Jordan David M. Blei, Andrew Y. Ng. 2003. Latent dirichlet allocation. *Journal of Machine Learning Research*.

Munmun De Choudhury, Scott Counts, and Eric Horvitz. 2013. Social media as a measurement tool of depression in populations. In *Proceedings of the 5th annual ACM web science conference*, pages 47–56.

Ed Diener and Martin EP Seligman. 2002. Very happy people. *Psychological science*, 13(1):81–84.

Jonas Dora, Marilyn Piccirillo, Katherine T Foster, Kelly Arbeau, Stephen Armeli, Marc Auriacombe, Bruce D Bartholow, Adriene Beltz, Shari Blumenstock, Krysten Bold, et al. 2022. The daily association between affect and alcohol use: A meta-analysis of individual participant data.

Johannes C Eichstaedt, Robert J Smith, Raina M Merchant, Lyle H Ungar, Patrick Crutchley, Daniel Preoţiuc-Pietro, David A Asch, and H Andrew Schwartz. 2018. Facebook language predicts depression in medical records. *Proceedings of the National Academy of Sciences*, 115(44):11203–11208.

et al. Falcon, WA. 2019. Pytorch lightning. *GitHub. Note: https://github.com/PyTorchLightning/pytorch-lightning*, 3.

Kamel Gana, Guillaume Broc, and Nathalie Bailly. 2019. Does the boredom proneness scale capture traitness of boredom? results from a six-year longitudinal trait-state-occasion model. *Personality and Individual Differences*, 139:247–253.

Adithya V Ganesan, Matthew Matero, Aravind Reddy Ravula, Huy Vu, and H Andrew Schwartz. 2021. Empirical evaluation of pre-trained transformers for human-level nlp: The role of sample size and dimensionality. *arXiv preprint arXiv:2105.03484*.

Ben Baumberg Geiger and George MacKerron. 2016. Can alcohol make you happy? a subjective wellbeing approach. *Social Science & Medicine*, 156:184–191.

Carsten Grimm, Simon Kemp, and Paul E Jose. 2015. Orientations to happiness and the experience of everyday activities. *The Journal of Positive Psychology*, 10(3):207–218.

Kishaloy Halder, Lahari Poddar, and Min-Yen Kan. 2017. Modeling temporal progression of emotional status in mental health forum: A recurrent neural net approach. In *Proceedings of the 8th Workshop on Computational Approaches to Subjectivity, Sentiment and Social Media Analysis*, pages 127–135.

Larry V Hedges. 1994. Fixed effects models. *The handbook of research synthesis*, 285:299.

Joop Hox. 1998. Multilevel modeling: When and why. In *Classification, data analysis, and data highways: proceedings of the 21st Annual Conference of the Gesellschaft für Klassifikation eV, University of Potsdam, March 12–14, 1997*, pages 147–154. Springer.

J Aaron Johnson, Anna Lee, Daniel Vinson, and J Paul Seale. 2013. Use of audit-based measures to identify unhealthy alcohol use and alcohol dependence in primary care: A validation study. *Alcoholism: Clinical and Experimental Research*, 37:E253–E259.

John A Johnson. 2014. Measuring thirty facets of the five factor model with a 120-item public domain inventory: Development of the ipip-neo-120. *Journal of research in personality*, 51:78–89.

Rupa Jose, Matthew Matero, Garrick Sherman, Brenda Curtis, Salvatore Giorgi, Hansen Andrew Schwartz, and Lyle H Ungar. 2022. Using facebook language to predict and describe excessive alcohol use. *Alcoholism: Clinical and Experimental Research*, 46(5):836–847.

Kenneth S Kendler, Henrik Ohlsson, Jan Sundquist, and Kristina Sundquist. 2016. Alcohol use disorder and mortality across the lifespan: a longitudinal cohort and co-relative analysis. *JAMA psychiatry*, 73(6):575–581.

Margaret L Kern, Gregory Park, Johannes C Eichstaedt, H Andrew Schwartz, Maarten Sap, Luke K Smith, and Lyle H Ungar. 2016. Gaining insights from social media language: Methodologies and challenges. *Psychological methods*, 21(4):507–525.

Matthew A Killingsworth and Daniel T Gilbert. 2010. A wandering mind is an unhappy mind. *Science*, 330(6006):932–932.

Rachel Kornfield, Catalina L. Toma, Dhavan V. Shah, Troy J. Moon, and David H. Gustafson. 2018. What do you say before you relapse? how language use in a peer-to-peer online discussion forum predicts risky drinking among those in recovery. *Health Communication*, 33:1184–1193.

Yinhan Liu, Myle Ott, Naman Goyal, Jingfei Du, Mandar Joshi, Danqi Chen, Omer Levy, Mike Lewis, Luke Zettlemoyer, and Veselin Stoyanov. 2019. Roberta: A robustly optimized bert pretraining approach. *arXiv preprint arXiv:1907.11692*.

Minh-Thang Luong, Hieu Pham, and Christopher D Manning. 2015. Effective approaches to attention-based neural machine translation. *arXiv preprint arXiv:1508.04025*.

Veronica Lynn, Youngseo Son, Vivek Kulkarni, Niranjan Balasubramanian, and H Andrew Schwartz. 2017. Human centered nlp with user-factor adaptation. In *Proceedings of the 2017 Conference on Empirical Methods in Natural Language Processing*, pages 1146–1155.

Davide Marengo, Debora Azucar, Fabrizia Giannotta, Valerio Basile, and Michele Settanni. 2019. Exploring the association between problem drinking and language use on facebook in young adults. *Heliyon*, 5:e02523.

Sophie Massin and Pierre Kopp. 2011. Alcohol consumption and happiness: an empirical analysis using russian panel data. *Centre d'Economie de la Sorbonne*, pages 1–19.

Sophie Massin and Pierre Kopp. 2014. Is life satisfaction hump-shaped with alcohol consumption? evidence from russian panel data. *Addictive behaviors*, 39(4):803–810.

Matthew Matero, Salvatore Giorgi, Brenda Curtis, Lyle H. Ungar, and H. Andrew Schwartz. 2023. Opioid death projections with AI-based forecasts using social media language. *npj Digital Medicine*, 6(1):35.

Matthew Matero, Albert Hung, and H Andrew Schwartz. 2021a. Evaluating contextual embeddings and their extraction layers for depression assessment. *arXiv preprint arXiv:2112.13795*.

Matthew Matero and H Andrew Schwartz. 2020. Autoregressive affective language forecasting: A self-supervised task. In *Proceedings of the 28th International Conference on Computational Linguistics*, pages 2913–2923.

Matthew Matero, Nikita Soni, Niranjan Balasubramanian, and H Andrew Schwartz. 2021b. Melt: Message-level transformer with masked document representations as pre-training for stance detection. In *Findings of the Association for Computational Linguistics: EMNLP 2021*, pages 2959–2966.

Lorenzo Menculini, Andrea Marini, Massimiliano Proietti, Alberto Garinei, Alessio Bozza, Cecilia Moretti, and Marcello Marconi. 2021. Comparing prophet and deep learning to arima in forecasting wholesale food prices. *Forecasting*, 3(3):644–662.

Megan A. Moreno, Alaina Arseniev-Koehler, Dana Litt, and Dimitri Christakis. 2016. Evaluating college students' displayed alcohol references on facebook and twitter. *Journal of Adolescent Health*, 58:527–532.

NIH. 2023. *Alcohol Use Disorder (AUD) in the United States: Age Groups and Demographic Characteristics*. NIH.

Annick Parent-Lamarche, Alain Marchand, and Sabine Saade. 2021. A multilevel analysis of the role personality play between work organization conditions and psychological distress. *BMC psychology*, 9(1):1–15.

Adam Paszke, Sam Gross, Francisco Massa, Adam Lerer, James Bradbury, Gregory Chanan, Trevor Killeen, Zeming Lin, Natalia Gimelshein, Luca Antiga, Alban Desmaison, Andreas Kopf, Edward Yang, Zachary DeVito, Martin Raison, Alykhan Tejani, Sasank Chilamkurthy, Benoit Steiner, Lu Fang, Junjie Bai, and Soumith Chintala. 2019. Pytorch: An imperative style, high-performance deep learning library. In H. Wallach, H. Larochelle, A. Beygelzimer, F. d'Alché-Buc, E. Fox, and R. Garnett, editors, *Advances in Neural Information Processing Systems 32*, pages 8024–8035. Curran Associates, Inc.

Ricardo Andrés Sánchez Gavilanes. 2022. *Univariate time series forecasting: comparing ARIMA & LSTM neural network to the random walk benchmark for exchange rates*. Ph.D. thesis, Instituto Superior de Economia e Gestão.

H Andrew Schwartz, Johannes Eichstaedt, Margaret Kern, Gregory Park, Maarten Sap, David Stillwell, Michal Kosinski, and Lyle Ungar. 2014. Towards assessing changes in degree of depression through facebook. In *Proceedings of the workshop on computational linguistics and clinical psychology: from linguistic signal to clinical reality*, pages 118–125.

H Andrew Schwartz, Johannes C Eichstaedt, Margaret L Kern, Lukasz Dziurzynski, Stephanie M Ramones, Megha Agrawal, Achal Shah, Michal Kosinski, David Stillwell, Martin EP Seligman, et al. 2013. Personality, gender, and age in the language of social media: The open-vocabulary approach. *PloS one*, 8(9):e73791.

H Andrew Schwartz, Salvatore Giorgi, Maarten Sap, Patrick Crutchley, Lyle Ungar, and Johannes Eichstaedt. 2017. Dlatk: Differential language analysis toolkit. In *Proceedings of the 2017 conference on empirical methods in natural language processing: System demonstrations*, pages 55–60.

Nikita Soni, Matthew Matero, Niranjan Balasubramanian, and H Andrew Schwartz. 2022. Human language modeling. *arXiv preprint arXiv:2205.05128*.

Rong Su, Gundula Stoll, and James Rounds. 2019. The nature of interests: Toward a unifying theory of trait-state interest dynamics. In *Vocational interests in the workplace*, pages 11–38. Routledge.

Adam Tsakalidis, Jenny Chim, Iman Munire Bilal, Ayah Zirikly, Dana Atzil-Slonim, Federico Nanni, Philip Resnik, Manas Gaur, Kaushik Roy, Becky Inkster, et al. 2022. Overview of the clpsych 2022 shared task: Capturing moments of change in longitudinal user posts. In *Proceedings of the Eighth Workshop on Computational Linguistics and Clinical Psychology*, pages 184–198.

Lisa Van der Werff, Yseult Freeney, Charles E Lance, and Finian Buckley. 2019. A trait-state model of trust propensity: Evidence from two career transitions. *Frontiers in Psychology*, 10:2490.

Lyn M. van Swol, Chia T. Chang, Brianna Kerr, and Megan Moreno. 2020. Linguistic predictors of problematic drinking in alcohol-related facebook posts. *Journal of Health Communication*, 25:214–222.

Ashish Vaswani, Noam Shazeer, Niki Parmar, Jakob Uszkoreit, Llion Jones, Aidan N Gomez, Łukasz Kaiser, and Illia Polosukhin. 2017. Attention is all you need. In *Advances in neural information processing systems*, pages 5998–6008.

Yu Zhu, Hao Li, Yikang Liao, Beidou Wang, Ziyu Guan, Haifeng Liu, and Deng Cai. 2017. What to do next: Modeling user behaviors by time-lstm. In *IJCAI*, volume 17, pages 3602–3608.

A Appendix

A.1 EMA Question Details

The exact phrasings of the relevant EMA questions, number of drinks, and experienced well-being essays are as follows:

- How many standard drinks did you have in the past 24 hours?
- Using the box below, please describe in 2 to 3 sentences how you are currently feeling.

A description of "standard drink" is given alongside the question describing the typical definitions in beer, malt liquor, wine, and distilled spirits. Such that the following are defined as a standard drink: (1) 12 fl oz of a 5% beer, (2) 8-9 fl oz of a 7% malt liquor, (3) 5 fl oz of 12% wine, and (4) 1.5 fl oz of a 40% spirit.

A.2 Implementation Details

All models were built using PyTorch (Paszke et al., 2019) and Lightning (Falcon, 2019) with hyperparameter tuning using Optuna (Akiba et al., 2019). Hyperparameters explored were learning rate between $5e-2$ and $5e-5$ and weight decay between 0.01 and 1.0. 10% of users were selected as a held-out validation set for hyperparameter tuning by random sampling. For these users, their last 2 days of drinking were only used for parameter tuning and thus were not included in the test set. However, their first k days of responses were included in training data using an out-of-sample time configuration (Matero and Schwartz, 2020). A random seed of 1337 was used for all training experiments.

Prevalent Frequency of Emotional and Physical Symptoms in Social Anxiety using Zero Shot Classification: An Observational Study

Muhammad Rizwan
Department of Information Technology,
Khwaja Fareed University of Engineering
and Information Technology,
Rahim Yar Khan, Pakistan
rizwan2phd@gmail.com

Jure Demšar
Faculty of Computer and
Information Studies,
University of Ljabljana, Slovenia
Jure.Demsar@fri.uni-lj.si

Abstract

Social anxiety represents a prevalent challenge in modern society, affecting individuals across personal and professional spheres. Left unaddressed, this condition can yield substantial negative consequences, impacting social interactions and performance. Further understanding its diverse physical and emotional symptoms becomes pivotal for comprehensive diagnosis and tailored therapeutic interventions. This study analyze prevalence and frequency of social anxiety symptoms taken from Mayo Clinic, exploring diverse human experiences from utilizing a large Reddit dataset dedicated to this issue. Leveraging these platforms, the research aims to extract insights and examine a spectrum of physical and emotional symptoms linked to social anxiety disorder. Upholding ethical considerations, the study maintains strict user anonymity within the dataset. By employing a novel approach, the research utilizes BART-based multi-label zero-shot classification to identify and measure symptom prevalence and significance in the form of probability score for each symptom under consideration. Results uncover distinctive patterns: "Trembling" emerges as a prevalent physical symptom, while emotional symptoms like "Fear of being judged negatively" exhibit high frequencies. These findings offer insights into the multifaceted nature of social anxiety, aiding clinical practices and interventions tailored to its diverse expressions.

1 Introduction

Social anxiety is prevalent in our society, posing a significant and widespread difficulty for individuals. The impact is deep and goes beyond limits, affecting both personal and professional aspects. If not addressed, this illness can have a significant impact, leading to a series of negative consequences. Going beyond just being shy, its enduring nature can result in significant repercussions (Hur et al., 2020; Lépine and Pelissolo, 2000), spanning from limited social contacts to compromised performance in several areas of life. The consistent existence of this phenomenon in the lives of many emphasises the importance of understanding its complexities and identifying its various forms in order to provide appropriate intervention and assistance. Social anxiety is a mental health problem that can have long-term consequences (Blood and Blood, 2016). The long-lasting character of the phenomenon emphasises the crucial importance of thoroughly analysing its physical and emotional symptoms, in order to fully comprehend its frequency and influence on the individuals afflicted (Liu and Tan, 2023; Zech et al., 2023). Understanding these symptoms not only helps to make the diagnosis clear but also facilitates the development of customised therapies, enabling prompt and accurate assistance for individuals struggling with this incapacitating condition.

In order to gain a comprehensive understanding of this complex subject, this study undertakes an investigative exploration into the realm of symptoms associated with social anxiety. This study aims to extract insights by analysing the diverse range of human experiences reported on Reddit subreddits dedicated to this issue. These platforms provide an unedited view of the real-life experiences of people dealing with the intricacies of social anxiety, including a large amount of text data that is suitable for research. By utilising this highly important resource, the research seeks to examine and define the intricate range of physical and emotional symptoms linked to social anxiety disorder. We strictly ensured that ethical and privacy consideration during our analysis, does not reveal any reddit user identity in the study.

This work utilises a new method by applying a multi-class zero-shot classification strategy assisted by BART (Bidirectional and Auto-Regressive Transformers). This framework utilises NLP and deep learning to identify and measure

Proceedings of the 9th Workshop on Computational Linguistics and Clinical Psychology (CLPsych 2024), pages 145–152
March 21, 2024

common symptoms, leading to a better understanding of the complex nature of social anxiety with respect to different emotional and physical symptoms. BART zero shot classification has already been used for such studies e.g. in (Farruque et al., 2021; Yang et al., 2023). This research aims to provide which symptoms are more frequent than the others comparatively using deep context provided by the BART language model. This study can further be used to inform clinical practices, interventions, and support mechanisms specifically designed to address the various ways in which social anxiety is expressed.

2 Social Anxiety Symptoms

This study considers the following common symptoms facing by common people during social anxiety disorder in order to analysis their prevalence frequency in reddit social anxiety dataset.

2.1 Physical Symptoms

We selected common physical symptoms associated with social anxiety disorder, as listed on the Mayo Clinic website (May, 2021) mentioned in Table 1 and 2, for deeper analysis within the Reddit dataset. These symptoms encompass a range of experiences, including blushing, a rapid heartbeat, trembling, sweating, upset stomach or nausea, difficulty breathing, feelings of dizziness or lightheadedness, experiencing mental blankness, and muscle tension. These specific manifestations represent key indicators of the physical impact that social anxiety can exert on individuals, prompting our exploration within the Reddit dataset to glean insights and understand the prevalence frequency of these symptoms in real life.

2.2 Emotional Symptoms

We have also extracted common emotional symptoms associated with social anxiety disorder from the Mayo Clinic website. These symptoms encompass a range of experiences, including a pervasive fear of negative judgment in social situations, concerns about potential embarrassment or humiliation, and an intense fear of interacting with strangers. Additionally, these symptoms encompass a fear of others noticing anxious behavior, avoidance of social interactions due to fear of embarrassment, and evading situations where attention might be directed toward oneself. The anticipation of anxiety-inducing activities, intense fear or anxiety during social interactions, and expecting the worst possible outcomes from negative experiences within social settings also form part of these emotional symptoms. These descriptors serve as crucial elements for further analysis within the Reddit dataset, providing a comprehensive understanding of the emotional complexities experienced by individuals grappling with social anxiety disorder.

3 Method

In this methodology section, we'll first outline the Reddit dataset chosen for the study on social anxiety disorder. This dataset forms the core of our investigation. Next, we introduce and examine the emotional and physical symptoms associated with social anxiety disorder, employing a zero-shot classification approach. This method allows us to explore a wide array of symptoms without requiring specific training data. Finally, we provide a detailed explanation of BART (Bidirectional and Auto-Regressive Transformers) and its utilization in a multi-label zero-shot classification setup. This methodology enables us to calculate the average probability of each social anxiety symptom within the dataset, offering a comprehensive insight into their prevalence and significance within the scope of this research.

3.1 Social Anxiety Reddit Dataset

The dataset utilized in this research, as detailed by (Low et al., 2020), was acquired using the pushshift API of Reddit. Researchers gathered posts from 15 distinct subreddits dedicated to various mental health communities. These subreddits encompassed a wide range of mental health concerns, including communities like r/EDAnonymous, r/addiction, r/alcoholism, r/adhd, r/anxiety, r/autism, r/BipolarReddit, r/bpd, r/depression, r/healthanxiety, r/lonely, r/ptsd, r/schizophrenia, r/socialanxiety, and r/SuicideWatch.

In the context of our study's specific objectives, we narrow our focus to the subreddit r/socialanxiety, honing in on discussions related to social anxiety disorder. The dataset under consideration comprises 12,277 text documents or subreddits, capturing social anxiety-related content posted between 2018 and 2019. Within the dataset of the r/socialanxiety Reddit community, individuals engage in discussions about their real-life experiences, opinions, and symptoms related to social anxiety. Notably, each document is associated with

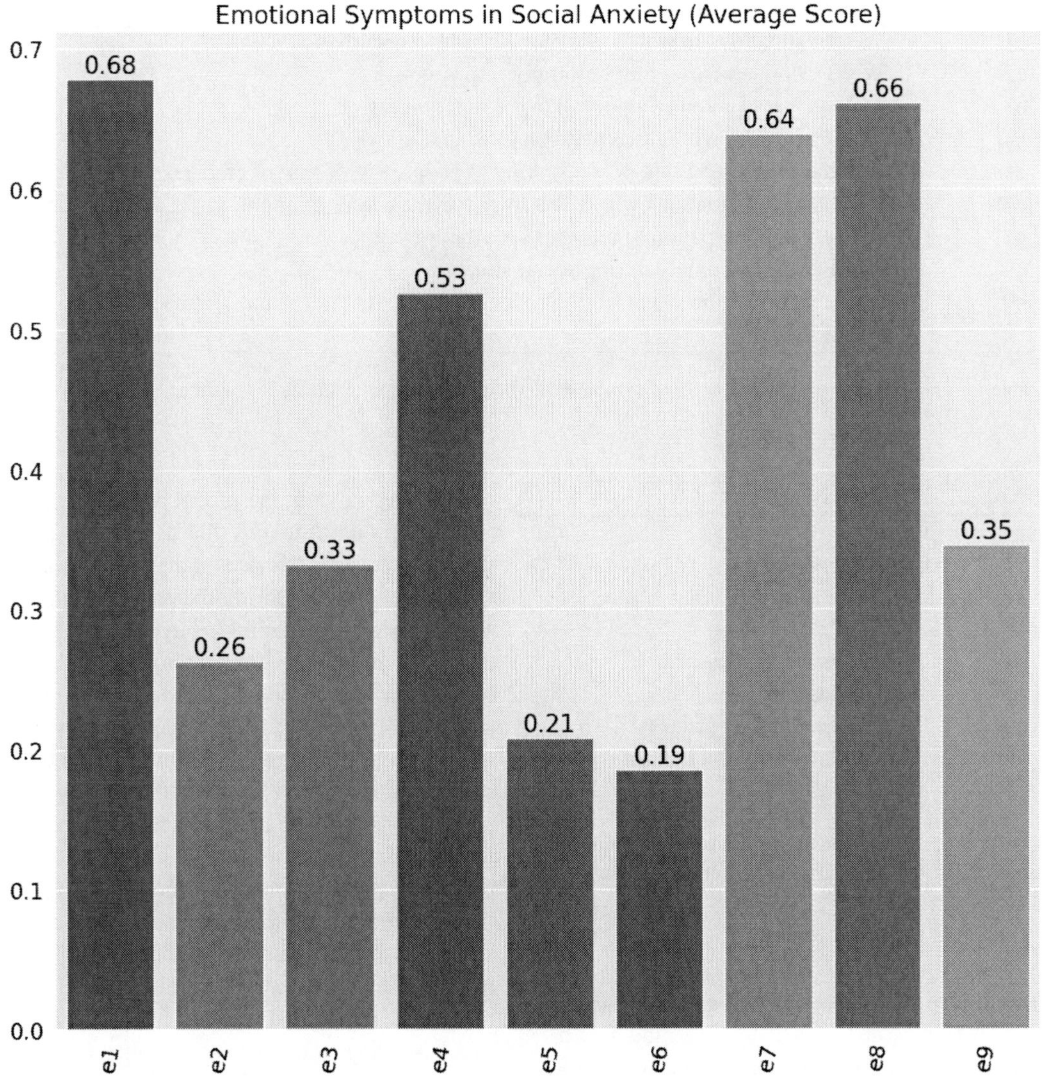

Figure 1: The bar chart illustrates the average zero-shot classification probability scores for emotional symptoms mentioned in Table 1 related to social anxiety. The scores were computed by averaging all individual scores for all 12,277 subreddits text documents / subreddits.

a distinct user, resulting in a dataset intentionally diversified with contributions from 12,277 unique users—a deliberate choice to enhance reliability in the context of crowd-sourcing tasks.

Our purpose in utilizing this dataset is to delve into the unique perspectives and challenges voiced by individuals within these online communities. The central objective is to conduct a thorough analysis, aiming to comprehend the intricate interplay and associations among various prevalent symptoms discussed within the r/socialanxiety subreddit. Our exploration involves examining the diverse experiences shared within this particular online community, with the primary goal of uncovering and scrutinizing the complex relationships between different symptoms linked to social anxiety disorder. This investigative approach provides a distinctive opportunity to gain valuable insights into the multifaceted nature of social anxiety, as perceived and expressed by members of this specific online community.

3.2 BART Based Multi-Label Zero Shot Classification

Facebook AI Research (FAIR) is accountable for the development of BART (Bidirectional and Auto

No.	Emotional Symptoms
e1	Fear of situations in which you may be judged negatively
e2	Worry about embarrassing or humiliating yourself
e3	Intense fear of interacting or talking with strangers
e4	Fear that others will notice that you look anxious
e5	Avoidance of doing things or speaking to people out of fear of embarrassment
e6	Avoidance of situations where you might be the center of attention
e7	Anxiety in anticipation of a feared activity or event
e8	Intense fear or anxiety during social situations
e9	Expectation of the worst possible consequences from a negative experience during a social situation

Table 1: The table illustrates the emotional symptoms associated with social anxiety as outlined on the Mayo Clinic (May, 2021)

No.	Physical Symptoms
p1	Blushing
p2	Fast heartbeat
p3	Trembling
p4	Sweating
p5	Upset stomach or nausea
p6	Trouble catching your breath
p7	Dizziness or lightheadedness
p8	Feeling that your mind has gone blank
p9	Muscle tension

Table 2: The table illustrates the physical symptoms associated with social anxiety as outlined on the Mayo Clinic (May, 2021)

Regressive Transformer), a progressive language model (Lewis et al., 2019). The model is pre-trained using a combination of denoising autoencoding and sequence-to-sequence tasks, and it is based on the Transformer architecture. The architecture of the BART model consists of encoders and decoders. The encoder receives the input sequence and proceeds to process it through a sequence of transformer layers. Every transformer layer includes position-wise feed-forward neural networks alongside multi-head self-attention approaches. The model can effectively capture the relationships between individual words in the input sequence through a technique known as self-attention.

The encoder generates an encoded representation, which is subsequently handed to the decoder. The decoder then produces the output sequence in an autoregressive manner. In addition to utilising transformer layers, it also has a cross-attention mechanism that focuses on the encoded input sequence. As a result, the model has the capability to produce output tokens that depend not just on the input sequence but also on the tokens it has previously generated. During the pre-training phase, BART undergoes training using vast amounts of data, which can be either monolingual or parallel. It gains the capacity to reconstruct the initial sequence of input data from damaged copies, allowing it to better capture significant representations of the entered data. The versatility of BART in performing various text generation tasks, including text summarization, machine translation, and text completion, is a very notable feature of this application. By conducting fine-tuning on specific downstream tasks and adjusting the model accordingly, it is feasible to optimise the pre-trained BART model to generate high-quality outputs for a diverse range of natural language processing applications.

(Yin et al., 2019) introduced an innovative technique harnessing the capabilities of pre-trained Natural Language Inference (NLI) models as adept zero-shot sequence classifiers. (Tesfagergish et al., 2022; Chae and Davidson, 2023) This approach involves structuring the sequence under examination as the NLI premise, then formulating a hypothesis for each potential label. For instance, when scrutinizing whether a sequence aligns with a specific social anxiety symptom, such as "Trembling," a corresponding hypothesis might read, "This text is about Trembling." Following this framing, the probabilities associated with entailment (alignment) and contradiction (misalignment) undergo transformation into probabilities specifically linked to each symptom label (Patadia et al., 2021; Basile et al., 2021). In instances where multiple labels could be pertinent, activating the multi-label setting, uti-

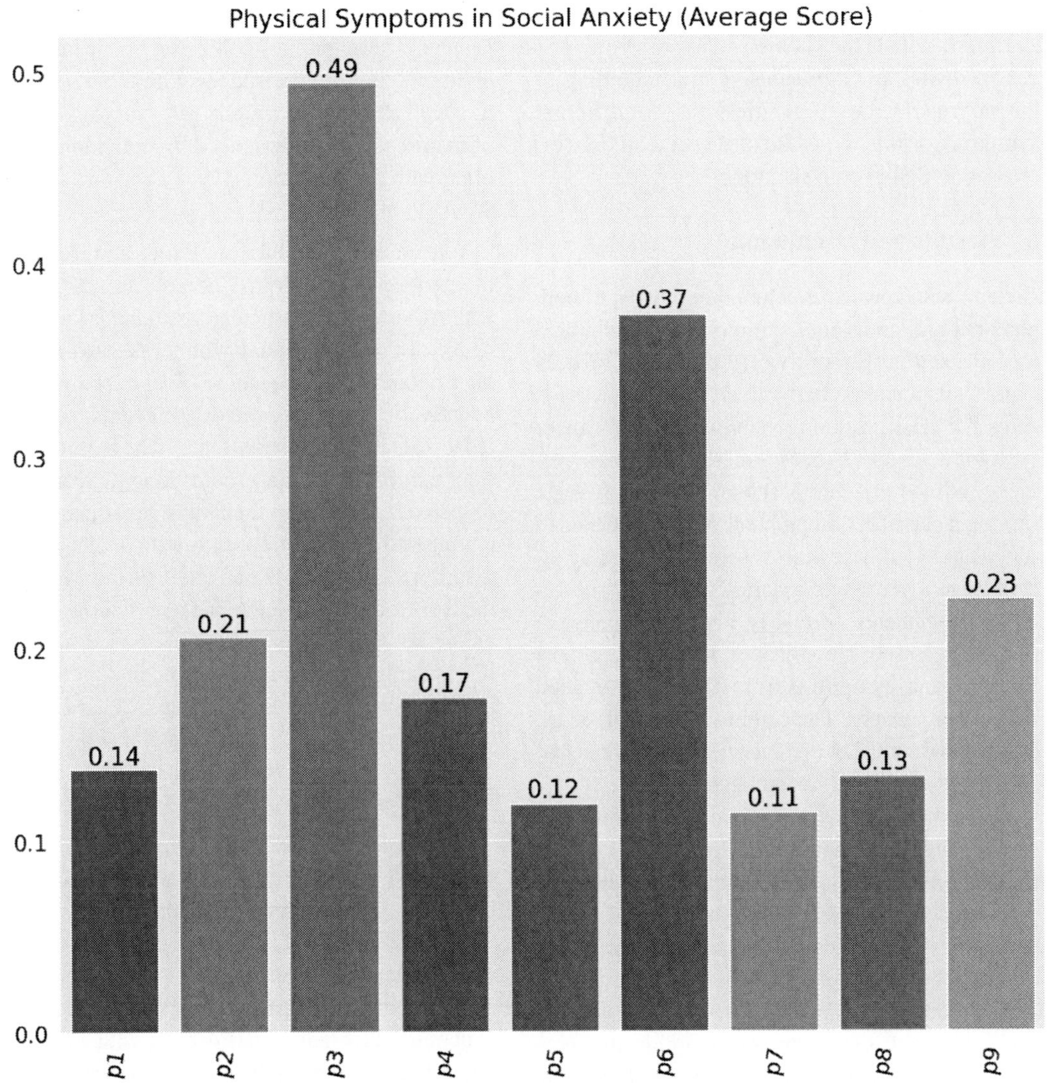

Figure 2: The bar chart illustrates the average zero-shot classification probability scores for physical symptoms mentioned in Table 2 related to social anxiety. The scores were computed by averaging all individual scores for all 12,277 subreddits text documents / subreddits.

lizing the huggingface BART implementation, enables the independent computation of probabilities for each symptom class.

The BART-based zero-shot classification solutions distinguish themselves from traditional supervised learning classification approaches by leveraging pre-trained language models. In contrast to supervised learning, which necessitates labeled training data for each class, BART-based zero-shot classification can generalize to new, unseen classes without specific training on them (Moreno-Garcia et al., 2023). This adaptability renders BART-based solutions superior to traditional classification algorithms. It proves particularly advantageous when dealing with evolving or dynamic datasets where labeled examples for all potential classes may not be readily accessible.

In our study, we employ this methodology to calculate the probabilities for each label representing various social anxiety symptoms within each individual Reddit text document. This meticulous analysis allows us to determine the relative strength of association between the document and each symptom label. Subsequently, by computing the arithmetic mean of these probabilities across all documents for each symptom label, we unveil the prevalence frequency of each social anxiety symptom within the dataset. This rigorous process provides a comprehensive understanding of the varying degrees of manifestation for different symptoms within the context of social anxiety expressed in Reddit conversations.

4 Results and Discussion

Tables 1 and 2 present a comprehensive list of both physical and emotional symptoms of social anxiety utilized in this study. Additionally, Figures 1 and 2 display bar charts illustrating the average zero-shot classification probability scores for these symptoms. Figure 1 focuses on the physical symptoms outlined in Table 2, showcasing the average zero-shot classification probability scores related to social anxiety. These scores were calculated by averaging individual scores across all 12,277 subreddit text documents. Similarly, Figure 2 depicts the average zero-shot classification probability scores for emotional symptoms from Table 1 associated with social anxiety. The computation involved averaging individual scores across the entire set of 12,277 subreddit text documents.

Beginning with an analysis of the results concerning physical symptoms, the data reveals intriguing patterns. Notably, the most prevalent physical symptom observed within social anxiety disorder emerges as "Trembling," boasting significantly, average probability score of 49 percent. Trembling, an outward manifestation characterized by body shaking, stands out prominently within this context, reflecting its substantial association with social anxiety experiences.

Following closely after Trembling, the subsequent prominent physical symptom is the sensation of catching one's breath. This finding reinforces the study's validity by mirroring the reality experienced by numerous individuals worldwide grappling with social anxiety. Moreover, the data highlights additional moderately prevalent symptoms, including rapid heartbeat, sweating, and muscle tension, each scoring approximately around 20 percent. This categorization positions Trembling and catching breath as higher-frequency symptoms, while the trio of rapid heartbeat, sweating, and muscle tension forms the middle tier in terms of prevalence. Conversely, the analysis also unveils relatively lower-frequency physical symptoms of social anxiety. Symptoms such as blushing, mental blankness, and upset stomach emerge with probability scores ranging from approximately 11 to 14 percent. These findings collectively delineate a gradient of symptom prevalence within the spectrum of social anxiety, showcasing the varying degrees of manifestation experienced by individuals grappling with this condition (Heerey and Kring, 2007; Weeks et al., 2008).

When examining the prevalence and frequency of emotional symptoms, notable trends surface within the dataset. Particularly striking is the prominence of three emotional symptoms, each registering a notably high frequency: "Fear of being judged negatively," "Anxiety or fear of events," and "Intense fear of social situations." These three emotions exhibit probability scores ranging from 64 to 68 percent, signifying their substantial occurrence among individuals grappling with social anxiety disorder. Additionally, the analysis uncovers that the fear of others noticing one's nervousness ranks as the second-highest emotional concern among respondents. Following closely behind, in the third position, are two emotional states: "Fear of worst consequences due to negative social experiences" and "Fear of talking with strangers," each carrying a notable probability score of 33 to 35 percent.

Conversely, the emotional symptoms exhibiting the lowest probability scores are "Avoidance of situations where attention might be drawn" and "Avoidance of speaking to people due to fear of embarrassment." These findings offer nuanced insights into the varying degrees of emotional distress experienced by individuals dealing with social anxiety disorder. These intriguing discoveries (Beard and Amir, 2008), obtained through observational studies, hold significant potential for fostering a deeper understanding of social anxiety from a community perspective. Moreover, they pave the way for crowd-sourced insights, potentially contributing to the development of innovative remedies and interventions aimed at alleviating the challenges posed by social anxiety. The insights gleaned from these emotional symptom prevalence patterns can serve as a valuable resource in guiding future research and therapeutic strategies aimed at addressing this prevalent mental health issue.

As previously stated, the findings presented herein are derived from a comprehensive analysis of 12,277 subreddits belongs to social anxiety, each associated with distinct users. It is crucial to acknowledge the potential for bias in the information gathered from these diverse sources. However, to mitigate this concern, we have adopted a methodological approach that involves averaging the prevalent scores. This calculation entails determining the probability score for each symptom across all subreddits. In doing so, we strive to enhance the authenticity of the information, particularly in the context of crowd-sourced data.

Nevertheless, to further bolster the credibility and reliability of these observational results, it is imperative to seek validation through clinical verification. The integration of clinical assessments would provide a more robust foundation for the findings, ensuring a comprehensive and well-rounded evaluation of the presented information.

5 Limitations

This study explores the experiences of individuals coping with social anxiety disorder, utilising user-generated content from Reddit. Nevertheless, it is crucial to recognise the inherent limitations associated with this observational methodology. The collected data includes self-reported experiences obtained from an open platform, which may introduce biases in terms of accuracy and completeness. Moreover, the absence of clinical validation or expert assessment of these symptoms could affect the precision and clinical significance of the collected information. This study solely captures experiences that are unique to the Reddit platform, perhaps disregarding a wide range of opinions or individuals, which in future may be verified from the clinical point of view for the further validation of this study.

Ethics Statement

This study upholds stringent ethical and privacy considerations throughout its entirety. Specifically, the dataset sourced from Reddit is rigorously maintained under the Public Domain Dedication and License v1.0, ensuring the preservation of Reddit users' privacy. Importantly, the study maintains a strict adherence to anonymity, refraining from disclosing any user identities within the article or its findings. This commitment to confidentiality and privacy safeguards the individuals contributing to the dataset, upholding their anonymity and confidentiality in line with ethical standards.

References

2021. [link].

Angelo Basile, Guillermo Pérez-Torró, and Marc Franco-Salvador. 2021. Probabilistic ensembles of zero-and few-shot learning models for emotion classification. In *Proceedings of the International Conference on Recent Advances in Natural Language Processing (RANLP 2021)*, pages 128–137.

Courtney Beard and Nader Amir. 2008. A multi-session interpretation modification program: Changes in interpretation and social anxiety symptoms. *Behaviour research and therapy*, 46(10):1135–1141.

Gordon W Blood and Ingrid M Blood. 2016. Long-term consequences of childhood bullying in adults who stutter: Social anxiety, fear of negative evaluation, self-esteem, and satisfaction with life. *Journal of fluency disorders*, 50:72–84.

Youngjin Chae and Thomas Davidson. 2023. Large language models for text classification: From zero-shot learning to fine-tuning. *Open Science Foundation.*

Nawshad Farruque, Randy Goebel, Osmar R Zaïane, and Sudhakar Sivapalan. 2021. Explainable zero-shot modelling of clinical depression symptoms from text. In *2021 20th IEEE International Conference on Machine Learning and Applications (ICMLA)*, pages 1472–1477. IEEE.

Erin A Heerey and Ann M Kring. 2007. Interpersonal consequences of social anxiety. *Journal of abnormal psychology*, 116(1):125.

Juyoen Hur, Kathryn A DeYoung, Samiha Islam, Allegra S Anderson, Matthew G Barstead, and Alexander J Shackman. 2020. Social context and the real-world consequences of social anxiety. *Psychological Medicine*, 50(12):1989–2000.

Jean-Pierre Lépine and Antoine Pelissolo. 2000. Why take social anxiety disorder seriously? *Depression and Anxiety*, 11(3):87–92.

Mike Lewis, Yinhan Liu, Naman Goyal, Marjan Ghazvininejad, Abdelrahman Mohamed, Omer Levy, Ves Stoyanov, and Luke Zettlemoyer. 2019. Bart: Denoising sequence-to-sequence pre-training for natural language generation, translation, and comprehension. *arXiv preprint arXiv:1910.13461.*

Pan Liu and Jaron XY Tan. 2023. Behavioral and erp indices of self-schematic processing show differential associations with emerging symptoms of depression and social anxiety in late childhood: Evidence from a community-dwelling sample. *Biological Psychology*, page 108594.

Daniel M Low, Laurie Rumker, Tanya Talkar, John Torous, Guillermo Cecchi, and Satrajit S Ghosh. 2020. Natural language processing reveals vulnerable mental health support groups and heightened health anxiety on reddit during covid-19: Observational study. *Journal of medical Internet research*, 22(10):e22635.

Carlos Francisco Moreno-Garcia, Chrisina Jayne, Eyad Elyan, and Magaly Aceves-Martins. 2023. A novel application of machine learning and zero-shot classification methods for automated abstract screening in systematic reviews. *Decision Analytics Journal*, page 100162.

Devika Patadia, Shivam Kejriwal, Pashva Mehta, and Abhijit R Joshi. 2021. Zero-shot approach for news and scholarly article classification. In *2021 International Conference on Advances in Computing, Communication, and Control (ICAC3)*, pages 1–5. IEEE.

Senait Gebremichael Tesfagergish, Jurgita Kapočiūtė-Dzikienė, and Robertas Damaševičius. 2022. Zero-shot emotion detection for semi-supervised sentiment analysis using sentence transformers and ensemble learning. *Applied Sciences*, 12(17):8662.

Justin W Weeks, Richard G Heimberg, and Thomas L Rodebaugh. 2008. The fear of positive evaluation scale: Assessing a proposed cognitive component of social anxiety. *Journal of anxiety disorders*, 22(1):44–55.

Kailai Yang, Tianlin Zhang, Ziyan Kuang, Qianqian Xie, and Sophia Ananiadou. 2023. Mentalllama: Interpretable mental health analysis on social media with large language models. *arXiv preprint arXiv:2309.13567*.

Wenpeng Yin, Jamaal Hay, and Dan Roth. 2019. Benchmarking zero-shot text classification: Datasets, evaluation and entailment approach. *arXiv preprint arXiv:1909.00161*.

James M Zech, Tapan A Patel, and Jesse R Cougle. 2023. Safety behaviors predict long-term treatment outcome following internet-based treatment of adults with social anxiety disorder. *Cognitive Therapy and Research*, 47(3):412–422.

Comparing panic and anxiety on a dataset collected from social media

Sandra Mitrović[1]
Oscar William Lithgow-Serrano[1]
Carlo Schillaci[2]
[1]IDSIA - USI/SUPSI, Switzerland
[2]SUPSI, Switzerland
sandra.mitrovic@idsia.ch, oscarwilliam.lithgow@idsia.ch
carlo.schillaci@student.supsi.ch

Abstract

The recognition of mental health's crucial significance has led to a growing interest in utilizing social media text data in current research trends. However, there remains a significant gap in the study of panic and anxiety on these platforms, despite their high prevalence and severe impact. In this paper, we address this gap by presenting a dataset consisting of 1,930 user posts from Quora and Reddit specifically focusing on panic and anxiety. Through a combination of lexical analysis, emotion detection, and writer attitude assessment, we explore the unique characteristics of each condition. To gain deeper insights, we employ a mental health-specific transformer model and a large language model for qualitative analysis. Our findings not only contribute to the understanding digital discourse on anxiety and panic but also provide valuable resources for the broader research community. We make our dataset, methodologies, and code available to advance understanding and facilitate future studies.

ANXIETY: "I honestly don't think it can be even described in words. I think anxiety comes in different ways in different people, so i am just going to say about my experience. Having anxiety is not being able to remember the last time that you were relaxed without a disturbing thought in your head. Having anxiety means that your brain is extremely creative with coming up with the worst improbable almost impossible scenario. It is like having a brain that thinks every minor chest pain as a heart attack, every headache a brain tumor and every numbness ms. Having anxiety means to always overthink every action and saying and every situation. It means that you have to forget about having fun and enjoying life. It means that you have always to doubt yourself. I can literally go on forever."
PANIC: "Picture yourself sitting on the couch enjoying a television show. You feel relaxed and decide to get up and get something to drink. You open the cabinet door to get a glass when... our of nowhere you feel this big surge of suffocating fear.. your heart starts pounding out of your chest, reality suddenly doesn't feel real. All you know is that you must be alone. You feel like you are free falling faster and faster into the dark pit of hell. You feel depressed and defeated and when it passes you feel exhausted."

Figure 1: An example of an ANXIETY and a PANIC post extracted from Quora website.

Source	Panic	Anxiety	*Total*
Quora	526	976	1502
Reddit	187	241	428
Total	**713**	**1217**	**1930**

Table 1: Number of samples per source and per class.

1 Introduction

The indisputable importance of mental health is recently reflecting in the increased research interest, putting the emphasis on identifying related issues in the textual sources in social media and focusing mainly on depression (William and Suhartono, 2021; Bhadra and Kumar, 2022; Parapar et al., 2023) and suicide (Bayram and Benhiba, 2022; Malhotra and Jindal, 2022). We contend that anxiety and panic, despite being understudied, are equally significant. Panic is conventionally described as a sudden, overwhelming fear (Bloom et al., 2009), while anxiety is marked by persistent unease and uncontrollable worry (Stein and Sareen, 2015). Despite their shared characteristics, the literature indicates that the differentiation between generalized anxiety and panic is valid (Russell Noyes et al., 1992). While anxiety, in the related literature, is typically coupled with depression (Burkhardt et al., 2022; Tasnim et al., 2023), panic is, in general and with few exceptions (Mitrović and Kanjirangat, 2022), (Mitrović et al., 2023), far less studied. Discriminating between anxiety and panic is important, given that individuals experiencing panic face a higher risk of more profound psychological and psychiatric issues, including acute suicidality and agoraphobia. Moreover, the study of panic can be instrumental in identifying individuals with PTSD, making it a highly worthwhile topic. Thus, the ability to identify patients undergoing panic is crucial, carrying substantial clini-

Proceedings of the 9th Workshop on Computational Linguistics and Clinical Psychology (CLPsych 2024), pages 153–165
March 21, 2024 ©2024 Association for Computational Linguistics

cal implications. Nevertheless, to the best of our knowledge, current literature lacks computational approaches for discerning panic and anxiety in social media textual resources. To bridge this gap, we collected a related dataset of 1,930 user posts originating from two well-known websites, Quora[1] and Reddit[2], and we conduct a versatile analysis to address the following research questions:

[RQ1]: How (dis)similar are panic-annotated to the anxiety-annotated posts? And how different are the posts coming from different blogs?

[RQ2]: How successfully can a classifier discern a panic post from an anxiety one?

[RQ3]: What a qualitative NLP-assisted analysis on this dataset can tell about mental health and related context?

Besides the insights of various lexical, emotion, writers' attitudes, classical machine learning and (large) language models-based approaches, we contribute the literature by providing the dataset, analysis and code[3].

We anticipate that certain discoveries from our research may contribute to practical applications. In particular, distinguishing between anxiety and panic triggers holds potential clinical utility and could guide the deployment of emergency medical assistance. Additionally, it may encourage individuals to reach out to their designated support person. In general, the paper could aid in screening posts on social media displaying indications of anxiety or panic, thereby contributing to a better mental health understanding and practice.

2 Dataset collection

We web scraped the data[4], starting from the well-known question answering website Quora and a set of questions related primarily to panic (attacks), extending it to similar questions related to anxiety (or other anxiety-related questions that we came upon in Quora). We then switched to another popular blogging website, Reddit, and looked for semantically similar questions and answers. We only collected the original question and the first reply to it, without tracking the whole conversation (replying to a reply is frequently common in Reddit). Question could contain either "anxiety" or "panic" keyword and we applied rule-based annotation based on the keyword presence (considering panic class as positive). It is important noting that questions, albeit used for determining class label, are not considered as the integral part of the dataset.

Tab. 1 presents basic distribution of posts per class per blog, while the questions used for data collection can be found in Appendix A.2, Tab. 4. It is noteworthy to mention that we adhered to this predetermined set of questions to guarantee the distinct separation of classes, guided by the rule-based strategy driven by question formulation.

3 [RQ1] How (dis)similar are panic- to the anxiety-annotated posts? And is there any difference wrt the post source (originating blog)?

To this end, we conducted a multifaceted analysis.

Linguistic Perspective Using LIWC-22 (Pennebaker et al., 2022) features, we could see than panic posts have on average more words than those of anxiety (169.87 vs. 160.83), also containing more pronouns and verbs. Anxiety posts, on the other hand, contain on average more words per sentence (20.64 vs 18.47) and longer words (23.17 vs. 17.45) than panic (see A.2, Fig. 5). Quora posts contain more words in general (191.64 vs. 67.77), more words per sentence and longer words than Reddit ones, which, on the contrary, are richer in verbs, adverbs and pronouns (see A.2, Fig. 6).

Readability Perspective Upon calculating different readability scores we have noticed prominent difference between two classes on average Flesch score (FS) for Quora posts, with 49.84 for anxiety versus 63.72 for panic, meaning that in Quora, posts denoted as anxiety are more difficult to read than those denoted as panic (see A.2, Fig. 9). Reddit texts are in general, more similar with respect to readability and also easier to read (with average FS per both classes being around 70).

Emotion Perspective We analyzed two different aspects related to emotions: their presence and their intensity. To determine how represented the emotions are in a post, we employed a pretrained HuggingFace language model (Demszky et al., 2020) and used inferred emotion probabilities relative to 28 different emotions, from the Go-Emotions dataset, as a proxy.

When considering only 5 most represented emotions per post (Fig. 2), we can notice that gratitude, nervousness and pride have higher average rank in the anxiety posts than in the panic ones. Similar

[1] https://www.quora.com/

[2] https://www.reddit.com/

[3] https://github.com/SandraMNE/QRPanicAnxiety

[4] For implementation details see Appendix A.1.

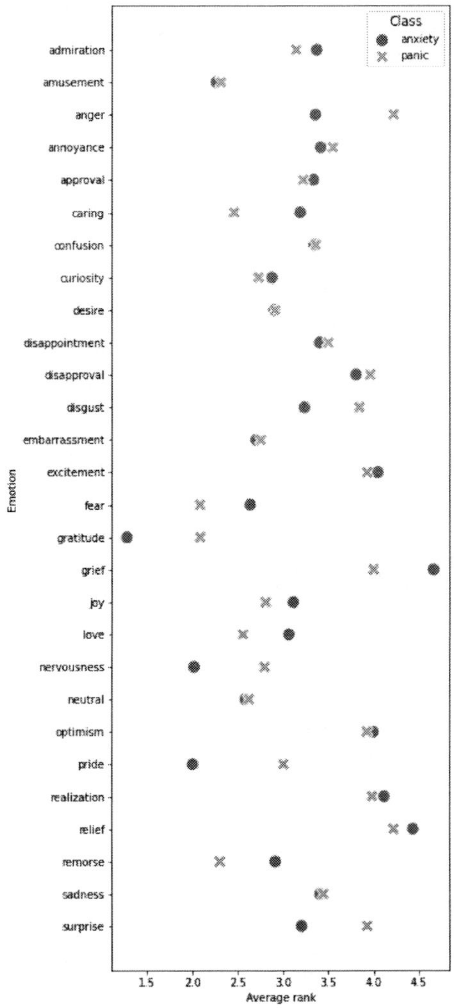

Figure 2: Average rank of emotions, calculated based on the 5 most important emotions per post.

pattern, although with much less important average rank, can be observed for disgust and surprise, while fear, remorse, caring and love have higher average rank in the panic posts. Within the top 5 most represented emotions per post, the 5 most frequent are neutral emotion, nervousness, fear and approval for both panic and anxiety; realization for panic and caring for anxiety (see A.2, Fig. 4).

When considering all the emotions per post, the Mann-Whitney U-test revealed a statistically significant difference in the mean ranks of fear, admiration, amusement, approval, disgust, gratitude, optimism, realization and surprise emotions between panic and anxiety posts, with a significance level set at $\alpha = 0.05$.

To assess emotion intensities, we used intensity lexicon (Mohammad, 2018) considering only 8 emotions: anger, anticipation, disgust, fear, joy, sadness, surprise, trust. As expected, fear is the emotion with the highest intensity in both classes. In panic posts, fear and anger have higher intensity on average than in anxiety posts (fear intensity: 0.46 in anxiety vs. 0.53 in panic posts; anger intensity: 0.34 in anxiety vs. 0.40 in panic posts). Conversely, anticipation and sadness have higher average intensity in anxiety posts than in the panic ones (see Fig. 7). With regard to the post sources, as displayed in A.2, Fig. 8, all considered emotion intensities are amplified in Quora as compared to Reddit.

Writer's Attitude Perspective We investigate writer's attitude from the perspective of convincingness (Gretz et al., 2019), persuasiveness and usage of irony (Barbieri et al., 2020). While almost no difference could be noted in the irony and persuasiveness average scores between the two classes, average score for convincingness somewhat differs (0.76 for anxiety vs. 0.73 for panic). When considering the sources, we observe that panic posts in both sources have similar convincingness level. However, on overall Quora posts exhibit higher average convincingness (0.78 vs. 0.7) and persuasiveness scores (0.36 vs. 0.29) than Reddit. On the contrary, Reddit posts contain more irony (average score 0.17) than Quora's (0.12).

4 [RQ2] How successfully can a classifier discern panic from anxiety posts?

In order to answer this question, we build a Gradient Boosting classifier. Apart from already mentioned LIWC variables (denoted as L), emotion probabilities (denoted as M), emotion intensities (denoted as I), convincingness, persuasiveness and irony scores (denoted together as W), we calculated also the embeddings (B) of the posts and included them as input features. The obtained results can be seen in Tab. 2. Fairly good performance of classifier, low variance across 10 runs and relatively small discrepancy between F1-macro and F1-weighted/F1-micro scores, despite the strong class imbalanceness, showcase the good predictive power of features and classifier robustness. Additionally, sacrificing a bit of performance by excluding embeddings we can obtain an explainable model. The latter, as depicted in A.2, Fig. 10, showcases that LIWC mental, fear intensity and LIWC long words are considered important in all

10 runs.

Features	F1-weighted	F1-macro	F1-micro	ROC AUC	MCC
B	0.896 (0.01)	0.889 (0.01)	0.897 (0.01)	0.960 (0.01)	0.780 (0.02)
L+M+I+W	0.816 (0.02)	0.801 (0.02)	0.819 (0.02)	0.891 (0.02)	0.609 (0.03)
B+L+M+I+W	0.899 (0.01)	0.891 (0.01)	0.898 (0.01)	0.960 (0.01)	**0.783 (0.02)**

Table 2: XGBoost classifier average performance in terms of F1-score, ROC AUC and MCC (and standard deviation) across 10 runs. Notation: B - embedding, L - LIWC, M - emotion probabilities, I - emotion intensities, W - writer's attitude.

Probing the rule-based annotation One might argue that the rule-based class separation used for annotation makes the two classes easily distinguishable based on the two keywords. We therefore perform two straightforward yet efficient analysis.

First, we investigated whether the imposed one-question-one-keyword pattern holds for the answers as well. It turned out that it was not the case. More specifically, out of total 1930 blog posts, as much as 386 (20%) contain both "panic"and "anxiety" keywords. The co-occurrence of "panic"and "anxiety" keywords is specifically prominent in Quora where 343 out of 1502 posts (22.84%) contain both keywords, while in Reddit this is less frequent (only 43 out of 428 posts or 14.06%).

Second, we replaced all the occurrences of the two keywords with "MASKEDCONTENT" token, recalculated the respective features on the obtained texts and retrained the classifier. As could be seen from Tab. 3, although, as expected, the performances drop in terms of all considered metrics, the downgrade in the performance is not prominent. This indicates that the presence of the "panic" and "anxiety" keywords in not crucial for classification.

5 [RQ3] What a qualitative NLP-assisted analysis on this dataset can tell about mental health and related context?

We conduct a two-fold analysis. First, we aim to determine what the posters were experiencing. To this end, we prompted language model pretrained on mental health discussions (Ji et al., 2021)), requesting a YES/NO answer related to stress and open answers related to "experiencing". Results are depicted in A.2, Fig. 12 and 11 respectively.

Second, we leveraged Large Language Models (LLM), specifically ChatGPT-3.5. We initially used it to assess the dataset annotation quality, finding that only 8.4% of collected panic posts were misclassified as anxiety by ChatGPT, and merely 3.8% of original anxiety posts were erroneously labeled

Features	Dataset	F1-weighted	F1-macro	F1-micro	ROC AUC	MCC
B	Original	0.896 (0.01)	0.889 (0.01)	0.897 (0.01)	0.960 (0.01)	**0.780 (0.02)**
	Masked	0.875 (0.01)	0.866 (0.01)	0.876 (0.01)	0.940 (0.01)	0.734 (0.02)
B+L+M+W	Original	0.896 (0.01)	0.889 (0.01)	0.897 (0.01)	0.960 (0.01)	0.779 (0.02)
	Masked	0.873 (0.01)	0.864 (0.01)	0.874 (0.01)	0.940 (0.01)	0.730 (0.02)

Table 3: XGBoost classifier average performance (and standard deviation) in terms of F1-score, ROC AUC and MCC across 10 runs on the original and masked dataset. Notation: B - embedding.

as panic. We then conducted a comprehensive multidimensional thematic and content analysis. This involved automated coding and key-phrase extraction across various dimensions (see A.2 for details). Several noteworthy observations emerged from our investigation. Notably, panic attacks exhibited a higher "Strong" intensity (21%) compared to anxiety attacks (7%). In the context of relationships, the top four categories were shared among classes. However, the fifth differed, with "Work" for anxiety and "Romantic partners" for panic. Location-wise, the prevalent places were Home, School, Work, and Public places. In the triggers category, social events constituted 33% of anxiety triggers, contrasting with only 9% for panic attacks. Traumatic experiences accounted for 11% of panic triggers, as opposed to 5.6% for anxiety. Notably, financial stress was among the top five anxiety triggers but was absent in panic (see Fig. 3). Understanding anxiety and panic triggers is vital for uncovering their root causes and informing targeted interventions (Johnson et al., 2014; Craske, 1991; Barzegar et al., 2021). Examining specific triggering events helps elucidate factors contributing to distress. Focusing on locations where these experiences occur provides insights into environmental influences (Swee et al., 2021), aiding the development of strategies for supportive environments. Investigating relationships contributes valuable insights into the impact of social interactions on these conditions (Tonge et al., 2020), facilitating interventions to improve social relationships and support systems. Figure 3 emphasizes these dimensions to enhance comprehension.

In the category of other_medical_conditions, stress-related conditions were prevalent in both anxiety and panic. However, panic exhibited a unique pattern, with breath-related conditions like asthma, COPD, sinus infections, nasal congestion, and COVID-19 being the most frequently mentioned. More details on different distributions, including professional inteventions, is provided in A.2, Tab. 5.

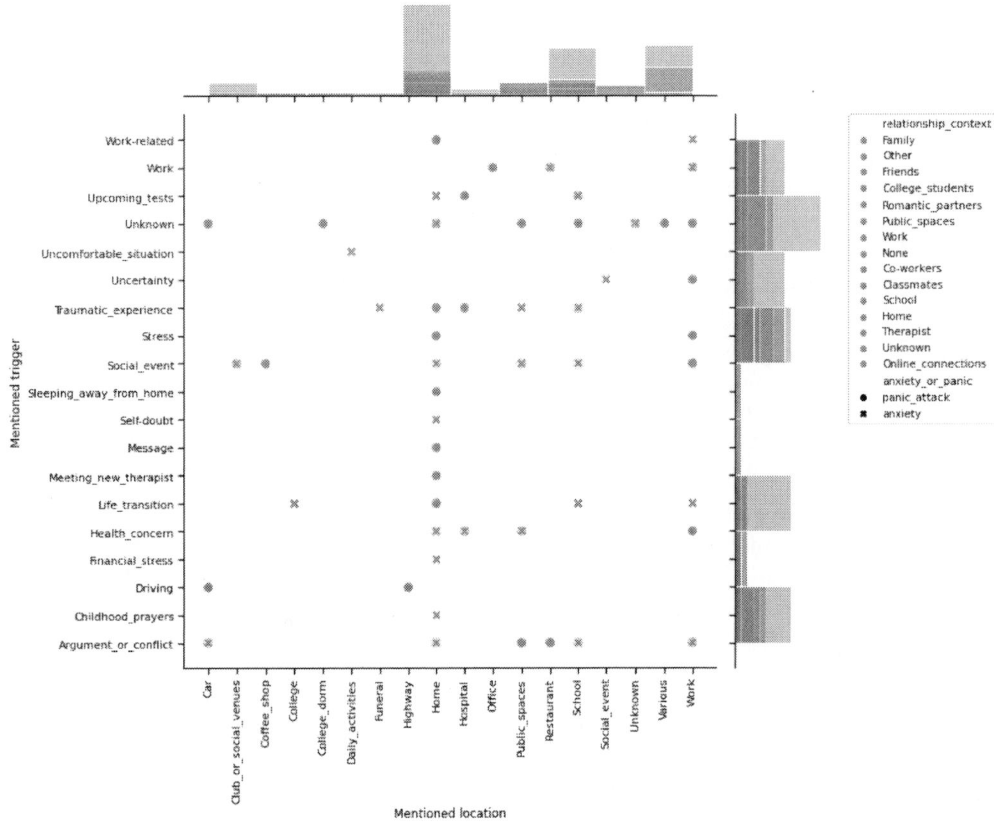

Figure 3: Context mentioned (Location, Social relationship and Trigger) in posts of personal experiences. Posts coded as "None" or "Other" on a specific axis were disregarded to enhance the readability.

6 Conclusion

In this study, we collected a dataset on two prevalent and closely related mental disorders: panic and anxiety. Our analytical exploration centered around three primary questions. Firstly, we focused into uncovering the distinctions and similarities, both in content and sources, between the anxiety and panic classes. To address this, we conducted lexical analyses, emotion assessments, and evaluations of writers' attitudes. Secondly, we assessed the efficacy of a classical machine learning classifier, leveraging combinations of the various extracted features, in distinguishing between posts belonging to these classes. Importantly, we conducted experiments to ensure the classifiers did not rely solely on the presence of explicit "panic"/"anxiety" keyword. Lastly, we sought insights into these disorders through a qualitative analysis of the dataset, leveraging a bidirectional transformer model trained on mental health texts (Mental-RoBERTa) and a large-language model (ChatGPT-3.5).

As a part of our contribution, we provide the entire output resulting from the NLP processes, including the collected codings and key-phrase extractions derived from the qualitative analysis. We hope that the obtained insights could be further exploited by domain experts. Looking ahead, future explorations aim to contribute to bring more layers of understanding within the context of these mental health disorders, for example, including a more in-depth analysis and clustering of key-phrase excerpts, with a particular focus on those associated with coping strategies, negative behavioral changes, and the impact on daily life.

7 Acknowledgements

The work of Oscar Lithgow-Serrano was partially supported by the project "Risk Identification and Prevention of Work-Related Stress Disorders" (Innosuisse 62423.1 IP-LS).

8 Limitations

As with any research, our study is not without limitations. With respect to data collection, the limitations are manifold. First, we considered limited number of questions which additionally have not been very well balanced between panic and anxiety. Second, the collected dataset is quite small and also the class distribution is quite skewed, hence we have to be very careful in assuming its generalizability. Third, as with all studies relying on the social media data, there is no possibility to know who is posting or how accurately. Fourth, we acknowledge that individuals writing may be experiencing anxiety, but they are unlikely to be blogging during a panic attack. Therefore, their narratives or teachings are more likely to revolve around recounting or educating about panic, rather than experiencing it in real-time.

Additionally, the emotion intensities were not calculated for all 28 emotions considered for the analysis of the emotions presence. Moreover, despite the small dataset size, we could have still tried to train a classifier with deep architecture.

9 Ethical considerations

Although Quora and Reddit data are publicly available, we do understand that the collected content is privacy-sensitive and that we might, even involuntarily, expose person's mental health-related privacy. To prevent easy backtrack to the author, we decided to delete not only users' usernames but also the original questions posed.

References

Francesco Barbieri, Jose Camacho-Collados, Luis Espinosa Anke, and Leonardo Neves. 2020. TweetEval: Unified Benchmark and Comparative Evaluation for Tweet Classification. In *Findings of the Association for Computational Linguistics: EMNLP 2020*, pages 1644–1650, Online. Association for Computational Linguistics.

Habibeh Barzegar, Mostafa Farahbakhsh, Hosein Azizi, Sepideh Aliashrafi, Hossein Dadashzadeh, and Ali Fakhari. 2021. A descriptive study of agoraphobic situations and correlates on panic disorder. *Middle East Current Psychiatry*, 28(1):31.

Ulya Bayram and Lamia Benhiba. 2022. Emotionally-informed models for detecting moments of change and suicide risk levels in longitudinal social media data. In *Proceedings of the Eighth Workshop on Computational Linguistics and Clinical Psychology*, pages 219–225.

Sweta Bhadra and Chandan Jyoti Kumar. 2022. An insight into diagnosis of depression using machine learning techniques: a systematic review. *Current medical research and opinion*, 38(5):749–771.

Floyd E Bloom, Nicholas C Spitzer, Fred Gage, and Tom Albright. 2009. *Encyclopedia of Neuroscience, Volume 1*, volume 1. Academic Press.

Hannah Burkhardt, Michael Pullmann, Thomas Hull, Patricia Areán, and Trevor Cohen. 2022. Comparing emotion feature extraction approaches for predicting depression and anxiety. In *Proceedings of the eighth workshop on computational linguistics and clinical psychology*, pages 105–115.

Michelle G. Craske. 1991. Phobic fear and panic attacks: The same emotional states triggered by different cues? *Clinical Psychology Review*, 11(5):599–620.

Dorottya Demszky, Dana Movshovitz-Attias, Jeongwoo Ko, Alan Cowen, Gaurav Nemade, and Sujith Ravi. 2020. GoEmotions: A Dataset of Fine-Grained Emotions. pages 4040–4054.

Shai Gretz, Roni Friedman, Edo Cohen-Karlik, Assaf Toledo, Dan Lahav, Ranit Aharonov, and Noam Slonim. 2019. A Large-scale Dataset for Argument Quality Ranking: Construction and Analysis.

Shaoxiong Ji, Tianlin Zhang, Luna Ansari, Jie Fu, Prayag Tiwari, and Erik Cambria. 2021. MentalBERT: Publicly Available Pretrained Language Models for Mental Healthcare.

Philip L. Johnson, Lauren M. Federici, and Anantha Shekhar. 2014. Etiology, triggers and neurochemical circuits associated with unexpected, expected, and laboratory-induced panic attacks. *Neuroscience & Biobehavioral Reviews*, 46:429–454.

Anshu Malhotra and Rajni Jindal. 2022. Deep learning techniques for suicide and depression detection from online social media: A scoping review. *Applied Soft Computing*, page 109713.

Sandra Mitrović, Fabio Frisone, Suryam Gupta, Chiara Lucifora, Dragana Čarapić, Carlo Schillaci, Samuele Di Giovanni, and Ayushi Singh. 2023. Annotating panic in social media using active learning, transformers and domain knowledge. In *2023 IEEE International Conference on Data Mining Workshops (ICDMW)*, pages 1269–1278. IEEE.

Sandra Mitrović and Vani Kanjirangat. 2022. Enhancing bert performance with contextual valence shifters for panic detection in covid-19 tweets. In *Proceedings of the 2022 6th International Conference on Natural Language Processing and Information Retrieval*, pages 89–92.

Saif M. Mohammad. 2018. Word affect intensities. In *Proceedings of the 11th Edition of the Language Resources and Evaluation Conference (LREC-2018)*, Miyazaki, Japan.

Javier Parapar, Patricia Martín-Rodilla, David E Losada, and Fabio Crestani. 2023. erisk 2023: Depression, pathological gambling, and eating disorder challenges. In *European Conference on Information Retrieval*, pages 585–592. Springer.

JW Pennebaker, RL Boyd, RJ Booth, A Ashokkumar, and ME Francis. 2022. Linguistic inquiry and word count: Liwc-22. pennebaker conglomerates.

Jr Russell Noyes, Catherine Woodman, Michael J Garvey, Brian L Cook, Michael Suelzer, John Clancy, and Dorothy J Anderson. 1992. Generalized anxiety disorder vs. panic disorder: Distinguishing characteristics and patterns of comorbidity. *The Journal of nervous and mental disease*, 180(6):369–379.

Murray B Stein and Jitender Sareen. 2015. Generalized anxiety disorder. *New England Journal of Medicine*, 373(21):2059–2068.

Michaela B. Swee, Rachel M. Butler, Brennah V. Ross, Arielle Horenstein, Emily B. O'Day, and Richard G. Heimberg. 2021. Interpersonal Patterns in Social Anxiety Disorder: Predictors and Outcomes of Cognitive-Behavioral Therapy. *Cognitive Therapy and Research*, 45(4):614–627.

Mashrura Tasnim, Malikeh Ehghaghi, Brian Diep, and Jekaterina Novikova. 2023. Depac: a corpus for depression and anxiety detection from speech. *arXiv preprint arXiv:2306.12443*.

Natasha A. Tonge, Michelle H. Lim, Marilyn L. Piccirillo, Katya C. Fernandez, Julia K. Langer, and Thomas L. Rodebaugh. 2020. Interpersonal problems in social anxiety disorder across different relational contexts. *Journal of Anxiety Disorders*, 75:102275.

David William and Derwin Suhartono. 2021. Text-based depression detection on social media posts: A systematic literature review. *Procedia Computer Science*, 179:582–589.

A Appendix

A.1 Implementation details

Web scraping To collect the data, we employed Octoparse: `https://www.octoparse.com/`, a web scraping tool that is capable of recognising the structure of a web page and allows a user to select which specific content from the web page to extract.

Linguistic and psychometric features were obtained using LIWC-22, `https://www.liwc.app/` (Pennebaker et al., 2022).

Readability scores were calculated using Python library: `https://pypi.org/project/py-readability-metrics/`.

Emotion probabilities were inferred using a pretrained HuggingFace language model SamLowe/roberta-base-go_emotions that can be found at: `https://huggingface.co/SamLowe/roberta-base-go_emotions` (Demszky et al., 2020). The list of 28 different emotions that are considered can be found at: `https://github.com/google-research/google-research/blob/master/goemotions/data/emotions.txt`.

Emotion intensities were calculated using intensity lexicon from: `https://saifmohammad.com/WebPages/AffectIntensity.htm`(Mohammad, 2018).

Writer's Attitude: **Convincingness** class softmax scores were obtained using fine-tuned HuggingFace model: `https://huggingface.co/jakub014/bert-base-\uncased-IBM-argQ-30k-finetuned-\convincingness-acl2016` (Gretz et al., 2019). **Persuasiveness** class softmax scores were obtained using pretrained HuggingFace model: `https://huggingface.co/paragon-analytics/roberta_persuade`. **Irony** class softmax scores were obtained using HuggingFace model specifically fine-tuned for irony detection: `https://huggingface.co/cardiffnlp/twitter-roberta-base-irony` (Barbieri et al., 2020).

Classifier was implemented using XGBoost library `https://xgboost.readthedocs.io/en/stable/`. Training was done using 100 boosting rounds, logloss as evaluation metric, 0.1 as eta (learning rate) and setting 5 as maximum depth of each tree. The procedure was repeated 10 times.

Embeddings were obtained using Hugging Face model: `https://huggingface.co/sentence-transformers/all-distilroberta-v1`.

Stressor scores: We utilized a bidirectional masked language model known as Mental-RoBERTa (Ji et al., 2021), trained on a corpus collected from social forums dedicated to mental health discussions. We prompted the pretrained model with each post appending the query "Consider this post on social media to answer the question. Is the poster of this post stressed? Return Yes or No. mask ". We collected the predicted next token and its probability for inference. Additionally, we explored the experiences of the posters using a similar approach, prompting Mental-RoBERTa with: "Consider this post on social media to answer the question. The poster of this post is experiencing mask ", without guiding the model with expected responses.

Analysis using LLM: LLM analysis involved automated coding and key-phrase extraction across various dimensions. Within the coded dimensions, we inferred classifications such as determining whether the poster experienced anxiety, a panic attack, or none at all. Additionally, we classified posts into main types related to mental disorders, encompassing Personal experience, Giving information, Advocacy and awareness, Support and encouragement, Tips and strategies, as well as Question and discussion. Furthermore, we coded information related to the poster's diagnosis by a professional, ongoing treatment, and mentions of medications.

Among the other coded axes, we explored the relationship context and triggers associated with panic attacks, categorizing them into Financial stress, Argument or conflict, Traumatic experience, Social event, Life transition, Upcoming tests, Health concern, and Other. We also considered free mentions of stressors associated with these triggers.

The location (physical place) mentioned in relation to the occurrence of panic attacks was also coded into classes such as School, Work, Home, Hospital, Public spaces, Club or social venues, and Other. Additionally, we used codes for First time, Few times, and Recurrent to analyze mentions of the frequency of panic attacks.

In the realm of free-form text extraction, we focused on five axes: Mentions of physical symptoms, Cognitive symptoms, Behavioral changes, Emotional well-being, and Impact on daily life. These axes allowed us to categorize explicit or implicitly conveyed information related to the individual's experiences.

Furthermore, we extracted two additional types of shared knowledge. First, we delved into coping mechanisms individuals use to deal with panic attacks. Second, we explored perceived signs of distress that others can observe to identify when someone close is suffering from anxiety or a panic attack.

A.2 Additional material

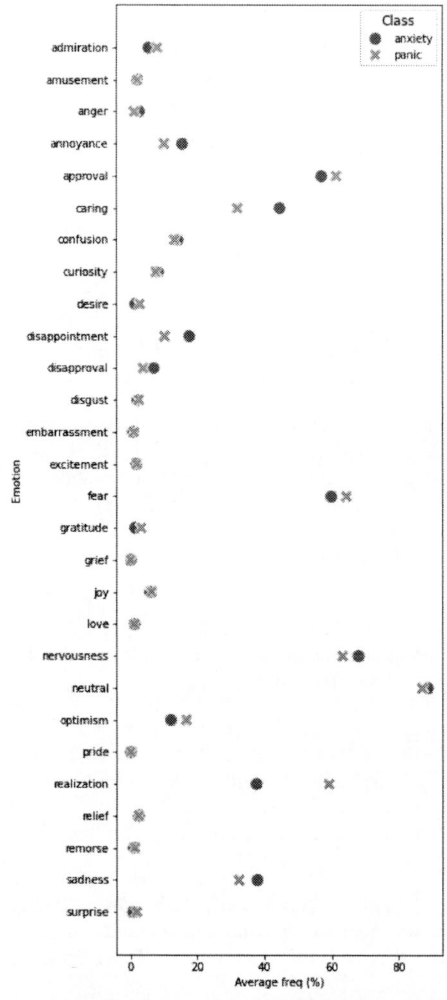

Figure 4: Average frequency of emotions, calculated based on the 5 most important emotions per post.

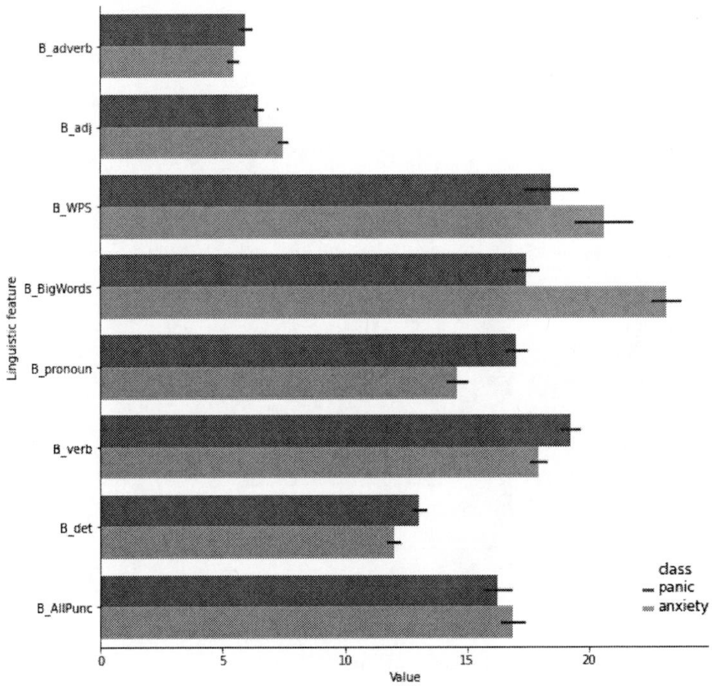

Figure 5: Linguistic features of panic and anxiety classes

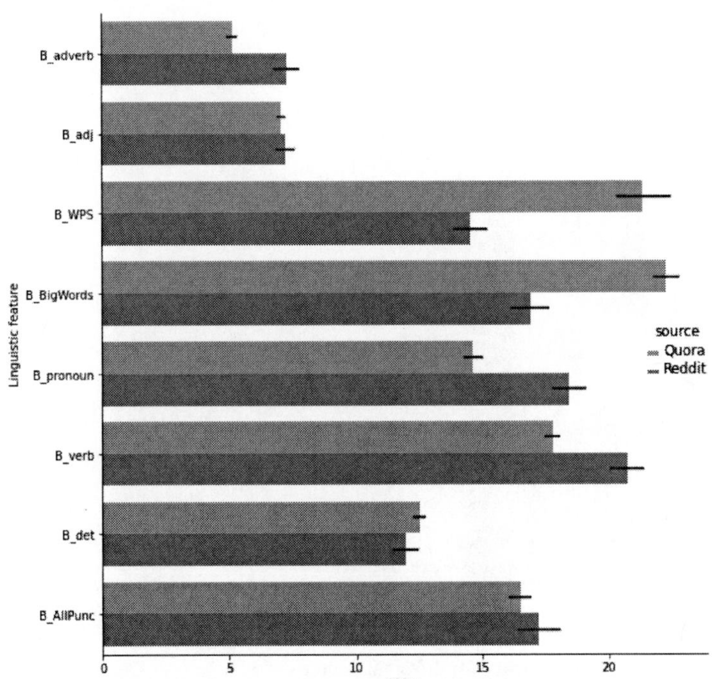

Figure 6: Linguistic features of two sources

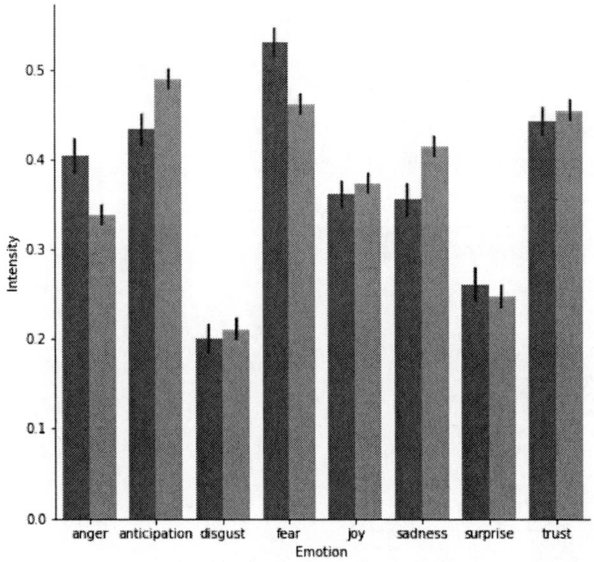

Figure 7: Emotion intensity on panic and anxiety class

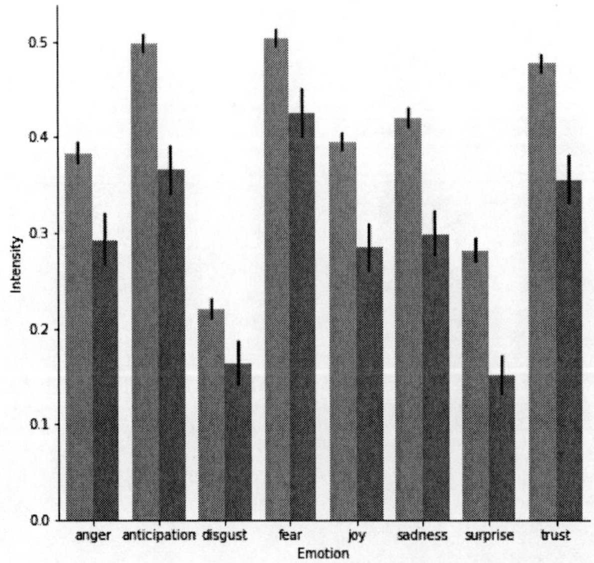

Figure 8: Emotion intensity for different sources

Category	Question
Panic	*What are panic attacks like?*
	Whats the worst panic attack you've ever had?
	How can I try to calm myself down while I'm having a panic attack?
	What was your first panic attack?
	What is it like to have a panic attack in public
	How does it feel like to have a panic attack at work?
	How can I tell if I had a panic attack?
	What do you do when you get panic attacks
	How to overcome panic attacks
	When was your last panic attack and how bad was it
	How-can-you-best-control-a-panic-attack-before-it-gets-out-of-control
	What is happening in the brain during a panic attack?
	Why can't I stop having panic attacks?
	How do i prevent panic attacks from happening when I'm sleeping?
	What do you take for panic attacks?
	How can I handle panic attacks at school?
	Have you ever seen someone having panic attacks?
Anxiety	*What is an anxiety?*
	Is anxiety disorder a mental illness?
	What are anxiety disorders
	Is there any difference between anxiety and social anxiety?
	Chemically and biologically what is anxiety?
	What is anxiety? What are its symptoms and its treatments?
	Why is anxiety so common today?
	What does anxiety feel like?
	What are the symptoms of anxiety
	How do you calm down when feeling anxious
	What is the real cause behind anxiety?
	How do i beat anxiety permanently?
	What did you first anxiety attack feel like?
	How do I know if I suffer from anxiety?
	How do I beat social anxiety?

Table 4: Questions used to retrieve posts per class (panic and anxiety) from two sources

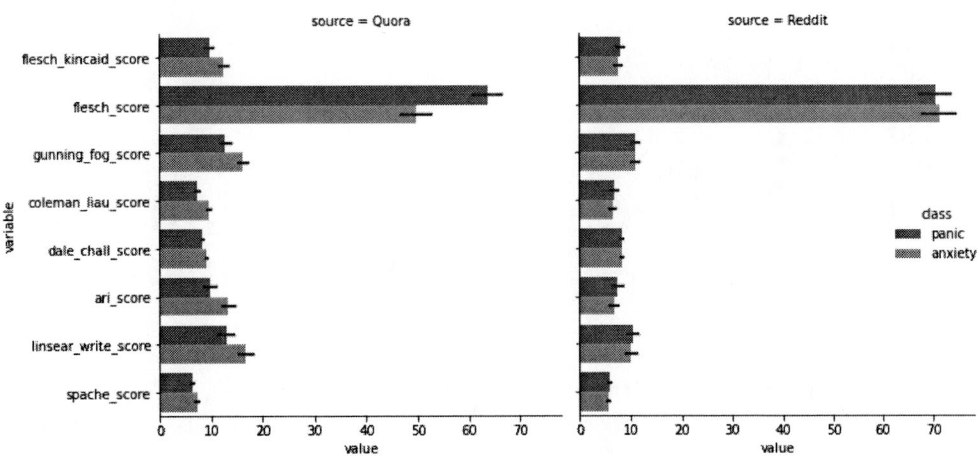

Figure 9: Different readability scores per class per source

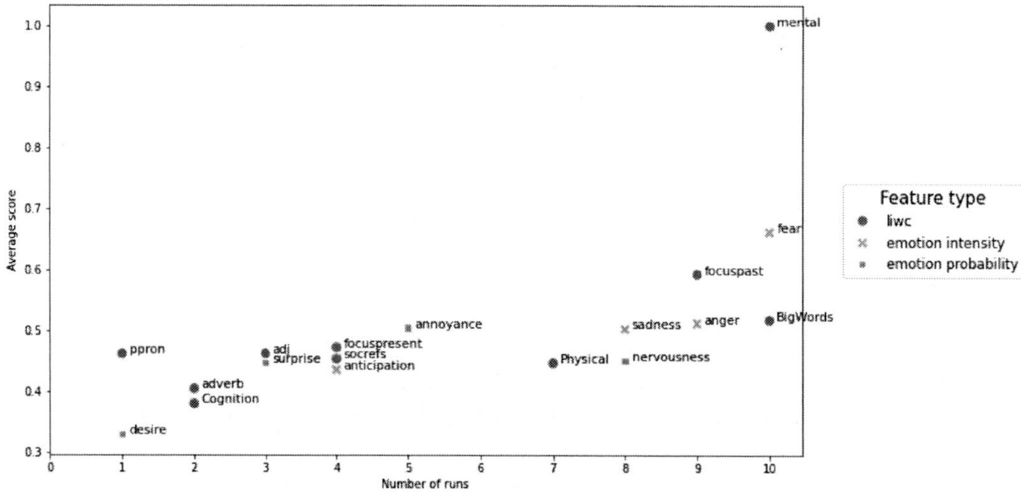

Figure 10: Most important features according to XGB feature importance across 10 runs, when considering L+M+I+W as input features. The x axis represents the number of runs where the features was considered among the top 10 most important features, while the y axis displays the average score across 10 runs.

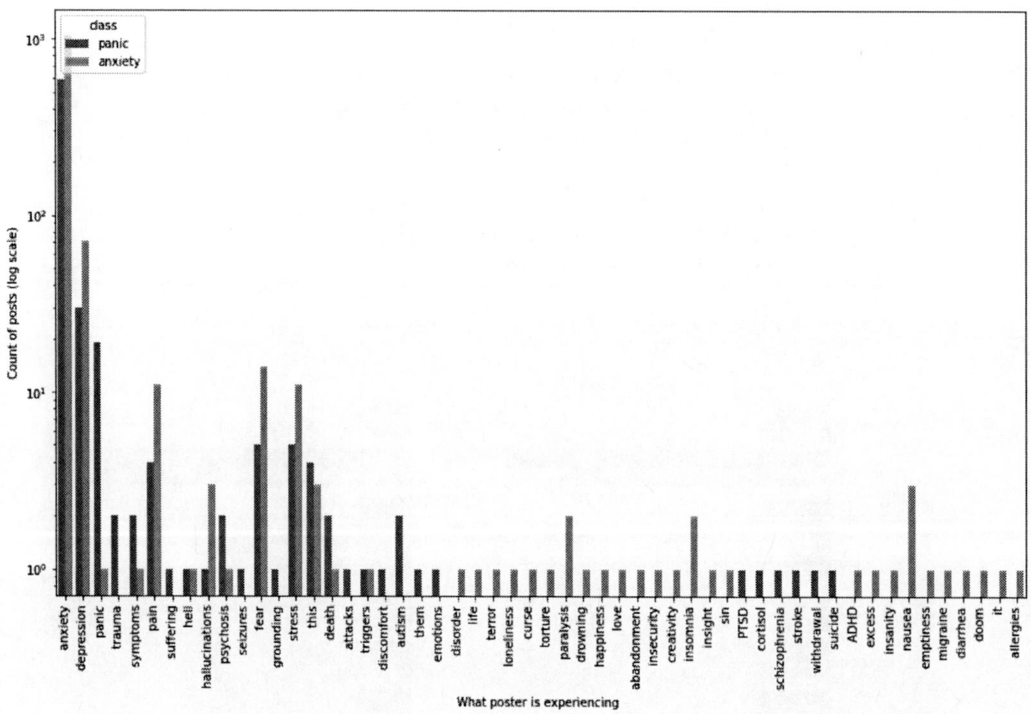

Figure 11: Variations in the distribution of anxiety and panic within the context of the poster's experiences (i.e., What is experiencing), obtained by prompting Mental_RoBERTa, are illustrated with counts presented on a logarithmic axis.

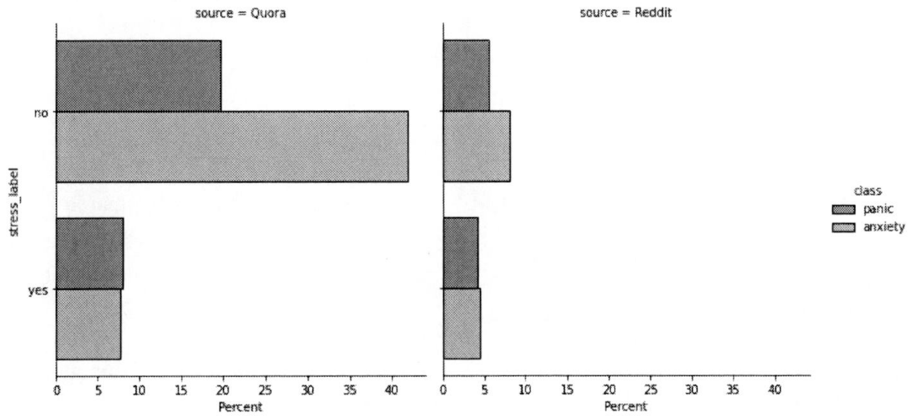

Figure 12: Stress labels per different classes and sources

Type_of_post	Counts	Response	Anxiety Profesionally_diagnosed	Anxiety Profesionally_treated	Anxiety Taking_medication	Panic Profesionally_diagnosed	Panic Profesionally_treated	Panic Taking_medication
Personal_experience	1,024	N/A	215	215	209	129	131	117
		NO	370	360	371	239	232	224
		YES	36	46	41	35	40	62
Giving_information	457	N/A	307	311	308	93	93	89
		NO	59	56	53	12	12	12
		YES	5	4	10	1	1	5
Tips_and_strategies	183	N/A	63	63	63	92	93	92
		NO	15	15	15	13	11	11
		YES	0	0	0	0	1	2
Support_and_encouragement	150	N/A	47	47	49	49	48	46
		NO	20	20	18	29	30	26
		YES	0	0	0	5	5	11
Advocacy_and_awareness	14	N/A	7	8	8	3	3	3
		NO	3	3	3	0	0	0
		YES	1	0	0	0	0	0
Question_and_discussion	17	N/A	11	11	11	1	1	1
		NO	2	2	2	3	3	3
Other	59	N/A	50	50	50	9	9	9
			Quora: 976	Reddit 241		Quora: 526	Reddit: 187	
			1,217			**713**		

Table 5: Dataset distribution with respect to post type and professional intervention, as identified by ChatGPT-3.5.

Your Model Is Not Predicting Depression Well And That Is Why: A Case Study of PRIMATE Dataset

Kirill Milintsevich[1,2] and **Kairit Sirts**[2] and **Gaël Dias**[1]
[1]Normandie Univ, UNICAEN, ENSICAEN, CNRS, GREYC, France
[2]Institute of Computer Science, University of Tartu, Estonia
{first_name}.{last_name}@{unicaen.fr[1]|ut.ee[2]}

Abstract

This paper addresses the quality of annotations in mental health datasets used for NLP-based depression level estimation from social media texts. While previous research relies on social media-based datasets annotated with binary categories, i.e. depressed or non-depressed, recent datasets such as D2S and PRIMATE aim for nuanced annotations using PHQ-9 symptoms. However, most of these datasets rely on crowd workers without the domain knowledge for annotation. Focusing on the PRIMATE dataset, our study reveals concerns regarding annotation validity, particularly for the lack of interest or pleasure symptom. Through reannotation by a mental health professional, we introduce finer labels and textual spans as evidence, identifying a notable number of false positives. Our refined annotations, to be released under a Data Use Agreement, offer a higher-quality test set for anhedonia detection. This study underscores the necessity of addressing annotation quality issues in mental health datasets, advocating for improved methodologies to enhance NLP model reliability in mental health assessments.

1 Introduction

Applying various NLP techniques to automatically estimate the depression level from social media texts has been a widely researched topic in the field of NLP applied for mental health. Most of these datasets consist of online posts gathered from popular social media platforms, such as Twitter or Reddit. These posts are usually annotated by crowd workers who had only a brief training with a mental health professional (MHP) or sometimes only had access to the annotation instructions.

While there exist multiple depression-related datasets based on social media texts, most of them only present binary annotation, i.e. whether the user is depressed or not. The most common sources of data are Reddit (Losada and Crestani, 2016; Yates et al., 2017; Pirina and Çöltekin, 2018) and X (former Twitter) (Coppersmith et al., 2014; Syarif et al., 2019). Most of the studies use automatic methods of annotations, such as regular expression matching of self-reported terms, like "I have been diagnosed with depression". Some of them perform manual verification and annotation either via layman crowd workers (Yates et al., 2017) or by the authors themselves (Coppersmith et al., 2014; Losada and Crestani, 2016).

Recently, the interest in more fine-grained depression annotation has emerged. In particular, the two recent datasets D2S (Yadav et al., 2020) and PRIMATE (Gupta et al., 2022), identify depressed social media posts from X and Reddit, respectively and annotate them with PHQ-9 symptoms (Kroenke and Spitzer, 2002). Both datasets have been annotated with the help of crowd workers and later verified by MHPs. However, the verification process was different. For D2S, conflicting annotations were resolved with the majority voting, and the psychiatrist resolved the ties. After that, 100 random samples were selected for quality control and verified by a psychiatrist. Additionally, Zirikly and Dredze (2022) annotated a random sample of D2S with the explanations for each symptom with the help of two MHPs[1], increasing the validity of the data. In the case of PRIMATE, no information is given on the quality control procedure. This raises concerns about the validity of the annotations; thus, we selected PRIMATE for our case study.

In this study, on the example of the PRIMATE dataset, we show that the validity of the annotations for the mental health data is a concern when performed by layman crowd workers. Our MHP reannotated 170 posts from the PRIMATE dataset for the lack of interest or pleasure (anhedonia) symp-

[1]Zirikly and Dredze (2022) did not report any conflicts between their annotation and the labels provided with D2S.

Proceedings of the 9th Workshop on Computational Linguistics and Clinical Psychology (CLPsych 2024), pages 166–171
March 21, 2024

tom. The MHP is the second author of the paper, who is also a practising clinical psychology intern. Our annotations include more fine-grained labels ("mentioned" vs "answerable", as well as an additional "writer's symptom" label) as well as spans of texts that serve as evidence of the labels. We observe a high number of false positives in the PRIMATE labels, which can be related to the high difficulty of conceptualizing anhedonia (Rizvi et al., 2016). The annotations are to be released under a Data Use Agreement (DUA), and we believe that it can serve as a higher-quality test set for anhedonia detection.

2 Dataset

PRIMATE (Gupta et al., 2022) is a dataset based on the Reddit posts from the r/depression_help subreddit. Each post is annotated with binary labels for each PHQ-9 question, where "yes" means that a post contains the answer to a PHQ-9 question and "no" otherwise. The nine symptoms are shortly described as follows: lack of interest or pleasure in doing things (LOI), feeling down or depressed (DEP), sleeping disorder (SLE), lack of energy (ENE), eating disorder (EAT), low self-esteem (LSE), problems with concentrating (CON), hyper or lower activity (MOV), suicidal thoughts (SUI).

The annotation was performed by five crowd workers with additional quality control by an MHP. The information about the annotation procedure or crowd worker training, as well as how exactly the MHPs were involved in the quality control, are not provided in the paper. The only metric on the annotation process is an annotator agreement using Fleiss' kappa, which is reported to be 67% for initial annotation and 85% after involvement of the MHPs.

In total, the dataset consists of 2003 posts. Table 1 shows the distribution of the labels[2]. Note that the exact numbers of labels are slightly different from the ones presented by Gupta et al. (2022). The dataset is not pre-split into train, validation and test sets; thus, we randomly sample 200 posts for validation and another 200 posts for testing.

PHQ-9 Symptom	Number of Posts	
	Present	Absent
LOI	949	1054
DEP	1664	339
SLE	374	1629
ENE	688	1315
EAT	194	1809
LSE	1680	323
CON	195	1808
MOV	527	1476
SUI	743	1260

Table 1: Label distribution in PRIMATE.

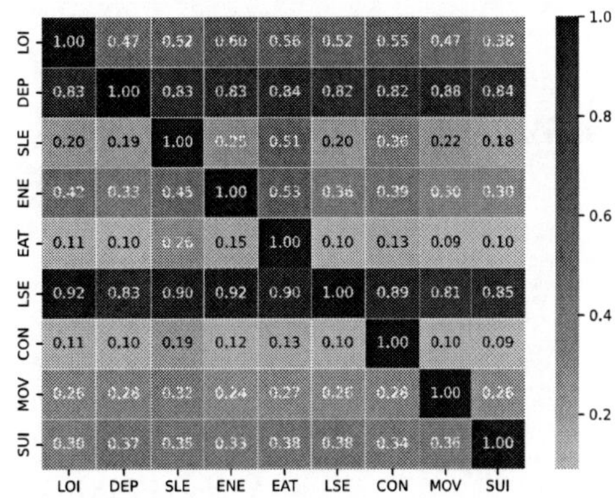

Figure 1: Symptom label co-occurrence matrix of the PRIMATE training set. Each value is normalized column-wise by dividing it by the highest value in the column.

Figure 1 shows the label co-occurrence matrix of the training set. Two symptoms, DEP and LSE, co-occur the most with all the other symptoms, which can be explained by their general prevalence in the dataset. The connection between the lack of interest or pleasure (LOI) and lack of energy (ENE) is also seen in the dataset, which reflects high comorbidity of these symptoms (van Borkulo et al., 2015; Park and Kim, 2020).

3 Experimental Setup

In our experiments, we aimed to test how well current pre-trained language models can model the depression symptom detection problem using the PRIMATE dataset. We first chose DistilBERT (Sanh et al., 2019) as a baseline and BERT-Base (Devlin et al., 2018), RoBERTa-Base, RoBERTa-Large (Liu et al., 2019), DeBERTa-Base, and DeBERTa-Large (He et al., 2020) as higher-performing models. In particular, DeBERTa has shown constant improvements in various NLP tasks and replaced BERT and RoBERTa as the state-of-the-art model for many of them[3].

For fine-tuning, we used the implementation from Transformers library (Wolf et al., 2020). Each

[2]The order of the symptoms in the original work by Gupta et al. (2022) is different from the one of PHQ-9. In our work, we reordered the symptoms to match PHQ-9.

[3]https://gluebenchmark.com/leaderboard

Model	LOI	DEP	SLE	ENE	EAT	LSE	CON	MOV	SUI
DistilBERT	.64	.88	.67	.58	.60	.90	.50	.67	.81
BERT-Base	.55	.88	.66	.55	.63	.90	.46	.66	.79
RoBERTa-Base	.54	.88	.70	.57	.57	.90	.51	.69	.85
RoBERTa-Large	.57	.86	.75	.63	.65	.91	.52	.71	.85
DeBERTa-Base	.58	.91	.69	.52	.42	.90	.36	.61	.81
DeBERTa-Large	.60	.90	.68	.64	.47	.91	.50	.73	.83

Table 2: Symptom-wise F1-scores on the validation set.

`Mentioned:`

`I simply want everything to finish.` **`I have no drive to do anything.`** `I am very irritable. Nothing is going as I want to and even if it was I probably wouldn't appreciate it.`

`Answerable:`

`I feel like I'm spending my life for nothing.` **`I used to escape my problems by browsing Youtube and Reddit for hours, but now I don't even find that enjoyable anymore.`**

`Not author's symptoms:`

`I've tried to talk about looking for other options or just ways to deal with the stress, but he's not really interested now.`

Figure 2: Examples of reannotated posts. Evidences are highlighted in **bold**.

Predictions	Against PRIMATE				Against "mentioned"				Against "answerable"			
	A	P	R	F1	A	P	R	F1	A	P	R	F1
DistilBERT	.58	.56	.62	.58	.56	.30	.71	.42	.51	.10	.75	.18
PRIMATE Labels	-	-	-	-	.56	.27	.58	.37	.54	.09	.58	.15

Table 3: Results on the reannotated part of the validation set. Here, **A** stands for Accuracy, **P** for Precision, **R** for Recall, and **F1** for F1-score for the positive class.

model consists of a pre-trained encoder with a classification head on the top of the `[CLS]` token. The classification head is represented by a linear layer; in the case of DeBERTa, another linear layer followed by GELU (Hendrycks and Gimpel, 2016) is added before the classification head. We trained each model for 20 epochs using AdamW optimizer with the learning rate of $2e^{-5}$, ϵ of $1e^{-6}$, β_1, β_2 of $(0.9, 0.999)$, and weight decay λ of 0.01. Additionally, a linear learning rate scheduler is applied with a warmup ratio of 0.1. Finally, the training batch size was set to 16.

4 Results and Discussion

Table 2 shows that larger models, such as RoBERTa-Large and DeBERTa-Large, perform better for `ENE`, `LSE`, `MOV`, and `SUI`. Additionally, `DEP` shows slight improvement with DeBERTa models, however, decreased performance for `EAT`. RoBERTa models perform better for `SLE` and `SUI` prediction. Nevertheless, DistilBERT sets a strong baseline and performs on par with larger models overall. Finally, `LOI` shows a decrease in performance for all the models compared to the DistilBERT.

We investigate the diminished performance of the `LOI` symptom since it is a core symptom of a major depressive disorder (Association, 2013) and shows unstable results for our models. Furthermore, `LOI` is one of the symptoms of schizophrenia (Association, 2013) and is associated with both anxiety and depression (Winer et al., 2017). Thus, we selected a subset of 170 posts from the validation set based on the DistilBERT predictions: if at least one symptom was predicted incorrectly, the post was selected. Next, an MHP read all the posts in the subset and labelled them for the presence of loss of interest or pleasure (`LOI`). The MHP assigned three labels to each post: a) "mentioned" if the symptom is talked about in the text, but it is not possible to infer its duration or intensity; b) "answerable" if there is clear evidence of anhedonia; c) "writer's symptoms" which shows whether the author of the post discusses themselves or a third person. Additionally, the MHP selected the part of the text that supports the positive label.

Figure 2 shows examples for the reannotated posts[4]. The first example is labelled as "mentioned" since it contains evidence of a symptom but does not contain information about the *loss* of interest. The second example is labelled as "answerable" because it is possible to infer that the person used to have interest in what they were doing before but lost it at some point in time. Finally, the last example shows the post without signs of LOI that describes the condition of another person.

Table 3 shows accuracy, precision, recall and F1-score for positive class against different sets of labels on our manually reannotated subset. DistilBERT, when measured against "mentioned" and "answerable" labels, performs considerably worse than against original labels from PRIMATE. It is unsurprising given the extremely low agreement between these sets of labels with Cohen's kappa of 9% and 3%, respectively. Furthermore, the most common error type is a false positive, i.e., a symptom marked as present in PRIMATE when our MHP found no evidence of it in the text. Additionally, using PRIMATE labels as predictions and comparing their performance against our labels shows lower performance than the DistilBERT model.

Considering the "writer's symptom" label, in 18 out of 170 selected posts, the author describes a symptom of another person rather than themselves. This raises the question of how these posts should be annotated and whether they should be included in the dataset at all. We suspect that the language of describing one's condition or feelings in the first person is different from the third person. We leave this question for future debate and assign "mentioned" and "answerable" labels to the posts describing a third person in the same manner as to the personal posts.

Our findings are consistent with the original results presented by Gupta et al. (2022). Similar to our experiment, they also trained a classifier based on the BERT-Base model and reported low MCC for LOI. However, we provided the evidence that this might be caused by annotation errors. Additionally, we noticed that many posts that were mistakenly labelled with LOI are more closely related to the "inner tension" symptom from the Montgomery-Åsberg Depression Rating Scale (MADRS) (Montgomery and Åsberg, 1979).

While we agree that our reannotated test set is also, to some extent, susceptible to errors, we believe that it serves as a more reliable benchmark for the anhedonia symptom. A more fine-grained, evidence-based labelling scheme reduces the risk of mislabelling and is more transparent for further verification. Finally, it lays the foundation for future collaboration to produce a higher-quality Reddit-based dataset for depression symptom estimation.

5 Conclusion

In conclusion, this study highlights the importance of evaluating and enhancing the quality of annotations in mental health datasets, particularly within the context of automated depression level estimation from social media texts. While recent datasets such as PRIMATE introduce commendable efforts toward nuanced annotations using PHQ-9 symptoms, our examination of the PRIMATE dataset reveals concerns about annotation validity, specifically regarding the lack of interest or pleasure symptom. Through careful reannotation by a mental health professional, we discerned a considerable number of false positives among the original labels indicative of challenges in conceptualizing anhedonia.

The findings presented here advocate for a more rigorous and standardized approach to mental health dataset annotation, emphasizing the need for greater involvement of domain experts in the annotation process. The release of our refined annotations under a Data Use Agreement (DUA) contributes a valuable resource for future research, offering a higher quality test set for anhedonia detection. Moving forward, a concerted effort toward refining annotation methodologies and promoting collaboration between domain experts and NLP practitioners is imperative to foster advancements in this crucial intersection of technology and mental health research.

6 Availability of Data

The instructions for accessing the annotations presented in this paper can be found here: https://github.com/501Good/primate-anhedonia.

[4]All example posts are paraphrased for privacy.

7 Ethical Considerations

According to Benton et al. (2017), studies involving user-generated content are exempt from Institutional Review Board (IRB) requirements if the data source is public and user identities are not identifiable. We access and use the data according to the Data Use Agreement provided with the PRIMATE dataset. Finally, we are going to release our annotations under another Data Use Agreement and separate them from the original PRIMATE data. We also acknowledge that no automatic system can replace a real mental health professional and cannot be used as a sole instrument of diagnostics.

8 Limitations

We acknowledge the limitations inherent in our work and findings. First, the manually annotated explanations serve as a proxy for what clinicians might find informative in assessing Reddit posts flagged as depressive. While evaluating the informativeness of explanations in a true clinical setting would provide more insight, it falls beyond the scope of this paper. Furthermore, our reannotation was carried out by only one mental health professional, which does not allow for performing an inter-annotator agreement analysis. However, we believe that our evidence-based labelling scheme partially mitigates this problem. Finally, anhedonia is extremely challenging to conceptualize and binary labels may not be the best choice in situations when the difference between the presence or absence of the symptom is marginal. In this case, labels based on the Likert scale, as in PHQ-9, would be more appropriate and allow us to capture the intensity of the symptom more accurately. Furthermore, different demographics, for example, adolescents and adults, express signs of anhedonia differently (Watson et al., 2020).

Acknowledgements

This research was supported by the Estonian Research Council Grant PSG721 and the FHU A^2M^2P project funded by the G4 University Hospitals of Amiens, Caen, Lille and Rouen (France). The calculations for model's training and inference were carried out in the High Performance Computing Center of the University of Tartu (University of Tartu, 2018).

References

American Psychiatric Association. 2013. *Diagnostic and statistical manual of mental disorders: DSM-5™ (5th ed.)*. American Psychiatric Publishing, Inc.

Adrian Benton, Glen Coppersmith, and Mark Dredze. 2017. Ethical research protocols for social media health research. In *Proceedings of the First ACL Workshop on Ethics in Natural Language Processing*, pages 94–102, Valencia, Spain. Association for Computational Linguistics.

Glen Coppersmith, Mark Dredze, and Craig Harman. 2014. Quantifying mental health signals in Twitter. In *Proceedings of the Workshop on Computational Linguistics and Clinical Psychology: From Linguistic Signal to Clinical Reality*, pages 51–60, Baltimore, Maryland, USA. Association for Computational Linguistics.

Jacob Devlin, Ming-Wei Chang, Kenton Lee, and Kristina Toutanova. 2018. Bert: Pre-training of deep bidirectional transformers for language understanding. *arXiv preprint arXiv:1810.04805*.

Shrey Gupta, Anmol Agarwal, Manas Gaur, Kaushik Roy, Vignesh Narayanan, Ponnurangam Kumaraguru, and Amit Sheth. 2022. Learning to automate follow-up question generation using process knowledge for depression triage on Reddit posts. In *Proceedings of the Eighth Workshop on Computational Linguistics and Clinical Psychology*, pages 137–147, Seattle, USA. Association for Computational Linguistics.

Pengcheng He, Xiaodong Liu, Jianfeng Gao, and Weizhu Chen. 2020. Deberta: Decoding-enhanced bert with disentangled attention. *arXiv preprint arXiv:2006.03654*.

Dan Hendrycks and Kevin Gimpel. 2016. Gaussian error linear units (gelus). *arXiv preprint arXiv:1606.08415*.

Kurt Kroenke and Robert L Spitzer. 2002. The PHQ-9: a new depression diagnostic and severity measure.

Yinhan Liu, Myle Ott, Naman Goyal, Jingfei Du, Mandar Joshi, Danqi Chen, Omer Levy, Mike Lewis, Luke Zettlemoyer, and Veselin Stoyanov. 2019. Roberta: A robustly optimized bert pretraining approach. *arXiv preprint arXiv:1907.11692*.

David E Losada and Fabio Crestani. 2016. A test collection for research on depression and language use. In *International conference of the cross-language evaluation forum for European languages*, pages 28–39. Springer.

Stuart A Montgomery and MARIE Åsberg. 1979. A new depression scale designed to be sensitive to change. *The British journal of psychiatry*, 134(4):382–389.

Seon-Cheol Park and Daeho Kim. 2020. The centrality of depression and anxiety symptoms in major depressive disorder determined using a network analysis. *Journal of affective disorders*, 271:19–26.

Inna Pirina and Çağrı Çöltekin. 2018. Identifying depression on Reddit: The effect of training data. In *Proceedings of the 2018 EMNLP Workshop SMM4H: The 3rd Social Media Mining for Health Applications Workshop & Shared Task*, pages 9–12, Brussels, Belgium. Association for Computational Linguistics.

Sakina J Rizvi, Diego A Pizzagalli, Beth A Sproule, and Sidney H Kennedy. 2016. Assessing anhedonia in depression: Potentials and pitfalls. *Neuroscience & Biobehavioral Reviews*, 65:21–35.

Victor Sanh, Lysandre Debut, Julien Chaumond, and Thomas Wolf. 2019. Distilbert, a distilled version of bert: smaller, faster, cheaper and lighter. *arXiv preprint arXiv:1910.01108*.

Iwan Syarif, Nadia Ningtias, and Tessy Badriyah. 2019. Study on mental disorder detection via social media mining. In *2019 4th International conference on computing, communications and security (ICCCS)*, pages 1–6. IEEE.

University of Tartu. 2018. UT rocket.

Claudia van Borkulo, Lynn Boschloo, Denny Borsboom, Brenda WJH Penninx, Lourens J Waldorp, and Robert A Schoevers. 2015. Association of symptom network structure with the course of depression. *JAMA psychiatry*, 72(12):1219–1226.

Rebecca Watson, Kate Harvey, Ciara McCabe, and Shirley Reynolds. 2020. Understanding anhedonia: A qualitative study exploring loss of interest and pleasure in adolescent depression. *European Child & Adolescent Psychiatry*, 29:489–499.

E Samuel Winer, Jessica Bryant, Gregory Bartoszek, Enrique Rojas, Michael R Nadorff, and Jenna Kilgore. 2017. Mapping the relationship between anxiety, anhedonia, and depression. *Journal of affective disorders*, 221:289–296.

Thomas Wolf, Lysandre Debut, Victor Sanh, Julien Chaumond, Clement Delangue, Anthony Moi, Pierric Cistac, Tim Rault, Remi Louf, Morgan Funtowicz, Joe Davison, Sam Shleifer, Patrick von Platen, Clara Ma, Yacine Jernite, Julien Plu, Canwen Xu, Teven Le Scao, Sylvain Gugger, Mariama Drame, Quentin Lhoest, and Alexander Rush. 2020. Transformers: State-of-the-art natural language processing. In *Proceedings of the 2020 Conference on Empirical Methods in Natural Language Processing: System Demonstrations*, pages 38–45, Online. Association for Computational Linguistics.

Shweta Yadav, Jainish Chauhan, Joy Prakash Sain, Krishnaprasad Thirunarayan, Amit Sheth, and Jeremiah Schumm. 2020. Identifying depressive symptoms from tweets: Figurative language enabled multitask learning framework. In *Proceedings of the 28th International Conference on Computational Linguistics*, pages 696–709, Barcelona, Spain (Online). International Committee on Computational Linguistics.

Andrew Yates, Arman Cohan, and Nazli Goharian. 2017. Depression and self-harm risk assessment in online forums. In *Proceedings of the 2017 Conference on Empirical Methods in Natural Language Processing*, pages 2968–2978, Copenhagen, Denmark. Association for Computational Linguistics.

Ayah Zirikly and Mark Dredze. 2022. Explaining models of mental health via clinically grounded auxiliary tasks. In *Proceedings of the Eighth Workshop on Computational Linguistics and Clinical Psychology*, pages 30–39, Seattle, USA. Association for Computational Linguistics.

Detecting a Proxy for Potential Comorbid ADHD in People Reporting Anxiety Symptoms from Social Media Data

Claire S. Lee
Princeton University
skclairelee@gmail.com

Noelle Lim
University of Toronto
LinkedIn Corporation
arinlim@gmail.com

Michael Guerzhoy
University of Toronto
guerzhoy@cs.toronto.edu

Abstract

We present a novel task that can elucidate the connection between anxiety and ADHD; use Transformers to make progress toward solving a task that is not solvable by keyword-based classifiers; and discuss a method for visualization of our classifier illuminating the connection between anxiety and ADHD presentations.

Up to approximately 50% of adults with ADHD may also have an anxiety disorder and approximately 30% of adults with anxiety may also have ADHD. Patients presenting with anxiety may be treated for anxiety without ADHD ever being considered, possibly affecting treatment. We show how data that bears on ADHD that is comorbid with anxiety can be obtained from social media data, and show that Transformers can be used to detect a proxy for possible comorbid ADHD in people with anxiety symptoms.

We collected data from anxiety and ADHD online forums (subreddits). We identified posters who first started posting in the Anxiety subreddit and later started posting in the ADHD subreddit as well. We use this subset of the posters as a proxy for people who presented with anxiety symptoms and then became aware that they might have ADHD. We fine-tune a Transformer architecture-based classifier to classify people who started posting in the Anxiety subreddit and then started posting in the ADHD subreddit vs. people who posted in the Anxiety subreddit without later posting in the ADHD subreddit. We show that a Transformer architecture is capable of achieving reasonable results (76% correct for RoBERTa vs. under 60% correct for the best keyword-based model, both with 50% base rate).

1 Introduction

Up to 53% of adults with ADHD may also have an anxiety disorder (Children and with Attention-Deficit/Hyperactivity Disorder Report, 2018) (Quinn and Madhoo, 2014) and up to 28% of adults who have an anxiety disorder may also have ADHD (Van Ameringen et al., 2011). However, patients presenting with anxiety or depressive symptoms may be treated for these disorders without ADHD ever being considered (Quinn and Madhoo, 2014) (Katzman et al., 2017). Misdiagnosis of ADHD is common, as many clinicians are still not aware that ADHD is a valid diagnosis in adults (Quinn and Madhoo, 2014) and physicians are more familiar with mood and anxiety disorders (Katzman et al., 2017). The danger of misdiagnosed comorbid ADHD and anxiety is that only the symptoms for anxiety will be treated and ADHD will be left untreated (Katzman et al., 2017). Social media such as Reddit provides publicly available text data of anonymous first-person experiences (Low et al., 2020).

We analyze people talking about their mental health on the forum website Reddit. We propose classifying posts from people who only posted in the Anxiety subreddit (forum) and never in the ADHD subreddit vs people who posted in the Anxiety subreddit and will later have started posting in the ADHD subreddit. This way, we can distinguish text from users whose posting will show interest/concern with ADHD in the future from people whose posting will not do that. Posting about ADHD is a proxy for being concerned about ADHD. Showing that this task is possible indicates that there is a systematic difference between the two groups of Reddit users. Our hope is that analyzing the classifier can elucidate the connection between anxiety and anxiety-comorbid ADHD. A limitation is that posting on Reddit is a proxy for concern with ADHD, and there can be both false positives and false negatives if Reddit posting is used as a proxy for identifying patients with ADHD.

We demonstrate that the task above is not solvable using keyword-based methods such as Naive Bayes and logistic regression. We then demonstrate

Proceedings of the 9th Workshop on Computational Linguistics and Clinical Psychology (CLPsych 2024), pages 172–176
March 21, 2024 ©2024 Association for Computational Linguistics

that the task is better solved using RoBERTa (Liu et al., 2019), indicating that the connection between anxiety and anxiety-comorbid ADHD is more complex than what can be captured with keywords. We report on visualizing the "explanation" for the classifier's prediction. In future work, we plan to use this visualization to gain insight into the connection between anxiety and anxiety-comorbid ADHD.

Transformer models such as RoBERTa have been used to classify mental health disorders from social media text (Ameer et al., 2022) (Murarka et al., 2020). However, we are not aware of research published of using transformers to classify comorbid anxiety with ADHD.

In the rest of the paper, we expand on comorbid ADHD and anxiety (Section 2.1), and using learned classifiers on mental health-related text (Section 2.2). We then discuss our data collection process (Section 3) and report on our experiments showing that it is possible to predict which posts in the Anxiety subreddit come from people who will never post in the ADHD subreddit vs. people who will post in the ADHD subreddit (Section 5). We discuss the limitations of our work in Section 7 and ethical considerations in Section 8.

2 Background

2.1 Comorbid ADHD and Anxiety

Up to 53% of adults with ADHD may also have an anxiety disorder (Children and with Attention-Deficit/Hyperactivity Disorder Report, 2018) and about 3 in 10 children with ADHD had anxiety [1]. ADHD and anxiety are frequently seen together; however, ADHD and anxiety are separate conditions (Ellis, 2017). ADHD is a common mental health disorder with symptoms such as inattention (not being able to keep focus), hyperactivity, and impulsivity (Elmaghraby and Garayalde, 2022). Anxiety disorders may involve symptoms of excessive fear (Muskin, 2022) which does not go away over time (NIMH, 2023). People who have anxiety disorders may struggle with intense and uncontrollable feelings of anxiety, fear, worry, or panic (American Psychiatric Association et al., 2013).

Although ADHD and anxiety have different symptoms, there are instances when the two conditions have overlapping symptoms, making it difficult to distinguish between the two conditions (Story, 2022). For instance, individuals with anxiety may have trouble concentrating in situations that trigger anxiety. Those with ADHD may have trouble concentrating in any type of situation (Story, 2022).

It is important to correctly diagnose patients with ADHD and anxiety, as the co-occurrence of ADHD and anxiety may make the symptoms of both conditions seem more extreme (Koyuncu et al., 2022). For example, anxiety can make it even more difficult for someone with ADHD to pay attention and follow through on tasks (Story, 2022).

Misdiagnosed comorbid ADHD and anxiety may lead to treating only the symptoms for anxiety while the root of the problem, which is ADHD, remains untreated (Katzman et al., 2017) (Hallowell, 2018). Undiagnosed ADHD can cause anxiety and depression which, in turn, can mask ADHD, making it more difficult to diagnose accurately (Kistler, 2022).

Diagnosis of ADHD typically occurs in children; however, ADHD is now recognized to be persistent to adulthood in 50-66% of people (Johnson et al., 2020). Misdiagnosis of ADHD is common as many clinicians are still not aware that ADHD is a valid diagnosis in adults (Johnson et al., 2020).

2.2 Classification of Mental Health-related texts with Deep Learning

Machine learning techniques have been utilized for multi-class classification of mental health condition-related text, particularly on Reddit. (Ameer et al., 2022) trained various models to detect texts related to anxiety, ADHD, bipolar disorder, depression, and PTSD. Ameer et al. observed that a pre-trained and then fine-tuned RoBERTa classifiers achieved the best performance. (Murarka et al., 2020) used RoBERTa to detect and classify texts related to mental health conditions and observed better accuracy and F-1 scores than BERT or LSTM models. However, their model performed poorly in classifying anxiety, partially due to the term "anxiety" occurring in 12% of ADHD posts.

The dataset that was used for both papers was data scraped from 13 subreddits using the Reddit API: 17,159 posts and title texts. Of the 13 subreddits, 5 were directly associated with a mental illness: `"bipolar"`, `"adhd"`, `"anxiety"`, `"depression"`, and `"ptsd"` while the remaining were chosen from a wide range of subreddit topics

[1] `https://www.cdc.gov/ncbddd/adhd/data.html`

and assigned the class label of "none".

Previously, work such as (Shen and Rudzicz, 2017) applied machine learning to classifying text by associated mental health condition.

Note that, in our work, we aim to distinguish finer-grained categories than in previous work: we are specifically interested in disintguishing posts in the Anxiety subreddit into two classes: posts from people who will and will not later post in the ADHD subreddit. That is a more difficult task than distinguishing posts in the Anxiety subreddit from posts in the ADHD subreddit, as in previous work.

3 Data Collection

Text data was collected from the Anxiety and ADHD subreddits on Reddit. Although Reddit posts are not formal clinical diagnoses, Reddit data offers advantages such as being immediately and publicly available, including a timeframe to track historical data, and anonymous posts documenting vulnerable first-person experiences (Low et al., 2020).

All posts were scraped from the Anxiety and ADHD subreddits from the dates February 16, 2020 to Nov 28, 2022.

3.1 Data Preprocessing

The data was cleaned by removing empty or removed posts. The data was filtered to only contain posts from users that only ever posted in the Anxiety subreddit or who first posted on the Anxiety subreddit only then in the ADHD subreddit.

For users who started posting in the ADHD subreddit eventually, we only kept posts from the Anxiety subreddit that were posted 6 months or more before the first post in the ADHD subreddit. No posts from the ADHD subreddit were used.

In total, 47482 posts were downloaded from the ADHD and Anxiety subreddits. 33% were retained for the test set.

4 Models

4.1 Baseline Model

Our baseline models were regularized logistic regression and binomial Naive Bayes.

4.1.1 Transformer Model

We fine-tined the pre-trained RoBERTa model from HuggingFace (Huggingface, 2020) with the RoBERTa tokenizer, the cross-entropy loss function, the Adam optimizer with a learning rate of $1e-5$, and a dropout layer with $p = 0.3$.

5 Results

5.1 Baseline Results

With a baserate of 50%, the best logistic regression model achieved a correct classification rate of 54% and the best Naive Bayes model achieved a correct classification rate of 59%.

As seen, Logistic Regression models performed at 54% accuracy and Naive Bayes performed at 58.6% accuracy. Attributing to its performance, as seen in Figure 6, the majority of samples fell correctly into the true positive and true negative class.

5.2 RoBERTa Results

With a test set baserate of 50%, the RoBERTa model achieved a correct classification rate of 76%.

5.3 Discussion

Our results demonstrate that, for posts in the Anxiety subreddit, it is possible to predict which posts come from people who will later post in the ADHD subreddit as well from posts that come from people who will not, without using any information "from the future."

Further, we have shown that keyword-based methods, Naive Bayes and logistic regression, are not sufficient for this task, while it is possible to make progress with RoBERTa. This indicates that complex cues can be used to detect which posters will later post in the ADHD subreddit.

6 Experiments with explainability

One application of our trained classifier is obtaining further insight into the relationship between anxiety disorders and ADHD.

To enable qualitative analysis, we have experimented with visualizing the reason that the RoBERTa classifier outputs "will post in ADHD" or "will not post in ADHD" for a given post. We visualize the difference in output caused by masking out each individual word and each individual phrase in the post.

Aggregate analysis will be available in the future.

7 Limitations

Our primary goal is to gain insight into the connection between anxiety and ADHD, as well as

Model	(Ameer et al., 2022)	(Murarka et al., 2021)
LSTM	76%	72%
BERT	78%	82%
RoBERTa	83%	86%

Table 1: Multiclass classification accuracy for Reddit posts

ADHD co-morbid with anxiety. We use a particular social media platform (Reddit), which is primarily English-speaking and whose audience is known to skew male [2]. Conclusions about symptoms drawn from Reddit therefore are likely biased by language, gender, and culture. We do not have specific demographic information about the Anxiety and ADHD subreddits, so that conclusion is itself tentative.

The classifier we train is not intended as a diagnostic tool and should not be used as such.

Classification results on text from outside of Reddit and outside of the Anxiety subreddit would likely not match what we report.

8 Ethical considerations

We use public data, and as such the research is not human-subjects research, as confirmed by our IRB.

Owing to the sensitivity of the topic, we have decided not to include samples from our data in the paper.

Creating classifiers whose output is mental health conditions is fraught with the danger that such a classifier would be used without consent on users' text. Care should be taken that this does not happen. Our classifier is not diagnostically useful.

9 Conclusions

We present a novel task: predicting whether internet text that comes from a person discussing their anxiety comes from a person who in the future will also discuss ADHD. We demonstrate that this task is not solvable using keyword-based methods, while it progress can be made using RoBERTa.

The immediate application of our method is for obtaining qualitative insight into the connection between anxiety and ADHD by visualizing the reason that the RoBERTa classifier outputs "will post in ADHD" or "will not post in ADHD" for a given post.

[2]https://www.statista.com/statistics/1255182/distribution-of-users-on-reddit-worldwide-gender/

References

I. Ameer, M. Arif, G. Sidorov, H. Gòmez-Adorno, and A. Gelbukh. 2022. Mental illness classification on social media texts using deep learning and transfer learning. In *8th World Conference on Soft Computing*.

DSMTF American Psychiatric Association, American Psychiatric Association, et al. 2013. *Diagnostic and statistical manual of mental disorders: DSM-5*, volume 5. American psychiatric association Washington, DC.

Children and Adults with Attention-Deficit/Hyperactivity Disorder Report. 2018. Coexisting conditions. https://chadd.org/about-adhd/coexisting-conditions/. Accessed: 2023-04-14.

Rachel Reiff Ellis. 2017. What's the link between anxiety and adhd? https://www.webmd.com/add-adhd/anxiety-adhd-link. Accessed: 2022-10-10.

Rana Elmaghraby and Stephanie Garayalde. 2022. What is adhd? In *American Psychiatric Association Physician Review*. Accessed: 2022-10-10.

Edward Hallowell. 2018. When depression and anxiety are really adhd. https://www.additudemag.com/depression-adhd-symptoms-misdiagnosis/. Accessed: 2023-01-29.

Huggingface. 2020. Transformers. https://huggingface.co/docs/transformers/index. Accessed: 2023-01-29.

J. Johnson, S. Morris, and S. George. 2020. Misdiagnosis and missed diagnosis of adult attention-deficit hyperactivity disorder. *BJPsych Advances*, 27(1):60–61.

Martin A. Katzman, Terrence S. Bilkey, Pratap R. Chokka, Angelo Fallu, and Laureen J. Klassen. 2017. Adult adhd and comorbid disorders: clinical implications of a dimensional approach. *BMC Psychiatry*, 17(1).

R. Kistler. 2022. Trouble sitting still disorder: Adhd through the social model of disability. https://cedar.wwu.edu/wwu_honors/587/. Accessed: 2023-01-29.

Ahmet Koyuncu, Tuğçe Ayan, Elvin Ince Guliyev, Şule Erbilgin, and Erdem Deveci. 2022. Adhd and anxiety disorder comorbidity in children and adults: Diagnostic and therapeutic challenges. *Current Psychiatry Reports*, 24(2):129–140.

Y. Liu et al. 2019. Roberta: A robustly optimized bert pretraining approach.

Daniel M. Low, Laurie Rumker, Tanya Talkar, John Torous, Guillermo Cecchi, and Soumya S. Ghosh. 2020. Natural language processing reveals vulnerable mental health support groups and heightened health anxiety on reddit during covid-19: Observational study. *Journal of Medical Internet Research*, 22(10):e22635.

A. Murarka, B. Radhakrishnan, and S. Ravichandran. 2020. Detection and classification of mental illnesses on social media using roberta. http://arxiv.org/abs/2011.11226.

Ankit Murarka, Balaji Radhakrishnan, and Sushma Ravichandran. 2021. Classification of mental illnesses on social media using roberta. In *Proceedings of the 12th international workshop on health text mining and information analysis*, pages 59–68.

Philip Muskin. 2022. What are anxiety disorders? In *American Psychiatric Association Physician Review*. Accessed: 2022-10-10.

NIMH. 2023. Anxiety disorders. In *National Institute of Mental Health Information Resource Center*. Accessed: 2023-04-15.

Patricia O. Quinn and Manisha Madhoo. 2014. A review of attention-deficit/hyperactivity disorder in women and girls. *The Primary Care Companion For CNS Disorders*, 16(3).

Judy Hanwen Shen and Frank Rudzicz. 2017. Detecting anxiety through reddit. In *Proceedings of the Fourth Workshop on Computational Linguistics and Clinical Psychology—From Linguistic Signal to Clinical Reality*, pages 58–65.

Colleen M. Story. 2022. Relationship between adhd and anxiety. https://www.healthline.com/health/adhd-and-anxiety#symptoms. Accessed: 2023-01-29.

Michael Van Ameringen, Catherine Mancini, William Simpson, and Beth Patterson. 2011. Adult attention deficit hyperactivity disorder in an anxiety disorders population. *CNS neuroscience & therapeutics*, 17(4):221–226.

Overview of the CLPsych 2024 Shared Task: Leveraging Large Language Models to Identify Evidence of Suicidality Risk in Online Posts

Jenny Chim[1*], **Adam Tsakalidis**[1,2*], **Dimitris Gkoumas**[1], **Dana Atzil-Slonim**[3], **Yaakov Ophir**[4,5], **Ayah Zirikly**[6], **Philip Resnik**[7], **Maria Liakata**[1,2]
[1]Queen Mary University of London (UK), [2]The Alan Turing Institute (UK), [3]Bar Ilan University (Israel), [4]Ariel University (Israel), [5]University of Cambridge (UK), [6]Johns Hopkins University (US), [7]University of Maryland (US)
{c.chim; a.tsakalidis; m.liakata}@qmul.ac.uk

Abstract

We present the overview of the CLPsych 2024 Shared Task, focusing on leveraging open source Large Language Models (LLMs) for identifying textual evidence that supports the suicidal risk level of individuals on Reddit. In particular, given a Reddit user, their pre-determined suicide risk level ('Low', 'Moderate' or 'High') and all of their posts in the *r/SuicideWatch* subreddit, we frame the task of identifying relevant pieces of text in their posts supporting their suicidal classification in two ways: (a) on the basis of evidence highlighting (extracting sub-phrases of the posts) and (b) on the basis of generating a summary of such evidence. We annotate a sample of 125 users and introduce evaluation metrics based on (a) BERTScore and (b) natural language inference for the two sub-tasks, respectively. Finally, we provide an overview of the system submissions and summarise the key findings.

1 Introduction

Recent statistics on mental health related problems during and after the COVID-19 pandemic are striking. In the US, almost 50% of adults aged 18-44 reported a mental illness in 2023,[1] whereas similar rates of the EU population had experienced emotional or psychosocial problems between June 2022-23.[2] Partially due to the limited accessibility of support services, individuals often seek support in online social media by sharing their thoughts and concerns and engaging in discussions with their peers. Research at the intersection of natural language processing (NLP) and mental health has focused on exploiting such user generated content in order to automatically detect vulnerable users (Coppersmith et al., 2015; Shing et al., 2018; Zirikly et al., 2019) or monitor their well-being over time (Tsakalidis et al., 2022b; Tseriotou et al., 2023). However, in real-world scenarios, detection is only part of the need: downstream evaluation and intervention would be facilitated by an understanding of *why* a user's text led them to be flagged (Ophir et al., 2022).

Large language models (LLMs) (Brown et al., 2020; Sanh et al., 2022; Chowdhery et al., 2022; Touvron et al., 2023) are currently dominating the field of NLP. Work at the intersection of NLP and mental health has leveraged such models for classification (Amin et al., 2023), data augmentation (Liyanage et al., 2023) or reasoning (Xu et al., 2023), among others. Recent research explores the language understanding and mental health reasoning capabilities of LLMs using instruction fine-tuning and Chain-of-Thought prompting (CoT) (Yang et al., 2023; Xu et al., 2023). Instead of direct phrase extraction, LLMs are instructed to provide step-by-step reasoning, leveraging inherent knowledge to generate human-like language (Xu et al., 2023). Such approaches pose the risk of incorrect predictions and flawed reasoning, especially in complex conversations (Li et al., 2023).

This year's CLPsych Shared Task focused on *leveraging open source LLMs for the purpose of finding evidence in online posts that supports the level of suicidal risk of their author*. In particular, we define two sub-tasks (thereafter 'tasks') on the basis of (a) highlighting and (b) summarising such supporting evidence. Working with the UMD Reddit Suicidality dataset (Shing et al., 2018; Zirikly et al., 2019), we present the process of defining the task (Section 3), selecting and annotating a subset of 125 Reddit users (Section 4), introducing our evaluation metrics (Section 5) and summarising the approaches and the best-performing system of each team (Section 7).

In this overview paper we make the following

*Denotes equal contribution.

[1]https://www.apa.org/news/press/releases/2023/11/psychological-impacts-collective-trauma

[2]https://europa.eu/eurobarometer/surveys/detail/3032

Proceedings of the 9th Workshop on Computational Linguistics and Clinical Psychology (CLPsych 2024), pages 177–190
March 21, 2024 ©2024 Association for Computational Linguistics

contributions:

- we introduce two novel tasks on identifying evidence that supports the suicidal risk level of a particular user;
- we describe the annotation process;
- we provide an overview of the approaches followed by the participating teams, our evaluation approach and an overview of the results.

2 Related Work

2.1 NLP and Mental Health

Related work during the last decade has been primarily focusing on classifying documents (Sawhney et al., 2022a) or users, with the latter being performed at a static (Coppersmith et al., 2015; Shing et al., 2018; Zirikly et al., 2019; Sawhney et al., 2022b) (e.g., suicide level of an individual) or a longitudinal basis (Tsakalidis et al., 2022b,a; Hills et al., 2023). Recent work has started paying attention to more fine-grained analysis with respect to mental health as well as explaining model predictions. The 2023 eRisk Task 1 focused on ranking of sentences based on their relevance to depressive symptoms (Parapar et al., 2023). Nguyen et al. (2022) proposed a spectrum of BERT-based methods for depression detection that are constrained by the presence of PHQ-9 symptoms for improved generalizability and interpretability of the models. Nemesure et al. (2021) used SHAP values (Lundberg and Lee, 2017) to explain predictions for generalized anxiety and major depressive disorder prediction models. Zirikly and Dredze (2022) used the PHQ-9 questions as auxiliary tasks to provide explanations for a depression detection model using LIME (Ribeiro et al., 2016) and measured performance on a manually annotated sample of highlighted text spans. Garg (2024) also annotated a dataset with highlighted text spans over several 'wellness' dimensions. In this year's Shared Task we also highlight text spans of online posts, which serve as evidence for an online user's suicide risk level, and we further accompany this with a summarisation of such evidence found at the user level. The task then sets out to explore to what extent such text spans and summaries can be obtained by leveraging open source LLMs.

2.2 LLMs for evidence extraction

The use of Large Language Models (LLMs) in evidence extraction is an ongoing area of research and discussion. LLMs have shown promise in retrieving supporting evidence for generated responses and in self-detecting hallucinations within them (Huo et al., 2023). In the context of medical evidence, domain-agnostic LLMs, like GPT-3, have been found to be potentially precise at zero- and few-shot information extraction from clinical unstructured texts (Agrawal et al., 2022), yet prone to inconsistent generated summaries, raising concerns about potential harm due to misinformation (Tang et al., 2023). In NLP for mental health, existing work has predominantly explored the capabilities of LLMs to predict critical mental states (e.g., stress and depression) or high-risk actions (suicide) by forcing LLaMA-2 or GPT3 to act as an expert in a zero- or few-shot setting (Lamichhane, 2023; Amin et al., 2023; Yang et al., 2023). Other work has systematically explored the mental health reasoning capabilities of various LLMs in an instruction fine-tuning setting, employing CoT prompting to elucidate the reasoning behind their predictions (Yang et al., 2023; Xu et al., 2023). However, these approaches do not directly extract precise phrases from the text. Instead, they instruct LLMs to provide step-by-step reasoning or explanations for their output, leveraging inherent knowledge and paraphrasing the text to generate human-like natural language based on embedded knowledge (Xu et al., 2023). This could result not only in incorrect predictions but also in flawed reasoning processes, particularly in more complex conversation contexts (Li et al., 2023).

2.3 LLMs for Summarisation

LLMs have demonstrated promising summarisation performance across document types including news articles (Goyal et al., 2022; Zhang et al., 2023b) and instructional texts (Maynez et al., 2023), and have shown significant improvements in challenging areas such as meeting transcripts (Laskar et al., 2023) and long narratives (Chang et al., 2024). While most use simple prompts (e.g. "*Summarize the following article:*"), prior work on news (Wang et al., 2023) and social media (Song et al., 2024) suggest that multi-step prompting strategies with prompt design informed by domain expertise can steer models to produce improved information-rich summaries. Nonetheless, how to effectively leverage the generative capabilities of LLMs while ensuring outputs are grounded in supporting evidence and consistent with expert knowledge remains an ongoing research problem, especially in high stake applications such as mental health.

3 Task Definition and Instructions

We define two tasks aimed at leveraging LLMs in order to find evidence within text that has been shared by particular online social media users supporting their pre-assigned Suicide Risk Level ('Low', 'Moderate' or 'High'). The distinction between the two tasks is based on the way that this evidence is expected to be provided.

Task A For our first task, participants were asked to provide the evidence supporting the pre-defined Suicide Risk Level of a user by *highlighting* relevant phrases within the text posted by the user. Each user could have multiple posts in the dataset; Task A was defined at the post (document) level – i.e., highlighting relevant phrases within each post made by a particular user.

Task B Our second task required *generating a summary* of evidence supporting a user's assigned risk level, across multiple posts made by the user. As opposed to Task A, Task B was performed at the user level – i.e., generating a single summary per user. Summaries were limited to 300 tokens.

No ground truth data were provided to the teams, except for a single example of a user with a pre-assigned Suicide Risk Level for whom we shared the expected highlights (Task A) and summary (Task B), as annotated by our experts (see Section 4.2). Compared to the latest CLPsych Shared Tasks, where the expected outputs were a class label either at the user level (Zirikly et al., 2019) or on a longitudinal basis (Tsakalidis et al., 2022a), this year's edition was considerably more open-ended. We therefore provided a list of 'aspects to consider' to the teams, which were compiled on the basis of our internal annotation instructions. These aspects, which were based on literature on suicidal risk (see Section 4.2), included, but were not limited to, the following:

- **Emotions**: How does the individual feel? From feeling sad to experiencing unbearable psychological pain, the self-disclosed emotions of the user could play an important role in the risk level assigned to the individual.
- **Cognitions**: What are the individual's thoughts and perceptions about suicide? For example, what is the level and frequency of suicidal thoughts? Does the individual intend to self-harm/suicide? Does the individual have a plan about it?
- **Behaviour and Motivation**: What are the individual's acts or behavior related to suicide? For example, do they have access to means and a concrete plan? What is the user's ability to handle difficult/stressful situations ('behaviour')? What is the motivation behind their wish to be dead?
- **Interpersonal and social support**: Does the individual have social support/stable relationships? How does the individual feel towards significant others?
- **Mental health-related issues**: Consider psychiatric diagnoses associated with suicide such as schizophrenia, bipolar/anxiety/eating disorder, previous self-harm/suicidal attempts and others.
- **Context/additional risk factors**: For example, socioeconomic and demographic factors, exposure to suicide behaviour by others, chronic medical condition, ...

Each team was allowed to provide (up to) three submissions for each task. Additional submissions were also allowed in order to facilitate ablation and further analysis by the teams, but were not included in our official results presented in this overview paper. Upon receiving the submissions, we returned the results based on our evaluation metrics (see Section 5) on a test set of 125 users (see Section 4).

4 Data and Annotation

4.1 Data

We use a subset of the The University of Maryland (UMD) Reddit Suicidality Dataset, Version 2 (Shing et al., 2018; Zirikly et al., 2019) for both tasks. The dataset contains posts made by a larger number of Reddit users.[3] The data was previously annotated at the user level with respect to level of suicide risk ('No', 'Low', 'Moderate' or 'Severe' risk labels), where the main difference between Moderate and Severe is that the latter indicates imminent or crisis-level risk. This annotation was performed in two ways (by (a) crowdsourcing and

[3]https://www.reddit.com/

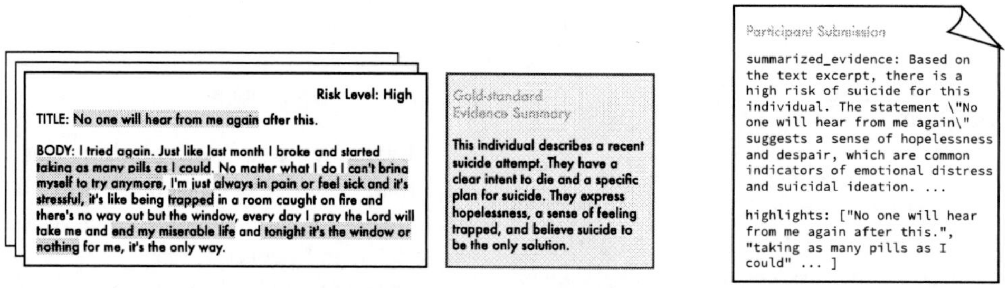

Figure 1: Example posts, gold evidence spans and summary, and corresponding submission data. Texts have been paraphrased for privacy. Participants are provided with posts and user-level risk labels, then asked to predict supporting evidence spans (Task A) and synthesise summaries (Task B). Each user can have multiple posts.

(b) experts, where the experts annotated a subset of the users) and it involved an annotator reading all of the posts that a user had made in the *r/SuicideWatch* subreddit in order to make a labelling decision for that particular user.

The inter-annotator agreement was higher amongst the expert annotators (Shing et al., 2018); we therefore ignored the crowdsourced annotations for this Shared Task and focused strictly on the 245 users annotated by the experts. Since our task involves finding evidence about the suicide risk level of a particular user, we only kept the 'Low', 'Moderate' and 'Severe' classes (209 users) and ignored the 'No risk' category. Also, since the original annotation was performed on the basis of the *r/SuicideWatch* posts only, we further focused explicitly on those 332 posts made by the 209 users. Lastly, we selected 125/209 users (162/332 posts) to be annotated by our annotators (see Section 4.2) and serve as our ground truth during the evaluation stage of the Shared Task. This final selection was based on (a) filtering out any users whose posts were very short, (b) ignoring users with more than 3 posts in *r/SuicideWatch* to accommodate faster annotation (i.e., prioritising more users instead of more posts in our evaluation data) and (c) prioritising the inclusion of 'Severe', followed by 'Moderate' risk users. In the end, 93 users had only one post, 27 users had two posts and five users had three posts. Table 1 shows the overall numbers of users and posts in *r/SuicideWatch* that were selected for annotation purposes (and therefore, our gold standard during evaluation), as described next.

	No	Low	Moderate	Severe	**Total**
Original (users)	36	50	115	44	245
Annotated (users)	–	13	74	38	125
Original (posts)	45	77	162	93	377
Annotated (posts)	–	17	91	54	162

Table 1: Summary of the data that was annotated in this Shared Task and used as our ground truth, compared to the original UMD Reddit Suicidality Dataset.

4.2 Annotation

The annotators were two graduate students (fluent English speakers) in a clinical psychology training program at Bar-Ilan University. Their task was to read the posts of each user on *r/SuicideWatch*, and highlight text spans as evidence supporting the suicide risk level previously assigned by experts in Shing et al. (2018). Next, they were asked to synthesize the textual evidence and related clinical observations in a short summary.

Annotators were provided with detailed guidelines and expert annotated examples. The guidelines for the annotations were based on the clinical literature about suicidal risk (Posner et al., 2011; Turecki et al., 2019; Rogers et al., 2023) and their main aspects are provided as a list in Section 4.1. We conducted two rounds of training supervised by a senior clinical psychology expert. In each round, annotators labelled posts independently. We manually checked the agreement on these posts, then addressed areas of disagreement and clarified task guidelines in training meetings. Next, the team was asked to refine their existing annotations and work on new ones. We repeated this process until satisfactory agreement levels were obtained upon manual inspection, where the most important key phrases were captured by both annotators, and the summarised evidences were mutually consistent. Out of the 125 posts, 13 were labeled twice by both annotators. The final pairwise relaxed F1 (Hripcsak and Rothschild, 2005; Deléger et al., 2012) over evidence spans from these doubly annotated instances is .96.

5 Evaluation Metrics

5.1 Task A

The main metric we consider is the recall of evidence spans. For a given user, given predicted evidence spans E and gold evidence spans H, we average the maximum recall-oriented BERTScore (Zhang et al., 2020):

$$\text{Recall} = \frac{1}{|E|}\sum_{e\in E}\max_{h\in H} R_{\text{BERT}}(e,h)$$

To provide a more holistic view of evidence identification performance, we compute precision by averaging the maximum precision-oriented BERTScore for each predicted evidence span $e \in E$ against each gold evidence span $h \in H$:

$$\text{Precision} = \frac{1}{|H|}\sum_{h\in H}\max_{e\in E} P_{\text{BERT}}(e,h)$$

We also report a weighted version of recall, which is sensitive to predicted evidence lengths relative to gold evidence lengths. For a given user with gold evidence spans of cumulative token count n_{gold} and predicted spans with cumulative token count n_{pred}, if the predicted evidence spans are longer than the gold-standard ones, we apply weight w to the user-level recall:

$$w = \begin{cases} \frac{n_{\text{gold}}}{n_{\text{pred}}} & \text{if } n_{\text{pred}} > n_{\text{gold}} \\ 1 & \text{otherwise} \end{cases}$$

Finally, we report F1, the harmonic mean between precision and unweighted recall, $\frac{2\times\text{Precision}\times\text{Recall}}{\text{Precision}+\text{Recall}}$.

5.2 Task B

Following prior work in general domain (Maynez et al., 2020) and mental health summarisation (Song et al., 2024), we leverage predictions from a natural language inference (NLI) model (Laurer et al., 2024) for summary evaluation.[4] We consider consistency to be the absence of contradiction. For each sentence in a submitted summary $s \in S$, we use the NLI model to compute its mean probability of contradicting each sentence in the corresponding gold-standard evidence summary $g \in G$, taking the gold sentence as premise and the submitted sentence as hypothesis:

$$\text{CS} = \tfrac{1}{|S|\cdot|G|}\textstyle\sum_{s\in S}\sum_{g\in G}(1-\text{NLI}(\text{Contradict}|g,s))$$

To complement consistency, we also evaluate summaries by their contradiction to expert summaries. We expect there to be some natural contradictory information in most summaries, since summarised evidence can include both risk factors and protective factors. We compute the contradiction score by averaging the *maximum* contradiction probability of a predicted sentence against gold evidence summary sentences:

$$\text{CT} = \frac{1}{|S|}\sum_{s\in S}\max_{g\in G}\text{NLI}(\text{Contradict}|g,s).$$

6 Participating Process & Teams

6.1 Registration Process

The registration process included (a) a team member initialising the process by filling an online form as the team representative, (b) reading and signing a data sharing agreement and (c) receiving instructions on how to download the data in a password protected zip folder. Each team member would also sign up for their team upon completing an individual registration form. The (b) data sharing agreement (among others) prohibited transferring any part of the data to third party providers in order to use their LLMs.

6.2 Participating Teams

Overall 23 teams (75 members) registered for the task. Members of four teams mentioned that they had participated in a previous CLPsych Shared Task, whereas members of three teams stated that they had previous experience with the UMD Suicidality Dataset. 15 out of 23 teams submitted their outputs for either of the two tasks – a percentage of 65% compared to 60% for Shared Task 2022 (Tsakalidis et al., 2022a) – and 13 teams submitted a paper at the end of the Shared Task (see Table 2).

7 Results

7.1 Overview

Task A The results are summarised in Table 3. The highest evidence recall comes from systems employing different approaches, including relying on smaller expert models for sentence-level predictions (SophiaADS), CoT prompting (UoS NLP), and prompting then post-processing (UniBuc Archeology). To improve precision and reduce incorrect outputs (e.g., hallucinations and unintended text normalisation where LLM corrects

[4] https://huggingface.co/MoritzLaurer/DeBERTa-v3-large-mnli-fever-anli-ling-wanli

Team Name	#Members	#Submissions Task A	Task B	Paper submitted
CSIRO	6	3	–	✓
DONUTS Colaboratory	6	2	2	
INF@UoS	2	1	1	✓
ISM	2	3	3	✓
LAMA	3	3	3	✓
MHNLP	1	1	1	
SBC	1	3	3	✓
SCALAR-NITK	3	1	1	✓
SKKU-DSAIL	5	3	3	✓
sophiaADS	3	3	3	✓
SWELL	11	3	3	✓
UniBuc Archaeology	3	3	3	✓
UoS NLP	4	3	3	✓
UZH_CLyp	2	1	1	✓
Xinhai	3	3	3	✓
Total (sum)	**55**	**36**	**33**	**13/15**

Table 2: Summary of the team information and submissions for the CLPsych Shared Task 2024.

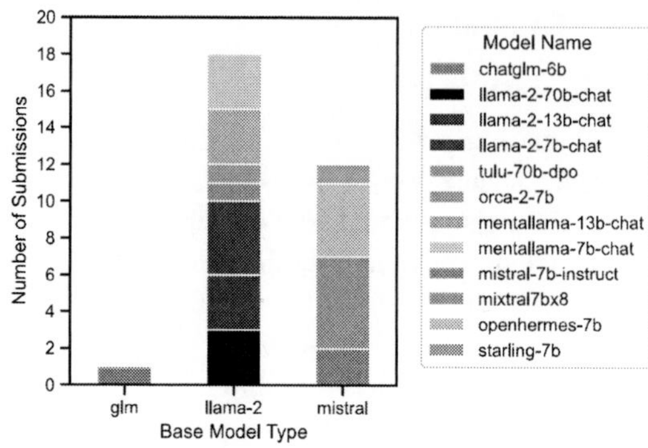

Figure 2: LLMs used in official submissions, grouped by model family and lineage.

typos in noisy user text), most teams applied post-processing procedures to align predicted spans to the original text, and some employed formal grammars to constrain model outputs (CSIRO, SBC).

Task B Submissions that achieved the highest consistency scores commonly incorporated domain knowledge, such as using expert models to retrieve emotionally charged text before summarising (UZH_CLyp), designing detailed instructions around the Shared Task guidelines (SBC, SWELL), and summarising evidence spans that were extracted based on psychology theory, e.g. Joiner's Interpersonal Theory of Suicide (SWELL). While there was no definitively superior LLM, top performing submissions on this task used Mistral (Jiang et al., 2023) and its derivative Openhermes[5], as well as LLaMA-2 (Touvron et al., 2023) and its mental health oriented derivative MentaLLaMA (Yang et al., 2023).

LLM Characteristics and Resources. As per the data use agreement, participants were forbidden from using Cloud APIs, relying on private and self-hosted instances. Figure 2 outlines the employed models. All submissions used instruction-tuned LLMs. The majority of submissions used models that are 7B or smaller (52%), the rest includes 13B and 8x7B mixture-of-expert models (35%) and 70B models (13%). Models were typically deployed with quantization, in some cases using libraries such as llama.cpp to run on consumer hardware.[6]

7.2 Individual Team Submissions

UoS_NLP Singh et al. (2024) explored prompting strategies with Mixtral7bx8 (Jiang et al., 2024), a LLM with the same high-level architecture as Mistral (Jiang et al., 2023) but utilising mixture-of-experts layers, and Tulu-2-DPO-70B (Ivison et al., 2023), LLaMA-2 further instruction finetuned using direct preference optimisation (Rafailov et al., 2023). Their best performing evidence extraction approach involved few-shot CoT prompting Tulu, choosing exemplars by embedding posts with social media fine-tuned RoBERTA (Barbieri et al., 2020) then applying k-means clustering and manually selecting representative examples. For evidence summarisation, their best approach involved zero-shot instruction prompting Mixtral with additional meta-information, i.e. inferred emotion, inferred sentiment, and suicide risk label.

SCALAR-NITK Koushik et al. (2024) used attention weights from hierarchical attention networks (Yang et al., 2016) to extract evidence spans. For evidence summarisation, they zero-shot prompted LLaMA-2-7B-chat, providing the content of the user's post(s) concatenated with their extracted evidence spans as input.

LAMA Alhamed et al. (2024) used LLaMA-7B-chat with instruction prompting. For evidence extraction, they zero-shot prompted the LLM and combined the outputs with keywords extracted using a suicide lexicon (Alhamed et al., 2022) as well as manually curated depression-related keywords. Evidence summaries were separately obtained by first prompting to provide explanations of the individual's suicide risk level then synthesising them.

[5] `https://huggingface.co/teknium/OpenHermes-2-Mistral-7B`

[6] `https://github.com/ggerganov/llama.cpp`

Team	Task A: Evidence Extraction					Task B: Evidence Summarisation		
	Hybrid	Recall	Precision	Weighted Recall	Harmonic Mean	Hybrid	Mean Consistency	Max Contradiction
SophiaADS	✓	**.944**	.906	.489	.924	✓	.944	.175
UoS NLP	✓	.943	.916	.527	**.929**		.966	.107
UniBuc Archaeology		.939	.890	.390	.914		.973	.081
ISM	✓	.935	.911	.564	.923	✓	.961	.125
SKKU-DSAIL	✓	.922	.912	.549	.917		.970	.096
CSIRO		.919	**.917**	.701	.917		–	–
SWELL	✓	.915	.892	.542	.903	✓	.973	.081
UZH_CLyp		.910	.916	.742	.913	✓	**.979**	.064
MHNLP	✓	.910	.888	.197	.909		.873	.204
SBC		.907	.912	.738	.909		.976	.079
Xinhai		.887	.906	.617	.911		.958	.126
SCALAR-NITK	✓	.886	.893	**.784**	.889		.901	.233
DONUTS Colaboratory		.872	.900	.626	.907		.942	.159
INF@UoS	✓	.850	.893	.630	.896	✓	.934	.165
LAMA	✓	.577	.899	.513	.888		.964	**.060**

Table 3: Evaluation scores for Task A, by selecting the top-performing submission of each team on the basis of Recall. The associated Task B evaluation scores are shown on the right. 'Hybrid' denotes that the shown submission incorporated non-LLM techniques, including using inputs derived via non-LLM methods, and excluding standard post-processing. For details and methods explored in other submissions, please refer to Section 7.2.

Team	Mean Consistency	Max Contradiction
UZH_CLyp	**.979**	.064
UoS NLP	.977	.079
SBC	.977	.083
SKKU-DSAIL	.973	.086
SWELL	.973	.081
UniBuc Archaeology	.973	.081
LAMA	.964	**.060**
ISM	.961	.125
Xinhai	.959	.121
SophiaADS	.944	.175
DONUTS Colaboratory	.942	.159
INF@UoS	.934	.165
SCALAR-NITK	.901	.233
MHNLP	.873	.204

Table 4: Evaluation scores for Task B, by selecting the top-performing submission of each team on the basis of Mean Consistency.

Xinhai Zhu et al. (2024) used instruction prompting on a version of the open-source ChatGLM-3-6B (Du et al., 2022) model adapted to healthcare data. They revised their prompt using GPT-4. For evidence span extraction, they ensured LLM predictions obtained from instruction prompting were text spans directly present in the input texts using regular expressions and aligning phrases by their semantic similarity.

SophiaADS Tanaka and Fukazawa (2024) proposed a hybrid solution comprising task-specific models, handcrafted rules, and MentaLLaMA-chat-7b. For evidence extraction, they first picked sentences corresponding to high probabilities of suicide risk, as predicted by a bert-base-uncased classifier (Devlin et al., 2019). The latter was fine-tuned on a binary sentence-level suicide ideation dataset heuristically developed from the Shared Task data. In cases of insufficient evidence, they added the most negative sentences as predicted by a Tweet sentiment classifier (Barbieri et al., 2020), and supplemented with predictions from instruction-prompting MentaLLaMA as necessary. To summarise evidence, the team combined LLM summaries with rules that produce descriptions of risk level, posting behaviour, and several mental health related risk factors.

ISM Tran and Matsui (2024) leveraged Mixtral-8-7B-Instruct (Jiang et al., 2024) in two distinct stages: a) knowledge self-extraction and b) output refinement. During the knowledge self-extraction phase, participants provided users' posts along with the associated risk levels, prompting the model to address the task. The resulting output comprises a set of generated highlights, summaries, and identifications of suicide risks. Next, they selected the most optimal generated outputs aligned with the risk level to enrich the model's knowledge in stage 2, creating an enhanced and knowledge-rich representation (i.e., concatenation of the best knowledge responses). In the final step, the model underwent an iterative refinement process, continuously prompting for adjustments to the newly generated summaries and highlights until no further changes were observed.

CSIRO Chen et al. (2024) introduced instructive prompting for a range of psychological and socioeconomic factors to extract evidence aligned with users' suicidal risk from LLaMA-2-70b-chat in a zero-shot setting. They investigated prompt engineering approaches across three different variations: a) A naive approach, instructing the model to extract phrases as evidence supporting suicide risk, thereby evaluating the inherent knowledge of the model. b) They enhanced the input content with a collection of psychological and socioeconomic factors, namely factor-orientied instruction. c) Finally, they reformulated the risk levels provided by annotators into a set of selected risk factors. The model was then guided by rules to choose the most appropriate prompt based on a user's risk level.

SBC Blanco-Cuaresma (2024) investigated opensource LLMs – OpenHermes, Orca2, Starling 7B alpha – in a one-shot setting. They employed the same crafted prompts, consisting in prefixed psychological and social factors provided by the organizers, to extract evidence from users' posts or to summarize evidence associated with their risk level. When extracting evidence, they utilized Backus-Naur Form (BNF), which is a metasyntactic notation for context-free grammars. This approach ensured that the order of words in the generated output matched the order of those in the users' posts.

INF@UoS Preiss and Chen (2024) proposed a two-stage pipeline to address span extraction and summarization related to suicidal risk levels. In the first stage, they fine-tuned a suicide risk classifier, i.e., MentalRoBERTa (Ji et al., 2022). Additionally, they employed Linguistic Inquiry and Word Count (LIWC-22) to extract informative features from the language, including desire for connection, certainty, negative tones, emotions, negative emotions, sadness emotions, mental health behavior, persuasiveness, and feelings. The additional extracted information was integrated with users' posts to train the classifier. Subsequently, SHAP was utilized to identify crucial phrases from the input content that contributed to the classifier's decision. In stage two, they prompted Mistral-7B-Instruct to generate summaries across five diverse factors—emotion, cognition, social support, mental health issues, and conceptual risk—using the extracted phrases from stage one.

SKKU-DSAIL For Task A, Jeon et al. (2024) prompted MentaLLaMA by assigning it a 'psychiatrist' identity and further providing it with (a) an example (partially highlighted) post, (b) a list of suicide-related words present in the post (Lee et al., 2022), (c) the post under consideration and (d) the suicide risk level of its author. For Task B, they used a similar setting, followed by two methods ('extract-then-generate' (Zhang et al., 2023a), integrating the highlighted phrases from Task A, and SOLAR (Kim et al., 2023)) for tackling hallucinations and inconsistencies in the generated summaries.

UZH_CLyp Uluslu et al. (2024) provided Mistral-7B-Instruct with the post and the author's label, asking it to extract the highlights for Task A as a suicide prevention therapist expert. For Task B, the levels of three emotions were calculated at the post-level and the top-5 saddest posts were included in the prompt (alongside the post, the user's risk level and the emotions) in order to generate the summary. In their ablation analysis, the authors showed that selecting the top-5 saddest posts had a large (positive) impact on model performance.

SWELL For Task A, Varadarajan et al. (2024) followed three approaches: (a) they constructed 'suicidality archetypes' on the basis of Joiner's IPTS (Joiner, 2007) in order to calculate their similarity against the sentence embeddings of a given post and extract the spans with the highest similarity; (b) they fine-tuned separate LMs using data from users with different suicidal risk levels and calculated the difference in entropy between these models for each sentence in a given post (Lahnala et al., 2021); (c) they prompted LLaMA-2 to extract sentences signalling any of the three main Joiner's IPTS constructs. For Task B they prompted LLaMA-2 in a few-shot setting, providing it with highlights and asking it to generate a summary by considering the six aspects present in Section 3.

UniBuc Archaeology Sandu et al. (2024) experimented with 'traditional' NLP approaches and LLMs: (a) for Task A, they used SHAP (Lundberg and Lee, 2017) on the outputs of a logistic regression trained to split 'No' vs 'Low/Moderate/High' risk users on the basis of tfidf ngrams and performed Task B as an extractive summarisation task; (b) they prompted OpenHermes 2.5 based on Mistral for extracting highlights and summarising the evidence.

7.3 Performance by Risk Level

Figure 3 summarises performance on test users at each risk level aggregated over all submissions. For the complete table of performance per team, see Table 3. While mean evidence recall values are relatively similar, for precision and metrics assessing summary consistency the lower the risk level the lower the average performance. This suggests that linguistic cues for lower to moderate risk can be subtler compared to those of higher risk levels, and it may be more challenging to describe protective factors and the *absence* of risk factors. Future approaches should aim to more fully capture the nuances within the spectrum of suicide risk factors.

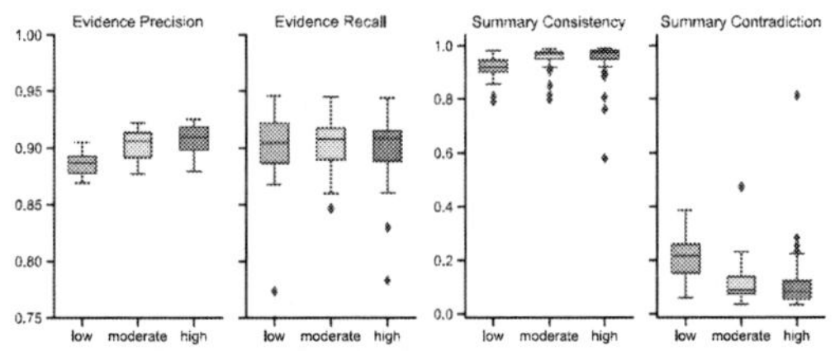

Figure 3: Mean performance by user's risk level. From left to right: evidence precision, recall, summary consistency, summary contradiction. Higher is better except for summary contradiction.

8 Conclusion

This work presented the overview of the CLPsych Shared Task 2024, focusing on leveraging open source LLMs to find supporting textual evidence for the suicide risk level of an online user, based on their online posts. We defined two tasks for finding such evidence – based on (a) text highlighting of relevant spans at the post-level and (b) summarising the evidence at the user-level. We generated a dataset of 125 social media users to facilitate evaluation and introduced the associated evaluation metrics for measuring system performance. Lastly, we have summarised the approaches taken by 13 teams and provided an overview of their results, their commonalities and novel aspects of their work.

Limitations

As in the vast majority of prior work on leveraging social media for user-level mental health assessments, this year's Shared Task involved users who were classified with respect to their suicide risk level on the basis of content they generated. This implies that the annotation of their suicidality risk level, as well as this Shared Task's additional annotations (see Section 4.2), have been made on the basis of self-report. Moreover, the present tasks were conducted using social media posts made on a particular subreddit in the English language, by users who willingly self-disclosed their thoughts and feelings. Generalisation of the approaches presented in this work to other contexts (e.g., in psychotherapy sessions) remains an open question. Lastly, we have examined the presence of evidence around suicidality at the post-level; importantly longitudinal linguistic cues that might be present in the data cannot be captured by our annotations – and therefore, by the approaches outlined in this work.

Ethics

This task explored the extent to which evidence for suicidal risk from online posts can be obtained by leveraging information inherent in open source LLMs, and how this information can be further summarised. However, the task cannot make any claims about the potential evidence providing explanations for suicidal risk and neither do the aggregate summaries constitute such explanations. The motivation behind the task was to explore the possibilities for evidence extraction provided by LLMs and the corresponding limitations. We hope that this is a first step to research that can actually make causal links between evidence and suicidality and augment models with symbolic of inference methods that can reveal reasoning processes.

The task also does not promote in any way the notion that LLMs could provide evidence for diagnosis that would not involve a human. Any such evidence would need to be reviewed by a human expert and our intuition is that better models could help augment the capacity of clinical experts by providing information that would not otherwise be available to them.

The UMD Reddit Suicidality Dataset was made available for the shared task following a determination by the University of Maryland College Park IRB that doing so was exempt from IRB review according to U.S. federal regulations. All of the data have been provided to the participants in an anonymised fashion. An application form was required to be signed by each of the teams before accessing the data, clarifying that only the listed members could have access to the dataset and the location where it would be hosted locally had to be stated. Even though we are using publicly available data from Reddit, we prohibited the use of any third-party LLMs that would require sending (part of) the data in the provider's servers, as to protect the suicide risk label of each user in the UMD Reddit Suicidality Dataset.

Acknowledgements

This work was supported by a UKRI/EPSRC Turing AI Fellowship to Maria Liakata (grant ref EP/V030302/1) and the Alan Turing Institute (grant ref EP/N510129/1). Philip Resnik was supported by U.S. NSF award 2124270. The shared task organizers would like to express their gratitude to the anonymous users of Reddit whose data feature in this year's shared task dataset; to the clinical experts from Bar-Ilan University who annotated the data for both tasks; to the American Association of Suicidology; to all team members for their participation; and to EACL for its support for CLPsych.

References

Monica Agrawal, Stefan Hegselmann, Hunter Lang, Yoon Kim, and David Sontag. 2022. Large language models are few-shot clinical information extractors. In *Proceedings of the 2022 Conference on Empirical Methods in Natural Language Processing*, pages 1998–2022.

Falwah Alhamed, Julia Ive, and Lucia Specia. 2022. Predicting moments of mood changes overtime from imbalanced social media data. In *Proceedings of the Eighth Workshop on Computational Linguistics and Clinical Psychology*, pages 239–244, Seattle, USA. Association for Computational Linguistics.

Falwah Alhamed, Julia Ive, and Lucia Specia. 2024. Using large language models (llms) to extract evidence from pre-annotated social media data. In *Proceedings of the Ninth Workshop on Computational Linguistics and Clinical Psychology*. Association for Computational Linguistics.

Mostafa M Amin, Erik Cambria, and Björn W Schuller. 2023. Will affective computing emerge from foundation models and general ai? a first evaluation on chatgpt. *arXiv preprint arXiv:2303.03186*.

Francesco Barbieri, Jose Camacho-Collados, Luis Espinosa Anke, and Leonardo Neves. 2020. TweetEval: Unified benchmark and comparative evaluation for tweet classification. In *Findings of the Association for Computational Linguistics: EMNLP 2020*, pages 1644–1650, Online. Association for Computational Linguistics.

Sergi Blanco-Cuaresma. 2024. Psychological assessments with large language models: A privacy-focused and cost-effective approach. In *Proceedings of the Ninth Workshop on Computational Linguistics and Clinical Psychology*. Association for Computational Linguistics.

Tom Brown, Benjamin Mann, Nick Ryder, Melanie Subbiah, Jared D Kaplan, Prafulla Dhariwal, Arvind Neelakantan, Pranav Shyam, Girish Sastry, Amanda Askell, Sandhini Agarwal, Ariel Herbert-Voss, Gretchen Krueger, Tom Henighan, Rewon Child, Aditya Ramesh, Daniel Ziegler, Jeffrey Wu, Clemens Winter, Chris Hesse, Mark Chen, Eric Sigler, Mateusz Litwin, Scott Gray, Benjamin Chess, Jack Clark, Christopher Berner, Sam McCandlish, Alec Radford, Ilya Sutskever, and Dario Amodei. 2020. Language models are few-shot learners. In *Advances in Neural Information Processing Systems*, volume 33, pages 1877–1901. Curran Associates, Inc.

Yapei Chang, Kyle Lo, Tanya Goyal, and Mohit Iyyer. 2024. Booookscore: A systematic exploration of book-length summarization in the era of LLMs. In *The Twelfth International Conference on Learning Representations*.

Jiyu Chen, Vincent Nguyen, Xiang Dai, Diego Molla-Aliod, Cecile Paris, and Sarvnaz Karimi. 2024. Exploring instructive prompts for large language models in the extraction of evidence for supporting assigned suicidal risk levels. In *Proceedings of the Ninth Workshop on Computational Linguistics and Clinical Psychology*. Association for Computational Linguistics.

Aakanksha Chowdhery, Sharan Narang, Jacob Devlin, Maarten Bosma, Gaurav Mishra, Adam Roberts, Paul Barham, Hyung Won Chung, Charles Sutton, Sebastian Gehrmann, Parker Schuh, Kensen Shi, Sasha Tsvyashchenko, Joshua Maynez, Abhishek Rao, Parker Barnes, Yi Tay, Noam M. Shazeer, Vinodkumar Prabhakaran, Emily Reif, Nan Du, Benton C. Hutchinson, Reiner Pope, James Bradbury, Jacob Austin, Michael Isard, Guy Gur-Ari, Pengcheng Yin, Toju Duke, Anselm Levskaya, Sanjay Ghemawat, Sunipa Dev, Henryk Michalewski, Xavier García, Vedant Misra, Kevin Robinson, Liam Fedus, Denny Zhou, Daphne Ippolito, David Luan, Hyeontaek Lim, Barret Zoph, Alexander Spiridonov, Ryan Sepassi, David Dohan, Shivani Agrawal, Mark Omernick, Andrew M. Dai, Thanumalayan Sankaranarayana Pillai, Marie Pellat, Aitor Lewkowycz, Erica Moreira, Rewon Child, Oleksandr Polozov, Katherine Lee, Zongwei Zhou, Xuezhi Wang, Brennan Saeta, Mark Díaz, Orhan Firat, Michele Catasta, Jason Wei, Kathleen S. Meier-Hellstern, Douglas Eck, Jeff Dean, Slav Petrov, and Noah Fiedel. 2022. Palm: Scaling language modeling with pathways. *J. Mach. Learn. Res.*, 24:240:1–240:113.

Glen Coppersmith, Mark Dredze, Craig Harman, Kristy Hollingshead, and Margaret Mitchell. 2015. Clpsych 2015 shared task: Depression and ptsd on twitter. In *Proceedings of the 2nd workshop on computational linguistics and clinical psychology: from linguistic signal to clinical reality*, pages 31–39.

Louise Deléger, Qi Li, Todd Lingren, Megan Kaiser, Katalin Molnár, Laura Stoutenborough, Michal Kouril, Keith A. Marsolo, and Imre Solti. 2012. Building gold standard corpora for medical natural language processing tasks. *AMIA ... Annual Symposium proceedings. AMIA Symposium*, 2012:144–53.

Jacob Devlin, Ming-Wei Chang, Kenton Lee, and Kristina Toutanova. 2019. BERT: Pre-training of deep bidirectional transformers for language understanding. In *Proceedings of the 2019 Conference of the North American Chapter of the Association for Computational Linguistics: Human Language Technologies, Volume 1 (Long and Short Papers)*, pages 4171–4186, Minneapolis, Minnesota. Association for Computational Linguistics.

Zhengxiao Du, Yujie Qian, Xiao Liu, Ming Ding, Jiezhong Qiu, Zhilin Yang, and Jie Tang. 2022. GLM: General language model pretraining with autoregressive blank infilling. In *Proceedings of the 60th Annual Meeting of the Association for Computational Linguistics (Volume 1: Long Papers)*, pages 320–335, Dublin, Ireland. Association for Computational Linguistics.

Muskan Garg. 2024. Wellxplain: Wellness concept extraction and classification in reddit posts for mental health analysis. *Knowledge-Based Systems*, 284:111228.

Tanya Goyal, Junyi Jessy Li, and Greg Durrett. 2022. News summarization and evaluation in the era of gpt-3. *arXiv preprint arXiv:2209.12356*.

Anthony Hills, Adam Tsakalidis, and Maria Liakata. 2023. Time-aware predictions of moments of change in longitudinal user posts on social media. In *International Workshop on Advanced Analytics and Learning on Temporal Data*, pages 293–305. Springer.

George Hripcsak and Adam S Rothschild. 2005. Agreement, the f-measure, and reliability in information retrieval. *Journal of the American medical informatics association*, 12(3):296–298.

Siqing Huo, Negar Arabzadeh, and Charles LA Clarke. 2023. Retrieving supporting evidence for llms generated answers. *arXiv preprint arXiv:2306.13781*.

Hamish Ivison, Yizhong Wang, Valentina Pyatkin, Nathan Lambert, Matthew Peters, Pradeep Dasigi, Joel Jang, David Wadden, Noah A. Smith, Iz Beltagy, and Hannaneh Hajishirzi. 2023. Camels in a changing climate: Enhancing lm adaptation with tulu 2.

Hyolim Jeon, Dongje Yoo, Daeun Lee, Sejung Son, Seungbae Kim, and Jinyoung Han. 2024. A dual-prompting for interpretable mental health language models. In *Proceedings of the Ninth Workshop on Computational Linguistics and Clinical Psychology*. Association for Computational Linguistics.

Shaoxiong Ji, Tianlin Zhang, Luna Ansari, Jie Fu, Prayag Tiwari, and Erik Cambria. 2022. MentalBERT: Publicly available pretrained language models for mental healthcare. In *Proceedings of the Thirteenth Language Resources and Evaluation Conference*, pages 7184–7190, Marseille, France. European Language Resources Association.

Albert Q Jiang, Alexandre Sablayrolles, Antoine Roux, Arthur Mensch, Blanche Savary, Chris Bamford, Devendra Singh Chaplot, Diego de las Casas, Emma Bou Hanna, Florian Bressand, et al. 2024. Mixtral of experts. *arXiv preprint arXiv:2401.04088*.

Albert Qiaochu Jiang, Alexandre Sablayrolles, Arthur Mensch, Chris Bamford, Devendra Singh Chaplot, Diego de Las Casas, Florian Bressand, Gianna Lengyel, Guillaume Lample, Lucile Saulnier, L'elio Renard Lavaud, Marie-Anne Lachaux, Pierre Stock, Teven Le Scao, Thibaut Lavril, Thomas Wang, Timothée Lacroix, and William El Sayed. 2023. Mistral 7b. *ArXiv*, abs/2310.06825.

T. Joiner. 2007. *Why people die by suicide*. Harvard University Press, Cambridge, Mass.

Dahyun Kim, Chanjun Park, Sanghoon Kim, Wonsung Lee, Wonho Song, Yunsu Kim, Hyeonwoo Kim, Yungi Kim, Hyeonju Lee, Jihoo Kim, et al. 2023. Solar 10.7 b: Scaling large language models with simple yet effective depth up-scaling. *arXiv preprint arXiv:2312.15166*.

L Koushik, M Vishruth, and M Anand Kumar. 2024. Detecting suicide risk patterns using hierarchical attention networks with large language models. In *Proceedings of the Ninth Workshop on Computational Linguistics and Clinical Psychology*. Association for Computational Linguistics.

Allison Lahnala, Yuntian Zhao, Charles Welch, Jonathan K. Kummerfeld, Lawrence C An, Kenneth Resnicow, Rada Mihalcea, and Verónica Pérez-Rosas. 2021. Exploring self-identified counseling expertise in online support forums. In *Findings of the Association for Computational Linguistics: ACL-IJCNLP 2021*, pages 4467–4480, Online. Association for Computational Linguistics.

Bishal Lamichhane. 2023. Evaluation of chatgpt for nlp-based mental health applications. *arXiv preprint arXiv:2303.15727*.

Md Tahmid Rahman Laskar, M Saiful Bari, Mizanur Rahman, Md Amran Hossen Bhuiyan, Shafiq Joty, and Jimmy Huang. 2023. A systematic study and comprehensive evaluation of ChatGPT on benchmark datasets. In *Findings of the Association for Computational Linguistics: ACL 2023*, pages 431–469, Toronto, Canada. Association for Computational Linguistics.

Moritz Laurer, Wouter Van Atteveldt, Andreu Casas, and Kasper Welbers. 2024. Less annotating, more classifying: Addressing the data scarcity issue of supervised machine learning with deep transfer learning and bert-nli. *Political Analysis*, 32(1):84–100.

Daeun Lee, Migyeong Kang, Minji Kim, and Jinyoung Han. 2022. Detecting suicidality with a contextual graph neural network. In *Proceedings of the eighth workshop on computational linguistics and clinical psychology*, pages 116–125.

Yucheng Li, Bo Dong, Chenghua Lin, and Frank Guerin. 2023. Compressing context to enhance inference efficiency of large language models. *arXiv preprint arXiv:2310.06201*.

Chandreen Liyanage, Muskan Garg, Vijay Mago, and Sunghwan Sohn. 2023. Augmenting Reddit posts to determine wellness dimensions impacting mental health. In *The 22nd Workshop on Biomedical Natural Language Processing and BioNLP Shared Tasks*, pages 306–312, Toronto, Canada. Association for Computational Linguistics.

Scott M. Lundberg and Su-In Lee. 2017. A unified approach to interpreting model predictions. In *Proceedings of the 31st International Conference on Neural Information Processing Systems*, NIPS'17, page 4768–4777, Red Hook, NY, USA. Curran Associates Inc.

Joshua Maynez, Priyanka Agrawal, and Sebastian Gehrmann. 2023. Benchmarking large language model capabilities for conditional generation. In *Proceedings of the 61st Annual Meeting of the Association for Computational Linguistics (Volume 1: Long Papers)*, pages 9194–9213, Toronto, Canada. Association for Computational Linguistics.

Joshua Maynez, Shashi Narayan, Bernd Bohnet, and Ryan McDonald. 2020. On faithfulness and factuality in abstractive summarization. In *Proceedings of the 58th Annual Meeting of the Association for Computational Linguistics*, pages 1906–1919, Online. Association for Computational Linguistics.

Matthew D Nemesure, Michael V Heinz, Raphael Huang, and Nicholas C Jacobson. 2021. Predictive modeling of depression and anxiety using electronic health records and a novel machine learning approach with artificial intelligence. *Scientific reports*, 11(1):1980.

Thong Nguyen, Andrew Yates, Ayah Zirikly, Bart Desmet, and Arman Cohan. 2022. Improving the generalizability of depression detection by leveraging clinical questionnaires. In *Proceedings of the 60th Annual Meeting of the Association for Computational Linguistics (Volume 1: Long Papers)*, pages 8446–8459, Dublin, Ireland. Association for Computational Linguistics.

Yaakov Ophir, Refael Tikochinski, Anat Brunstein Klomek, and Roi Reichart. 2022. The hitchhiker's guide to computational linguistics in suicide prevention. *Clinical Psychological Science*, 10(2):212–235.

Javier Parapar, Patricia Martín-Rodilla, David E Losada, and Fabio Crestani. 2023. Overview of erisk 2023: Early risk prediction on the internet. In *International Conference of the Cross-Language Evaluation Forum for European Languages*, pages 294–315. Springer.

Kelly Posner, Gregory K Brown, Barbara Stanley, David A Brent, Kseniya V Yershova, Maria A Oquendo, Glenn W Currier, Glenn A Melvin, Laurence Greenhill, Sa Shen, et al. 2011. The columbia–suicide severity rating scale: initial validity and internal consistency findings from three multisite studies with adolescents and adults. *American journal of psychiatry*, 168(12):1266–1277.

Judita Preiss and Zenan Chen. 2024. Incorporating word count information into depression risk summary generation: Inf@uos clpsych 2024 submission. In *Proceedings of the Ninth Workshop on Computational Linguistics and Clinical Psychology*. Association for Computational Linguistics.

Rafael Rafailov, Archit Sharma, Eric Mitchell, Christopher D Manning, Stefano Ermon, and Chelsea Finn. 2023. Direct preference optimization: Your language model is secretly a reward model. In *Thirty-seventh Conference on Neural Information Processing Systems*.

Marco Tulio Ribeiro, Sameer Singh, and Carlos Guestrin. 2016. " why should i trust you?" explaining the predictions of any classifier. In *Proceedings of the 22nd ACM SIGKDD international conference on knowledge discovery and data mining*, pages 1135–1144.

Megan L Rogers, Min Eun Jeon, Sifan Zheng, Jenelle A Richards, Thomas E Joiner, and Igor Galynker. 2023. Two sides of the same coin? empirical examination of two proposed characterizations of acute suicidal crises: Suicide crisis syndrome and acute suicidal affective disturbance. *Journal of psychiatric research*, 162:123–131.

Anastasia Sandu, Teodor Mihailescu, and Sergiu Nisioi. 2024. Cheap ways of extracting clinical markers from texts. In *Proceedings of the Ninth Workshop on Computational Linguistics and Clinical Psychology*. Association for Computational Linguistics.

Victor Sanh, Albert Webson, Colin Raffel, Stephen Bach, Lintang Sutawika, Zaid Alyafeai, Antoine Chaffin, Arnaud Stiegler, Arun Raja, Manan Dey, M Saiful Bari, Canwen Xu, Urmish Thakker, Shanya Sharma Sharma, Eliza Szczechla, Taewoon Kim, Gunjan Chhablani, Nihal Nayak, Debajyoti Datta, Jonathan Chang, Mike Tian-Jian Jiang, Han Wang, Matteo Manica, Sheng Shen, Zheng Xin Yong, Harshit Pandey, Rachel Bawden, Thomas Wang, Trishala Neeraj, Jos Rozen, Abheesht Sharma, Andrea Santilli, Thibault Fevry, Jason Alan Fries, Ryan Teehan, Teven Le Scao, Stella Biderman, Leo Gao, Thomas Wolf, and Alexander M Rush. 2022. Multitask prompted training enables zero-shot task generalization. In *International Conference on Learning Representations*.

Ramit Sawhney, Shivam Agarwal, Atula Tejaswi Neerkaje, Nikolaos Aletras, Preslav Nakov, and Lucie Flek. 2022a. Towards suicide ideation detection through online conversational context. In *Proceedings of the 45th international ACM SIGIR conference on research and development in information retrieval*, pages 1716–1727.

Ramit Sawhney, Atula Tejaswi Neerkaje, and Manas Gaur. 2022b. A risk-averse mechanism for suicidality assessment on social media. *Association for Computational Linguistics 2022 (ACL 2022)*.

Han-Chin Shing, Suraj Nair, Ayah Zirikly, Meir Friedenberg, Hal Daumé III, and Philip Resnik. 2018. Expert, crowdsourced, and machine assessment of suicide risk via online postings. In *Proceedings of the Fifth Workshop on Computational Linguistics and Clinical Psychology: From Keyboard to Clinic*, pages 25–36, New Orleans, LA. Association for Computational Linguistics.

Loitongbam Gyanendro Singh, Junyu Mao, Rudra Mutalik, and Stuart E Middleton. 2024. Extracting and summarizing evidence of suicidal ideation in social media contents using large language models. In *Proceedings of the Ninth Workshop on Computational Linguistics and Clinical Psychology*. Association for Computational Linguistics.

Jiayu Song, Jenny Chim, Adam Tsakalidis, Julia Ive, Dana Atzil-Slonim, and Maria Liakata. 2024. Clinically meaningful timeline summarisation in social media for mental health monitoring.

Rika Tanaka and Yusuke Fukazawa. 2024. Suicide risk assessment and summarization using bert and mentallama. In *Proceedings of the Ninth Workshop on Computational Linguistics and Clinical Psychology*. Association for Computational Linguistics.

Liyan Tang, Zhaoyi Sun, Betina Idnay, Jordan G Nestor, Ali Soroush, Pierre A Elias, Ziyang Xu, Ying Ding, Greg Durrett, Justin Rousseau, et al. 2023. Evaluating large language models on medical evidence summarization. medrxiv.

Hugo Touvron, Louis Martin, Kevin Stone, Peter Albert, Amjad Almahairi, Yasmine Babaei, Nikolay Bashlykov, Soumya Batra, Prajjwal Bhargava, Shruti Bhosale, et al. 2023. Llama 2: Open foundation and fine-tuned chat models. *arXiv preprint arXiv:2307.09288*.

Vu Tran and Tomoko Matsui. 2024. Team ism at clpsych 2024: Extracting evidence of suicide risk from reddit posts with knowledge self-generation and output refinement using a large language model. In *Proceedings of the Ninth Workshop on Computational Linguistics and Clinical Psychology*. Association for Computational Linguistics.

Adam Tsakalidis, Jenny Chim, Iman Munire Bilal, Ayah Zirikly, Dana Atzil-Slonim, Federico Nanni, Philip Resnik, Manas Gaur, Kaushik Roy, Becky Inkster, Jeff Leintz, and Maria Liakata. 2022a. Overview of the CLPsych 2022 shared task: Capturing moments of change in longitudinal user posts. In *Proceedings of the Eighth Workshop on Computational Linguistics and Clinical Psychology*, pages 184–198, Seattle, USA. Association for Computational Linguistics.

Adam Tsakalidis, Federico Nanni, Anthony Hills, Jenny Chim, Jiayu Song, and Maria Liakata. 2022b. Identifying moments of change from longitudinal user text. In *Proceedings of the 60th Annual Meeting of the Association for Computational Linguistics (Volume 1: Long Papers)*, pages 4647–4660.

Talia Tseriotou, Adam Tsakalidis, Peter Foster, Terence Lyons, and Maria Liakata. 2023. Sequential path signature networks for personalised longitudinal language modeling. In *Findings of the Association for Computational Linguistics: ACL 2023*, pages 5016–5031.

G Turecki, DA Brent, D Gunnell, RC O'Connor, MA Oquendo, J Pirkis, and BH Stanley. 2019. Suicide and suicide risk. nature reviews disease primers, 5 (1), 1-22.

Ahmet Yavuz Uluslu, Andrianos Michail, and Simon Clematide. 2024. Utilizing large language models to identify evidence of suicidality risk through analysis of emotionally charged posts. In *Proceedings of the Ninth Workshop on Computational Linguistics and Clinical Psychology*. Association for Computational Linguistics.

Vasudha Varadarajan, Allison Lahnala, Adithya V Ganesan, Gourab Dey, Siddharth Mangalik, Ana-Maria Bucur, Nikita Soni, Rajath Rao, Kevin Lanning, Isabella Vallejo, Lucie Flek, H. Andrew Schwartz, Charles Welch, and Ryan Boyd. 2024. Archetypes and entropy: Theory-driven extraction of evidence for suicide risk. In *Proceedings of the Ninth Workshop on Computational Linguistics and Clinical Psychology*. Association for Computational Linguistics.

Yiming Wang, Zhuosheng Zhang, and Rui Wang. 2023. Element-aware summarization with large language models: Expert-aligned evaluation and chain-of-thought method. In *Proceedings of the 61st Annual Meeting of the Association for Computational Linguistics (Volume 1: Long Papers)*, pages 8640–8665, Toronto, Canada. Association for Computational Linguistics.

Xuhai Xu, Bingshen Yao, Yuanzhe Dong, Hong Yu, James Hendler, Anind K Dey, and Dakuo Wang. 2023. Leveraging large language models for mental health prediction via online text data. *arXiv preprint arXiv:2307.14385*.

Kailai Yang, Shaoxiong Ji, Tianlin Zhang, Qianqian Xie, Ziyan Kuang, and Sophia Ananiadou. 2023. Towards interpretable mental health analysis with large language models. In *Proceedings of the 2023 Conference on Empirical Methods in Natural Language Processing*, pages 6056–6077, Singapore. Association for Computational Linguistics.

Zichao Yang, Diyi Yang, Chris Dyer, Xiaodong He, Alex Smola, and Eduard Hovy. 2016. Hierarchical attention networks for document classification. In *Proceedings of the 2016 Conference of the North American Chapter of the Association for Computational Linguistics: Human Language Technologies*, pages 1480–1489, San Diego, California. Association for Computational Linguistics.

Haopeng Zhang, Xiao Liu, and Jiawei Zhang. 2023a. Extractive summarization via ChatGPT for faithful summary generation. In *Findings of the Association for Computational Linguistics: EMNLP 2023*, pages 3270–3278, Singapore. Association for Computational Linguistics.

Tianyi Zhang, Varsha Kishore, Felix Wu, Kilian Q. Weinberger, and Yoav Artzi. 2020. Bertscore: Evaluating text generation with bert. In *International Conference on Learning Representations*.

Tianyi Zhang, Faisal Ladhak, Esin Durmus, Percy Liang, Kathleen McKeown, and Tatsunori B Hashimoto. 2023b. Benchmarking large language models for news summarization. *arXiv preprint arXiv:2301.13848*.

Jingwei Zhu, Ancheng Xu, Minghuan Tan, and Min Yang. 2024. Xinhai@clpsych 2024 shared task: Prompting healthcare-oriented llms for evidence highlighting in posts with suicide risk. In *Proceedings of the Ninth Workshop on Computational Linguistics and Clinical Psychology*. Association for Computational Linguistics.

Ayah Zirikly and Mark Dredze. 2022. Explaining models of mental health via clinically grounded auxiliary tasks. In *Proceedings of the Eighth Workshop on Computational Linguistics and Clinical Psychology*, pages 30–39.

Ayah Zirikly, Philip Resnik, Özlem Uzuner, and Kristy Hollingshead. 2019. CLPsych 2019 shared task: Predicting the degree of suicide risk in Reddit posts. In *Proceedings of the Sixth Workshop on Computational Linguistics and Clinical Psychology*.

Team ISM at CLPsych 2024: Extracting Evidence of Suicide Risk from Reddit Posts with Knowledge Self-Generation and Output Refinement using A Large Language Model

Vu Tran
The Institute of Statistical Mathematics
Tokyo, Japan
vutran@ism.ac.jp

Tomoko Matsui
The Institute of Statistical Mathematics
Tokyo, Japan
tmatsui@ism.ac.jp

Abstract

This paper presents our approach to the CLPsych 2024 shared task: utilizing large language models (LLMs) for finding supporting evidence about an individual's suicide risk level in Reddit posts. Our framework is constructed around an LLM with knowledge self-generation and output refinement. The knowledge self-generation process produces task-related knowledge which is generated by the LLM and leads to accurate risk predictions. The output refinement process, later, with the selected best set of LLM-generated knowledge, refines the outputs by prompting the LLM repeatedly with different knowledge instances interchangeably. We achieved highly competitive results comparing to the top-performance participants with our official recall of 93.5%, recall–precision harmonic-mean of 92.3%, and mean consistency of 96.1%.

1 Introduction

In the unprecedented rapid evolution of large language models (LLMs), the ninth workshop on Computational Linguistics and Clinical Psychology (CLPsych 2024) introduced the shared task of utilizing LLMs for finding supporting evidence about an individual's suicide risk level in Reddit posts (Chim et al., 2024). It is evident that recent work on LLMs suggest their potential applications on clinical tasks such as information extraction (Agrawal et al., 2022) and question answering (Singhal et al., 2023).

The CLPsych 2024 shared task uses the same Reddit dataset as the CLPsych 2019 shared task (Shing et al., 2018; Zirikly et al., 2019) which consisted of Reddit posts and annotated users' suicide risk labels at 4 levels: no risk, low risk, moderate risk, and high (severe) risk. The annotations were performed by both experts and crowd-source workers. The CLPsych 2024 shared task focuses on the expert annotations of users and posts on the subreddit 'r/SuicideWatch', where users are annotated with risk labels at 3 levels: low risk, moderate risk or high risk. From the user posts and annotations, the task's goal is to find supporting evidence in the form of post highlights and a summarized evidence given a user. It is important to note that the ground-truth evidence is not available for the task participants, so no direct optimization using ground-truth evidence is possible.

Task Definition. Formally, given a user i who was assessed with either low risk, moderate risk, or high risk of committing suicide, a set of their Reddit posts V_i, and their suicide risk assessment A_i in 3 risk levels (low risk, moderate risk, high risk), the goal is to identify the evidence supporting the assessment A_i in the form of post highlights and a summary: $\{H_i, S_i\}$.

Overview of Our Approach. Our framework is constructed around an LLM with knowledge self-generation and output refinement. Inspired by MedPrompt (Nori et al., 2023) where using LLM-generated knowledge of solving a task as a part of task prompting can help boost the performance of such task, we ask the LLM to respond with its knowledge of how to make suicide risk assessment and find supporting evidence from social media posts. The best set of LLM-generated knowledge is selected based on the prediction accuracy. Now we have output candidates from potential knowledge leading to accurate predictions. We design an output refinement process to aggregate and refine the output candidates to obtain the final output. In the refinement process, the LLM is prompted with interchanging knowledge on the same input repeatedly, so when finished, we obtained an output with more agreement among different knowledge instances. Similar to our idea of output refinement, Madaan et al. (2023) proposed a self-refinement process where the output is put back to the same LLM, albeit the same conversation, to get feedback

Proceedings of the 9th Workshop on Computational Linguistics and Clinical Psychology (CLPsych 2024), pages 191–196
March 21, 2024

and refined output. Our approach, instead of going in-depth with one conversation, collectively refines the output under various input knowledge.

2 Method

2.1 Framework

Our framework is constructed around an LLM and consists of two stages: 1) knowledge self-generation, and 2) output refinement. In stage 1 - knowledge self-generation, we ask the LLM to generate its knowledge of how to handle the task and use the LLM's generated responses as a part of the inputs for finding evidence, i.e. extracting highlights and generating summaries, and making suicide risk predictions. We, then, find the best set of the LLM's generated knowledge responses leading to accurate predictions. In stage 2 - output refinement, with the best set of knowledge, outputs are aggregated and refined by repeatedly prompting the LLM with each instance in the best set of the generated knowledge until no further change is observed. Our framework is illustrated in Figure 1.

Stage 1. We sample responses from the LLM to a knowledge prompt with our pre-defined knowledge generation instructions I^g asking for the LLM's understanding of the task:

$$K^l = g_{\text{LLM}}(I^g) \tag{1}$$

and obtain a set of generated knowledge responses to be used as knowledge inputs: $\{K^l\}$.

For each user i, we prompt the LLM with knowledge input K^l, the user's posts V_i, and our pre-defined instructions I^h for extracting highlights $\hat{H}_i^l$, generating a summary $\hat{S}_i^l$ and making a risk-level prediction $\hat{A}_i^l$ as following:

$$\{\hat{H}_i^l, \hat{S}_i^l, \hat{A}_i^l\} = h_{\text{LLM}}(K^l, V_i, I^h) \tag{2}$$

After that, for each user i, we select a subset of knowledge inputs $\{K^l\}$ leading to top-k accurate predictions with the following scoring:

$$\text{score}_i(K^l) = (1_{\hat{A}_i^l = A_i} + \varepsilon) \times \sum_j 1_{\hat{A}_j^l = A_j} \tag{3}$$

where ε is a very small positive number to avoid zero-scoring. It means that given a user, the selected knowledge inputs yield accurate predictions for that specific user and overall high accuracy for all users[1].

[1]Tie-breaks are decided by the earlier time order.

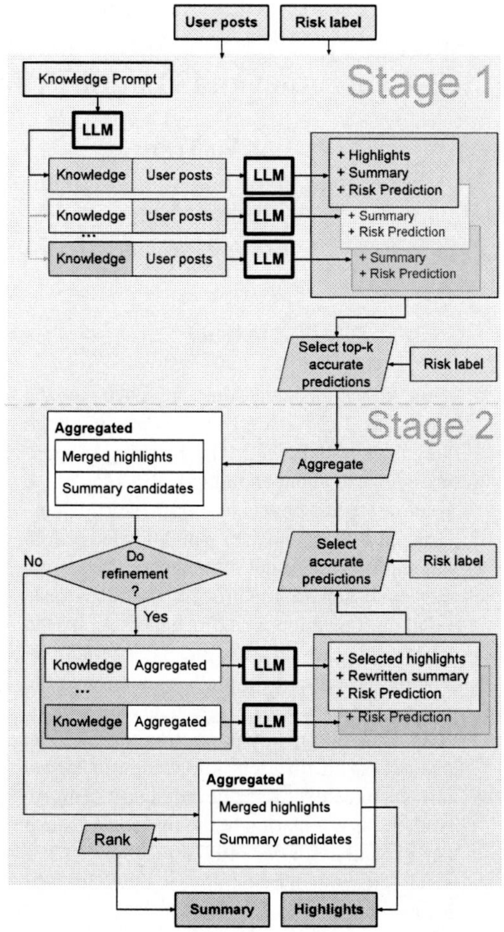

(a) Not using risk labels in stage 2 prompts.

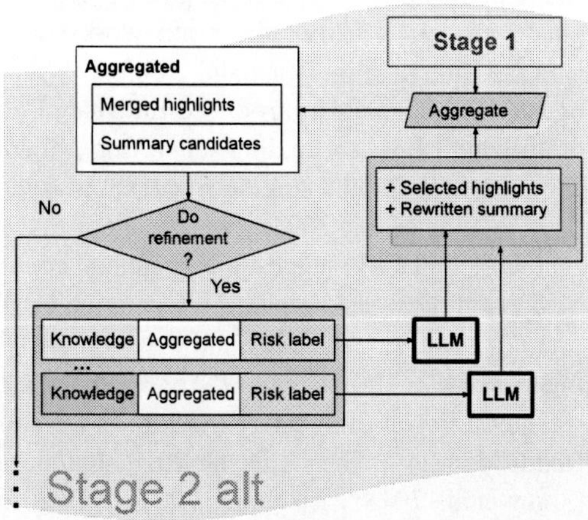

(b) Using risk labels in stage 2 prompts.

Figure 1: Our framework with and without using ground-truth assessments, i.e. risk labels, in stage 2 prompts.

Stage 2. Instead of the user posts V_i as in stage 1, we input the extracted highlights and generated summaries $\bigcup_l \{\hat{H}_i^l, \hat{S}_i^l\}$ aggregated over all $\{K^l\}$ selected in stage 1, and our pre-defined instructions I^f to select new highlights, generate a new summary and make a new risk-level prediction. The procedure is repeated with newly extracted/generated highlights/summaries as inputs for further refinement as following:

$$\{\hat{H}_i^l, \hat{S}_i^l, \hat{A}_i^l\}_t = f_{\text{LLM}}(K^l, \bigcup_m \{H_i^m, S_i^m\}_{t-1}, I^f) \quad (4)$$

After each step t, we filter out knowledge inputs with inaccurate predictions $\hat{A}_i^l \neq A_i$.

We also investigate an alternative procedure of the refinement process. In addition to the highlights and summaries, we input the ground-truth risk assessment instead of predicting it as following:

$$\{\hat{H}_i^l, \hat{S}_i^l\}_t = f'_{\text{LLM}}(K^l, \bigcup_m \{\hat{H}_i^m, \hat{S}_i^m\}_{t-1}, A_i, I^{f'}) \quad (5)$$

where our pre-defined instructions $I^{f'}$ are for additionally using ground-truth risk assessment to select new highlights and generate a new summary.

We repeat the refinement process until $\bigcup_m \{\hat{H}_i^m\}_t = \bigcup_m \{\hat{H}_i^m\}_{t-1}$ for a maximum number of iterations T. Let $\tau \leq T$ be the stopped iteration, the final set of highlights is $\bigcup_m \{\hat{H}_i^m\}_\tau$, and the final summary is selected from the summary candidates $\{\hat{S}_i^m\}_\tau$ using TextRank (Mihalcea and Tarau, 2004) with BERTScore-F1 (Zhang et al., 2019) for measuring summary-pair similarity. As the results, the final set of highlights can be seen as a stable extraction across different knowledge inputs, and the final summary can be seen as the best summary over plausible summaries.

2.2 Experimental Settings

We used the LLM named Mixtral[2] with the specific version Mixtral-8x7B-Instruct-v0.1[3] trained to follow instructions. We used the original model weights and didn't further train the LLM. For efficient utilization of the LLM, we used the Huggingface transformers library[4] and loaded the LLM with 4-bit quantization (Dettmers et al., 2023). The temperature of the LLM is set to 1 for prompting knowledge (Equation 1) and is set to 0 for finding evidence and making predictions (Equations 2, 4, and 5). We set top-k = 3 for stage 1. For the final summary ranking in stage 2, we computed BERTScore-F1 using roberta-large (Liu et al., 2019).

In stage 1, to obtain the set of knowledge responses, we prompted the LLM with instructions I^g as following:

1. *"Suppose you are a mental health care professional, describe in details steps to assess suicide risk of a person by reading their public posts on social media."*
2. *"Response"* from LLM, which describes abstractly about professional suicide risk analysis.
3. *"According to that, what are the cues to look for where the assessment is one of the 3 levels of risk (low, moderate, and high). Explain the cues for each of the level."*
4. *"Response"* from LLM to use as the generated knowledge response.

In addition to the generated knowledge responses, we also use manual provided by the shared task organizer, "aspects to consider" specifically, as an instruction of the aspects to focus on during finding evidence.

Other instructions are:

- I^h: *"Firstly, do a step-by-step analysis of the user posts. Secondly, give a list of extracted text spans from the TITLE and the BODY, which serve as evidence for your assessment. Thirdly, give a summary of the evidence in less than 100 words. Finally, give your assessment in just one of the three options: low risk, moderate risk, or high risk."*
- I^f: *"Firstly, select all important highlights linked to the suicide risk level. Secondly, in less than 100 words, write a summary given the selected highlights and the above summary candidates. Finally, give your assessment in just one of the three options: low risk, moderate risk, or high risk. "*
- $I^{f'}$: *"The mentioned user has been assessed with a suicide risk level of* ***{risk-level}****. Firstly,*

[2] https://mistral.ai/news/mixtral-of-experts/

[3] https://huggingface.co/mistralai/Mixtral-8x7B-Instruct-v0.1

[4] https://huggingface.co/

select all important highlights linked to the suicide risk level. Secondly, in less than 100 words, write a summary given the selected highlights and the above summary candidates." Where **{risk-level}** is filled with the user's suicide risk level annotated.

For the final submission, we submitted 3 runs with the following options:

- Run 1: Skipping the refinement process. The highlights/summaries from stage 1 are merged/ranked to obtain the final outputs.
- Run 2: Not using ground-truth risk labels as input of the refinement process (Equation 4).
- Run 3: Using ground-truth risk labels as input of the refinement process (Equation 5).

3 Results & Discussions

The results are obtained with the metrics briefly described below.

- Highlights: recall, precision, and recall–precision harmonic-mean. Recall weighted by length-ratio of gold highlights vs. submitted highlights is also reported.
- Summary: mean consistency and max contradiction between submitted summary (hypothesis) and gold summary (premise) using a natural language inference model.

Please refer to the organizer's paper (Chim et al., 2024) for the details of the evaluation metrics.

As the official results shown in Table 1, we achieved a recall of 0.935 (4th rank), a harmonic-mean of 0.923 (3rd rank) and a mean consistency of 0.961 (8th rank). The top results are pretty close with the best recall of 0.944, the best harmonic-mean of 0.929 and the best mean consistency of 0.979.

In stage 1, we acquired 320 knowledge responses, averaging 55.4% accuracy in risk prediction, with a peak accuracy of 72.8%. An example of the responses is shown in Appendix A.

In stage 2, we observed convergence with stopped iteration τ not going over 5 and having an average of 1.4 for run 2 and 1.9 for run 3.

The refinement process helps reduce the length of extracted highlights from 53% to 32–33%, which leads to a big improvement of weighted recall despite the cost of lower recall (Table 2). The process is, however, shown to reduce mean consistency and increase max contradiction. The problem could be because of the lack of context when using only highlights to generate a summary.

Team Name	Rec	HM	MeC
CSIRO (baseline)	.919	.917	-
DONUTS Colaboratory	.872	.907	.942
INF@UoS	.850	.896	.934
LAMA	.577	.888	.964
MHNLP	.910	.909	.873
SBC	.907	.909	.976
SCALAR-NITK	.886	.889	.901
SKKU-DSAIL	.922	.917	.970
sophiaADS	**.944**	.924	.944
SWELL	.915	.903	.973
UniBuc Archaeology	.939	.914	.973
UoS NLP	.943	**.929**	.966
UZH_CLyp	.910	.913	**.979**
Xinhai	.887	.911	.958
ISM (Ours)	.935	.923	.961
Our ranking	4	3	8

Table 1: Official results. Rec: recall, HM: recall–precision harmonic-mean, MeC: mean consistency.

Run	Rec	Prec	WR	HM	MeC	MaC
1	**.935**	.911	.564	**.923**	**.961**	**.125**
2	.910	**.918**	.715	.913	.952	.145
3	.904	.917	**.744**	.910	.957	.127

Table 2: Our results for different runs. Rec: recall, Prec: precision, WR: weighted recall, HM: recall–precision harmonic-mean, MeC: mean consistency, MaC: maximum contradiction (lower is better).

Although we achieved high (>90%) recall, precision, and consistency in finding evidence, risk level classification accuracy is at most 72.8%, a recognizable discrepancy between finding evidence and matching it with a correct risk level.

4 Conclusion

In the concept of the CLPsych 2024 shared task, we have constructed a framework for extracting evidence of suicide risk from Reddit posts with knowledge-self generation and output refinement using an LLM. We achieved competitive results among the top participants. Our future work needs to focus on improving output refinement, and tackling consistency problems in matching supporting evidence with risk prediction.

Limitations

- No guarantee of adequate domain understanding. Mixtral, the LLM used in this paper was pre-trained on data extracted from the open Web, which means the model is not guaranteed to be trained on high-quality professional data needed to understand the domain data in this task.
- No guarantee of a strong consistency between finding evidence and making predictions. Our framework relies on the prediction accuracy measurement as a critical part of our evidence finding mechanism. However, our framework has no mechanism for checking the consistency between the prediction and the evidence found.

Ethics Statement

Secure access to the shared task dataset was provided with IRB approval under University of Maryland, College Park protocol 1642625 and approval by the Biomedical and Scientific Research Ethics Committee (BSREC) at the University of Warwick (ethical application reference BSREC 40/19-20).

Acknowledgements

The authors are particularly grateful to the anonymous users of Reddit whose data feature in this year's shared task dataset, to the crowdsource annotators and to the clinical experts from BarIlan University for the data annotation, to the American Association of Suicidology for their assistance in making the dataset available, to the CLPsych organizers for holding this meaningful shared task, to the reviewers for their constructive comments. This work was supported by "Strategic Research Projects" grant from ROIS (Research Organization of Information and Systems), Japan and JSPS KAKENHI Grant Number JP23K16954. Any opinions, findings, and conclusions or recommendations expressed in this material are those of the author(s) and do not necessarily reflect the views of the author(s)' organization, JSPS or MEXT.

References

Monica Agrawal, Stefan Hegselmann, Hunter Lang, Yoon Kim, and David Sontag. 2022. Large language models are few-shot clinical information extractors. In *Proceedings of the 2022 Conference on Empirical Methods in Natural Language Processing*, pages 1998–2022, Abu Dhabi, United Arab Emirates. Association for Computational Linguistics.

Jenny Chim, Adam Tsakalidis, Dimitris Gkoumas, Dana Atzil-Slonim, Yaakov Ophir, Ayah Zirikly, Philip Resnik, and Maria Liakata. 2024. Overview of the clpsych 2024 shared task: Leveraging large language models to identify evidence of suicidality risk in online posts. In *Proceedings of the Ninth Workshop on Computational Linguistics and Clinical Psychology*. Association for Computational Linguistics.

Tim Dettmers, Artidoro Pagnoni, Ari Holtzman, and Luke Zettlemoyer. 2023. Qlora: Efficient finetuning of quantized llms. *arXiv preprint arXiv:2305.14314*.

Yinhan Liu, Myle Ott, Naman Goyal, Jingfei Du, Mandar Joshi, Danqi Chen, Omer Levy, Mike Lewis, Luke Zettlemoyer, and Veselin Stoyanov. 2019. Roberta: A robustly optimized BERT pretraining approach. *CoRR*, abs/1907.11692.

Aman Madaan, Niket Tandon, Prakhar Gupta, Skyler Hallinan, Luyu Gao, Sarah Wiegreffe, Uri Alon, Nouha Dziri, Shrimai Prabhumoye, Yiming Yang, et al. 2023. Self-refine: Iterative refinement with self-feedback. *arXiv preprint arXiv:2303.17651*.

Rada Mihalcea and Paul Tarau. 2004. TextRank: Bringing order into text. In *Proceedings of the 2004 Conference on Empirical Methods in Natural Language Processing*, pages 404–411, Barcelona, Spain. Association for Computational Linguistics.

Harsha Nori, Yin Tat Lee, Sheng Zhang, Dean Carignan, Richard Edgar, Nicolo Fusi, Nicholas King, Jonathan Larson, Yuanzhi Li, Weishung Liu, Renqian Luo, Scott Mayer McKinney, Robert Osazuwa Ness, Hoifung Poon, Tao Qin, Naoto Usuyama, Chris White, and Eric Horvitz. 2023. Can generalist foundation models outcompete special-purpose tuning? case study in medicine.

Han-Chin Shing, Suraj Nair, Ayah Zirikly, Meir Friedenberg, Hal Daumé III, and Philip Resnik. 2018. Expert, crowdsourced, and machine assessment of suicide risk via online postings. In *Proceedings of the Fifth Workshop on Computational Linguistics and Clinical Psychology: From Keyboard to Clinic*, pages 25–36, New Orleans, LA. Association for Computational Linguistics.

Karan Singhal, Shekoofeh Azizi, Tao Tu, S Sara Mahdavi, Jason Wei, Hyung Won Chung, Nathan Scales, Ajay Tanwani, Heather Cole-Lewis, Stephen Pfohl, et al. 2023. Large language models encode clinical knowledge. *Nature*, 620(7972):172–180.

Tianyi Zhang, Varsha Kishore, Felix Wu, Kilian Q Weinberger, and Yoav Artzi. 2019. Bertscore: Evaluating text generation with bert. In *International Conference on Learning Representations*.

Ayah Zirikly, Philip Resnik, Özlem Uzuner, and Kristy Hollingshead. 2019. CLPsych 2019 shared task: Predicting the degree of suicide risk in Reddit posts. In

Proceedings of the Sixth Workshop on Computational Linguistics and Clinical Psychology, pages 24–33, Minneapolis, Minnesota. Association for Computational Linguistics.

A Self-Generated Knowledge Responses

Below is an illustration of knowledge responses in stage 1. Potentially sensitive contents are omitted.

```
Sure, I'd be happy to explain the cues to look for when assessing the level of suicide risk (low, moderate, or high) based on a social media post. Here are some possible cues to look for at each level:
1. Low Risk:
Cues to look for at this level may include:
* Expressions of vague or fleeting suicidal thoughts, such as "I feel [OMITTED]" or "I don't know [OMITTED]"
* Indirect references to suicide, such as "I wish [OMITTED]" or "I'm tired [OMITTED]"
* Ambivalent or inconsistent statements about wanting to live or die.
* Statements that suggest a willingness to seek help or talk to someone about their feelings.
* A support system that is actively engaged and responsive.
2. Moderate Risk:
Cues to look for at this level may include:
* Specific plans or intentions to commit suicide, such as "I've been thinking [OMITTED]" or "I've been looking for [OMITTED]"
* Preparations for suicide, such as giving away prized possessions or putting affairs in order.
* A history of previous suicide attempts or self-harm.
* Access to means of suicide, such as firearms or medications.
* A lack of social support or a sense of isolation.
* Statements that suggest a belief that there is no other way out or no hope for the future.
3. High Risk:
Cues to look for at this level may include:
* A specific and imminent plan to commit suicide, such as "I have a [OMITTED]" or "I'm going to [OMITTED]"
* Recent suicide attempts or self-harm that required medical attention.
* Active suicidal ideation with a sense of calm or determination.
* A lack of impulse control or a sense of hopelessness or desperation.
* Substance abuse or intoxication that increases the risk of impulsive or dangerous behavior.
* A lack of social support or a sense of burdensomeness on others.
It is important to note that these cues are not exhaustive and may vary depending on the individual and their unique circumstances. If you are concerned about an individual's suicide risk, it is important to involve trained professionals in the assessment and intervention process.
```

This knowledge response led to the best risk prediction accuracy of 72.8%.

B Organizer Manual: Aspects to Consider

In addition to the generated knowledge responses, we also use manual provided by the shared task organizer. Specifically, we input the contents of "aspects to consider" to the LLM as an instruction of what to focus on during finding supporting evidence. A part of the "aspects to consider" is:

```
1. Emotions: How does the individual feel? ...

2. Cognitions: What are the individual's thoughts and perceptions about suicide? ...

3. Behaviour and Motivation: What are the individual's acts or behavior related to suicide? ...

4. Interpersonal and social support: Does the individual have social support/stable relationships? ...

5. Metal health-related issues: Consider psychiatric diagnoses associated with suicide ...

6. Context/additional risk factors: ... socioeconomic and demographic factors ...
```

Exploring Instructive Prompts for Large Language Models in the Extraction of Evidence for Supporting Assigned Suicidal Risk Levels

Jiyu Chen[1] and **Vincent Nguyen**[1] and **Xiang Dai**[1] and **Cécile Paris**[1,2] and **Sarvnaz Karimi**[1]
CSIRO's Data61[1]
Sydney, Australia
firstname.lastname@csiro.au

Diego Mollá[2,1]
Macquarie University[2]
Sydney, Australia
diego.molla-aliod@mq.edu.au

Abstract

Monitoring and predicting the expression of suicidal risk in individuals' social media posts is a central focus in clinical NLP. Yet, existing approaches frequently lack a crucial explainability component necessary for extracting evidence related to an individual's mental health state. We describe the CSIRO Data61 team's evidence extraction system submitted to the CLPsych 2024 shared task. The task aims to investigate the zero-shot capabilities of open-source LLM in extracting evidence regarding an individual's assigned suicide risk level from social media discourse. The results are assessed against ground truth evidence annotated by psychological experts, with an achieved recall-oriented BERTScore of 0.919. Our findings suggest that LLMs showcase strong feasibility in the extraction of information supporting the evaluation of suicidal risk in social media discourse. Opportunities for refinement exist, notably in crafting concise and effective instructions to guide the extraction process.

1 Introduction

The intersection between NLP and mental health research has provided valuable insights, uncovering the diagnostic potential inherent in language (Agrawal et al., 2022; Singhal et al., 2023). Previous research has primarily concentrated on static classifications of individuals' social media posts, with studies, for example, focusing on predicting the level of suicide risk within social media posts (O'dea et al., 2015; Shing et al., 2018; Zirikly et al., 2019) and tracking changes in emotion over time (Paris et al., 2015; Larsen et al., 2015; Tsakalidis et al., 2022b,a). Despite these advancements, the increasing reliance on computational models in mental health assessments unveils a prominent gap — the lack of an essential explainability component. This absence is critical for the nuanced extraction of evidence that explains an individual's mental health state. This deficiency assumes significance in supporting practitioners' decision-making as they navigate the intricacies of mental health diagnostics.

In response to this problem, a shared task is organised as part of the CLPsych 2024 workshop (Chim et al., 2024). In our participation, we investigate the application of an open-source Large Language Model (LLM), namely Llama-2 (Touvron et al., 2023) within a zero-shot learning framework. The principal objective is to systematically extract text spans that can be treated as evidence of an individual's assigned suicide risk level from their social media posts. Beyond the mere evaluation of LLM viability, we assume a proactive stance, aiming to formulate instructive prompts that guide the model in extracting accurate and semantically rich evidence. We use a sub-sample of the University of Maryland Reddit Suicidality Dataset, Version 2, which includes 125 randomly selected Reddit users and their $r/SuicideWatch$ posts (Shing et al., 2018; Zirikly et al., 2019), provided by the task organisers. The suicide risk levels of these users are annotated by psychologists.

The robustness and validity of our findings are ensured through evaluation against ground truth evidence annotated by domain experts, employing BERTScore (Zhang et al., 2020). Overall, we found instructing LLM with factor-oriented and risk-level-specific prompts achieved the best recall-oriented BERTScore of 0.919 among our experimented approaches.

2 Dataset

A sub-sample of 125 users and their posts on the $r/SuicideWatch$ subreddit was selected from the University of Maryland Reddit Suicidality Dataset (UMD Subset) (Shing et al., 2018; Zirikly et al., 2019). Each user in the subset creates 1.3 posts on average, with a maximum of three posts.

Proceedings of the 9th Workshop on Computational Linguistics and Clinical Psychology (CLPsych 2024), pages 197–202
March 21, 2024

Psychology experts conducted annotations of the suicidal risk level for each user, classifying them as low, moderate, or high (or severe) risk through a comprehensive review of all posts associated with a particular user. Note that the risk level annotation is performed at the user level rather than the post level. Specifically, each user receives an annotation based on the highest risk level expressed throughout their entire collection of posts. To provide clarity, in instances where a user conveys high-risk suicidal thoughts in an initial post followed by expressing low risk in a subsequent post, the user's annotation reflects the highest risk level.

We utilise the provided UMD Subset, consisting of 125 users, to investigate the application of LLMs for evidence extraction using zero-shot learning. For development, we randomly select nine users from the broader UMD dataset, where the suicide risk levels are annotated through crowd-sourcing, focusing on posts from $r/SuicideWatch$. This ensures their distinction from the 125 users in the provided UMD Subset.

3 Method

We design three approaches: (1) a baseline, (2) a factor-oriented, and (3) a risk level & factor-oriented approach. Each method varies in the design of the prompt in the zero-shot learning setting.

Baseline

The baseline employs a basic prompt (Listing 1) to instruct the LLM in extracting evidence supporting the annotation of a specific user's expression of suicidal thoughts. It is important to note that we do not explicitly indicate the risk level associated with users in specific posts. Two special linguistic markers are utilised in the pre-training stage of Llama-2 (Touvron et al., 2023). These linguistic markers, `[INST]` and `<<SYS>>`, are added during zero-shot learning to indicate the structure of the prompt. The `[INST]` token marks the boundary of the prompt instruction, while the `<<SYS>>` token marks the boundary of the system message used for setting the context for LLM.

Listing 1: Basic Prompt Template

```
[INST] <<SYS>> Here is a post containing
 suicidal ideation:{{post content}} <</
SYS>> Extract phrases as evidence that
support the suicide risk[/INST]
```

Factor-oriented Instruction

The factor-oriented approach depends on more instructive prompts, carefully designed with instructions that explicitly address the consideration of diverse psychological and socioeconomic factors when evaluating the risks of suicide. A study (Corbitt-Hall et al., 2016; Jones et al., 2003) indicates that humans tend to classify a post as having a high level of risk if it includes explicit expressions of self-harm, prolonged severe depression, and a lack of support from family or friends. Conversely, a user is less likely to have suicide risk if the post minimally contains overly dramatic complaints. A set of risk factors formed the foundation for creating these guidelines. We synthesised our compilation of risk factors and crafted prompts to instruct the LLM in extracting evidence related to specific factors. Table 1 shows the synthesised factors and their indication of suicide risk. Subsequently, We crafted a factor-oriented prompt (Listing 2) instructing the LLM in extracting evidence that supports each risk factor.

Listing 2: Factor-oriented Prompt Template

```
[INST] <<SYS>> Here is a post written
     by an individual: {{post content
     }} <</SYS>> Extract phrases if
     they covers any of the following
     aspects:

1. signs of fear, anger, or sadness
2. expression of thoughts or
   intention in self-harm or suicide
3. expression of difficulties in
   handling stress
4. expression of lacking support or
   connection from families or
   friends
5. diagnosis of chronic psychiatric
   disease, such as schizophrenia,
   bipolar, anxiety, eating
   disorder
6. signs of seeking public attention
[/INST]
```

Risk Level & Factor-oriented Instruction

Identifying evidence specific to various risk levels might present a challenge for LLMs. Hence, in the design of the baseline and factor-oriented approach, we did not explicitly specify the risk level associated with users in certain posts. Consequently, any text spans, irrespective of the expression of the risk level, will be extracted as evidence. To address this limitation, we propose a new approach that focuses on extracting evidence directly aligned with annotated risk levels in users' posts, providing a concise

Risk factors	Explanation
Emotion	Individual's emotional state, encompassing feelings such as fear, anger, or intense psychological distress.
Cognition	Individual's expression of the intention, the severity, and the frequency of self-harm or suicide thoughts.
Behavior	Individuals access to means or proposal of concrete plans to commit suicide
Motivation	The triggering events of individual's suicidal thoughts
Support	The unstable relationship and lack of support
Mental	The psychiatric diagnosis associated suicide risk, such as schizophrenia, bipolar, severe anxiety, or eating disorder
Environment	Exposure to suicide behaviour by others

Table 1: A collection of risk factors referred for the design of instructive factor-oriented prompt.

perspective for practitioners. To achieve this, we developed three prompt variations to guide the LLM. Specifically, our instruction emphasises extracting evidence indicative of acute situations that demand immediate interventions for users annotated with high risk. We incorporated selected risk factors to formulate risk level & factor-oriented prompts. For the formulation of risk factors, we referred to a previous study (Corbitt-Hall et al., 2016), in which researchers engaged college students in identifying socio-economic factors linked to various levels of suicide risk.

Additionally, we established rules for choosing one of the three prompts based on the associated risk level. To illustrate the distinctions in prompt design for guiding evidence extraction concerning low and high risk, we present the covered risk factors in Listing 3.

Post-processing

We employ a set of Backus-Naur form grammars (Listing 4), which is the standard mechanism, to

Listing 3: Risk level & Factor-oriented Prompt Template

```
#low risk:
Extract phrases if they cover one or more of the
    following aspects:
1. expression of difficulties in handling stress
2. expression of lacking support or connection
   from families or friends
3. expression of emotion
4. action of overly dramatic reaction
5. seeking attentions
6. exposure to other people who commit suicide


#high risk:
Extract phrases if they cover one or more of the
    following aspects:
1. expression of self-harm or suicide plans
2. expression of serious warnings
3. calling for help
4. expression of emotional states, especially
   depression, anger, and fear
5. diagnosis of mental disorders, such as
   schizophrenia, bipolar, anxiety, eating
   disorder
6. expression of taking medicines or
   prescriptions for psychiatric treatment
```

regulate the output of Llama, directing it to generate only the extracted content from the original text, without including descriptions or explanations. We observed that Llama can automatically correct spelling errors within the original text and may slightly rephrase the content. For instance, it rectifies "beleive" to its correct form "believe" or omits certain words, such as "just" in the extracted evidence of phrases like "I just feel so trapped". Nevertheless, the occurrences of auto-correction or rephrasing are intermittent and unpredictable, posing challenges in making strategies to revert the modified extracted text back to its original form. We propose a solution by instructing Llama to extract only concise phrases as evidence. In post-processing, we discard any extraction that does not match the content of the original post, ignoring capitalization.

Experiments

LLM	llama-2-70b-chat.Q4_0.gguf [1]
GPU	NVIDIA RTX 3500 Ada
context size	4096
batch size	4096
temperature	0

Table 2: The key environment setting and parameters for running the experiment.

[1]https://huggingface.co/TheBloke/Llama-2-70B-Chat-GGUF

We utilise Llama-2-70B-Chat (Touvron et al., 2023) as our LLM for the task and implement it using the Llama C++ framework [2] and 4-bits quantisation. A detailed parameters and hardware settings for running Llama is shown in Table 2.

4 Evaluation Metrics

The evaluation was conducted by the shared task organisers using BERTScore (Zhang et al., 2020). Assume G is a set of 4 gold highlights $G = \{g_1, g_2, g_3, g_4\}$ and H is a set of 2 submitted highlights $H = \{h_1, h_2\}$. Then, the evaluation metrics are:

- *Recall*: For a given user, take the average of the maximum BERTScore from each g_* to each h_*.
- *Precision*: For a given user, find the g_* with the maximum BERTScore to each each h_*, and then take the average over H.
- weighted-*Recall*: For a given user, sum the token count (tokenised by Zhuang et al.) of G as $len(G)$ and of H as $len(H)$. Weigh the user-level *Recall* by the $\frac{len(G)}{len(H)}$, if $len(H) > len(G)$.

The overall submission-level score is the mean across all test users.

5 Results

Table 3 demonstrates that the risk & factor-oriented (RF-oriented) approach is the most effective in extracting evidence associated with all three levels of pre-annotated risks when measured under recall-oriented BERTScore (+0.015 to baseline and +0.007 to factor-oriented approach). Specifically, we observed that the RF-oriented approach notably facilitates the extraction of evidence for user annotations with low risks (0.924). The extraction of this risk level presents a greater challenge, as the scores for high-risk tend to be higher than those for medium and low risks. This discrepancy is likely attributed to the fact that posts with lower risk levels tend to employ lexicons that express suicidal ideation less explicitly. In contrast, posts with a high risk level may explicitly include contents like "I cannot stop thinking of kill myself" or "I want to commit suicide". Shifting to precision-oriented BERTScore, its deficiency compared to the Baseline is minimal (0.01) and remains consistent with the factor-oriented approach, showcasing its robust nature. Nevertheless, the RF-oriented approach extracts longer context as evidence to support low-risk annotations (0.504 in weighted-*Recall*). Consequently, it yields worse weighted recall than the baseline and factor-oriented approach.

The baseline demonstrated excellent *Precision* (0.918) in extracting evidence. This observation suggests that while the LLM may not comprehensively grasp the causative factors for evaluating suicide risk levels in context, and may fail to cover all aspects, it has embedded enough knowledge to accurately identify relevant context. It also achieved the best weighted-*Recall* of 0.740 among the experimented approaches, indicating its extraction length is closer to the human annotation compared to the instruction that explicitly covers the risk factors as guidance.

Upon comparing the RF-oriented approach to the factor-oriented approach, we noticed that refining instructions to the LLM for conciseness led to improved performance (+0.007 in *Recall*; +0.002 in *Precision*; +0.022 in weighted-*Recall*) in evidence extraction. Specifically, when excluding the extraction of evidence for low-risk annotations, the RF-oriented approach, with instructions tailored for different risk levels, demonstrated the ability to extract shorter context and achieved better weighted-*Recall*.

6 Conclusions

We investigated three approaches with varying levels of instruction detail to guide LLMs in extracting evidence related to users exhibiting low, moderate, or high suicide risk levels. All approaches demonstrated strong effectiveness, with the baseline excelling in precision for shorter text pieces. However, the factor-oriented and RF-oriented approaches, equipped with detailed instructions covering diverse mental health factors tailored to different risk levels, proved more effective in capturing comprehensive evidence, with the RF-oriented approach performing the best. Our findings highlight the robust feasibility of LLMs in extracting information supporting the evaluation of suicidal risk in social media discourse. There is room for improvement by creating clear and effective instructions to steer the extraction process. This could involve adapting existing manual annotation guidelines for evidence extraction into instructive prompts. Ad-

[2] https://github.com/ggerganov/llama.cpp

	Recall			*Precision*			weighted-*Recall*		
	low	moderate	high	low	moderate	high	low	moderate	high
Median		0.910			0.906			0.617	
Baseline		0.904			**0.918**			**0.740**	
	0.910	0.904	0.902	<u>0.900</u>	0.904	0.903	<u>0.686</u>	<u>0.753</u>	0.736
Factor-oriented		0.912			0.915			0.679	
	0.906	0.910	0.918	0.899	0.904	0.919	0.602	0.680	0.708
RF-oriented		**0.919**			0.917			0.701	
	<u>0.924</u>	<u>0.919</u>	<u>0.920</u>	0.899	<u>0.917</u>	<u>0.923</u>	0.504	0.721	<u>0.737</u>

Table 3: Results of baseline, Factor-oriented, and RF-oriented (Risk Level & Factor) approaches on submission level. The median denotes the score of the 8-th ranked participant in the shared task from the total of 15 participants. The median by risk level is not disclosed by the task organisers. The top row of each cell denotes the overall submission-level score across all three risk levels, with the greatest value presented in bold; The bottom row of each cell denotes the overall submission-level score by risk level, with the greatest value marked by underline.

dressing the auto-correction behaviour of the generative LLM is crucial for further improving *Recall*. The model's generative settings occasionally auto-correct spelling errors or rephrase extracted text, posing challenges in recovering the originally expressed content and impacting the fidelity of evidence. This unpredictability introduces complexities in formulating strategies to revert the modified text to its original form, adding an additional layer of intricacy to the evidence extraction process.

In future, we will conduct a more comprehensive qualitative analysis. We aim to refine the instructional prompts given to the model, adapting existing manual annotation guidelines to ensure clearer and more effective guidance. We will explore the integration of contextual information, aiming to enhance the model's ability to capture broader situational cues for improved risk assessment. Addressing the auto-correction behavior, especially in terms of spelling errors, will be a priority, involving fine-tuning the model or implementing post-processing steps to preserve the original expressions in extracted text.

Limitations

The effectiveness of our approach heavily relies on the performance of the leveraged LLM in accurately processing mental health information. We noticed that when changing the Llama-2-70B model to Llama-2-7B, many text spans with the expression of evidence failed to be extracted.

Another limitation is the comprehensibility of the instructive prompts provided to the LLM. The design of prompts plays a crucial role in guiding the model's behaviour. However, achieving optimal prompt design is a challenging task, and variations in prompt comprehension could influence the accuracy and relevance of evidence extraction. We have noticed that slightly changing the order of the covered risk factors in the prompt may lead to a varied output. Due to the time constraints associated with this shared task, and the lack of labelled development and test data at the time of submission, we could not thoroughly analyze the impact of variations in the prompt text.

Besides, the extraction granularity cannot be systematically controlled. For some posts, the model tends to extract full sentences as evidence, while others may only extract single keywords. This inconsistency in extraction granularity poses challenges in achieving consistent and precise evidence granularity, requiring further exploration.

Lastly, our approach is based on zero-shot learning. This inherently limits the real-time adaptability of the model to evolving patterns in user behaviour or language expression. More advanced approaches, such as in-context learning, could be explored in the future.

Ethics Consideration

We affirm that the data utilised in this study is not shared with any external entities, including cloud services, third-party organizations, or companies. All data processing is conducted within our organization, ensuring a secure and protected environment. Our commitment includes presenting findings and insights responsibly, and avoiding potential harm. This involves careful interpretation of results and avoiding stigmatization based on extracted information.

Acknowledgments

Acknowledging the assistance of the American Association of Suicidology in making the UMD dataset available.

References

Monica Agrawal, Stefan Hegselmann, Hunter Lang, Yoon Kim, and David Sontag. 2022. Large language models are few-shot clinical information extractors. In *Proceedings of the 2022 Conference on Empirical Methods in Natural Language Processing*, pages 1998–2022.

Jenny Chim, Adam Tsakalidis, Dimitris Gkoumas, Dana Atzil-Slonim, Yaakov Ophir, Ayah Zirikly, Philip Resnik, and Maria Liakata. 2024. Overview of the clpsych 2024 shared task: Leveraging large language models to identify evidence of suicidality risk in online posts. In *Proceedings of the Ninth Workshop on Computational Linguistics and Clinical Psychology*. Association for Computational Linguistics.

Darcy J Corbitt-Hall, Jami M Gauthier, Margaret T Davis, and Tracy K Witte. 2016. College students' responses to suicidal content on social networking sites: An examination using a simulated facebook newsfeed. *Suicide and Life-Threatening Behavior*, 46(5):609–624.

Jana E Jones, Bruce P Hermann, John J Barry, Frank G Gilliam, Andres M Kanner, and Kimford J Meador. 2003. Rates and risk factors for suicide, suicidal ideation, and suicide attempts in chronic epilepsy. *Epilepsy & Behavior*, 4:31–38.

Mark E Larsen, Tjeerd W Boonstra, Philip J Batterham, Bridianne O'Dea, Cecile Paris, and Helen Christensen. 2015. We feel: mapping emotion on twitter. *IEEE journal of biomedical and health informatics*, 19(4):1246–1252.

Bridianne O'dea, Stephen Wan, Philip J Batterham, Alison L Calear, Cecile Paris, and Helen Christensen. 2015. Detecting suicidality on twitter. *Internet Interventions*, 2(2):183–188.

Cécile Paris, Helen Christensen, Philip Batterham, and Bridianne O'Dea. 2015. Exploring emotions in social media. In *2015 IEEE Conference on Collaboration and Internet Computing (CIC)*, pages 54–61. IEEE.

Han-Chin Shing, Suraj Nair, Ayah Zirikly, Meir Friedenberg, Hal Daumé III, and Philip Resnik. 2018. Expert, crowdsourced, and machine assessment of suicide risk via online postings. In *Proceedings of the fifth workshop on computational linguistics and clinical psychology: from keyboard to clinic*, pages 25–36.

Karan Singhal, Shekoofeh Azizi, Tao Tu, S Sara Mahdavi, Jason Wei, Hyung Won Chung, Nathan Scales, Ajay Tanwani, Heather Cole-Lewis, Stephen Pfohl, et al. 2023. Large language models encode clinical knowledge. *Nature*, 620(7972):172–180.

Hugo Touvron, Louis Martin, Kevin Stone, Peter Albert, Amjad Almahairi, Yasmine Babaei, Nikolay Bashlykov, Soumya Batra, Prajjwal Bhargava, Shruti Bhosale, et al. 2023. Llama 2: Open foundation and fine-tuned chat models. *arXiv preprint arXiv:2307.09288*.

Adam Tsakalidis, Jenny Chim, Iman Munire Bilal, Ayah Zirikly, Dana Atzil-Slonim, Federico Nanni, Philip Resnik, Manas Gaur, Kaushik Roy, Becky Inkster, et al. 2022a. Overview of the clpsych 2022 shared task: Capturing moments of change in longitudinal user posts. In *Proceedings of the Eighth Workshop on Computational Linguistics and Clinical Psychology*, pages 184–198.

Adam Tsakalidis, Federico Nanni, Anthony Hills, Jenny Chim, Jiayu Song, and Maria Liakata. 2022b. Identifying moments of change from longitudinal user text. In *Proceedings of the 60th Annual Meeting of the Association for Computational Linguistics (Volume 1: Long Papers)*, pages 4647–4660. Association for Computational Linguistics.

Tianyi Zhang, Varsha Kishore, Felix Wu, Kilian Q. Weinberger, and Yoav Artzi. 2020. Bertscore: Evaluating text generation with bert. In *International Conference on Learning Representations*.

Liu Zhuang, Lin Wayne, Shi Ya, and Zhao Jun. 2021. A robustly optimized BERT pre-training approach with post-training. In *Proceedings of the 20th Chinese National Conference on Computational Linguistics*, pages 1218–1227. Chinese Information Processing Society of China.

Ayah Zirikly, Philip Resnik, Ozlem Uzuner, and Kristy Hollingshead. 2019. Clpsych 2019 shared task: Predicting the degree of suicide risk in reddit posts. In *Proceedings of the sixth workshop on computational linguistics and clinical psychology*, pages 24–33.

A Appendix

Listing 4: Backus-Naur Form Grammars for Post-processing

```
root ::= Post
Post ::= "{" ws "\"highlights\":" ws
    stringlist "}"
Postlist ::= "[]" | "[" ws Post (","
    ws Post)* "]"
string ::= "\"" ([^"][^\t]*)␣"\""
boolean ::= "true" | "false"
ws ::= "\n\t"
number ::= [0-9]+ "."? [0-9]*
stringlist ::= "[" ws "]" | "[" ws
    string ("," ws string)* ws "]"
numberlist ::= "[" ws "]" | "[" ws
    string ("," ws number)* ws "]"
```

Psychological Assessments with Large Language Models: A Privacy-Focused and Cost-Effective Approach

Sergi Blanco-Cuaresma
Harvard-Smithsonian Center for Astrophysics, 60 Garden Street, Cambridge, MA 02138, USA
Laboratoire de Recherche en Neuroimagerie, University Hospital (CHUV) and
University of Lausanne (UNIL), Lausanne, Switzerland
sblancocuaresma@cfa.harvard.edu

Abstract

This study explores the use of Large Language Models (LLMs) to analyze text comments from Reddit users, aiming to achieve two primary objectives: firstly, to pinpoint critical excerpts that support a predefined psychological assessment of suicidal risk; and secondly, to summarize the material to substantiate the preassigned suicidal risk level. The work is circumscribed to the use of "open-source" LLMs that can be run locally, thereby enhancing data privacy. Furthermore, it prioritizes models with low computational requirements, making it accessible to both individuals and institutions operating on limited computing budgets. The implemented strategy only relies on a carefully crafted prompt and a grammar to guide the LLM's text completion. Despite its simplicity, the evaluation metrics show outstanding results, making it a valuable privacy-focused and cost-effective approach. This work is part of the Computational Linguistics and Clinical Psychology (CLPsych) 2024 shared task.

1 Introduction

Large Language Models (LLMs) like GPT (Generative Pre-trained Transformer; OpenAI et al., 2023), Llama (Large Language Model Meta AI; Touvron et al., 2023a,b), Mistral/Mixtral (Jiang et al., 2024, 2023), and others (based on the transformer architecture and its attention mechanism, made popular thanks to BERT and derivatives; Vaswani et al., 2017; Devlin et al., 2018; Grezes et al., 2021, 2022) represent a significant advancement in the field of artificial intelligence, specifically within natural language processing (NLP). These models have transformed how machines understand, generate, and interact with human language, enabling a wide range of applications.

During the "pre-training" phase, LLMs learn a wide range of language patterns and they encode knowledge from a vast corpora of text data. In a posterior phase, they can be "fine-tuned" on smaller/alternate datasets to become specialized on specific tasks such as psychological assessments. The fine-tuning can also be restricted to a smaller number of parameters using techniques such as LoRA (Hu et al., 2021) or QLoRA (Dettmers et al., 2023) for quantized models (Kim et al., 2023). However, fine-tuning can still be costly in terms of computational resources and time investment, requiring a high level of expertise.

Models with a higher number of parameters are more sophisticated, encode more accurate knowledge and are capable of performing more advanced tasks with optimal results. This reduces the need for fine-tuning, but it increases the requirements for computational resources. There is also the option of not running the models locally, but relying on external services such as OpenAI's API and their chatGPT interface[1]. Regrettably, this approach may not be viable due to the involvement of third parties, which might not ensure adequate data protection or adhere to the stringent privacy standards and ethical codes mandated by healthcare and medical institutions, along with other legal obligations.

Given this context, in this study I explore the use of "open-source" LLMs that can be run locally in current commodity hardware (thus, 4-bit quantized models with a maximum 7 billion parameters), and I do not fine-tune these models to specialize in any specific task or to incorporate new knowledge relevant to the domain of clinical psychology. This evaluation is focused on the shared task proposed by the Computational Linguistics and Clinical Psychology (CLPsych) 2024 workshop (Chim et al., 2024) at the 18th Conference of the European Chapter of the Association for Computational Linguistics (ACL).

[1] https://openai.com/

Proceedings of the 9th Workshop on Computational Linguistics and Clinical Psychology (CLPsych 2024), pages 203–210
March 21, 2024

2 Task and Data

The CLPsych 2024 shared task consisted on finding evidence within Reddit comments that support a preassigned suicide risk level. The organizers provided access the University of Maryland Reddit Suicidality Dataset (UMD version 2; Shing et al., 2018; Zirikly et al., 2019), which includes posts to the *"r/SuicideWatch"* subreddit plus crowdsourced and expert risk level assessments. The risk levels to be considered are low, moderate and high.

The evidence supporting the preassigned risk level can take two different forms: 1) highlights (i.e., snippets) from the user's comments; 2) a summary that aggregates the evidence that justifies the assigned risk level. In this study, both forms of evidence were generated for a selection of 162 posts (by 125 users) that the organizers used to evaluate each submitted result.

3 Methods

This study considered six different LLMs, which were selected based on their ranking on the Open LLM Leaderboard[2], and the LMSys Chatbot Arena Leaderboard[3] as of January 15th (2024). The models were obtained from Tom Jobbins's huggingface repository[4] in GGUFv2 format ("Q4_K_M" quant method). The inference code was run locally using the NASA SciX Brain software (Blanco-Cuaresma et al., 2023) on a MacBook Air with the Apple M1 chip (released on November 2020) and 16GB of RAM. The concrete models were:

1. OpenHermes 2.5[5], based on Mistral 7B and further trained on mainly GPT-4 generated data, and other open datasets.

2. Orca 2 (Mitra et al., 2023), based on Llama 2, designed to excel in reasoning, trained on a censored synthetic dataset. Human preference alignment techniques such as Reinforcement learning from human feedback (RLHF; Ziegler et al., 2019) or Direct Preference Optimization (DPO; Rafailov et al., 2023) were not used.

3. Starling 7B alpha (Zhu et al., 2023), based on OpenChat 3.5 which is refinement of Mistral 7B using C(onditioned)-RLFT (Wang et al., 2023), trained by Reinforcement Learning from AI Feedback (RLAIF; Lee et al., 2023).

4. Dolphin 2.6, based on Mistral 7B, trained following LASER (Sharma et al., 2023) and aligned to human preferences using DPO.

5. Mistral 7B instruct 0.2 (Jiang et al., 2024), based on Mistral 7B, trained with a variety of publicly available conversation datasets.

6. Zephyr 7B beta (Tunstall et al., 2023), based on Mistral 7B, trained on on a mix of publicly available, synthetic datasets using DPO.

Each model is requested to either extract evidences from user's comments as text highlights or to generate a comprehensive summary, both with the goal of justifying a preassigned suicidal risk level. The request is done with a crafted prompt that sets the scene (e.g., act as a psychologist specializing in suicidal ideation), and includes a fake interaction where the user has shared the reddit comment and a preassigned risk level, and the model (i.e., the assistant) has already provided an answer. This is a one-shot prompt from where the model can infer what we expect it to generate after a user request. Subsequently, the real comment to be analyzed is included, and the model's response is left empty for it to be completed.

My evaluation of various prompts was not exhaustive, but rather a manual and subjective process based on a limited set of examples. The tests (inspired by a previous work; Blanco-Cuaresma et al., 2023) suggested that a prompt in which a user outlines the entire task and includes an example generally yields slightly inferior results compared to a prompt that simulates an initial round of interaction between the user and the assistant, as if the assistant had already responded to a previous request. All the tested prompts directed the model to adopt the role of an expert and incorporated a description of what constitutes evidence for supporting a suicidal risk assessment, based on the assumption that the LLM will rely more heavily on this provided information than on the knowledge it has gained through its training.

The structure of the final prompt used for extracting text highlights can be found in Appendix A. For

[2]https://huggingface.co/spaces/HuggingFaceH4/open_llm_leaderboard

[3]https://huggingface.co/spaces/lmsys/chatbot-arena-leaderboard

[4]https://huggingface.co/TheBloke

[5]https://huggingface.co/teknium/OpenHermes-2.5-Mistral-7B

this particular subtask, I use a formal grammar (feature included in llama.cpp[6]) to constraint the possible tokens that can be sampled (i.e., discarding tokens that would break the rules defined by the grammar). The grammar is in GBNF format, which is an extension of BNF (Backus–Naur/Normal form, a metasyntax notation for context-free grammars) that primarily adds a few modern regex-like features. The grammar imposes the generation of a list (surrounded by square brackets) of strings (surrounded by double quotes), and the string can only contain words present in the user's comment in their original order (see a concrete example in Appendix B).

Regarding the summarization subtask, the structure of the used prompt can be found in Appendix C. In this case, there is no imposed grammar, the model is free to complete the response but it is primed by providing already the first sentence, which states what the preassigned suicidal risk level is.

For both subtasks, a top-p sampling (aka nucleus sampling; Holtzman et al., 2019) approach is followed (after the grammar constrains have been applied in the case of the highlights subtask), where only the top tokens will be considered (up to a cumulative score of 0.95), and a temperature of 0.7 to favor precision over creativity (low values makes top tokens more likely) and a repeat penalty of 1.1 is used to prevent loops.

Thanks to the workshop organizers, the generated text highlights and summaries that support the preassigned suicidal risk level were automatically evaluated against a test set annotated by domain experts (who manually generated gold highlights and summaries). The computed metrics to evaluate highlights are:

- Recall: For every gold highlight, find the generated highlight with the highest semantic similarity (based on BERTScore; Zhang et al., 2019) and compute the average across users. It measures how relevant the highlights are as supporting evidence.

- Precision: For every generated highlight, find the gold highlight with the highest semantic similarity and compute the average across users. It measures the quality of the generated highlights.

- Weighted Recall: Sum the gold and generated highlights lengths (i.e., number of tokens) per user. If the generated length is greater than the gold one, correct the calculated recall value R with the length ratio: $R_{\text{weighted}} = R \times \frac{L_{\text{gold}}}{L_{\text{candidate}}}$. It measures how relevant the highlights are as supporting evidence and if lengths are similar to human-highlighted ones.

- Harmonic Mean: Balances between precision and recall (the unweighted version).

Regarding the evaluation of summaries, the computed metrics are:

- Consistency: Using a natural language inference (NLI) model, obtain the probability p of each generated sentence (hypothesis) contradicting the gold sentence (premise). Then average $1 - p$ across all sentences and users. It measures lack of contradiction.

- Contradiction: Similar to the previous one, but directly takes the maximum contradiction probability and averages all sentences and users. Hence, it penalizes information that contradicts the gold summary, and lower scores are better.

4 Results

The CLPsych 2024 shared task only accepted three submissions per team, but the organizers were kind enough to evaluate additional submissions that are not considered for the workshop ranking. For the competition, I submitted the output from OpenHermes, Orca 2, and Starling. Orca 2 was selected as it is the sole model based on Llama 2, while the other two were chosen for their standings in the LLM leaderboards. In the final official ranking, OpenHermes produced the best results. For highlights, based on recall and harmonic mean metrics, it ended in the modest 10th position (out of 15). However, if the weighted recall were considered instead, it would have ended in the 3rd position. This shows that OpenHermes' length of its generated highlights are closer to human-highlighted ones compared to other systems. Regarding summaries, based on the consistency metrics, OpenHermes ended in an outstanding 2nd position (out of 14). If the organizer would have considered the contradiction metrics, then it would have fallen to a (still honorable) 3rd position.

[6]https://github.com/ggerganov/llama.cpp

	Highlights				Summaries	
Model	Recall	Precision	Weighted Recall	Harmonic Mean	Consistency	Contradiction
OpenHermes	0.907	0.912	0.738	0.909	0.976	**0.079**
Orca 2	0.904	**0.914**	0.777	0.909	0.971	0.104
Starling	0.907	0.913	0.766	0.910	**0.977**	0.083
Dolphin	**0.910**	0.913	0.736	**0.911**	0.971	0.093
Mistral	0.902	0.913	0.799	0.907	0.969	0.105
Zephyr	0.894	**0.914**	**0.803**	0.903	0.974	0.085

Table 1: Performance metrics for all the evaluated models. The last three models did not enter the CLPsych 2024 shared task competition. The best scores per metric are highlighted in bold.

Beyond the workshop competition, and in the interest of better assessing all the considered LLMs, the performance metrics for all the evaluated models can be found in Table 1. For the highlights, the best performing models are Dolphin and Zephyr, depending if we consider the weighted or unweighted recall metrics. Zephyr produces highlights of a length that is more similar to the human-made highlights, but Dolphin generates highlights that are more relevant. Regarding summaries, OpenHermes and Starling are in the lead, depending if we give a higher importance to being consistent or minimizing contradictions. OpenHermes generates summaries with the lowest level of contradiction, and its consistency level is only slightly below Starling, hence it would be fair to claim that it is the best model for this subtask.

It is also worth exploring the evaluation metrics split by the preassigned suicidal risk level (see Table 2 and Table 3). There is no single model that excels at all risk levels, suggesting that a combined strategy could lead to even better overall results. Additionally, almost for all models and metrics, the performance correlates with the suicidal risk level: the higher the risk, the better the performance of the model.

Finally, in terms of computation, the average inference time was of 40 minutes to extract highlights from 162 posts ($\sim$14.8 seconds per post), and 30 minutes to generate summaries for 125 users ($\sim$14.4 seconds per user). These are extremely competitive numbers for LLMs running on a consumer-grade machine.

5 Discussion

The OpenHermes' generated highlights and summaries, when compared to other submitted systems to the CLPsych 2024 shared task competition, ended up with remarkable comparative metrics for an approach that has used cost-effective "open-source" LLMs without any specific fine-tuning for these specific tasks. The highlights subtask seems to be the one with more margin of improvement, especially if we only consider the unweighted recall (where matching highlight lengths are not taken into account). It would have been interesting to make a manual human-based evaluation, comparing the generated highlights with the golden ones (which has not been released publicly), to better understand the discrepancy between the unweighted and weighted recall metrics (10th vs 3rd position in the final ranking, respectively) and justify selecting one over the other. In any case, these extraordinary results seem to signal the potential that this approach may have at other relatively similar tasks such as Named Entity Recognition. Regarding the generation of summaries, both evaluation metrics placed this approach in the top 3 ranking, a stunning result for a model that has not been trained specifically for psychological assessments.

OpenHermes seems to be the best well-balance model and one of the best for summarization, but if we consider all the evaluated LLMs, Dolphin and Zephyr perform better in the highlights subtask. However, these results would likely change if other prompt templates were used. For instance, the crafted prompt includes only one example with a high suicidal risk level, and we observed that almost all models perform better for comments from high risk users. Expanding the prompt to include more examples of different risk levels could potentially improve the overall performance.

6 Conclusion

Six different "open-source" Large Language Models were evaluated to accomplish the shared task proposed by the CLPsych 2024 workshop. This work demonstrated that following a relatively simple approach, mainly consisting on a well structured prompt with one single example, can be used with cost-effective LLMs to extract highlights and generate comprehensive and consistent summaries

	Recall			Precision			Weighted Recall			Harmonic Mean		
Model / Risk	**Low**	**Mod.**	**High**	**Low**	**Mod.**	**High**	**Low**	**Mod.**	**High**	**Low**	**Mod.**	**High**
OpenHermes	0.900	0.904	**0.915**	0.896	0.909	0.922	0.677	0.739	0.759	0.898	0.906	**0.919**
Orca 2	0.902	0.903	0.905	**0.907**	**0.914**	0.919	0.723	0.785	0.778	**0.905**	0.908	0.911
Starling	0.892	0.909	0.907	0.893	0.911	0.924	0.705	0.763	0.794	0.892	0.910	0.915
Dolphin	0.901	**0.912**	0.912	0.894	0.913	0.920	0.632	0.748	0.750	0.897	**0.912**	0.915
Mistral	**0.905**	0.898	0.909	0.898	0.910	**0.925**	0.658	**0.816**	**0.813**	0.901	0.904	0.917
Zephyr	0.890	0.893	0.896	0.900	**0.914**	0.917	**0.792**	0.811	0.791	0.895	0.903	0.906

Table 2: Performance metrics for the highlights subtask, split by users with different suicidal risk level (low, moderate, or high). The best scores per metric and risk level are highlighted in bold.

	Consistency			Contradiction		
Model / Risk	**Low**	**Mod.**	**High**	**Low**	**Mod.**	**High**
OpenHermes	0.937	0.977	**0.986**	0.178	**0.078**	**0.045**
Orca 2	0.958	0.975	0.970	0.125	0.092	0.119
Starling	**0.962**	**0.978**	0.979	**0.113**	0.079	0.079
Dolphin	0.948	0.973	0.975	0.165	0.084	0.087
Mistral	0.931	0.976	0.968	0.205	0.084	0.110
Zephyr	0.944	0.976	0.981	0.161	0.081	0.068

Table 3: Performance metrics for the summarization subtask, split by users with different suicidal risk level (low, moderate, or high). The best scores per metric and risk level are highlighted in bold.

that justify a preassigned suicidal risk level of users who participate in online text-based forums. This approach does not rely on complex operations such as further training or fine-tuning the models to adapt them to the goal in hand. Hence, existing "open-source" models with moderate hardware requirements can successfully run locally to support psychological assessments. This approach facilitates respecting privacy rules, best ethical practices and other local, national, and international regulations.

7 Limitations

This study has considered a selection of six models based on two existing public rankings, but there are many more "open-source" LLMs available. In particular, there are models with even larger number of parameters that could still be run in advanced commodity hardware such as gaming computers. It would have been interesting to evaluate how differently these larger models perform compared to the selected 7 billion parameter models. The presented approach is also highly dependent on the prompt template, this work has not explored and compared other prompts with more embedded examples or different prompt wording.

It is important to recognize that LLMs are trained on datasets that are not necessarily representative of the global population (e.g., many biases may be present), and they may not always accurately interpret the nuances of human psychology and emotions, leading to potential misinterpretation with severe implications. Hence, using LLMs for psychological assessments has associated risks that need to be properly handled and mitigated.

Finally, not having direct access to the golden highlights and summaries makes understanding certain results a bit more difficult.

8 Ethics

Secure access to the shared task dataset was provided with IRB approval under University of Maryland, College Park protocol 1642625 and approval by the Biomedical and Scientific Research Ethics Committee (BSREC) at the University of Warwick (ethical application reference BSREC 40/19-20). The author[7] signed a data use agreement that establishes multiple requirements such as the strict use of the dataset for only the CLPsych shared task, protecting its content and the users privacy.

9 Acknowledgements

The author is particularly grateful to the anonymous users of Reddit whose data feature in this year's shared task dataset, the American Association of Suicidology for making the dataset available, the individuals involved in manually annotating the dataset, and to the organizers of the CLPsych 2024 workshop/shared task. This work could not have been possible without the support of NASA Science Explorer[8] and its brilliant team at the Harvard-Smithsonian Center for Astrophysics (USA), as well as Dr. Marzia De Lucia's support at the Lausanne University Hospital/University of Lausanne (Switzerland).

[7] `https://blancocuaresma.com/s/`
[8] `https://scixplorer.org/`

References

Sergi Blanco-Cuaresma, Ioana Ciucă, Alberto Accomazzi, Michael J. Kurtz, Edwin A. Henneken, Kelly E. Lockhart, Felix Grezes, Thomas Allen, Golnaz Shapurian, Carolyn S. Grant, Donna M. Thompson, Timothy W. Hostetler, Matthew R. Templeton, Shinyi Chen, Jennifer Koch, Taylor Jacovich, Daniel Chivvis, Fernanda de Macedo Alves, Jean-Claude Paquin, Jennifer Bartlett, Mugdha Polimera, and Stephanie Jarmak. 2023. Experimenting with Large Language Models and vector embeddings in NASA SciX. *arXiv e-prints*, page arXiv:2312.14211.

Jenny Chim, Adam Tsakalidis, Dimitris Gkoumas, Dana Atzil-Slonim, Yaakov Ophir, Ayah Zirikly, Philip Resnik, and Maria Liakata. 2024. Overview of the clpsych 2024 shared task: Leveraging large language models to identify evidence of suicidality risk in online posts. In *Proceedings of the Ninth Workshop on Computational Linguistics and Clinical Psychology*. Association for Computational Linguistics.

Tim Dettmers, Artidoro Pagnoni, Ari Holtzman, and Luke Zettlemoyer. 2023. QLoRA: Efficient Finetuning of Quantized LLMs. *arXiv e-prints*, page arXiv:2305.14314.

Jacob Devlin, Ming-Wei Chang, Kenton Lee, and Kristina Toutanova. 2018. BERT: Pre-training of Deep Bidirectional Transformers for Language Understanding. *arXiv e-prints*, page arXiv:1810.04805.

Felix Grezes, Thomas Allen, Sergi Blanco-Cuaresma, Alberto Accomazzi, Michael J. Kurtz, Golnaz Shapurian, Edwin Henneken, Carolyn S. Grant, Donna M. Thompson, Timothy W. Hostetler, and et al. 2022. Improving astroBERT using Semantic Textual Similarity. *arXiv e-prints*, page arXiv:2212.00744.

Felix Grezes, Sergi Blanco-Cuaresma, Alberto Accomazzi, Michael J. Kurtz, Golnaz Shapurian, Edwin Henneken, Carolyn S. Grant, Donna M. Thompson, Roman Chyla, Stephen McDonald, and et al. 2021. Building astroBERT, a language model for Astronomy & Astrophysics. *arXiv e-prints*, page arXiv:2112.00590.

Ari Holtzman, Jan Buys, Li Du, Maxwell Forbes, and Yejin Choi. 2019. The Curious Case of Neural Text Degeneration. *arXiv e-prints*, page arXiv:1904.09751.

Edward J. Hu, Yelong Shen, Phillip Wallis, Zeyuan Allen-Zhu, Yuanzhi Li, Shean Wang, Lu Wang, and Weizhu Chen. 2021. LoRA: Low-Rank Adaptation of Large Language Models. *arXiv e-prints*, page arXiv:2106.09685.

Albert Q. Jiang, Alexandre Sablayrolles, Arthur Mensch, Chris Bamford, Devendra Singh Chaplot, Diego de las Casas, Florian Bressand, Gianna Lengyel, Guillaume Lample, Lucile Saulnier, Lélio Renard Lavaud, Marie-Anne Lachaux, Pierre Stock, Teven Le Scao, Thibaut Lavril, Thomas Wang, Timothée Lacroix, and William El Sayed. 2023. Mistral 7B. *arXiv e-prints*, page arXiv:2310.06825.

Albert Q. Jiang, Alexandre Sablayrolles, Antoine Roux, Arthur Mensch, Blanche Savary, Chris Bamford, Devendra Singh Chaplot, Diego de las Casas, Emma Bou Hanna, Florian Bressand, Gianna Lengyel, Guillaume Bour, Guillaume Lample, Lélio Renard Lavaud, Lucile Saulnier, Marie-Anne Lachaux, Pierre Stock, Sandeep Subramanian, Sophia Yang, Szymon Antoniak, Teven Le Scao, Théophile Gervet, Thibaut Lavril, Thomas Wang, Timothée Lacroix, and William El Sayed. 2024. Mixtral of Experts. *arXiv e-prints*, page arXiv:2401.04088.

Sehoon Kim, Coleman Hooper, Thanakul Wattanawong, Minwoo Kang, Ruohan Yan, Hasan Genc, Grace Dinh, Qijing Huang, Kurt Keutzer, Michael W. Mahoney, Yakun Sophia Shao, and Amir Gholami. 2023. Full Stack Optimization of Transformer Inference: a Survey. *arXiv e-prints*, page arXiv:2302.14017.

Harrison Lee, Samrat Phatale, Hassan Mansoor, Thomas Mesnard, Johan Ferret, Kellie Lu, Colton Bishop, Ethan Hall, Victor Carbune, Abhinav Rastogi, and Sushant Prakash. 2023. RLAIF: Scaling Reinforcement Learning from Human Feedback with AI Feedback. *arXiv e-prints*, page arXiv:2309.00267.

Arindam Mitra, Luciano Del Corro, Shweti Mahajan, Andres Codas, Clarisse Simoes, Sahaj Agarwal, Xuxi Chen, Anastasia Razdaibiedina, Erik Jones, Kriti Aggarwal, Hamid Palangi, Guoqing Zheng, Corby Rosset, Hamed Khanpour, and Ahmed Awadallah. 2023. Orca 2: Teaching Small Language Models How to Reason. *arXiv e-prints*, page arXiv:2311.11045.

OpenAI, :, Josh Achiam, Steven Adler, Sandhini Agarwal, Lama Ahmad, Ilge Akkaya, Florencia Leoni Aleman, Diogo Almeida, Janko Altenschmidt, Sam Altman, Shyamal Anadkat, Red Avila, Igor Babuschkin, Suchir Balaji, Valerie Balcom, Paul Baltescu, Haiming Bao, Mo Bavarian, Jeff Belgum, Irwan Bello, Jake Berdine, Gabriel Bernadett-Shapiro, Christopher Berner, Lenny Bogdonoff, Oleg Boiko, Madelaine Boyd, Anna-Luisa Brakman, Greg Brockman, Tim Brooks, Miles Brundage, Kevin Button, Trevor Cai, Rosie Campbell, Andrew Cann, Brittany Carey, Chelsea Carlson, Rory Carmichael, Brooke Chan, Che Chang, Fotis Chantzis, Derek Chen, Sully Chen, Ruby Chen, Jason Chen, Mark Chen, Ben Chess, Chester Cho, Casey Chu, Hyung Won Chung, Dave Cummings, Jeremiah Currier, Yunxing Dai, Cory Decareaux, Thomas Degry, Noah Deutsch, Damien Deville, Arka Dhar, David Dohan, Steve Dowling, Sheila Dunning, Adrien Ecoffet, Atty Eleti, Tyna Eloundou, David Farhi, Liam Fedus, Niko Felix, Simón Posada Fishman, Juston Forte, Isabella Fulford, Leo Gao, Elie Georges, Christian Gibson, Vik Goel, Tarun Gogineni, Gabriel Goh, Rapha Gontijo-Lopes, Jonathan Gordon, Morgan Grafstein, Scott Gray, Ryan Greene, Joshua Gross, Shixiang Shane Gu, Yufei Guo, Chris Hallacy, Jesse

Han, Jeff Harris, Yuchen He, Mike Heaton, Johannes Heidecke, Chris Hesse, Alan Hickey, Wade Hickey, Peter Hoeschele, Brandon Houghton, Kenny Hsu, Shengli Hu, Xin Hu, Joost Huizinga, Shantanu Jain, Shawn Jain, Joanne Jang, Angela Jiang, Roger Jiang, Haozhun Jin, Denny Jin, Shino Jomoto, Billie Jonn, Heewoo Jun, Tomer Kaftan, Łukasz Kaiser, Ali Kamali, Ingmar Kanitscheider, Nitish Shirish Keskar, Tabarak Khan, Logan Kilpatrick, Jong Wook Kim, Christina Kim, Yongjik Kim, Hendrik Kirchner, Jamie Kiros, Matt Knight, Daniel Kokotajlo, Łukasz Kondraciuk, Andrew Kondrich, Aris Konstantinidis, Kyle Kosic, Gretchen Krueger, Vishal Kuo, Michael Lampe, Ikai Lan, Teddy Lee, Jan Leike, Jade Leung, Daniel Levy, Chak Ming Li, Rachel Lim, Molly Lin, Stephanie Lin, Mateusz Litwin, Theresa Lopez, Ryan Lowe, Patricia Lue, Anna Makanju, Kim Malfacini, Sam Manning, Todor Markov, Yaniv Markovski, Bianca Martin, Katie Mayer, Andrew Mayne, Bob McGrew, Scott Mayer McKinney, Christine McLeavey, Paul McMillan, Jake McNeil, David Medina, Aalok Mehta, Jacob Menick, Luke Metz, Andrey Mishchenko, Pamela Mishkin, Vinnie Monaco, Evan Morikawa, Daniel Mossing, Tong Mu, Mira Murati, Oleg Murk, David Mély, Ashvin Nair, Reiichiro Nakano, Rajeev Nayak, Arvind Neelakantan, Richard Ngo, Hyeonwoo Noh, Long Ouyang, Cullen O'Keefe, Jakub Pachocki, Alex Paino, Joe Palermo, Ashley Pantuliano, Giambattista Parascandolo, Joel Parish, Emy Parparita, Alex Passos, Mikhail Pavlov, Andrew Peng, Adam Perelman, Filipe de Avila Belbute Peres, Michael Petrov, Henrique Ponde de Oliveira Pinto, Michael, Pokorny, Michelle Pokrass, Vitchyr Pong, Tolly Powell, Alethea Power, Boris Power, Elizabeth Proehl, Raul Puri, Alec Radford, Jack Rae, Aditya Ramesh, Cameron Raymond, Francis Real, Kendra Rimbach, Carl Ross, Bob Rotsted, Henri Roussez, Nick Ryder, Mario Saltarelli, Ted Sanders, Shibani Santurkar, Girish Sastry, Heather Schmidt, David Schnurr, John Schulman, Daniel Selsam, Kyla Sheppard, Toki Sherbakov, Jessica Shieh, Sarah Shoker, Pranav Shyam, Szymon Sidor, Eric Sigler, Maddie Simens, Jordan Sitkin, Katarina Slama, Ian Sohl, Benjamin Sokolowsky, Yang Song, Natalie Staudacher, Felipe Petroski Such, Natalie Summers, Ilya Sutskever, Jie Tang, Nikolas Tezak, Madeleine Thompson, Phil Tillet, Amin Tootoonchian, Elizabeth Tseng, Preston Tuggle, Nick Turley, Jerry Tworek, Juan Felipe Cerón Uribe, Andrea Vallone, Arun Vijayvergiya, Chelsea Voss, Carroll Wainwright, Justin Jay Wang, Alvin Wang, Ben Wang, Jonathan Ward, Jason Wei, CJ Weinmann, Akila Welihinda, Peter Welinder, Jiayi Weng, Lilian Weng, Matt Wiethoff, Dave Willner, Clemens Winter, Samuel Wolrich, Hannah Wong, Lauren Workman, Sherwin Wu, Jeff Wu, Michael Wu, Kai Xiao, Tao Xu, Sarah Yoo, Kevin Yu, Qiming Yuan, Wojciech Zaremba, Rowan Zellers, Chong Zhang, Marvin Zhang, Shengjia Zhao, Tianhao Zheng, Juntang Zhuang, William Zhuk, and Barret Zoph. 2023. GPT-4 Technical Report. *arXiv e-prints*, page arXiv:2303.08774.

Rafael Rafailov, Archit Sharma, Eric Mitchell, Stefano Ermon, Christopher D. Manning, and Chelsea Finn. 2023. Direct Preference Optimization: Your Language Model is Secretly a Reward Model. *arXiv e-prints*, page arXiv:2305.18290.

Pratyusha Sharma, Jordan T. Ash, and Dipendra Misra. 2023. The Truth is in There: Improving Reasoning in Language Models with Layer-Selective Rank Reduction. *arXiv e-prints*, page arXiv:2312.13558.

Han-Chin Shing, Suraj Nair, Ayah Zirikly, Meir Friedenberg, Hal Daumé III, and Philip Resnik. 2018. Expert, crowdsourced, and machine assessment of suicide risk via online postings. In *Proceedings of the Fifth Workshop on Computational Linguistics and Clinical Psychology: From Keyboard to Clinic*, pages 25–36, New Orleans, LA. Association for Computational Linguistics.

Hugo Touvron, Thibaut Lavril, Gautier Izacard, Xavier Martinet, Marie-Anne Lachaux, Timothée Lacroix, Baptiste Rozière, Naman Goyal, Eric Hambro, Faisal Azhar, Aurelien Rodriguez, Armand Joulin, Edouard Grave, and Guillaume Lample. 2023a. LLaMA: Open and Efficient Foundation Language Models. *arXiv e-prints*, page arXiv:2302.13971.

Hugo Touvron, Louis Martin, Kevin Stone, Peter Albert, Amjad Almahairi, Yasmine Babaei, Nikolay Bashlykov, Soumya Batra, Prajjwal Bhargava, Shruti Bhosale, Dan Bikel, Lukas Blecher, Cristian Canton Ferrer, Moya Chen, Guillem Cucurull, David Esiobu, Jude Fernandes, Jeremy Fu, Wenyin Fu, Brian Fuller, Cynthia Gao, Vedanuj Goswami, Naman Goyal, Anthony Hartshorn, Saghar Hosseini, Rui Hou, Hakan Inan, Marcin Kardas, Viktor Kerkez, Madian Khabsa, Isabel Kloumann, Artem Korenev, Punit Singh Koura, Marie-Anne Lachaux, Thibaut Lavril, Jenya Lee, Diana Liskovich, Yinghai Lu, Yuning Mao, Xavier Martinet, Todor Mihaylov, Pushkar Mishra, Igor Molybog, Yixin Nie, Andrew Poulton, Jeremy Reizenstein, Rashi Rungta, Kalyan Saladi, Alan Schelten, Ruan Silva, Eric Michael Smith, Ranjan Subramanian, Xiaoqing Ellen Tan, Binh Tang, Ross Taylor, Adina Williams, Jian Xiang Kuan, Puxin Xu, Zheng Yan, Iliyan Zarov, Yuchen Zhang, Angela Fan, Melanie Kambadur, Sharan Narang, Aurelien Rodriguez, Robert Stojnic, Sergey Edunov, and Thomas Scialom. 2023b. Llama 2: Open Foundation and Fine-Tuned Chat Models. *arXiv e-prints*, page arXiv:2307.09288.

Lewis Tunstall, Edward Beeching, Nathan Lambert, Nazneen Rajani, Kashif Rasul, Younes Belkada, Shengyi Huang, Leandro von Werra, Clémentine Fourrier, Nathan Habib, Nathan Sarrazin, Omar Sanseviero, Alexander M. Rush, and Thomas Wolf. 2023. Zephyr: Direct Distillation of LM Alignment. *arXiv e-prints*, page arXiv:2310.16944.

Ashish Vaswani, Noam Shazeer, Niki Parmar, Jakob Uszkoreit, Llion Jones, Aidan N. Gomez, Lukasz Kaiser, and Illia Polosukhin. 2017. Attention Is All You Need. *arXiv e-prints*, page arXiv:1706.03762.

Guan Wang, Sijie Cheng, Xianyuan Zhan, Xiangang Li, Sen Song, and Yang Liu. 2023. OpenChat: Advancing Open-source Language Models with Mixed-Quality Data. *arXiv e-prints*, page arXiv:2309.11235.

Tianyi Zhang, Varsha Kishore, Felix Wu, Kilian Q. Weinberger, and Yoav Artzi. 2019. BERTScore: Evaluating Text Generation with BERT. *arXiv e-prints*, page arXiv:1904.09675.

Banghua Zhu, Evan Frick, Tianhao Wu, Hanlin Zhu, and Jiantao Jiao. 2023. Starling-7b: Improving llm helpfulness & harmlessness with rlaif.

Daniel M. Ziegler, Nisan Stiennon, Jeffrey Wu, Tom B. Brown, Alec Radford, Dario Amodei, Paul Christiano, and Geoffrey Irving. 2019. Fine-Tuning Language Models from Human Preferences. *arXiv e-prints*, page arXiv:1909.08593.

Ayah Zirikly, Philip Resnik, Özlem Uzuner, and Kristy Hollingshead. 2019. CLPsych 2019 shared task: Predicting the degree of suicide risk in Reddit posts. In *Proceedings of the Sixth Workshop on Computational Linguistics and Clinical Psychology*, pages 24–33, Minneapolis, Minnesota. Association for Computational Linguistics.

A Prompt for Highlights Extraction

The specific text included as an example in the following prompt has been altered and paraphrased to safeguard user privacy (the actual prompt contained a real example):

```
<|im_start|>system
As a psychologist specializing in suicidal ideation, you are adept
at identifying key evidences within brief online text comments
that assess an individual's risk of suicide. These evidences
encompass various aspects: Emotions (the individual's feelings),
Cognitions (thoughts and perceptions about suicide), Behavior and
Motivation (actions or behaviors linked to suicide), Interpersonal
and Social Support (availability of social support and stable
relationships), Mental Health-Related Issues (potential
psychiatric diagnoses), and Risk Factors (including socioeconomic
and demographic aspects). The risk levels are categorized as low
(indicating minimal perceived risk of suicide), moderate
(suggesting a tangible risk of a suicide attempt), and high
(implying a strong likelihood of a suicide attempt in the near
future). You will now analyze several texts to extract pertinent
excerpts as evidences that effectively evaluate the individual's
risk of suicide.<|im_end|>
<|im_start|>user
Risk level: high
Text: Recently, I attempted suicide by consuming an unspecified
amount of prescription medications. After realizing that the pills
were not lethal, I desperately prayed for an end to my suffering,
wishing to escape the torment inflicted by those who profess their
love yet demonstrate indifference through their actions.<|im_end|>
<|im_start|>assistant
["Recently, I attempted suicide", "I desperately prayed for an
end", "those who profess their love yet demonstrate indifference
through their actions"]
<|im_start|>user
Risk level: risk_level
Text: user_comment
<|im_start|>assistant
```

The prompt above follows the Chat Markup Language (ChatML) format, which is used by OpenHermes, Orca 2, and Dolphin. The prompt format was adapted to follow the appropriate one for the rest of the models (e.g., Starling uses *GPT4 User:*, *GPT4 Assistant*, and no tag for the system message).

B Grammar for Highlights Extraction

Simplified example of a grammar used to extract highlights from the following text: *'Recently, I attempted suicide by consuming an unspecified amount of prescription medications.'*.

```
root ::= "[" h (", " h)* "]"
h ::= "\"" (t0 | t1 | t2 | t3 | t4 | t5 | t6 | t7 | t8 | t9 | t10 |
t11) "\""
t0 ::= "Recently," (" " t1)?
t1 ::= "I" (" " t2)?
t2 ::= "attempted" (" " t3)?
t3 ::= "suicide" (" " t4)?
t4 ::= "by" (" " t5)?
t5 ::= "consuming" (" " t6)?
t6 ::= "an" (" " t7)?
t7 ::= "unspecified" (" " t8)?
t8 ::= "amount" (" " t9)?
t9 ::= "of" (" " t10)?
t10 ::= "prescription" (" " t11)?
t11 ::= "medications." (" " t12)?
t12 ::= ""
```

A response that respects this grammar would be: *'["I attempted suicide", "prescription medication"]'*. However, the grammar does not prevent the model from extracting repetitive strings or out of order strings (e.g., *'["suicide", "I attempted suicide", "medications.", "I attempted suicide"]'*), but this behavior was not observed (probably thanks to the repeat penalty).

C Prompt for Summarization

As in Appendix A, the specific text included as an example in the following prompt was altered and paraphrased to safeguard user privacy:

```
<|im_start|>system
As a psychologist specializing in suicidal ideation, you excel in
crafting concise summaries that collate evidences supporting a
designated suicide risk level for online texts. These evidences
encompass various aspects: Emotions (the individual's feelings),
Cognitions (thoughts and perceptions about suicide), Behavior and
Motivation (actions or behaviors linked to suicide), Interpersonal
and Social Support (availability of social support and stable
relationships), Mental Health-Related Issues (potential
psychiatric diagnoses), and Risk Factors (including socioeconomic
and demographic aspects). The risk levels are categorized as low
(indicating minimal perceived risk of suicide), moderate
(suggesting a tangible risk of a suicide attempt), and high
(implying a strong likelihood of a suicide attempt in the near
future). You will now analyze various texts and succinctly
summarize the evidence that substantiates the assigned risk level
for each case.<|im_end|>
<|im_start|>user
Risk level: high
Text: Recently, I attempted suicide by consuming an unspecified
amount of prescription medications. After realizing that the pills
were not lethal, I desperately prayed for an end to my suffering,
wishing to escape the torment inflicted by those who profess their
love yet demonstrate indifference through their actions. I am
prone to anxiety, and for the past two weeks, I've been coerced
into tolerating the intrusive presence of my housemate's
girlfriend. Despite my patience, my attempt to diplomatically
express the need for boundaries was met with coercion,
exacerbating my sense of violation.<|im_end|>
<|im_start|>assistant
This person is at high risk because they describe a recent suicide
attempt. They express a wish to be dead, extreme hopelessness, and
a sense of feeling trapped. Their overall tone is aroused and
agitated. They feel disconnected from others, and bullied by
others. They experience extreme anxiety.<|im_end|>
<|im_start|>user
Risk level: risk_level
Text: user_comments<|im_end|>
<|im_start|>assistant
This person is at risk_level risk.
```

Incorporating Word Count Information into Depression Risk Summary Generation: INF@UoS CLPsych 2024 Submission

Judita Preiss and **Zenan Chen**
University of Sheffield, Information School
The Wave, 2 Whitham Rd, Sheffield S10 2SJ, United Kingdom
judita.preiss@sheffield.ac.uk and zchen249@sheffield.ac.uk

Abstract

Large language model classifiers do not directly offer transparency: it is not clear why one class is chosen over another. In this work, summaries explaining the suicide risk level assigned using a fine-tuned `mental-roberta-base` model are generated from key phrases extracted using SHAP explainability using Mistral-7B. The training data for the classifier consists of all Reddit posts of a user in the University of Maryland Reddit Suicidality Dataset, Version 2, with their suicide risk labels along with selected features extracted from each post by the Linguistic Inquiry and Word Count (LIWC-22) tool. The resulting model is used to make predictions regarding risk on each post of the users in the evaluation set of the CLPsych 2024 shared task, with a SHAP explainer used to identify the phrases contributing to the top scoring, correct and severe risk categories. Some basic stoplisting is applied to the extracted phrases, along with length based filtering, and a locally run version of Mistral-7B-Instruct-v0.1 is used to create summaries from the highest value (based on SHAP) phrases.

1 Introduction

With the ability to use large language models (LLMs) to classify people's suicide risk level comes the need for transparency: artificial intelligence (AI) has been known to learn incorrect patterns and make incorrect generalizations (Narla et al., 2018). To this end, especially in a sensitive domain such as mental health, insight into the reasons for the prediction made is required to allow an expert to look through the output and correct it as needed. In this work, we employ SHAP values to extract phrases contributing to the LLM's decision regarding suicide level risk which we further summarize using locally run generative AI to offer an explanation for the suicide risk level assigned.

The CLPsych 2024 shared task (Chim et al., 2024) explores the use of LLMs in order to find evidence within text supporting an assigned suicide risk level. The University of Maryland Reddit Suicidality Dataset version 2 dataset, which was made available to participants, contains user-linked posts from Reddit annotated for level of suicide risk labelled on a four point scale (no risk, low, moderate, and severe risk) as described in (Shing et al., 2018) and (Zirikly et al., 2019). The evidence supporting the risk level could be supplied in one of two ways:

1. By highlighting the relevant portions of posts.
2. By summarizing the evidence into a short explanation.

For the first task, we fine-tune a pre-trained Reddit based mental health model for suicide risk level classification and extract SHAP value based phrases which represent the highest contributors to the decision. For the second task, a subset of the phrases extracted from the first task is used as part of a prompt to a generative AI algorithm which is instructed to produce a summary focusing on the aspects highlighted in the task definition, namely: emotions, cognitions, behaviour and motivation, interpersonal and social support, mental health related issues and additional risk factors.

2 Related work

The approach is composed of two distinct phases: (1) fine-tuning of a suicide risk classifier, and (2) generation of a summary. The work also explores the integration of additional psycholinguistic based information and transparency via explainability.

2.1 Detection of mental health state

Online social media is increasingly used by users to share a variety of user-generated or user-curated information, including publishing of personal status updates and engaging in topic-specific channels (Wongkoblap et al., 2017). Language use

Proceedings of the 9th Workshop on Computational Linguistics and Clinical Psychology (CLPsych 2024), pages 211–217
March 21, 2024

has been shown to change depending on a person's mental health state (Coppersmith et al., 2015), fuelling the creation of classifiers based on social media posts with Reddit forming a frequently used resource due to the presence of topic-specific channels, subreddits, such as r/SuicideWatch, r/depression.

Increased prediction performance has been observed when language models (LMs) used targetted texts in training, for example PsychBERT, a specialized BERT model trained on PubMed papers in the domain of psychology, psychiatry, mental health, and behavioral health and social media conversations about mental health (Vajre et al., 2021), or MentalBERT and MentalRoBERTa, which trained BERT and RoBERTa models respectively based on data from social forums for mental health discussion (Ji et al., 2022). The models were fine-tuned for classification of a number of mental health conditions and evaluated on standard datasets, and therefore lend themselves to fine-tuning for suicide risk level classification.

2.2 Generative AI system

Generative AI is frequently used in chatbots, where an AI system is generating its own, new, responses to hold a conversation with a human participant. The knowledge they hold stems from the wide variety of training data used to create such models; non-open-source models, such as GPT-4 (OpenAI et al., 2023) or PaLM (Chowdhery et al., 2022), do not share exact details of their training data or their architectures, however open source models, such as LLaMA-2 (Touvron et al., 2023) or Mistral (Jiang et al., 2023) can be deployed in local environments, enabling customisation with particular datasets while preserving data privacy. Their suitability for the mental health domain can be observed, for example, in the number of mental-health chatbot apps (Haque and Rubya, 2023).

2.3 Linguistic Inquiry Word Count

Linguistic Inquiry Word Count (LIWC) is a computing software used to extract features for mental health studies (Pennebaker and King, 1999). It has been used widely in research related to mental health condition identification. Chen et al. (2018) trained a log-linear classier, using LIWC as one of the feature sets to detect mental issues, while Sekulic et al. (2018) used LIWC features to predict bipolar disorder. In the social media domain, Coppersmith et al. (2015) extracted LIWC features from Twitter data to examine various mental health conditions.

2.4 Transparency of LMs

Surrogate models, such as LIME (Ribeiro et al., 2016) and SHAP (Lundberg and Lee, 2017), tweak a model's input slightly to explore the change in prediction. This enables them to highlight words / phrases which are particularly significant to a specific decision within a black box model such as a LM, with SHAP enabling straightforward extraction of important phrases from multi-class text based classifiers.

3 Method

The creation of short summaries describing the mental health state and depression risk of users is of a two step design: (1) a deep learning classifier is built for risk level prediction, which provides access to important phrases in each post, and (b) a subset of such phrases is summarized by a generative AI system.

3.1 Classification of suicide risk level

The provided data contains an expert assigned suicide risk level alongside numerous Reddit posts made by these users. The posts span a relatively short time frame, with the earliest posts in the data from 2015-09-01 and the latest 2016-01-29. While a person's mental health state may change over time, we make the assumption that over the time period covered by the data, their mental health state, and specifically their suicide risk level, has not changed. Therefore, each post made by the user is assigned the same risk level label. The data is balanced and a stratified 70 / 30 split is created to yield training and evaluation datasets: the data is only stratified by risk level, not user, as (a) individual posts of a user are not linked, and (b) the ultimate goal is not risk level prediction. Each post is converted to a single text, by concatenating the title and body as follows: *Title: ... Body: ...*

The classifier is built by fine-tuning `mental/mental-roberta-base`, a moderately-sized pre-trained language model which has been trained using mental health-related posts on top of RoBERTa-Base (cased_L-12_H-768_A-12) (Ji et al., 2022). Early stopping is applied, which allows (limited) exploration of hyperparameters, specifically the learning rate, as well as the (best portion of) input data.

LIWC	Description
affiliation	Desire for connection
allnone	Certainty
tone_neg	Negative tone
emotion	Emotion
emo_neg	Negative emotion
emo_sad	Sadness emotion
mental	Mental health behaviour
allure	Persuasiveness
feeling	Feeling

Table 1: Selected LIWC features with description

3.1.1 Inclusion of LIWC information

LIWC-22 (Boyd et al., 2022) is used to extract additional information from each post. The most informative of these features (see below) are integrated into the training phase of the classifier. LIWC uses word counting to determine the percentage of words indicative of specific psychological constructs or categories within a text. The words of interest (such as personal pronouns) are based on internal dictionaries, with LIWC-22's dictionary containing over over 12,000 words associated with the selected psychologically relevant categories, resulting in values for 119 different features output for each post.

Many of the features are relatively sparse for the current dataset, enabling feature reduction to be performed. Standard statistics of each feature were explored, as were correlations with risk categories. Statistical information was extracted from data constrained to specific risk categories: i.e. all posts of a user were assigned the user's risk category, and the mean value of each LIWC feature was computed. Features with a monotonically increasing mean across risk categories were included in the final selection shown in Table 1; the description was used to construct a phrase which was prepended to the post information. Since LMs do not interpret numbers well, values below a feature's mean were converted to *low* and above the mean were considered *high*. Thus a post with the title *"I feel sad"* and body *"It's that time of year"* with an associated LIWC score of 0.3 for the *emo_sad* feature (which has a mean of 0.12) becomes: *High emotional sadness. Title: I feel sad. Body: It's that time of year.* This augmented input is used to train a suicide risk classifier as described in Section 3.1.

3.1.2 Extraction of important phrases

SHAP values are a game theory based approach to gaining insights into the predictions made by machine learning by producing an explanation based on feature contributions towards the final decision (Lundberg and Lee, 2017). The approach is model agnostic and can be applied to all machine learning models including neural networks. For a multiclass problem, such as suicide risk classification, the partition explainer can be used to compute the SHAP values for each text. These values explain the impact of unmasking each word to the final prediction (see official SHAP example in Figure 1 from `https://shap.readthedocs.io`).

For a given user, phrases highlighted by SHAP as contributing to the highest suicide risk prediction were extracted from each post in the r/SuicideWatch subreddit.[1] Words between selected phrases were added if their contribution was low to other classes, increasing the quantity of continuous text. I.e. for the example shown in Figure 1, *feeling* and *hopeless* would be extracted initially and *so* would be added to produce the highlighted phrase *feeling so hopeless*. Any phrases consisting of at most a single content word alongside 0 or more (nltk) stoplist words are removed.

3.2 Generation of summary

Locally run generative AI was explored for the purpose of building a summary based on the important phrases extracted in Section 3.1.2. For each user, the phrases were ordered by decreasing length and the longest phrases were retained until a pre-specified length limit was reached. A number of prompts was explored with the `meta-llama/Llama-2-13b-chat-hf` model (Touvron et al., 2023), however, the model was found to be hard to (a) restrict to a specific maximum length, and (b) stop from deteriorating into a more social media style. The `mistralai/Mistral-7B-Instruct-v0.1` model (Jiang et al., 2023), which uses sliding-window attention, did not suffer from the same problems. The instruction given to the model was

> Summarize the (1) emotions, (2) cognitions, (3) social support, (4) mental health issues and (5) conceptual risk factors (one average length sentence for

[1] Note that posts were uniformly shortened for the explainer until post length matched the explainer's expectations – for the majority of posts, this corresponded to 512 tokens.

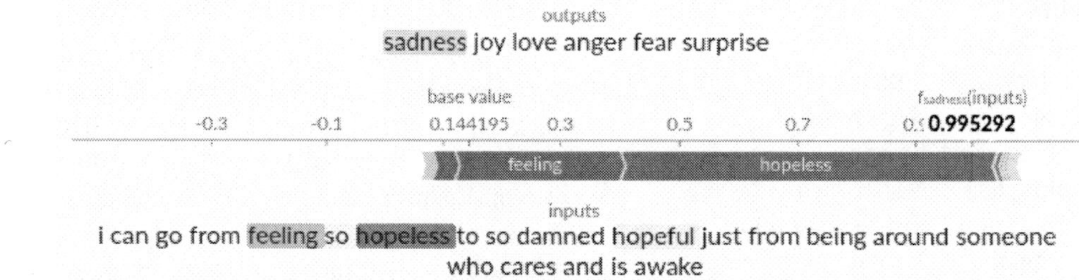

Figure 1: Example showing contributions of words towards final prediction of emotion (example from `https://shap.readthedocs.io`, not CLPsych dataset)

> each of the five factors) indicating depressed or suicidal thoughts in following phrases:

followed by the subset of phrases identified above. The prompt may be considered relatively complex, however prompts such as *Generate a 250 word summary based on the following excerpts explaining why the following phrases may indicate depressed or suicidal thought:* frequently failed to address one or more of the requested five aspects. Since no data was available for optimization, the model was used with its default parameter values.

4 Results and discussion

Optimization, with early stopping, was performed over learning rate, the quantity of data used in training and inclusion or exclusion of LIWC information. The training data was balanced and the best performing model, at 51% (over a balanced evaluation dataset which included all 4 classes), was found to be using expert data only with LIWC information included with a learning rate of $2 - e6$.

The pipeline, starting from risk level classification, through extraction of important phrases and ending with summary generation, was run for all 125 users in the evaluation set. While important phrases were extracted from all posts, only the highlights that were used in summary generation were submitted, alongside summaries, resulting in some submissions having empty highlights for specific posts (but having a non empty summary, as this was generated from posts which were deemed more informative). Fourteen users were therefore submitted with empty highlights for at least one post (21 posts, out of 166 posts, in total): this affects the overall metrics for the system shown in Table 2. When computed only over the 111 users with a submitted set of complete highlights, the recall increases to 0.958.[2] Interestingly, mean consistency is identical (to 2 d.p.) for users where posts other than those in the test set were used to summarize evidence (i.e. users with empty highlights). To reiterate, empty highlights forming part of the submission do not mean that SHAP failed to extract important phrases from the appropriate post, only that other posts by the same author were selected for summary generation – extracted SHAP phrases were not submitted if they were not used for evidence generation.

	Recall	HM	Mean consistency
Value	0.850	0.896	0.934

Table 2: Results of the INF@UoS system

After the competition, manual analysis was performed of the summarized evidence and the extracted highlights. Note that the official summaries and highlights were not released, so the results presented are only our judgements. The evaluation set contained 125 users: 39% of the submitted summaries were complete sentences summarizing the requested aspects of its inputs, 39% were also good summaries, but rather than sentences, they consisted of lists (such as "Emotions: hopelessness, loneliness"). 4% answered each point with an exact quote from the SHAP phrases and 8% were a mix of quotes from posts and generated text. Also relevant were 3% of summaries which in addition contained information which wasn't linked to the required points – such as a basic sentence containing only the person's age (e.g. "They are 30 years old."). The remaining summaries were either partial (2%), or probably too general, appearing to outline importance of the various aspects for suicide risk evaluation. Only one summary was nonsensi-

[2]Note that this is not comparable to the overall results for other teams.

cal and all summaries were within the permitted length, with a mean of 85 words.

Since the summarized evidence is generated from SHAP extracted phrases, 25% of these (136 highlights) were also manually explored. While 88% appeared OK (in this we include highlights which were not clearly supporting suicide risk judgement alone, but they complemented other selected highlights), a large portion contained fragments within the highlight: such as portions of a previous or following sentence, or ending at a point where is was clear how the fragment continued but with the end missing (e.g. "... one way or"). Some fragment highlights were also not entire sentences from the original post, but they were a self contained sentence. The remaining sources of error were either fragments that were too short to carry enough meaning (5%), fragments that - due to their selection - were inconsistent (1%), and highlights which didn't appear pertinent to the assessment of someone's risk of suicide (6%).

5 Conclusion and future work

We have shown the utility of SHAP explainability for the extraction of important phrases from text for the purpose of transparency within a text based suicide risk level classifier. Mistral 7B performs well for summary generation in this domain, retaining text integrity and producing minimal hallucinations.

Further investigations are required as to the contribution of the LIWC tool to the changes of SHAP extracted phrases, alongside a comparison with a one step (rather than the two step, SHAP + Mistral) summary generation process. Ablation tests evaluating changes to each step of the pipeline would also bring more insights.

In future work, the quality of highlights selected by SHAP could be improved by ensuring complete sentences surrounding the highlight are extracted.

6 Limitations

Some assumptions are made in this work, resulting in a number of limitations. We assume that the user's mental health state has not changed over the period of time the posts are from. While the period from which the posts were gathered was deemed short, this may not always hold. In addition, all posts of a user were included in training, including posts from subreddits other than r/SuicideWatch. It is unclear whether the variability in length as well as topic and emphasis may not be affecting the performance of the resulting classifier. Currently, the length of posts is limited to the max length of the model; recent models (such as MentalXLNet and MentalLongformer (Ji et al., 2023)), which allow longer contexts should be explored.

The integration of LIWC data is not optimized: large language models are not designed for interpreting numeric content, and the integration of an approach capable of understanding numeric values may result in better classifier results. The SHAP values produced highlight correlations between features (words) and the classification category. However, individual behaviours may be different, and a feature which is indicative of a low risk with other person may not be so with another.

Lastly, using generative AI in a sensitive domain is risky due to its ability to hallucinate.

7 Ethics

Secure access to the shared task dataset was provided with the task's approval under University of Maryland, College Park and approval by the University of Sheffield Information School Ethics Committee (ethical application reference 058377).

Acknowledgements

We would like to acknowledge the assistance of the American Association of Suicidology in making the dataset available.

References

Ryan L. Boyd, Ashwini Ashokkumar, Sarah Seraj, and James W. Pennebaker. 2022. The development and psychometric properties of LIWC-22. Technical report, Austin, TX: University of Texas at Austin.

Xuetong Chen, Martin Sykora, Thomas Jackson, Suzanne Elayan, and Fehmidah Munir. 2018. Tweeting your mental health: An exploration of different classifiers and features with emotional signals in identifying mental health conditions. In *Proceedings of the 51st Hawaii International Conference on System Sciences*. Hawaii International Conference on System Sciences.

Jenny Chim, Adam Tsakalidis, Dimitris Gkoumas, Dana Atzil-Slonim, Yaakov Ophir, Ayah Zirikly, Philip Resnik, and Maria Liakata. 2024. Overview of the clpsych 2024 task: Leveraging large language models to identify evidence of suicidality risk in online posts. In *Proceedings of the Ninth Workshop on Computational Linguistics and Clinical Psychology*. Association for Computational Linguistics.

Aakanksha Chowdhery, Sharan Narang, Jacob Devlin, Maarten Bosma, Gaurav Mishra, Adam Roberts, Paul Barham, Hyung Won Chung, Charles Sutton, Sebastian Gehrmann, Parker Schuh, Kensen Shi, Sasha Tsvyashchenko, Joshua Maynez, Abhishek Rao, Parker Barnes, Yi Tay, Noam Shazeer, Vinodkumar Prabhakaran, Emily Reif, Nan Du, Ben Hutchinson, Reiner Pope, James Bradbury, Jacob Austin, Michael Isard, Guy Gur-Ari, Pengcheng Yin, Toju Duke, Anselm Levskaya, Sanjay Ghemawat, Sunipa Dev, Henryk Michalewski, Xavier Garcia, Vedant Misra, Kevin Robinson, Liam Fedus, Denny Zhou, Daphne Ippolito, David Luan, Hyeontaek Lim, Barret Zoph, Alexander Spiridonov, Ryan Sepassi, David Dohan, Shivani Agrawal, Mark Omernick, Andrew M Dai, Thanumalayan Sankaranarayana Pillai, Marie Pellat, Aitor Lewkowycz, Erica Moreira, Rewon Child, Oleksandr Polozov, Katherine Lee, Zongwei Zhou, Xuezhi Wang, Brennan Saeta, Mark Diaz, Orhan Firat, Michele Catasta, Jason Wei, Kathy Meier-Hellstern, Douglas Eck, Jeff Dean, Slav Petrov, and Noah Fiedel. 2022. PaLM: Scaling language modeling with pathways.

Glen Coppersmith, Mark Dredze, Craig Harman, and Kristy Hollingshead. 2015. From ADHD to SAD: Analyzing the language of mental health on Twitter through self-reported diagnoses. In *Proceedings of the 2nd Workshop on Computational Linguistics and Clinical Psychology: From Linguistic Signal to Clinical Reality*, Stroudsburg, PA, USA. Association for Computational Linguistics.

M D Romael Haque and Sabirat Rubya. 2023. An overview of chatbot-based mobile mental health apps: Insights from app description and user reviews. *JMIR Mhealth Uhealth*, 11:e44838.

Shaoxiong Ji, Tianlin Zhang, Luna Ansari, Jie Fu, Prayag Tiwari, and Erik Cambria. 2022. MentalBERT: Publicly Available Pretrained Language Models for Mental Healthcare. In *Proceedings of LREC*.

Shaoxiong Ji, Tianlin Zhang, Kailai Yang, Sophia Ananiadou, Erik Cambria, and Jörg Tiedemann. 2023. Domain-specific continued pretraining of language models for capturing long context in mental health.

Albert Q. Jiang, Alexandre Sablayrolles, Arthur Mensch, Chris Bamford, Devendra Singh Chaplot, Diego de las Casas, Florian Bressand, Gianna Lengyel, Guillaume Lample, Lucile Saulnier, Lélio Renard Lavaud, Marie-Anne Lachaux, Pierre Stock, Teven Le Scao, Thibaut Lavril, Thomas Wang, Timothée Lacroix, and William El Sayed. 2023. Mistral 7b.

Scott M Lundberg and Su-In Lee. 2017. A unified approach to interpreting model predictions. In *Advances in Neural Information Processing Systems*, volume 30. Curran Associates, Inc.

Akhila Narla, Brett Kuprel, Kavita Sarin, Roberto Novoa, and Justin Ko. 2018. Automated classification of skin lesions: From pixels to practice. *Journal of Investigative Dermatology*, 138(10):2108–2110.

OpenAI, :, Josh Achiam, Steven Adler, Sandhini Agarwal, Lama Ahmad, Ilge Akkaya, Florencia Leoni Aleman, Diogo Almeida, Janko Altenschmidt, Sam Altman, Shyamal Anadkat, Red Avila, Igor Babuschkin, Suchir Balaji, Valerie Balcom, Paul Baltescu, Haiming Bao, Mo Bavarian, Jeff Belgum, Irwan Bello, Jake Berdine, Gabriel Bernadett-Shapiro, Christopher Berner, Lenny Bogdonoff, Oleg Boiko, Madelaine Boyd, Anna-Luisa Brakman, Greg Brockman, Tim Brooks, Miles Brundage, Kevin Button, Trevor Cai, Rosie Campbell, Andrew Cann, Brittany Carey, Chelsea Carlson, Rory Carmichael, Brooke Chan, Che Chang, Fotis Chantzis, Derek Chen, Sully Chen, Ruby Chen, Jason Chen, Mark Chen, Ben Chess, Chester Cho, Casey Chu, Hyung Won Chung, Dave Cummings, Jeremiah Currier, Yunxing Dai, Cory Decareaux, Thomas Degry, Noah Deutsch, Damien Deville, Arka Dhar, David Dohan, Steve Dowling, Sheila Dunning, Adrien Ecoffet, Atty Eleti, Tyna Eloundou, David Farhi, Liam Fedus, Niko Felix, Simón Posada Fishman, Juston Forte, Isabella Fulford, Leo Gao, Elie Georges, Christian Gibson, Vik Goel, Tarun Gogineni, Gabriel Goh, Rapha Gontijo-Lopes, Jonathan Gordon, Morgan Grafstein, Scott Gray, Ryan Greene, Joshua Gross, Shixiang Shane Gu, Yufei Guo, Chris Hallacy, Jesse Han, Jeff Harris, Yuchen He, Mike Heaton, Johannes Heidecke, Chris Hesse, Alan Hickey, Wade Hickey, Peter Hoeschele, Brandon Houghton, Kenny Hsu, Shengli Hu, Xin Hu, Joost Huizinga, Shantanu Jain, Shawn Jain, Joanne Jang, Angela Jiang, Roger Jiang, Haozhun Jin, Denny Jin, Shino Jomoto, Billie Jonn, Heewoo Jun, Tomer Kaftan, Łukasz Kaiser, Ali Kamali, Ingmar Kanitscheider, Nitish Shirish Keskar, Tabarak Khan, Logan Kilpatrick, Jong Wook Kim, Christina Kim, Yongjik Kim, Hendrik Kirchner, Jamie Kiros, Matt Knight, Daniel Kokotajlo, Łukasz Kondraciuk, Andrew Kondrich, Aris Konstantinidis, Kyle Kosic, Gretchen Krueger, Vishal Kuo, Michael Lampe, Ikai Lan, Teddy Lee, Jan Leike, Jade Leung, Daniel Levy, Chak Ming Li, Rachel Lim, Molly Lin, Stephanie Lin, Mateusz Litwin, Theresa Lopez, Ryan Lowe, Patricia Lue, Anna Makanju, Kim Malfacini, Sam Manning, Todor Markov, Yaniv Markovski, Bianca Martin, Katie Mayer, Andrew Mayne, Bob McGrew, Scott Mayer McKinney, Christine McLeavey, Paul McMillan, Jake McNeil, David Medina, Aalok Mehta, Jacob Menick, Luke Metz, Andrey Mishchenko, Pamela Mishkin, Vinnie Monaco, Evan Morikawa, Daniel Mossing, Tong Mu, Mira Murati, Oleg Murk, David Mély, Ashvin Nair, Reiichiro Nakano, Rajeev Nayak, Arvind Neelakantan, Richard Ngo, Hyeonwoo Noh, Long Ouyang, Cullen O'Keefe, Jakub Pachocki, Alex Paino, Joe Palermo, Ashley Pantuliano, Giambattista Parascandolo, Joel Parish, Emy Parparita, Alex Passos, Mikhail Pavlov, Andrew Peng, Adam Perelman, Filipe de Avila Belbute Peres, Michael Petrov, Henrique Ponde de Oliveira Pinto, Michael, Pokorny, Michelle Pokrass, Vitchyr Pong, Tolly Powell, Alethea Power, Boris Power, Elizabeth Proehl, Raul Puri, Alec Radford, Jack Rae, Aditya Ramesh, Cameron Raymond, Francis Real, Kendra Rimbach, Carl Ross, Bob Rotsted, Henri Roussez, Nick Ryder, Mario Saltarelli, Ted Sanders, Shibani Santurkar, Girish Sastry, Heather Schmidt, David Schnurr, John Schulman, Daniel Selsam, Kyla Sheppard, Toki Sherbakov, Jessica Shieh, Sarah Shoker, Pranav Shyam, Szymon Sidor, Eric Sigler, Maddie Simens, Jordan Sitkin, Katarina Slama, Ian Sohl, Benjamin Sokolowsky, Yang Song, Natalie Staudacher, Felipe Petroski Such, Natalie Summers, Ilya Sutskever, Jie Tang, Nikolas Tezak, Madeleine Thompson, Phil Tillet, Amin Tootoonchian, Elizabeth Tseng, Preston Tuggle, Nick Turley, Jerry Tworek, Juan Felipe Cerón Uribe, Andrea Vallone, Arun Vijayvergiya, Chelsea Voss, Carroll Wainwright, Justin Jay Wang, Alvin Wang, Ben Wang, Jonathan Ward, Jason Wei, C J Weinmann, Akila Welihinda, Peter Welinder, Jiayi Weng, Lilian Weng, Matt Wiethoff, Dave Willner, Clemens Winter, Samuel Wolrich, Hannah Wong, Lauren Workman, Sherwin Wu, Jeff Wu, Michael Wu, Kai Xiao, Tao Xu, Sarah Yoo, Kevin Yu, Qiming Yuan, Wojciech Zaremba, Rowan Zellers, Chong Zhang, Marvin Zhang, Shengjia Zhao, Tianhao Zheng, Juntang Zhuang, William Zhuk, and Barret Zoph. 2023. GPT-4 technical report.

J W Pennebaker and L A King. 1999. Linguistic styles: language use as an individual difference. *J. Pers. Soc. Psychol.*, 77(6):1296–1312.

Marco Tulio Ribeiro, Sameer Singh, and Carlos Guestrin. 2016. "why should i trust you?": Explaining the predictions of any classifier. In *Proceedings of the 22nd ACM SIGKDD International Conference on Knowledge Discovery and Data Mining*, KDD '16, page 1135–1144, New York, NY, USA. Association for Computing Machinery.

Ivan Sekulic, Matej Gjurković, and Jan Šnajder. 2018. Not just depressed: Bipolar disorder prediction on reddit. In *Proceedings of the 9th Workshop on Computational Approaches to Subjectivity, Sentiment and Social Media Analysis*, Stroudsburg, PA, USA. Association for Computational Linguistics.

Han-Chin Shing, Suraj Nair, Ayah Zirikly, Meir Friedenberg, Hal Daumé III, and Philip Resnik. 2018. Expert, crowdsourced, and machine assessment of suicide risk via online postings. In *Proceedings of the Fifth Workshop on Computational Linguistics and Clinical Psychology: From Keyboard to Clinic*, pages 25–36, New Orleans, LA. Association for Computational Linguistics.

Hugo Touvron, Louis Martin, Kevin Stone, Peter Albert, Amjad Almahairi, Yasmine Babaei, Nikolay Bashlykov, Soumya Batra, Prajjwal Bhargava, Shruti Bhosale, Dan Bikel, Lukas Blecher, Cristian Canton Ferrer, Moya Chen, Guillem Cucurull, David Esiobu, Jude Fernandes, Jeremy Fu, Wenyin Fu, Brian Fuller, Cynthia Gao, Vedanuj Goswami, Naman Goyal, Anthony Hartshorn, Saghar Hosseini, Rui Hou, Hakan Inan, Marcin Kardas, Viktor Kerkez, Madian Khabsa, Isabel Kloumann, Artem Korenev, Punit Singh Koura, Marie-Anne Lachaux, Thibaut Lavril, Jenya Lee, Diana Liskovich, Yinghai Lu, Yuning Mao, Xavier Martinet, Todor Mihaylov, Pushkar Mishra, Igor Molybog, Yixin Nie, Andrew Poulton, Jeremy Reizenstein, Rashi Rungta, Kalyan Saladi, Alan Schelten, Ruan Silva, Eric Michael Smith, Ranjan Subramanian, Xiaoqing Ellen Tan, Binh Tang, Ross Taylor, Adina Williams, Jian Xiang Kuan, Puxin Xu, Zheng Yan, Iliyan Zarov, Yuchen Zhang, Angela Fan, Melanie Kambadur, Sharan Narang, Aurelien Rodriguez, Robert Stojnic, Sergey Edunov, and Thomas Scialom. 2023. Llama 2: Open foundation and fine-tuned chat models.

Vedant Vajre, Mitch Naylor, Uday Kamath, and Amarda Shehu. 2021. PsychBERT: A mental health language model for social media mental health behavioral analysis. In *2021 IEEE International Conference on Bioinformatics and Biomedicine (BIBM)*. IEEE.

Akkapon Wongkoblap, Miguel A Vadillo, and Vasa Curcin. 2017. Researching mental health disorders in the era of social media: Systematic review. *J. Med. Internet Res.*, 19(6):e228.

Ayah Zirikly, Philip Resnik, Özlem Uzuner, and Kristy Hollingshead. 2019. CLPsych 2019 task: Predicting the degree of suicide risk in Reddit posts. In *Proceedings of the Sixth Workshop on Computational Linguistics and Clinical Psychology*, pages 24–33, Minneapolis, Minnesota. Association for Computational Linguistics.

Extraction and Summarization of Suicidal Ideation Evidence in Social Media Content Using Large Language Models

Loitongbam Gyanendro Singh*, Junyu Mao*, Rudra Mutalik, Stuart E. Middleton
School of Electronics and Computer Science,
University of Southampton, Southampton, UK
{gyanendro.loitongbam, j.mao, rudra.mutalik, sem03}@soton.ac.uk

Abstract

This paper explores the use of Large Language Models (LLMs) in analyzing social media content for mental health monitoring, specifically focusing on detecting and summarizing evidence of suicidal ideation. We utilized LLMs *Mixtral7bx8* and *Tulu-2-DPO-70B*, applying diverse prompting strategies for effective content extraction and summarization. Our methodology included detailed analysis through Few-shot and Zero-shot learning, evaluating the ability of *Chain-of-Thought* and *Direct* prompting strategies. The study achieved notable success in the CLPsych 2024 shared task (ranked top for the evidence extraction task and second for the summarization task), demonstrating the potential of LLMs in mental health interventions and setting a precedent for future research in digital mental health monitoring.

1 Introduction

Large Language Models (LLMs) such as GPT (Generative Pre-trained Transformer) (Brown et al., 2020) have become cornerstones in the field of natural language processing domain. Their ability to process and generate human-like text, learned from extensive datasets, empowers them to recognize and interpret complex language patterns on various reasoning tasks, such as arithmetic, commonsense, and symbolic reasoning (Kojima et al., 2022; Wei et al., 2022). One of the critical abilities of LLMs is text span extraction from unstructured data, such as social media posts (e.g. Reddit, Twitter, Facebook, etc.) (Srivastava et al., 2023; Xu et al., 2023; Yang et al., 2023). This process involves identifying and extracting specific segments of text that contain relevant information or unique characteristics. In the mental health context, this capability becomes indispensable for spotting signs of mental illness, such as depression, anxiety, and particularly suicidal thoughts or tendencies in online conversations.

Given the increasing prevalence of mental health issues and the growing tendency of individuals to express their thoughts and emotions on social media platforms, accurately recognizing signs of suicidal ideation and other mental health concerns from individual posts shared online becomes imperative (Singh et al., 2024; Azim et al., 2022). Since LLMs can process and interpret such complex language patterns, they are essential for identifying early signs of mental health concerns, including suicidal ideation, and thus play a crucial role in mental health interventions (Xu et al., 2023; Yang et al., 2023).

Addressing the need for effective mental health monitoring on social media, this study attempts to make the best use of LLMs to scrutinize user-generated content focusing specifically on identifying and summarizing potential indicators of suicidal ideation. We employ two LLMs, *Mixtral7bx8* (Jiang et al., 2024) and *Tulu-2-DPO-70B* (Ivison et al., 2023), utilizing diverse prompting strategies to extract and summarize the text that signifies suicidal thoughts, thereby gaining insights into users' mental states. Our team (UoS_NLP) participated in the CLPsych 2024 shared task (Chim et al., 2024), where we excelled, securing first place in the evidence extraction task with an F1 score of 0.929 and second in the summarization task with a mean consistency score of 0.977. Our methodology encompassed in-depth post-by-post analysis, incorporating both Few-shot (Wei et al., 2022; Zhang et al., 2022) and Zero-shot (Kojima et al., 2022; Wei et al., 2021) learning techniques, and further evaluate the ability of *Chain-of-Thought* and *Direct* prompting strategies (Kojima et al., 2022; Zhang et al., 2022). For the summarization aspect, we adopted a Zero-shot approach, exploring the impact of including meta-information such as sentiments and user suicide risk labels in the prompts and showcasing the potent application of LLMs in mental health analysis and intervention.

*Equal contributions.

Proceedings of the 9th Workshop on Computational Linguistics and Clinical Psychology (CLPsych 2024), pages 218–226
March 21, 2024

Instruction prompt	As a mental health assistant, your task is to [TASK] directly from the provided input text to highlight the mental health issues. For the [TASK] task, consider the following aspects: • **Emotions**: Evaluate expressed emotions, from sadness to intense psychological pain, as they may influence the assigned risk level. • **Cognitions**: Explore the individual's thoughts and perceptions about suicide, including the level and frequency of suicidal thoughts, intentions of suicide, and any existing plans. • **Behavior and Motivation**: Evaluate the user's actions related to suicide, such as access to means and concrete plans. Consider their ability to handle difficult/stressful situations and the motivations behind their desire to die. • **Interpersonal and Social Support**: Investigate the individual's social support or stable relationships, and understand their feelings toward significant others. • **Mental Health-Related Issues**: Consider psychiatric diagnoses associated with suicide such as schizophrenia, bipolar, anxiety, eating disorder, previous suicidal attempts, and others. • **Additional Risk Factors**: Consider other factors like socioeconomic and demographic factors, exposure to suicide behavior by others, chronic medical conditions, etc.
Meta-information	The opinion holder has an indication of [Risk] suicidal risk, with probable [Emotion] emotion and [Sentiment] sentiment.
Input	[USER POST]
Output	[TASK OUTPUT]

Table 1: Instruction prompt for Mental Health Analysis Task Using Large Language Models (LLMs). The [TASK] placeholder is adapted based on whether the focus is on evidence extraction or summarization. The [TASK OUTPUT] is considered for the *Few-shot* prompting strategy.

The rest of the paper is organized as follows: Section 2 provides an overview of the shared task. Section 3 discusses the experiment designs. Section 4 presents the results and discussion, and finally, the study concludes in Section 5.

2 CLPsych 2024 Shared Task and Dataset

The CLPsych 2024 Shared Task (Chim et al., 2024) centers on employing Large Language Models (LLMs) to identify supporting evidence of an individual's suicide risk level from their social media posts. The challenge requires using an LLM to extract and coherently present evidence from posts that align with the pre-assigned risk levels of low, moderate, or severe suicide risk(Zirikly et al., 2019). This task aims to utilize the generative capabilities of LLMs in producing supportive evidence for clinical assessments.

For this shared task, we were provided UMD Suicidality Dataset (Shing et al., 2018; Zirikly et al., 2019). This dataset includes social media posts from users on the Reddit platform, specifically from the r/SuicideWatch subreddit. These posts have been annotated with suicide risk levels by experts and crowdsource workers, categorizing them into no, low, moderate, or severe risk. Participants are tasked with using LLMs to identify and extract text spans from these posts that support the assigned risk levels. This dataset provides a unique opportunity to explore the application of LLMs in mental health analysis, particularly in assessing and understanding suicide risk from online interactions.

3 Prompting Strategies

In this section, we explore various prompting strategies for text span extraction and summarization in the realm of mental health analysis, utilizing Large Language Models (LLMs). Focusing specifically on two LLMs, *Mixtral7bx8* (Jiang et al., 2024) and *Tulu-2-DPO-70B* (Ivison et al., 2023), this part of the study examines how diverse prompting techniques can enhance the extraction and summarization of relevant information from large datasets in the context of mental health.

3.1 Zero-shot Prompting

This approach utilizes the inherent knowledge of the LLMs without relying on task-specific training. We assess its effectiveness by providing the LLMs with carefully crafted instruction prompts that include the context of the task. Table 1 presents the instruction prompt used for this study. The aim is to guide the LLMs to concentrate on six crucial aspects when identifying text spans related to suicide risk: Emotions, Cognitions, Behavior and Motivation, Interpersonal and Social Support,

Mental Health-Related Issues, and Additional Risk Factors. The instruction is designed to guide the LLMs in utilizing their pre-trained knowledge to identify key text spans that may indicate mental health issues. By giving precise and contextualized prompts, we aim to measure the inherent capabilities of the LLMs in extracting meaningful information without additional training or examples.

3.2 Few-Shot Prompting

To enhance the understanding of Large Language Models (LLMs) beyond Zero-shot prompting, this approach incorporates context examples (referred to as demonstrations), enabling the use of few-shot prompting for *In-Context Learning* (ICL). We integrate *k*-number of input-output pairs with the instruction prompts in Table 1 for effective ICL. Our methodology involves selecting posts that display a range of sentiments, emotions, and levels of user-suicidal risk for annotation, ensuring a comprehensive coverage of contexts for ICL. This selection aids the LLMs in gaining a deeper grasp of the task.

For the preparation of ICL, we utilize Sentence-BERT (Thakur et al., 2021) and pre-trained RoBERTa-base models (Barbieri et al., 2020) to represent user posts in a vector space, incorporating semantic, emotional, and sentiment dimensions. These post representations are then categorized into eight clusters via K-means clustering[1]. In each cluster, the top three posts nearest to the centroid are identified for further analysis. These posts are manually reviewed to determine the user's suicidal risk levels, and three are manually selected for the annotation process in ICL. Our study considers two prompting strategies for ICL: *Direct Prompting* and *Chain-of-Thoughts Prompting*, to evaluate their effectiveness in this context.

3.2.1 Direct Prompting

In *Direct Prompting* strategy, the focus is on presenting clear, explicit instructions or queries that directly correspond with the text span extraction task. This method hinges on the clarity of the prompt to effectively guide the model's response. Additionally, we incorporate few-shot demonstrations within these prompts. These examples are intended to provide more context, thereby enhancing the LLM's ability to discern and extract the relevant text spans accurately. An example of a direct prompting instruction template with input and output is shown in Appendix Table 4.

3.2.2 Chain-of-Thought Prompting

In the *Chain-of-Thoughts Prompting* (CoT) strategy, we direct LLMs through a step-by-step logical reasoning process, thereby enhancing their ability to handle complex tasks. This method involves designing prompts that not only present a problem but also guide the model in a structured thought process towards a solution, exemplified by the phrase *"Let's think step by step"*. The goal is to encourage the LLMs to effectively identify text spans that are relevant to critical aspects such as Emotions, Cognitions, Behavior and Motivation, Interpersonal and Social Support, Mental Health-Related Issues, and Additional Risk Factors. It is important to note that some text spans might be relevant to multiple aspects. For example, the phrase *"I just want to die"* could be indicative of both an emotional state and a cognitive condition. In these instances, we carefully avoid redundant text spans in our final extraction task to maintain a clear and focused representation of each aspect. An example of a CoT template with one demonstration example is shown in Appendix Table 5.

By implementing these prompting strategies, we aim to harness the full potential of LLMs in the domain of text span extraction, addressing both simple and complex extraction requirements with high precision and contextual relevance.

4 Result analysis

In this section, we conduct a comprehensive analysis comparing Zero-shot and few-shot prompting strategies, assessing their effectiveness in enabling in-context learning for text span extraction tasks. Additionally, we examine the performance of direct prompting and chain-of-thought prompting strategies, highlighting their impact on precision and coherence in text span extraction. We also investigate how the inclusion of meta-information such as sentiment, emotion, and suicide risk levels influences the LLMs' ability to identify and summarize mental health-related content. This evaluation provides insights into the strengths and weaknesses of these strategies in the evidence extraction and summarization tasks. Table 2 and 3 showcase the performance of our LLMs in the evidence extraction and summarization tasks, along with the top-ranked competitors from the shared task.

[1] https://en.wikipedia.org/wiki/K-means_clustering

LLMs	Prompt Strategies	Evidences extraction task			
		Recall	Precision	W-Recall	F1-score
Mixtral7bx8	0-shot	0.914	0.911	0.675	0.912
Mixtral7bx8	Direct	0.914	0.907	0.651	0.910
Tulu-2-DPO-70B	CoT	**0.943**	0.916	0.527	**0.929**
BERT-finetuned	–	**0.944**	0.906	0.489	0.924

Table 2: Performance Comparison of Large Language Models (LLMs) in Evidence Extraction Task using various prompting strategies. *sophiaADS* is noted as the top competitor against our models in the evidence extraction task.

LLMs	Include Meta information?	Evidences summarization	
		Mean Consistency	Max Contradict
Mixtral7bx8	–	0.951	0.127
Mixtral7bx8	✓	**0.977**	**0.079**
Tulu-2-DPO-70B	✓	0.966	0.107
mistral-7b-instruct-v0.2	–	**0.979**	**0.064**

Table 3: Performance Comparison of Large Language Models (LLMs) in Evidence Summarization Tasks Using Zero-Shot Prompting, with and without Meta-Information. ✓indicates the inclusion of meta-information like sentiments and suicide risk labels in the prompts. *UZH_CLyp* is noted as the top competitor against our model in the summarization task.

4.1 Evidence extraction task

In the evidence extraction task, the *Mixtral7bx8* model shows no significant difference between its Few-Shot (Direct) and Zero-shot prompting strategies, with both achieving a recall and F1-score of 0.914 and 0.912, respectively shown in Table 2. This suggests that the model's performance in identifying relevant textual evidence does not depend on the additional context provided by a Few-Shot approach. On the other hand, the *Tulu-2-DPO-70B* model benefits from a Few-Shot (CoT) strategy, leading to the highest recall of 0.943 and F1-score of 0.929 among the listed approaches, indicating that the Chain-of-Thought prompting substantially enhances its evidence extraction capabilities. This is expected as *Tulu-2-DPO-70B* is an instruction-tuned model that incorporates chain-of-thought data within its training mixture dataset, endowing it with robust reasoning abilities. While the BERT-finetuning model by *sophiaADS* (Tanaka and Fukazawa, 2024), a competitor in this evidence extraction task, marginally surpasses the *Tulu-2-DPO-70B* in recall. However, the *Tulu-2-DPO-70B* model achieves a higher F1 score. This superior F1 score indicates a more optimal balance between precision and recall, underscoring the *Tulu-2-DPO-70B* model's enhanced effectiveness in evidence extraction when compared to its competitor.

4.2 Evidence summarization task

For the evidence summarization task, we utilized a Zero-shot prompting strategy with a focus on incorporating specific types of meta-information: emotion, sentiment, and user risk label, derived from multiple posts of a user, as outlined in Appendix Table 6. This process involved aggregating all posts from a single user, analyzing the emotion and sentiment for each post, and then selecting the most prevalent emotion and sentiment to represent the overall state of the user. The user risk label was determined based on an assessment of all the user's posts. Table 3 presents the effectiveness of LLMs using Zero-shot strategies both with and without this meta-information. Notably, the *Mixtral7bx8* model incorporating meta-information attains a high mean consistency score of 0.977, indicating its strong capability in generating accurate and coherent summaries aligned with the extracted evidence. This underscores the effectiveness of Zero-shot strategies in mental health analysis on social media. Notably, the *mistral-7b-instruct-v0.2* used by *UZH_CLyp* (Uluslu et al., 2024), as our top competitor in the shared task, slightly outperforms the *Mixtral7bx8* model with meta-information in terms of mean consistency, highlighting their marginally superior summarization reliability.

5 Conclusion

This study demonstrates the significant potential of Large Language Models (LLMs) in mental health analysis, particularly in identifying and summarizing suicidal ideation from social media content. Through the CLPsych 2024 Shared Task, we successfully applied advanced LLMs using both Few-shot and Zero-shot prompting strategies, achieving notable performance in evidence extraction and summarization tasks. Our findings emphasize the efficacy of LLMs in handling complex mental health data and highlight the impact of Chain-of-Thought (CoT) prompting on evidence extraction. The study also highlights the importance of incorporating meta-information to enhance the evidence summarization tasks. Our success in the CLPsych 2024 shared task highlights the practical application of LLMs in mental health interventions, paving the way for future advancements in digital mental health monitoring.

6 Limitation

The study has a few key limitations. First, it focuses mainly on two models, *Mixtral7bx8* and *Tulu-2-DPO-70B*, which might not represent how other Large Language Models would perform. Second, it only looks at Few-Shot and Zero-shot prompting, missing out on other possible methods. Third, the datasets used for this study might not be diverse or large enough, which could make the findings less applicable to real-world situations. Additionally, the reliance on manual annotation for Few-Shot prompting introduces subjectivity and potential scalability issues. Lastly, analyzing only two competitor models may not fully capture the competitive landscape, potentially leading to an incomplete comparative assessment. These factors highlight the need for a more inclusive approach in model selection, diverse prompting strategies, comprehensive datasets, and objective competitor analysis in future research.

Ethical Statement

We adhere to the ethical standards of the CLPsych 2024 Shared Task by ensuring a secure environment and user anonymity. All parties involved have signed agreements to protect data privacy and prohibiting data sharing with any unauthorized entities. Our approach is designed to prioritize responsible use, with strict access controls and guidelines to prevent misuse.

Acknowledgements

This work was supported by the Natural Environment Research Council (NE/S015604/1), Economic and Social Research Council (ES/V011278/1), and Engineering and Physical Sciences Research Council (EP/S024298/1), and the Alan Turing Institute's Turing Enrichment Scheme. The authors acknowledge the use of the IRIDIS High Performance Computing Facility, and associated support services at the University of Southampton, which significantly contributed to the completion of this work. The authors are particularly grateful to the anonymous users of Reddit whose data feature in this year's shared task dataset, to the clinical experts from Bar-Ilan University who annotated the data, and the assistance of the American Association of Suicidology for making the dataset available.

References

Tayyaba Azim, Loitongbam Singh, and Stuart Middleton. 2022. Detecting moments of change and suicidal risks in longitudinal user texts using multi-task learning. In *Proceedings of the Eighth Workshop on Computational Linguistics and Clinical Psychology*, pages 213–218.

Francesco Barbieri, Jose Camacho-Collados, Luis Espinosa Anke, and Leonardo Neves. 2020. TweetEval: Unified benchmark and comparative evaluation for tweet classification. In *Findings of the Association for Computational Linguistics: EMNLP 2020*, pages 1644–1650, Online. Association for Computational Linguistics.

Tom Brown, Benjamin Mann, Nick Ryder, Melanie Subbiah, Jared D Kaplan, Prafulla Dhariwal, Arvind Neelakantan, Pranav Shyam, Girish Sastry, Amanda Askell, et al. 2020. Language models are few-shot learners. *Advances in neural information processing systems*, 33:1877–1901.

Jenny Chim, Adam Tsakalidis, Dimitris Gkoumas, Dana Atzil-Slonim, Yaakov Ophir, Ayah Zirikly, Philip Resnik, and Maria Liakata. 2024. Overview of the clpsych 2024 shared task: Leveraging large language models to identify evidence of suicidality risk in online posts. In *Proceedings of the Ninth Workshop on Computational Linguistics and Clinical Psychology*. Association for Computational Linguistics.

Hamish Ivison, Yizhong Wang, Valentina Pyatkin, Nathan Lambert, Matthew Peters, Pradeep Dasigi, Joel Jang, David Wadden, Noah A. Smith, Iz Beltagy, and Hannaneh Hajishirzi. 2023. Camels in a changing climate: Enhancing lm adaptation with tulu 2.

Albert Q Jiang, Alexandre Sablayrolles, Antoine Roux, Arthur Mensch, Blanche Savary, Chris Bamford, Devendra Singh Chaplot, Diego de las Casas, Emma Bou Hanna, Florian Bressand, et al. 2024. Mixtral of experts. *arXiv preprint arXiv:2401.04088*.

Takeshi Kojima, Shixiang Shane Gu, Machel Reid, Yutaka Matsuo, and Yusuke Iwasawa. 2022. Large language models are zero-shot reasoners. *Advances in neural information processing systems*, 35:22199–22213.

Han-Chin Shing, Suraj Nair, Ayah Zirikly, Meir Friedenberg, Hal Daumé III, and Philip Resnik. 2018. Expert, crowdsourced, and machine assessment of suicide risk via online postings. In *Proceedings of the fifth workshop on computational linguistics and clinical psychology: from keyboard to clinic*, pages 25–36.

Loitongbam Gyanendro Singh, Stuart E Middleton, Tayyaba Azim, Elena Nichele, Pinyi Lyu, and Santiago De Ossorno Garcia. 2024. Conversationmoc: Encoding conversational dynamics using multiplex network for identifying moment of change in mood and mental health classification. In *Proceedings of the Machine Learning for Cognitive and Mental Health Workshop (ML4CMH) @ AAAI 2024*.

Aarohi Srivastava, Abhinav Rastogi, Abhishek Rao, Abu Awal Md Shoeb, Abubakar Abid, Adam Fisch, Adam R Brown, Adam Santoro, Aditya Gupta, Adrià Garriga-Alonso, et al. 2023. Beyond the imitation game: Quantifying and extrapolating the capabilities of language models. *Transactions on Machine Learning Research*.

Rika Tanaka and Yusuke Fukazawa. 2024. Integrating supervised extractive and generative language models for suicide risk evidence summarization. In *Proceedings of the Ninth Workshop on Computational Linguistics and Clinical Psychology*. Association for Computational Linguistics.

Nandan Thakur, Nils Reimers, Johannes Daxenberger, and Iryna Gurevych. 2021. Augmented SBERT: Data augmentation method for improving bi-encoders for pairwise sentence scoring tasks. In *Proceedings of the 2021 Conference of the North American Chapter of the Association for Computational Linguistics: Human Language Technologies*, pages 296–310, Online. Association for Computational Linguistics.

Ahmet Yavuz Uluslu, Andrianos Michail, and Simon Clematide. 2024. Utilizing large language models to identify evidence of suicidality risk through analysis of emotionally charged posts. In *Proceedings of the Ninth Workshop on Computational Linguistics and Clinical Psychology*. Association for Computational Linguistics.

Jason Wei, Maarten Bosma, Vincent Zhao, Kelvin Guu, Adams Wei Yu, Brian Lester, Nan Du, Andrew M Dai, and Quoc V Le. 2021. Finetuned language models are zero-shot learners. In *International Conference on Learning Representations*.

Jason Wei, Xuezhi Wang, Dale Schuurmans, Maarten Bosma, Fei Xia, Ed Chi, Quoc V Le, Denny Zhou, et al. 2022. Chain-of-thought prompting elicits reasoning in large language models. *Advances in Neural Information Processing Systems*, 35:24824–24837.

Xuhai Xu, Bingshen Yao, Yuanzhe Dong, Hong Yu, James Hendler, Anind K Dey, and Dakuo Wang. 2023. Leveraging large language models for mental health prediction via online text data. *arXiv preprint arXiv:2307.14385*.

Kailai Yang, Tianlin Zhang, Ziyan Kuang, Qianqian Xie, and Sophia Ananiadou. 2023. Mentalllama: Interpretable mental health analysis on social media with large language models. *arXiv preprint arXiv:2309.13567*.

Zhuosheng Zhang, Aston Zhang, Mu Li, and Alex Smola. 2022. Automatic chain of thought prompting in large language models. In *The Eleventh International Conference on Learning Representations*.

Ayah Zirikly, Philip Resnik, Ozlem Uzuner, and Kristy Hollingshead. 2019. Clpsych 2019 shared task: Predicting the degree of suicide risk in reddit posts. In *Proceedings of the sixth workshop on computational linguistics and clinical psychology*, pages 24–33.

A Appendix

The subsequent Tables 4 and 5 provide detailed examples illustrating the process of inputting instruction prompts into LLM models for the purpose of evidence extraction and summarization tasks related to suicidal thought ideation. These tasks are executed using both direct and Chain-of-Thought (CoT) prompting strategies, incorporating meta-information alongside the given input. Furthermore, Table 6 specifically displays the outputs generated by the LLM for the summarization tasks, highlighting the effectiveness of the applied prompting strategies.

Instruction prompt	As a mental health assistant, your task is to extract evidence directly from the provided input text to highlight the mental health issues. For the evidence extraction task, consider the following aspects: • **Emotions**: Evaluate expressed emotions, from sadness to intense psychological pain, as they may influence the assigned risk level. • **Cognitions**: Explore the individual's thoughts and perceptions about suicide, including the level and frequency of suicidal thoughts, intentions of suicide, and any existing plans. • **Behavior and Motivation**: Evaluate the user's actions related to suicide, such as access to means and concrete plans. Consider their ability to handle difficult/stressful situations and the motivations behind their desire to die. • **Interpersonal and Social Support**: Investigate the individual's social support or stable relationships, and understand their feelings toward significant others. • **Mental Health-Related Issues**: Consider psychiatric diagnoses associated with suicide such as schizophrenia, bipolar, anxiety, eating disorder, previous suicidal attempts, and others. • **Additional Risk Factors**: Consider other factors like socioeconomic and demographic factors, exposure to suicide behavior by others, chronic medical conditions, etc.
Meta-information	The opinion holder indicates Severe suicidal risk, with probable sad emotion and negative sentiment.
Input	Today marks a particularly challenging point in my life. My relationship is going through significant dificulties, and academically, I'm failing to keep up in five subjects. The mornings bring with them a profound struggle to even leave my bed. At 16 years old, a high school student, I'm begining to feel the weight of life's hardships acutely. This period marks two years of battling depression , and after trying eight diferent medications without success, I've reached a state of despair. In my pain, I've contemplated ending my life, beleiving it to be a release from this seemingly endless suffering. I've even gone as far as to plan for it in a way that minimizes the impact on my loved ones, whom I care deeply about. I've prepared a farewell note . This post is a manifestation of my internal conflict; part of me questions if it's truely my time to go. I recognize that suicide is not the solution, yet the immense pain I'm experiencing makes it appear as the only option for temporary relief.
Output	[*relationship is going through significant dificulties, failing to keep up in five subjects, profound struggle to even leave my bed, two years of battling depression, I've reached a state of despair., contemplated ending my life, endless suffering, prepared a farewell note, suicide is not the solution, the immense pain I'm experiencing, the only option for temporary relief*]

Table 4: Illustration of Instruction Prompt for evidence extraction task using Direct Prompting strategy. The output text spans are provided as a demonstration.

As a mental health assistant, your task is to extract relevant spans directly from the provided input text to support the assigned Suicide Risk Level. When highlighting evidence, consider the following aspects:
Emotions: Evaluate expressed emotions, from sadness to intense psychological pain, as they may influence the assigned risk level.
Cognitions: Explore the individual's thoughts and perceptions about suicide, including the level and frequency of suicidal thoughts, intentions of suicide, and any existing plans.
Behavior and Motivation: Evaluate the user's actions related to suicide, such as access to means and concrete plans. Consider their ability to handle difficult/stressful situations and the motivations behind their desire to die.
Interpersonal and Social Support: Investigate the individual's social support or stable relationships, and understand their feelings toward significant others.
Mental Health-Related Issues: Consider psychiatric diagnoses associated with suicide such as schizophrenia, bipolar, anxiety, eating disorder, previous suicidal attempts and others.
Additional Risk Factors: Consider other factors like socioeconomic and demographic factors, exposure to suicide behaviour by others, chronic medical condition, etc.

Input: Today marks a particularly challenging point in my life. My relationship is going through significant dificulties, and academically, I'm failing to keep up in five subjects. The mornings bring with them a profound struggle to even leave my bed. At 16 years old, a high school student, I'm begining to feel the weight of life's hardships acutely. This period marks two years of battling depression , and after trying eight diferent medications without success, I've reached a state of despair. In my pain, I've contemplated ending my life, beleiving it to be a release from this seemingly endless suffering. I've even gone as far as to plan for it in a way that minimizes the impact on my loved ones, whom I care deeply about. I've prepared a farewell note . This post is a manifestation of my internal conflict; part of me questions if it's truely my time to go. I recognize that suicide is not the solution, yet the immense pain I'm experiencing makes it appear as the only option for temporary relief.
The opinion holder indicates Severe suicidal risk, with probable sad emotion and negative sentiment.
Output: Let's think step by step.
Emotions:

* "I've reached a state of despair."
* "endless suffering"
* "the immense pain I'm experiencing"

Cognitions:

* "contemplated ending my life"
* "prepared a farewell note"
* "suicide is not the solution"
* "the only option for temporary relief"

Behaviour and Motivation:

* "relationship is going through significant dificulties"
* "failing to keep up in five subjects"
* "profound struggle to even leave my bed"
* "prepared a farewell note"

Interpersonal and Social Support:

* "relationship is going through significant dificulties"

Mental Health-Related Issues:

* "two years of battling depression"

Additional Risk Factors:

* (Not applicable or lacking information)

...

Table 5: Illustration of Instruction Prompt for evidence extraction task using Chain-of-Thought Prompting with one demonstration.

Instruction prompt	As a mental health assistant, your task is to summarize directly from the provided input text that highlights the mental health issues. For the summarization task, consider the following aspects: • **Emotions**: Evaluate expressed emotions, from sadness to intense psychological pain, as they may influence the assigned risk level. • **Cognitions**: Explore the individual's thoughts and perceptions about suicide, including the level and frequency of suicidal thoughts, intentions of suicide, and any existing plans. • **Behavior and Motivation**: Evaluate the user's actions related to suicide, such as access to means and concrete plans. Consider their ability to handle difficult/stressful situations and the motivations behind their desire to die. • **Interpersonal and Social Support**: Investigate the individual's social support or stable relationships, and understand their feelings toward significant others. • **Mental Health-Related Issues**: Consider psychiatric diagnoses associated with suicide such as schizophrenia, bipolar, anxiety, eating disorder, previous suicidal attempts, and others. • **Additional Risk Factors**: Consider other factors like socioeconomic and demographic factors, exposure to suicide behavior by others, chronic medical conditions, etc.
Meta-information	The opinion holder indicates Severe suicidal risk, with probable sad emotion and negative sentiment.
Input	Today marks a particularly challenging point in my life. My relationship is going through significant dificulties, and academically, I'm failing to keep up in five subjects. The mornings bring with them a profound struggle to even leave my bed. At 16 years old, a high school student, I'm begining to feel the weight of life's hardships acutely. This period marks two years of battling depression , and after trying eight diferent medications without success, I've reached a state of despair. In my pain, I've contemplated ending my life, beleiving it to be a release from this seemingly endless suffering. I've even gone as far as to plan for it in a way that minimizes the impact on my loved ones, whom I care deeply about. I've prepared a farewell note . This post is a manifestation of my internal conflict; part of me questions if it's truely my time to go. I recognize that suicide is not the solution, yet the immense pain I'm experiencing makes it appear as the only option for temporary relief.
Summary output without Meta-information	The individual, a 16-year-old high school student, is grappling with severe depression, which has persisted for two years despite multiple medication trials. Academic struggles in five subjects and relationship difficulties exacerbate their emotional distress. They have considered suicide, planning it to minimize harm to loved ones, and have drafted a farewell note. Despite understanding that suicide is not a solution, the intensity of their pain leads them to consider it as a potential escape..
Summary output with Meta-information	The user is at Severe suicidal risk because they have been struggling with depression for two years, despite trying various medications. They are currently experiencing academic difficulties and relationship issues, which exacerbate their feelings of hopelessness. Their morning struggles suggest possible sleep disturbances or lack of motivation, common in depression. Despite recognizing that suicide is not a solution, they have planned for it, indicating a serious level of distress. Their use of language like 'endless suffering' and 'temporary relief' suggests intense emotional pain.

Table 6: Illustration of Instruction Prompt Variations for the Suicidal Ideation Evidence Summarization Task. This table compares the results of instruction prompts when incorporating meta information against those without it.

Detecting Suicide Risk Patterns using Hierarchical Attention Networks with Large Language Models

L. Koushik[1], Vishruth M[2], Anand Kumar M[3]
Department of Information Technology,
National Institute of Technology Karnataka, Surathkal
koushik.201it131@nitk.edu.in[1],
vish.201it167@nitk.edu.in[2],
m_anandkumar@nitk.edu.in[3]

Abstract

Suicide has become a major public health and social concern in the world . This Paper looks into a method through use of LLMs (Large Language Model) to extract the likely reason for a person to attempt suicide , through analysis of their social media text posts detailing about the event , using this data we can extract the reason for the cause such mental state which can provide support for suicide prevention. This submission presents our approach for CLPsych Shared Task 2024. Our model uses Hierarchical Attention Networks (HAN) and Llama2 for finding supporting evidence about an individual's suicide risk level.

1 Introduction

Suicide is a common and very serious concern that affects many lives globally (Picardo et al., 2020). Detecting signs of suicide early is important to provide timely help and support to those at risk. Even though many current methods for identifying suicide risk exist, they have their limitations in terms of efficiency and accuracy. Traditional methods focus on factors such as psychiatric diagnoses, agitation, past suicidal behavior or even self-reported questionnaire surveys (Maclean et al., 2023). However, these methods sometimes struggle to predict suicidal thoughts accurately, and there's a need for more effective tools.

Social media platforms have become a valuable source for understanding and identifying suicide risk. People often share their thoughts and emotions on platforms like Twitter, Facebook, and Reddit. Diagnosing these posts on these platforms can be very helpful to get insights into the lives of the individuals who might be struggling with suicidal thoughts. In recent years, there's been exciting progress in the use of technology to enhance suicide detection, particularly the use artificial intelligence. Many researches have used various machine learning (Lekkas et al., 2021) and deep learning algorithms (Sourirajan et al., 2020) to detect signs of suicide risk with varying levels of success. Improving the current models could end up being very helpful to prevent many suicide cases.

Based on reddit data, in this paper we use LLMs for extracting suicidal thoughts from the user. LLMs use advanced natural language processing algorithms to analyze vast amounts of textual data, including social media posts, to identify patterns and linguistic cues associated with suicidal thoughts. By leveraging the power of LLMs, researchers and mental health professionals can develop more sophisticated and accurate tools for detecting and understanding the individual.

2 Related Work

There is a rising number of research being done in suicide risk detection. This has been a key focus in the field of Natural Language Processing. This task has been done using a lot of methods, but the key focus keeps evolving over time as the field of Machine Learning and Artificial Intelligence keeps expanding. Various Machine Learning algorithms have been used for this task like Long Short Term Memory (LSTM) and Convolutional Neural Networks (CNN) in (Chatterjee et al., 2019) or ensemble learning methods using Convolutional Neural Networks (CNN) and XGBoost used by (Kim et al., 2020). There has also been an increase in the use of transformer based models (Poświata and Perełkiewicz, 2022).

Recent work on large language models (LLMs) suggest that they can perform well on NLP tasks such as information extraction (Agrawal et al., 2022) and question answering (Singhal et al., 2022) which could help us in identifying evidence supporting individual's suicide risk level from a given social media post. We used a hierarchical attention network (HAN) (Yang et al., 2016) in our model to capture the importance of the words and the sen-

Proceedings of the 9th Workshop on Computational Linguistics and Clinical Psychology (CLPsych 2024), pages 227–231
March 21, 2024 ©2024 Association for Computational Linguistics

tences of the post to find the portions of the text which indicate the presence of suicide risk.

3 Dataset

This paper discusses our involvement in CLPsych 2024 Shared Task (Chim et al., 2024). The problem statement was to use an open source LLM to provide evidence for the assigned suicide risk level of a person on the basis of their linguistic content. Our task was to highlight the parts of the text which indicate evidence of suicide risk and explain the assignment of a particular suicide risk level using our model.

The dataset we used is from the 2019 CLPsych Shared Task A (Shing et al., 2018),(Zirikly et al., 2019) (University of Maryland Reddit Suicidality Dataset, Version 2). This includes a collection of data from Reddit posts within the r/SuicideWatch community. A careful selection process is employed to focus exclusively on posts where individuals openly share personal experiences related to suicide attempts. The dataset includes Reddit users and their r/SuicideWatch posts, alongside their suicide risk levels in four classes: No, Low, Moderate and Severe risk. However we were asked to exclude posts and users labeled as no risk. The task participants were required to sign data sharing agreements and abide by ethical practice during the competition.

4 Methodology

The architecture of the process followed in this paper can be mainly divided into two parts ,first being use of Hierarchical Attention Modeling to get highlights from the posts from the user and then using these highlights with the post , using this as LLAMA-2 LLM for generating the summarized reason for suicide attempt .

4.1 Hierarchical Attention Modeling for highlights

Hierarchical Attention Networks (HAN) are basically a type of neural network architecture that are used to capture the importance of sequential data present in various hierarchical levels. These work especially well for tasks involving text or document classification. The aim behind using HAN in this paper is to address the challenge of understanding context at different levels such as words, sentences, and entire documents. This architecture is especially very useful for tasks where the meaning of a document is affected not only by individual words but also by the hierarchical structure of sentences and paragraphs.

There can be multiple levels to this attention mechanism: word-level attention mechanism consists of an attention mechanism which assigns different weights to words based on their relevance to the overall document. This helps the model to focus on important words. We use this representation with its respective attention weights to get a context vector representing the document-level information for each word. Similarly sentence-level attention mechanism consists of an attention mechanism which assigns different weights to each sentence based on their importance to the document. We use this representation with its respective attention weights to get a context vector representing the document-level information for each sentence.

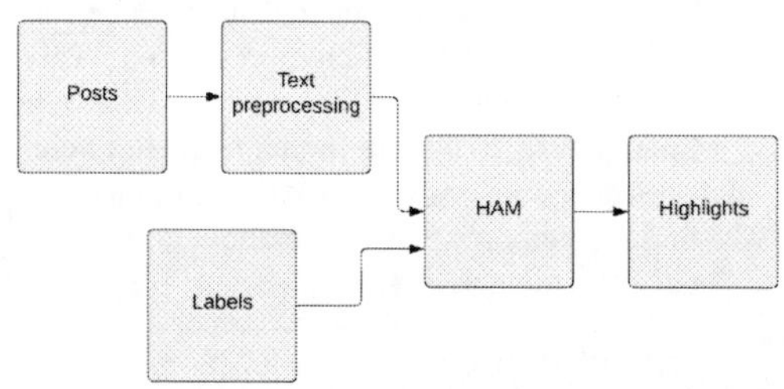

Figure 1: Architecture of the HAN for highlights

Our model architecture uses a Hierarchical Attention Network (HAN) for text extraction. The input sequences undergo embedding, converting them into fixed-size vectors. A bidirectional LSTM layer processes the embedded sequences, capturing word-level contextual information. The attention mechanism then focuses on specific words, forming a context vector. Afterwards, another bidirectional LSTM layer processes these word representations to capture sentence-level context. This hierarchical approach that integrates word and sentence attention mechanisms, allows the model to find out important features at varying levels of detail, improving its capacity for accurate text classification.

4.2 Using Llama2 for summarization

Here in this work we utilize an Large Language Model (LLM) named LLAMA2 as a key component, particularly for the pivotal task of generating concise and summarized insights into the likely reasons behind suicide attempts. The selection of LLAMA2 as it's an auto-regressive language model that uses an optimized transformer architecture. The tuned versions use supervised fine-tuning (SFT) and reinforcement learning with human feedback (RLHF) to align to human preferences for helpfulness and safety with this it gives it remarkable proficiency in processing and comprehending extensive textual data, making it a well-suited candidate for the task to be done in the paper.

Data from 2 trillion tokens publicly accessible sources were used to pretrain Llama 2. The fine-tuning data consists of more than a million newly annotated human cases in addition to publicly accessible instruction datasets.

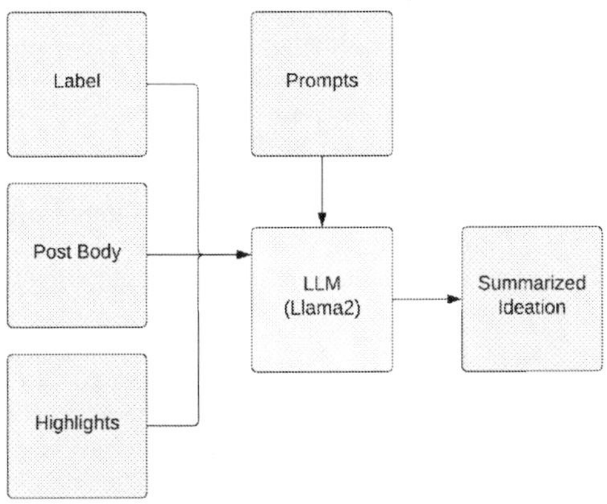

Figure 2: Architecture with LLM model

In this paper, we employ a 4-bit quantization technique to load the Llama 2 7b chat hf version of the model. This approach lowers the computational and memory expenses associated with inference by representing weights using low-precision data types such as 8-bit integer, rather than the customary 32-bit floating point.By lowering the bit count, the resulting model uses less energy and requires less memory, which enables us to make better use of the huge LLM model.

The highlight extractions from the Hierarchical Attention Networks (HAN) procedure and the original post bodies are the two essential components that are concatenated and fed into the model in the next phase. The LLM is able to obtain a thorough representation of all the pertinent information included in the Reddit postings thanks to collective participation. With the help of its pre-trained knowledge gained from exposure to a variety of language patterns and the development of suicidal content expertise, the LLM demonstrates a remarkable capacity to extract the finer features contained in the concatenated input.

The LLM using it's trained architecture helps to create brief summaries that capture the most likely causes of the reported suicide attempts after it receives the concatenated input. The interpretability and accessibility of the research findings are improved by the model's ability to condense complex information into brief and insightful outputs. The produced summaries function as combined representation that provide insightful information about the underlying causes of people's experiences with suicidal thoughts.

Finally we can see that, Llama 2 here is a potent model to help in the study for psychiatrists and researchers, helping to provide complex and educational summaries that facilitate comprehension of the multidimensional character of suicide-related narratives posted users in social media sites.

5 Results

The results of our methodology demonstrate strong performance, with high precision and recall values indicating accurate and comprehensive summarization of suicide-related content within the dataset. The generated summaries not only provide meaningful insights into likely reasons behind suicide attempts but also maintain interpretability. Overall, these results suggest the potential of our method in extracting and understanding sensitive content within online communities, contributing to both research and mental health support systems.

article multirow booktabs

Table 1: Highlights Results-1

Recall	Precision
0.886	0.893

Table 2: Highlights Results-2

Mean Consistency	Max Contradiction
0.784	0.889

Table 3: Summarized text Results

Mean Consistency	Max Contradiction
0.901	0.233

6 Conclusion

In conclusion, our research endeavors to address the intricate challenges of understanding and summarizing suicide-related narratives within the r/SuicideWatch community. The utilization of advanced techniques, including Hierarchical Attention Networks (HAN) and the Large Language Model (LLM) LLAMA2, has yielded promising results. The application of HAN facilitates the extraction of critical information, while LLAMA2's proficiency in processing extensive textual data ensures the generation of concise and insightful summaries.

7 Ethics and Limitations

We obtained our dataset from the University of Maryland and adhered to ethical standards throughout the research process. The dataset, comprising sensitive information, has been handled with utmost confidentiality, and no sharing has occurred to maintain participant privacy and comply with ethical guidelines. Time constraints posed challenges in conducting a more extensive research. This constraint affected the depth of our analysis and the ability to explore additional variables. Despite these limitations, we believe our study provides valuable insights within the given constraints.

Acknowledgements

We would like to express our sincere gratitude to the American Association of Suicidology for their invaluable assistance in making the dataset available for this study. We appreciate the Institute's commitment to promoting scientific research in the field of suicidology.

References

Monica Agrawal, Stefan Hegselmann, Hunter Lang, Yoon Kim, and David Sontag. 2022. Large language models are few-shot clinical information extractors. In *Proceedings of the 2022 Conference on Empirical Methods in Natural Language Processing*, pages 1998–2022.

Ankush Chatterjee, Umang Gupta, Manoj Kumar Chinnakotla, Radhakrishnan Srikanth, Michel Galley, and Puneet Agrawal. 2019. Understanding emotions in text using deep learning and big data. *Computers in Human Behavior*, 93:309–317.

Jenny Chim, Adam Tsakalidis, Dimitris Gkoumas, Dana Atzil-Slonim, Yaakov Ophir, Ayah Zirikly, Philip Resnik, and Maria Liakata. 2024. Overview of the clpsych 2024 shared task: Leveraging large language models to identify evidence of suicidality risk in online posts. In *Proceedings of the Ninth Workshop on Computational Linguistics and Clinical Psychology*. Association for Computational Linguistics.

Jina Kim, Jieon Lee, Eunil Park, and Jinyoung Han. 2020. A deep learning model for detecting mental illness from user content on social media. *Scientific reports*, 10(1):1–6.

Damien Lekkas, Robert J Klein, and Nicholas C Jacobson. 2021. Predicting acute suicidal ideation on instagram using ensemble machine learning models. *Internet interventions*, 25:100424.

Brant R Maclean, Tahni Forrester, Jacinta Hawgood, John O'Gorman, and Jurgita Rimkeviciene. 2023. The personal suicide stigma questionnaire (pssq): relation to self-esteem, well-being, and help-seeking. *International journal of environmental research and public health*, 20(5):3816.

Jacobo Picardo, Sarah K McKenzie, Sunny Collings, and Gabrielle Jenkin. 2020. Suicide and self-harm content on instagram: A systematic scoping review. *PloS one*, 15(9):e0238603.

Rafał Poświata and Michał Perełkiewicz. 2022. Opi@ lt-edi-acl2022: Detecting signs of depression from social media text using roberta pre-trained language models. In *Proceedings of the Second Workshop on Language Technology for Equality, Diversity and Inclusion*, pages 276–282.

Han-Chin Shing, Suraj Nair, Ayah Zirikly, Meir Friedenberg, Hal Daumé III, and Philip Resnik. 2018. Expert, crowdsourced, and machine assessment of suicide risk via online postings. In *Proceedings of the Fifth Workshop on Computational Linguistics and Clinical Psychology: From Keyboard to Clinic*, pages 25–36, New Orleans, LA. Association for Computational Linguistics.

Karan Singhal, Shekoofeh Azizi, Tao Tu, S Sara Mahdavi, Jason Wei, Hyung Won Chung, Nathan Scales, Ajay Tanwani, Heather Cole-Lewis, Stephen Pfohl, et al. 2022. Large language models encode clinical knowledge. *arXiv preprint arXiv:2212.13138*.

Vaibhav Sourirajan, Anas Belouali, Mary Ann Dutton, Matthew Reinhard, and Jyotishman Pathak. 2020. A machine learning approach to detect suicidal ideation in us veterans based on acoustic and linguistic features of speech. *arXiv preprint arXiv:2009.09069*.

Zichao Yang, Diyi Yang, Chris Dyer, Xiaodong He, Alex Smola, and Eduard Hovy. 2016. Hierarchical attention networks for document classification. In *Proceedings of the 2016 conference of the North American chapter of the association for computational linguistics: human language technologies*, pages 1480–1489.

Ayah Zirikly, Philip Resnik, Özlem Uzuner, and Kristy Hollingshead. 2019. CLPsych 2019 shared task: Predicting the degree of suicide risk in Reddit posts. In *Proceedings of the Sixth Workshop on Computational Linguistics and Clinical Psychology*, pages 24–33, Minneapolis, Minnesota. Association for Computational Linguistics.

Using Large Language Models (LLMs) to Extract Evidence from Pre-Annotated Social Media Data

Falwah AlHamed[1,3], **Julia Ive**[2], and **Lucia Specia**[1]

[1]Department of Computing, Imperial College London, London, UK
[1]{f.alhamed20,l.specia}@imperial.ac.uk
[2]Queen Mary University of London, London, UK
[2]j.ive@qmul.ac.uk
[3]King Abdulaziz City for Science and Technology(KACST), Riyadh, Saudi Arabia

Abstract

For numerous years, researchers have employed social media data to gain insights into users' mental health. Nevertheless, the majority of investigations concentrate on categorizing users into those experiencing depression and those considered healthy, or on detection of suicidal thoughts. In this paper, we aim to extract evidence of a pre-assigned gold label. We used a suicidality dataset containing Reddit posts labeled with the suicide risk level. The task is to use Large Language Models (LLMs) to extract evidence from the post that justifies the given label. We used Meta Llama 7b and lexicons for solving the task and we achieved a precision of 0.96.

1 Introduction

In today's world, many people use social media platforms. These platforms allow individuals to express themselves openly, sharing daily details about their activities and thoughts. Researchers have been studying social media data for years to understand users' mental health.

Natural Language Processing (NLP) is often applied to social media data in research that focuses on classifying the presence or absence of depression (Boinepelli et al., 2022; Chancellor and De Choudhury, 2020). Researchers also examine how to detect the transition from depression to suicidal ideation (De Choudhury et al., 2016; Gong et al., 2019; Matero et al., 2019; Sawhney et al., 2020).

In this paper, we explain our approach to the CLPsych 2024 shared task. The goal of this shared task is to utilize Large Language Models (LLMs) to detect textual cues that support the designated Suicide Risk Level, which may be classified as Low, Moderate, or High. This "evidence" could be provided in two ways, either highlighting (or "extracting") relevant spans within the text or by providing a summary, aggregating evidence that supports the assigned suicide risk level.

2 Dataset

Data used for this shared task was from (Zirikly et al., 2019; Shing et al., 2018). It was pulled from Reddit. This well-known social media platform contains communities known as "subreddits", each of which covers a different topic. Access has been granted to the UMD Suicidality Dataset v2, encompassing multiple Reddit users and their corresponding posts on the platform, along with the associated Suicide Risk Level labels. The dataset incorporates annotations for Suicide Risk Levels across subsets of posts within the r/SuicideWatch subreddit, categorized as follows:

- No Risk (or "None"): Absence of evidence indicating the person (post author) is at risk of suicide;
- Low Risk: Some factors may suggest a level of risk, but the likelihood of suicide is deemed low;
- Moderate Risk: Indications exist that the person could genuinely be at risk of attempting suicide;
- High ("Severe") Risk: The belief that the person is at a high risk of attempting suicide in the near future.

This shared task exclusively concentrates on the assessment of Low, Moderate, and High risk levels. It is essential to note that, although the term "suicidal crisis" was not employed in the original risk labeling by (Shing et al., 2018), the High category closely aligns with this concept, denoting an acute situation necessitating immediate intervention. All authors have signed the Data User Agreement (as requested by the organisers) to have access to the dataset.

Proceedings of the 9th Workshop on Computational Linguistics and Clinical Psychology (CLPsych 2024), pages 232–237
March 21, 2024

3 Methods

In this section, we will describe the methods we developed to address the shared tasks. The main instruction for this task was to use Large Language Models (LLMs) to extract the evidence. LLMs have demonstrated superior performance in understanding human language and generating text resembling it.

3.1 Task Description

The task (Chim et al., 2024) is to detect textual cues that support the annotated Suicide Risk Level to Reddit users who wrote posts on the r\suicideWatch subreddit. The "evidence" critical to our analysis can be presented through two approaches. The first method involves providing a comprehensive summary. This entails aggregating and synthesizing the identified evidence into a cohesive overview that captures essential information throughout the text. The second method centers on highlighting or extracting specific, relevant spans within the text, focusing on essential details that contribute to the assigned suicide risk level. This method includes extracting key textual segments indicative of the individual's suicide risk level. The granularity of requirements of the tasks is as follows: the risk is annotated at user-level, the summary evidence is required at user-level, and the highlights evidence is required at post-level. Some rules were identified for accomplishing this task, including that the summary does not exceed 300 words, and that highlights are extracted as exact quotes from the posts. In addition, it is not allowed to use APIs as transmitting the data to other servers raises a concern of data leaks. Thus, we are not allowed to use OpenAI GPT models [1] or Google Bard model [2].

3.2 Model

We used the open-source Meta Llama 2 7B chat LLM (Touvron et al., 2023). Llama is built on a transformer architecture and underwent pre-training on openly accessible online data sources. Subsequently, the fine-tuned model, Llama Chat, utilizes publicly available instructional datasets, incorporating input from over 1 million human annotations. The Hugging face library (Wolf et al., 2019) is used, namely the `'Llama-2-7b-chat-hf'` model card. We experiment using a zero-shot learning approach with different prompts.

[1]https://platform.openai.com/docs/libraries/python-library

[2]https://bard.google.com/chat

3.3 Evidence 1: Summary

Prompts are questions or statements that are provided to the model to initiate and guide a conversation or specific task or to generate desired text.

We experimented with Llama 2 7b to find the summarized text evidence in two rounds with different prompts. In the first round, we are seeking an explanation of the state of the user who wrote the post. A set of the prompts used in extracting evidence 1 (the summary) round 1 is illustrated in Table 1. After receiving the response, we then prompt the model again aiming at summarizing the paragraphs received from the first round. The prompt used for the second round is: `Rewrite this text as a descriptive paragraph of the person who wrote it in less than 300 words starting with This person is at [suicide level] risk because Text:...`

Table 1: A set of the prompts used finding evidence 1 (the summary)

Explain the suicide risk level of the person who wrote this text
Explain why the user who wrote this text has [suicide level] suicide risk level.
Explain why the user who wrote this text has depressive episodes.
Why do you think who wrote this text has [suicide level] suicide risk level?
A psychologist identifies the person who wrote the following text as having a [suicide level] risk of suicide, can you explain why?
Write a paragraph on why this text might contain [suicide level] suicide risk.
Can you let me know in a paragraph why this text is considered low mood?

3.4 Evidence 2: Highlights

Llama Prompts. We experimented with Llama 2 7b to extract the highlights evidence from the posts using different prompts, a set of the prompts used in extracting highlights evidence is illustrated in Table 2.

Lexical Extraction. Previous studies indicate that enhancing prediction outcomes can be achieved by incorporating lexical features in conjunction with machine learning models (AlHamed and AlGwaiz, 2020; Carvalho and Plastino, 2021). Thus, we inspected the posts of the three classes

Table 2: A set of the prompts used finding evidence 2 (the highlights)

Can you identify pieces of text that indicate low mood in the following text and answer with a list of texts?
A psychologist identifies the person who wrote the following text as having a [suicide level] risk of suicide, can you identify pieces of text that indicate that
Identify all quotes of low mood in this text
Identify all quotes about suicide risk in this text
Can you identify all text spans of depressive symptoms in this text?

Table 3: List of suicidal words for Task B

Suicidal Words	
kill	die
knife	survive
dead	end my life
I'm gone	live anymore
I'm done	taking my life
killing	overdose
jump	suicide
wrist	hang
burn	self-harm
self harm	pesticide
death	take my life
call for help	
Depressive Words	
depression	depressive
depressed	sad
mood	cry

and found that they contain many words related to suicide attempts and depressive thoughts. Thus, in addition to the highlights extracted by Llama, we used the list of suicidal words created by (Alhamed et al., 2022) and we added other words of depression inferred from manual posts' inspection. The word list is shown in Table 3. For each word from the text found in a post, we retrieved the sentence as two words before and 2 words after the word found in the lexicon (5 words window size). This sentence was added to the highlights list.

4 Evaluation

As per task organizers (Chim et al., 2024), submissions are evaluated against a test set annotated by two domain experts. Each test set example comprises (i) the risk level label of an individual, (ii) a list of posts written by the individual, (iii) text spans highlighted by annotators from the posts with evidence that support the risk level label, and (iv) a human-written summary that aggregates the highlighted evidence and observations into a single piece of text. Evaluation metrics are as follows:

Summarized Evidence

- **Consistency** is the lack of contradiction. At a user-level, score each sentence in the submitted evidence summary by running a natural language inference (NLI) model on it and every gold summary sentence, using it as hypothesis and the gold sentence as a premise, to obtain the probability of it contradicting the gold sentence. The sentence-level consistency score is thus `1 - (the probability of the "contradiction" prediction)`. Then, take the average consistency score across all sentences for the user. Overall submission-level score is the mean consistency score across all users.

- **Contradiction** Penalizes information that contradicts the gold evidence summary. Lower scores are better. Note that some contradictions are expected, since the same text can describe both risk and protective factors. At a user-level, the organaizer score each sentence in the submitted evidence summary by running an NLI model on it (hypothesis) and every gold summary sentence (premise), taking the maximum contradiction probability. Then, average across all submitted sentences. Overall submission-level score is the mean contradiction score across all users.

Highlights

- **Recall** Measures how much relevant supporting evidence information was predicted. For a given user, for every gold highlight, find the candidate highlight with the highest semantic similarity (based on BERTScore (Zhang et al., 2019)). Take the average similarity across all gold highlights. Overall submission-level score is the mean recall across all test users.

- **Precision** Measures the quality of predicted supporting evidence. For a given user, for every candidate highlight, find the gold highlight with the highest semantic similarity (based on BERTScore). Take the average similarity across all candidate highlights. Overall submission-level score is the mean precision across all test users.

- **Weighted Recall** A length-sensitive version of recall. Measures how much relevant supporting evidence information was predicted and whether the evidence lengths are similar to human-highlighted ones. At a user-level, sum the length (token count) of gold highlights and of submitted highlights. If the number of submitted highlight tokens exceeds the number of gold highlight tokens, weigh the user-level recall score by the ratio of gold:candidate tokens. Overall submission-level score is the mean weighted recall across all test users.

- **Harmonic Mean** Balances between precision and recall when evaluating how well the submission identified supporting evidence. The user-level harmonic mean between unweighted recall and precision is mean-averaged across all test users.

5 Results

We applied prompts to Llama, and it responded to the majority of them with an explanation for the given post. Although Large Language Models (LLMs) are known for their robust language processing capabilities, they have encountered difficulties in addressing specific aspects of mental health. In some cases, Llama refuses to answer and responds with "`It is important to note that this is just one text message, and it is not possible to make a definitive assessment of the person's suicide risk level based on this one message`" or "`It is important to note that these are just a few potential indicators of suicide risk, and that each person's situation is unique. However, if you are concerned about someone's safety, it is important to take their concerns seriously and offer support and resources..`" The prompt that provides us with the best matching summary evidence for all of the posts was "`Can you let me know in a paragraph why this text is considered low mood?`" as it scored 0.964 consistency with the gold standard, where the prompts "`Explain why the user who wrote this text has [suicide level] suicide risk level`" and "`Write a paragraph on why this text might contain [suicide level] suicide risk`" scored 0.873 and 0.878, respectively.

The prompt that provides the best matching highlights evidence was "`Can you identify pieces of text that indicate low mood in the following text and answer with a list of texts?`"

In this shared task, it was imperative to extract direct quotes, or highlights, from the text of posts. Our model adeptly performed this task while also rectifying any spelling mistakes within these quotes. However, during the subsequent validity check phase before submission, this spell-checking process inadvertently led to errors, resulting in some posts being submitted with empty quotes due to the approaching deadline. Consequently, this issue contributed to a lower overall recall (0.577). Nevertheless, it's worth noting that our model maintained a high level of recall (0.887) for all posts that did not contain empty quotes.

The incorporation of a lexicon in our work enhances the results by expanding the list of highlights, identified during the extraction process. This integration contributes to an increased recall rate as the lexicon serves as a valuable reference, allowing the model to recognize and include additional relevant quotes that align with predefined criteria. By leveraging the lexicon, our approach not only captures a broader spectrum of highlights but also augments the comprehensiveness of the extracted information in the summary, thereby improving the overall performance of the system.

The results obtained using our proposed method are illustrated in Table 4

Table 4: Results

Summarized Evidence	Mean Consistency	0.964
	Max Contradiction	0.060
Highlights	Precision	0.899
	Harmonic Mean	0.888

6 Conclusions and Future Work

In conclusion, researchers have extensively utilized social media data over the years to gain valuable insights into users' mental health. However, the predominant focus of many investigations has been on categorizing users into those with depression and those deemed healthy, or on detecting suicidal ideation. In this study, our objective was to extract evidence corresponding to pre-assigned gold labels. To achieve this, we utilized a suicidality dataset comprising Reddit posts labeled with suicide risk levels. Our task involved employing Large Language Models (LLMs) to extract evidence from the posts justifying the assigned labels. Through the utilization of Meta Llama 7b and lexicons, we attained commendable results, achieving a precision rate of 0.96. These findings underscore the efficacy of utilizing advanced language models and lexicon-based approaches in extracting evidence pertinent to the assigned suicide risk levels from social media posts. In the future, we aim to try other LLM models such as OpenAI GPT and Google Bard. We also aim to expand the suicidal words list and extract additional features from the text that could enhance the obtained results.

7 Limitations

Llama2 7b is limited to handling a maximum of 4096 tokens, which resulted in trimmed posts, leading to potential information loss and truncation of longer posts that possibly caused incomplete understanding and biased sampling. In addition, the llama2 model used in this paper is trained using extensive datasets collected from the internet. Although it can produce human-like text, it is worth noting that training it on domain-specific data (mental health data) could improve its performance.

8 Ethical Consideration

The collected dataset contains only publicly available posts from Reddit, and we have signed a data user agreement not to share or distribute any data outside the team. We are also committed to following ethical practices to protect users' privacy and anonymity. This includes not using commercial LLMs to protect user privacy, not submitting all or part of the data to any platform that may use the data for training, and data is only stored on password protected servers and computers.

Acknowledgements

The authors are particularly grateful to the anonymous users of Reddit whose data feature in this year's shared task dataset, to the clinical experts from BarIlan University who annotated the data. We extend our acknowledgements to the American Association of Suicidology for making the dataset available.

References

Falwah AlHamed and Aljohara AlGwaiz. 2020. A Hybrid Social Mining Approach for Companies Current Reputation Analysis. In *Recent Advances on Soft Computing and Data Mining*, pages 429–438, Cham. Springer International Publishing.

Falwah Alhamed, Julia Ive, and Lucia Specia. 2022. Predicting moments of mood changes overtime from imbalanced social media data. In *Proceedings of the Eighth Workshop on Computational Linguistics and Clinical Psychology*, pages 239–244, Seattle, USA. Association for Computational Linguistics.

Sravani Boinepelli, Tathagata Raha, Harika Abburi, Pulkit Parikh, Niyati Chhaya, and Vasudeva Varma. 2022. Leveraging mental health forums for user-level depression detection on social media. In *Proceedings of the Thirteenth Language Resources and Evaluation Conference*, pages 5418–5427.

Jonnathan Carvalho and Alexandre Plastino. 2021. On the evaluation and combination of state-of-the-art features in Twitter sentiment analysis. *Artificial Intelligence Review*, 54(3):1887–1936.

Stevie Chancellor and Munmun De Choudhury. 2020. Methods in predictive techniques for mental health status on social media: a critical review. *npj Digital Medicine*, 3(1):43.

Jenny Chim, Adam Tsakalidis, Dimitris Gkoumas, Dana Atzil-Slonim, Yaakov Ophir, Ayah Zirikly, Philip Resnik, and Maria Liakata. 2024. Overview of the clpsych 2024 shared task: Leveraging large language models to identify evidence of suicidality risk in online posts. In *Proceedings of the Ninth Workshop on Computational Linguistics and Clinical Psychology*. Association for Computational Linguistics.

Munmun De Choudhury, Emre Kiciman, Mark Dredze, Glen Coppersmith, and Mrinal Kumar. 2016. Discovering shifts to suicidal ideation from mental health content in social media. *Conference on Human Factors in Computing Systems - Proceedings*, pages 2098–2110.

Jue Gong, Gregory E. Simon, and Shan Liu. 2019. Machine learning discovery of longitudinal patterns of depression and suicidal ideation. *PLoS ONE*, 14(9):1–15.

Matthew Matero, Akash Idnani, Youngseo Son, Sal Giorgi, Huy Vu, Mohammad Zamani, Parth Limbachiya, Sharath Chandra Guntuku, and H. Andrew Schwartz. 2019. Suicide Risk Assessment with Multi-level Dual-Context Language and. pages 39–44.

Ramit Sawhney, Harshit Joshi, Saumya Gandhi, and Rajiv Ratn Shah. 2020. A Time-Aware Transformer Based Model for Suicide Ideation Detection on Social Media. pages 7685–7697.

Han-Chin Shing, Suraj Nair, Ayah Zirikly, Meir Friedenberg, Hal Daumé III, and Philip Resnik. 2018. Expert, crowdsourced, and machine assessment of suicide risk via online postings. In *Proceedings of the Fifth Workshop on Computational Linguistics and Clinical*

Psychology: From Keyboard to Clinic, pages 25–36, New Orleans, LA. Association for Computational Linguistics.

Hugo Touvron, Thibaut Lavril, Gautier Izacard, Xavier Martinet, Marie-Anne Lachaux, Timothée Lacroix, Baptiste Rozière, Naman Goyal, Eric Hambro, Faisal Azhar, et al. 2023. Llama: Open and efficient foundation language models. *arXiv preprint arXiv:2302.13971*.

Thomas Wolf, Lysandre Debut, Victor Sanh, Julien Chaumond, Clement Delangue, Anthony Moi, Pierric Cistac, Tim Rault, Rémi Louf, Morgan Funtowicz, et al. 2019. Huggingface's transformers: State-of-the-art natural language processing. *arXiv preprint arXiv:1910.03771*.

Tianyi Zhang, Varsha Kishore, Felix Wu, Kilian Q Weinberger, and Yoav Artzi. 2019. Bertscore: Evaluating text generation with bert. *arXiv preprint arXiv:1904.09675*.

Ayah Zirikly, Philip Resnik, Özlem Uzuner, and Kristy Hollingshead. 2019. CLPsych 2019 shared task: Predicting the degree of suicide risk in Reddit posts. In *Proceedings of the Sixth Workshop on Computational Linguistics and Clinical Psychology*, pages 24–33, Minneapolis, Minnesota. Association for Computational Linguistics.

XinHai@CLPsych 2024 Shared Task: Prompting Healthcare-oriented LLMs for Evidence Highlighting in Posts with Suicide Risk

Jingwei Zhu[1], **Ancheng Xu**[2], **Minghuan Tan**[2*] and **Min Yang**[2*]
[1] University of Science and Technology of China.
[2] Shenzhen Key Laboratory for High Performance Data Mining,
Shenzhen Institutes of Advanced Technology, Chinese Academy of Sciences.
jingweizhu@mail.ustc.edu.cn,{mh.tan,ac.xu,min.yang}@siat.ac.cn

Abstract

In this article, we introduce a new method for analyzing and summarizing posts from *r/SuicideWatch* on Reddit, overcoming the limitations of current techniques in processing complex mental health discussions online. Existing methods often struggle to accurately identify and contextualize subtle expressions of mental health problems, leading to inadequate support and intervention strategies. Our approach combines the open-source Large Language Model (LLM), fine-tuned with health-oriented knowledge, to effectively process Reddit posts. We also design prompts that focus on suicide-related statements, extracting key statements, and generating concise summaries that capture the core aspects of the discussions. The preliminary results indicate that our method improves the understanding of online suicide-related posts compared to existing methodologies.

1 Introduction

Suicide prevention is a key aspect of psychological research that addresses a critical need in mental health care. There have been different approaches to the research on suicide prevention. The Suicide Risk Level Prediction Task uses machine learning algorithms to assess and predict suicide risk levels in individuals, offering a significant advancement in the field of mental health and preventive care. The recent evolution of Large Language Models (LLMs) (OpenAI:, 2023; Touvron et al., 2023) has brought about a paradigm shift in computer-based language understanding, profoundly improving the capacity to uncover latent meanings and intricacies within the language.

In this paper, we explore an innovative approach that synergizes traditional Natural Language Processing (NLP) techniques with the advanced capabilities of LLM. Our study explores the potential benefits of integrating LLMs with established NLP techniques to extract supporting evidence for an identified user at risk of suicide. By applying this method, our aim is to better interpret the linguistic cues that may signify mental health risks. This approach contributes to ongoing efforts in suicide prevention by providing a refined tool for analysis. The implications of this research suggest a promising direction for future investigation in psychological health monitoring.

2 Task

The CLPsych 2024 Shared Task (Chim et al., 2024) aims at utilizing LLMs for finding supporting evidence about an individual's suicide risk level.

2.1 Data

The UMD Suicidality Dataset v2 (University of Maryland Reddit Suicidality Dataset, Version 2) (Shing et al., 2018; Zirikly et al., 2019) contains the assessment of suicide risk of users who post to the sub-Reddit *r/SuicideWatch*.

Suicide Risk Level is annotated with a four-point scale (*No Risk*, *Low Risk*, *Moderate Risk* and *High Risk*). The annotations for the dataset were performed by crowd-sourced workers and experts.

The dataset has been used for Suicide Risk Level Prediction in the CLPsych 2019 Shared Task (Zirikly et al., 2019).

For this task, only the *expert* split is used and only users with *Low Risk*, *Moderate Risk* and *High Risk* are considered. The posts to highlight evidence are all from the *r/SuicideWatch* subreddit.

2.2 Definition

Given posts from *r/SuicideWatch* posted by users identified by experts with *Low Risk*, *Moderate Risk* and *High Risk*, the system: (1) uses offline LLMs to extract evidence as text spans in the post, (2) generates a summary of evidence. In cases where a user has multiple posts, the system is expected

*Corresponding author.

Proceedings of the 9th Workshop on Computational Linguistics and Clinical Psychology (CLPsych 2024), pages 238–246
March 21, 2024

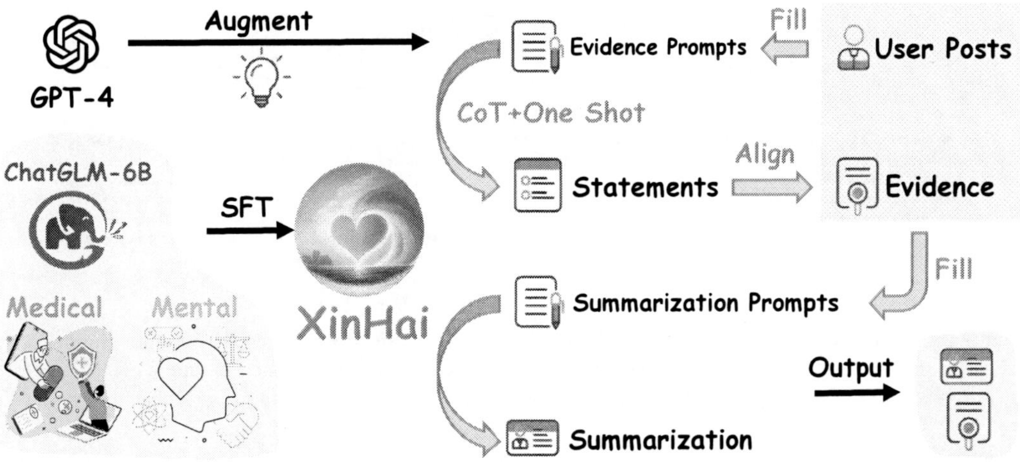

Figure 1: Overview of our system. On the left, we display the Supervised Fine-Tuning (SFT) sketch of our XinHai LLM. On the right, we outline the structured pipeline developed for this specific task.

to generate a single summary but highlights text spans in each post.

2.3 Evaluation

The evaluation of the task is conducted from two perspectives:

Evidence Highlights For each post, the maximum recall-oriented BERTScore (Zhang et al., 2020) will be computed between each expert-provided evidence highlight and all submitted highlights for that post.

Summarized Evidence For each post, a natural language inference (NLI) model will be used to calculate the mean probabilities of sentences in the summarized evidence submitted that contradicts or involves the summarized evidence provided by experts.

3 System

Our system is a pipeline built using a healthcare-oriented LLM, which accepts Reddit posts from users at risk of suicide and prompts for formatted output to extract evidence accordingly. The overview of the system is shown in Figure 1. The implementation details and source code of our system are available in our online repository[1].

3.1 Healthcare-Oriented LLM

The core of the system is the healthcare-oriented LLM XinHai, which has been fine-tuned from the ChatGLM3-6B model. This fine-tuning includes specific enhancements with medical and psychological knowledge. Supervised Fine-Tuning (SFT) details for XinHai can be found in the Appendix B.

3.2 Tailored Prompts

To guide the model effectively, we utilize custom prompts. These well-designed prompts are meticulously crafted to direct the model's focus toward identifying statements in the post that are relevant to suicide. This step is essential to extract the key statements of the posts and filter out irrelevant information, ensuring that the output of the model is both relevant and precise.

Prompt with Chain-of-Thought for Analysis In our pursuit to enhance the functionality of LLMs, we have meticulously developed a series of tailored prompts. These prompts are intricately designed to direct the LLMs to read and analyze user posts with care. This focused reading enables accurate identification and extraction of phrases or words that indicate the user's mental state.

To further refine the reasoning capabilities of our LLM, we have incorporated the Chain of Thought prompting technique (Wei et al., 2022). This technique provides a structured framework for the LLM to follow a logical progression of intermediate steps when formulating responses, thereby improving its ability to identify and utilize relevant evidence. The prompts designed using the Chain of Thought method are exemplified in Figure4.

[1]https://github.com/CAS-SIAT-XinHai/XinHai-at-CLPsych2024/

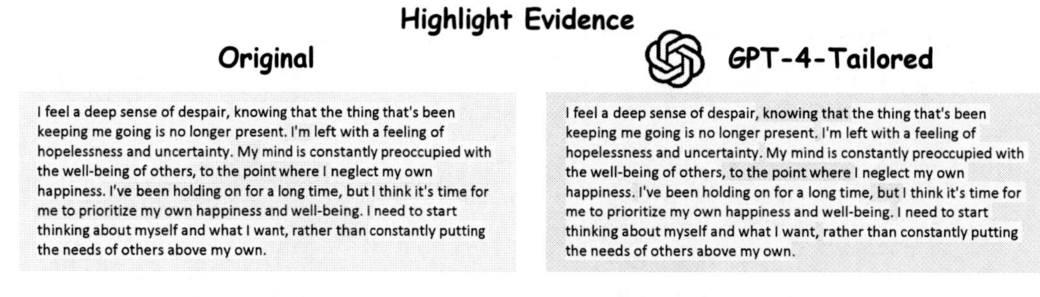

Figure 2: Side-by-side Comparison of Prompt Outputs: The left panel displays results from the original prompt, while the right panel features results from the GPT-4 augmented prompt. Both panels highlight evidence extracted by our local LLM, illustrating the nuanced differences elicited by the two prompting approaches.

Enhancing Prompt Effectiveness with GPT4 Furthermore, we leverage OPENAI's GPT-4 (OpenAI:, 2023) to augment the effectiveness of our prompts. Comparing the original and GPT-4 fine-tuned prompts reveals significant simplifications in structure and clarity. The GPT-4 tailored prompts not only refine the language but also enhance the analytical capabilities to distill complex meanings. During this enhancement process, it's crucial to note that no part of our dataset was shared with GPT-4, this approach ensures the utmost respect for data privacy and integrity. The comparative effects on prompt structure and response quality are encapsulated in Figure 2, with the left side showing the original prompt's output and the right side displaying the GPT-4 tailored prompt's results. The latter is further detailed in Figure 4, demonstrating the model's ability to produce more targeted and coherent outputs. In both figures, results have been rephrased by our local language model to safeguard user privacy.

Prompt with One-shot Demonstration In our approach, we observed challenges with instruction-following, particularly when generating structured outputs like JSON, using our language model. To mitigate these issues, we employed a one-shot learning strategy (Brown et al., 2020), which involves the integration of a single instructive example within the prompt. This example serves as a guide for the language model, illustrating how to format its responses in JSON structure effectively. By incorporating this one-shot demonstration, we can direct the model's output towards structured JSON data, aligning with the requirements of our subsequent processing stages. This method demonstrates the specific application of one-shot learning in enhancing the model's capability to produce formatted outputs based on a singular, illustrative example.

3.3 Evidence Matching

Despite the model's effectiveness in extracting evidence, the uncontrollable nature of model output means that we can only strive to extract relevant information from the phrases or sentences generated by the model. Consequently, we choose to perform evidence matching with the original text.

Segment Alignment As mandated by the task requirements, our objective is to highlight evidence within original Reddit posts. However, a pivotal requirement in our system is to accurately match the original text, stemming from the inherent unpredictability of model outputs, which often do not align precisely with the source text.

To meet this challenge, we leverage Spacy[2], a Natural Language Processing toolkit, to convert sentences or phrases into vector representations. This conversion facilitates the computation of similarity scores between vectors, allowing us to pinpoint the segments in the original text that most closely match in meaning.

After processing through our LLM, words or sentences in the user's original text might transform. For instance, the original phrase *"comparing myself to person A and person B"* could be altered by the LLM to *"comparing to the rest of the world."* In such cases, SpaCy plays a crucial role in finding the best match for these transformed phrases in the original text. It analyzes the vector representations of the LLM's output and aligns them with those of the original text. In our example, despite the

[2] https://spacy.io/

significant change in wording, SpaCy successfully identifies the underlying similarity in meaning, ensuring accurate and contextually relevant highlights in the original post.

This methodology underscores the synergy between LLM's text processing capabilities and SpaCy's precision in matching, enabling our system to interpret and relate the nuances of user-generated content effectively.

Regular Processing Regular expressions are a versatile tool in text processing, capable of identifying complex patterns and structures within large volumes of text. In our system, regex plays a dual role.

(1) **Handling Incomplete Words**: By designing specific regex patterns, we can detect words that are cut off or incomplete. This pattern recognition enables the system to intelligently infer the complete form of a word based on its partial appearance and the surrounding context. This is crucial in ensuring the integrity and comprehensiveness of the text analysis.

(2) **Ensuring Semantic Consistency**: The same regex approach is adopted to maintain semantic similarity between extracted text and the original content. By identifying and extracting key phrases and sentences through pattern matching, the system ensures that the essence and context of the original post are preserved.

3.4 Summary Generation

Alongside the extraction and matching of key statements, our system is equipped to generate concise and coherent summaries of user posts. This feature plays a critical role in providing mental health professionals with quick, comprehensive reviews of the posts. The summaries, crafted by our LLM, encompass both the titles and bodies of the posts, ensuring that no crucial detail or nuance is overlooked.

To achieve this, we utilize a sophisticated process where the LLM engages with the content, analyzing it in the context of the assessed risk levels. Our technical approach involves sending structured prompts to the LLM, which guide it to not only parse the content but also to synthesize it into a coherent summary. For instance, a typical prompt might read *"Evaluate this post for indicators of mental health risks and generate a summary, including key phrases and assigned risk levels."* This prompt initiates a detailed analysis by the LLM, resulting in summaries that are both accurate and context-aware.

4 Results

Figure 3 in the appendix and Table 1 together demonstrate the effectiveness of our two distinct text-matching approaches: the phrase-level and the sentence-level extraction methods.

Highlights metrics include *Recall*, gauging the extent to which relevant evidence was captured. The *Precision* metric assesses the accuracy of the evidence extracted. Additionally, *Weighted Recall* provides insight into the length appropriateness of the evidence. Lastly, the *Harmonic Mean* of precision and recall offers a balanced view of both metrics.

Summarized Evidence is evaluated based on *Consistency*, reflecting the absence of contradictions in the summaries compared to expert-written narratives. The *Contradiction* metric further refines this analysis by penalizing any contradicting information, acknowledging the complexity inherent in texts that encompass both risk and protective factors.

The table captures the essence of our comparative study, where phrase-level extractions (V3-phrase and V4-phrase) were generally more precise—adept at identifying pivotal information, as reflected by their precision scores. Sentence-level extractions (V2-sentence), while offering comprehensive insights, often included additional context that did not always contribute to the assessment's focus, as evidenced by the weighted recall scores. This distinction underscores the importance of selecting the appropriate extraction level depending on the desired balance between detail and breadth in evidence gathering.

4.1 Phrase-Level

Phrase-level extraction has proven to be a superior method for identifying nuanced emotions and specific sentiments within a text. This method is precise because it can isolate impactful phrases that directly convey the user's emotional state, without the confusion of surrounding context.

4.2 Sentence-Level

Sentence-level extraction is a method that captures the context in which the user's emotions are expressed. This approach provides a broader view, but it can also include irrelevant information that

Version	Recall	Precision	Weighted Recall	Harmonic Mean	Mean Consistency	Max Contradiction↓
v2-sentence	**0.887**	**0.906**	0.617	**0.911**	0.958	0.126
v3-phrase	0.834	0.884	0.772	0.876	**0.959**	**0.121**
v4-phrase	0.868	0.884	**0.807**	0.876	0.956	0.132

Table 1: Comparative Results of Text-Matching Approaches

might make it difficult to understand the core sentiment. Therefore, additional processing may be required to extract the relevant emotions from the sentence.

5 Conclusion

In conclusion, we constructed a prompt-based evidence highlighting and summarization system for the suicide risk evaluation task utilizing the healthcare-oriented LLM XinHai. We utilized GPT-4 to further enhance our prompt design and conducted experiments at phrase-level and sentence-level highlighting.

Limitations

Our system's performance is heavily reliant on the quality of the prompts and the base generative AI model. Without a range of comparative baselines, the precise contribution of each factor to the overall performance remains unclear.

A clear limitation of our study is the uncertainty surrounding the effect of SFT on the model's performance for the shared task. Without baselines using models without SFT, such as ChatGLM3-6B, we cannot definitively ascertain the impact of this process.

Ethics

The dataset used for the investigation may contain sensitive data and is not available to the public. We obey the rules of using the data restrictively and adopt group access control for each project member. All the experiments have been conducted on a local GPU server of the lab.

We confirm that we have not shared any part of the dataset with external entities, including but not limited to GPT-4 or any other service. Our commitment to ensuring the confidentiality of the data is of utmost importance throughout the research process.

Acknowledgements

We commit to acknowledging the assistance of the American Association of Suicidology in making the dataset available, in any publications.

References

Ashwag Alasmari, Luke Kudryashov, Shweta Yadav, Heera Lee, and Dina Demner-Fushman. 2023. CHQ-SocioEmo: Identifying Social and Emotional Support Needs in Consumer-Health Questions. *Scientific Data*, 10(1):329.

Zhijie Bao, Wei Chen, Shengze Xiao, Kuang Ren, Jiaao Wu, Cheng Zhong, Jiajie Peng, Xuanjing Huang, and Zhongyu Wei. 2023. DISC-MedLLM: Bridging General Large Language Models and Real-World Medical Consultation.

Nicolas Bertagnolli. 2020. Counsel chat: Bootstrapping high-quality therapy data.

Tom B. Brown, Benjamin Mann, Nick Ryder, Melanie Subbiah, Jared Kaplan, Prafulla Dhariwal, Arvind Neelakantan, Pranav Shyam, Girish Sastry, Amanda Askell, Sandhini Agarwal, Ariel Herbert-Voss, Gretchen Krueger, Tom Henighan, Rewon Child, Aditya Ramesh, Daniel M. Ziegler, Jeffrey Wu, Clemens Winter, Christopher Hesse, Mark Chen, Eric Sigler, Mateusz Litwin, Scott Gray, Benjamin Chess, Jack Clark, Christopher Berner, Sam McCandlish, Alec Radford, Ilya Sutskever, and Dario Amodei. 2020. Language Models are Few-Shot Learners.

Sven Buechel, Anneke Buffone, Barry Slaff, Lyle Ungar, and João Sedoc. 2018. Modeling empathy and distress in reaction to news stories.

Nan Chen, Xiangdong Su, Tongyang Liu, Qizhi Hao, and Ming Wei. 2020. A benchmark dataset and case study for Chinese medical question intent classification. *BMC Medical Informatics and Decision Making*, 20(3):125.

Jenny Chim, Adam Tsakalidis, Dimitris Gkoumas, Dana Atzil-Slonim, Yaakov Ophir, Ayah Zirikly, Philip Resnik, and Maria Liakata. 2024. Overview of the CLPsych 2024 Shared Task: Leveraging Large Language Models to Identify Evidence of Suicidality Risk in Online Posts. In *Proceedings of the Ninth Workshop on Computational Linguistics and Clinical Psychology*. "Association for Computational Linguistics".

Linh D. Dang, Uyen T.P. Phan, and Nhung T.H. Nguyen. 2023. GENA: A knowledge graph for nutrition and mental health. *Journal of Biomedical Informatics*, 145:104460.

Junqing He, Mingming Fu, and Manshu Tu. 2019. Applying deep matching networks to Chinese medical question answering: A study and a dataset. *BMC Medical Informatics and Decision Making*, 19(2):52.

Xuehai He, Shu Chen, Zeqian Ju, Xiangyu Dong, Hongchao Fang, Sicheng Wang, Yue Yang, Jiaqi Zeng, Ruisi Zhang, Ruoyu Zhang, Meng Zhou, Penghui Zhu, and Pengtao Xie. 2020. MedDialog: Two Large-scale Medical Dialogue Datasets.

Di Jin, Eileen Pan, Nassim Oufattole, Wei-Hung Weng, Hanyi Fang, and Peter Szolovits. 2020. What Disease does this Patient Have? A Large-scale Open Domain Question Answering Dataset from Medical Exams. *arXiv preprint arXiv:2009.13081*.

Qiao Jin, Bhuwan Dhingra, Zhengping Liu, William W. Cohen, and Xinghua Lu. 2019. PubMedQA: A Dataset for Biomedical Research Question Answering.

Dongfang Li, Baotian Hu, Qingcai Chen, Weihua Peng, and Anqi Wang. 2020. Towards medical machine reading comprehension with structural knowledge and plain text. In *Proceedings of the 2020 Conference on Empirical Methods in Natural Language Processing (EMNLP)*, pages 1427–1438, Online. Association for Computational Linguistics.

Jing Li, Shangping Zhong, and Kaizhi Chen. 2021. MLEC-QA: A Chinese Multi-Choice Biomedical Question Answering Dataset. In *Proceedings of the 2021 Conference on Empirical Methods in Natural Language Processing*, pages 8862–8874, Online and Punta Cana, Dominican Republic. Association for Computational Linguistics.

Siyang Liu, Chujie Zheng, Orianna Demasi, Sahand Sabour, Yu Li, Zhou Yu, Yong Jiang, and Minlie Huang. 2021. Towards emotional support dialog systems. In *Proceedings of the 59th Annual Meeting of the Association for Computational Linguistics and the 11th International Joint Conference on Natural Language Processing (Volume 1: Long Papers)*, pages 3469–3483, Online. Association for Computational Linguistics.

Do June Min, Verónica Pérez-Rosas, Kenneth Resnicow, and Rada Mihalcea. 2022. PAIR: Prompt-aware margIn ranking for counselor reflection scoring in motivational interviewing. In *Proceedings of the 2022 Conference on Empirical Methods in Natural Language Processing*, pages 148–158, Abu Dhabi, United Arab Emirates. Association for Computational Linguistics.

Damilola Omitaomu, Shabnam Tafreshi, Tingting Liu, Sven Buechel, Chris Callison-Burch, Johannes Eichstaedt, Lyle Ungar, and João Sedoc. 2022. Empathic conversations: A multi-level dataset of contextualized conversations.

OpenAI:. 2023. GPT-4 Technical Report.

Ankit Pal, Logesh Kumar Umapathi, and Malaikannan Sankarasubbu. 2022. MedMCQA: A Large-scale Multi-Subject Multi-Choice Dataset for Medical domain Question Answering. In *Proceedings of the Conference on Health, Inference, and Learning*, volume 174 of *Proceedings of Machine Learning Research*, pages 248–260. PMLR.

Huachuan Qiu, Hongliang He, Shuai Zhang, Anqi Li, and Zhenzhong Lan. 2023. SMILE: Single-turn to Multi-turn Inclusive Language Expansion via ChatGPT for Mental Health Support.

Hannah Rashkin, Eric Michael Smith, Margaret Li, and Y-Lan Boureau. 2019. Towards Empathetic Open-domain Conversation Models: a New Benchmark and Dataset.

Ashish Sharma, Adam S Miner, David C Atkins, and Tim Althoff. 2020. A Computational Approach to Understanding Empathy Expressed in Text-Based Mental Health Support. In *EMNLP*.

Han-Chin Shing, Suraj Nair, Ayah Zirikly, Meir Friedenberg, Hal Daumé III, and Philip Resnik. 2018. Expert, crowdsourced, and machine assessment of suicide risk via online postings. In *Proceedings of the Fifth Workshop on Computational Linguistics and Clinical Psychology: From Keyboard to Clinic*, pages 25–36, New Orleans, LA. Association for Computational Linguistics.

Hao Sun, Zhenru Lin, Chujie Zheng, Siyang Liu, and Minlie Huang. 2021. PsyQA: A Chinese dataset for generating long counseling text for mental health support. In *Findings of the Association for Computational Linguistics: ACL-IJCNLP 2021*, pages 1489–1503, Online. Association for Computational Linguistics.

Hugo Touvron, Thibaut Lavril, Gautier Izacard, Xavier Martinet, Marie-Anne Lachaux, Timothée Lacroix, Baptiste Rozière, Naman Goyal, Eric Hambro, Faisal Azhar, Aurelien Rodriguez, Armand Joulin, Edouard Grave, and Guillaume Lample. 2023. Llama: Open and efficient foundation language models.

David Vilares and Carlos Gómez-Rodríguez. 2019. HEAD-QA: A healthcare dataset for complex reasoning.

Hai Liang Wang, Zhi Zhi Wu, and Jia Yuan Lang. 2020. 派特心理：心理咨询问答语料库.

Xidong Wang, Guiming Hardy Chen, Dingjie Song, Zhiyi Zhang, Zhihong Chen, Qingying Xiao, Feng Jiang, Jianquan Li, Xiang Wan, Benyou Wang, et al. 2023. CMB: A Comprehensive Medical Benchmark in Chinese. *arXiv preprint arXiv:2308.08833*.

Jason Wei, Xuezhi Wang, Dale Schuurmans, Maarten Bosma, E. Chi, Quoc Le, and Denny Zhou. 2022. Chain of Thought Prompting Elicits Reasoning in Large Language Models. *ArXiv*, abs/2201.11903.

Anuradha Welivita, Yubo Xie, and Pearl Pu. 2021. A large-scale dataset for empathetic response generation. In *Proceedings of the 2021 Conference on Empirical Methods in Natural Language Processing*, pages 1251–1264, Online and Punta Cana, Dominican Republic. Association for Computational Linguistics.

Sheng Zhang, Xin Zhang, Hui Wang, Lixiang Guo, and Shanshan Liu. 2018. Multi-scale attentive interaction networks for chinese medical question answer selection. *IEEE Access*, 6:74061–74071.

Tianyi Zhang, Varsha Kishore, Felix Wu, Kilian Q. Weinberger, and Yoav Artzi. 2020. BERTScore: Evaluating Text Generation with BERT. In *International Conference on Learning Representations*.

Chujie Zheng, Sahand Sabour, Jiaxin Wen, Zheng Zhang, and Minlie Huang. 2023a. AugESC: Dialogue augmentation with large language models for emotional support conversation. In *Findings of the Association for Computational Linguistics: ACL 2023*, pages 1552–1568, Toronto, Canada. Association for Computational Linguistics.

Zhonghua Zheng, Lizi Liao, Yang Deng, and Liqiang Nie. 2023b. Building Emotional Support Chatbots in the Era of LLMs.

Ayah Zirikly, Philip Resnik, Özlem Uzuner, and Kristy Hollingshead. 2019. CLPsych 2019 shared task: Predicting the degree of suicide risk in Reddit posts. In *Proceedings of the Sixth Workshop on Computational Linguistics and Clinical Psychology*, pages 24–33, Minneapolis, Minnesota. Association for Computational Linguistics.

A Prompts

Figure 4 displays the full-length versions of the prompt used in our study compared to those finetuned for GPT-4. This side-by-side presentation allows for a detailed view of the prompt structures, showcasing the specific instructions tailored to guide the language model's analysis for suicide risk assessment in online posts.

B XinHai LLM

XinHai LLM is fine-tuned from ChatGLM3-6B, utilizing a comprehensive SFT process that integrates extensive medical knowledge to enhance its proficiency in the healthcare domain. Our SFT process involves curating a diverse range of healthcare datasets, which includes dialogues, question-answering pairs, and specialized content from both mental and physical health disciplines. This rich dataset compilation ensures that XinHai LLM is exposed to a wide array of medical terminologies, conditions, treatments, and patient interactions, fostering a deeper understanding of medical contexts. To accommodate multilingual capabilities, we also acknowledge the availability of healthcare datasets in various languages, such as Spanish from HeadQA (Vilares and Gómez-Rodríguez, 2019) and French from French MedMCQA (Pal et al., 2022). However, for the XinHai model, we specifically focus on datasets in English and Chinese to align with our target demographic and application requirements. The open-accessible datasets employed for our SFT are meticulously listed in Table 2, ensuring transparency in our fine-tuning resources. The integration of this targeted medical knowledge aims to provide XinHai LLM with a nuanced understanding of the healthcare sector, thereby improving its performance on related tasks.

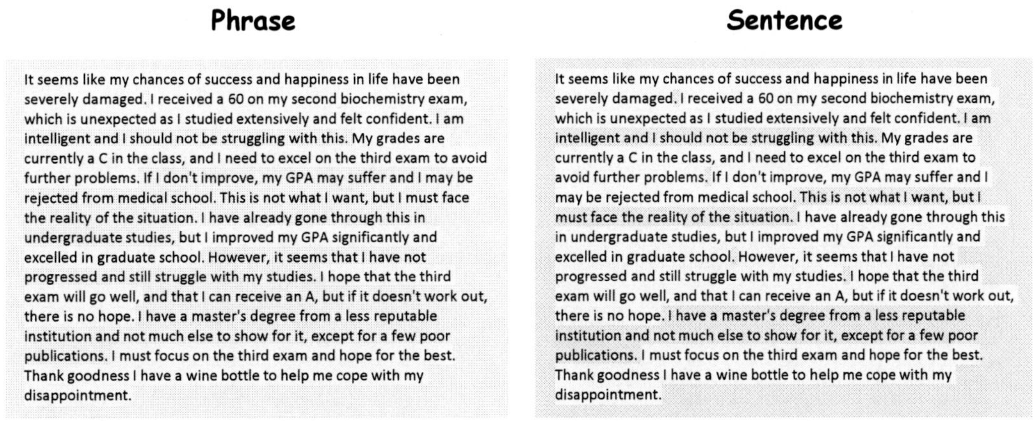

Figure 3: The figure compares the extracted results at phrase and sentence levels, highlighting evidence identified by the local LLM. The examples have been rephrased for privacy reasons. This demonstrates the impact of phrase-level versus sentence-level prompting on output clarity and structure.

Language	Domain	Dataset	Style	Size	Instructions
English	Medical	PubMedQA (Jin et al., 2019)	QA	273,518	273,518
		MedMCQA (Pal et al., 2022)	MCQA	182,822	182,822
	Mental	EmpathicReactions (Buechel et al., 2018)		1,860	916
		EmpatheticDialogues (Rashkin et al., 2019)	Dialogue	84,170	35,535
		EmpathyMentalHealth (Sharma et al., 2020)	QA	2,775	1,344
		CounselChat (Bertagnolli, 2020)	QA	2,775	2,775
		ESConv (Liu et al., 2021)	Dialogue	15,395	15,325
		EDOS (Welivita et al., 2021)	Dialogue	1,000,000	569,328
		EmpathicConversations (Omitaomu et al., 2022)	Dialogue	8,776	4,360
		PAIR (Min et al., 2022)	Dialogue	318	636
		CHQ-SocioEmo (Alasmari et al., 2023)	QA	1,500	593
		GENA (Dang et al., 2023)	KG	40,805	40,805
		ExTES (Zheng et al., 2023b)	Dialogue	11,178	78,131
		AugESC (Zheng et al., 2023a)	Dialogue	65,077	797,783
		HeadQA (Vilares and Gómez-Rodríguez, 2019)	QA	2,657	2657
		MedQAJin (Jin et al., 2020)	QA	48,876	48,876
Chinese	Medical	cMedQA2 (Zhang et al., 2018)	QA	100,000	188,783
		cMedDialogue[a]	QA	792,099	792,099
		webMedQA (He et al., 2019)	QA	252,850	50,570
		MedicalDialog (He et al., 2020)	Dialogue	2,725,989	4,503,475
		CMID (Chen et al., 2020)	NER	12,254	11,786
		NLPEC (Li et al., 2020)	MCQA	18,703	18,703
		MLEC-QA (Li et al., 2021)	MCQA	108,988	108,988
		DISCMed (Bao et al., 2023)	Dialogue	464,898	1,362,307
		CMB (Wang et al., 2023)	MCQA	269,359	269,359
	Mental	PsyQA (Sun et al., 2021)	QA	50,471	50,471
		EFAQA (Wang et al., 2020)	QA	20,000	56,743
		SMILE (Qiu et al., 2023)	Dialogue	355,732	355,732

Table 2: Public datasets for medical domain and psychological domain. The table shows their size with the original format and numbers of instructions constructed for the XinHai LLM.

[a] https://github.com/Toyhom/Chinese-medical-dialogue-data

Before

You are a medical language model trained to analyze Reddit posts for suicide risk assessment. Your task is to identify key phrases or sentences that indicate suicidal ideation or distress and to evaluate the suicide risk level based on specified criteria.

1. Read the Reddit post.
2. Use Chain of Thought reasoning to identify and extract sentences or some words that suggest suicidal thoughts, distress, or related issues.
3. Assess the suicide risk level based on the identified criteria
4. Assign a risk level: No Risk, Low Risk, Moderate Risk, High Risk.
5. Briefly summary extraced sentences and explain why you are assign a risk level to it.

Assigned Risk Level:
- No Risk: I don't see evidence that this person [the author of the post(s)] is at risk of suicide;
- Low Risk: There may be some factors here that could suggest risk, but I don't really think this person is at much of a risk of suicide
- Moderate Risk: I see indications that there could be a genuine risk of this person making a suicide attempt
- High Risk: I believe this person is at high risk of attempting suicide in the near future

identified criteria:
(a) Emotions: How does the individual feel? From feeling sad to experiencing unbearable psychological pain, the self-disclosed emotions of the user could play an important role in the risk level assigned to the individual.
(b) Cognitions: What are the individual's thoughts and perceptions about suicide? For example, what is the level and frequency of suicidal thoughts? Does the individual intend to self-harm/suicide? Does the individual have a plan about it?
(c) Behaviour and Motivation: What are the individual's acts or behavior related to suicide? For example, do they have access to means and a concrete plan? What is the user's ability to handle difficult/stressful situations ("behaviour"); what is the motivation behind their wish to be dead?
(d) Interpersonal and social support: Does the individual have social support/stable relationships? How does the individual feel towards significant others?
(e) Mental health-related issues: Consider psychiatric diagnoses associated with suicide such as schizophrenia, bipolar/anxiety/eating disorder, previous self-harm/suicidal attempts and others.
(f) Context/additional risk factors: For example, socioeconomic and demographic factors, exposure to suicide behaviour by others, chronic medical condition, ...

Output format: JSON format with three fields: 'Evidences', 'Assigned Risk Level', and 'Summary'. Only output these fields.The 'Evidences' field should be a list of sentences extracted from the Reddit post that suggest suicide risk.
{
"Extracted Evidences": ["Extracted sentence 1", "Extracted sentence 2", "..."\],
"Label": "An assigned risk level according to identified criteria.",
"Example summarized evidence": "A summary of evidence and explain the risk level briefly"
}

GPT-4-Tailored

"Role: Specialized Medical Language Model for Suicide Risk Assessment in Online Posts

Instructions for the AI:

1. Carefully examine the provided Reddit post. Focus on identifying phrases or words that suggest suicidal ideation, distress, or related mental health issues.

2. Employ Chain of Thought reasoning to discern and highlight specific phrases or words from the post that are indicative of the user's mental state, considering the following criteria:

(a) Emotions: Assess the emotions expressed, ranging from sadness to unbearable psychological pain.
(b) Cognitions: Analyze thoughts and perceptions about suicide, including frequency of suicidal thoughts, intentions to self-harm, and the presence of a plan.
(c) Behaviour and Motivation: Examine behaviors or actions related to suicide, access to means, coping abilities, and motivations behind suicidal ideation.
(d) Interpersonal and Social Support: Evaluate the user's social support and relationship stability.
(e) Mental Health-related Issues: Consider any mentioned psychiatric diagnoses, history of self-harm, or suicidal attempts.
(f) Context/Additional Risk Factors: Take into account socioeconomic, demographic factors, exposure to suicidal behavior, chronic medical conditions, etc.

3. Based on the identified evidences, assign a suicide risk level from the options: No Risk, Low Risk, Moderate Risk, High Risk.

4. Provide a concise summary explaining the reasoning behind the assigned risk level. This summary should elaborate on how the extracted phrases or words align with the identified criteria.

5. Format the output in a JSON structure with fields for 'Extracted Evidences', 'Assigned Risk Level', and 'Summary'. Ensure that the 'Extracted Evidences' field comprehensively lists the specific phrases or words identified from the Reddit post.

Example JSON Output Format:

{
"Extracted Evidences": ["Specific phrase or word 1", "Specific phrase or word 2", "..."\],
"Assigned Risk Level": "An assigned risk level according to identified criteria.",
"Summary": "A brief explanation of the evidence and the reasoning behind the assigned risk level"
}

Now, process the input case into the specified output format, paying special attention to the structured list output in the case."

Figure 4: Full-length prompts.

A Dual-Prompting for Interpretable Mental Health Language Models

Hyolim Jeon[1,2*], **Dongje Yoo**[3*], **Daeun Lee**[1],
Sejung Son[1], **Seungbae Kim**[4], **Jinyoung Han**[1,2†]

[1]Department of Applied Artificial Intelligence, Sungkyunkwan University, Seoul, South Korea
[2]Department of Human-AI Interaction, Sungkyunkwan University, Seoul, South Korea
[3]Department of Computer Engineering, Chung-Ang University, Seoul, South Korea
[4]Computer Science & Engineering Department, University of South Florida, Tampa, FL, USA
{gyfla1512, maze0717}@g.skku.edu {delee12, jinyounghan}@skku.edu
pass12@cau.ac.kr, seungbae@usf.edu

Abstract

Despite the increasing demand for AI-based mental health monitoring tools, their practical utility for clinicians is limited by the lack of interpretability. The CLPsych 2024 Shared Task[1] aims to enhance the interpretability of Large Language Models (LLMs), particularly in mental health analysis, by providing evidence of suicidality through linguistic content. We propose a dual-prompting approach: (i) Knowledge-aware evidence extraction by leveraging the expert identity and a suicide dictionary with a mental health-specific LLM; and (ii) Evidence summarization by employing an LLM-based consistency evaluator. Comprehensive experiments demonstrate the effectiveness of combining domain-specific information, revealing performance improvements and the approach's potential to aid clinicians in assessing mental state progression.

1 Introduction

The global healthcare system faces significant challenges from mental health conditions such as depression and suicidal ideation (Darrudi et al., 2022), emphasizing the need for an advanced monitoring system for early intervention (Galea et al., 2020).

In response, NLP researchers have paid attention to identifying mental states, often leveraging social media data (Chen et al., 2023; Liu et al., 2023; Lee et al., 2023). Notably, the most recent development involves the application of Large Language Models (LLMs), which have demonstrated robust capabilities in general language processing in mental health analysis (Yang et al., 2023a,b; Xu et al., 2023b). Specifically, Amin et al. (2023) conducted a comparison of ChatGPT's zero-shot capability in identifying suicide and depression, contrasting it with previous methods that relied on previous Pretrained Language Models (PLMs). Furthermore, Lamichhane (2023) evaluated ChatGPT's effectiveness in recognizing stress, depression, and suicide, emphasizing its strong grasp of language in texts related to mental health.

However, these studies have focused on identifying mental health status through a black box model, posing a challenge in interpreting the rationale behind their outcomes (Schoene et al., 2023; Zhang et al., 2022). Accordingly, efforts have been made to enhance the interpretability of mental health analysis, such as guiding LLMs to emphasize emotional cues (Yang et al., 2023a) and developing open-source LLMs by training them with data from mental health-related social media (Yang et al., 2023b). Nevertheless, a lack of reliability still remains; recent LLMs are often unreliable or inconsistent (Agrawal et al., 2022), potentially due to the lack of mental health-related knowledge (Yang et al., 2023a). This problem has significantly delayed the practical use of LLMs in clinical settings (Malhotra and Jindal, 2024).

To address this issue, the CLPsych 2024 Shared Task (Chim et al., 2024) introduces the challenge of utilizing open-source LLMs to enhance their interpretability in mental health analysis, specifically focusing on detecting suicidality through linguistic content in social media data. Particularly, the shared task includes two subtasks: (i) *Task A* requires finding key phrases from each post to support suicide risk, and (ii) *Task B* aims to provide a summary of evidence related to the user's suicide risk across multiple posts.

In this paper, we design an enhanced prompt for the extraction task (Task A) by assigning an expert identity, enabling LLMs to function as an expected agent (Xu et al., 2023a), and leveraging a suicide dictionary (Lee et al., 2022) to capture suicide-related context. Here, we utilize mental health-specific LLM, MentaLLaMA (Yang et al., 2023a). For the summarization task (Task B), we employ a consistency evaluator (Luo et al., 2023) to

* Equal contribution.
† Corresponding author.
[1]https://clpsych.org/shared-task-2024/

Proceedings of the 9th Workshop on Computational Linguistics and Clinical Psychology (CLPsych 2024), pages 247–255
March 21, 2024

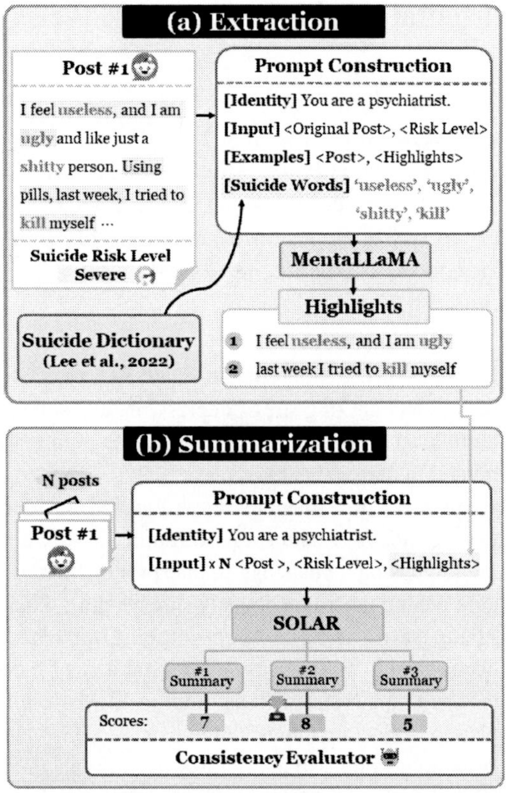

Figure 1: The overall architecture of the proposed approach: (a) Knowledge-aware Evidence Extraction (§2.1) and (b) Evidence Summarization with LLM-based Consistency Evaluator (§2.2)

improve the consistency of outcomes with multiple summaries.

The extensive experiments illustrate that combining domain-specific information with few-shot learning enhances the extraction of evidence, resulting in an improvement in recall from 91.0% to 92.2%. Additionally, our findings indicate that an LLM trained with general datasets is more effective in mitigating hallucination in summarization tasks than a domain-specific LLM. We believe our approach can support clinicians in assessing mental state progression.

2 Methodology

Our aim is (i) to extract evidence supporting the user's suicide risk from each post and (ii) to summarize all the evidence across multiple posts. To this end, we design two prompting strategies to instruct LLMs for trustworthy reasoning in mental health analysis. These strategies include Knowledge-aware Evidence Extraction (§2.1) and Evidence Summarization with an LLM-based Consistency Evaluator (§2.2). The overall proposed approach is depicted in Figure 1, and the full text of each prompt is available in Appendix A.

Table 1: Example of suicide words (Lee et al., 2022).

Suicide Risk	# of Words	Examples
Low	48	emptiness, overthink
Moderate	83	psychiatric, pain
Severe	111	cutting, die

2.1 Knowledge-aware Evidence Extraction

As shown in Figure 1(a), the prompt for the extraction task includes the original post and the assigned user's suicide risk level. For few-shot learning, we incorporate examples that are not included in the evaluation dataset. Moreover, we apply the three prompting strategies to address the unreliability issue of LLMs arising from the lack of mental health-related knowledge (Yang et al., 2023a).

A. Mental health-specific LLM. In order to tackle the zero-shot challenge in LLMs (Han et al., 2023), we utilize MentaLLaMA-chat-13B (Yang et al., 2023b), fine-tuned with 105K mental health-related social media data, demonstrating its efficacy in mental health-related tasks.

B. Assigning expert identity. As LLMs tend to provide insight into their cognitive processes when assigning predefined roles (Li et al., 2023; Xu et al., 2023a), we employ prompts to allocate the domain expert identity (e.g., *'You are a psychiatrist'*).

C. Utilizing a suicide dictionary. Since a domain-specific dictionary can aid LLMs in capturing relevant context (Yang et al., 2023a), we utilize a suicide dictionary (Lee et al., 2022), which has proven effective in identifying suicidal ideation on social media data. As shown in Table 1, the dictionary uses the UMD Reddit Suicidality Dataset (Shing et al., 2018), comprising 279 words validated by domain experts. If the given post includes words from the suicide dictionary (Lee et al., 2022), the model identifies and incorporates these words into our prompt, instructing the LLM to consider these words attentively.

2.2 Evidence Summarization with LLM-based Consistency Evaluator

As shown in Figure 1(b), the prompt for the summarization incorporates multiple posts and the assigned user's suicide risk level. Additionally, an expert identity is assigned, similar to the previous step. However, despite the advancements in LLMs,

Table 2: Statistics of the evaluation dataset.

	Highlights	Summarization
Suicide Risk	**# posts (avg. # length)**	**# users (avg. # posts)**
Low	17 (1,149)	13 (1.31)
Moderate	91 (1,132)	75 (1.21)
Severe	54 (1,178)	37 (1.46)
Total	**162 posts**	**125 users**

hallucination and inconsistency still remain significant concerns (Tang et al., 2023a,b). To mitigate this issue, we apply the two following strategies that can enhance consistency.

A. Extract-then-Generate. Zhang et al. (2023) demonstrated the effectiveness of prompts that incorporate an extractive summary for abstractive summarization. Following this approach, the proposed prompt integrates the extracted phrases obtained from the preceding step (§2.1). The full text of each prompt is available in Appendix A.2.1.

B. Consistency Evaluator. We adopt a consistency evaluator proposed by Luo et al. (2023). Initially, multiple candidate answers are generated through the LLM. We then compute consistency scores (ranging from 1 to 10) for each candidate, assessing the extent to which the generated summary aligns with the original posts, utilizing the consistency evaluator. In the end, the answer with the highest score from multiple candidates is selected as the final result. Here, we adopt SOLAR (Kim et al., 2023) as the summarizer and evaluator, known for its recent outstanding performance[2]. Further details comparing summarizer and evaluator are provided in §4.2.

3 Experiments

3.1 Evaluation Dataset

The CLPsych 2024 shared task (Chim et al., 2024) provides the UMD Reddit Suicidality Dataset (Zirikly et al., 2019; Shing et al., 2018), consisting of 79,569 posts from 37,083 subreddits by 866 Reddit users who posted on r/SuicideWatch between 2008 and 2015. Each user in the dataset is assigned a label that indicates the severity of suicidality (i.e., No, Low, Moderate, or Severe), determined by crowdsourcers and domain experts.

The evaluation dataset comprises a subset of users labeled with *Low*, *Moderate*, and *Severe* risks validated by domain experts. It includes 162 posts distributed among 125 users and the statistics of the dataset are summarized in Table 2.

[2]`https://huggingface.co/spaces/HuggingFaceH4/open_llm_leaderboard`

Table 3: Comparison of performance between zero-shot and few-shot learning for the extraction task (Task A) using the evaluation dataset.

Model	Highlights (Task A)		
	Pre.↑	Rec.↑	F1↑
Ours w/ Zero-shot	**0.913**	0.910	0.911
Ours w/ Few-shot	0.912	**0.922**	**0.917**

3.2 Experimental Settings

All experiments are conducted on a GeForce RTX 3090 Ti GPU with 26GB of memory. To minimize the memory cost of 16-bit weights, we employ the bitsandbytes library (Dettmers et al., 2022a), converting them to int8 using vector-wise quantization (Dettmers et al., 2022b) without significant quality loss. Each prompt is processed independently to mitigate the impact of dialogue history.

3.3 Evaluation Metrics

Note that the ground truth dataset was not provided to the participants. Therefore, all the evaluation metrics and reported results are supplied by the organizers of the CLPsych 2024 Shared Task.

(1) Similarity: BERTScore (Zhang et al., 2019) is employed for the extraction task to assess token similarity using contextual embeddings.

(2) Consistency: For the summarization task, a natural language inference (NLI) model (Laurer et al., 2024) is applied to assess the consistency of individual sentences in the provided evidence summary. Specifically, the contradiction scores are calculated between the predicted outcomes and each ground truth summary sentence. The resulting sentence-level consistency score is then determined as 1 minus the probability of the contradiction prediction.

4 Results & Analysis

To demonstrate the effectiveness of the proposed method, we compare its performance with various approaches and conduct the case study where our proposed approach performs better. Note that due to the absence of ground truth from the organizer, quantitative analysis was limited, leading us to focus on qualitative analysis instead. Additionally, we manually paraphrase any examples from the data to preserve user anonymity.

4.1 Analysis on Knowledge-aware Evidence Extraction

Table 3 shows the results of our approach on the evaluation dataset, with precision, recall, and F1 scores, for the highlights task (Task A).

Analysis on few-shot learning. We find an improvement in recall from 91.0% to 92.2% by integrating few-shot learning. This suggests the importance of providing examples for few-shot learning in domain-specific tasks, particularly in clinical settings (Han et al., 2023).

Analysis on suicide-dictionary. We find integrating a suicide dictionary (Lee et al., 2022) also improves domain knowledge in extracting evidence. Specifically, it allows thorough consideration of suicide risk factors that might be overlooked due to their general meaning, such as *'family'* and *'credit'*, which have been validated by domain experts as suicide-related words. Examples of the results are provided below.

> ***Response w/ Suicide Dictionary:*** ["Fear of failing.","Fear of hurting."], ["working as of credit problems."], ["Don't want to be a burden or face my friends and family."]

Analysis on expert identity. We explore the performance of the LLM by employing different expert identities, such as psychology, counseling, and psychiatry. This analysis aims to understand how the model's behavior varies depending on the assigned role. For example, when the role is assigned as a psychologist, the LLM tends to prioritize the user's negative self-perception (e.g., *'ugly'* and *'hate'*) to a greater extent. Conversely, adopting the identity of a counselor enables the model to focus on the relationship (e.g., *'broke up'* and *'divorce'*), which may contribute to feelings of isolation. Additionally, we observe that assigning a psychiatrist role is likely to focus on clinical markers, such as emotional distress (e.g., *'anxiety'*) and history of abuse (e.g., *'assaulted'*), which can be connected to suicidal ideation. Hence, we suggest that selecting an appropriate identity aligned with the research objective can offer valuable insights.

> ***Response w/ Psychology Identity:*** ["I am ugly, I am annoying, I am unwanted"], ["I hate me"]
>
> ***Response w/ Counselor Identity :*** ["Fuck, we broke up three weeks ago"], ["disconnected from everybody"]

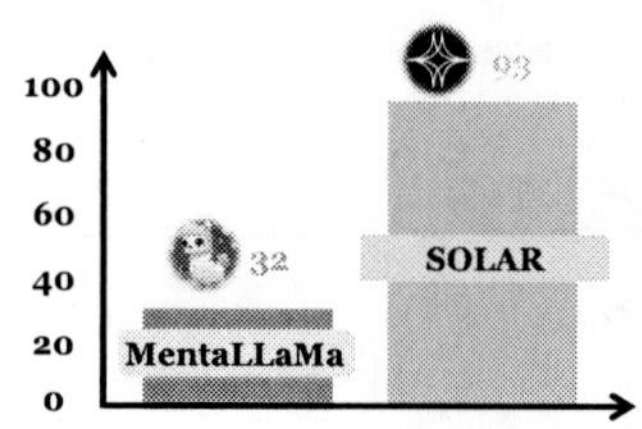

Figure 2: Winner count comparison for MentaLLaMA (Yang et al., 2023b) and SOLAR (Kim et al., 2023) in 125 evaluation dataset using evaluator.

> ***Response w/ Psychiatry Identity:*** ["I will never go to school because of my depression."], ["I am feeling anxious/angry and constantly lonely"], ["When I was 4 years old, I was sexually abused"]

4.2 Analysis on Evidence Summarization with LLM-based Consistency Evaluator

Analysis on Extract-then-Generate. We explore the efficacy of incorporating extractive summaries from Task A for the evidence summarization task. We observe that the hallucination issue frequently arises when extractive summaries are absent. This indicates that our approach enhances consistency by providing contextual information (Zhang et al., 2023). For a better understanding, we provide an example below. We notice that the LLM misinterprets the expression *'wishing to do it'* as a desire for success, resulting in generating *'self-distrust in achievements'* by the LLM.

> ***Posts:*** I was thinking about when I tried to hang myself, wishing to do it now.
> ***Response w/o Extract-then-Generate:*** They exhibit risk due to cognitions (self-distrust in achievements).

Comparison LLMs with Consistency Evaluator. Table 4 shows the results of our approach on the evaluation dataset, along with the mean consistency scores for the summarization task (Task B). We find that using only SOLAR (Kim et al., 2023) as a summarizer performed better than using both SOLAR (Kim et al., 2023) and MentaLLaMA (Yang et al., 2023b). This also can be found in Figure 2, when we use both summarizers, the evaluator selects 93 results from SOLAR (Kim et al., 2023) and 32 from MentaLLaMA (Yang et al., 2023b) as the final outputs from the 125 evaluation set. This implies that domain-specific models tend to perform worse than general LLMs, like

Table 4: Comparison of performance among different summarizers for the summarization task (Task B) using the evaluation dataset.

Summarizer	Summarization (Task B)
	Consistency↑
SOLAR & MentaLLaMa	0.970
SOLAR	**0.973**

ChatGPT (Luo et al., 2023) or SOLAR (Kim et al., 2023), on general linguistic tasks such as abstractive summarization (Wu et al., 2023). Moreover, MentaLLaMA (Yang et al., 2023b) exhibits biased hallucination issues by generating mental-health-related words like '*stuck*' or '*bother*' regardless of original contexts, leading to inconsistency. In future work, we plan to explore the comparison of evaluators and summarizers using a broader range of LLMs to gain additional insights.

> ***Posts:*** If I couldn't return, I would jump on the train, or my dad wouldn't take me to the TV show ...
> ***Response w/ MentaLLaMa:*** The user shows a feeling of being stuck and bothered by others.

4.3 Error Analysis

While our proposed approach demonstrates outstanding performance, there are a few cases where the model fails to recognize crucial evidence supporting the suicide risk level and extracts sentences that are irrelevant to the potential suicide risk. Concerning practical utility, the lack of reliability has considerably impeded the implementation of LLMs in clinical settings (Malhotra and Jindal, 2024).

> ***Response w/ Expert Identity:*** ["This subreddit is a fantastic place."]

> ***Response w/ Suicide Dictionary:*** ["I love everyone in this subreddit."]

5 Conclusion

In this study, we introduced promising prompting strategies that can provide evidence supporting suicide risk levels on social media data. We enhanced the LLM interpretability by incorporating domain-specific elements like assigning a psychiatrist identity and combining a suicide word. Additionally, we improved the consistency in summarization by using a consistency evaluator with multiple candidates. The proposed dual-prompting approach provides reliable reasoning, making it suitable for monitoring mental health-related risks.

Limitations

Since ground truth is not provided, quantitative comparisons are limited. Therefore, we rely on qualitative comparisons, which may be subjective. Our experiments use only the smallest version of LLMs due to limited resources. Providing inferences about suicidality using social media data is inherently subjective, allowing for various interpretations among researchers (Keilp et al., 2012). Moreover, the experimental data may be sensitive to demographic and media-specific biases (Hovy and Spruit, 2016). While the effectiveness of leveraging social media data for mental health analysis may be constrained in specific clinical settings (Ernala et al., 2019), adopting a practical model promises the potential to discern diverse statistical patterns and biases across various objectives (Jacobson et al., 2020). Although the suicide dictionary (Lee et al., 2022) has demonstrated effectiveness in predicting suicide risk, its reliance on social media data for construction might restrict its generalizability. Furthermore, the dictionary was constructed using the same dataset as the one utilized in the Shared Task, which is anticipated to introduce a certain degree of bias.

Future Work. In future work, we plan to explore a wider range of prompt templates to enhance overall performance further. For instance, the prompts could be diversified by applying various LLM-based consistency evaluators, including ChatGPT and LLaMa2. Our ultimate objective is to expand the scope to cover diverse mental health domains, such as depression and bipolar disorder, and validate its effectiveness comprehensively. To achieve this, we plan to investigate domain-specific fine-tuning methods for LLMs in the mental health field, thereby extending the model to a more interpretable context.

Ethical Statement

The CLPsych 2024 shared task (Chim et al., 2024) prioritized responsible data utilization by providing exclusive access to the dataset for researchers aligned with ethical principles. Consequently, all task participants must adhere to data use agreements and ethical practices during the competition. Our research strongly emphasizes ethics, particularly in (i) protecting the privacy of Reddit users and (ii) preventing potential misuse of the dataset. We strictly adhered to Reddit's privacy policy[3] to ensure user anonymity (Benton et al., 2017; Williams et al., 2017).

Acknowledgments

We commit to acknowledging the assistance of the American Association of Suicidology in making the dataset available, in any publications.

This research was supported by the Ministry of Education of the Republic of Korea and the National Research Foundation (NRF) of Korea (NRF-2022S1A5A8054322) and the International Research & Development Program of the National Research Foundation of Korea (NRF) funded by the Ministry of Science and ICT (RS-2023-00265683).

References

Monica Agrawal, Stefan Hegselmann, Hunter Lang, Yoon Kim, and David Sontag. 2022. Large language models are few-shot clinical information extractors. In *Proceedings of the 2022 Conference on Empirical Methods in Natural Language Processing*, pages 1998–2022.

Mostafa M Amin, Erik Cambria, and Björn W Schuller. 2023. Will affective computing emerge from foundation models and general ai? a first evaluation on chatgpt. *IEEE Intelligent Systems*, 38:2.

Adrian Benton, Glen Coppersmith, and Mark Dredze. 2017. Ethical research protocols for social media health research. In *Proceedings of the first ACL workshop on ethics in natural language processing*, pages 94–102.

Siyuan Chen, Zhiling Zhang, Mengyue Wu, and Kenny Zhu. 2023. Detection of multiple mental disorders from social media with two-stream psychiatric experts. In *Proceedings of the 2023 Conference on Empirical Methods in Natural Language Processing*, pages 9071–9084, Singapore. Association for Computational Linguistics.

Jenny Chim, Adam Tsakalidis, Dimitris Gkoumas, Dana Atzil-Slonim, Yaakov Ophir, Ayah Zirikly, Philip Resnik, and Maria Liakata. 2024. Overview of the clpsych 2024 shared task: Leveraging large language models to identify evidence of suicidality risk in online posts. In *Proceedings of the Ninth Workshop on Computational Linguistics and Clinical Psychology*. Association for Computational Linguistics.

Alireza Darrudi, Mohammad Hossein Ketabchi Khoonsari, and Maryam Tajvar. 2022. Challenges to achieving universal health coverage throughout the world: a systematic review. *Journal of preventive medicine and public health*, 55(2):125.

[3]`https://www.reddit.com/policies/privacy-policy`

Tim Dettmers, Mike Lewis, Younes Belkada, and Luke Zettlemoyer. 2022a. GPT3.int8(): 8-bit matrix multiplication for transformers at scale. In *Advances in Neural Information Processing Systems*.

Tim Dettmers, Mike Lewis, Sam Shleifer, and Luke Zettlemoyer. 2022b. 8-bit optimizers via block-wise quantization. *9th International Conference on Learning Representations, ICLR*.

Sindhu Kiranmai Ernala, Michael L Birnbaum, Kristin A Candan, Asra F Rizvi, William A Sterling, John M Kane, and Munmun De Choudhury. 2019. Methodological gaps in predicting mental health states from social media: triangulating diagnostic signals. In *Proceedings of the 2019 chi conference on human factors in computing systems*, pages 1–16.

Sandro Galea, Raina M Merchant, and Nicole Lurie. 2020. The mental health consequences of covid-19 and physical distancing: the need for prevention and early intervention. *JAMA internal medicine*, 180(6):817–818.

Tianyu Han, Lisa C Adams, Jens-Michalis Papaioannou, Paul Grundmann, Tom Oberhauser, Alexander Löser, Daniel Truhn, and Keno K Bressem. 2023. Medalpaca–an open-source collection of medical conversational ai models and training data. *arXiv preprint arXiv:2304.08247*.

Dirk Hovy and Shannon L Spruit. 2016. The social impact of natural language processing. In *Proceedings of the 54th Annual Meeting of the Association for Computational Linguistics (Volume 2: Short Papers)*, pages 591–598.

Nicholas C Jacobson, Kate H Bentley, Ashley Walton, Shirley B Wang, Rebecca G Fortgang, Alexander J Millner, Garth Coombs III, Alexandra M Rodman, and Daniel DL Coppersmith. 2020. Ethical dilemmas posed by mobile health and machine learning in psychiatry research. *Bulletin of the World Health Organization*, 98(4):270.

John G Keilp, Michael F Grunebaum, Marianne Gorlyn, Simone LeBlanc, Ainsley K Burke, Hanga Galfalvy, Maria A Oquendo, and J John Mann. 2012. Suicidal ideation and the subjective aspects of depression. *Journal of affective disorders*, 140(1):75–81.

Dahyun Kim, Chanjun Park, Sanghoon Kim, Wonsung Lee, Wonho Song, Yunsu Kim, Hyeonwoo Kim, Yungi Kim, Hyeonju Lee, Jihoo Kim, et al. 2023. Solar 10.7 b: Scaling large language models with simple yet effective depth up-scaling. *arXiv preprint arXiv:2312.15166*.

Bishal Lamichhane. 2023. Evaluation of chatgpt for nlp-based mental health applications. *arXiv preprint arXiv:2303.15727*.

Moritz Laurer, Wouter Van Atteveldt, Andreu Casas, and Kasper Welbers. 2024. Less annotating, more classifying: Addressing the data scarcity issue of supervised machine learning with deep transfer learning and bert-nli. *Political Analysis*, 32(1):84–100.

Daeun Lee, Migyeong Kang, Minji Kim, and Jinyoung Han. 2022. Detecting suicidality with a contextual graph neural network. In *Proceedings of the eighth workshop on computational linguistics and clinical psychology*, pages 116–125.

Daeun Lee, Sejung Son, Hyolim Jeon, Seungbae Kim, and Jinyoung Han. 2023. Towards suicide prevention from bipolar disorder with temporal symptom-aware multitask learning. In *Proceedings of the 29th ACM SIGKDD Conference on Knowledge Discovery and Data Mining*, pages 4357–4369.

Guohao Li, Hasan Abed Al Kader Hammoud, Hani Itani, Dmitrii Khizbullin, and Bernard Ghanem. 2023. CAMEL: Communicative agents for "mind" exploration of large language model society. In *Thirty-seventh Conference on Neural Information Processing Systems*.

Yujian Liu, Laura Biester, and Rada Mihalcea. 2023. Improving mental health classifier generalization with pre-diagnosis data. In *Proceedings of the International AAAI Conference on Web and Social Media*, volume 17, pages 566–577.

Zheheng Luo, Qianqian Xie, and Sophia Ananiadou. 2023. Chatgpt as a factual inconsistency evaluator for abstractive text summarization. *arXiv preprint arXiv:2303.15621*.

Anshu Malhotra and Rajni Jindal. 2024. Xai transformer based approach for interpreting depressed and suicidal user behavior on online social networks. *Cognitive Systems Research*, 84:101186.

Annika Marie Schoene, John Ortega, Silvio Amir, and Kenneth Church. 2023. An example of (too much) hyper-parameter tuning in suicide ideation detection. In *Proceedings of the International AAAI Conference on Web and Social Media*, volume 17, pages 1158–1162.

Han-Chin Shing, Suraj Nair, Ayah Zirikly, Meir Friedenberg, Hal Daumé III, and Philip Resnik. 2018. Expert, crowdsourced, and machine assessment of suicide risk via online postings. In *Proceedings of the fifth workshop on computational linguistics and clinical psychology: from keyboard to clinic*, pages 25–36.

Liyan Tang, Tanya Goyal, Alex Fabbri, Philippe Laban, Jiacheng Xu, Semih Yavuz, Wojciech Kryscinski, Justin Rousseau, and Greg Durrett. 2023a. Understanding factual errors in summarization: Errors, summarizers, datasets, error detectors. In *Proceedings of the 61st Annual Meeting of the Association for Computational Linguistics (Volume 1: Long Papers)*, pages 11626–11644, Toronto, Canada. Association for Computational Linguistics.

Liyan Tang, Zhaoyi Sun, Betina Idnay, Jordan G Nestor, Ali Soroush, Pierre A Elias, Ziyang Xu, Ying Ding, Greg Durrett, Justin F Rousseau, et al. 2023b. Evaluating large language models on medical evidence summarization. *npj Digital Medicine*, 6(1):158.

Matthew L Williams, Pete Burnap, and Luke Sloan. 2017. Towards an ethical framework for publishing twitter data in social research: Taking into account users' views, online context and algorithmic estimation. *Sociology*, 51(6):1149–1168.

Shijie Wu, Ozan Irsoy, Steven Lu, Vadim Dabravolski, Mark Dredze, Sebastian Gehrmann, Prabhanjan Kambadur, David Rosenberg, and Gideon Mann. 2023. Bloomberggpt: A large language model for finance. *arXiv preprint arXiv:2303.17564*.

Benfeng Xu, An Yang, Junyang Lin, Quan Wang, Chang Zhou, Yongdong Zhang, and Zhendong Mao. 2023a. Expertprompting: Instructing large language models to be distinguished experts. *arXiv preprint arXiv:2305.14688*.

Xuhai Xu, Bingshen Yao, Yuanzhe Dong, Saadia Gabriel, Hong Yu, Marzyeh Ghassemi, James Hendler, Anind K Dey, and Dakuo Wang. 2023b. Mental-llm: Leveraging large language models for mental health prediction via online text data. *arXiv preprint arXiv:2307.14385*.

Kailai Yang, Shaoxiong Ji, Tianlin Zhang, Qianqian Xie, Ziyan Kuang, and Sophia Ananiadou. 2023a. Towards interpretable mental health analysis with large language models. In *Proceedings of the 2023 Conference on Empirical Methods in Natural Language Processing*, pages 6056–6077.

Kailai Yang, Tianlin Zhang, Ziyan Kuang, Qianqian Xie, and Sophia Ananiadou. 2023b. Mentalllama: Interpretable mental health analysis on social media with large language models. *arXiv preprint arXiv:2309.13567*.

Haopeng Zhang, Xiao Liu, and Jiawei Zhang. 2023. Extractive summarization via ChatGPT for faithful summary generation. In *Findings of the Association for Computational Linguistics: EMNLP 2023*, pages 3270–3278, Singapore. Association for Computational Linguistics.

Tianlin Zhang, Annika M Schoene, Shaoxiong Ji, and Sophia Ananiadou. 2022. Natural language processing applied to mental illness detection: a narrative review. *NPJ digital medicine*, 5(1):46.

Tianyi Zhang, Varsha Kishore, Felix Wu, Kilian Q Weinberger, and Yoav Artzi. 2019. Bertscore: Evaluating text generation with bert. In *International Conference on Learning Representations*.

Ayah Zirikly, Philip Resnik, Ozlem Uzuner, and Kristy Hollingshead. 2019. Clpsych 2019 shared task: Predicting the degree of suicide risk in reddit posts. In *Proceedings of the sixth workshop on computational linguistics and clinical psychology*, pages 24–33.

A Appendix

A.1 Prompt of Knowledge-aware Evidence Extraction

Knowledge-aware Evidence Extraction

You are a psychiatrist.
<Examples>
Suicide Risk Level: [**Example's Label**]
Post: [**Example's Post**]
Highlights:
1. [**Highlights of Example**]
...

Referring to the <Examples> , Identify the original phrases in the post that express or reference suicide risk factors and list them without modification about <Question>.

<Question>
Suicide Risk Level: [**Label**]
Post : [**Post**]
- The answer must be in numbering format [examples of formatting]
- Phrases should be included in the given <Question>'s post.
- You MUST refer <Question>'s given post.
- Highlight only necessary phrases, not full sentences.
- Select the parts that haves the suicide-related words like [**Suicide Word List**]
- Select as many phrases as possible related to suicide even a little.

Highlights:

A.2 Evidence Summarization with LLM-based Consistency Evaluator

A.2.1 Prompt of Evidence Summarization

Extract-then-Generate

You are a psychiatrist.
You are willing to do an abstractive summary about the evidence that shows the user is at **[Label]** suicide risk.
There are suicide risk assessment aspects when seeing Reddit posts.

[GROUND TRUTH]
The suicide risk level of this user is [**Label**].
Here are Reddit posts and extractive evidence that supports the user is at **[Label]** suicide risk based on aspects.

[**Posts and Highlights**] Regarding the user's posts and extracted evidence and aspects of suicide risk assessments, Explain why the user is at [**Label**] suicide risk.
The revised summary should include the information in the extractive evidence and aspects.
The summary should be shorter than 300 letters.
The summary MUST be less than 300 letters.

Summarized evidence explain:

A.2.2 Prompt of Evaluating Consistency

Consistency Evaluator

You are an expertise psychiatry evaluator.
There are **[Label]** suicide risk user's posts and explain the reason for diagnosis based on posts.

[Posts]
Explain and summary of evidence: **[Summary]**
Score the following summary given the user posts concerning consistency from 1 to 10. Note that consistency measures how much information the summary includes in the source posts. 10 points indicate that the summary contains only statements that are entailed by the source posts. 1 point indicates that the summary does not contain any word or statement that is entailed by the source posts.

Scores choices: from [1] to [10]

Give me a clear mark score and explain about it.
Keep the answer format
- Format: The score is [1]

to
- Format: The score is [10]

Scores:

Cheap Ways of Extracting Clinical Markers from Texts

Anastasia Sandu anastasiasandu777@gmail.com
Teodor Mihailescu teomihailescu@yahoo.com
Sergiu Nisioi sergiu.nisioi@unibuc.ro

Human Language Technologies Research Center
Faculty of Mathematics and Computer Science
University of Bucharest

Abstract

This paper describes the work of the UniBuc Archaeology team for CLPsych's 2024 Shared Task, which involved finding evidence within the text supporting the assigned suicide risk level. Two types of evidence were required: highlights (extracting relevant spans within the text) and summaries (aggregating evidence into a synthesis). Our work focuses on evaluating Large Language Models (LLM) as opposed to an alternative method that is much more memory and resource efficient. The first approach employs a good old-fashioned machine learning (GOML) pipeline consisting of a tf-idf vectorizer with a logistic regression classifier, whose representative features are used to extract relevant highlights. The second, more resource intensive, uses an LLM for generating the summaries and is guided by chain-of-thought to provide sequences of text indicating clinical markers.

1 Introduction

Suicidal-themed messages on social media platforms can represent an indicator of suffering and mental health issues. According to Harmer et al. (2022), 6% of individuals aged 18-25 responded affirmatively to the survey questions on suicide ideation. Interdisciplinary work on psychology and computational linguistics (Zirikly et al., 2019; Uban et al., 2022) uses statistical models to identify various risks based on the content of social media posts or based on multi-modal characteristics such as time of post, user gender and class (Yang et al., 2022). Gaining awareness of the risk of suicide is essential, as it allows state organizations to offer support to those in need, and consequently, preventive measures can be taken, potentially saving the lives of those contemplating suicide. Therefore, it may be beneficial from multiple perspectives to develop methods through which the presence of suicidal thoughts can be determined on the basis of text posts on social networks. However, as Rezapour (2023) suggests, relying solely on algorithmic methods can introduce biases, risks, and, ultimately, case-by-case analyses must be carried out by experts.

In this paper, as part of the shared task of the 2024 Workshop on Computational Linguistics and Clinical Psychology (Chim et al., 2024), we address the identification of suicidal evidence in users' posts on Reddit by extracting phrases, expressions, key-words, and various types of summaries that can explain such labels. The shared task has been framed from the perspective of large language models (LLMs) with a suggestive title in this sense: "Utilising LLMs for finding supporting evidence about an individual's suicide risk level". Although LLMs are the current standard in natural language processing (McCoy et al., 2023; Hosseini et al., 2024), deploying such models at scale can be prohibitively expensive, while the pre-trainig can often be resource- and data-intensive, making such models available only for well-resourced languages and large research laboratories.

We address this task from the perspective of finding solutions for fast inference, and propose two variants: 1) to create a straightforward and *cheap* (as in time-efficient) pipeline for training and identifying suicidal evidence and 2) to use prompting with quantized LLMs (Dettmers et al., 2023) executed locally on CPU. The former is based on traditional machine learning classification techniques consisting of a tf-idf vectorizer over word ngrams paired with a feature importance selection process from a linear logistic regression classifier.

Our results in the shared task show that a machine learning pipeline can achieve competitive evaluation scores (top 3 recall) by leveraging the risk assement annotations from the provided dataset (Shing et al., 2018; Zirikly et al., 2019). However, our best-performing model is a combination of LLMs used to generate good-quality summarizations and machine learning to detect highlights.

Proceedings of the 9th Workshop on Computational Linguistics and Clinical Psychology (CLPsych 2024), pages 256–263
March 21, 2024

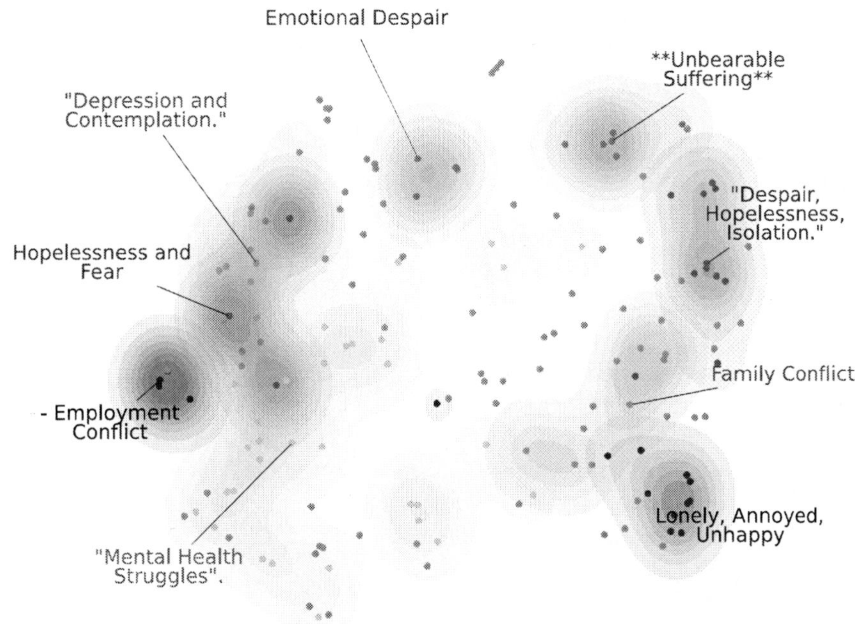

Figure 1: Major topics extracted from expert data labeled with openhermes-2.5-mistral-7b-q4_k_m.

2 Data Analysis

The annotated data provided for the shared task participants is identical to the previous edition CLPsych 2019 Shared Task: Predicting the Degree of Suicide Risk in Reddit Posts (Shing et al., 2018; Zirikly et al., 2019) and here we include a brief summary of its subdivisions: Task A: users on r/SuicideWatch Reddit annotated based on their risk level across multiple posts using crowd-sourced annotations. Expert: user posts annotated by experts of different specialties. Tasks B and C of annotations that we did not use in this work.

All data annotations contain suicide risk categories (Corbitt-Hall et al., 2016) marked with letters signifying different degrees: (a) no risk, (b) low, (c) moderate, and (d) severe risk. Expert data is of higher quality, it consists of 332 posts, the majority (49%) are labeled medium risk, followed by 28% high risk and 23% low risk. The 2024 Shared Task (Chim et al., 2024) evaluation data (not released to participants) contains additional annotations of suicide risk evidence (highlights and summaries) for 125 users of the expert subset. Our work only uses Task A and the expert subsets.

2.1 Topic Modelling

To have a first glance over the expert-annotated data, we use the BERTopic library (Grootendorst, 2022) and embed the documents with `BAAI/bge-small-en` a pre-trained English model (Xiao et al., 2023) which has the advantage of being relatively small and achieving good performance on the MTEB benchmark (Muennighoff et al., 2022). All document embeddings are projected into a bi-dimensional plane using a 5-neighbour UMAP (McInnes et al., 2018) configured to optimize the cosine similarity. The representations are clustered using HDBSCAN (McInnes et al., 2017) with a minimum cluster size of four. In a typical BERTopic pipeline, the topics are extracted using cTF-IDF and further fine-tuned using a representation model from openhermes-2.5-mistral-7b-q4_k_m[1]. The representation model is prompted with the following statement: *I have a topic that contains the following documents: [DOCUMENTS]. The topic is described by the following keywords: '[KEYWORDS]'. As an expert psychologist and therapist, provide a brief 5 word phrase to summarize the reason:.*

Figure 1 shows a result of this process with documents grouped by topic. Several key phrases are extracted using LLM prompts. Upon close inspection, the main topics in the dataset revolve around feelings of *despair*, *hopelessness*, socioeconomic hardships, and family conflicts. Our brief analyses

[1] `https://huggingface.co/TheBloke/OpenHermes-2.5-Mistral-7B-GGUF`

indicate that the texts contain strong signals for suicide and that very few subtleties can be observed in the assessment of risk degrees.

3 Good Old-fashioned Machine Learning (GOML)

The first approach, which also obtained the highest recall amongst submissions, is based on the following steps.

1. Begin with Task A crowd-annotated data and map the labels to binary, i.e., assigning the label 'a' to the value -1, and the labels 'b', 'c', and 'd' to the value +1. We fit a scikit learn logistic regression classifier on tf-idf features (Pedregosa et al., 2011). Tokenization is done using a regular expression of the form `r'\b[^\d\W]+\b'` and we employ a range of n-grams between 2 and 4 words. We cross-validate several models on different subsamples of risk annotations labeled as follows: **1.1 Test** - a model trained solely on Task A test set (186 posts), **1.2 TaskA** a model trained on the entire Task A, and **1.3 A+E** a model trained on both expert and TaskA data. Table 3 in the appendix contains the 5-fold cross-validation results that show relatively poor classifier performance.

2. SHAP SHapley Additive exPlanations (Lundberg and Lee, 2017) is an explainability library that implements several techniques to attribute individual contributions of each feature to a classifier's prediction. In our case, we use a simple linear explainer that assumes feature independence and ranks features based on a score computed as: $s_i = w_i(x_i - \hat{m}_i)$, where w_i is the classifier coefficient of feature i, x_i is the feature value in a post and $\hat{m}_i$ the mean of the feature value across all posts.

3. Selecting the highlights requires matching the tokenized features from our tf-idf extractor to the text. We do so by aligning the different tokenizations using the Natural Language Toolkit (Bird et al., 2009) and retrieving the original verbatim strings. For highlight selection, we test **option 3.1** - highlights consisting of a context window of 14 words before and after each matched feature, not exceeding the sentence boundary. And **option 3.2** highlights consisting of entire sentences where important features are discovered in the original text.

4. The summarization consists of two options: **4.1** take the sentences found previously in step 3.2 and use an extractive summarization technique such as TextRank (Mihalcea and Tarau, 2004; Nathan, 2016) to generate a summary. This method is the fastest, but performed relatively poorly, obtaining high contradiction rates (0.238) and relatively low mean consistency (0.901). **Option 4.2 GOML+LLM** achieved the best overall performance and requires taking the sentences found previously and prompting a language model to generate an abstractive summary. Our best performing system in the official ranking is configured with option 3.2 (to extract full sentences as highlights) and option 4.2 (to generate summaries using LLM).

4 Language Models

For efficient text generation, we use a 4-bit quantized model (Q4_K_M) together with llama-cpp[2] and langchain (Chase, 2022) libraries. We use OpenHermes 2.5 based on Mistral (Jiang et al., 2023) that has been fine-tuned on code. According to the authors[3] training on a good ratio of code instruction of around 7-14% of the total dataset boosted several noncode benchmarks, including TruthfulQA, AGIEval, and GPT4All suite. The language models approach can be summarized in the following steps:

(a) prompt the model using langchain to extract highlights from the texts for a number of $K = 8$ times

(b) parse the LLM output and extract highlights from between quotation marks

(c) post-process responses: ensure the highlights are actually in the texts, remove duplicates, keep the longest matching highlights

(d) concatenate all posts and prompt the model without langchain to do a summary analysis of maximum 300 words

Text generation parameters are set to a temperature of 0.75, top-p nucleus sampling 1, and a maximum context size of 32000. To obtain as much data as possible, the LLM was run eight times on each post. The langchain prompt for extracting highlights is: *Provide sequences of text that indicate that this person is suicidal? \n \n Post Body: {post_body}*. Each response is saved and post-processed to extract valid highlights present in the text, to remove duplicates, and to preserve the longest matching highlight. The model tends to

[2]`https://github.com/ggerganov/llama.cpp`

[3]`https://huggingface.co/teknium/OpenHermes-2.5-Mistral-7B`

submission	recall	precision	recall_w	harmonic
Test[1]	0.921	0.888	0.513	0.904
Test + LLM[2]	**0.939**	0.890	0.390	0.914
LLM[3]	0.935	**0.905**	**0.553**	**0.919**
TaskA_3.1 + LLM	0.919	0.891	0.560	0.905
A+E_3.1 + LLM	0.918	0.892	**0.578**	0.905
LLM duplicates	**0.941**	**0.907**	0.398	**0.924**
UoS NLP	0.943	**0.916**	0.527	**0.929**
sophiaADS	**0.944**	0.906	0.489	0.924
UZH_CLyp	0.910	**0.916**	**0.742**	0.913

Table 1: Highlights evaluation scores of our systems in comparison to other participants in the Shared Task. The first three rows marked with superscript are the official versions we submitted during competition. The next 3 are additional experiments with highlights 3.1 or without removing duplicates and overlaps from LLM output. The last three rows are submissions from other participants.

submission	consistency	contradiction
Test[1]	0.901	0.238
Test + LLM[2]	**0.973**	**0.081**
LLM[3]	0.964	0.104
TaskA_3.1	0.910	0.217
A+E_3.1	0.908	0.218
TaskA_3.1 + LLM	0.971	0.085
A+E_3.1 + LLM	**0.974**	**0.076**
UoS NLP	0.966	0.107
sophiaADS	0.944	0.175
UZH_CLyp	**0.979**	**0.064**

Table 2: Summary evaluation scores of our systems in comparison to other participants in the Shared Task.

be more verbose, no matter how much we change the prompt, so the post-processing step proved to be essential.

To extract summaries, we run the model only once with the following prompt: *As a psychologist and expert therapist, summarize the content by identifying any indications of suicidal thoughts. Provide evidence from the text to support your analysis. \n \n Post Body: {content_body}\n \n Analysis:*. When using GOML with Option 4.2, the content body consists in the concatenation of important sentences instead of the post bodies. We found that the model tends to hallucinate and copy paste content from the text, unless the word *Analysis* is explicitly mentioned at the end.

5 Results and Discussion

Our three official submissions for the Shared Task in this order are:

- Test[1] - GOML fit on the Task A test set (1.1), highlights consisting of a 14 word context window (3.1), and extractive summaries generated from important sentences (4.1)
- Test + LLM[2] - [our best submission] GOML fit on the Task A test set (1.1), highlights consisting of entire sentences with important features (3.2), and LLM-generated abstractive summaries from combined sentences (4.2)
- LLM[3] - pipeline as described in section 4

Recall is computed as the average of the maximal semantic similarity between each gold highlight and all predicted highlights based on BERTScore (Zhang et al., 2019). A point of critique that we can raise here is that introducing duplicate highlights of different sizes will generate a better overall recall score. In practice, such a system could potentially slow down an expert looking for indicators of suicide. For example, our submission "LLM duplicates" from Table 1 does not remove highlights extracted from multiple runs of the LLM that are substrings of each other, and therefore obtains the highest recall. Similarly, systems that have shorter highlights (such as those that use the context around important features) achieve a lower recall than systems that return entire sentences as highlights. We do not know whether this is an artifact of BERTScore or from the way the annotations have been created. For example, the sophiaADS team (Tanaka and Fukazawa, 2024) returns complete sentences using a fine-tuned BERT model and their method obtains the highest recall score in the competition. In both their case and ours, we can observe that the weighted recall penalizes results in which highlights are entire sentences.

For this downstream task of identifying highlights, we did not observe significant improvements in performance when training the logistic regression classifier with more data, nor did we observe a degradation of performance when training on the smallest amount of samples consisting only of the test set of Task A. This is encouraging for potential extensions of the GOML methodology to less-resourced languages.

The generated summaries are evaluated by taking the probability scores (from an external NLI tool) of having a summary that contradicts the gold sentence as a premise. In terms of consistency and contradiction Table 2, the best results were obtained by Test + LLM[2] which combines the efficacy of extracting highlights of high recall (albeit low precision) with the ability of LLMs to generate adequate and coherent summary content. This is confirmed by the additional results combining LLM with GOML + option 3.1 with shorter summaries (Table 1 rows four and five). These models achieve the highest consistency (.974) and lowest contradiction scores (.076) of our systems. Team UZH_CLyp (Uluslu et al., 2024) uses retrieval augmented generation and provides additional context to the model when generating the summary to obtain the best results in the competition (given this criterion). This corroborates our observations that giving more concise or more focused content to LLMs leads to better generated summaries than providing the complete (and possibly noisy) post bodies from users to the LLM. The results of the team UoS NLP (Singh et al., 2024) are relatively similar to our LLM submissions that use chain-of-thought prompting to extract highlights and remove duplicates. Their LLM is based on Mixtral model quantized to 8 bits, which might explain the slight increase in evaluation scores across different metrics.

While GOML performs competitively to more resource-intensive approaches in detecting highlights, the same cannot be said about summaries. Our Test[1] model that used TextRank for extractive summarization obtained one of the worst contradiction and consistency scores in the entire competition. Its main advantage remains that it can run the entire machine learning pipeline to train the classifier and generate all the evidence (highlights and summaries) for the 125 users in less than 60 seconds. In contrast, our quantized LLM on CPU runs in 3.5 hours for the same set of users. To be consistent with our comparisons, in all of our approaches, we have only used a CPU server with 7 cores and 64 GB of memory to compute the results.

Given the surprising efficacy of the traditional machine learning model, we ask whether sentences containing important features have specific linguistic characteristics. Sentences are divided into two categories: **important** if they contain important features for classification and with the label **other** otherwise. Our statistical analyses visible also in Figure 2 indicate that important sentences are generally more likely to have pronouns, verbs, and adjectives. In terms of mean value, pronouns and verbs are statistically different at a p-value < 0.05 in important sentences more often than in the rest. Similarly, mean sentence lengths are statistically larger in important sentences than in the other ones. Adverbs show no difference between the two classes, and adjectives and nouns obtain a p-value of 0.6 after 100,000 permutations. Given the nature of permutation tests, this is equivalent to saying that there is a 6% chance of observing a difference in means for adjectives and nouns due to chance.

Our brief analyses show that important sentences have different (statistically significant) linguistic patterns that can distinguish them from the rest. We believe that this could be one of the reasons behind the good evaluation scores and the suitability of the GOML approach to extract highlights from this particular dataset.

6 Conclusions

To conclude, our results show that a classifier paired with a machine learning explainability method can be a useful tool for identifying important sentences, phrases, and highlights that are representative of a given class. This is encouraging for languages where current LLMs do not perform as well or where the amount of data and compute resources is limited. Additionally, our experiments show that noisy generated output containing duplicates achieves better recall, leading to the conclusion that relying on a single metric can be detrimental to this task. We believe that ultimately expert human judgments would be the best measure for evaluating and selecting the most useful systems based on multiple criteria.

In general, when investigating the output of LLM-based approaches, we could observe better quality in terms of the generated text and langchain reasoning. Our work shows that these results can be further improved by combining LLMs with good old-fashioned machine learning methods.

7 Ethics

Working with user posts that talk about inflicting self-harm is a difficult endeavor. Although our methods bring about a small contribution in the interdisciplinary field of suicidology, we must recognize that technological solutions are not always helpful in an impactful way for people who suffer. Our work was carried out with the greatest care for the privacy and management of this data. During human analyses, repeated exposure to suicide-related content can be triggering and potentially harmful. The authors have double-checked each other on their mental health and ability to work during the entire time of doing this work.

8 Limitations

- Preserving duplicates or generating too many highlights can lead to an artificial increase in recall. The score increase can be misleading, since such a system can generate duplicates that are hard to interpret and not user-friendly.
- LLM-generated summaries may include sexist biases, we have not observed these in a systematic manner, but on occasion the LLM would assign gendered pronouns to users who did not explicitly mention this in their posts. Further research is required to integrate multi-modal variables such as class, race, gender in the prediction mechanism.
- The data that we have to work with had strong signals of suicide risk, therefore, we wonder whether such an approach would still be suitable in cases where the linguistic signal is more subtle or whether our models are able to generalize on out-of-domain data.

Acknowledgements

We acknowledge the assistance of the American Association of Suicidology in making the dataset available. This work is supported by the Faculty of Mathematics and Computer Science, University of Bucharest, as part of the Archaeology of Intelligent Machines course.

References

Steven Bird, Ewan Klein, and Edward Loper. 2009. *Natural language processing with Python: analyzing text with the natural language toolkit.* " O'Reilly Media, Inc.".

Ricardo Campos, Vítor Mangaravite, Arian Pasquali, Alípio Jorge, Célia Nunes, and Adam Jatowt. 2020. YAKE! Keyword extraction from single documents using multiple local features. *Information Sciences*, 509:257–289.

Harrison Chase. 2022. LangChain. Software. Released on 2022-10-17.

Jenny Chim, Adam Tsakalidis, Dimitris Gkoumas, Dana Atzil-Slonim, Yaakov Ophir, Ayah Zirikly, Philip Resnik, and Maria Liakata. 2024. Overview of the CLPsych 2024 Shared Task: Leveraging Large Language Models to Identify Evidence of Suicidality Risk in Online Posts. In *Proceedings of the Ninth Workshop on Computational Linguistics and Clinical Psychology*. Association for Computational Linguistics.

Darcy J Corbitt-Hall, Jami M Gauthier, Margaret T Davis, and Tracy K Witte. 2016. College students' responses to suicidal content on social networking sites: An examination using a simulated facebook newsfeed. *Suicide and Life-Threatening Behavior*, 46(5):609–624.

Tim Dettmers, Artidoro Pagnoni, Ari Holtzman, and Luke Zettlemoyer. 2023. Qlora: Efficient finetuning of quantized llms. *arXiv preprint arXiv:2305.14314*.

Maarten Grootendorst. 2022. Bertopic: Neural topic modeling with a class-based tf-idf procedure. *arXiv preprint arXiv:2203.05794*.

Bonnie Harmer, Sarah Lee, Abdolreza Saadabadi, et al. 2022. Suicidal Ideation. In *StatPearls [Internet]*. StatPearls Publishing.

Eghbal A. Hosseini, Martin Schrimpf, Yian Zhang, Samuel R. Bowman, Noga Zaslavsky, and Evelina Fedorenko. 2024. Artificial neural network language models predict human brain responses to language even after a developmentally realistic amount of training. *Neurobiology of Language*, pages 1–50.

Albert Qiaochu Jiang, Alexandre Sablayrolles, Arthur Mensch, Chris Bamford, Devendra Singh Chaplot, Diego de Las Casas, Florian Bressand, Gianna Lengyel, Guillaume Lample, Lucile Saulnier, L'elio Renard Lavaud, Marie-Anne Lachaux, Pierre Stock, Teven Le Scao, Thibaut Lavril, Thomas Wang, Timothée Lacroix, and William El Sayed. 2023. Mistral 7B. *ArXiv*, abs/2310.06825.

Scott M Lundberg and Su-In Lee. 2017. A unified approach to interpreting model predictions. In I. Guyon, U. V. Luxburg, S. Bengio, H. Wallach, R. Fergus, S. Vishwanathan, and R. Garnett, editors, *Advances in Neural Information Processing Systems 30*, pages 4765–4774. Curran Associates, Inc.

R Thomas McCoy, Paul Smolensky, Tal Linzen, Jianfeng Gao, and Asli Celikyilmaz. 2023. How much do language models copy from their training data? evaluating linguistic novelty in text generation using raven. *Transactions of the Association for Computational Linguistics*, 11:652–670.

Leland McInnes, John Healy, and Steve Astels. 2017. hdbscan: Hierarchical density based clustering. *The Journal of Open Source Software*, 2(11).

Leland McInnes, John Healy, Nathaniel Saul, and Lukas Grossberger. 2018. Umap: Uniform manifold approximation and projection. *The Journal of Open Source Software*, 3(29):861.

Rada Mihalcea and Paul Tarau. 2004. TextRank: Bringing order into text. In *Proceedings of the 2004 Conference on Empirical Methods in Natural Language Processing*, pages 404–411, Barcelona, Spain. Association for Computational Linguistics.

Niklas Muennighoff, Nouamane Tazi, Loïc Magne, and Nils Reimers. 2022. MTEB: Massive Text Embedding Benchmark. *arXiv preprint arXiv:2210.07316*.

Paco Nathan. 2016. PyTextRank, a Python implementation of TextRank for phrase extraction and summarization of text documents.

F. Pedregosa, G. Varoquaux, A. Gramfort, V. Michel, B. Thirion, O. Grisel, M. Blondel, P. Prettenhofer, R. Weiss, V. Dubourg, J. Vanderplas, A. Passos, D. Cournapeau, M. Brucher, M. Perrot, and E. Duchesnay. 2011. Scikit-learn: Machine Learning in Python. *Journal of Machine Learning Research*, 12:2825–2830.

Mahdi Rezapour. 2023. Contextual evaluation of suicide-related posts. *Humanities and Social Sciences Communications*, 10(1):1–10.

Han-Chin Shing, Suraj Nair, Ayah Zirikly, Meir Friedenberg, Hal Daumé III, and Philip Resnik. 2018. "Expert, Crowdsourced, and Machine Assessment of Suicide Risk via Online Postings". In *"Proceedings of the Fifth Workshop on Computational Linguistics and Clinical Psychology: From Keyboard to Clinic"*, pages 25–36, New Orleans, LA. Association for Computational Linguistics.

Loitongbam Gyanendro Singh, Junyu Mao, Rudra Mutalik, and Stuart E Middleton. 2024. Extraction and Summarization of Suicidal Ideation Evidence in Social Media Content Using Large Language Models. In *Proceedings of the Ninth Workshop on Computational Linguistics and Clinical Psychology*. Association for Computational Linguistics.

Rika Tanaka and Yusuke Fukazawa. 2024. Integrating Supervised Extractive and Generative Language Models for Suicide Risk Evidence Summarization. In *Proceedings of the Ninth Workshop on Computational Linguistics and Clinical Psychology*. Association for Computational Linguistics.

Ana-Sabina Uban, Berta Chulvi, and Paolo Rosso. 2022. Explainability of depression detection on social media: From deep learning models to psychological interpretations and multimodality. In *Early Detection of Mental Health Disorders by Social Media Monitoring: The First Five Years of the eRisk Project*, pages 289–320. Springer.

Ahmet Yavuz Uluslu, Andrianos Michail, and Simon Clematide. 2024. Utilizing Large Language Models to Identify Evidence of Suicidality Risk through Analysis of Emotionally Charged Posts. In *Proceedings of the Ninth Workshop on Computational Linguistics and Clinical Psychology*. Association for Computational Linguistics.

Shitao Xiao, Zheng Liu, Peitian Zhang, and Niklas Muennighoff. 2023. C-pack: Packaged resources to advance general chinese embedding.

Bing Xiang Yang, Pan Chen, Xin Yi Li, Fang Yang, Zhisheng Huang, Guanghui Fu, Dan Luo, Xiao Qin Wang, Wentian Li, Li Wen, et al. 2022. Characteristics of high suicide risk messages from users of a social network—sina weibo "tree hole". *Frontiers in psychiatry*, 13:789504.

Tianyi Zhang, Varsha Kishore, Felix Wu, Kilian Q Weinberger, and Yoav Artzi. 2019. Bertscore: Evaluating text generation with bert. *arXiv preprint arXiv:1904.09675*.

Ayah Zirikly, Philip Resnik, Özlem Uzuner, and Kristy Hollingshead. 2019. "CLPsych 2019 shared task: Predicting the degree of suicide risk in Reddit posts". In *"Proceedings of the Sixth Workshop on Computational Linguistics and Clinical Psychology"*, pages 24–33, Minneapolis, Minnesota. Association for Computational Linguistics.

A Appendix

The first text classification training scenario involves only the test set from Task A, because it is the smallest (186 posts), and one should expect it to generate the weakest classifier. We gradually increase the data to see whether there are changes in the results by adding the entire Task A data (labeled in the results section as "TaskA"). Lastly, we include the entire Task A and expert data, referred to in the results section as "A+E".

When running the tf-idf vectorizer we set the minimum document frequency to one, no limit on maximum features, Unicode strip accents, minimum number of documents set to one, enable the use of inverse document frequency (IDF) reweighting, smoothing to the IDF weights, and sublinear scaling to term frequency.

Logistic regression is set with balanced class weight, and we do not perform any hyperparameter optimization. Nevertheless, classifiers tend to predict only the majority class Table 3, so the balanced accuracy score never increases significantly, regardless of the fold or amount of data used.

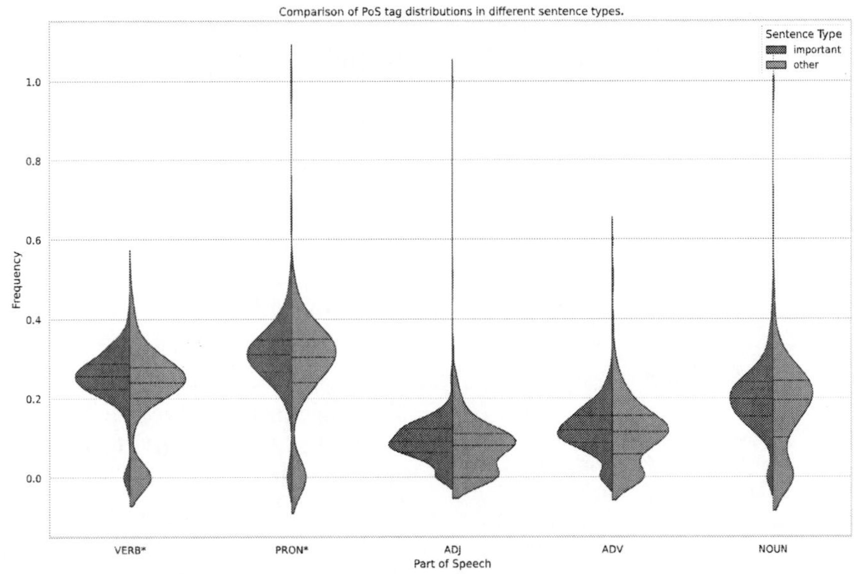

Figure 2: PoS tag distributions in sentences containing highlighted features (important) vs. other. Marked with * are PoS tags that have statistically significant means in a bootstrap permutation test at a p-value of 0.05.

Approach	Bal. Acc	Acc	F1
test → Test	.5	.82	.74
+train → TaskA	.5	.82	.74
+expert → A+E	.5	.86	.8

Table 3: Stratified 5-fold cross-validation for binary risk prediction on different subsets of Task A and expert data. The first row represents cross-validation only on the test set, the second row adds the training set over the test set thus using the entire Task A, and the third row adds the expert data over all the previous. All values can vary between $\pm .05$ at different random shuffles.

B What did Not Work

- Fine-tuning a LLM for classification with LoRA and unsloth library [4] using mistral-7b-bnb-4bit quantized model to classify the suicide risk by responding verbally; we were hoping to guide the model's attention towards important features for generating the content; after fine-tuning, the model was not able to produce good highlights.

- Given that OpenHermes 2.5 is fine-tuned on code, we were expecting to use grammars[5] to constrain the generation of highlights in the form of a list of strings, but the model proved not to perform very well in some of our empirical small-scale tests and we eventually abandoned this direction.

- We also tried to use Yake (Campos et al., 2020) to extract keywords from the titles and posts and then use this list of words as a parameter in TF-IDF. This approach did not work well because the list of extracted important features was too limited.

[4] https://github.com/unslothai/unsloth

[5] https://github.com/ggerganov/llama.cpp/blob/master/grammars

Utilizing Large Language Models to Identify Evidence of Suicidality Risk through Analysis of Emotionally Charged Posts

Ahmet Yavuz Uluslu*
University of Zurich
ahmetyavuz.uluslu@uzh.ch

Andrianos Michail*
University of Zurich
andrianos.michail@cl.uzh.ch

Simon Clematide
University of Zurich
simon.clematide@cl.uzh.ch

Abstract

This paper presents our contribution to the CLPsych 2024 shared task, focusing on the use of open-source large language models (LLMs) for suicide risk assessment through the analysis of social media posts. We achieved first place (out of 15 participating teams) in the task of providing summarized evidence of a user's suicide risk. Our approach is based on Retrieval Augmented Generation (RAG), where we retrieve the top-k (k=5) posts with the highest emotional charge and provide the level of three different negative emotions (sadness, fear, anger) for each post during the generation phase.

1 Introduction

While healthcare systems are crucial in identifying suicide risk, the limited time available to clinicians often hinders a comprehensive assessment of all risk factors (Knipe et al., 2022). Expressions of suicidal thoughts are among the most significant warning signs. However, the standard practice of clinicians inquiring about these thoughts has not been reliably effective in predicting and preventing suicide (Hawton et al., 2022). It was revealed that the majority of patients who commit suicide had not reported suicidal thoughts to their healthcare providers (Chan et al., 2016).

The CLPsych 2024 shared task (Chim et al., 2024) addresses the significant challenge of generating supporting evidence for clinical assessments, with a specific focus on suicide risk assessment using open-source large language models (LLMs). This task concentrates on analyzing linguistic content from social media posts to substantiate the assigned suicide risk levels of individuals (Shing et al., 2018a). By examining users' posting activities on online forums, the goal is to extract, in an unsupervised manner, evidence within these posts that supports the pre-assigned risk levels.

Our approach aims to develop a scalable and efficient system that utilizes the state-of-the-art open-source LLM Mistral 7B (Jiang et al., 2023) for mental health assessment. It uses 4-bit quantization and Retrieval Augmented Generation (RAG) (Lewis et al., 2020) to effectively select the most emotional and relevant extracts from the user history with minimal resource requirements. We use emotional insights, which have been shown to correlate with mental illnesses such as depression, to improve our task by recognizing emotional patterns that could indicate suicidality (Zhang et al., 2023). We engage with both Task A (Highlighting Suicidal Evidence) and Task B (User's Summarized Suicidal Evidence). The two main contributions of this work, which were instrumental in achieving the top performance in Task B, are as follows:

- We retrieve the top-k ($k = 5$) emotionally charged user posts to include as context to the model to summarize evidence of suicidal risks.
- We enriched the prompt context with the regression-predicted percentage levels of three different negative emotions (sadness, fear, anger) alongside the selected posts.

2 Related Work

The CLPsych Shared Tasks 2019 (Zirikly et al., 2019) and 2022 (Tsakalidis et al., 2022) were mainly focused on suicide risk prediction and mood swing detection, which was predominantly considered a multi-class classification problem. The top approaches in the previous shared task have predominantly utilized transformer-based models and multitask learning, yet the capabilities of prompting-based approaches in this context remains largely unexplored. There is a growing interest in the responsible use of LLMs in healthcare, including in psychotherapy and mental health as-

*Equal contribution

Proceedings of the 9th Workshop on Computational Linguistics and Clinical Psychology (CLPsych 2024), pages 264–269
March 21, 2024 ©2024 Association for Computational Linguistics

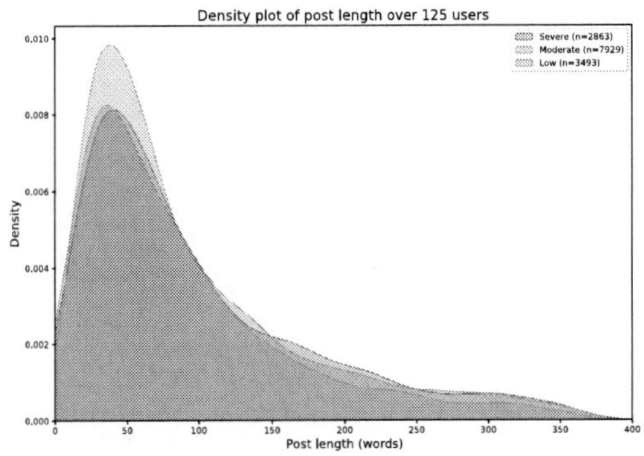

Figure 1: Kernel density estimation plot, grouped by post's author assigned risk level. n denotes the number of posts among all subreddits written by users of the assigned risk level. On average, the 125 users contributed to 131 posts each.

System: You are a suicide prevention therapist expert.

You are performing psychological analysis of suicidality risks of the author of the following Reddit post:
title: {postTitle}
content: {postContent}
It is estimated that the author has at least {riskLevel} risk of suicidality.
Extract ALL relevant evidence (snippets) of at least {riskLevel} suicidality exclusively from the post's content.
Formatting: Strictly provide each snippet and only the snippets delimited by a semicolon(';')

Figure 2: Task A: Zero-shot prompt template (Step 1) given to Mistral7B for the extraction of relevant spans.

sessment (Stade et al., 2023). The recent advancements have seen a significant increase in the zero-shot classification abilities of LLMs, alongside a deepened understanding of mental health issues (Xu et al., 2023). These models are increasingly recognized for their effectiveness in extracting information, especially in identifying mental health crises. They have demonstrated the ability to generate explainable findings and exhibit reasoning capabilities, which significantly enhances their utility in mental health assessments (Yang et al., 2023). This evolution in the capabilities of LLMs sets a new precedent for our approach and underscores the potential of these models in contributing to mental health assessments.

3 Data and Tasks

We use the Reddit suicidality dataset provided by the organizers of the 2019/2024 CLPsych Workshop (Shing et al., 2018b; Zirikly et al., 2019; Chim et al., 2024). Our team's utilization of this data and our participation in the associated tasks adhere to the ethical review standards outlined by the organizers. The dataset comprises posts from 125 Reddit users on various subreddits where each user has at least one post in r/SuicideWatch. All users are categorized by experts into four risk levels: *No Risk*, *Low Risk*, *Moderate Risk*, and *Severe Risk*. The distribution of the length of posts is shown in Figure 1.

The participants of the shared task were asked to contribute to the following two methods of extracting evidence of suicidality from the users' posts:

- **Task A – Highlighting Suicidal Evidence:** focuses on extracting highlights (snippets) exclusively from r/SuicideWatch posts that have been assigned a risk level by an expert.
- **Task B – User's Summarized Suicidal Evidence:** Using any content available from a person, the task is to find evidence for a person's suicidality risk level and report it, either extractive or abstractive.

4 Methods

4.1 Model & Computational Resources

Our approach exclusively employs the open-source LLM Mistral-7B-Instruct-v0.2 (Jiang et al., 2023) in zero-shot setting with 4-bit quantization. Detailed parameters used for the text generation can be found in Table A1. All of our experiments, including inference over all posts and users, were carried out locally for a total of less than two hours using a MacBook Pro with an M2 Pro with a 10-core GPU.

4.2 Task A – Highlighting Suicidal Evidence

To extract and highlight relevant snippets from a user's post, we deploy a multistep procedure:

1. Prompting the LLM to extract relevant passages from the text (see Figure 2).
2. Prompting to remove unwanted text output (e.g., explanations) from Step 1 and reorganize snippets (see Figure A1).
3. Segmenting the snippets and applying up to 4-character replacement string substitutions

Team	Rank	Recall	Precision	Weighted Recall	Harmonic Mean
sophiaADS	1	0.944	0.906	0.489	0.924
UoS NLP	2	0.943	0.916	0.527	0.929
UniBuc Arch	3	0.939	0.890	0.390	0.914
SWELL	7	0.915	0.892	0.542	0.903
Our Official Submission	8	0.910	0.916	0.742	0.913
MHNLP	9	0.910	0.888	0.197	0.909

Table 1: Shared Task Results for Task A – Highlighting Suicidal Evidence. Our team name is UZH_CLyp and Rank denotes the subtask's ranking that is based on the primary score, Recall.

to restore the exact text form of the original post.[1] Unmatched evidence, often arising from rewritten or reordered user texts as well as from hallucinated insertions, is then discarded.

This method of using LLMs for an extractive task, while laborious, was explored to determine the feasibility of accomplishing this task solely through the use of generative AI. However, in doing so, we required two separate rounds of inference and an additional string matching, compromising the efficiency of our solution.

The primary evaluation metric for this task is a variation of BERTScore (Zhang et al., 2019), focusing on recall, weighted recall and precision, benchmarked against snippets extracted by human experts. Our submission for Task A achieved 8th place out of the 15 best team submissions (42 submissions in total). Detailed results for Task A can be found in Table 1.

System: You are a suicide prevention therapist expert.

You are performing psychological analysis of suicidality risks in online forums. Here are the most emotional posts of the same author for analysis: {postTitle, content and estimations(in percentages) of sadness, fear and anger separated by new lines, for all five posts retrieved by the highest sadness estimation} Aspects of text to consider are the emotions, cognitions as well as behaviours and mentions of the author related to things like self-harm or suicide.
It was confirmed that the author has a {riskLevel} risk of suicidality. Provide your hypothesis of {riskLevel} suicidality from the post contents and general online behaviour.

Figure 3: Task B: Zero-shot prompt template given to Mistral7B to generate the summarized evidence.

[1]This was necessary for the submission as the LLM would fix small grammar errors, typing nuances or irregular punctuation usage.

4.3 Task B – User's Summarized Suicidal Evidence

Emotion Regression Models In addition to using our generative Suicidal Evidence predictions, we apply Encoder Transformer models to regress the emotional load of a text. We fine-tuned the Muppet RoBERTa (Aghajanyan et al., 2021) Large Encoder models on the SemEval2018 Affect dataset (Mohammad et al., 2018) to function as Emotion Regressors for emotions like anger, sadness, and fear, each with its separately trained model. These models are fine-tuned using the Head First Fine-Tuning method as described in Michail et al. (2023). The Pearson r correlation coefficient on its test set is 0.856, 0.832 and 0.808 for anger, fear and sadness respectively. Before prompting Mistral7B, we compute predictions with our emotion regression models for all posts of the studied users.

Prompting To generate the summarized evidence, we perform a zero-shot query by concatenating the title, the post and the predicted emotions to the five most sad posts (in descending order), similar to a Retrieval Augmented Generation (RAG) approach (Lewis et al., 2020). In addition to the post information, we provide the model with the following system message "You are a suicide prevention therapist expert", and some information and hints about aspects to consider when performing the task. Figure 3 presents the complete prompt template.

5 Results

The official results of Task B are shown in Table 2. Our submission (UZH_CLyp) achieved first place out of the 42 submitted runs according to the official scores. The official score of the Shared Task attempts to measure agreement between the model-generated summary and the human expert analysis (Chim et al., 2024) using a model trained on Natu-

Team	Rank	Mean Consistency ↑	Max Contradiction ↓
Our Official Submission	1	**0.979**	0.064
Our Ablation: No Emotion Regression	-	0.976	0.074
SBC	2	0.976	0.079
SWELL	3	0.973	0.081
UniBuc-Arch	4	0.973	0.081
SKKU-DSAIL	5	0.970	0.096
Our Ablation: No Emotion RAG	-	0.947	0.120
sophiaADS	12	0.944	0.175

Table 2: Shared Task Results for Task B – User's Summarized Suicidal Evidence. Italics denote our additional evaluations for the ablation study. Our team name is UZH_CLyp and Rank denotes the Subtask's ranking that is based on the primary score, Mean Consistency.

ral Language Inference (Wang et al., 2021). This agreement is measured with two scores: the **Mean Consistency**, defined as the average sentence-level probability of consistency, 1 - P(Contradiction), and the **Max Contradiction**, which represents the average maximum probability of a contradiction occurring, $\max(P(\text{Contradiction}))$. Our submission performed best within Task B among all submissions.

It is worth noting that the top teams achieve promising performance, with only minor differences between them. However, another interesting insight from this generally high performance is that it demonstrates the ability of today's LLMs to generate analyses that align closely with the assessments of human experts.

5.1 Ablation Study

To better understand the relevant factors for the performance of our system, we asked the organizers to evaluate two additional post-submission runs for our ablation study. We have included the results of these variants in the main results table 2.

In the *No Emotion Regression* ablation experiment, we omitted information about the emotionality levels of each post. This leads to a very minor performance decrease, showing that the actual predictions of the emotions are not crucial to the model.

In the *No Emotion RAG* ablation experiment, we omitted information about the emotions and also replaced the retrieval procedure that selected the most emotional posts with a heuristic to retrieve the five longest posts. This results in a large performance decrease and showcases the value of the emotion regressions as a selection criterion for retrieving relevant posts.

6 Conclusion

The system presented in this paper demonstrates the potential of using open-source LLMs to identify evidence of suicidality utilizing emotionally charged social media posts. Our main innovation is the combination of RAG with emotional regression of posts. This technique was found to be effective, as evidenced by the first-place performance in Shared Task B and the insights from our ablation experiments. Our results highlight the ability of current LLMs to accurately summarize evidence of a user's suicide risk from online posts that closely align with human expert assessments.

In conclusion, this study highlights the potential of LLMs in healthcare, particularly for mental health assessments. While the approach shows promise, especially in suicide risk analysis from social media posts, it also poses challenges, such as the risk of inaccurate content generation. Future research should aim to enhance the accuracy of these models and consider the ethical implications of applying AI in sensitive health contexts. This research opens up new possibilities for the application of LLMs in mental health services, suggesting a path towards integrating them with traditional healthcare methods for more effective outcomes.

Limitations

While our approach leveraging open-source LLMs shows promising results in both Task A and Task B of the CLPsych 2024 Shared Task, it is important to recognize inherent limitations when using LLMs in sensitive contexts of mental health assessment. We acknowledge the possibility of hallucinations and generation of inaccurate content, which can lead to misinterpretation of a user's mental state. During a manual inspection, we inspected the hallucination factor in scenarios where the model encounters posts with low/medium pre-assigned risk levels. In these cases, it often fails to pick up relevant clinical cues such as an intent to self-harm, thus underlining the crucial role of pre-assigned risk levels in guiding the model's explanation. Furthermore, the shared task is assessed using automated metrics, which may lead to significant discrepancies between these results and the evaluations of human expert annotations.

Ethics

We used publicly available data that was stripped of identifiable information and collected in a non-intrusive manner for mental health research. All researchers working on the project have signed a non-disclosure agreement with the dataset providers. The data was stored securely at the storage services of the Department for Computational Linguistics at the University of Zurich and was only accessible to the parties involved during the project. The open-source language models used in the project were hosted locally without any potential data disclosure to third parties. The results of this work are intended for fellow researchers in the fields of computational linguistics and psychology to improve mental health assessment technology. It is part of the growing body of mental health research aimed at applications to improve well-being. However, it should not be used without collaboration with clinical practitioners.

Acknowledgements

Ahmet Yavuz Uluslu was partially supported by the Innosuisse innovation project AUCH (103.188 IP-ICT). We are thankful to the organisers of the CLPsych 2024 Shared Task and the American Association of Suicidology for preparing the dataset.

References

Armen Aghajanyan, Anchit Gupta, Akshat Shrivastava, Xilun Chen, Luke Zettlemoyer, and Sonal Gupta. 2021. Muppet: Massive multi-task representations with pre-finetuning. In *Proceedings of the 2021 Conference on Empirical Methods in Natural Language Processing*, pages 5799–5811, Online and Punta Cana, Dominican Republic. Association for Computational Linguistics.

Melissa KY Chan, Henna Bhatti, Nick Meader, Sarah Stockton, Jonathan Evans, Rory C O'Connor, Nav Kapur, and Tim Kendall. 2016. Predicting suicide following self-harm: systematic review of risk factors and risk scales. *The British Journal of Psychiatry*, 209(4):277–283.

Jenny Chim, Adam Tsakalidis, Dimitris Gkoumas, Dana Atzil-Slonim, Yaakov Ophir, Ayah Zirikly, Philip Resnik, and Maria Liakata. 2024. Overview of the clpsych 2024 shared task: Leveraging large language models to identify evidence of suicidality risk in online posts. In *Proceedings of the Ninth Workshop on Computational Linguistics and Clinical Psychology*. Association for Computational Linguistics.

Keith Hawton, Karen Lascelles, Alexandra Pitman, Steve Gilbert, and Morton Silverman. 2022. Assessment of suicide risk in mental health practice: shifting from prediction to therapeutic assessment, formulation, and risk management. *The Lancet Psychiatry*, 9(11):922–928.

Albert Q Jiang, Alexandre Sablayrolles, Arthur Mensch, Chris Bamford, Devendra Singh Chaplot, Diego de las Casas, Florian Bressand, Gianna Lengyel, Guillaume Lample, Lucile Saulnier, et al. 2023. Mistral 7b. *arXiv preprint arXiv:2310.06825*.

Duleeka Knipe, Prianka Padmanathan, Giles Newton-Howes, Lai Fong Chan, and Nav Kapur. 2022. Suicide and self-harm. *The Lancet*, 399(10338):1903–1916.

Patrick Lewis, Ethan Perez, Aleksandra Piktus, Fabio Petroni, Vladimir Karpukhin, Naman Goyal, Heinrich Küttler, Mike Lewis, Wen-tau Yih, Tim Rocktäschel, et al. 2020. Retrieval-augmented generation for knowledge-intensive nlp tasks. *Advances in Neural Information Processing Systems*, 33:9459–9474.

Andrianos Michail, Stefanos Konstantinou, and Simon Clematide. 2023. UZH_CLyp at SemEval-2023 task 9: Head-first fine-tuning and ChatGPT data generation for cross-lingual learning in tweet intimacy prediction. In *Proceedings of the 17th International Workshop on Semantic Evaluation (SemEval-2023)*, pages 1021–1029, Toronto, Canada. Association for Computational Linguistics.

Saif Mohammad, Felipe Bravo-Marquez, Mohammad Salameh, and Svetlana Kiritchenko. 2018. Semeval-2018 task 1: Affect in tweets. In *Proceedings of the 12th international workshop on semantic evaluation*, pages 1–17.

Han-Chin Shing, Suraj Nair, Ayah Zirikly, Meir Friedenberg, Hal Daumé III, and Philip Resnik. 2018a. Expert, crowdsourced, and machine assessment of suicide risk via online postings. In *Proceedings of the fifth workshop on computational linguistics and clinical psychology: from keyboard to clinic*, pages 25–36.

Han-Chin Shing, Suraj Nair, Ayah Zirikly, Meir Friedenberg, Hal Daumé III, and Philip Resnik. 2018b. Expert, crowdsourced, and machine assessment of suicide risk via online postings. In *Proceedings of the Fifth Workshop on Computational Linguistics and Clinical Psychology: From Keyboard to Clinic*, pages

25–36, New Orleans, LA. Association for Computational Linguistics.

Elizabeth C Stade, Shannon W Stirman, Lyle H Ungar, Cody L Boland, H. A Schwartz, David B Yaden, João Sedoc, Robert DeRubeis, Robb Willer, and johannes C Eichstaedt. 2023. Large language models could change the future of behavioral healthcare: A proposal for responsible development and evaluation.

Adam Tsakalidis, Jenny Chim, Iman Munire Bilal, Ayah Zirikly, Dana Atzil-Slonim, Federico Nanni, Philip Resnik, Manas Gaur, Kaushik Roy, Becky Inkster, et al. 2022. Overview of the clpsych 2022 shared task: Capturing moments of change in longitudinal user posts. In *Proceedings of the Eighth Workshop on Computational Linguistics and Clinical Psychology*, pages 184–198.

Sinong Wang, Han Fang, Madian Khabsa, Hanzi Mao, and Hao Ma. 2021. Entailment as few-shot learner. *CoRR*, abs/2104.14690.

Xuhai Xu, Bingshen Yao, Yuanzhe Dong, Hong Yu, James Hendler, Anind K Dey, and Dakuo Wang. 2023. Leveraging large language models for mental health prediction via online text data. *arXiv preprint arXiv:2307.14385.*

Kailai Yang, Shaoxiong Ji, Tianlin Zhang, Qianqian Xie, Ziyan Kuang, and Sophia Ananiadou. 2023. Towards interpretable mental health analysis with large language models. In *Proceedings of the 2023 Conference on Empirical Methods in Natural Language Processing*, pages 6056–6077, Singapore. Association for Computational Linguistics.

Tianlin Zhang, Kailai Yang, Shaoxiong Ji, and Sophia Ananiadou. 2023. Emotion fusion for mental illness detection from social media: A survey. *Information Fusion*, 92:231–246.

Tianyi Zhang, Varsha Kishore, Felix Wu, Kilian Q Weinberger, and Yoav Artzi. 2019. BERTScore: Evaluating text generation with BERT. *arXiv preprint arXiv:1904.09675.*

Ayah Zirikly, Philip Resnik, Ozlem Uzuner, and Kristy Hollingshead. 2019. Clpsych 2019 shared task: Predicting the degree of suicide risk in reddit posts. In *Proceedings of the sixth workshop on computational linguistics and clinical psychology*, pages 24–33.

A Appendix – Supplementary Material

System: You are a helpful assistant.

We have the original text and a set of extracted snippets mixed in text. We want to extract ONLY all snippets (not numbered) without any further discussion or comments
Original: {postContent}
Mixed Extracted Snippets: {Step 1 Output}
Follow the following format for all snippets (each on a new line): \nsnippet text as presented in the original

Figure A1: Task A: Zero-shot prompt template (Step 2) given to Mistral7B to extract the relevant spans.

Model Parameter	Value
Temperature	0.8
Top-P	0.8
Top-K	40
Max Tokens	512
Context Size	4096

Table A1: The main parameters used for Mistral7B (mistral7binstructv0.2.Q4_K_M)

Integrating Supervised Extractive and Generative Language Models for Suicide Risk Evidence Summarization

Rika Tanaka[*] **Yusuke Fukazawa**[*]
Graduate Degree Program of Applied Data Sciences
Sophia University Graduate School
Tokyo, JAPAN

Abstract

We propose a method that integrates supervised extractive and generative language models for providing supporting evidence of suicide risk in the CLPsych 2024 shared task. Our approach comprises three steps. Initially, we construct a BERT-based model for estimating sentence-level suicide risk and negative sentiment. Next, we precisely identify high suicide risk sentences by emphasizing elevated probabilities of both suicide risk and negative sentiment. Finally, we integrate generative summaries using the MentaLLaMa framework and extractive summaries from identified high suicide risk sentences and a specialized dictionary of suicidal risk words. SophiaADS, our team, achieved 1st place for highlight extraction and ranked 10th for summary generation, both based on recall and consistency metrics, respectively.

1 Introduction

Identifying suicide risk from online discussions is crucial problem. The 2018 and 2019 Shared Task at CLPsych posed the task of predicting the level of suicide risk annotated by experts from Reddit posts (Shing et al., 2018; Zirikly et al., 2019).

In the 2024 Shared Task (Chim et al., 2024), the task is further developed to provide supporting evidence about an individual's suicide risk level on the basis of their linguistic content. There are two related subtasks. First subtask is to provide highlights; relevant evidence spans supporting the expert-assigned risk level. Second subtask is to provide evidence summaries which synthesizes the identified evidence into insights that are consistent with human-written summaries.

Two main approaches for text summarization exist: extractive and generative. The extractive approach focuses on selecting significant portions of the original text, often using techniques like sentence extraction and machine learning-based sentence ranking (Ferreira et al., 2013; Aliaksei et al., 2015). In contrast, the generative approach involves creating coherent summaries by understanding the context and meaning of the input text, employing advanced neural network architectures such as Transformer models pre-trained for language understanding and generation (Vaswani et al., 2017; Brown et al., 2019).

The extractive approach excels in selecting crucial sentences based on supervised learning and explicit extraction criteria. In contrast, the generative approach is advantageous for understanding context and generating summaries without the need for explicit guidance. While the extractive approach struggles with the holistic contextual consideration, the generative approach faces challenges in reliably extracting desired evidence through prompt engineering. Consequently, when clear criteria are present, the extractive approach is preferable; however, for generating contextually comprehensive summaries, the generative approach is more suitable.

Given the dual requirements of this year's shared task – identifying high suicide risk sentences and comprehensively considering various aspects of the entire post, including emotions, cognitions, behavior, and motivation – we propose an integrated method combining both extractive and generative approaches. Our contributions include: (1) Developing a BERT (Devlin et al., 2019) based model for sentence-level suicide risk and negative sentiment estimation. (2) Identifying high suicide risk sentences precisely by focusing on elevated probabilities of both suicide risk and negative

[*] Both authors contributed equally, with Ms. Tanaka on MentaLLaMa and Prof. Fukazawa on BERT.

Proceedings of the 9th Workshop on Computational Linguistics and Clinical Psychology (CLPsych 2024), pages 270–277
March 21, 2024

sentiment. (3) Integrating generative summaries using the MentaLLaMa (Yang et al., 2023) framework and extractive summaries from identified high-risk sentences and a specialized suicidal risk words dictionary. The following sections detail our proposed method, results, and conclusion.

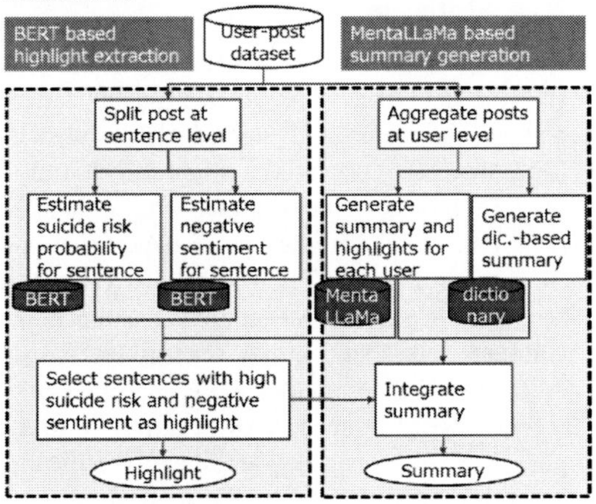

Figure 1: Overall process of proposed model.

2 Proposed method

The proposed method, outlined in Fig. 1, comprises two parts: highlight extraction and summary generation. To identify sentences indicating suicide risk, we employ a supervised extractive approach, leveraging BERT's fine-tuning capabilities for enhanced contextual understanding. Our model, fine-tuned on BERT, estimates suicide risk and negative sentiment at the sentence level. For summary generation, we combine extractive and generative approaches. Extractive summaries are crafted using patterns derived from high suicide risk sentences and associated keywords. Generative summaries are produced using MentaLLaMa. The overall summary is an integration of both approaches.

In the following, we detailed sentence level suicide risk classification, sentiment classification, highlight extraction, and summary generation.

2.1 Sentence level suicide risk classification

2.1.1 Extraction level

The decision of extraction level, be it word, phrase, sentence, or paragraph, is crucial. To capture effective contextual information, a minimum consideration of the phrase level is necessary. Examining words around the phrase is vital for strengthening the evidentiary basis for suicide risk. However, paragraph-level extraction introduces the risk of irrelevant context, prompting our choice of sentence-level extraction in this study. Each post is divided into sentences by punctuation marks (.,!?;:).

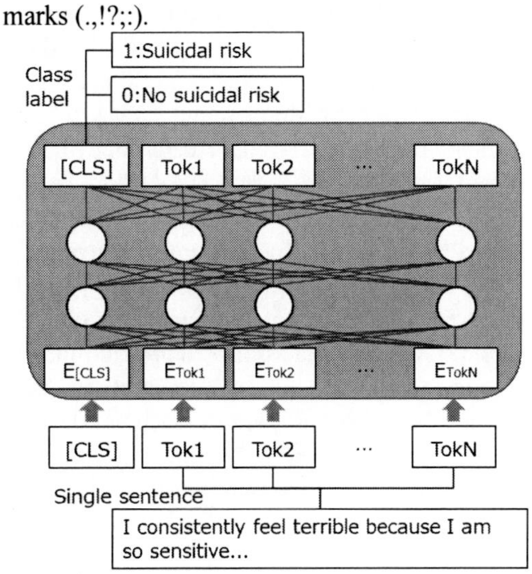

Figure 2: BERT finetuning for sentence level assessment of suicide risk.

2.1.2 BERT finetuning

To assess sentence level suicide risk estimation, we adopt BERT finetuning approach. We prepared training data for finetuning by collecting sentences that refer to suicide in direct expressions. We found that suicide risk sentences contained characteristic phrases as shown in Appendix A. We collected sentences containing the phrases in Appendix A as suicide risk sentences. As a result, the number of sentences containing those phrases was 557 (label 1), and the number of other sentences (label 0) was 31,428. In order to balance the number of labels, we down sampled the one with label 0. As a result, we acquired the training data (label 1: 449, label 0: 412) and validation data (label 1: 108, label 0: 115).

We utilize the BERT model[1] as depicted in Fig. 2. The finetuning process involves inserting a [CLS] token at the text's start, tokenizing the data, and using the Transformer architecture to abstract sentence representations (E) for each token. The E[CLS] representation of the [CLS] token captures the sentence's meaning and context. A fully-connected layer (classifier) applies a softmax function to E[CLS] to generate class probabilities. Both the embedded representation and the

[1] https://huggingface.co/bert-base-uncased

classifier's parameters are adjusted to predict the golden labels (suicide risk: 1, no suicide risk: 0) for the input text.

The parameters used for training are as follows; The batch size utilized during the training phase is set to 8. The learning rate, a crucial hyperparameter governing the model's weight updates during training is 2e-5. Warmup ratio controlling the initial gradual increase of the learning rate is 0.1. The evaluation metric utilized to determine the best model is accuracy.

Fig. 3 displays the learning curve, with training halted at epoch=50 for presumed convergence. Using the model with the highest accuracy (0.996), we predicted labels for all sentences, obtaining suicide risk labels and associated probabilities. The results revealed the model's capability to detect previously undetected phrases, such as "Dying is the only way to make it better" and "fall asleep and never wake up," which were not identified by the phrases listed in Appendix A.

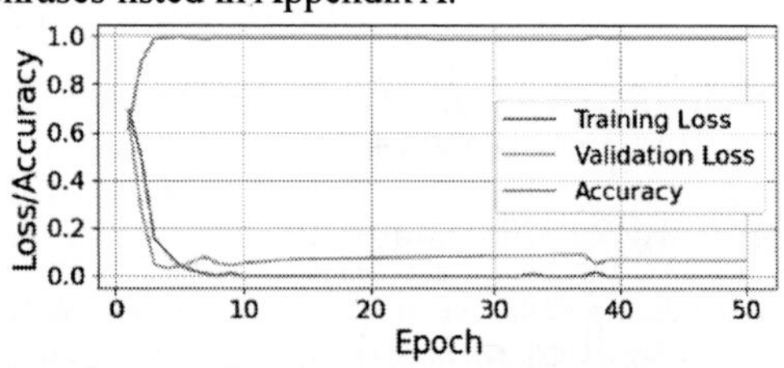

Figure 3: Learning curve of finetuning

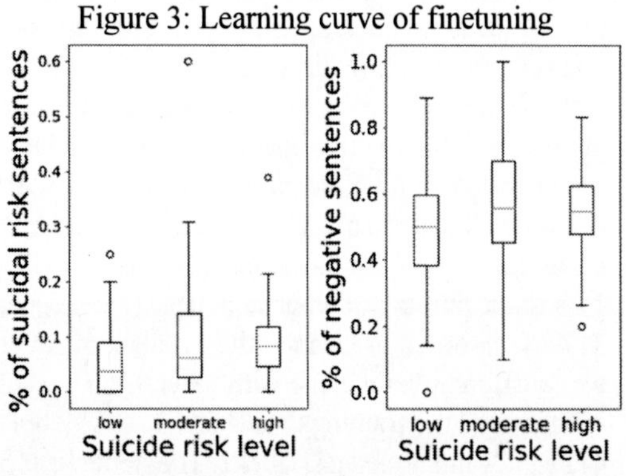

Figure 4: Boxplots of the number of suicide risk / negative sentiment sentences across user's post for each suicide risk level.

2.1.3 Correlation to suicide risk level

The data provided are flagged by experts on the levels of suicide risk: low, moderate, and high risk. In Fig.4 (left), we examine the correlation between ratio of suicide risk sentences in user's post and suicide risk level of corresponding user. We can see that the ratio of suicide risk sentences increases as the levels judged by experts increases. Consequently, the sentences classified as high suicidal risk demonstrates a high potential for the evidence of suicide risk.

2.2 Sentiment classification

In this section, we extract sentences with high suicide risk in terms of sentiment. The link between negative emotions and suicide risk is debated. Monselise et al. observed a slight increase in the proportion of negative sentiments before and just after the first suicidal ideation in Reddit user posts (Monselise et al., 2022). In contrast, Gaur et al. found no significant variation in sentiment and emotions across suicide risk severity levels using AFINN and LabMT in C-SSRS (Gaur et al., 2021).

We classify sentence into negative, neutral or positive sentiments using sentiment classification. We used the finetuned BERT model[2], which is currently the latest model trained on short sentences of X posts (Loureiro et al., 2022). X is a social network platform that allows users to post short sentences about their daily events and thoughts. Reddit, on the other hand, is a social network platform where users can post long sentences about their problems and troubles. Although the contents of X and Reddit are different, in this study, we decompose the long sentences of Reddit and perform sentiment classification on a sentence level. For this reason, we used fine-tuned BERT with the X data as the teacher data for the classification.

In Fig.4 (right), we examine the correlation between ratio of negative sentiment sentences in user's post and suicide risk level of corresponding user. We can see that the ratio of negative sentiment sentences increases as the levels judged by experts increases from low to moderate. Consequently, sentences with negative sentiment may be evidence of suicide risk.

2.3 Highlight extraction

First, we select all sentences classified as high suicide risk as highlights. Then, we sort sentences in order of probability of negative sentiment and get sentences as highlights from the top to the bottom until the total word count is within 300. If

[2] https://huggingface.co/cardiffnlp/twitter-roberta-base-sentiment-latest

still short of 300 words, we add highlights by MentaLLaMa[3], which is a LLaMA2 (Touvron et al., 2023) finetuned by large collection of social media data related to mental health. We make a query prompt to MentaLLaMa like "The text below implies a risk of suicide. Extract only the necessary and sufficient phrases and keywords indicating the risk exactly as they appear in the original text. Present the extracted words in a list format, separated by commas." with the post aggregated on a per-user basis.

We observe that the format of output was unstable as there were a mixture of asterisks, numbering, and comma-separated lists. Therefore, instead of parsing the output, we created all the possible phrase candidates consisting of continuous three or more words from the output text. Then we select the sentence of user post that included one of phrase candidates as highlights.

We used the tokenizer to encode the input text without adding special tokens. For text generation, we set the max_length parameter to 1024 tokens, limiting the output size. Additionally, max_new_token was set to 128 tokens, controlling the number of newly generated tokens. To enhance text diversity, we activated do_sample, enabling random sampling. Temperature and repetition penalty were not adjusted.

2.4 Summary generation

Our summary consists of 4 parts as shown in Fig. 5. First, we create the opening summary about the level judged by experts. For low suicide risk user, we output "This person is at low risk of suicide."; for moderate suicide risk user, "This person is at moderate risk of suicide."; and for high suicide risk user, "This person is at high risk of suicide.".

Second, we generate a rule-based summary using the number of sentences classified as high suicide risk across multiple posts by a user. When the number of sentences is 1, we output "This person made a post implying suicide.", when the number of sentences is 2, we output "This person made multiple posts implying suicide.", and when the number of sentences is more than 3, output "This person made lots of posts implying suicide.".

Third, we also generate a dictionary-based summary by collecting important phrases leading to suicide ideation across multiple posts by a user. The phrases are shown in Appendix B. We define those phrases from several websites on suicide feelings. We generate the summary by connecting prefixes and phrases. We also do same procedure for phrases defined in Appendix A. In this case, we use "This person implies suicide such as" as prefix.

Fourth, we generate summaries using MentaLLaMA. We employ a query prompt "Please summarize the next post in 300 words" with user-aggregated posts. The well-crafted output summaries, capturing user behavior and context, are used as-is.

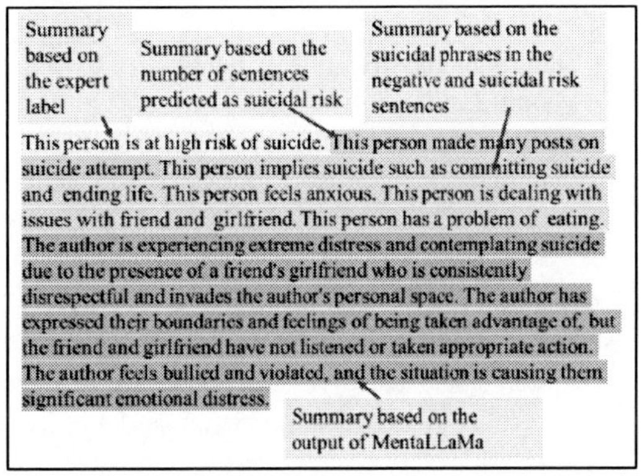

Figure 5: The contents of summary.

3 Results

Organizers assess submitted highlights based on recall and precision, with recall measuring gold highlight prediction using BERT-score semantic similarity (Zhang et al., 2019). Precision gauges the quality of predicted supporting evidence. Summarized evidence is evaluated for consistency, indicating the absence of contradiction by calculating the probability of it conflicting with the gold summary. Further details can be found in the paper (Chim et al., 2024).

Two highlight submission patterns were employed - one using only suicide risk classification and the other combining suicide risk classification, sentiment classification, and MentaLLaMa. Table 1 shows results for both patterns. The former achieved the highest precision among all teams, and the latter attained the highest recall among all teams. This underscores the effectiveness of sentence-level suicide extraction for evidence extraction. Sentence-level sentiment classification and MentaLLaMa-based highlight extraction complement in covering additional

[3] https://huggingface.co/klyang/MentaLLaMA-chat-7B

evidence of suicide risk. Further analysis is provided in the next section.

In the summary generation subtask, it achieved the 10th rank with a consistency metric of 0.944. The lower score is attributed to two reasons: insufficient attention to consistency when integrating multiple summaries and the absence of prompt engineering to incorporate shared task background, relevant aspects, and evaluation metrics into the prompts, despite using simple prompts.

	Recall	Precision
Suicide risk classification	0.912	**0.919**
+Sentiment classification +MentaLLaMa	**0.944**	0.906

Table 1: Results of highlight extraction subtask for two submission patterns.

3.1 Analysis on highlight extraction

For every submitted highlight, we received the semantic similarity between the golden highlight as precision calculated by BERT-Score. We analyzed the correlation between precision and predicted suicide risk/negative sentiment probability for each highlight. Figs. 6 and 7 show the average suicide risk and negative sentiment probabilities for highlight precision. They also display the percentage of highlights with a suicide risk probability of 0.9 or higher and negative sentiment probability of 0.9 or higher. Fig. 6 indicates a correlation between suicide risk probability and precision as evaluated by the golden highlight. In contrast, Fig. 7 shows no correlation between negative sentiment probability and precision as assessed by the golden highlight. This suggests that while sentence-level suicide risk assessment significantly contributes to precise suicide risk evidence highlight extraction, negative sentiment classification does not.

Table 2 presents highlights with high and low precision. High precision highlights frequently articulate users' suicidal thoughts, consistent with previous studies (Rude et al., 2004; Jamil et al., 2017). On the other hand, low precision highlights discuss suicide but often lack actual suicide risk. Instances involve discussions about another person's suicide or expressing negativity towards suicide, such as "I'm not about to commit suicide" and "my best friend also tried to kill himself". This misclassification arises from our suicide risk classification model, which utilizes keyword matching. The training data may include denials of suicide or stories about others' suicides unrelated to personal suicide risk.

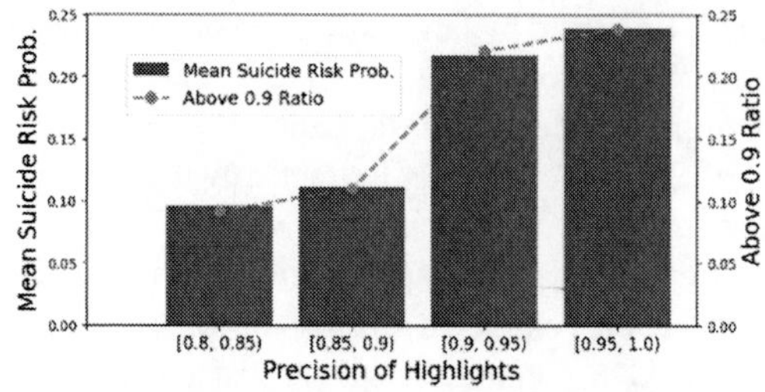

Figure 6: Mean suicide risk probability and above 0.9 ratio vs precision of highlights. We deleted error bar as most of values are close to 0 or 1.

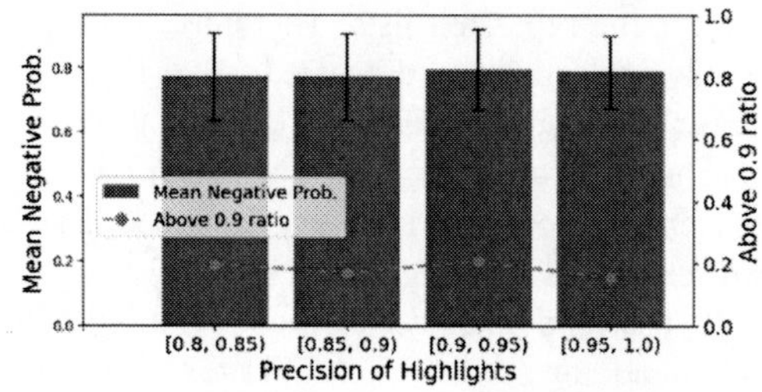

Figure 7: Mean negative sentiment probability and above 0.9 ratio vs precision of highlights.

	Phrases
Highlights with high precision	I want to die / i am suicidal / I've tried to hang myself two times / I don't know how to stop thinking of suicide
Highlights with low precision	I'm not about to commit suicide / I wasnt able to kill myself / My last objection to suicide is that/ losing someone to suicide / I haven't considered actually killing myself / my best friend also tried to kill himself / If you're close to killing yourself

Table 2: Example highlights that received high and low precision scores. The higher the score, the higher the semantic similarity to gold highlights.

4 Conclusion

We proposed integrating supervised extractive LLM (BERT fine-tuned for sentence-level suicide risk extraction) and generative LLM (MentaLLaMa) for summarizing suicide risk evidence. Sentence-level suicide risk assessment achieved the highest precision and recall. Future work will explore replicating these promising results with generative LLMs.

Limitations

This paper lacks meticulous teacher data creation for suicide risk estimation. Suicide risk has been labeled using keyword matching with the dictionary in Appendix A, potentially introducing noise data like sentences without suicidal thoughts or sentences about others' suicides. To enhance the accuracy of suicide risk classification, manual examination of the training data is necessary. Some participants such as (Sandu et al., 2024) take supervised approach, and we will reference their approaches.

This paper lacks a clear evaluation of why sentence-level surpasses other levels (e.g., word or paragraph) for highlight extraction. In the case of long sentences, there is a possibility that unnecessary parts are highlighted.

The methodology heavily depends on manual design, lacking automation by generative LLMs. While achieving excellent results in highlight extraction, the manual processes hinder scalability and efficiency. Exploring directions to replicate these promising results using generative LLMs is essential, emphasizing the need for automation. Many participating research teams in this shared task such as (Singh et al., 2024) utilized generative LLMs with prompt engineering, and we will reference their approaches.

Ethical Statement

We have signed a data usage agreement with organizer of CLPsych 2024 ensuring strict adherence to privacy protection and confidentiality. Secure access to the shared task dataset was provided with IRB approval under University of Maryland, College Park protocol 1642625 and approval by the Biomedical and Scientific Research Ethics Committee (BSREC) at the University of Warwick (ethical application reference BSREC 40/19-20). To reinforce the confidentiality of the data, it has been securely stored in an environment accessible exclusively by team members. We excluded API-related LLMs from consideration and focused only on downloadable LLMs.

Prof. Fukazawa, one of the authors, briefed the team on potential mental health impacts during tasks, addressing risks linked to individuals with a history of suicidal thoughts. The team is thoughtfully assembled with members free from mental health concerns, ensuring a supportive and safe work environment.

Acknowledgments

The authors are particularly grateful to the anonymous users of Reddit whose data feature in this year's shared task dataset, to the clinical experts who annotated the data, to the American Association of Suicidology in making the dataset available, to the CLPsych 2024 shared task organizers. This work was supported by Sophia University Special Grant for Academic Research.

References

Han-Chin Shing, Suraj Nair, Ayah Zirikly, Meir Friedenberg, Hal Daumé III, and Philip Resnik. 2018. Expert, Crowdsourced, and Machine Assessment of Suicide Risk via Online Postings, In *Proceedings of the Fifth Workshop on Computational Linguistics and Clinical Psychology: From Keyboard to Clinic*, pages 25–36.

Ayah Zirikly, Philip Resnik, Özlem Uzuner, and Kristy Hollingshead. 2019. CLPsych 2019 shared task: Predicting the degree of suicide risk in Reddit posts. In *Proceedings of the Sixth Workshop on Computational Linguistics and Clinical Psychology (CLPsych'19), Conference of the North American Chapter of the Association for Computational Linguistics (NAACL)*.

Jenny Chim, Adam Tsakalidis, Dimitris Gkoumas, Dana Atzil-Slonim, Yaakov Ophir, Ayah Zirikly, Philip Resnik, and Maria Liakata. 2024. Overview of the CLPsych 2024 Shared Task: Leveraging Large Language Models to Identify Evidence of Suicidality Risk in Online Posts, In *Proceedings of the Ninth Workshop on Computational Linguistics and Clinical Psychology, Association for Computational Linguistics*.

Rafael Ferreira, Luciano de Souza Cabral, Rafael Dueire Lins, Gabriel Pereira e Silva, Fred Freitas, George D.C. Cavalcanti, Rinaldo Lima, Steven J. Simske. 2013. Luciano Favaro, Assessing sentence scoring techniques for extractive text summarization. *Expert Systems with Applications*, Volume 40. Issue 14. pages 5755-5764.

Aliaksei Severyn and Alessandro Moschitti. 2015. Learning to Rank Short Text Pairs with Convolutional Deep Neural Networks. *SIGIR*. pages 373–382.

Ashish Vaswani, Noam Shazeer, Niki Parmar, Jakob Uszkoreit, Llion Jones, Aidan N. Gomez, Lukasz Kaiser, and Illia Polosukhin. 2017. Attention is all you need. *Advances in neural information processing systems*.

Tom B. Brown, Benjamin Mann, Nick Ryder, Melanie Subbiah, Jared Kaplan, Prafulla Dhariwal, Arvind Neelakantan, Pranav Shyam, Girish Sastry, Amanda Askell, Sandhini Agarwal, Ariel Herbert-Voss, Gretchen Krueger, Tom Henighan, Rewon Child, Aditya Ramesh, Daniel M. Ziegler, Jeffrey Wu, Clemens Winter, Christopher Hesse, Mark Chen, Eric Sigler, Mateusz Litwin, Scott Gray, Benjamin Chess, Jack Clark, Christopher Berner, Sam McCandlish, Alec Radford, Ilya Sutskever, and Dario Amodei. 2019. Language Models are Few-Shot Learners. *Advances in Neural Information Processing Systems*.

Jacob Devlin, Ming-Wei Chang, Kenton Lee, and Kristina Toutanova. 2018. BERT: Pre-training of Deep Bidirectional Transformers for Language Understanding. *arXiv*:1810.04805v2.

Kailai Yang, Tianlin Zhang, Ziyan Kuang, Qianqian Xie, Sophia Ananiadou, and Jimin Huang. 2023. MentaLLaMA: Interpretable Mental Health Analysis on Social Media with Large Language Models. *arXiv*:2309.13567.

Michal Monselise and Christopher C. Yang. 2022. “I'm always in so much pain and no one will understand”-Detecting Patterns in Suicidal Ideation on Reddit. In Companion Proceedings of the *Web Conference 2022*, pages 686-691.

Manas Gaur, Vamsi Aribandi, Amanuel Alambo, Ugur Kursuncu, Krishnaprasad Thirunarayan, Jonathan Beich, Jyotishman Pathak and Amit Sheth. 2021. Characterization of time-variant and time-invariant assessment of suicidality on Reddit using C-SSRS, *PLOS ONE*

Daniel Loureiro, Francesco Barbieri, Leonardo Neves, Luis Espinosa Anke, and Jose Camacho-collados. 2022. TimeLMs: Diachronic Language Models from Twitter, *ACL: System Demonstrations*. pages 251–260.

Hugo Touvron, Louis Martin, Kevin Stone, Peter Albert, Amjad Almahairi, Yasmine Babaei, Nikolay Bashlykov, Soumya Batra, Prajjwal Bhargava, Shruti Bhosale, Dan Bikel, Lukas Blecher, Cristian Canton Ferrer, Moya Chen, Guillem Cucurull, David Esiobu, Jude Fernandes, Jeremy Fu, Wenyin Fu, Brian Fuller, Cynthia Gao, Vedanuj Goswami, Naman Goyal, Anthony Hartshorn, Saghar Hosseini, Rui Hou, Hakan Inan, Marcin Kardas, Viktor Kerkez, Madian Khabsa, Isabel Kloumann, Artem Korenev, Punit Singh Koura, Marie-Anne Lachaux, Thibaut Lavril, Jenya Lee, Diana Liskovich, Yinghai Lu, Yuning Mao, Xavier Martinet, Todor Mihaylov, Pushkar Mishra, Igor Molybog, Yixin Nie, Andrew Poulton, Jeremy Reizenstein, Rashi Rungta, Kalyan Saladi, Alan Schelten, Ruan Silva, Eric Michael Smith, Ranjan Subramanian, Xiaoqing Ellen Tan, Binh Tang, Ross Taylor, Adina Williams, Jian Xiang Kuan, Puxin Xu, Zheng Yan, Iliyan Zarov, Yuchen Zhang, Angela Fan, Melanie Kambadur, Sharan Narang, Aurelien Rodriguez, Robert Stojnic, Sergey Edunov, Thomas Scialom. 2023. Llama 2: Open foundation and fine-tuned chat models. *arXiv*:2307.09288.

Tianyi Zhang, Varsha Kishore, Felix Wu, Kilian Q. Weinberger, and Yoav Artzi. 2019. BERTScore: Evaluating Text Generation with BERT. *arXiv* e-prints, page arXiv:1904.09675.

Stephanie Rude, Eva-Maria Gortner, and James Pennebaker. 2004. Language use of depressed and depression-vulnerable college students. *Cognition and Emotion*. Vol. 18, No. 8, pp. 1121-1133.

Zunaira Jamil, Diana Inkpen, Prasadith Buddhitha, and Kenton White. 2017. Monitoring tweets for depression to detect at-risk users. *ACL CLPsych*. pages 32-40.

Anastasia Sandu, Teodor Mihailescu, and Sergiu Nisioi. 2024. Cheap Ways of Extracting Clinical Markers from Texts, In *Proceedings of the Ninth Workshop on Computational Linguistics and Clinical Psychology, Association for Computational Linguistics*.

Loitongbam Gyanendro Singh, Junyu Mao, and Rudra Mutalik, and Stuart E. Middleton, 2024. Extraction and Summarization of Suicidal Ideation Evidence in Social Media Content Using Large Language Models, In *Proceedings of the Ninth Workshop on Computational Linguistics and Clinical Psychology, Association for Computational Linguistics*.

Appendix A. List of suicide risk phrases.

1. attempt suicide, attempted suicide, attempting suicide, attempts of suicide, suicide attempt, suicide attempts
2. commit suicide, committed suicide, committing suicide
3. consider suicide, considered suicide, considering suicide
4. want to die, wanted to die, don't want to live
5. end my life
6. hang myself, hanging myself, myself hanging
7. kill me, kill myself, killed myself, killing me, killing myself
8. means of suicide, ways of dying
9. shoot me, shooting me, shoot myself, shooting myself
10. suicide plan, plan suicide
11. suicide thoughts, think about suicide, thinking about suicide, thinking of suicide, thought of suicide, thoughts of suicide, suicidal thoughts, suicide thoughts

Appendix B. Prefix and phrases for generating summary

Prefix	Phrases
This person feels	pain, anxious, sad, angry, agitated, trapped, hopeless, empty, guilt, shame, helpless, worthless, enraged, alone, isolated, failure
This person is dealing with issues with	friend, girlfriend, boyfriend, family, brother, sister, father, mother
This person has a problem of	eating, money, drug, alcohol
This person is struggling with	depression, trauma
This person is experiencing	bullying, abused, raped

Archetypes and Entropy: Theory-Driven Extraction of Evidence for Suicide Risk

**Vasudha Varadarajan[1], Allison Lahnala[2], Adithya V Ganesan[1], Gourab Dey[1]
Siddharth Mangalik[1], Ana-Maria Bucur[3,4], Nikita Soni[1], Rajath Rao[1], Kevin Lanning[5]
Isabella Vallejo[5], Lucie Flek[2], H. Andrew Schwartz[1], Charles Welch[2], Ryan L Boyd[1]**

[1]Department of Computer Science, Stony Brook University
[2]Bonn-Aachen International Center for Information Technology (b-it), University of Bonn
[3]Interdisciplinary School of Doctoral Studies, University of Bucharest
[4]PRHLT Research Center, Universitat Politècnica de València
[5]Wilkes Honors College, Florida Atlantic University
{vvaradarajan, boyd}@cs.stonybrook.edu, alahnala@uni-bonn.de

Abstract

Sensitive content warning: This paper contains sensitive content related to suicide.

Psychological risk factors for suicide have been extensively studied for decades. However, combining explainable theory with modern data-driven language modeling approaches is non-trivial. Here, we propose and evaluate methods for identifying language patterns indicative of suicide risk by combining theory-driven suicidal *archetypes* with language model-based and *relative entropy*-based approaches. *Archetypes* are based on prototypical statements that evince risk of suicidality while *relative entropy* considers the difference between how probable the risk-familiar and risk-unfamiliar models find user language. Each approach performed well individually; combining the two strikingly improved performance, yielding our combined system submission with a BERTScore Recall of 0.906. Further, we find diagnostic language is distributed unevenly in posts, with titles containing substantial risk evidence. We conclude that a union between theory- and data-driven methods is beneficial, outperforming more modern prompt-based methods.

1 Introduction

With the advent of large language models (LLMs) (Brown et al., 2020), studies exploring their potential for estimating suicide risk from social media data have proliferated (Coppersmith et al., 2018; Matero et al., 2019; Nock et al., 2019; Coppersmith, 2022). Such studies, however, chiefly emphasize predictive accuracy over explainability and interpretability (Schafer et al., 2021), limiting both their clinical applicability and their utility in testing theories of suicide. Our team, SWELL, takes a psychological theory-informed approach to produce evidential explanations and summaries for the assigned suicide risk score of Reddit users.

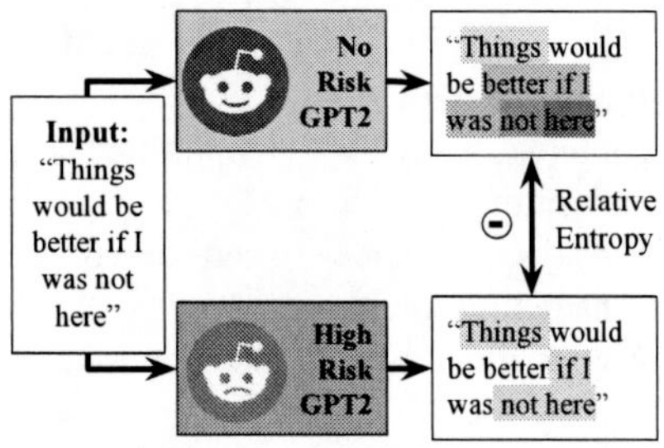

Figure 1: ***Relative entropy* method.** Two DistilGPT2 models were independently pretrained domain-adaptively (Gururangan et al., 2020) on posts from users having no suicide risk (*No Risk GPT2*) and users having high suicide risk (*High Risk GPT2*). The difference in the token entropy between the models is used as a measure of "surprisal" to extract the evidential highlights of at-risk suicide users. Highlighted spans indicate entropy values, with darker colors indicating higher entropy.

Despite substantial effort dedicated to extracting explanatory rationale for LLM answers for math, physics, and even theory of mind (Cobbe et al., 2021; Zheng et al., 2023; Saha et al., 2023), there has been limited work in building similar explanatory pipelines for mental health diagnostics. The CLPsych-2024 shared task asked teams to provide evidences and summaries for suicide risk from social media posts (Chim et al., 2024).

Our main contributions include three novel methods for suicide risk evidence extraction based on (1) theory-based *archetype* representations of suicidality including with Llama2-Chat (Touvron et al., 2023), (2) an LLM-based *relative entropy* method, and (3) a hybrid combination of *entropy* with *archetypes*. Additionally, we provide (4) a method for prompt-based explanation summaries, and (5) associations of theory-based *archetypes* with trained expert annotations. Further, we release the code associated with our submissions.[1]

[1]https://github.com/humanlab/clp24-arch-entropy

Proceedings of the 9th Workshop on Computational Linguistics and Clinical Psychology (CLPsych 2024), pages 278–291
March 21, 2024

2 Background

Conceptualizing Suicide Risk. One of the most prominent theoretical conceptualizations of suicide is Joiners' Interpersonal Theory of Suicide (IPTS) (Van Orden et al., 2010) which is comprised of 3 factors that jointly characterize suicide risk: 1) *Acquired Capability*, a person's increased tolerance for physical pain and fear of death, which can develop over time through suicidal ideation and repeated exposure to painful or fear-inducing experiences (Smith et al., 2010); 2) *Perceived Burdensomeness*, an individual's belief that their existence or presence is a burden on others (Joiner et al., 2002); 3) *Thwarted Belongingness*, the perception or experience of not belonging to, or feeling disconnected from, meaningful social relationships despite efforts to form connections (Silva et al., 2015). Prior work suggests that suicide becomes possible when an individual experiences high levels of all 3 constructs (Joiner, 2007).

Explainable Approaches for Suicide Risk Prediction. The evolution of language modeling techniques has led to improvements in risk prediction tasks (Sawhney et al., 2022; Xu et al., 2023; V Ganesan et al., 2021; Juhng et al., 2023; V Ganesan et al., 2022), yet very little has been focused on adapting these models to be more reliable or practical for real-world applications. Heckler et al. (2022) identified *interpretability and explainability* as one of the primary challenges in supporting specialists with understanding model inferences. A number of NLP tasks such as natural language inference (Camburu et al., 2018), hate speech detection (Mathew et al., 2021), discourse relation prediction (Son et al., 2022) and commonsense reasoning (Aggarwal et al., 2021) have made long strides in building explainable models. In the vein of improving the explainability of LLMs and addressing the particular need for suicide-risk assessment models, this year's CLPsych shared task investigates evidence extraction and summarization for suicide risk from social media posts, evaluating against highlights and summaries written by experts.

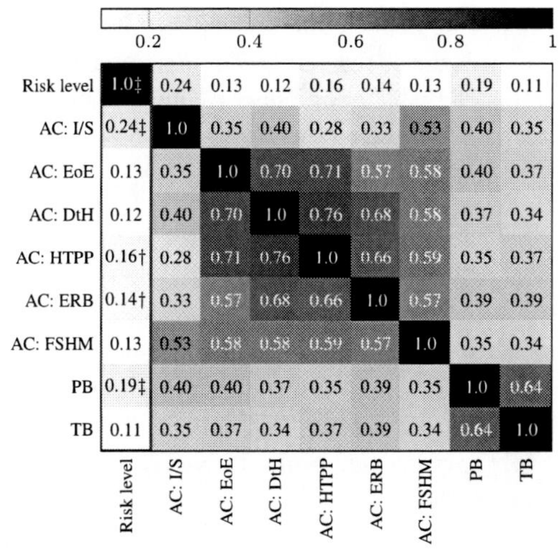

Figure 2: A descriptive Spearman correlation matrix between expert-labeled risk level from UMD Suicidality Dataset and maximum user-level *archetype* scores. Archetypes include Perceived Burdensomness (PB), Thwarted Belongingness (TB), and Acquired Capability (AC) with subtypes Ideation/Simulation (I/S), Experiences of Endurance (EoE), Desensitization to Harm (DtH), High Tolerance for Physical Pain (HTPP), Engagement in Risky Behaviors (ERB), and Familiarity with Self-Harm Methods (FSHM). Statistically significant correlations between the archetypes and risk levels are marked in the first column ($p < 0.05^{\dagger}$ and $p < 0.005^{\ddagger}$). Archetypes correlated with each other in theory-consistent ways and, additionally, were meaningfully related to expert evaluations.

3 Data & Tasks

Dataset. The CLPsych-2024 shared task uses the UMD Suicidality v2 dataset (Shing et al., 2018; Zirikly et al., 2019), which contains history of posts from all subreddits for a set of users who posted on `r/SuicideWatch` (SW), a support forum for people struggling with suicidal thoughts. For each SW poster, the dataset includes a suicide risk label and a list of posts from the user. Expert annotators further assessed the posts to highlight text spans that provide evidence supporting the risk label, and wrote cohesive summaries of all evidence selected for each user.

The SW posts came from 195 users whom experts labeled as having no risk, and 671 users whom experts labeled into 3 suicide risk categories (*any risk*): low, moderate, and high risk. There were 1,241 posts on SW and 59,933 posts on non-SuicideWatch (NSW) subreddits. 125 users from the expert-annotated set (162 SW posts; 19,894 NSW posts) were held out as the test set. From the 195 control (*no risk*) users, the dataset also included 19,631 NSW and 195 SW posts.

Shared Tasks. The first task was to automatically extract highlights from the SW posts that explain the assigned suicide risk level of the user. The second task was to generate cohesive summaries that aggregate the evidence supporting the users' assigned suicide risk levels. These summaries were evaluated by their consistency with human expert summaries based on the same users' SW posts.

4 Methods

4.1 Evidence Extraction

We designed three general approaches described below, and experimented with variants and compositions of each. Except for the prompt-based approach, we extract highlights at the sentence level, preprocessed with the NLTK sentence tokenizer (Bird and Loper, 2004).

4.1.1 Suicidality *Archetypes*.

Several extant theories of suicide have been proposed that explain various psychological states and trajectories of suicide. For the purposes of this paper, we focused specifically on constructs from Joiner's IPTS (Joiner, 2007). Psychologists on our team formalized prototypical statements reflecting patterns of cognition relevant to suicide risk (e.g., "I've intentionally exposed myself to pain to build up my resistance"). Prototype sentences were embedded using `RoBERTa-large` (Liu et al., 2019); all embeddings were then averaged, separately by factor, to create a representative *archetype* of each construct (see Table A3). As an example, for the Ideation/Simulation archetype, the average embedding of the three statements forms the representation of the archetype.

Inspired by Garten et al. (2018), we calculate the cosine similarity between the sentence embeddings of a post and each archetype. We compute Spearman's correlation between the expert risk assessments and archetypes of Joiner's IPTS, with the users' maximum scores for each archetype to reflect the maximum risk evidence. The correlation matrix is shown in Figure 2. We find statistically significant correlations between expert-labeled risk levels and Perceived Burdensomeness, AC: Engagement in Risky Behaviors, AC: High Tolerance for Physical Pain, and AC: Ideation/Simulation, the latter having the strongest, most significant relationship with $r = 0.238$ and $p < 0.001$.

For our *archetypes*-only method ("Archetypes" in Table 1), Principal Component Analysis (PCA) (Tipping and Bishop, 1999) was applied to all 8 archetype similarity scores, reducing them from 8 to 2 dimensions. After z-scoring the sum of component scores, we highlighted spans that were either in the top-ranking 25% of each post or ≥ 1.5 standard deviations from the mean sum of components.

4.1.2 Relative Entropy.

This method is based on Lahnala et al. (2021)'s approach for studying the language of mental health professionals and peer supporters in online support forums. The entropy (used to calculate perplexity) for a token in an LM is a signal of "surprisal" of that token given the context and domain (Jurafsky and Martin, 2023, Ch. 3). Figure 1 depicts this method adapted for this work, in which, the token "here" would be particularly unexpected in this context from a no-risk user.

Domain adaptation (Gururangan et al., 2020) of LLMs on low-risk or no-risk data leads to higher entropy for tokens signaling high-risk in the high-risk data. However, as out-of-domain expressions can also have high entropy, we calibrate the entropy by domain-adaptive pre-training of two LLMs; one with lower-risk data and one with higher-risk data. We hypothesize that higher differences from subtracting token entropies of higher-risk models from lower-risk models are signals of risk-associated language.

To calculate the relative entropy, we subtract the entropy of the token-level predictions of one model from the other. For a model, H, trained on high-risk data, we can subtract the entropy this model assigns to high-risk data from the entropy assigned by a model, L, trained on low-risk data. To obtain the entropy difference for a sequence of tokens, S, in a given sentence, we calculate the maximum[2] of token entropy differences within the sentence:

$$E_{L,H} = \max_{s \in S}\{log(p_L(s)) - log(p_H(s))\} \quad (1)$$

We applied domain-adaptive pretraining to DistilGPT2 (Sanh et al., 2019) for each of the risk categories: none (a), low (b), moderate (c), high (d) and any (b,c,d), and calculate the entropy differences between sentences for each language model pair. In our system, four pairs of models were considered: no-low, no-moderate, no-high and no-any. We applied PCA to reduce the dimensionality of these four elements to a single relative entropy score and qualitatively examined the scores to determine a threshold for selecting sentences as spans, resulting in the top 30% of sentences.

[2]We conducted a qualitative analysis and found that the maximum performed better than the mean or median.

	Highlighted Evidence				Summarized Evidence	
	Recall ↑	Precision ↑	W.Recall ↑	H.Mean ↑	Mean Consist. ↑	Max Contra. ↓
Random (25%)	0.887	0.894	0.790	0.891	0.969	0.094
Archetypes (25%)	0.897	**0.914**	**0.816**	0.905	**0.973**	**0.080**
ArchPrompts-Llama2c	0.884	**0.914**	0.741	**0.910**	0.972	0.082
Entropy-DistilGPT2 (30%)	0.901	0.884	0.621	0.892	0.967	0.094
Entropy-DGPT2 x Archs (30%)	**0.906**	0.897	0.648	0.901	0.970	0.092

Table 1: **Scores based on shared task's annotations.** The first row indicates a baseline which is a random selection of 25% of sentences from each post. Our submissions to the shared task were Archetypes, ArchPrompts-Llama2c (LLama2-chat 13b prompted to extract sentences evidential of the 3 major archetypes), and Entropy-DistilGPT2 x Archs (combining our Entropy based approach with Archetype scores). The scores on the right compare the gold evidence summaries with the evidence summaries generated by Llama2c with highlighted evidence spans from each method as the inputs.

We also applied similar techniques to another LM, HaRT (Human-aware Recurrent Transformer) (Soni et al., 2022) which is a user-level LM that models message-level context along with author-specific context, helping capture the surprisal of language specific to the author. The dataset for domain-adaptive pretraining included a limited number of historical posts from other subreddits for each user in the SW test set. We encode users' NSW and SW posts in a chronological order by concatenating them with a separator token. Two models were trained for none and any risk levels, and we followed the same entropy calculations. In §5, we discuss a comparison of this user-level variant of the entropy method against a combination of archetypes and entropy (see Table 3).

4.1.3 Prompt-based evidence highlights.

Our submission based on Llama2-Chat used Joiner's constructs in a few-shot setting to extract highlights from the posts. We created instructions that included a definition of each construct alongside five prototypical examples of highlights extracted from the posts for the respective construct. We then prompted a self-hosted instance of Llama2-Chat (13B) with these instructions to generate a list of highlights that correspond with each construct for each post. The full prompts are in Appendix B.

4.2 Evidence Summarization

For each system detailed in §4.1, we prompt Llama2-chat (13B) with detailed instructions to summarize the highlighted evidence of the user explaining the assigned risk level. The instruction was framed to incorporate different factors of language (Emotional State, Cognitive Processes, Behavior and Motivation, Interpersonal Relationships and Social Support, Mental Health Issues, and Other Risk Factors) while summarizing the highlights with the objective of explaining the risk category. For the prompt and more details about the method, please see Appendix B. Llama2-Chat was provided up to 10 highlights in order to avoid running into problems caused by long context (Liu et al., 2023) and the highlights were uniformly sampled from all posts for each user.

	Rec	Prec	*M/p*
Archetypes	**0.892**	**0.899**	**3.75**
ArchPrompt-Llama2c	0.789	0.797	4.39
Entropy-DGPT2	0.867	0.861	5.41
Entropy-DGPT2 x Archs	0.881	0.865	6.40

Table 2: Recall, Precision on the set of internal expert annotations and mean spans extracted per post (*M/p*). The *M/p* for the internal expert annotation was 6.35.

4.3 Internal Annotations

To support our experimental evaluations, we collected our own set of annotations of evidence from experts, based on Joiner's IPTS (§2). We selected 50 posts from 50 unique users that were not part of the heldout test set for the shared task. These were annotated by two clinical experts following the guidelines outlined in the Appendix (Table A6). We used the annotations to internally validate our systems and select the best models (see Table 2).

5 Results

We discuss the result of our experiments with the methods described in §4. We report the results of our official submissions in Appendix A.[3]

[3]We intended our first official submission to be Archetypes-based and the second to be based on Entropy x Archetypes. Instead, due to a couple of interesting bugs, we re-did experiments to validate our findings and report them in §5 and Table 1. The initial submissions are described in Appendix A.

Archetypes capture relevant highlights. Table 1 shows that theory-driven approaches such as Archetypes (1) outperform random chance; and (2) interestingly, we observe that small yet strong encoder language models (RoBERTa-large) generalize archetypal utterances of suicidal risk with few examples better than large generative models (Llama2c). Further, performance on internal expert annotations in Table 2 validates the generalizability of Archetypes from internal to shared task annotator pools. Archetypes also have an average of 3.75 highlights per post, which when coupled with the overall performance, indicates highly informative spans are selected as evidence.

Entropy combined with Archetypes further improves Recall. We find that entropy-based methods have a high recall owing to better coverage of highlights signaling suicide risk, however, this comes at a small cost of precision, as seen in Table 1. Since *Archetypes* reflect theory-driven signals and *Entropy* captures data-driven signals of suicide risk, we combine Archetypes with Entropy by multiplying the scores and selecting the top-scoring 30% of sentences. This produced the best recall and improved the precision of the entropy-based method by a significant margin in the case of shared task annotations. In the case of internal expert annotations, Archetypes fared better, likely due in part to our internal annotation schema being consistent with Joiner's IPTS theory. For summaries and extracted spans for each system for a paraphrased example, see Appendix A2.

	Recall	Precision	W.Recall
Post-structure experiments			
Random 25%	0.887	**0.894**	0.790
Title only	0.862	**0.894**	**0.840**
25% body	**0.884**	0.892	0.699
Title + 25% body	0.883	0.893	0.788
Entropy-variant experiments **(top 40%)**			
DGPT2 x Archs	**0.915**	**0.892**	**0.542**
HaRT	0.912	0.887	0.525

Table 3: Recall, precision, and weighted recall for the post-structure experiments and entropy-variant experiments for Task A.

We further compare the performance boost afforded by using Entropy-DGPT2 x Archetypes against better modeling of user-level context using Entropy-HaRT, selecting top 40% of sentences from both the methods as the suicide risk evidence. Table 3 (bottom) shows a comparison of the two entropy-variant experiments, and we find that the combination of Entropy-DGPT2 x Archetypes is better across all three performance metrics.

Title of a post is highly informative. In Table 3 (top), we explore the post structure of SuicideWatch posts to understand the effects of the title and body. We experiment with three conditions; using only the title, the first 25% of the body and the title and 25% body together. Our results from using the title and the first 25% of the posts show that they outperform a random sampling of 25% of posts. Interestingly, when using only the title, we get the highest weighted recall across all methods, supporting that titles are highly informative (Matero et al., 2019) and potentially pointing to signals of suicide being presented upfront in SW posts on platforms with a similar post structure.

Llama2-Chat is consistent with Summarization. Summaries generated by Llama2-chat (13B) had high consistency and low contradiction scores across all submissions. This may have resulted from (1) the model's ability to precisely identify the suicide risk from appropriate psychological dimensions inferred from the span(s), and (2) a prompt carefully crafted to consider the important psychological dimensions to provide the summary.

While these summarized explanations are more convincing for high-risk users, we also find that the model is extremely sensitive to the inputs. For example, posts with very few spans from low-risk users were still surmised to exhibit a "heightened risk of suicide."

6 Conclusion

We combined theory-driven archetypes with data-driven language models to extract evidence from users' social media posts that support the assigned suicide risk levels. We found that scores derived for Joiner's constructs show a significant correlation with assigned suicide risk. Combining the relative entropy scores with Joiner construct scores improves upon relative entropy alone, which is demonstrated in the experimental results on both the shared task test set as well as our set of internal annotations. These rigorous data-driven methods grounded in theory also outperformed extensive prompting of instruction-following LLMs. Still, archetypes alone yield the highest precision in both evaluations. This demonstrates the importance of theoretically derived constructs in language modeling approaches to build explainable approaches for mental health diagnosis.

Limitations

While often not characterized within the context of IPTS, research has identified numerous other, more specific factors and pathways to suicidality, such as an omnibus need for "escape" from aversive self-awareness (Baumeister, 1990) and substance dependence (Pompili et al., 2012). A comprehensive review of suicide risk factors is beyond the scope of this paper, however, several such risk factors played a role in our approach to understanding and capturing suicide risk. We limited our methods to the most prominent factors as described in §2.

For the scope of our work, we limited our study of prompt-based methods for both evidential highlighting as well as evidence summarization to a single modern large language model – Llama2-chat. While modern LLMs lack social (Choi et al., 2023; Ziems et al., 2023; Varadarajan et al., 2023; Lahnala et al., 2022) and personal understanding (Havaldar et al., 2023; V Ganesan et al., 2023) from language, experiments using the same prompting structure with other socially and human aware LMs (Dey et al., 2024) could potentially produce results that outperform the methods described in this paper.

The studied data is limited to the English-speaking Reddit and may contain other data-specific biases (Chancellor et al., 2019) such as sampling bias towards certain groups. Furthermore, the subjectivity of interpretation of suicidality across individuals (Keilp et al., 2012) and the possibility for annotator biases (Hovy and Spruit, 2016) could implicate limitations in model training and evaluation approaches.

Ethics Statement

While the essence of our work is to aid in the detection of at-risk users, it is imperative that any interventions be well-thought, failing which may lead to counter-productive outcomes, such as users moving to fringe platforms, which would make it harder to provide assistance (Kumar et al., 2015). Care should be taken so as not to create stigma, and interventions must be carefully planned by consulting relevant stakeholders such as clinicians, designers, and researchers (Chancellor et al., 2016), to maintain social media as a safe space for individuals looking to express themselves (Chancellor et al., 2019).

We do not seek to make any diagnostic claims with our work; rather, we aim to help prioritize individuals in need of immediate help. Our approach should hence not act as a standalone method in risk assessment (De Choudhury et al., 2016). It is critical to avoid misuse of algorithmic inferences by bad actors (Chancellor et al., 2019), as in the case of Samaritan's radar (Hsin et al., 2016), by only selectively sharing the evaluations made by our study (De Choudhury et al., 2016). It is also vital to incorporate accessible interpretations (Chancellor et al., 2019). While we highlight the role of NLP as part of forming a human-in-the-loop framework, it is further essential that clinicians are not overburdened (Chancellor et al., 2019).

Issues with summarization methods also suggest that today's open-source LLMs are still not at the stage to run post-hoc explanations for suicide risk associated with the text. These models need to be fine-tuned and could be guardrailed using RLHF (Ouyang et al., 2022).

Acknowledgements

We would like to thank Veerle Eijsbroek and Katarina Kjell for their efforts in creating high-quality and IPTS-based annotations of the SuicideWatch posts. These expert annotations were invaluable for allowing us to conduct internal evaluations. We also thank the American Association of Suicidology for their assistance in making the dataset available for conducting this study.

References

Shourya Aggarwal, Divyanshu Mandowara, Vishwajeet Agrawal, Dinesh Khandelwal, Parag Singla, and Dinesh Garg. 2021. Explanations for CommonsenseQA: New Dataset and Models. In *Proceedings of the 59th Annual Meeting of the Association for Computational Linguistics and the 11th International Joint Conference on Natural Language Processing (Volume 1: Long Papers)*, pages 3050–3065, Online. Association for Computational Linguistics.

Roy F. Baumeister. 1990. Suicide as escape from self. *Psychological Review*, 97(1):90–113. Place: US Publisher: American Psychological Association.

Steven Bird and Edward Loper. 2004. NLTK: The natural language toolkit. In *Proceedings of the ACL Interactive Poster and Demonstration Sessions*, pages 214–217, Barcelona, Spain. Association for Computational Linguistics.

Tom Brown, Benjamin Mann, Nick Ryder, Melanie Subbiah, Jared D Kaplan, Prafulla Dhariwal, Arvind Neelakantan, Pranav Shyam, Girish Sastry, Amanda Askell, et al. 2020. Language models are few-shot learners. *Advances in neural information processing systems*, 33:1877–1901.

Oana-Maria Camburu, Tim Rocktäschel, Thomas Lukasiewicz, and Phil Blunsom. 2018. e-snli: Natural language inference with natural language explanations. *Advances in Neural Information Processing Systems*, 31.

Stevie Chancellor, Michael L. Birnbaum, Eric D. Caine, Vincent M. B. Silenzio, and Munmun De Choudhury. 2019. A taxonomy of ethical tensions in inferring mental health states from social media. In *Proceedings of the Conference on Fairness, Accountability, and Transparency*, FAT* '19, pages 79–88, Atlanta, GA, USA.

Stevie Chancellor, Zhiyuan Lin, Erica L. Goodman, Stephanie Zerwas, and Munmun De Choudhury. 2016. Quantifying and predicting mental illness severity in online pro-eating disorder communities. In *Proceedings of the 19th ACM Conference on Computer-Supported Cooperative Work and Social Computing*, CSCW '16, pages 1171–1184, San Francisco, CA, USA.

Jenny Chim, Adam Tsakalidis, Dimitris Gkoumas, Dana Atzil-Slonim, Yaakov Ophir, Ayah Zirikly, Philip Resnik, and Maria Liakata. 2024. Overview of the clpsych 2024 shared task: Leveraging large language models to identify evidence of suicidality risk in online posts. In *Proceedings of the Ninth Workshop on Computational Linguistics and Clinical Psychology*. "Association for Computational Linguistics".

Minje Choi, Jiaxin Pei, Sagar Kumar, Chang Shu, and David Jurgens. 2023. Do LLMs understand social knowledge? evaluating the sociability of large language models with SocKET benchmark. In *Proceedings of the 2023 Conference on Empirical Methods in Natural Language Processing*, pages 11370–11403, Singapore. Association for Computational Linguistics.

Karl Cobbe, Vineet Kosaraju, Mohammad Bavarian, Mark Chen, Heewoo Jun, Lukasz Kaiser, Matthias Plappert, Jerry Tworek, Jacob Hilton, Reiichiro Nakano, et al. 2021. Training verifiers to solve math word problems. *arXiv preprint arXiv:2110.14168*.

Glen Coppersmith. 2022. Digital life data in the clinical whitespace. *Current Directions in Psychological Science*, 31(1):34–40.

Glen Coppersmith, Ryan Leary, Patrick Crutchley, and Alex Fine. 2018. Natural language processing of social media as screening for suicide risk. *Biomedical informatics insights*, 10:1178222618792860.

Munmun De Choudhury, Emre Kiciman, Mark Dredze, Glen Coppersmith, and Mrinal Kumar. 2016. Discovering shifts to suicidal ideation from mental health content in social media. In *Proceedings of the 2016 CHI Conference on Human Factors in Computing Systems*, CHI '16, pages 2098–2110, San Jose, CA, USA.

Gourab Dey, Adithya V Ganesan, Yash Kumar Lal, Manal Shah, Shreyashee Sinha, Matthew Matero, Salvatore Giorgi, Vivek Kulkarni, and H. Andrew Schwartz. 2024. SOCIALITE-LLAMA: An instruction-tuned model for social scientific tasks. In *18th Conference of the European Chapter of the Association for Computational Linguistics*, St. Julian's, Malta. Association for Computational Linguistics.

Justin Garten, Joe Hoover, Kate M. Johnson, Reihane Boghrati, Carol Iskiwitch, and Morteza Dehghani. 2018. Dictionaries and distributions: Combining expert knowledge and large scale textual data content analysis. *Behavior Research Methods*, 50(1):344–361.

Suchin Gururangan, Ana Marasović, Swabha Swayamdipta, Kyle Lo, Iz Beltagy, Doug Downey, and Noah A. Smith. 2020. Don't stop pretraining: Adapt language models to domains and tasks. In *Proceedings of the 58th Annual Meeting of the Association for Computational Linguistics*, pages 8342–8360, Online. Association for Computational Linguistics.

Shreya Havaldar, Bhumika Singhal, Sunny Rai, Langchen Liu, Sharath Chandra Guntuku, and Lyle Ungar. 2023. Multilingual language models are not multicultural: A case study in emotion. In *Proceedings of the 13th Workshop on Computational Approaches to Subjectivity, Sentiment, & Social Media Analysis*, pages 202–214, Toronto, Canada. Association for Computational Linguistics.

Wesllei Felipe Heckler, Juliano Varella de Carvalho, and Jorge Luis Victória Barbosa. 2022. Machine learning for suicidal ideation identification: A systematic literature review. *Computers in Human Behavior*, 128:107095.

Dirk Hovy and Shannon L. Spruit. 2016. The social impact of natural language processing. In *Proceedings of the 54th Annual Meeting of the Association for Computational Linguistics*, ACL '16, pages 591–598, Berlin, Germany.

Honor Hsin, John Torous, and Laura Roberts. 2016. An adjuvant role for mobile health in psychiatry. *JAMA Psychiatry*, 73(2).

T. Joiner. 2007. *Why people die by suicide*. Harvard University Press, Cambridge, Mass.

Thomas E. Joiner, Jeremy W. Pettit, Rheeda L. Walker, Zachary R. Voelz, Jacqueline Cruz, M. David Rudd, and David Lester. 2002. Perceived burdensomeness and suicidality: Two studies on the suicide notes of those attempting and those completing suicide. *Journal of Social and Clinical Psychology*, 21(5):531–545. Publisher: Guilford Publications Inc.

Swanie Juhng, Matthew Matero, Vasudha Varadarajan, Johannes Eichstaedt, Adithya V Ganesan, and H. Andrew Schwartz. 2023. Discourse-level representations can improve prediction of degree of anxiety. In

Proceedings of the 61st Annual Meeting of the Association for Computational Linguistics (Volume 2: Short Papers), pages 1500–1511, Toronto, Canada. Association for Computational Linguistics.

Dan Jurafsky and James H Martin. 2023. *Speech and Language Processing (3rd ed. draft)*.

John G Keilp, Michael F Grunebaum, Marianne Gorlyn, Simone LeBlanc, Ainsley K Burke, Hanga Galfalvy, Maria A Oquendo, and J John Mann. 2012. Suicidal ideation and the subjective aspects of depression. *Journal of Affective Disorders*, 140(1).

Mrinal Kumar, Mark Dredze, Glen Coppersmith, and Munmun De Choudhury. 2015. Detecting changes in suicide content manifested in social media following celebrity suicides. In *Proceedings of the 26th ACM Conference on Hypertext & Social Media*, HT '15, pages 85–94, Guzelyurt, TRNC, Cypru.

Allison Lahnala, Charles Welch, David Jurgens, and Lucie Flek. 2022. A critical reflection and forward perspective on empathy and natural language processing. In *Findings of the Association for Computational Linguistics: EMNLP 2022*, pages 2139–2158, Abu Dhabi, United Arab Emirates. Association for Computational Linguistics.

Allison Lahnala, Yuntian Zhao, Charles Welch, Jonathan K. Kummerfeld, Lawrence C An, Kenneth Resnicow, Rada Mihalcea, and Verónica Pérez-Rosas. 2021. Exploring self-identified counseling expertise in online support forums. In *Findings of the Association for Computational Linguistics: ACL-IJCNLP 2021*, pages 4467–4480, Online. Association for Computational Linguistics.

Nelson F Liu, Kevin Lin, John Hewitt, Ashwin Paranjape, Michele Bevilacqua, Fabio Petroni, and Percy Liang. 2023. Lost in the middle: How language models use long contexts. *arXiv preprint arXiv:2307.03172*.

Yinhan Liu, Myle Ott, Naman Goyal, Jingfei Du, Mandar Joshi, Danqi Chen, Omer Levy, Mike Lewis, Luke Zettlemoyer, and Veselin Stoyanov. 2019. Roberta: A robustly optimized bert pretraining approach. *ArXiv*, abs/1907.11692.

Matthew Matero, Akash Idnani, Youngseo Son, Salvatore Giorgi, Huy Vu, Mohammad Zamani, Parth Limbachiya, Sharath Chandra Guntuku, and H. Andrew Schwartz. 2019. Suicide risk assessment with multi-level dual-context language and BERT. In *Proceedings of the Sixth Workshop on Computational Linguistics and Clinical Psychology*, pages 39–44, Minneapolis, Minnesota. Association for Computational Linguistics.

Binny Mathew, Punyajoy Saha, Seid Muhie Yimam, Chris Biemann, Pawan Goyal, and Animesh Mukherjee. 2021. Hatexplain: A benchmark dataset for explainable hate speech detection. In *Proceedings of the AAAI conference on artificial intelligence*, volume 35, pages 14867–14875.

Matthew K Nock, Franchesca Ramirez, and Osiris Rankin. 2019. Advancing our understanding of the who, when, and why of suicide risk. *JAMA psychiatry*, 76(1):11–12.

Long Ouyang, Jeffrey Wu, Xu Jiang, Diogo Almeida, Carroll Wainwright, Pamela Mishkin, Chong Zhang, Sandhini Agarwal, Katarina Slama, Alex Ray, et al. 2022. Training language models to follow instructions with human feedback. *Advances in Neural Information Processing Systems*, 35:27730–27744.

Maurizio Pompili, Gianluca Serafini, Marco Innamorati, Massimo Biondi, Alberto Siracusano, Massimo Di Giannantonio, Giancarlo Giupponi, Mario Amore, David Lester, Paolo Girardi, and Anne Maria Möller-Leimkühler. 2012. Substance abuse and suicide risk among adolescents. *European Archives of Psychiatry and Clinical Neuroscience*, 262(6):469–485.

Swarnadeep Saha, Peter Hase, and Mohit Bansal. 2023. Can language models teach weaker agents? teacher explanations improve students via theory of mind. *arXiv preprint arXiv:2306.09299*.

Victor Sanh, Lysandre Debut, Julien Chaumond, and Thomas Wolf. 2019. Distilbert, a distilled version of bert: smaller, faster, cheaper and lighter. In *NeurIPS EMC^2 Workshop*.

Ramit Sawhney, Shivam Agarwal, Atula Tejaswi Neerkaje, Nikolaos Aletras, Preslav Nakov, and Lucie Flek. 2022. Towards suicide ideation detection through online conversational context. In *Proceedings of the 45th international ACM SIGIR conference on research and development in information retrieval*, pages 1716–1727.

Katherine M. Schafer, Grace Kennedy, Austin Gallyer, and Philip Resnik. 2021. A direct comparison of theory-driven and machine learning prediction of suicide: A meta-analysis. *PLOS ONE*, 16(4):e0249833. Publisher: Public Library of Science.

Han-Chin Shing, Suraj Nair, Ayah Zirikly, Meir Friedenberg, Hal Daumé III, and Philip Resnik. 2018. Expert, crowdsourced, and machine assessment of suicide risk via online postings. In *Proceedings of the Fifth Workshop on Computational Linguistics and Clinical Psychology: From Keyboard to Clinic*, pages 25–36, New Orleans, LA. Association for Computational Linguistics.

Caroline Silva, Jessica D. Ribeiro, and Thomas E. Joiner. 2015. Mental disorders and thwarted belongingness, perceived burdensomeness, and acquired capability for suicide. *Psychiatry Research*, 226(1):316–327.

Phillip N. Smith, Kelly C. Cukrowicz, Erin K. Poindexter, Valerie Hobson, and Lee M. Cohen. 2010. The acquired capability for suicide: A comparison of suicide attempters, suicide ideators, and non-suicidal controls. *Depression and Anxiety*, 27(9):871–877.

Youngseo Son, Vasudha Varadarajan, and H. Andrew Schwartz. 2022. Discourse relation embeddings:

Representing the relations between discourse segments in social media. In *Proceedings of the Workshop on Unimodal and Multimodal Induction of Linguistic Structures (UM-IoS)*, pages 45–55, Abu Dhabi, United Arab Emirates (Hybrid). Association for Computational Linguistics.

Nikita Soni, Matthew Matero, Niranjan Balasubramanian, and H. Andrew Schwartz. 2022. Human language modeling. In *Findings of the Association for Computational Linguistics: ACL 2022*, pages 622–636, Dublin, Ireland. Association for Computational Linguistics.

Michael E Tipping and Christopher M Bishop. 1999. Mixtures of probabilistic principal component analyzers. *Neural computation*, 11(2):443–482.

Hugo Touvron, Louis Martin, Kevin Stone, Peter Albert, Amjad Almahairi, Yasmine Babaei, Nikolay Bashlykov, Soumya Batra, Prajjwal Bhargava, Shruti Bhosale, et al. 2023. Llama 2: Open foundation and fine-tuned chat models. *arXiv preprint arXiv:2307.09288*.

Adithya V Ganesan, Yash Kumar Lal, August Nilsson, and H. Schwartz. 2023. Systematic evaluation of GPT-3 for zero-shot personality estimation. In *Proceedings of the 13th Workshop on Computational Approaches to Subjectivity, Sentiment, & Social Media Analysis*, pages 390–400, Toronto, Canada. Association for Computational Linguistics.

Adithya V Ganesan, Matthew Matero, Aravind Reddy Ravula, Huy Vu, and H. Andrew Schwartz. 2021. Empirical evaluation of pre-trained transformers for human-level NLP: The role of sample size and dimensionality. In *Proceedings of the 2021 Conference of the North American Chapter of the Association for Computational Linguistics: Human Language Technologies*, pages 4515–4532, Online. Association for Computational Linguistics.

Adithya V Ganesan, Vasudha Varadarajan, Juhi Mittal, Shashanka Subrahmanya, Matthew Matero, Nikita Soni, Sharath Chandra Guntuku, Johannes Eichstaedt, and H. Andrew Schwartz. 2022. WWBP-SQT-lite: Multi-level models and difference embeddings for moments of change identification in mental health forums. In *Proceedings of the Eighth Workshop on Computational Linguistics and Clinical Psychology*, pages 251–258, Seattle, USA. Association for Computational Linguistics.

Kimberly A. Van Orden, Tracy K. Witte, Kelly C. Cukrowicz, Scott Braithwaite, Edward A. Selby, and Thomas E. Joiner. 2010. The interpersonal theory of suicide. *Psychological review*, 117(2):575–600.

Vasudha Varadarajan, Swanie Juhng, Syeda Mahwish, Xiaoran Liu, Jonah Luby, Christian Luhmann, and H. Andrew Schwartz. 2023. Transfer and active learning for dissonance detection: Addressing the rare-class challenge. In *Proceedings of the 61st Annual Meeting of the Association for Computational Linguistics (Volume 1: Long Papers)*, pages 11923–11936, Toronto, Canada. Association for Computational Linguistics.

Xuhai Xu, Bingshen Yao, Yuanzhe Dong, Saadia Gabriel, Hong Yu, James Hendler, Marzyeh Ghassemi, Anind K. Dey, and Dakuo Wang. 2023. Mental-llm: Leveraging large language models for mental health prediction via online text data. *arXiv preprint arXiv:2307.14385*.

Yizhen Zheng, Huan Yee Koh, Jiaxin Ju, Anh TN Nguyen, Lauren T May, Geoffrey I Webb, and Shirui Pan. 2023. Large language models for scientific synthesis, inference and explanation. *arXiv preprint arXiv:2310.07984*.

Caleb Ziems, William Held, Omar Shaikh, Jiaao Chen, Zhehao Zhang, and Diyi Yang. 2023. Can Large Language Models Transform Computational Social Science? *Computational Linguistics*, pages 1–53.

Ayah Zirikly, Philip Resnik, Özlem Uzuner, and Kristy Hollingshead. 2019. CLPsych 2019 shared task: Predicting the degree of suicide risk in Reddit posts. In *Proceedings of the Sixth Workshop on Computational Linguistics and Clinical Psychology*, pages 24–33, Minneapolis, Minnesota. Association for Computational Linguistics.

Appendices

A Official Submissions to CLPsych 2024 Shared Task.

The results of our official submissions to both Shared Task A and B are shown in Table A1.

A.1 Task A: Evidence Extraction.

A.1.1 SWELL-1: First 25% Title + Body

For our first submission, we picked the first 25% of sentences from the concatenated title and body for each post as evidence of the assigned suicide risk level. As discussed in §5, the title of a post is highly informative, and with its inclusion, this system scored the highest weighted recall (0.808) among all the official submissions for Task A.

A.1.2 SWELL-2: Top 40% Archetypes + Entropy

In this approach, each sentence from the posts was scored by taking the product of the maximum archetype score and the relative entropy score (as described in §4.1). Spans were selected by using the top-scoring 40% of sentences. For the official submission, the training data was comprised of mostly crowd-annotated posts, while the validation set was comprised entirely of expert-annotated

	Highlighted Evidence				Summarized Evidence	
	Recall ↑	Precision ↑	W.Recall ↑	H.Mean ↑	Mean Consist. ↑	Max Contra. ↓
1. First 25%	0.881	0.895	**0.808**	0.888	0.972	0.080
2. 40% Entropy-DGPT2 x Archs	**0.915**	0.892	0.542	0.903	0.973	0.081
3. ArchPrompts-Llama2c	0.884	**0.914**	0.741	**0.910**	0.972	0.082

Table A1: **Official Submissions**: Recall, precision and weighted recall for our official submissions to CLPsych Shared Task 2024 Task A. The recall of entropy-based systems is much higher than Table 1 due to picking top 40% of the sentences rather than top 30%, which is reflected in the decreased weighted recall.

posts. This likely contributed to our model overfitting on the crowd-annotated domain. We mixed the distribution of crowd and expert-annotated data across the train and validation sets in our experiments after the official submission, which are the results we present in the main paper (with top 30%). Since the Shared Task emphasizes the importance of recall, our official submission included the top 40% highest-scoring sentences. While this method succeeds in improving recall, the weighted recall is much lower than SWELL-1's. This shows that the evidence selected by SWELL-2 captures most expert-annotated evidence of suicide risk but also many potentially irrelevant sentences. We find from other experiments in §5 that when we select top 30% instead of 40%, the recall is reduced too, indicating that a 40% cutoff yields some of the most evidential highlights, albeit with a higher false positive rate.

A.1.3 SWELL-3: ArchPrompts-LLaMA2c

The third submission included the highlights extracted using prompting, as explained in §4.1.3 and is same as the one reported in Table 1. The prompts were based on Joiner's IPTS theory as well (§4.1.3), instructing the model to find highlights relevant to each archetype. The exact instruction can be found in Table A4. This theory-based method yields precise spans that evince suicide risk much better than SWELL-1 and SWELL-2, while not trading off performance on weighted recall.

A.2 Task B: Evidence Summarization

The highlights from the Task A for SWELL-1, SWELL-2 and SWELL-3 were further prompted to be summarized, as explained in §4.2. The exact instruction can be found in Table A5. All the three methods yielded similar results, generating summaries highly consistent with the expert summaries.

B Prompts for Evidence Extraction and Summarizing

The instruction prompts we developed are shown in Table A4 for the evidence extraction task (Task A) and Table A5 for the summarization task (Task B).

C Paraphrased examples

The following are sample summaries generated based on the example post and highlighted evidence selected by each system shown in Table A2.

C.1 SWELL-1 (First 25% Title + Body)

Generated summary: "There is a high risk of suicide for this individual. The first excerpt reveals that they spent two hours trying to "man up" and hang themselves, and even wrote a note to their family. This suggests a high level of emotional distress and a possible loss of hope. The second excerpt highlights the individual's sobering reality of nearly killing themselves today, which further substantiates their emotional state. Additionally, the use of the phrase "man up" implies a sense of shame or stigma associated with their emotions, which may hinder their ability to seek help. The individual's cognitive processes may be impaired due to emotional distress, as evidenced by the length of time they spend attempting to take their own life. Their behavior and motivation have also changed, as they have lost interest in activities they once enjoyed. The lack of social support and mental health issues, such as depression or anxiety, may also contribute to their suicide risk. Overall, the text excerpts suggest a high risk of suicide for this individual."

C.2 SWELL-2 (Archetypes + Entropy)

Generated summary: "There is a high risk of suicide for this individual. They have expressed a desire to end their life, with a history of suicidal thoughts and a lack of motivation to engage in activities they once enjoyed. Their emotional state is characterized by sadness, hopelessness, and a sense of emptiness. They have also reported poor grades, social isolation, and a lack of close relationships, which can further exacerbate their risk of suicide. Additionally, their cognitive processes are impaired, as evidenced by their negative thought patterns and decision-making abilities. Overall, this individual is at a high risk of suicide and should be given immediate attention and support."

C.3 SWELL-3 (ArchPrompts-LLaMA2c)

Generated summary: "There is a high risk of suicide for this individual. They express feelings of emotional distress, hopelessness, and a lack of motivation to engage in activities they once enjoyed. They have a negative self-image, feeling like they have "piss poor grades" and are not amounting to anything. They have also considered suicide, spending two hours trying to "man up" and hang themselves. Additionally, they have no real friends and have never been close to a girl, which can further exacerbate their feelings of isolation and low self-esteem. These factors, combined with their mental health issues and lack of social support, contribute to a high risk of suicide."

SWELL1: First 25% Title + Body
I almost killed myself today. I wrote a note for my family and tried to man up and hang myself. I couldn't do it. For the past year my life has felt strange and just hasn't been worth living. Some days I'm great, and others I'm thinking about how to kill myself. My life just feels...empty. My grades suck, don't have any friends, never had a girlfriend. My life is meaningless, so what's even the point?

SWELL2: Entropy-DGPT2 x Archetype (Top 40%)
I almost killed myself today.$_{score=1.18}$ I wrote a note for my family and tried to man up and hang myself.$_{score=0.76}$ I couldn't do it.$_{score=0.49}$ For the past year my life has felt strange and just hasn't been worth living.$_{score=0.69}$ Some days I'm great, and others I'm thinking about how to kill myself.$_{score=1.28}$ My life just feels...empty.$_{score=1.50}$ My grades suck, don't have any friends, never had a girlfriend.$_{score=1.56}$ My life is meaningless, so what's even the point?$_{score=1.42}$

SWELL3: Prompt-LLaMA2c
I almost killed myself today. I wrote a note for my family and tried to man up and hang myself. I couldn't do it. For the past year my life has felt strange and just hasn't been worth living. Some days I'm great, and others I'm thinking about how to kill myself. My life just feels...empty. My grades suck, don't have any friends, never had a girlfriend. My life is meaningless, so what's even the point?

Table A2: A paraphrased example showing the highlighted evidence from each system.

Construct	Prototype Sentence	Relevant Work
Acquired Capability: Ideation/Simulation	I think about putting a rope around my neck. I want to put a gun in my mouth and pull the trigger. I plan on taking a bunch of pills and just fall asleep forever.	Smith et al. (2010)
Acquired Capability: Experiences of Endurance	I've been through so much pain in my life that I feel like nothing can hurt me anymore. Overcoming those challenges made me realize I can endure a lot more than I thought. I've become numb to the pain and it takes a lot to bother me now.	
Acquired Capability: Desensitization to Harm	I've seen and experienced so much violence that it doesn't faze me anymore. I can handle situations that used to terrify me, it's like I'm immune to the fear. I've become desensitized to the pain.	
Acquired Capability: High Tolerance for Physical Pain	I can tolerate physical pain much better now; it's almost like I've trained myself. I've intentionally exposed myself to pain to build up my resistance. I've been through so many injuries that pain doesn't bother me as much.	
Acquired Capability: Engagement in Risky Behaviors	I've taken risks that others wouldn't even consider; it's like I'm not afraid of consequences anymore. Engaging in extreme activities has made me less afraid of potential harm. I've deliberately put myself in dangerous situations, and it doesn't scare me like it used to.	
Acquired Capability: Familiarity with Self-Harm Methods	I've researched and learned about different ways to harm myself. Knowing about self-harm methods doesn't bother me. I'm not disturbed by the idea of self-harm anymore.	
Perceived Burdensomeness	Everyone would be better off without me. The world would be a better place without me. I add nothing to the world. Things would be better if I was not here.	Joiner et al. (2002)
Thwarted Belongingness	I am alone. I don't fit in anywhere. Everyone hates me.	Silva et al. (2015)

Table A3: The suicide-related constructs were composed into "archetypes" for the Shared Task. The primary archetypes of interest reflected Joiner's Interpersonal Theory of Suicide (acquired capability, perceived burdensomeness, and thwarted belongingness). Multiple rounds of evaluation and refinement were performed to ensure coherence and consistency with hypothesized aspects of suicidality.

Constructs	Instruction Prompt
Acquired Capability	Instruction: The Acquired Capability refers to a person's increased tolerance for physical pain and fear of death, which develops over time through repeated exposure to painful or fear-inducing experiences. People who experience high levels of Acquired Capability may have exposure to self-harm, previous suicide attempts, or experiences in environments where pain and death are commonplace.Read the user written input text provided below and highlight the text spans for Acquired Capability, if present. If it is not present, print 'Not Present'. Input: Running on empty I've gotten to the point in my life where I don't know what makes me happy anymore. I've been in this long term relationship, I've met new people, work is not bad. I have good things but they don't make happy anymore. This all happened a couple months back and its gotten worse and worse. I ended up cutting myself again. Lying to people and telling them I'm seeing help when I'm not. I've gotten to the point where I'll cut just because my life has nothing better to keep me busy. So I hurt myself. I feel empty except for the anxiety that one day, I will end it. I've traveled to try and spark new adventures and memories. Nothing has been able to remove this feeling in my stomach. This feeling of having nothing. If my life has no meaning. Of I can't give it meaning. It should end soon. Text Spans: Acquired Capability: 'I ended up cutting myself again', 'I've gotten to the point where I'll cut just because my life has nothing better to keep me busy', 'So I hurt myself', 'I feel empty except for the anxiety that one day, I will end it', 'If my life has no meaning. Of I can't give it meaning. It should end soon'
Perceived Burdensomeness	Instruction: Perceived Burdensomeness specifically refers to an individual's belief that their existence or presence is a burden on others. People who experience high levels of perceived burdensomeness believe that their family, friends, or society in general would be better off without them.Read the user written input text provided below and highlight the text spans for Perceived Burdensomeness, if present. If it is not present, print 'Not Present'. Input: Is life really worth living? Im not suicidal like at all... But i do question if life is even worth living. I know people die of cancer and this is extremely rude of me to say since i have a good crack at a happy life. But sorry not to sound depressing but i dont see how anyone can be happy in such a selfish world. This world just flat out sucks. So why am i here? Why are you here? Shouldn't there be a goal in the end? Besides getting married and having kids and being happy with a normal life? Text Spans: Perceived Burdensomeness: 'So why am i here? Why are you here? Shouldn't there be a goal in the end?'
Thwarted Belongingness	Instruction: Thwarted Belongingness refers to the perception or experience of not belonging or feeling disconnected from meaningful social relationships despite their efforts to form connections. People who experience thwarted belongingness feel isolated or excluded from social groups.Read the user written input text provided below and highlight the text spans for Thwarted Belongingness, if present. If it is not present, print 'Not Present'. Input: Running on empty I've gotten to the point in my life where I don't know what makes me happy anymore. I've been in this long term relationship, I've met new people, work is not bad. I have good things but they don't make happy anymore. This all happened a couple months back and its gotten worse and worse. I ended up cutting myself again. Lying to people and telling them I'm seeing help when I'm not. I've gotten to the point where I'll cut just because my life has nothing better to keep me busy. So I hurt myself. I feel empty except for the anxiety that one day, I will end it. I've traveled to try and spark new adventures and memories. Nothing has been able to remove this feeling in my stomach. This feeling of having nothing. If my life has no meaning. Of I can't give it meaning. It should end soon. Text Spans: Thwarted Belongingness: 'Lying to people and telling them I'm seeing help when I'm not'

Table A4: Prompt for Evidence Extraction

Task	Instruction Prompt
Summarization	Instruction: You are required to analyze and summarize text excerpts from an individual, who has been assigned a Moderate risk of suicide. In your summary, compile all the evidence that substantiates this level of risk. While preparing your summary, take into account the following aspects that can be deduced from their text: 1. Emotional State: Look for signs of emotional distress, sadness, or hopelessness. 2. Cognitive Processes: Pay attention to their thought patterns, decision-making abilities, and problem-solving skills. 3. Behavior and Motivation: Observe any changes in their behavior or lack of motivation to engage in activities they once enjoyed. 4. Interpersonal Relationships and Social Support: Assess the quality of their relationships and the level of social support they receive. 5. Mental Health Issues: Identify any signs of mental health disorders or issues, such as depression or anxiety. 6. Other Risk Factors: Consider any other potential risk factors that may contribute to their suicide risk. Your task is to provide a comprehensive summary that encapsulates all these factors, based on the evidence found in the individual's text. Write your summary in a single paragraph without numbering. Spans: 1. It would be so easy, and relieve me of this pain forever.You don't know what it's like going through life despising yourself, and everything you are.Everything in this world is against me even thought it isn't.I'm going to end it.Edit: In case anyone was wondering, I didn't go through with it. 2. I'm too apathetic to even kill myself anymore, I just don't know what to do at all. 3. I don't want to live anymore. 4. It would be so easy, and simple, and I could end all of this pain. 5. No one cares about me. Summary: Based on the text excerpts provided, the individual is at a Moderate risk of suicide. They express a strong desire to end their life, stating that it would be ""easy"" and ""relieve [them] of this pain forever"" (1). They also mention feeling ""despis[ed]"" and that ""everything in this world is against [them]"" (1), indicating a sense of hopelessness and isolation. Additionally, they mention being ""apathetic"" and not knowing what to do (2), which suggests a lack of motivation and problem-solving skills. The individual also expresses a belief that no one cares about them (5), further contributing to their feelings of isolation and despair. These factors, combined with the individual's explicit statements about wanting to end their life, substantiate a Moderate risk of suicide.</s>"

Table A5: Prompt for Summarization of selected spans

Joiner's Constructs	Definition	Facets/Symptoms
Thwarted belongingness	Thwarted belongingness refers to the perception or experience of not belonging or feeling disconnected from meaningful social relationships despite their efforts to form connections. People who experience thwarted belongingness feel isolated or excluded from social groups.	Loss of Social Support Isolation/Loneliness Perceived/Actual Rejection
Perceived burdensomeness	Perceived burdensomeness specifically refers to an individual's belief that their existence or presence is a burden on others. People who experience high levels of perceived burdensomeness believe that their family, friends, or society in general would be better off without them.	Belief in Being a Burden Failure to Contribute Perceived Lack of Worth
Acquired Capability	The Acquired Capability refers to a person's increased tolerance for physical pain and fear of death, which develops over time through repeated exposure to painful or fear-inducing experiences. People who experience high levels of Acquired Capability may have exposure to self-harm, previous suicide attempts, or experiences in environments where pain and death are commonplace.	Simulation Experiences of Endurance Desensitization to Harm High Tolerance for Physical Pain Engagement in Risky Behaviors Familiarity with Self-Harm Methods
Protective Factors	Protective Factor can be any factor that indicates an improvement in the person's mental health– for example, an expression of resilience, gratefulness, seeking therapy etc. It can be something that hints at the opposite of Joiner's constructs: good social support and belonging, feel worthy and grateful for life, feeling pain and being careful about their own life.	

Table A6: Annotation Schema for Internal Experts

Author Index

Agarwal, Navneet, 127
Alfi-Yogev, Tal, 61
Alhamed, Falwah, 232
Aragon, Mario, 12
Atzil-Slonim, Dana, 177

Bar, Kfir, 1
Bernardi, Giulio, 92
Bertolini, Lorenzo, 92
Blanco-Cuaresma, Sergi, 203
Boyd, Ryan, 278
Bucur, Ana-Maria, 278

Chen, Jiyu, 197
Chen, Zenan, 211
Chim, Jenny, 177
Cho, Young Min, 133
Clematide, Simon, 264
Cohen, Ben, 1

Dai, Xiang, 197
de la Fuente, Marie, 41
Demšar, Jure, 145
Dey, Gourab, 278
Dias, Gaël, 127, 166
Dollfus, Sonia, 127

Eichstaedt, johannes, 133
Elce, Valentina, 92

Flek, Lucie, 278
Friedman, Doron, 1
Fukazawa, Yusuke, 270

Gkoumas, Dimitris, 177
Guerzhoy, Michael, 172
Gyanendro Singh, Loitongbam, 218

Han, Jinyoung, 247
Hoang, Van, 23

Inkpen, Diana, 108
Ive, Julia, 232

Jeon, Hyolim, 247
Just, Sandra Anna, 41

Karimi, Sarvnaz, 197
Kim, Seungbae, 247
Kirinde Gamaarachchige, Prasadith, 108
Klomek Brunstein, Anat, 1

L, Koushik, 227
Lahnala, Allison, 278
Lanning, Kevin, 278
Lee, Claire, 172
Lee, Daeun, 247
Liakata, Maria, 177
Lim, Noelle, 172
Lithgow-Serrano, Oscar William, 153
Losada, David E, 12

M, Anand Kumar, 227
M, Vishruth, 227
Mahwish, Syeda, 133
Mangalik, Siddharth, 278
Mao, Junyu, 218
Matero, Matthew, 133
Matsui, Tomoko, 191
McKay, James, 133
Michail, Andrianos, 264
Michalak, Adriana, 92
Middleton, Stuart, 218
Mihailescu, Teodor, 256
Milintsevich, Kirill, 166
Mitrović, Sandra, 153
Molla-Aliod, Diego, 197
Montag, Christiane, 41
Mutalik, Rudra, 218

Nenchev, Ivan, 41
Nguyen, Vincent, 197
Nilsson, August, 133
Nisioi, Sergiu, 256

Ophir, Yaakov, 177
Orr, Martin, 74

Parapar, Javier, 12
Paris, Cecile, 197
Parry, David, 74
Preiss, Judita, 211

Rao, Rajath, 278
Resnik, Philip, 177
Rizwan, Muhammad, 145

Rogers, Eoin, 23
Rosenthal, Richard, 133
Ross, Robert, 23

Sandu, Anastasia, 256
Scheffler, Tatjana, 41
Schillaci, Carlo, 153
Schwartz, H. Andrew, 133, 278
Shapira, Natalie, 61
Sirts, Kairit, 166
Son, Sejung, 247
Soni, Nikita, 278
Specia, Lucia, 232
Stuke, Heiner, 41

Tan, Minghuan, 238
Tanaka, Rika, 270
Tran, Vu, 191
Tsakalidis, Adam, 177

Uluslu, Ahmet Yavuz, 264
Ungar, Lyle, 133

V Ganesan, Adithya, 278
Vallejo, Isabella, 278
Van Kessel, Kirsten, 74
Varadarajan, Vasudha, 278
Vu, Huy, 133

Wang, Yuxi, 108
Weeds, Julie, 92
Welch, Charles, 278
Widhoezl, Hanna-Sophia, 92
Wilck, Benjamin, 41

Xu, Ancheng, 238

Yang, Min, 238
Yoo, Dongje, 247
Yosef, Stav, 1

Zhu, Jingwei, 238
Zirikly, Ayah, 177
Zisquit, Moreah, 1

Association for Computational Linguistics
209 N. Eighth Street
Stroudsburg, Pennsylvania 18360

ISBN 978-1-7138-9450-6

9 781713 894506

CURRAN ASSOCIATES INC.
proceedings.com